LISTENING TO MUSIC

Listening to Music

SECOND EDITION

CRAIG WRIGHT
Yale University

WEST PUBLISHING COMPANY

St. Paul / Minneapolis   New York   Los Angeles   San Francisco

Copy Editor: Eliot Simon
Composition: Parkwood Composition
Musical Examples: Igor Popovic
Index: Terry Casey
Production, PrePress, Printing, and Binding: West Publishing Company

Cover Image: "Liszt at the Grand Piano" by Josef Danhauser, 1840 (Bildarchiv Preussischer Kulturbesitz, Berlin).

Art and photo credits begin on page A–10.

Student Study Guide
A study guide has been developed to assist students in mastering the concepts presented in this text. It reinforces chapter material, presenting it in a concise format with review questions. An examination copy is available to instructors by contacting West Publishing Company. Students can purchase the study guide from their local bookstore under the title *Study Guide to Accompany Listening to Music,* prepared by Timothy Roden.

West's Commitment to the Environment
In 1906, West Publishing Company began recycling materials left over from the production of books. This began a tradition of efficient and responsible use of resources. Today, up to 95 percent of our legal books and 70 percent of our college texts are printed on recycled, acid-free stock. West also recycles nearly 22 million pounds of scrap paper annually—the equivalent of 181,717 trees. Since the 1960s, West has devised ways to capture and recycle waste inks, solvents, oils, and vapors created in the printing process. We also recycle plastics of all kinds, wood, glass, corrugated cardboard, and batteries, and have eliminated the use of Styrofoam book packaging. We at West are proud of the longevity and the scope of our commitment to the environment

 TEXT IS PRINTED ON 10% POST CONSUMER RECYCLED PAPER

British Library Cataloguing-in-Publication Data. A catalogue record for this book is available from the British Library.

Copyright © 1992   By WEST PUBLISHING COMPANY
Copyright © 1996   By WEST PUBLISHING COMPANY
610 Opperman Drive
P.O. Box 64526
St. Paul, MN 55164-0526

Printed in the United States of America

03   02   01   00   99   98   8   7   6   5

Library of Congress Cataloging-in-Publication Data

Wright, Craig M.
      Listening to music/Craig Wright.—2nd ed.
         p.   cm.
      Includes bibliographical references and index.
      ISBN 0–314–06752–3 (soft : alk. paper)
         1. Music appreciation.   I. Title.
MT6.W94L6   1996   95–31764
781.1'7—dc20   CIP
                                                         MN

CONTENTS

Chapter 19 | CONTRASTS: WESTERN MUSIC AND NON-WESTERN MUSIC   408

Appendix A | FOR FURTHER LISTENING   423

LISTENING EXERCISE LIST

PREFACE

The painting that serves as the cover for this book is a fascinating artifact. Indeed, one could write a book about it alone. Executed in 1840 by a minor Austrian painter, Josef Danhauser, it is a fanciful depiction of a gathering of some of the greatest artistic luminaries of the nineteenth century. Engaged at the piano is the imposing figure of Franz Liszt, perhaps the most formidable pianist who ever lived. Standing immediately behind him are Gioachino Rossini, the famous opera composer, and Niccolò Paganini, a violin virtuoso whose playing was so extraordinary that he was widely thought to be in league with the devil. With arm on chair, book in hand, is the French nineteenth-century lion of letters, Victor Hugo. Below sits Alexandre Dumas, author of *The Three Musketeers* and *The Count of Monte Cristo*. To his left, cigar in hand, is Aurore Dudevant, the prototype of the nineteenth-century feminist and a novelist of more than two dozen volumes under her pen name George Sand. Reclining under the sway of the music is Marie d'Agoult, herself a novelist, playwright, and historian of distinction. Finally, radiating the very spirit of music from Olympian heights, a bust of the great Beethoven sits atop the piano—Beethoven the law-giver surrounded by his apostles. Although most of the listeners are poets, playwrights, and novelists, it is the art of music that dominates the scene. From the faces of the guests we can see that they are profoundly affected by what they hear. Music touches their emotions. They are transfixed by its power.

Pedagogical Goals

The aim of this textbook is to help the student of today discover and be moved by the great expressive power of music, as in the painting by Danhauser. As this scene suggests, music can be the most compelling of the arts. Yet ironically, most beginning students feel more comfortable with the visual arts than with music. The reason for this is not difficult to fathom: Painting, sculpture, and architecture have an immediate appeal to our visual senses. But music cannot be seen or held. It is intangible, ephemeral, and more mysterious. Because of this, our ways of thinking and talking about music are different from those used to address the visual arts. A new and separate set of concepts and vocabulary is needed. The notion of scales, chords, meters, and rhythms, for example, involves a technical understanding that can be intimidating to the beginning student. This book aims to present these concepts in simple, straightforward terms so as to remove this technical barrier. Pursuing the same desire for clarity, it will also use the language of the visual arts whenever possible to explain musical concepts. The more than two hundred lavish illustrations contained herein are present in great measure to help transfer concepts already understood in the visual arts to the art of music.

A course in music should be a qualitatively different experience than that which the student receives elsewhere in the university. It should involve feelings, imagination, notions of beauty, and personal taste, not precise formulas, equations, figures, or dates. The student should be encouraged to express feelings and to be sincerely moved by music as a way of developing the ability to judge this art more critically. But most textbooks of this sort treat music not as an expressive art, but more as a history of that art. The student is required to learn something of the technical workings of music (what a tonic chord is, for example) and specific facts (how many symphonies Beethoven wrote) but is not asked to become personally engaged in the act of listening to music. What listening there is is passive, not active and participatory.

This book makes use of a new and different approach, one that the author has used for many years in his own teaching. By means of forty-six Listening Exercises, the student is asked to embrace hundreds of specific passages of music and make critical decisions about them. The exercises begin by developing basic listening skills—recognizing rhythmic patterns, graphing melodies, distinguishing major keys from minor, differentiating various kinds of textures. They then move on to entire pieces in which the student is required to become a participant in a lengthy artistic exchange, the composer communicating with the listener, and the listener reacting over a long span of time. Ultimately, equipped with these listening skills and a new-found capacity for critical judgment, the student will move comfortably to the concert hall to listen to classical and popular music with equal facility and enjoyment.

Pedagogical Aids: Listening Exercises, Listening Guides, CDs and Tapes, and Computer Software

The Listening Exercises are the most novel and important part of this text, and the student should be assigned at least two of them each week. Once completed, they can be photocopied and handed to the instructor. Duplicate copies are also contained in the excellent Study Guide prepared by Professor Timothy Roden of Ohio Wesleyan University. (Many students will benefit from the additional drills, self-tests, and suggestions for further listening contained in Professor Roden's Study Guide.)

In addition to the Listening Exercises, a total of eighty-two Listening Guides appear regularly throughout the text to help the novice enjoy extended musical compositions. Within each guide is a "time log" that allows the listener to follow along as the piece unfolds. The compact disc makes this especially easy, since all that is required is a glance at the minute and second counter to know how far the piece has progressed. The discussion in the text, the Listening Exercises, and the Listening Guides have been carefully coordinated, minute by minute, second by second, with a set of six CDs. Whenever feasible, students should read the text and do their assignments at a CD player, using a set of CDs they have purchased or one available in the college library. By watching the minute and second counter, the student will easily be able to coordinate the description of the music in the text with what he or she hears. Repeated hearing also can be carried out quickly and accurately with CD players. Of course, many students will prefer to work with the less expensive set of tapes. This will require that they follow the music with a digital watch or a watch or clock with a sweep second hand. This is more awkward, but it is still workable. Tapes are available in a six-tape set (6Tape), which contains all of the music on the CDs, as well as in a more limited and selective three-tape set (3Tape).

New to this second edition is multimedia listening software developed by Professor Thomas Smialek of Pennsylvania State University at Hazelton. This software works with the set of three CDs, which can be wrapped with the text, to provide on-screen commentary and exercises for nineteen of the most commonly assigned pieces in the text. It can be used by the instructor in a computer-equipped classroom or individually by the student who has access to a CD-ROM personal computer. This software allows the instructor to enhance the text by means of supplementary materials and drills, just as it permits the student to access rapidly diverse sorts of information. For example, students can refer to the on-screen glossary in defining the term *legato* while simultaneously listening to a legato passage from the compact disc.

Finally, Professor Edmund Goehring of the University of Georgia has written an imaginative Instructor's Manual that includes core material for lectures as well as Listening Guides and Listening Exercises not found in the text. Suggestions for further reading are contained in both Prof. Goehring's Instructor's Manual and Prof. Roden's Student Study Guide.

Musical Terminology and the Glossary

As with every specialized discipline—be it medicine, architecture, or the art of painting—music has its own vocabulary to express concepts unique to the experience of composing and listening. To engage in a lively dialogue about music, we must all understand and be conversant with this musical vocabulary. All musical terms used in this book are defined in the Glossary (beginning on page 423). They appear in the text with an asterisk to remind the reader that definitions can be found in this Glossary. They also are set in boldface type, usually at their first appearance in the text, and are included in the appropriate list of Key Words found at the ends of chapters.

The Second Edition

Every book about music aims to present the very best musical repertoire. This goal—to improve the musical repertoire—has inspired the writing of the second edition of this book. Stravinsky's *The Rite of Spring* is surely a historically more significant ballet than his *Petrushka* (discussed in the first edition), just as Debussy's *Prelude to The Afternoon of a Faun* is more of a musical watershed than his *Nuages* (also in the first edition).

Keeping abreast of what the public perceives to be the core of classical music is likewise important. Students need to feel that what they learn in a music course has some connection to the music of today—even if that music of today, with regard to classical music, is the music they know as sound tracks for television commercials or movie scores. For this reason, this new edition includes pieces such as Vivaldi's "The Spring" Concerto from his *The Seasons,* Liszt's *Liebestraum,* and the "Largo" from Dvořák's *Symphony from the New World*—three pieces very much in the public consciousness today.

Similarly, students need to see that not all music worth hearing was composed by "dead white males," but that women have played an important role throughout history—as performers of music, as patrons of music, and, especially in our present century, as composers. The expanded coverage of Hildegard of Bingen and the Countess of Dia, as well as the introduction of pieces by Clara Schumann and Ellen Taaffe Zwilich, have been made to this end.

Finally, this same desire for inclusiveness has inspired, in this new edition, a discussion of the history of Broadway, a fuller treatment of opera and jazz, and an introduction to the music of sub-Saharan Africa. The final chapter now embraces representative works from Africa, Indonesia, China, and India.

Acknowledgments

Perhaps the greatest pleasure of preparing the second edition of this book has been the opportunity to engage in sometimes impassioned discussions with colleagues around the country on how to teach the great works of music to eager students who know little about music. What can students be reasonably expected to hear? What pieces are not only great works of art but also effective teaching pieces in the classroom? The colleagues whose input has been felt in this second edition include Prof. Anne Robertson of the University of Chicago, Prof. Michael Tusa of the University of Texas, Prof. Walter Kreyszig of the University of Saskatchewan, Prof. Keith Polk of the University of New Hampshire, as well as Profs. Timothy Roden and Edmund J. Goehring, the authors, respectively, of the Study Guide and the Instructor's Manual. Prof. Wilson Pickering of Del Mar College carefully reviewed the content of the Instructor's Manual of the first edition. Most important, the selection of pieces, the factual accuracy, and the general tone of this book were greatly improved by the always astute suggestions of Prof. James Ladewig of the University of Rhode Island and Prof. William E. Hettrick of Hofstra University.

The following reviewers also evaluated material or provided helpful information during the writing of this book:

K. Gary Adams
Bridgewater College

Jeff Brister
Sam Houston State University

Mary E. Burke
Framingham State College

Charles Carroll
Lake City Community College

Peggy Demers
Sam Houston State University

George Diehl
La Salle University

Jason Edwards
Northern Michigan University

John Faber,
Valdosta State University

Nancy Gamso
Ohio Wesleyan University

Michael Golden
Colby College

Tom Harris
Augustana College

Gregory Harwood
Georgia Southern University

Dirk Hillyer
Salem State College

S. Renee Jackson
Ashland University

Gladys Johnsen
Keene State College

Jeff Jordan
Paducah Community College

Steven Krantz
St. Anselm College

Jerome Laszloffy
University of Connecticut

William Mandle
University of the District of Columbia

Philip Morgan
Lebanon Valley College

Marc Moskovitz
University of Toledo

Edward Nagel
University of South Carolina

Manuel Prestamo
Marquette University

Alison Reynolds
Ashland University

Frederik Schuetze
Bradford College

Diana Skroch
Valley City State University

Terence Small
University of Florida

Todd Snyder
North Idaho College

James Stroud
University of Tennessee at Chattanooga

Mark Strunsky
Orange County Community College

David Thompson
Limestone College

Lucy Underwood
Georgia College

Thomas Wright
Florida State University

Finally, I also owe a debt of gratitude to several colleagues at Yale, including Profs. Jonathan Berger, Leon Plantinga, Ramon Satyendra, and Michael Tenzer, as well as to the staff of the Yale Music Library: Kathy Manzi, Eva Heater, Richard Warren, Suzanne Eggleston, Helen Bartlett, and Ken Crilly, librarian. Karl Schrom, record librarian at Yale, gave frequent good advice regarding the availability and quality of recordings, and Igor and Linda Popovic set the musical examples with a careful eye. My wife, Sherry, ironed out several troublesome passages in my prose; and my two oldest sons, Evan and Andrew, kept me abreast of the pop music scene. At the end of the process of publication Laurie Ongley of Southern Connecticut State University was an invaluable final editor. As always, it has been a privilege to work with the staff of West Publishing. Copyeditor Elliot Simon, Editorial Assistant Linda Poirier, and Production Editor Ann Rudrud have been paradigms of professionalism during the creation of this second edition. My editor, Clark Baxter, has for ten years been a constant source of amazement and delight. Without him this project would not have become the success that it is.

New Haven, Connecticut
October 1995

LISTENING TO MUSIC

"It is perhaps in music that the dignity of art is most eminently apparent, for it elevates and ennobles everything that it expresses."

Johann Wolfgang von Goethe (1749–1832)

"It don't mean a thing if it ain't got that swing."

Edward Kennedy "Duke" Ellington (1899–1974)

Why do we listen to music? Because it gives us pleasure. Why does it give us pleasure? We don't know, though psychologists have spent a great deal of time trying to find out. By some inexplicable means, music has the power to intensify and deepen our feelings, to calm our jangled nerves, to make us sad or cheerful, to incite us to dance, and even, perhaps, march proudly off to war. The ancient Greeks recognized the effective powers of music; indeed, Plato thought the proper sort of music would encourage the young men of Athens to study diligently and avoid the eternal temptations of wine, women, and wanton song. We in the modern world have made music a part of our most important religious, social, and artistic activities. Music adds to the solemnity of our ceremonies, arts, and entertainments, and thus "moves" or heightens the feelings of all those who watch and participate. If you doubt this is so, try looking at a motion picture without listening to the musical score, or imagine a parade or a funeral procession without music and think how empty these events would be.

When we listen to music, physically speaking, we are reacting to an organized disturbance of our environment. A voice or an instrument emits energized sounds that set the air in motion, creating waves that carry the sound to our ears. Inside the inner ear, these vibrations are transformed into electrochemical impulses that, in turn, are transferred to the brain. What happens there is not certain, but it appears that the impulses are sorted and recognized as patterns and shapes, perhaps not unlike visual patterns or geometric shapes. In the end, the way we perceive a musical composition may not be much different from our perception of an impressive work of architecture, the harmonious shapes of a beautiful painting, or the gently moving contours of a lovely landscape. We respond emotionally to, and are moved by, musical relationships that are pleasing, novel, or even disturbing. Responding to the endless patterns of music—by tapping our feet, moving our bodies, or humming along—is an experience common to all of us.

This book aims to improve your ability to listen to music and thus your enjoyment of it. "But I listen to music every day," you may say. "Why must I *learn* to listen?" Because hearing music in the way that most of us do and truly listening to music in an attentive, perceptive way are two different things. Ironically, the more we are surrounded by music—with the Walkman, car radio, or MTV, say—the less we actually hear. The very technology that has engulfed us with music

FIGURE 1–1

Outdoor concert at the Hollywood Bowl. The shell focuses sound and projects it to the listener. Although sound can also be picked up by microphones and electronically amplified, it is not as pleasing as natural, acoustical sound.

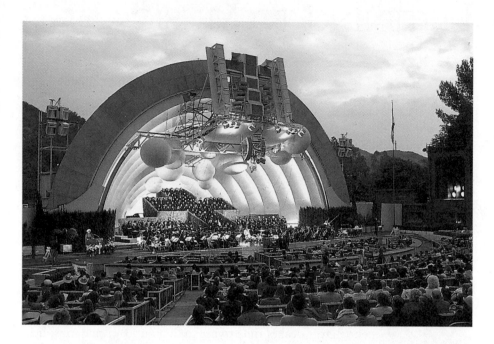

has tended to make us poor listeners. We are so accustomed to music in our daily lives that we pay little attention to it.

Now is your chance to tune into music and discover a whole new world of sound. Because music is everywhere, a course in listening to music is arguably the most useful you will take as a student in a college or university. You will never have to look far to apply what you have learned. Indeed, the music will find you, be it commercial music, film music, rock, jazz, blues, or classical.

BECOMING A GOOD LISTENER

Listening to music is an art, and like all the arts it requires preparation and discipline. Part of the preparation involves learning what to listen for and what to expect in music. For this, we must have some knowledge of how music works. How do melodies unfold? How do musical phrases work together to mark the progress of a piece? How does a composer get from one section to the next, and how does he or she signal that the conclusion is near? One of the aims of this book is to give you an understanding of what these common musical processes are so that you can make sense out of what you hear and can even anticipate what may come next. In this way, knowledge will increase your enjoyment.

improve listening skills

Along with learning how music works comes the development of good listening skills. We should be able to recognize which instruments are playing, sort out the melody from the harmony, identify how many distinctive layers or lines there are in the musical texture, feel the meter and the rhythm of the piece, and sense where we are in the formal design of the work. This will require active, not passive, listening. But once such skills have been mastered, they can be applied equally well to both classical and popular music. Hearing a bass line in a tune of R.E.M., for example, is not much different from hearing one in a symphony by Beethoven.

FIGURE 1–2

A musical instrument produces regular waves of sound that pass through the air to the listener's ear. The listener sorts and tries to make sense of the sound patterns.

Focus Solely on the Music

The first step toward improving your listening skills is to focus your attention solely on the music. You may be in the habit of listening to the radio or a CD while doing your class assignments. Some music, specifically the "easy listening music" that floods the FM airwaves, is in fact designed *not* to be heard, or at least not to be the object of heavy thinking. But for more serious music, this sort of "background" listening won't do. Similarly, for most popular music, we need only respond emotionally, and perhaps physically if we wish to dance. But classical music and much jazz requires that we open our minds as well as hearts to the music. We have to recognize specific musical events, retain these in our memory, and relate them to one another over a span of time. We must think critically about what we hear. For this, we must devote our full attention to the music.

Improve Your Memory

Memory, too, is important to good listening. Unlike the visual arts, music moves by in time. When we look at a painting, for example, it stands still before us, to be taken in all at once. The challenge to the viewer is to bring some knowledge

FIGURE 1–3

The early phonograph used a stylus, or needle, to cut the patterns of sound waves into a wax or vinyl disk.

FIGURE 1–4

Compact disc technology has replaced the phonograph and magnetic tape because of its greater fidelity. On a standard CD, 16,000 bits of encoded information specify the acoustical properties of each second of sound.

of painting techniques, subject matter, and symbolism to bear in order to appreciate the work of art in terms of its technical execution and its meaning. Our approach to a musical composition is much different. We are not given the entire object at once. Rather, it comes to us gradually, bit by bit, as the seconds and minutes go by. To make sense of the musical object, we have to remember what came before. Trying to remember and relate sounds that seem to pass by all too quickly is perhaps the greatest challenge for the beginning listener. How do we deal with this rush of musical ideas? Simply said, the listener must learn how to

seize the important ideas

seize a few key musical events and hold them firmly in the consciousness. The Listening Exercises in this book are designed to improve your capacity to remember sounds. And, like most physical and mental exercises, the more you use your musical memory, the better it becomes.

FIGURE 1–5

How a compact disc produces sound.

A violinist records music in a studio.

Incoming analog sound is sampled 44,100 times a second.

A digital version of the sound is created, by converting music into numerical "words" of 16 bits each. The encoded sound is then stored as digital data along an extremely narrow (1/100th the thickness of a human hair) spiral track. The track, if uncoiled, would extend for three miles.

The finished CD is coated with aluminum to give it a reflective surface and covered with ultraviolet lacquer.

Finally, a digital analog converter within the CD player changes numbers to electrical impulses that can be amplified and pushed through audio speakers.

CD player and speakers.

Hear the Important Sounds

Unless we happen to have a talent like Mozart's, our minds cannot retain all that our ears hear. The music simply passes too quickly, no matter how good our memory, how hard we concentrate, or how well prepared for listening we may be. But composers have central ideas or themes they wish to express, and they also have moments of preparation, transition, and just plain filler. Some parts of their music should be strongly locked in our consciousness and other parts less so. Being able to differentiate between the important and the unimportant in music is thus indispensable to good listening. The Listening Guides in this book are designed to sharpen your critical faculties by showing you what the author thinks you should listen for. But reading another's description of what is important is only a start toward hearing and evaluating by yourself. The Listening Exercises at the end of the chapters are intended to get you actively involved in the decision-making process. Both Guides and Exercises make use of tapes and the newer compact disc technology. With either, you can go back quickly to an important musical event and play it again and again. You have at your fingertips a way to listen, learn, and improve your critical skills in a controlled musical environment. Later, you will begin to make critical judgments about music by yourself, when you attend a concert or hear a new piece on the television or radio.

Listen Regularly

When everything is said and done, all this work on developing listening skills will be in vain if you do not listen to music regularly. We perceive music aurally, with our ears, not visually, with our eyes. And for some unknown reason, the rate at which we can absorb sounds is different from that of visually received information—facts and figures, dates, and abstract designs. The student of music cannot expect to cram large amounts of material in a few intense sessions, the way one might prepare for an exam in American history, for example. Learning to listen to music is much like learning the sounds of a foreign language. It must be done gradually, a small amount every day, and with much repetition.

FIGURE 1–6

Trumpeter Wynton Marsalis can record a collection of Vivaldi trumpet concertos one week and an album of Dixieland jazz the next. He has won eight Grammy awards, six for various jazz categories and two for classical discs.

CLASSICAL MUSIC—POPULAR MUSIC

There is an astonishing variety of music in the world, and there is good and bad in all of it. Most of the music that will be discussed in this book is what we refer to as "classical" music. It is also called "art" music or "serious" music. Whatever its name, this is the music that we hear in the concert hall, on certain FM radio stations, sometimes on public television, and occasionally as background music for movies, cartoons, and television commercials. Most of it was created by composers living in Europe and by Americans using European traditions. It also tends to be old. That is to say, most of what we hear in the way of classical music—the music of Bach, Handel, Mozart, Haydn, Beethoven, Schubert, and Tchaikovsky, for example—was written between 1700 and 1900, and thus was created at least a century ago. Indeed, one thing that makes a cultural artifact a "classic" is that it possesses certain qualities of expression, proportion, and balance that are timeless in their appeal. Classical music has given pleasure to music lovers generation after generation.

timeless appeal of classical music

Rock 'n' roll great Chuck Berry issues an "in your face" challenge to classical music in his popular song "Roll Over Beethoven."

popular music can help us to hear classical music

Popular music, which we also discuss here from time to time, can be just as artful and just as serious as classical music, and often the musicians who perform it are just as talented and skilled as classical musicians. Some performers are equally at home in both the classical and popular repertoire, as is the case with trumpeter Wynton Marsalis (Fig. 1–6). Popular music can be highly useful in learning good listening skills. When trying to hear how and when chords change in music, for example, it can be helpful to listen to a rock 'n' roll tune in which the chords are uncomplicated, the chords change at regular time intervals, and the bass, which carries the chords, is played very loud and thus is easy to hear.

But popular music, unlike classical, rarely contains multiple levels of musical activity, and for this reason does not require, and does not reward, concentrated thought. What we hear the first time is more or less what we get. Perhaps this inability to reward repeated hearings or to allow for a different interpretation each time we listen accounts for the fact that the listening public quickly tires of particular popular songs and then moves on to new ones. Only when a popular song does give pleasure to more than one generation, over a span of twenty or thirty years, do we say that that tune has become a "classic."

CLASSICAL CONCERTS

If this book is successful, you will find yourself listening to more and more classical music. You may discover yourself searching for classical music programs on the radio, buying a tape or CD of some new symphony you have learned, or perhaps going to a concert of classical music. Let's say you opt for a concert. What kinds of music are you likely to hear? That, of course, depends on where you go.

Some theaters are designed specifically for the production of operas and ballets. In these the action—whether sung or danced—takes place on the stage, and the musicians of the orchestra accompany this from beneath the front of the stage, in the orchestra pit, as it is called. A **ballet** is a dance form featuring one or more dancers who usually use conventional movements to tell a tale. An

ballet and opera

FIGURE 1–8

Opera Theater, Indiana University, with a production of Peter Tchaikovsky's opera *Eugene Onegin* in progress.

opera is a dramatic work in which the actors sing some or all of their words. It usually makes use of elaborate stage sets and costumes. Some operas have great dramatic content. Some are written solely to exploit, or showcase, the vocal skills of the principal singers. Yet when all of the elements of opera—music, word, drama, dance, and scenery—work together harmoniously, there is no more powerful medium of artistic expression.

Should you venture into a large concert hall, like the Concert Hall (Fig. 1–9) of the Kennedy Center in Washington, D.C., you will likely hear a symphony orchestra performing a symphony*, a concerto*, or an overture*. These are all genres, or general types, of symphonic music, which are explained in the chapters that follow. All are performed by a symphony orchestra that may have near-

symphonic music

*Terms marked with an asterisk are defined in the Glossary.

FIGURE 1–9

Concert Hall, Kennedy Center, with a concert in progress as played by the National Symphony Orchestra.

FIGURE 1–10

Kilbourn Hall, Eastman School of Music, Rochester, New York, is the site of many chamber music performances.

FIGURE 1–11

Maurice Ravel working at the piano ca. 1925. Ravel habitually composed at the piano, even when writing music for full orchestra.

ly a hundred players and in an auditorium that may seat as many as three thousand listeners. Concert halls can accommodate a large symphony orchestra on the stage, but they do not have the space or theatrical machinery to make possible the production of opera and ballet.

If more intimate classical music becomes your passion, then perhaps you will head for a recital hall where a few hundred connoisseurs might gather to hear a string quartet play string quartets* or a pianist play piano sonatas*. These more intimate genres of classical music make up what we call **chamber music,** because of the smaller, more personal surroundings in which they take place.

But why wait until the spirit moves you? Let's get started with the listening experience by discussing, and hearing, a piece that often opens a program of classical music in a large concert hall, Maurice Ravel's *Bolero*.

MAURICE RAVEL (1875–1937): *BOLERO*

The composer of *Bolero* came from the Basque region in southwestern France, though he spent most of his life in and around Paris. Diminutive in size—he was smaller than the five-foot-four-inch Napoleon—Maurice Ravel cultivated the image of a dandy, always appearing publicly in the latest, color-coordinated fashions. For the most part, he earned his living as a pianist, teacher, and composer. In many of his compositions Ravel tried to capture the musical flavor of far-off places: Spain, Arabia, ancient Greece, and the Far East. But Ravel had little personal knowledge of any of these distant lands. As one writer said of his life of the imagination, "He was the eternal traveler who never went there."

One trip that Ravel did make—and it was by far the longest of his life—was to the United States in 1928. Lured to America by the guarantee of $10,000 for a two-month visit, Ravel arrived in New York City and began to criss-cross the continent, playing and conducting his music before large, enthusiastic crowds in twenty-five different cities. He heard jazz in Harlem with American composer George Gershwin (1898–1937), and had breakfast in Hollywood with actor Charlie Chaplin (1889–1977); he visited Niagara Falls and the Grand Canyon. In the end, Ravel's American tour lasted nearly four months and earned him what was then the enormous sum of $27,000. He left the United States financially secure for the remainder of his life.

The first thing Ravel did on his return to Paris was to begin planning the music for a new ballet. It was to be called *Bolero* and to feature Spanish dancing. The work had been commissioned by ballerina Ida Rubinstein (1880–1960), a woman of legendary beauty and great wealth who used her money to sponsor new ballets in which she appeared (Fig. 1–13). *Bolero* had its premiere at the Paris Opera on November 22, 1928, with Ida Rubinstein dancing the principal role, a seductive gypsy.

Bolero draws its title from the stately Spanish dance of the same name. For the first performance in Paris, the stage was set to represent the interior of a Spanish inn of the sort found not far from Ravel's own Basque country. Located at center stage is a large table. Above it hangs a huge chandelier that not only casts bright light but also creates dark shadows on the colorful scene below. On the floor languishes a group of male dancers. At first they seem unaware of the gypsy dancer's presence, but as she mounts the table and moves with greater passion, they, too, join in her seductive dance. With growing abandon, the entire company is inspired to sway to the hypnotic music, moving toward a frenzied climax of sound, motion, and color.

Most of the audience that first night in Paris cheered the composer and his new work, but at least one woman yelled, "He's mad!" What excited the passions of the crowd was that Ravel had written a work with only one melody repeated over and over. It didn't develop or progress, as melodies in classical music usually do; it just got louder and louder each time it recurred. Ravel himself was ambivalent about his creation. "I have written only one masterpiece. That is the *Bolero*. Unfortunately, it contains no music." What Ravel meant by this paradox was that *Bolero* is an exercise in the creation of a gigantic orchestral **crescendo** (a progressive increase in volume), but is devoid of musical contrasts and melodic invention. Here the volume and color of the orchestra grow while the melody remains constant.

The first sound you hear when listening to Ravel's *Bolero* is a rhythmic pattern played on a snare drum. This represents the sound of the castanets carried by the ballerina. The rhythmic pattern is only two measures long, but it repeats over and over. (In the following examples, the variously shaped notes show the rhythm, while the long, vertical lines indicate the beginning of a new **measure**— a group of beats, or musical pulses. Musical notation will be explained much more fully in Chapter 2.)

EXAMPLE 1–1

While the drum moves inexorably forward, a few string instruments are heard plucking softly in the background. This accompaniment sets up a second two-measure rhythm.

EXAMPLE 1–2

Soon a flute enters and plays a soft, enchanting melody. This theme came to Ravel one day when he was working at the piano, perhaps inspired, as he said, by the Spanish folk songs his mother used to sing to him. The melody, or theme, actually appears in two different guises: One is somewhat bland as well as rhythmically square (we'll call it A); the other is more colorful and rhythmically complex (let's call that B):

EXAMPLE 1–3 Melody A:

EXAMPLE 1–4 Melody B:

FIGURE 1–12

Spanish dancer Lola de Valence painted by Manet, 1862. Spanish music and Spanish dancing had a powerful influence on French musicians and painters beginning in the 1860s.

FIGURE 1–13

Ida Rubenstein, who commissioned and first danced the role of the seductive gypsy in Ravel's *Bolero*.

Both versions of the melody are sixteen measures long, and they, too, repeat again and again, according to the following arrangement: **AABBAABB** (etc.) **AB.**

A rhythm, melody, or harmony that repeats over and over in music is called an **ostinato** (from the Italian word meaning "obstinate" or "stubborn"). We will have occasion to hear many musical ostinatos. Here in *Bolero* Ravel has created two rhythmic ostinatos (Exs. 1–1 and 1–2) and two melodic ostinatos (Exs. 1–3 and 1–4). As *Bolero* proceeds, more and more instruments join in playing these patterns, just as more and more of the men on stage enter excitedly into the dance. The music grows louder and more insistent, and a musical form begins to emerge. Form in music, simply said, is the general shape of a composition as perceived by the listener. The form of *Bolero* might be represented by the following diagram. The work not only increases in volume (gets louder) but also in density as more and more instruments are added.

Finally, after nearly fourteen minutes of repetition and rising tension, the melody changes (at 13:46). It is extended by several measures and moves up to a new, higher group of pitches. This shift breaks the hypnotic spell of the music, and soon the work comes to a crashing conclusion. Listen now to *Bolero* and follow the Listening Guide.

LISTENING GUIDE		Maurice Ravel Ballet music, *Bolero* (1928)	Intro CD (1)—Tape (A) 6CD 1/1

This is the first of eighty Listening Guides in this book. It is intended to lead you through the fourteen and a half minutes of *Bolero* and begin to give you a sense of what to listen for in music. *Bolero* is marked by the gradual appearance of several different instruments of the orchestra, each playing in turn as a soloist. Some of these instruments, like the trumpet and the flute, you may be familiar with already. Others, like the oboe and bassoon, are likely to be foreign to you. But don't worry too much about the sounds of the various instruments or what they look like. This will all be explained in Chapter 3. For the moment, just sit back and enjoy the music.

The numbers in the left-hand column tell you where you are in the composition. If you are listening to a CD, the numbers will appear on the machine and are easy to follow. If you are listening to a tape, you will need a digital watch or a watch or clock with a sweep hand. This "time log" is here to help you follow the music. It shouldn't detract or interfere with your listening pleasure.

0:00   Snare drum accompanied by low strings begin two-measure rhythmic ostinatos

0:10	Flute enters quietly with melody **A**
0:55	Clarinet presents melody **A**
1:42	Bassoon enters with melody **B,** harp added to accompaniment
2:29	High clarinet presents melody **B**
3:08	Bassoon joins with snare drum in playing rhythmic ostinato
3:13	Low oboe plays melody **A**
4:00	Trumpet (with mute) and flute together play melody **A**
4:45	Saxophone plays melody **B**
5:32	High saxophone repeats melody **B**
6:18	Two flutes, a French horn, and a celesta (a keyboard instrument that produces a sound like a bell) together play melody **A**
7:03	Several woodwind instruments play melody **A**
7:48	Trombone plays melody **B**
8:33	Woodwinds and French horn play melody **B** loud
9:13	Large drum (a timpani) added to accompaniment
9:19	First violins and woodwinds play melody **A**
10:03	First and second violins and woodwinds play melody **A**
10:48	Violins, woodwinds, and trumpets play melody **B**
11:33	Violins, violas, cellos, woodwinds, and trumpets play melody **B**
12:19	Melody **A** played mainly by first violins, trumpets, and piccolos (small, high flutes)
13:05	Same instruments, now with trombone added, play melody **B**
13:46	Musical climax: melody **B** moves to higher pitches and is extended
14:06	Melody settles back down to original pitch level
14:11	End: no melody, just rhythmic ostinato and cymbal crashes

popularity of Bolero

When Ravel completed his *Bolero,* he predicted that no symphony orchestra would dare to play the work. He was wrong. Its initial popularity was so great that symphony conductors jumped at the chance to perform it, though usually just as a musical work without the accompanying dance. One Hollywood producer, thinking mistakenly that *Bolero* was an opera, paid Ravel a handsome sum for the movie rights to the work; and in the end Ravel's score served as background music for a film entitled *Bolero* (1934). More recently, it was used in the same fashion for the movie *10* (1979), starring Dudley Moore and Bo Derek, in which Ida Rubinstein's sexually suggestive conception receives an updated treatment. Ravel's strikingly original way of whipping up tension and holding the listener in a trancelike state has lost none of its broad appeal: The allure of the endlessly repeating melody continues to fascinate lovers of both classical and popular music alike. Now do Listening Exercise 1, which asks you some specific questions about *Bolero* as well as about your general reaction to this unusual musical creation.

LISTENING EXERCISE

 Maurice Ravel
Ballet music, *Bolero* (1928)

Intro CD (1)—Tape (A)
6CD 1/1

Read the discussion of Maurice Ravel's *Bolero* in the text (pages 8–11) and listen to the piece while following the Listening Guide (page 10). Now listen to it again and answer the following questions. As we noted, your task will be easier if you are able to listen by means of a compact disc player that has a built-in clock to keep track of the minutes and seconds as the work unfolds. If you are listening to a tape, you will need a digital watch or a watch or clock with a sweep hand to follow the time. This first exercise is designed to be "user friendly"—the questions are not too difficult.

1. (0:00–0:50) Which is an accurate description of the opening of *Bolero?*
   a. opens with a solo flute playing the melody (**A**) loudly while snare drum and strings play loudly in the background
   b. opens with a loud melody (**A**) in the snare drum while flute and strings play loud accompaniment
   c. opens with a quiet background of snare drum and strings, and then a flute enters quietly with the melody (**A**)
2. (0:51–0:55) The melody in the flute ends at 0:50. Which of the following is true?
   a. There is a brief absence of melody before the clarinet enters.
   b. The clarinet enters immediately with the melody.

1:42 Bassoon enters with melody **B.**

3. (2:29–3:08) Clarinet enters with melody **B.** Is the sound of this clarinet higher or lower than that of the bassoon that just ended? _____

3:13 Oboe enters with melody **A.**

4. (4:00–4:40) A trumpet (with mute) and a flute play melody **A** together. Are the snare drum and the low strings still audible in the background, or have they stopped playing? _____
5. (4:45–5:26) A saxophone now enters with melody **B.** Which of the following is true?
   a. This is a true solo.
   b. This is not a true solo because another instrument joins with the saxophone on the melody.
6. (5:32–6:12) A higher saxophone plays melody **B.** What about now, have the snare drum and strings stopped playing their ostinato rhythm in the background? _____

6:18 Two flutes, a French horn, and a celesta (bell-like instrument) enter with melody **A.**

7:03 Several woodwind instruments play melody **A.**

7. (7:48–8:27) A trombone comes in with melody **B.** The trombone is an instrument provided with a slide. Does the performer make use of it by sliding between notes? _____

Now just listen to the music to the end and answer these questions.

8. As the music progresses, what is happening?
    a. Music gets louder and texture gets thicker as more and more instruments are added.
    b. Music gets softer and texture gets thinner as more and more instruments are added.
9. At the very end, which is true about the music?
    a. It sounds loud, harsh, and dissonant.
    b. It sounds soft, bland, and consonant.
10. Now on a scale of 10, how would you characterize your response to Ravel's *Bolero*? You are welcome to choose more than one response if you wish.
    1. Constant beating made me ill.
    2. Left me cold and a little bored.
    3. Found it interesting but unnecessarily repetitious.
    4. Would enjoy it more if I could see the dancers.
    5. Astonished that a musician can get so much mileage out of just one idea.
    6. Decided that Ravel had an odd notion of what erotic music ought to be.
    7. Liked the piece, but now can't get that ostinato rhythm out of my head.
    8. Found myself moving around the room in step with the beat.
    9. Vowed to learn how to dance a bolero.
    10. Felt a sense of exhilaration, even power as I listened to the growing swell of sound.

KEY WORDS

ballet	Ida Rubinstein	ostinato
Bolero	Maurice Ravel	Wynton Marsalis
chamber music	measure	
crescendo	opera	

2

RHYTHM, MELODY, AND HARMONY

Music can be defined as sound that moves through time in some organized fashion. Sounds and silences can be shaped, given a profile, as they pass through time. Durations can be organized in repeating patterns to form rhythms. And musical pitches can be placed one after the other in a purposeful way to form a melody. When more than one pitch sounds at a time, the potential exists for musical harmony. Rhythm, melody, and harmony, then, are the most basic musical elements. They are the building blocks of music, and how they are arranged determines the color, texture, and form of every musical composition.

In discussing rhythm, melody, and harmony, we depend greatly on a terminology that has grown up around the practice of notating music. Musical notation is simply music put down on paper by means of special signs or symbols. By recording a piece in musical notation, we, in effect, "freeze dry" the musical work so that it can be exactly reproduced by performers at some later date. In addition, musical notation allows us to stop at any point, to look at a composition as it is standing still, talk about its various parts, and learn something about how it is put together. You do not have to know musical notation to derive great pleasure from listening to music, nor will you have to read it to be highly successful in using this book. But the enjoyment of music can be enhanced if we understand how music works, and to explain this we need to know something of the technical language of music. This allows us to talk about the music we hear in a specific, meaningful way, rather than in vague generalities.

RHYTHM

Rhythm is arguably the most fundamental element of music. When asked to sing a favorite song, most of us will recall the rhythm better than the melody. Similarly, when hearing a piece of music for the first time, we are more likely to be struck by, and remember, a catchy rhythm than a catchy tune. We have a direct, even physical, response to rhythm.

Rhythm, in its broadest definition, is the organization of time in music. It divides up long spans of time into smaller, more easily comprehended units. It gives a shape, or profile, to the melody or tune. Basic to rhythm is the principle of the beat. The **beat** is an even pulse that divides the passing of time into equal segments. It may be strongly felt, as in a waltz or a straight-ahead rock 'n' roll tune, or it may be only dimly heard (because no instrument plays it strongly), as in much of the Impressionistic music of the late nineteenth century (Chapter 16). But whether immediately or distantly heard, almost all music has a beat to it. When we tap our foot to music, we are reacting to such a beat.

beat

The beat in music is most often carried by a unit of measurement called the quarter note (♩), a basic duration in music. Normally, the quarter note will move along roughly at the rate of the average person's heartbeat, sometimes faster, sometimes slower. As you might suspect from its name, the quarter note is shorter in length than the half and the whole note, but longer than the eighth and the sixteenth note. These other note values account for durations that are longer or shorter than the beat. Here are the symbols for the most-used musical notes and an indication of how they relate to one another in length:

note values

EXAMPLE 2–1

(whole note) 𝅝 = ♩ ♩ (2 half notes)

(half note) ♩ = ♩ ♩ (2 quarter notes)

(quarter note) ♩ = ♪ ♪ (2 eighth notes)

(eighth note) ♪ = ♬ ♬ (2 sixteenth notes)

FIGURE 2–1

Performers of traditional New Orleans jazz often play simultaneously in different rhythms.

To help the performer keep the beat when playing or singing, the smaller note values, specifically, those with flags on the vertical stem, are beamed, or joined together, in groups of two or four:

EXAMPLE 2–2

♩ ♪♪♪♩ ♪♪♪♪ becomes ♩ ♫♩ 𝅘𝅥𝅰𝅘𝅥𝅰

In vocal music, however, the beaming is broken when a syllable of text is placed below a note:

EXAMPLE 2–3

Jin‑gle bells, jin‑gle bells, jin‑gle all the way

In addition to notes that signify the duration of sound, there are other signs, called rests, that indicate silence. For each note there is a corresponding rest of the same value:

rests

FIGURE 2–2

Rhythms (1934) by Robert Delaunay (1885–1941).

EXAMPLE 2–4

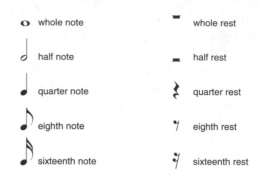

You will have noticed that, in their basic form, adjacent note values (and rests) in music all have a 2:1 ratio to one another: One half note equals two quarter notes, and so on. But triple relationships can and do exist, and these are created by means of the addition of a dot after a note, which increases the duration of the note to one and one-half its original value:

EXAMPLE 2–5

dotted notes

Let's take a look at how the various note values can reflect the rhythm of an actual piece of music. For this we choose a simple, well-known tune, *Yankee Doodle*. First the text is given to refresh your memory as to how the song goes, next the rhythm of the tune indicated by horizontal lines of different lengths to show how long each pitch lasts, then the rhythm in musical notation, and finally the position of the beat in *Yankee Doodle* as indicated by quarter notes:

EXAMPLE 2–6

Here's the patriotic song *America* (first known in England and Canada as *God Save the King*—or *Queen*) arranged the same way:

EXAMPLE 2–7

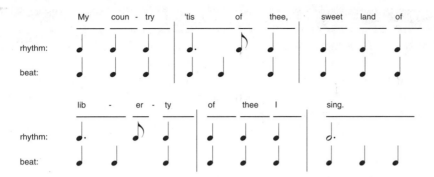

Listening Exercise 2a at the end of the chapter will help you to focus on the many musical rhythms you already have in your ear.

Meter

Notice how in the preceding examples vertical lines divide the music into groups of two beats, in the case of *Yankee Doodle*, and into groups of three beats in *America*. These strokes are called measure lines, or bar lines. A measure*, or bar, is a group of beats. Usually, there are two or three, sometimes four or more beats per measure. The gathering of beats into regular groups is called **meter.** Instead of having a steady stream of undifferentiated beats, we instinctively stress some more than others in a regular and repeating fashion. If we stress every other beat—ONE two, ONE two, ONE two—we have two beats per measure and therefore duple meter. The stressed beats are called strong beats and the unstressed beats weak beats. Similarly, if we emphasize every third beat—ONE two three, ONE two three, ONE two three—we have three beats per measure and thus triple meter. Triple meter has one strong beat and two weak beats per bar. In addition, there are other meters with four or six beats per measure. Here is a familiar folk song in the more common quadruple meter (four beats per measure):

duple and triple meters

EXAMPLE 2–8

And here is an equally well-known tune in sextuple meter:

EXAMPLE 2–9

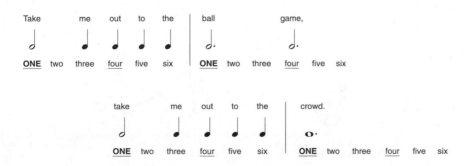

Most music, however, is written in duple ($\frac{2}{4}$), triple ($\frac{3}{4}$), or quadruple ($\frac{4}{4}$) meter. Meter in music is indicated by a **time signature,** two numbers, one on top of the other, placed at the beginning of the music to tell the performer how the beats of the music are to be grouped. The top number of the signature indicates how many beats there are per measure; the bottom number tells what note value is the beat. Since, as we have said, the quarter note most often carries the beat, most time signatures have a "4" on the bottom. The three most frequently encountered time signatures are given here:

time signatures

EXAMPLE 2–10

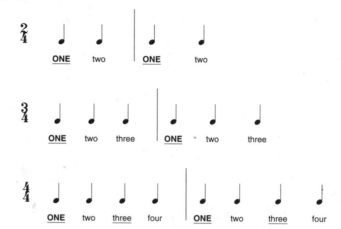

Having a time signature at the beginning of the music may be of great value to the performer, but it doesn't help the listener, unless he or she happens to be following along with the musical notation—following the **score,** as musicians call it. Without a score, the listener must of necessity hear and feel the meter. Most music, as we have said, is written in $\frac{2}{4}$, $\frac{3}{4}$, or $\frac{4}{4}$. Since $\frac{4}{4}$ is in most (but not all) ways merely a multiple or extension of $\frac{2}{4}$, there are really only two meters that the beginning listener should be aware of: duple meter ($\frac{2}{4}$) and triple meter ($\frac{3}{4}$). But how do we hear these and differentiate between them?

Hearing Meters

One way you can more easily come to hear a given meter is to establish some sort of physical response to the music: Obvious as it seems, start tapping the beat with your foot and moving with the music in a way that groups beats into measures of two or three. Perhaps the most graceful way to move with the music is to adopt the same patterns of motion that conductors use to lead symphony orchestras and other musical ensembles. These are patterns cut in the air with the right hand (a baton is optional!). Here are the patterns that conductors use to show $\frac{2}{4}$ and $\frac{3}{4}$ meter:

conducting duple and triple meters

EXAMPLE 2–11

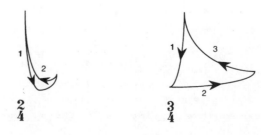

Notice that in both of these patterns, and indeed in all conducting patterns, the first beat is indicated by a downward movement of the hand. This is called the **downbeat.** It is always the first and by far the strongest beat in the measure. In $\frac{2}{4}$ the downbeat is stronger, or more accented, than the **upbeat** (the beat signaled by an upward motion); in $\frac{3}{4}$ it is more accented than either the middle beat (2) or the upbeat (3). When listening to a piece of music, then, tap the beat with your foot, listen for the downbeat, and try to get your conducting pattern synchronized with the music. If you hear only one weak beat between each strong beat, the music is in duple meter and you should be conducting in $\frac{2}{4}$ time. If you hear two weak beats between each downbeat, on the other hand, you are listening to a piece in triple meter and should be using the $\frac{3}{4}$ pattern. Try conducting *Yankee Doodle* and *America* in $\frac{2}{4}$ and $\frac{3}{4}$, respectively.

feel the downbeat

EXAMPLE 2–12

Yan - kee doo - dle	went to town	rid - ing on a	po - ny.
ONE two	**ONE** two	**ONE** two	**ONE** two

My coun - try	'tis of thee,	sweet land of	lib - er - ty	of thee I	sing.
ONE two three	**ONE** two three	**ONE** two three	**ONE** two three	**ONE** two three	**ONE** two three

One final observation about meters and conducting patterns: Almost all music that we hear, and especially dance music, has a clearly identifiable meter and a strong downbeat. But not all music *starts* with the downbeat. Often a piece will begin with an upbeat. An upbeat at the very beginning of a piece is called a pickup. The **pickup** is usually only a note or two, but it gives a little momentum or extra push into the first downbeat, as can be seen in the following examples:

pickup to the downbeat

EXAMPLE 2–13

She'll be	com - in' round the	moun - tain when she	comes
two	**ONE** two	**ONE** two	**ONE** two

Oh	say can you	see by the	dawn's ear - ly	light
three	**ONE** two three	**ONE** two three	**ONE** two three	**ONE** two

Turn now to the end of the chapter and complete Listening Exercise 2b. Then go on to Listening Exercises 3 and 4, which ask you to identify the meter of several musical works and give you a chance to practice conducting in $\frac{2}{4}$ and $\frac{3}{4}$ time.

Syncopation

One of the ways to add variety and excitement to music is by the use of syncopation. In most music the **accent,** or musical stress, falls on the beat with the downbeat getting the greatest accent of all. **Syncopation** places the accent either on a weak beat or between the beats. The note that is syncopated sounds accented because it is played louder or held longer than the surrounding notes. A good example of syncopation is found at the end of the first phrase of Stephen Foster's *Camptown Races*, where the "dah" of "doo-dah" is syncopated.

EXAMPLE 2–14

| Camp - town | la - dies | sing | this | song, | doo | **dah** ___ | doo | **dah** ___ |

rhythm:

beat: **ONE**   two   **ONE**   two   **ONE**   two   **ONE**   two

Syncopation gives an unexpected bounce or lift to the music and is a prominent feature in jazz. Indeed, part of the fun of playing jazz is to obscure the beat by means of syncopation and thereby to tease or tantalize the listener.

Tempo

tempo: the speed of the beat

If meter is the grouping of beats, and rhythm the durational patterns superimposed on the meter, **tempo** is the speed at which the beats occur. Obviously, the tempo, or speed, of the beat can be fast or slow, but it usually falls somewhere in the neighborhood of 60 to 100 beats per minute. Tempo is indicated to the performer by means of tempo markings placed at the beginning of the piece. Because they were first used in Italy in the seventeenth century, at the beginning of the Baroque period in music, tempo markings are most often written in Italian. The following are a few of the most common tempo indications, arranged from slow to fast:

grave (grave)	very slow
largo (broad)	
lento (slow)	slow
adagio (slow)	
andante (moving)	moderate
andantino (slightly faster than *andante*)	
moderato (moderate)	
allegretto (moderately fast)	fast
allegro (fast)	
vivace (fast and lively)	very fast
presto (very fast)	
prestissimo (as fast as possible)	

FIGURE 2–3

Leonard Bernstein (1918–1990), one of the most forceful, and flamboyant, conductors of the twentieth century.

Naturally, general terms such as these allow for a good deal of interpretive freedom. Conductors like Leonard Bernstein (1918–1990), Arturo Toscanini (1867–1957), and Seiji Ozawa (b. 1935), for example, have had different notions of just how fast a movement of Beethoven marked *allegro* (fast) should really go. In addition, composers often call for fluctuations in tempo within a piece by placing commands such as *accelerando* (getting faster) and *ritardando* (getting slower) in the score. One particularly colorful term is *rubato* (robbed), meaning that the performer is given license to steal some additional time for the passage of music in question and thus to slow it down. Frequent changes in tempo make it more difficult for the listener to follow the beat, but they add much in the way of expression and feeling to the music.

Melody

A **melody** is a series of notes arranged in order to form a recognizable unit. The more beautiful the melody, the more we are drawn to the music. When supported by its companions, rhythm and harmony, melody can produce an overwhelming emotional experience. Yet one of the wonders of music is that we are hard pressed to explain in precise terms why this is so. What is it about the shape of a melody, its balance and contour, that makes one so moving and another so very forgettable? The pursuit of this question, however, would carry us off into the realm of aesthetic theory. Instead, let us simply describe how melodies are put together so that we can more readily grasp them.

Pitch

Just as a grammatical sentence is made up of building blocks we call words, so a melody is composed of individual units called pitches. **Pitch** is the relative position, high or low, of a musical sound. When sound comes in regular vibrations, it produces a musical **tone.** If it occurs in irregular vibrations, then it is merely noise of the sort generated by a crashing plate or a barking dog. Musical tones are usually produced when a string or a column of air is set in motion on a musical instrument, and this motion, in turn, creates vibrating airwaves that reach the ear at equal time intervals. The faster a string vibrates, for example, the higher the pitch. Normally, humans will hear sounds produced in a range between a low of about 20 vibrations (or cycles) per second to a high of about 16,000. (Some animals can hear sounds twice this high.) In theory, pitch can occur anywhere on this wide band of sound—think of a fire siren starting low, rising, and then falling back down. But when making music, we take this broad spectrum of sound and divide it into individual steps or degrees of pitch. We then string these units together in time to produce a melody.

faster vibrations produce a higher pitch

Example 2–15

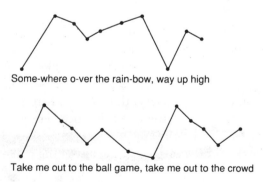

Some-where o-ver the rain-bow, way up high

Take me out to the ball game, take me out to the crowd

The Octave

One of the remarkable qualities of pitch is that, when singing or playing a succession of tones up or down, a performer often comes to a tone that sounds like an exact duplication of an earlier pitch, but at a higher or lower level. For a reason that will become clear shortly, the duplicating pitch is called an **octave.**

octave duplication used in all musical cultures

Pitches an octave apart sound similar because the frequency of vibration of the higher pitch, or note, is precisely twice that of the lower. Middle C on the piano, for example, vibrates at 256 cycles per second, while the C an octave above does so at 512 cycles. When men and women sing a song or hymn together without harmony, they invariably sing at the octave; it sounds as if they are all singing the same notes, but, in fact, the men are an octave below the women. Almost all musical cultures, Western and non-Western, make use of the principle of octave duplication in their melodies. But not all cultures agree as to how the octave should be divided, that is, how many notes there should be within an octave. In many traditional Chinese melodies, the octave is divided into five separate pitches. Some Arabic and Turkish melodies, however, make use of fourteen. Judging from our earliest written music, which dates back more than a thousand years, we in the West have always preferred melodies that were built on seven pitches within the octave. The eighth pitch duplicated, or doubled, the sound of the first, and thus it was called the octave.

dividing the octave

At first, the seven notes within the octave corresponded to the white keys of the keyboard. Eventually, five additional notes were inserted within the span of the octave, and these correspond to the black keys.

EXAMPLE 2–16

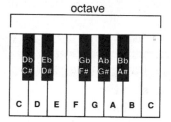

To get the sound of the octave in your ear, try singing *Over the Rainbow* and *Take Me Out to the Ball Game*. Both begin with a leap up an octave no matter on what pitch you choose to start.

Notating Melodies

The type of notation used for the two tunes in Ex. 2–15 is useful if you merely need to be reminded of how a melody goes, but it is not precise enough to allow a singer to produce the tune if he or she didn't know it already. When the melody goes up, how *far* up does it go? More precision for musical notation began to appear in the West as early as the eleventh century, when notes came to be situated on lines and spaces so that the exact distance between pitches could be judged immediately. This gridwork of lines and spaces came to be called a **staff.** The higher on the staff the note is placed, the higher the pitch.

EXAMPLE 2–17

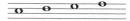

treble and bass clefs

The staff is always provided with a **clef sign** to indicate the range of pitch in which the melody is to be played or sung. One clef, called the **treble clef,** designates the upper range and is appropriate for high instruments like the trumpet and the violin, and a woman's voice. A second clef, called the **bass clef,** covers the lower range and is used for lower instruments like the trombone and the cello, and a man's voice.

EXAMPLE 2–18

For a single vocal part or a single instrument, a melody could easily be placed on either one of these two clefs. But for two-hand keyboard music with greater range, both clefs are used, one on top of the other. The performer looks at this combination of clefs, called the **great staff,** and relates the notes to the keys beneath the fingers. The space between the two clefs is filled in by a short, temporary line called a ledger line. On the keyboard it indicates middle C (the middle-most C key on the piano).

EXAMPLE 2–19

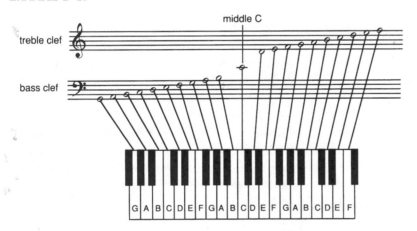

FIGURE 2–4
G *Clef* (1935) by Josef Albers
(1888–1976).

Each musical pitch can be referred to by a letter name, like C, as well as represented by a note placed on the great staff. Only seven letter names are used because, as we have said, melodies were originally made up of only seven pitches within each octave—corresponding to the seven white notes of the keyboard. When the pitch is duplicated at the octave, the letter name repeats (see Ex. 2–19). But gradually, the spaces between the white keys were divided and additional (black) keys inserted. This increased the number of pitches within the octave from seven to twelve. Since they were not originally part of the staff, the five additional pitches were not represented by a line or space, nor were they given a separate letter name. Instead, they came to be indicated by a symbol, either a sharp or a flat, applied to one of the existing notes. A **sharp** (♯) raises the note to the key immediately above, usually a black one, whereas a **flat** (♭) lowers it to the next key below, again usually a black one. A **natural** (♮), on the other hand, cancels either of the two previous signs. Here, as an example of musical notation on the great staff, is a well-known melody as it might be notated for a chorus of male and female voices, the women an octave higher than the men. To keep things simple, the melody is notated in equal whole notes (without rhythm).

names of the notes

EXAMPLE 2–20

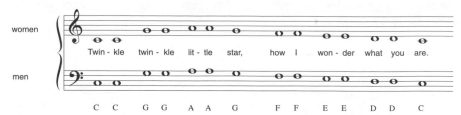

FIGURE 2–5

Contrasting Sounds (1924) by Wassily
Kandinsky (1866–1944).

Tonality, Keys, and Scales

Melodies have a central pitch, called the **tonic,** around which they gravitate and
on which they usually end. The organization of music around this central tone,
the tonic, is called **tonality.** In the case of *Twinkle, Twinkle,* C is the tonic—the
tune not only ends on C but happens to begin on C as well. A melody may, in
fact, have C or D or F♯, or any other of the twelve notes within the octave, as the
tonic. In addition, we say that *Twinkle, Twinkle* is written in the tonality, or key,
of C major, meaning that it has the tonic C, but also that it makes use of a C
major scale. A **key,** then, is a tonal center built on a tonic note and making use
of a scale.

But what is a scale? A **scale** is an arrangement of pitches that ascends and
descends in a fixed and unvarying pattern. Almost all Western melodies are written in one of two types of scales, either major or minor. To understand the difference between the major and minor scale, it's necessary to look at a keyboard
for a moment (see Ex. 2–19). Notice that there are no black keys between B and
C and between E and F. All the adjacent white notes of the keyboard are not the
same distance apart. The difference, or distance, in sound between B and C is
only half of that between C and D. B to C is the interval of a half step, while C
to D is the interval of a whole step. The major and minor scales, in turn, are built
on two distinctly different patterns of whole and half steps, each starting on a
tonic note. The **major scale** has a succession of whole and half steps that pro-
major and minor scales   ceeds 1–1–½–1–1–1–½. The **minor scale** goes 1–½–1–1–½–1–1. Every scale uses
only seven of the available twelve pitches within each octave; and once the
octave is reached, the pattern can start over again. A major or minor scale may
begin on any of the twelve notes within the octave, and thus there are twelve
major and twelve minor scales and keys. Here are the notes of the major and
minor scales as they start on C and then on A. Next time you pass by a piano,
try playing these to get the sound of major and minor in your ear.

EXAMPLE 2–21

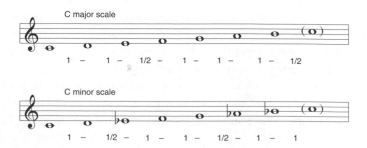

EXAMPLE 2–21 (CONTINUED)

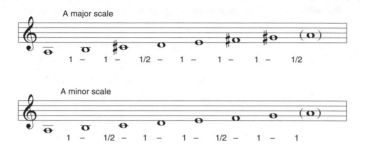

A major scale built on C uses only the white notes of the keyboard, as does a minor scale constructed on A. When begun on a note other than C (for the major scale) or A (for the minor scale), however, sharps and flats are needed so that the pattern of whole and half steps does not vary. For example, a major scale may begin on A and ascend up the octave; but to keep the major scale pattern intact, the notes C, F, and G must be sharped (see Ex. 2–21). Similarly, starting the minor scale pattern on C will require that E be lowered to E♭, A to A♭, and B to B♭ (see Ex. 2–21).

Composing a piece in A major would require writing out many sharps, just as one in C minor would require writing many flats. To avoid this labor, musicians have developed the custom of "preplacing" the sharps and flats at the beginning of the staff. The sharps and flats are then active throughout the piece. Preplaced sharps or flats are called a **key signature.**

key signatures

EXAMPLE 2–22

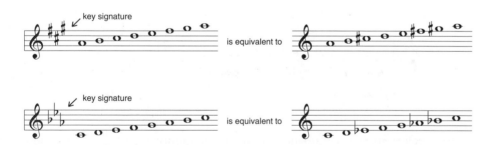

is equivalent to

is equivalent to

Key signatures indicate to the performer the key in which a piece is written; that is, they show what scale is about to be employed and what the tonic note is.

MODULATION. **Modulation** is the change from one key to another. Most short pieces—folk songs, hymns, and the like—don't modulate; they stay in one key. But longer pieces need to modulate or the listener is soon bored. Modulation gives a dynamic sense of movement to music. As the composer Arnold Schoenberg (1874–1951) has said, "Modulation is like a change of scenery." The beginning listener will find modulations difficult to hear. You may not recognize precisely when they occur, but you will sense, however subconsciously, that the music is changing from one key to another.

HEARING MAJOR AND MINOR. Scales are like colors on an artist's palette. A composer will choose what he or she believes is the right scale to achieve the desired musical mood or feeling for the composition. The differences in mood or color within each of the two principal melodic types, major and minor, are small and are not commonly agreed on even by professional musicians. Some say D major is a bright key, F major comfortable and restful, D♭ major dark and rich. But what may seem rich to one listener may sound bright to the next. Taste in music, as in the other arts, is a very personal matter.

One thing we can all agree on, however, is that a melody in a major key sounds decidedly different from one in minor. Major melodies seem bright, cheery, optimistic, while minor ones are dark, somber, even ominous. Try singing the beginning of the following familiar major and minor songs to establish firmly in your mind's ear the difference between major and minor:

EXAMPLE 2–23

Positive emotions (joy, confidence, triumph, tranquility, love, etc.) have traditionally been expressed in major, while negative feelings (fear, anxiety, sorrow, despair, etc.) have usually been played out in minor. Major and minor scales are constructed according to two distinctly different patterns of whole and half steps (see Ex. 2–21), and this is why they affect us in different ways. The change from a major key to a minor one with the same tonic (C major to C minor, for example), or from minor to major (F minor to F major, for example) is called a change of **mode.** Lest there be any doubt that a change in mode can change how you feel about a melody, listen to the following familiar tunes (your instructor will play them for you). The mode in each has been changed from major to minor by inserting a flat into the scale near the tonic note (C). Notice here how all the happiness, joy, and sunshine have disappeared from these formerly major tunes. Such shifts create the subtle emotional language of music.

changing the mode

EXAMPLE 2–24

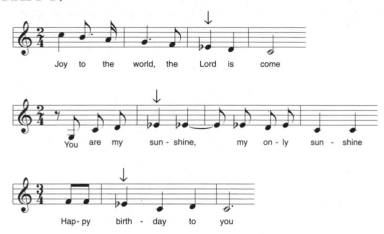

Now turn to Listening Exercise 5, which asks you to distinguish between melodies in the major and minor mode.

DIATONIC VERSUS CHROMATIC. Most of the melodies we know are what we call **diatonic** melodies, meaning that they make use only of the seven notes of the major or minor scale, the so-called diatonic notes. A scale using all twelve notes within the octave, however, is called a **chromatic** scale. In a chromatic scale all twelve pitches are a half step apart.

EXAMPLE 2–25

Chromatic (from the Greek *chroma,* "color") is a good word for this scale because the additional five pitches do indeed add color and richness to a melody. Here is a popular tune that begins by using a chromatic scale.

EXAMPLE 2–26

In general, chromatic melodies sound more intense, tight, and angular than diatonic ones.

Melodic Structure

Difficult as it is to say why some melodies are so pleasing and others so dull, all good melodies seem to have a few essential qualities: a strong tonic note, forward motion, a goal or climax, and ultimately a feeling of repose or completion. These qualities are all found in abundance in the *Ode to Joy* by Ludwig van Beethoven (1770–1827). Beethoven originally composed this music for the last movement of his Symphony No. 9 (1824), but in more recent times the melody has been

Beethoven's Ode to Joy

used as a Christmas carol, a hymn for the United Nations, a movie score (*Die Hard*), and even a pop-rock tune. Here the melody is notated in the bass clef in D major, the key in which Beethoven composed it.

EXAMPLE 2–27

FIGURE 2–6

A portrait of Ludwig van Beethoven painted in 1818–1819 by Ferdinand Schimon (1797–1852).

We can make a few general observations about Beethoven's melody: First, notice that it moves mainly by **step,** from one letter name of the scale to the next (D to E, for example), and rarely moves by **leap,** a jump of one or more letter names (D to F♯, or D to G, for example). Melodies that move predominantly by step are called **conjunct** melodies, while those that move mainly by leap are called **disjunct** ones. *Ode to Joy* may be the most conjunct melody ever written! The only leaps of any importance are the two at the end of phrase **c** (measure 12).

Next, notice that there are, in fact, four melodic phrases here. A **phrase** in music functions much like a dependent phrase or clause within a grammatical sentence. It constitutes a dependent idea within a melody. Here four four-measure phrases form a complete sixteen-bar melody. Let's concentrate for a moment on the first two phrases. The opening phrase (**a**) begins on the third step of the D major scale, F♯, and ends on the second step, E. If you try to sing, hum, or whistle this first phrase, you will notice that when you get to the end ("Elysium"), the music doesn't sound complete or finished—it wants to go on. By the end of the second phrase (**b**), however, you arrive on the tonic note ("welcome") and now do have a feeling of arrival and completion. Many melodies begin this way: The initial phrase opens the melody and ends on some note *other* than the tonic; the second phrase answers this idea and *antecedent and consequent phrases* returns the melody to the tonic. Two phrases that work in tandem this way are called **antecedent** and **consequent** phrases. Both end with a cadence. A **cadence** is a musical resting place at the end of a phrase. The cadence at the end of Beethoven's antecedent phrase does not sound final, and therefore is called a **half cadence;** the one at the end of his consequent phrase, because it ends on the tonic, does sound complete and is called a **full cadence.**

Ode to Joy then pushes off in a new direction (**c**). The music gains momentum by means of a repeating rhythm in measures 10–11 and reaches a musical climax in measure 12 with the two leaps. The fourth and final phrase is an almost exact repeat of the second phrase (**b**), with the exception of one interesting detail (see * in Ex. 2–27). Beethoven brings the return of this phrase in one beat early—a bit of rhythmic syncopation—thereby giving an unexpected lift to the melody.

The melodic structure of Beethoven's *Ode to Joy*—balanced groups of four-bar phrases arranged antecedent–consequent–extension–consequent—is found frequently in music, from the works of Haydn, Mozart, and Beethoven in the eighteenth and early nineteenth centuries to popular songs of nineteenth- and twentieth-century America. You may have been singing antecedent–consequent phrases and using full and half cadences all your life and not been aware of it. To prove the point, sing the following two well-known tunes:

The Saints Go Marching In (traditional)
"Oh when the saints, go marching in, oh when the saints go marching in"   (half cadence)
(antecedent phrase)
"Oh how I want to be in that number, when the saints go marching in."   (full cadence)
(consequent phrase)

Oh Suzanna (Stephen Foster)
"Oh I come from Alabama with my banjo on my knee"   (half cadence)
(antecedent phrase)
"I'm bound for Louisiana my true love for to see."   (full cadence)
(consequent phrase)

Now do Listening Exercise 6, which invites you to become more familiar with the melodic structure of Beethoven's famous *Ode to Joy*.

Hearing Melodies

Hearing melodies may be the single most important part of listening to music. Melodies contain the main musical ideas the composer wishes to communicate. Once a composer has hit on a good melody, he or she is likely to repeat or elaborate on it several times in the course of a composition. Beethoven, for example, brings back his *Ode to Joy* in various guises at least a half-dozen times in his Symphony No. 9. Indeed, by reintroducing a melody at certain important moments in a work, the composer reveals the form, or structure, of the musical creation. It is important, therefore, that the listener be able to seize on the melody, to remember it over a span of time, and to recognize its return, as if welcoming an old friend.

How do we improve our ability to hear melodies and recognize their return? The best way is perhaps not to try to take in an entire melody, or even a full phrase, at once. A melody can move by rapidly, and the beginning listener can expect to absorb only three to four seconds of it at a time. Instead of trying to grasp everything at once, grab hold of some small part of the melody. Find a distinctive rhythmic figure of three or four notes, or a salient melodic motive. A **motive** in music is a short, distinctive melodic figure that stands by itself. Concentrate on this one figure and lock it into your mind by asking: What is it doing?

melodic motives

FIGURE 2–7

Does it jump up rapidly? If so, by a lot or just a little? Does it move down by steps? Does it repeat a note in some distinctive way? Does it end on the same pitch as it began? To do this it is helpful to visualize, even draw a picture of, the melodic motive that you seize on. Listening Exercise 7 is designed to help you construct a visual image of the musical sounds you hear.

Harmony

Melody provides a lyrical voice for music, rhythm gives vitality and definition to that voice, while harmony adds depth and richness to it, just as the dimension of depth in painting adds a rich backdrop to that art. Although melody can and sometimes does stand by itself, most often it is closely bound to, and, indeed, grows out of, the harmony. The two work gracefully in tandem, the harmony supporting and amplifying the melody. Sometimes, however, discord arises—as when a folksinger strumming a guitar suddenly hits a wrong chord—and the result can be startling. The melody and harmony now clash: They are out of harmony. The double sense of this last statement shows that the term **harmony** has several meanings. Broadly speaking, harmony means the peaceful cohabitation of diverse elements; the ancient Greeks, for example, spoke of the unheard harmony of the planets and of the soul. When applied specifically to music, harmony is said to be the sounds that provide a support and enrichment—an accompaniment—for melody. Finally, we often speak of harmony as if it was a specific musical event, as when we say the harmony changes, meaning that one chord in the accompaniment changes to another. Thus, we say that the cowboy ballad *The Streets of Laredo* is a harmonious piece, harmonized in the key of F major, and that the harmony changes fifteen times:

EXAMPLE 2–28

Building Harmony

Chords are the building blocks of harmony. A **chord** is simply a group of two or more pitches that sound at the same time. When we learn to play guitar or jazz

FIGURE 2–8

In *New Harmony* (1936), the painter
Paul Klee (1879–1940) creates tonal
harmony by superimposing complementary blocks of color.

piano, we first learn mainly how to construct chords. The basic chord in music
is the **triad,** so called because it consists of three pitches arranged in a very specific way. Here is a C major triad:

EXAMPLE 2–29

Note that it comprises the first, third, and fifth notes of the C major scale. The
distance between each of these notes is called an **interval.** C to E, spanning three
letter names (C,D,E) is the interval of a third. E to G, again spanning three let-

ter names (E,F,G) is another third. Triads always consist of two intervals of a
third placed one on top of the other. Here are triads built on every note of the C
major scale:

EXAMPLE 2–30

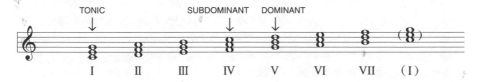

These triads provide all the basic chords necessary to harmonize a melody in C
major.

Notice that each of the chords is given a Roman numeral, indicating on
which note of the scale the triad is built, and that the triads built on I, IV, and
V are called the tonic, subdominant, and dominant chords. We have already

met the tonic note in our discussion of melody—it is the pitch around which a tune gravitates and on which it ends. Similarly, the tonic chord, or triad, is the "home" chord of the harmony. It is the most stable and the one toward which the other chords move. The **dominant** triad, always built on the fifth note of the scale, is next in importance. Note in *The Streets of Laredo* how most of the melody is harmonized simply by changing back and forth between tonic and dominant triads. Dominant triads are especially likely to move to tonic triads at the ends of musical phrases, where such a movement (V–I) helps create the strong effect of a full cadence*. The **subdominant** triad is built on the note *chord progressions* below the dominant, and it frequently moves to the dominant, which, in turn, moves to the tonic (IV–V–I). A movement of chords in a purposeful fashion like this is called a **chord progression.** The end of *The Streets of Laredo* is marked by a subdominant–dominant–tonic chord progression (IV–V–I), one that is heard frequently in music and, perhaps for that reason, gives a solid, reliable feeling to the harmony.

The notes of a triad need not always enter together but can be spaced out over time. Such a broken, or staggered, triad is called an **arpeggio.** Arpeggios can appear either as part of the melody or in the harmony that supports a melody. An arpeggio used in an accompaniment usually gives the listener the sense that the harmony has more substance than it really does. In Ex. 2–31, the beginning of *The Streets of Laredo* is harmonized with the triads spaced out as arpeggios (beneath the brackets). The supporting triads are the same as in Ex. 2–28, but now the accompaniment seems more active because one note of the triad is sounding on every beat:

EXAMPLE 2–31

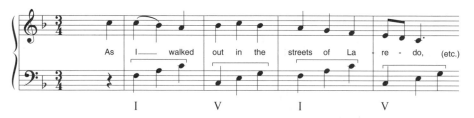

As I walked out in the streets of La re do, (etc.)

I   V   I   V

FIGURE 2–9

Henri Matisse, *Violinist at the Window* (1918). In his writings on art, Matisse often spoke of the "consonance and dissonance of color."

Consonance and Dissonance

You have undoubtedly noticed, when pressing the keys of the piano at one time or another, that some combinations of keys produce a harsh, jarring sound, while others are pleasing and harmonious. The former chords are characterized by **dissonance** (pitches sounding disagreeable and unstable) and the latter by **consonance** (pitches sounding agreeable and stable). Generally speaking, chords that contain pitches that are very close together, just a half or a whole step apart, sound dissonant. On the other hand, chords that involve a third, a somewhat larger interval, are usually consonant. Each of the triads built on the notes of the major scale (see Ex. 2–30), for example, contains two intervals of a third and therefore is consonant. Dissonant chords add a feeling of tension and anxiety to music; consonant ones produce a sense of rest and stability. Composers have traditionally used dissonant chords sparingly, like a hot spice. They prepare them carefully in a bed of consonance and then immediately resolve them—move them—back to a consonance. Our musical psyche demands this constant ebb and flow between the tension of dissonance and the stability of consonance.

Hearing the Harmony Change

Chords move from consonance to consonance, from consonance to dissonance, from dissonance to consonance, and sometimes, in modern music, from dissonance to dissonance. The rate of change may be rapid or slow, regular or irregular. In *The Streets of Laredo* (Ex. 2–28), the rate of harmonic change is moderately fast and regular. There are three beats for each chord and then a new chord appears, without exception, at the beginning of each group of three (each new measure). Composers can alter the rate at which new chords appear in order to achieve particular effects. A rapid rate of change communicates to the listener a feeling of movement and perhaps tension. A deceleration in the speed with which chords change from one to the next can convey a sense of slowing down and relaxation, even though the tempo of the piece (the real speed at which it is moving) remains the same. Handel (1685–1759) and Beethoven (1770–1827) were especially fond of slowing down the rate of harmonic change toward the end of a piece in order to give it a feeling of conclusion, to tell the listener that the piece, in fact, is at an end.

The first step to listening to harmony is to focus your attention on the bass, separating it from the higher melody line. Chords are often built upon the bass note, and a change in the bass from one pitch to another may signal a change in chord. Concentrating on the bass at first will not be easy. Most of us have always thought that listening to music is listening to melody. Certainly, hearing melody is crucial. But the bass is next in importance, and it rules supreme in a sort of subterranean world. It carries the chords and determines where the harmony is going, more so than the higher melody. Baroque music (1600–1750) usually has a clear, driving bass line, and hard rock music perhaps even more so. Next time you listen to a piece of rock, follow the bass guitar line instead of the melody and lyrics. See if you don't begin to sense when the chords are changing and when you have reached a chord that feels like the home key (the tonic triad). Listening Exercise 8 helps you to focus on the bass and begin to recognize when the harmony changes from one chord to the next.

listen to the bass

LISTENING EXERCISES

2a　　Identification of Rhythm

In this exercise you are asked to recall and listen to rhythms that are already in your musical memory. Following are the opening text and rhythm of several well-known songs. Place the correct note values above the unnotated portion of the text in order to complete the rhythm for the entire phrase. For example:

(If you are unfamiliar with one or more of these tunes, feel free to substitute your own. Simply write out the text and then try to indicate the musical rhythm above it by writing in the note values.)

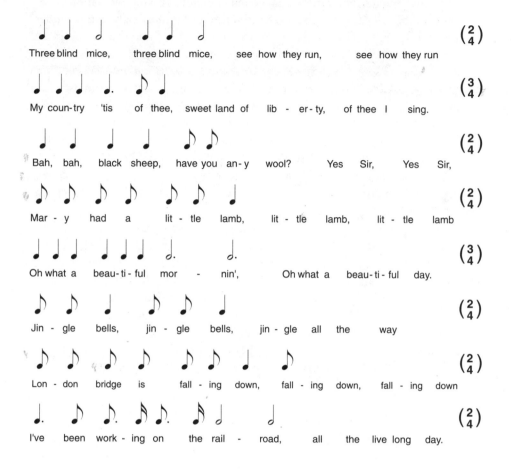

2b

Now that you have read about meters and time signatures (pages 17–18), complete this exercise by inserting the bar lines and beats (1 2 or 1 2 3) for each of the preceding examples. The meter for each example is either $\frac{2}{4}$ or $\frac{3}{4}$, and each begins with a downbeat, not a pickup. For example:

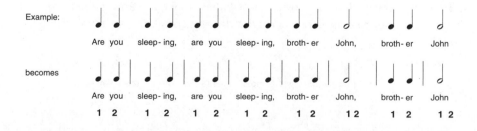

3   Identification of Meters

On your Introduction to Listening CD (tracks 2–11)—Tape (side A), you have ten short musical excerpts each played once (you'll probably want to replay them several times). Identify the meter of each excerpt. To do this, you should listen for the beat, count 1–2 or 1–2–3, and get your conductor's beat pattern in synchrony with the music (downbeat of the hand with the downbeat of the music). If you have done it correctly, the completion of each full conductor's pattern will equal one measure. All the pieces are in duple ($\frac{2}{4}$) or triple ($\frac{3}{4}$) meter, and all begin with the downbeat.

1. Meter ——————— (Chopin, *Grande Valse brilliante* in E♭)
2. Meter ——————— (Sousa, March: *Stars and Stripes Forever*)
3. Meter ——————— (Beethoven, Variations on *God Save the King*)
4. Meter ——————— (Schubert, Scottish Dance in A♭)
5. Meter ——————— (Johann Strauss, *Blue Danube Waltz*)
6. Meter ——————— (Beethoven, Symphony No. 8, first movement)
7. Meter ——————— (Beethoven, Symphony No. 8, second movement)
8. Meter ——————— (Mozart, Symphony No. 36, fourth movement)
9. Meter ——————— (Scott Joplin, *The Entertainer*)
10. Meter ——————— (Schubert, *Original Dance*, No. 36)

---

4   Identification of Meters

Below are listed eight pieces of classical music and jazz that are found on the CDs and tapes for this book. Your task is to listen to each and identify the meter of the piece. Find the music on the CDs or tapes and begin listening. Try to feel the beat. Then get your conducting pattern in sync with the music, making sure that your downbeat comes with the strongest beat in the music. Remember, if you have just one weak beat between each strong beat, then the piece is in duple meter ($\frac{2}{4}$); if you have two, it is in triple meter ($\frac{3}{4}$).

1. Ravel, *Bolero* (1928) (Intro CD [1]–Tape [A]; 6CD 1/1) meter _____ (N.B.: the tempo here, and hence the beat, is slow.)
2. Handel, "Hallelujah" chorus from *Messiah* (1741) (Intro CD [39]–Tape [B]) meter _____
3. Mozart, *A Little Night Music* (1787), First movement (6CD 2/7; 6Tape 2A; 3CD 2/9; 3Tape 2A) meter _____
4. Chopin, Polonaise in A major (1839) (6CD 4/4; 6Tape 4A; 3CD 3/2; 3Tape 3A) meter _____
5. Vivaldi, Violin Concerto in E major ("The Spring"), First movement (early 1700s) (6CD 1/15; 6Tape 1B; 3CD 2/5; 3Tape 2A) meter _____
6. Handel, Minuet from *Water Music* (1717) (Intro CD [32]–Tape [A]; 3CD 1/32; 3Tape 1A) meter _____
7. Jean-Joseph Mouret, *Rondeau* from *Suite de symphonies* (1729) (6CD 2/5; 6Tape 2A, 3CD 2/8; 3Tape 2A): meter _____

8. Musorgsky, *The Great Gate of Kiev* from *Pictures at an Exhibition* (1874) (6CD 5/5; 6Tape 5B; 3CD 3/6; 3Tape 3B) meter _____

---

 5   Hearing Major and Minor Melodies

On your Introduction to Listening CD (tracks 12–21)—Tape (side A), you will find ten musical excerpts that will help you begin to differentiate a piece in a major key from one in a minor key. Each is preceded by the major or minor scale that is used for the excerpt, so you can more readily identify whether the piece is in major or minor. For most listeners, melodies in major are bright, cheerful, sometimes bland, whereas those in minor tend to be darker, more somber, sometimes exotic, even oriental, in sound. Again, each excerpt is played just once, but you can replay them as many times as you like.

1. _____ (Mozart, Piano Sonata, K. 331)
2. _____ (Chopin, Mazurka, Opus 7, No. 3)
3. _____ (Beethoven, Variations on a theme of Paisiello)
4. _____ (Schumann, *Träumerei (Dreaming)* from *Kinderszenen*)
5. _____ (C. P. E. Bach, *Polonaise*)
6. _____ (J. S. Bach, Three-part Invention)
7. _____ (Schubert, Piano Sonata, D. 959)
8. _____ (Beethoven, Piano Sonata, Opus 13)
9. _____ (Chopin, Piano Sonata, Opus 35)
10. _____ (J. S. Bach, Prelude, *The Well-Tempered Clavier*, Book I)

---

 6   Hearing Melodic Structure
Ludwig van Beethoven, *Ode to Joy* from Symphony No. 9 (1824)

On your Introduction to Listening CD (track 22)—Tape (side A), you have an excerpt from the last movement of Beethoven's Symphony No. 9, in which his famous *Ode to Joy* can be heard. You are probably familiar with the tune already, but look at it again as it is given on page 28. Try to get the antecedent (**a**), consequent (**b**), and extension (**c**) phrases firmly in your ear. Now listen to the music on your tape. The melody is actually heard four times, first played softly by the low string instruments, then more loudly by the higher strings, then louder still by yet higher strings, and finally loudest of all by the trumpets and full orchestra.

Your task is to prepare a listening guide indicating when each phrase occurs. Indicate in the blanks the minute and second when each phrase occurs. (Notice that Beethoven actually repeats the extension (**c**) and consequent (**b**) phrases at the end of each of the four presentations of the melody.) Some of the timings have already been inserted to help you along.

After you have filled in the blanks, go back and treat yourself to one final hearing in which you listen unencumbered to the growing power of Beethoven's melody.

Playing Number:	1	2	3	4
	Low strings (double basses)	Higher strings (2nd violins)	Higher strings (1st violins)	Trumpets with full orchestra
Antecedent	a 0:00	a 0:49	a 1:40	a 2:30
Consequent	b 0:08	b : ___	b : ___	b : ___
Extension	c : ___	c : ___	c : ___	c : ___
Consequent	b : ___	b : ___	b : ___	b : ___
	(repeat)	(repeat)	(repeat)	(repeat)
Extension	c 0:32	c 1:23	c 2:13	c 3:03
Consequent	b : ___	b : ___	b : ___	b : ___

7   Melodic Graphing

One of the biggest challenges for any listener is to lock onto the important motives and melodies as they unfold in a musical composition. Constructing a visual image of the music is often a good way of grasping more surely what you hear. In this assignment we once again make use of melodies that you know. For the following melodies, sing, whistle, or hum the tune and then try to construct a melodic graph that shows the relative distance between the pitches. You don't have to get the exact proportions between pitches, just the general contour or shape of the tune. Nor do you have to be concerned at this point with the rhythm. Here are two completed examples to give you the idea. Later, when you listen to a symphony of Mozart or Beethoven, you will be better prepared to draw a picture, either actual or mental, of the melody that you hear. *Again, if you don't know one or more of these tunes, substitute one of your own.* Simply write down the text and draw a melodic graph of the melody above it.

Sing a song of six-pence

My bon-nie lies o-ver the o-cean

1. Joy to the world, the Lord has come

2. Jin-gle bells, jin-gle bells, jin-gle all the way

3. Hap-py birth-day to you, hap-py birth-day to you

4. Row, row, row your boat gent-ly down the stream

5. Yes-ter-day, all my trou-bles seemed so far a-way (Lennon/McCartney)

6. Ru-dolph the red-nosed rein-deer, had a ver-y shin-y nose

7. The hills are a-live, with the sound of mu-sic (*Sound of Music*)

8. Oh say can you see, by the dawn's ear-ly light (*Star Spangled Banner*)

9. Oh beau-ti-ful, for spa-cious skies (*America*)

10. For he's a jol-ly good fel-low

8 Hearing Chord Changes in the Harmony
Listening to Music Blues

The following exercise encourages you to focus on the bass line and the chords that support a melody, rather than the melody itself. The music you hear (Introduction to Listening CD [track 23]—Tape [side A]) consists of three improvisations on a standard blues chord progression. The rate at which the chords of the harmony change is slow to moderately slow. It is also irregular, meaning that a chord is held sometimes for many beats and sometimes only for a few. In this performance the left hand of the electronic keyboard player holds one chord until it is time to move on to the next. Each time it stops holding and moves elsewhere, we have a new chord. Below you are asked to fill in a time log for the chord changes in this repeating blues harmony. Record the minute and second that each chord changes. A few of the correct times are already filled in to make your task easier.

There are several traditional blues harmonies. The one employed here is an old standard that uses the repeating chord progression tonic (I), subdominant (IV), tonic (I), dominant (V), subdominant (IV), tonic (I) to carry the blues tune. The blues and its history are discussed in Chapter 18, but for now let's just concentrate on the harmony.

1. 0:00 ____ ____ ____ ____ ____
   I   IV   I   V   IV   I
2. 0:25 ____ ____ ____ ____ ____
   I   IV   I   V   IV   I
3. 0:50 ____ ____ ____ ____ 1:10
   I   IV   I   V   IV   I

KEY WORDS

arpeggio	harmony	pickup
bass clef	key	rhythm
beat	key signature	subdominant chord
cadence	major scale	syncopation
chord	melody	tempo
chord progression	meter	tonality
chromatic	minor scale	tonic
diatonic	mode	treble clef
dominant chord	modulation	triad
downbeat	motive	upbeat
great staff	octave	

3

MUSICAL COLOR, TEXTURE, AND FORM

Every musical composition is made up of a number of elements, just as every painting has a number of components to it. Color, texture, and form are important in both these arts. They are the broad, general qualities of a work that help give it its meaning and structure. Form in music is the general shape of a composition as perceived by the listener. It usually becomes apparent only gradually as the work progresses from beginning to end. Color and texture, on the other hand, are qualities that may be obvious to the listener immediately. We may be struck by a particular melody, not so much because of its pitches or rhythm, but because it is played on a brilliant-sounding instrument like the trumpet. Or we may be captivated by a musical climax, not because the melody at that point is particularly original, but because the full sound of a large orchestra is heard for the first time—the musical texture has gained impressive substance. Color and texture, then, are less musical ideas in themselves and more ways of expressing ideas. Nonetheless, color and texture can be crucial to the success of a work. Imagine how boring Ravel's *Bolero* would be if the melody returned each time in the same instrument or if the texture remained the same because no new instruments were added. The interest in *Bolero* lies not in the melody itself but in the changing colors and textures in which that melody is clothed (see page 8).

Color

Simply said, **color** in music is the tone quality of any sound produced by a voice or an instrument. **Timbre** is another term for the tone quality of musical sound. Instruments produce sounds of different colors, or timbres, because they are constructed in different ways and of different materials. We need not go into the acoustical reasons why this is so—instinctively, we all recognize that the sound of a flute has a different tone quality from that of a trombone. Similarly, the voice of pop singer Michael Jackson has a different timbre to it from that of opera star Luciano Pavarotti (Fig. 3–2), even when the two produce the same pitches. Since the human voice was probably the first "instrument" to make music, let's start our investigation of musical color with it.

The Voice

The human voice is an instrument of a very special sort that naturally generates sound without the aid of any kind of mechanical contrivance. It is highly expressive, in part because it can produce an enormously wide range of sounds.

When we sing we force air up through our vocal cords, causing them to vibrate. Men's vocal cords are longer and thicker than women's, and for that reason the sound of the mature male voice is lower. (This principle is also at work with the string instruments: The longer and thicker the string, the lower the pitch.) Voices are classified by range into four principal parts. The two women's vocal parts are the **soprano** and the **alto,** and the two men's parts the **tenor** and the **bass.** The soprano is the highest voice and the bass the lowest. When many voices join together, they form a **chorus;** the soprano, alto, tenor, and bass constitute the four standard choral parts. In addition, the area of pitch shared by the soprano and alto is sometimes designated as a separate vocal range called the **mezzo-soprano,** just as the notes adjoining the tenor and bass are said to be encompassed by the **baritone** voice.

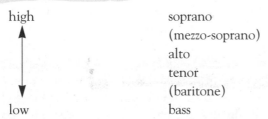

high   soprano

       (mezzo-soprano)

       alto

       tenor

       (baritone)

low   bass

The voice is capable of producing many different styles of singing: the raspy sound of a blues singer, the twang of the country balladeer, the gutsy belt of a Broadway songster, or the lyrical tones of an operatic soprano. We all try to sing, and we would like to sing well. How well we do, and what kind of sound we produce, depends on our training and our physical makeup—the lungs, vocal cords, throat, nose, and mouth are all involved in the production of vocal sound.

FIGURE 3–1

(Above, left) Color, texture, and form are all essential components in Picasso's Cubist painting *Three Musicians* (1921). Here color works rigidly to elucidate form.

FIGURE 3–2

(Above, right) Opera singer Luciano Pavarotti, perhaps the greatest tenor voice of the twentieth century.

FIGURE 3–3
Violinist Midori.

Musical Instruments

Musical instruments come in groups, or families. The symphony orchestra traditionally includes four such groups. The first is the string family, so called because these instruments produce sound by plucking or bowing a string. The second and third groups are the woodwind and brass families, both of which generate music by blowing air through a pipe or tube of one sort or another. The fourth group is the percussion family, which makes music—and sometimes just plain noise—usually by striking a suspended membrane (a drum), a block of wood, or a piece of metal with a stick of some kind. In addition, there is a fifth group of instruments, the keyboard instruments, which are not normally part of the symphony orchestra. The organ, harpsichord, and piano are the main keyboard instruments, and they make sound by means of keys and pipes (organ) or keys and strings (harpsichord and piano). The organ is usually played alone, while the piano is most often heard either by itself or as an accompaniment to another solo instrument.

Why does a composer choose a particular instrument to present a melody and not some other? In general, one instrument is chosen over another because of its capacity to express what the composer feels about the music that he or she intends to create. Invariably, the instrument with the tone color best able to portray the composer's feeling about a given musical line—and what the composer wishes to express to the listener—is the one selected. To be able to hear these subtle emotional shadings in music, it is important that we sharpen our awareness of the separate tone colors of the various instruments.

STRINGS. Generally speaking, when we speak of string instruments we broadly include all instruments that produce sound by means of vibrating strings: the guitar, banjo, ukulele, and the harp, as well as the violin and its close relatives, the viola, cello, and double bass. But the guitar, banjo, ukulele, and harp usually produce their sound when plucked, whereas the violin and its relatives are normally played with a bow, not just plucked. Indeed, it is their use of a bow, along with their distinctive shape, that identifies the four members of the violin group. We traditionally associate these instruments with classical music. The guitar, banjo, ukulele, and harp, on the other hand, have their origins in folk music.

Violin Group. The violin group constituted the original core of the symphony orchestra when it was first formed during the Baroque era (1600–1750). In numbers of players, the violins, violas, cellos, and double basses still make up the largest part of any orchestra. A large symphony orchestra can easily include as many as a hundred members, at least sixty of whom play one of these four instruments.

The **violin** is chief among the string instruments. It is also the smallest—it has the shortest strings and therefore the highest pitch. Because of its high range and singing tone, it often is assigned the melody in orchestral and chamber music. The violins are usually divided into groups known as firsts and seconds. The seconds play a part slightly lower in pitch and subordinate in function to the firsts.

The sound of the violin is produced when a bow is pulled across one of four strings held tightly in place by tuning pegs at one end of the instrument and by a tailpiece at the other (Fig. 3–3 and page 117). The strings are slightly elevated above the wooden body by means of a supporting bridge. Different sounds or pitches are produced when a finger of the left hand shortens, or "stops," a string

by pressing it against the fingerboard—again, the shorter the string, the higher the pitch. Because each of the four strings can be stopped quickly in many different places, the violin possesses both great range and agility. The strings themselves are made either of animal gut or of metal wire. The singing tone of the violin, however, comes not so much from the strings as from the wooden body, known as the sound box, which amplifies and enriches the sound. The better the design, wood, glue, and varnish of the sound box, the better the tone.

The **viola** (Fig. 3–4) is about six inches larger than the violin and it produces a somewhat lower sound. If the violin is the string counterpart of the soprano voice, then the viola has its parallel in the alto voice. Its tone is darker, richer, and more somber than the brilliant violin.

You can easily spot the **cello** (violoncello) in the orchestra because the player sits with the instrument placed between the legs (Fig. 3–5). The pitch of the cello is well below that of the viola. It can provide a low bass sound as well as a singing melody. When played in its middle range by a skilled performer, the cello is capable of producing an indescribably rich, expressive tone.

The **double bass** (Fig. 3–6) gives weight and power to the bass line in the orchestra. Since at first it merely doubled the notes of the cello an octave* below, it was called the double bass. As you can see, the double bass is the largest, and hence lowest sounding, of the string instruments. Its job in the orchestra, and even in jazz bands, is to help set a firm base for the musical harmony.

String Techniques. The members of the violin group all generate pitches in the same way: A bow is drawn across a tight string. This produces the traditional, penetrating string sound. In addition, a number of other effects can be created by using different playing techniques.

pizzicato: Instead of bowing the strings, the performer plucks them. With this technique, the resulting sound has a sharp attack, but it dies away quickly. For a good example of pizzicato, listen again to the beginning of Ravel's *Bolero* where the soft string accompaniment is plucked rather than bowed (Intro CD [1]–Tape [A]; 6CD 1/1).

FIGURES 3–4, 3–5, AND 3–6
(left) Violist Yuri Bashmet. (*center*) Cellist Yo-Yo Ma. (right) Double bass player Gary Karr.

FIGURE 3–7

A harp.

vibrato: By shaking the left hand as it stops the string, the performer can produce a sort of controlled wobble in the pitch. This adds richness to the tone of the string because, in effect, it creates a blend of two or more pitches.

tremolo: The performer creates a musical "tremor" by rapidly repeating the same pitch with quick up and down strokes of the bow. Tremolo creates a feeling of heightened tension and excitement when played loudly, and a velvety, shimmering backdrop when performed quietly.

mute: If a composer wants to dampen the penetrating tone of a string instrument, he or she can instruct the player to place a mute (a metal or rubber clamp) on the strings of the instrument.

Harp. Although originally a folk instrument, one found in virtually every musical culture, the **harp** (Fig. 3–7) is sometimes added to the modern symphony orchestra. Its role is to add color to the orchestral sound and sometimes to create special effects, the most striking of which is a rapid run up or down the strings called a **glissando.**

WOODWINDS. The name "woodwind" was originally given to this family of instruments because they emit sound when air is blown through a wooden tube or pipe. The pipe has holes along its length, and the player covers or uncovers these to change the pitch. Nowadays, however, some of these woodwind instruments are made entirely of metal. Flutes, for example, are constructed of silver, and sometimes of gold or even platinum. As with the violin group, there are four principal woodwind instruments in every modern symphony orchestra: flute, oboe, clarinet, and bassoon. In addition, each of these has a close relative that is larger or smaller in size and which possesses a somewhat different timbre and range. The larger the instrument or length of pipe, the lower the sound.

The lovely, silvery tone of the **flute** is probably familiar to you. The instrument can be rich in the lower register and then light and airy on top. It is especially agile, capable of playing tones rapidly and moving quickly from one range to another.

FIGURE 3–8

(from left to right) A flute, two clarinets, an oboe, and a bassoon. The flute, clarinet, and oboe are about the same length. The bassoon is nearly twice their size.

The smaller cousin of the flute is the **piccolo.** ("Piccolo" comes from the Italian *flauto piccolo*, meaning "little flute".) It can produce higher notes than any other orchestral instrument. And though very small, its sound is so shrill that it can always be heard, even when the full orchestra is playing loudly.

The **clarinet** produces sound when the player blows against a single reed fitted to the mouthpiece. The tone of the clarinet is more mellow than that of the other woodwinds, especially in the lower register of the instrument. It also has the capacity to slide or glide smoothly between pitches, and this allows for a highly expressive style of playing. The flexibility and expressiveness of the instrument have made it a favorite with jazz musicians. A lower, larger version of the clarinet is the **bass clarinet.**

The **oboe** is equipped with a double reed—two reeds tied together with an air space in between. When the player blows into the instrument through the double reed, a nasal, slightly exotic sound is created. It is invariably the oboe that gives the pitch at the beginning of every symphony concert. Not only was the oboe the first nonstring instrument to be added to the orchestra, but it is a difficult instrument to tune. Better have the other instruments tune to it than to try to have it adjust to them.

Related to the oboe is the **English horn.** Unfortunately, it is wrongly named, for the English horn is neither English nor a horn. It is simply a larger variety of the oboe that originated on the continent of Europe. The English horn produces a dark, haunting sound, one that was especially favored by composers of the Romantic period (1820–1900).

The **bassoon** functions among the woodwinds much as the cello does among the strings. It can serve as a bass instrument, adding weight to the lowest sound, or it can act as a soloist in its own right. When playing moderately fast or rapid passages as a solo instrument, it has a dry, almost comic tone. If you are unfamiliar with the sound of the bassoon, go back and listen to *Bolero* where the bassoon presents the melody (at 1:42).

There is also a double bassoon, usually called the **contrabassoon.** Its sound is deep and sluggish. Indeed, the contrabassoon can play notes lower than any other orchestral instrument.

The bassoon, contrabassoon, and English horn are all double-reed instruments, just like the oboe. Their tones, therefore, may sound more vibrant, even exotic, than those of the single-reed instruments like the clarinet and saxophone.

Strictly speaking, the single-reed **saxophone** is not a member of the symphony orchestra, though it can be added on occasion, as Ravel chose to do in *Bolero* (at 4:45). Its sound can be mellow and expressive but also, if the player wishes, shrill and raucous. The expressiveness of the saxophone makes it a welcome member of most jazz ensembles, while the shrill, penetrating tone of the instrument is prized by rock musicians.

BRASSES. Like the woodwind and string groups of the orchestra, the brass family consists of four primary instruments: French horn, trumpet, trombone, and tuba. Brass players use no reeds but instead blow into their instruments through a cup-shaped **mouthpiece** (Fig. 3–10). By adjusting valves or moving a slide, the performer can make the length of pipe on the instrument longer or shorter, and hence the pitch lower or higher.

FIGURE 3–9

Members of the Canadian Brass, with the French horn player at the left and the tuba player at the right.

The **French horn** was the first brass instrument to join the orchestra. Its sound is rich and mellow, yet somewhat veiled or covered. Because of this, composers have traditionally used the horn to add warmth and fullness to the orchestral texture. During the Romantic period (1820–1900), the horn not only provided a sonorous glue to bind the tones of the other instruments but also began to emerge as a solo instrument in its own right.

Everyone has heard the high, bright, cutting sound of the **trumpet.** Whether on a parade ground or in an orchestral hall, the trumpet is an excellent solo instrument because of its agility and penetrating tone. When provided with a mute (a hollow plug placed in the bell of the instrument to dampen the sound), it can produce a softer tone that blends well with other instruments. Witness the effective combination of muted trumpet with flute early on in *Bolero* (at 4:00).

Although distantly related to the trumpet, the **trombone** plays in the middle range of the brass family. Sometimes it is possible to confuse the sound of the trombone with that of the French horn, because they are both full and majestic. But the tone of the trombone is somewhat clearer and more focused than that of the horn. Because of its slide, the trombone also has the capacity to glide easily between pitches. A good example of the slide at work can be heard in the trombone solo, once again, in *Bolero* (at 7:48).

The **tuba** is the lowest-sounding instrument of the brass family. It produces a full, though surprisingly muffled tone. Like the double bass of the violin group, the tuba is most often used for setting a base, or foundation, of sound, but not for serving as a solo melodic instrument. In fact, the tuba is perhaps more spectacular in the way it looks, concealing the performer as it does, than in the way it sounds.

FIGURE 3–10

Mouthpieces for brass instruments.

PERCUSSION. Percussion instruments are those that are struck in some way, either by hitting the head of a drum with a stick or by banging or scraping a piece of metal or wood in one fashion or another. Some percussion instruments, like the timpani (kettledrums), produce a specific pitch, while others just generate noise without a recognizable musical tone. It is the job of the percussion instruments to sharpen the rhythmic contour of the music. They can also add color to the sounds of other instruments and, when they play loudly, can heighten the sense of climax in a piece. In *Bolero* the snare drum is used to carry the primary rhythmic pattern from beginning to end, the timpani (starting at 9:13) adds color to the accompaniment in the low strings, while the cymbals heighten the intensity of the final climax.

The **timpani** (Fig. 3–11) is the percussion instrument most often heard in classical music. Whether struck in single, detached strokes or hit rapidly to produce a thunderlike roll, the function of the timpani is usually to add depth, tension, and drama to the music. Timpani usually come in pairs, one instrument to play the tonic* note and the other to play the dominant*.

The crashing ring of the **cymbals,** the dull thud of the **bass drum,** and the rat-ta-tat-tat of the **snare drum** are sounds well known from marching bands and jazz ensembles, as well as the classical orchestra. None of these instruments produces a specific musical tone.

On the other hand, a wide spectrum of musical pitches are created by a trio of instruments that generate sound in a rather similar way: the xylophone, glockenspiel, and celesta (Fig. 3–12). The **xylophone** is a set of wooden bars that, when struck by two hard mallets, produce a dry, wooden sound. The **glockenspiel** works the same way, but the bars are made of metal so that the tone is brighter and more ringing. The **celesta,** too, produces sound when hammers strike metal bars, but the hammers are activated by keys, as in a piano; the tone of the celesta is bright and tinkling—a delightful, "celestial" sound, as the name of the instrument suggests.

KEYBOARD INSTRUMENTS. The pipe organ, harpsichord, and piano are our most familiar keyboard instruments. The **pipe organ** (Fig. 3–13), which traces its ancestry back to ancient Greece, is by far the oldest. It works according to a simple principle: The player depresses a key that allows air to rush into a pipe, there-

FIGURES 3–11 AND 3–12
(left) Timpanist Marvin Dahlgren of the Minnesota Orchestra. (right) A xylophone, a celesta, and a glockenspiel.

FIGURE 3–13

A pipe organ in the Chapel of St. Thomas Aquinas at the University of St. Thomas, Minnesota.

FIGURES 3–14 AND 3–15

(left) A two-manual harpsichord built by Pascal Taskin (Paris, 1770), preserved in the Yale University Collection of Musical Instruments. (right) Pianist André Watts.

by producing sound. The pipes are arranged in separate groups according to their shape and material. Each group produces a full range of musical tones with one special tone quality or color. When the organist wants to bring a particular group of pipes into play, he or she simply pulls a switch, called a **stop.** The most colorful, forceful sound occurs when all the stops have been activated (thus the expression "pulling out all the stops"). The several keyboards of the organ make it possible to play several musical lines at once, each with its own timbre. There is even a keyboard for the feet!

The **harpsichord** (Fig. 3–14) was known in northern Italy as early as 1400, but it reached its heyday during the Baroque era (1600–1750). It produces sound not by means of pipes but by strings. When a key is depressed, it drives a lever upward that, in turn, forces a pick to pluck a string. The plucking creates a bright, jangling sound. Some harpsichords are equipped with two keyboards so that the player can change from one group of strings to another, each with its particular tone color and volume of sound. The harpsichord has one important shortcoming, however: The lever mechanism does not allow the performer to control the force with which the string is plucked, so each string always sounds at the same volume. (For more on the harpsichord, see page 103.)

The **piano** (Fig. 3–15) was invented in Italy in 1709, in part to remove the dynamic limitations of the harpsichord. In a piano, strings are not plucked but hit by soft hammers. A lever mechanism makes it possible for the player to regulate how hard each string is struck, thus producing softs and louds (the original piano was called the *pianoforte,* the "soft-loud"). During the lifetime of Mozart (1756–1791), the piano replaced the harpsichord as the favorite domestic musical instrument. By the nineteenth century every aspiring household had to have a piano, whether as an instrument for real musical enjoyment or as a symbol of affluence.

If the organ's familiar home is the church, where it is heard in association with religious services, the versatile piano is found almost everywhere. With equal success it can accompany a school chorus or an opera singer; it can harmonize with a rock band when in the hands of an Elton John or a Billy Joel; or it can become a powerful, yet expressive, solo instrument when played by a master such as

Vladimir Horowitz or André Watts. The harpsichord, on the other hand, is used mainly to recreate the music of the time of Johann Sebastian Bach (1685–1750).

ELECTRONIC INSTRUMENTS. In addition to these natural musical instruments—acoustical instruments as they are called—machines that produce musical sounds by electronic means have been invented in the twentieth century. The electric keyboard synthesizer has recently gained great favor among rock and jazz musicians because of the variety of sounds it can create and the ease with which it can be moved from job to job. Electronic instruments such as the keyboard synthesizer and electric organ and electric guitar, as well as the sound-processing computer, are discussed in Chapter 17.

The Orchestra

The modern symphony orchestra is one of the largest and certainly the most colorful of all musical ensembles. It originated in the seventeenth century and has continually grown in size since then. When at full strength, the symphony orchestra can include upward of one hundred performers and nearly thirty different instruments, from the high piping of the piccolo down to the rumble of the contrabassoon. A typical seating plan for an orchestra is given in Fig. 3–16. Strings are placed toward the front, and the more powerful brasses at the back.

FIGURE 3–16

Seating plan of an orchestra.

ORCHESTRAL SEATING PLAN

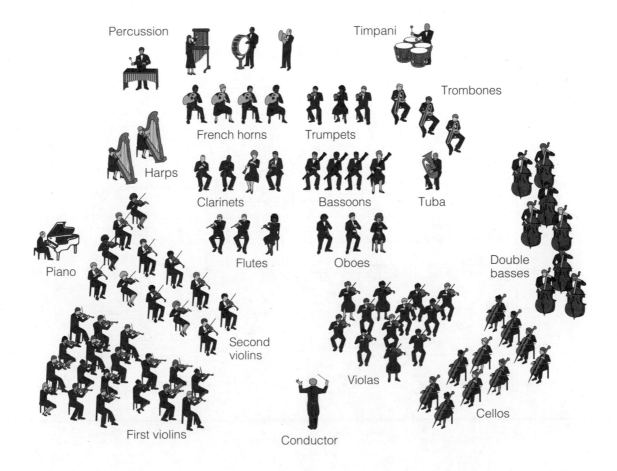

Other seating arrangements are also used, according to the composition to be played and the personal preferences of the conductor.

the conductor

Surprisingly, a separate conductor was not originally part of the orchestra. For the first two hundred years of its existence (1600–1800), the symphony was led by one of the performers, either a keyboard player or the principal first violinist. By the time of Beethoven (1770–1827), however, the group had so grown in size that it was thought necessary to have someone stand before it and lead, not only to keep the players together, but also to help draw out and elucidate the important musical ideas. The conductor follows an **orchestral score,** a composite notation of all the instrumental parts for a particular piece (Fig. 3–17).

When hearing a symphony orchestra perform, the listener's first task is to pick out the instruments that are playing the melodies, or main themes, and to differentiate them from the instruments that provide an accompaniment or play some other subordinate role. If you are fortunate enough to attend a "live" performance, the gestures of the conductor can be an aid to your listening, for he or she will usually turn to, and communicate directly with the instruments that are playing the most important musical lines (Fig. 3–18). Listening Exercise 9 gives you the chance to gain greater familiarity with the instruments of the orchestra.

FIGURE 3–17

The orchestral score of the beginning of Beethoven's Symphony No. 5, first page, with instruments listed.

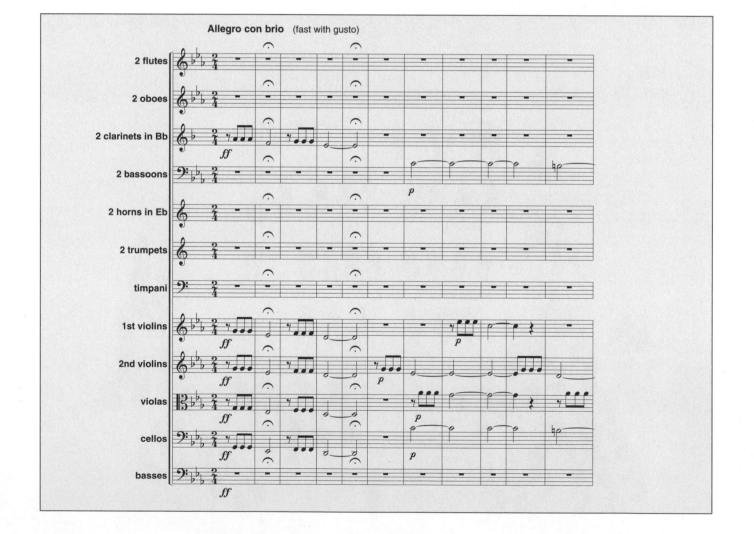

Dynamics

Dynamics in music are the various levels of volume, loud and soft, at which sounds are produced. Dynamics work together with tone colors to affect the way we hear and react to musical sound. A high note in the clarinet has one quality—shrill and harsh—when played *fortissimo* (very loud) and quite another—vague and otherworldly—when played *pianissimo* (very soft). Following are the names of the most common musical dynamics. Since they were first used by composers working in Italy, these terms are traditionally written in Italian.

Term	Musical Symbol	Definition
fortissimo	*ff*	very loud
forte	*f*	loud
mezzo forte	*mf*	moderately loud
mezzo piano	*mp*	moderately soft
piano	*p*	soft
pianissimo	*pp*	very soft

Conductor Seiji Ozawa of the Boston Symphony Orchestra. By watching the gestures of the conductor, the listener is often able to follow the principal themes as they are passed from player to player or section to section.

Dynamics sometimes change abruptly, for special effects. Most common among these quick changes is the **sforzando,** a sudden, loud attack on one note or chord. A famous *sforzando* occurs in the second movement of Joseph Haydn's "Surprise" Symphony (1792), for example, in which the composer interrupts a soft melody with a thunderous crash on a single chord (6CD 2/9; 6Tape 2B)—his intent was apparently to awaken those listeners who might have dozed off!

But changes in dynamics need not be sudden and abrupt. They can be gradual and extend over a long period of time. A gradual increase in the intensity of sound is called a crescendo, while a gradual decrease is called either a decrescendo or diminuendo.

Term	Musical symbol	Definition
crescendo		growing louder
decrescendo or *diminuendo*		growing softer

Ludwig van Beethoven was a master at writing long crescendos. The transition to the last movement of his Symphony No. 5 comes upon the listener like a great tidal wave of sound (6CD 3/8–9; 6Tape 3B). The epitome of the crescendo, as you have heard, is Ravel's *Bolero* (Intro CD [1]–Tape [A]; 6CD 1/1). It begins quietly, gains greater volume as more and more instruments are added, and ultimately, after fourteen minutes of growing intensity, crashes to a *fortissimo* conclusion.

FIGURE 3–19

Piet Mondrian's *Composition with Red, Yellow and Blue* (1939–1942) has a rather thin texture with uneven linear spacing and occasional zones of dense color.

TEXTURE

Texture in music is the density and disposition of the musical lines that make up a musical composition. To understand this better, picture in your mind a tapestry or some other type of woven material. The individual strands, or lines, can be dense or thin; colors can be bunched toward the center or spread out more or less evenly; the lines may have either a strong vertical or a horizontal thrust. Just as a weaver or painter can fabricate a particular texture—dense, heavy, light, or thin, with independent or interdependent strands—so, too, can the composer create similar effects with musical lines. *Bolero* begins with a few, well-spaced lines and hence a thin texture. As more and more instruments are added, the density of the texture increases. By the end, the texture is dense, with the density being about equal from the top instruments to the bottom ones.

Monophonic, Polyphonic, and Homophonic Textures

There are three primary textures in music—monophonic, polyphonic, and homophonic—depending on the number of musical lines and the way they relate to one another. Often we call these lines, or parts, "voices" even though they may not actually be sung.

Monophony is the easiest to hear. As the name "one sounding" indicates, there is only a single line of music, with no accompaniment. When you sing by yourself, you are creating monophonic music. The largest body of monophonic music in the West is Gregorian chant*, one-line melodies created during the Middle Ages as music for the Church (see page 70). Most Gregorian chants were intended to be sung by a group of clerics, all chanting the same pitches together—singing in **unison** as it is called. This adds richness to the otherwise sparse sound of monophonic music.

As you may suppose from the name "many sounding," **polyphony** requires two or more lines in the musical fabric. In addition, the term "polyphonic" also implies that each of the lines will be autonomous and independent. They compete equally for the listener's attention. Usually, they move against one another, and when this happens they create what is called counterpoint. ***counterpoint*** **Counterpoint** is simply the harmonious opposition of two or more independent musical lines. Because counterpoint presupposes polyphony, the terms "contrapuntal texture" and "polyphonic texture" are often used interchangeably.

What is more, there are two types of counterpoint: imitative and free. In imitative counterpoint the individual voices enter separately and the followers duplicate at least a part of what the first, or lead, voice had presented. If they ***canon*** reproduce exactly, note for note, what the first part plays or sings, then a **canon** results. Think of *Three Blind Mice, Are You Sleeping?*, or *Row, Row, Row Your Boat*, and remember how each voice enters in turn and then exactly imitates the first voice from beginning to end. These are all short canons, or rounds. Among the more famous longer canons in music is the well-known canon of Johann Pachelbel (1653–1706) that goes on for several minutes. Example 3–1 shows the beginning of a brief canon for three voices:

EXAMPLE 3–1

Are you sleep-ing, are you sleep-ing, broth-er John, *etc.*

Are you sleep-ing, are you sleep-ing, broth-er John, *etc.*

Are you sleep-ing, are you sleep-ing,

Free counterpoint is counterpoint without any sort of imitation among the voices. The voices, or lines, may begin all together or begin separately, but they go their separate ways. Much jazz improvisation is done in free counterpoint.

free counterpoint

Homophony means "same sounding." In this texture the voices, or lines, move to new pitches at roughly the same time. Homophony, then, differs from polyphony in that the strands are not independent but interdependent; they proceed in a tight, interlocking fashion. Usually, the lines form harmonious blocks of sound, called chords*, which support and draw attention to a higher voice that carries the melody. Hymns, Christmas carols, popular songs, and folk songs almost always have a homophonic texture because they consist of a simple melody and blocks of accompanying chords below. Melody plus accompaniment then—perhaps the most common musical arrangement—produces homophonic texture. As the arrows in Exs. 3–1 and 3–2 show, in polyphonic texture the musical fabric has lines with a strong linear (horizontal) thrust, whereas in homophonic texture the fabric is marked by lines that are more vertically conceived, as blocks of accompanying chords.

EXAMPLE 3–2

Are you sleep-ing, are you sleep-ing, broth - er John,

Of course, composers are not limited to just one of these three musical textures within any given work. They can change from one texture to another to add variety and contrast to their music. A monophonic solo can be saved for a particularly expressive moment, a homophonic passage may be needed to create a feeling of comfort and solidity, and a polyphonic section may be desirable to give the piece a sudden sense of movement and tension owing to the independent action of several parts. Usually, the longer the piece, the greater the number of changes. But changes of texture can come in rapid succession in short pieces as well. George Frideric Handel (1685–1759) is perhaps best known as the composer of *Messiah*, a large work for chorus and orchestra usually performed just

changing textures

before Christmas. By far the most familiar number within *Messiah* is the "Hallelujah" chorus, for which the audience traditionally rises to its feet.[†] To get the sound of the various textures securely in your ear, listen to this famous chorus. Notice how rapidly and how smoothly the composer moves back and forth among homophonic, polyphonic, and monophonic textures. The following Listening Guide makes it clear where the changes come.

LISTENING GUIDE	George Frideric Handel "Hallelujah" Chorus from *Messiah* (1741)	Intro CD (39)—Tape (B) 6CD 2/4; 6Tape 2A

0:01	"Hallelujah! Hallelujah!"—homophony
0:25	"For the Lord God Omnipotent reigneth"—monophony
0:32	"Hallelujah! Hallelujah"—homophony
0:37	"For the Lord God Omnipotent reigneth"—monophony
0:44	"Hallelujah! Hallelujah!"—homophony
0:49	"For the Lord God Omnipotent reigneth" together with "Hallelujah"—polyphony
1:16	"The Kingdom of this world is become"—homophony
1:35	"And He shall reign for ever and ever"—polyphony
1:58	"King of Kings and Lord of Lords" together with "Hallelujah"—homophony
2:39	"And He shall reign for ever and ever"—polyphony
2:51	"King of Kings and Lord of Lords" together with "Hallelujah"—homophony
3:01	"And He shall reign for ever and ever"—polyphony
3:07	"King of Kings and Lord of Lords" together with "Hallelujah"—homophony

When you have finished, turn to Listening Exercises 10 and 11, which provide additional practice in hearing musical textures.

FORM

Form in art is the purposeful organization of the artist's materials. It is present in every medium of creative expression. In architecture, sculpture, and painting, for example, the formal design imposes a shape and a definition on physical space. In poetry the meter, the rhyme, and the stanza give a sense of logic and coherence to the sounds, ideas, and images. And in music the melody, harmony, rhythm, tone color, and texture can be arranged to create a sequence of events that the composer and listener find pleasing and convincing.

the composer needs a plan

A composer needs formal principles to help in the process of selecting and arranging materials. Nothing is more frightening to a creator than absolute freedom of choice. How to begin? What to write now? What next? When and how to end? The selection of a musical form can help with these decisions by suggesting an overall shape as well as a set of operating procedures. Sometimes a composer will create a unique design because the musical material seems to develop in new and surprising ways. Ravel's *Bolero*, for example, continues to grow in the shape of an ever-enlarging wedge. But more often a composer will fall back on a time-honored form. Using a traditional form does not tell the composer what to do at every step, but it does suggest plausible paths that might be taken—paths that other composers at other times have used and with which the listener is likely to be familiar.

[†] It seems that King George II (ruled 1727–1760) stood up at this point during a performance of *Messiah* in London. If the King stood, so did everyone else; hence the tradition of the audience standing.

From the listener's standpoint, an awareness of form is perhaps the most important tool he or she can employ while listening to music. If the composer needs help in setting a broad musical plan, the listener needs formal guideposts as a means of following what the composer is trying to communicate. What has happened? Where am I? What is about to come? These questions are invariably asked, consciously or unconsciously, when hearing a piece for the first time. By working through the discussion and diagrams that follow, you will acquire a mental picture of the most commonly used musical forms. You will more easily comprehend the material that you hear, and be comfortable with it, because you will have met these forms before and now know what to expect. You may also gain satisfaction from hearing the composer deviate from your expectations by treating the traditional time-honored form in some new and surprising fashion.

the listener needs to know the plan

Creating Formal Designs: Repetition, Contrast, and Variation

How are formal designs created in music? By means of repetition, contrast, and variation. **Repetition** establishes the most obvious formal units. When a distinctive melody returns, for example, it strikes the ear as an important event. Such repeating events set forth the outlines of a musical design in the same way that a steel framework outlines and holds together the materials of a building. Repetition is essential to music, perhaps because music is the most abstract of all the arts. Instead of creating tedium or boredom, each return helps to establish weight, balance, and symmetry. Because the musical material is familiar, repetition conveys to the listener a feeling of comfort and security.

repetition

Contrast, on the other hand, takes us away from the familiar and into the unknown. A quiet melody in the strings can suddenly be followed by an insistent theme blasting from the French horns, as happens, for example, in the third movement of Beethoven's well-known Symphony No. 5 (6CD 3/8; 6Tape 3B). Contrasting melodies, rhythms, textures, and moods can be both exciting and disquieting. They are most effective when used as a foil to familiar material, to provide variety, even conflict. In many aspects of our lives we have a need to balance comfort and security with novelty and excitement. In music this human need is given expression through the juxtaposition of the familiar and the unknown—through the interplay of repeating and contrasting musical units.

contrast

Variation stands midway between repetition and contrast. The original melody returns, but it is altered in some way. For example, the tune may now be more complex, or new instruments may be added against it to create counterpoint. The listener has the satisfaction of hearing the familiar melody, yet is challenged to recognize in what way it has been changed.

variation

Needless to say, memory plays an important role in hearing musical form. In architecture, painting, and sculpture, form is taken in all at once by a single glance. But in music, as to some extent in poetry and literature, formal relationships only become obvious over the course of time. Here our memory must put the pieces together and show us the relationships. For this to happen, we must be able to recognize an exact repetition, a varied repetition, and a contrasting musical event. To help in this process, musicians have developed a simple system to visualize forms by labeling musical units with letters. The first prominent musical idea is designated **A.** Subsequent contrasting sections are each labeled **B, C, D,** and so on. If the first or any other musical unit returns in varied form,

the role of memory

then that variation is indicated by a superscript number: A^1, B^2, for example. Subdivisions of each large musical unit are shown by lowercase letters (**a, b,** etc.). How this works will become clear in the following examples.

Musical Forms

Most musical forms transcend musical epochs—they are not unique to any one period in the history of music. The following musical forms are universal as well as timeless.

STROPHIC FORM. This is the most familiar of all musical forms because our hymns, carols, folk tunes, and patriotic songs invariably make use of it. In **strophic form** the composer sets the words of the first stanza and then uses the same entire melody for all subsequent stanzas. A good example is the Welsh holiday carol *Deck the Halls*. Notice how the first phrase (**a**) of the musical unit (**A**), or stanza, is repeated.

	a	Deck the halls with boughs of holly, fa, la, la, la, etc.
A	**a**	'Tis the season to be jolly, fa, la, la, la, la, etc.
	b	Don we now our gay apparel, fa, la, la, la, la, etc.
	c	Troll the ancient Yule-tide carol, fa, la, la, la, etc.

The basic musical unit, **A,** with the subdivisions **a, a, b, c,** is then heard four more times for each of the remaining stanzas, or strophes, of text. The overall form is thus:

A	A	A	A	A
a a b c	a a b c	a a b c	a a b c	a a b c

THEME AND VARIATIONS. If, in the preceding example, the music of the first stanza (**A**) is altered in some way each time it returns, then **theme-and-variations** form is present. Additions to the melody, new chords in the supporting accompaniment, and more density in the texture are the sort of changes that might occur. The return of the basic musical unit (**A**) provides a unifying element, while the changes add variety. Theme and variations form can be visualized in the following scheme:

FIGURE 3–20

Sydney Opera House seen from Sydney harbor. There is a theme, the rising pointed arch, and many variations of it.

Statement of theme A	Variation 1 A¹	Variation 2 A²	Variation 3 A³	Variation 4 A⁴

A good example of theme-and-variations form can be found in the second movement of Joseph Haydn's String Quartet, Opus 76, No. 3. Here the composer created a theme (**A**), which was later to become the Austrian national anthem, and then wrote a set of four variations on it. (For more on this piece, see page 194).

LISTENING GUIDE

Joseph Haydn
String Quartet, Opus 76, No. 3 (1797)
Second movement

6CD 2/14; 6Tape 2B
3CD 2/12; 3Tape 2B

0:00	**A**	Theme: theme in first violin supported by homophonic accompaniment
1:19	**A¹**	Variation 1: theme in second violin
2:35	**A²**	Variation 2: theme in cello
4:04	**A³**	Variation 3: theme in viola
5:31	**A⁴**	Variation 4: theme in first violin supported by polyphonic accompaniment

---

BINARY FORM. As the name indicates, **binary form** consists of two contrasting units, **A** and **B**. In length and general shape, **A** and **B** are constructed so as to balance and complement each other. Variety is usually introduced in **B** by means of a dissimilar mood, key*, or melody. Sometimes in binary form, both **A** and **B** are immediately repeated, note for note. Musicians indicate exact repeats by means of the following sign: ‖: :‖. Thus, when binary form appears as ‖:A:‖ ‖:B:‖ it is performed **AABB.**

George Frideric Handel's Hornpipe from his *Water Music* (1717) is a jaunty country dance in binary form. There are no repeats, and hence the form is simply **AB.** The beginning of **B** is easy to hear because the melody jumps to a high range and the texture is suddenly thinner so the music sounds quieter. Because Handel's Hornpipe is very short—it lasts only forty seconds—he required that it be performed three times: On our recording it is played first by strings alone, then by woodwinds and percussion, and finally by all these instruments together. Therefore, in this example you will hear the same dance in binary form (**AB**) played three times, each with a different orchestration.

LISTENING GUIDE

George Frideric Handel
Hornpipe from *Water Music* (1717)

Intro CD (33)—Tape (A)

First playing (strings alone)
| 0:00 | **A** section |
| 0:18 | Sudden *piano* signals beginning of the **B** section |

Second playing (woodwinds and percussion)
| 0:41 | **A** section |
| 0:58 | Sudden *piano* signals beginning of the **B** section |

Third playing (strings, woodwinds, and percussion together)
| 1:19 | **A** section |
| 1:37 | Sudden *piano* signals beginning of the **B** section |

FIGURES 3–21 AND 3–22

(left) Barbara Hepworth, *Two Figures (Menhirs)* (1964). Here the two units of sculpture are distinctly different, yet mutually harmonious. This is the essence of binary form. (right) The cathedral of Salzburg, Austria, where Mozart and his father frequently performed during the 1760s and 1770s. It clearly reflects a ternary, or **ABA,** form.

TERNARY FORM. **Ternary form** in music is even more common than binary. It consists of three sections. The second is a contrasting unit, and the third is a repeat of the first—hence the formal pattern is **ABA**. As we will see later (page 166), ternary form has appeared at many different times in the history of music. It is an especially satisfying arrangement because it is simple yet rounded and complete. It, too, sometimes uses musical repeats, first of the **A** section, then of both **B** and **A** together (‖: A :‖ ‖: B A :‖).

Listen now to the opening Minuet and Trio from Handel's *Water Music*. The Minuet (**A**) is in a major key and has a sprightly melody consisting of two phrases, here introduced in turn by the French horns and the trumpets. The Trio (**B**) is in a contrasting minor key and is played softly by the strings alone. The return of the Minuet completes the ternary form: **ABA.**

LISTENING GUIDE	George Frideric Handel Minuet and Trio from *Water Music* (1717)	Intro CD (32)—Tape (A)

0:00	French horns play phrase 1	
0:13	Trumpets play phrase 2	**A**
0:29	Phase 1 heard twice more	
0:55	Phrase 2 heard twice more	
1:28	Shift to minor key and soft dynamics; only strings play	**B**
2:19	Full orchestra returns with phrases 1 and 2	**A**

RONDO FORM. **Rondo form** is almost as old as music itself. It uses a simple principle: A refrain alternates with contrasting music. Perhaps because of this simplicity, rondo form has been favored by musicians of every age—Medieval songsters, Classical symphonists like Mozart and Haydn, and even contemporary rock stars like Elton John and Sting. Although the principle of a recurring refrain is a constant, composers have written rondos in several different formal patterns, including the following ones:

ABABA   ABACA   ABACABA

You may already be familiar with a rondo composed by Jean-Joseph Mouret (1682–1738), for it is used as the theme music for "Masterpiece Theater" on PBS-TV. Mouret was a composer at the French court during the reign of Louis XV (1715–1774), and his well-known *Rondeau* typifies the ceremonial splendor of the royal household during the Baroque era (1600–1750). Here the refrain (**A**), played by full orchestra with brilliant trumpets and drums, alternates with two contrasting ideas (**B** and **C**) to form a neatly symmetrical pattern. The divisions between sections are clearly audible because each unit is played by a distinctive group of instruments. As you listen to Mouret's rondo, perhaps you will agree that a simple, effective formal principle is at work here.

FIGURE 3–23

The château of Chambord, France, has a formal design equivalent to **ABACABA** structure, a pattern often encountered in music in the rondo.

LISTENING GUIDE		Jean-Joseph Mouret *Rondeau* from *Suite de symphonies* (1729)	6CD 2/5; 6 Tape 2A 3CD 2/8; 3 Tape 2A

0:00	**A**	Refrain played by full orchestra, including trumpets and drums, and then repeated (at 0:12)
0:24	**B**	Quieter contrasting section played by organ
0:37	**A**	Refrain returns but without repeat
0:50	**C**	New contrasting section played by organ
1:21	**A**	Refrain returns and is repeated (at 1:33)

Although these examples of musical form are all short, they clearly show that an internal logic and cohesiveness is at work in each piece. More complex musical forms, of course, do exist, and these give rise to longer, more complex compositions. Sonata–allegro form and fugal form are the principal ones. These we will discuss when we come to the music of the Baroque and Classical periods. In addition, there are also free musical forms, such as the fantasy and the prelude, which give free reign to the composer's imagination without tight formal restraints. These, too, we will meet in good time.

LISTENING EXERCISES

9 Instruments of the Orchestra
Benjamin Britten, *The Young Person's Guide to the Orchestra* (1946)

On your Introduction to Listening CD (track 34)—Tape (side B), you will find a performance of Benjamin Britten's *The Young Person's Guide to the Orchestra*. Britten (1913–1976) composed this piece in 1946, though he used as his main theme a melody written in 1695 by another English composer, Henry Purcell (1659–1695). *The Young Person's Guide* was originally written to provide musical examples for a film entitled *The Instruments of the Orchestra*. Britten's intent was to demonstrate first the sounds of the four instrumental families of the orchestra and then the distinctive colors of the individual instruments.

The work begins with the full orchestra playing the theme. This is followed by a presentation of the same theme, in turn, by the woodwind family alone, by the brasses, by the strings (including harp), and finally by the percussion (1–4). After the percussion holds forth, the full orchestra returns with a sweeping statement of the theme (5).

Next comes a series of thirteen variations of the theme (6–18), each of which exposes the special tone colors of one or two instruments. We begin with the flutes (6) and work our way to the percussion (18).

Finally, *The Young Person's Guide* ends with all of the instruments of the orchestra engaged in a fugue. We discuss the fugue at length in Chapter 7. For now, notice simply that the texture of the fugue is polyphonic, meaning that there are several quickly moving lines and they proceed independently of one another.

Your task is to fill in the blanks by indicating the time at which each musical event occurs, specifically, the minute and second at which the various families of instruments or individual instruments enter.

Introduction to the theme:

	0:00	Full orchestra
1.	_____	Woodwinds
2.	_____	Brass
3.	_____	Strings (with harp)
4.	_____	Percussion
5.	_____	Full orchestra

Short transition (string tremolo and harp)

Variations on the theme:

6.	1:56	Flutes and piccolo (with harp accompaniment)
7.	_____	Oboes (with string accompaniment)
8.	_____	Clarinets (with tuba accompaniment)

9. _____ Bassoons (with string accompaniment)

10. 5:00 Violins sweep forward

11. _____ Violas play more quietly (with brass and woodwind accompaniment)

12. _____ Cellos offer lovely melody (with clarinet/string accompaniment)

13. _____ Double basses play comical melody (with light woodwind and percussion accompaniment)

14. _____ Harp solo (with string tremolo accompaniment)

15. _____ French horns (with string and harp accompaniment)

16. _____ Trumpets play a light gallop

17. _____ Trombones blast forth with tuba down below (with woodwind accompaniment)

18. _____ Percussion, beginning with the timpani, and then cymbals, snare drum, xylophone, and so on; ends with xylophone solo

Fugue based on the theme:

13:39 (very fast) Fugue begins with piccolo and flutes, followed by clarinets, bassoons, violins, violas, cellos, double basses, harp, horns, trumpets, trombones, and tuba

---

10 Hearing Musical Textures

This exercise asks you to become familiar with the three basic textures of music: monophonic, polyphonic, and homophonic. On your Introduction to Listening CD (tracks 24–31)—Tape (side A), you have eight excerpts that represent these various textures. Monophonic texture, you will find, is easy to hear because it has only one line of music. More difficult is to differentiate between polyphonic texture and homophonic texture. Polyphonic texture embodies many active, independent lines. Homophonic texture, on the other hand, usually uses blocks of chords that accompany and support a single melody. Identify the texture of each of the excerpts in the spaces.

1. _____ (Saint-Säens, *Carnival of the Animals*)
2. _____ (Schubert, Overture to *Rosamunde*)
3. _____ (Bach, Fugue, *The Well-Tempered Clavier*, Book I)
4. _____ (Mahler, Symphony No. 5, first movement)
5. _____ (Strauss, *Blue Danube Waltz*)
6. _____ (Beethoven, Piano Sonata, Opus 110)
7. _____ (Brahms, Rhapsody for Piano, Opus 119)
8. _____ (Beethoven, Symphony No. 8, fourth movement)

---

11 Hearing Musical Textures

This assignment asks you to listen to three different pieces performed by three different musical forces. All are found on your Listening CDs or tapes. The following questions will help you to focus on the texture of each.

A. Let's return for a moment to Ravel's *Bolero* (Intro CD[1]—Tape [A]; 6CD 1/1). Instead of commencing at the beginning, this time start the music somewhere toward the end, perhaps two or three minutes from the end.
   1. Is Ravel's *Bolero* performed by one instrument or many? _____
   2. Does the texture involve just one melody at a time and an accompaniment or many different melodies played simultaneously? _____
   3. How would you describe this melody-plus-accompaniment texture of *Bolero:* monophonic, homophonic, or polyphonic? _____

B. Now find the Organ Fugue in G minor of Baroque composer Johann Sebastian Bach (6CD 2/2; 6Tape 2A; 3CD 2/7; 3 Tape 2A). Listen to just the first minute of the music. Can you hear four musical lines or voices enter during this opening passage (at 0:00, 0:18, 0:42, and 1:00)?
   1. Are they all being played on one instrument or several? _____
   2. As the individual lines, or voices, enter, does each come in with the same melody or does each enter with a new and different tune? _____
   3. How would you characterize the texture of this piece: monophonic, homophonic, or polyphonic? _____
   4. Is this an example of imitative or nonimitative counterpoint? _____

C. Finally, turn to 6CD 6/19, or 6Tape 6B, and listen to the opening (the first forty-seven seconds, to be precise) of Louis Armstrong's rendition of *Droppin' Shucks.* This is a fine example of classic New Orleans–style jazz. Can you hear the three principal melodic instruments: trumpet, trombone, and clarinet?
   1. Are the three melodic instruments all playing the same melody, or are they playing different-sounding lines? _____
   2. How would you characterize the texture of this piece: monophonic, homophonic, or polyphonic? _____
   3. Is this imitative or nonimitative counterpoint? _____

(Listening Exercise 32, centering on Frédéric Chopin's "Military" Polonaise, provides additional drill in hearing musical form, dynamics, tempo, meter, and texture.)

KEY WORDS

binary form	mute	ternary form
canon	orchestral score	texture
color	*piano*	theme and variations
counterpoint	*pianissimo*	timbre
forte	pizzicato	tremolo
fortissimo	polyphony	vibrato
glissando	rondo form	unison
homophony	*sforzando*	
monophony	strophic form	

HEARING MUSICAL STYLES

One of the pleasures of learning more about music is being able to evaluate and appreciate what we hear. But before we can make value judgments about a musical composition and begin to enjoy its beauty, we must have a sense of what it is. When we hear an unknown work for the first time, we try to make an educated guess, however subconsciously, to identify the period of the music and perhaps the composer. Is it Baroque music or Romantic music, New Orleans–style jazz or bebop, Bach or Beethoven? Identifying the period of a composition, and even the composer, is the first step toward true musical enjoyment. This recognition is mainly an exercise in hearing musical style. But what is musical style?

Style in music is the surface sound produced by the inner action of the elements of music: melody, rhythm, harmony, color, texture, and form. It is the shape of the melody, the arrangement of the rhythm, the choice of the harmony, the disposition of the texture, the treatment of form, and the use of instrumental color that, taken in sum, determine musical style. Each composer, like each painter and poet, has a personal style, one that makes his or her music different from all the rest. Take a work by Mozart (1756–1791), for example. A trained listener will recognize it as a piece from the Classical period (1750–1820) because of its generally symmetrical melodies, light texture, and dynamic ebb and flow. A truly experienced ear will identify Mozart as the composer, perhaps by recognizing the sudden shifts to minor keys, the intensely chromatic melodies, or the colorful writing for bassoon or clarinet—all hallmarks of Mozart's musical style.

each composer possesses a personal style

Each period in the history of music has a musical style, too. That is to say, the music of one epoch will possess qualities common to much other music of that same time. A common set of musical practices and procedures is at work. Many symphonies* of the Romantic period (1820–1900), for example, exhibit long, vocally inspired melodies, chromatic* harmonies, languid rhythms, and uniformly dense orchestral textures. A *sinfonia** from the late Baroque period (1710–1750), on the other hand, is more likely to possess an instrumentally inspired melody, diatonic* harmonies, driving rhythms, and a texture that is heavy on both top and bottom but thin in the middle.

each historical period has a style

As you might suspect, the boundaries between any two periods in the history of music are arbitrarily drawn. Musical styles do not change overnight; usually they evolve and overlap. Composers can stand midway between periods. For example, Guillaume Dufay (ca. 1400–1474) is a composer of the Middle Ages in his use of texture, but of the Renaissance in regard to his harmonies. Ludwig van Beethoven (1770–1827) straddles the Classical and Romantic periods, being somewhat conservative in his choice of harmonies but radically progressive in his use of form and rhythm. Despite such contradictions, historians of music, like historians of art, find it useful to discuss style in terms of historical periods. It makes it possible to conceptualize and speak about these arts in a more convenient way. Here are the stylistic periods that are discussed in the following chapters:

Middle Ages: 400–1475   Classical: 1750–1820
Renaissance: 1475–1600   Romantic: 1820–1900
Early Baroque: 1600–1710   Impressionist: 1880–1920
Late Baroque: 1710–1750   Twentieth Century: 1900–present

Check List of Musical Style by Periods

Middle Ages: 400–1475

Representative composers: Hildegard of Bingen, Leoninus, Perotinus, Machaut, Countess of Dia, Dufay, Binchois

Principal genres: Gregorian chant, polyphonic Mass, *troubadour* and *trouvère* songs, secular polyphonic chanson, instrumental dance

Melody:	Moves mostly by step within a narrow range; uses diatonic and not chromatic notes of the scale
Harmony:	Most surviving medieval music is monophonic Gregorian chant or monophonic *troubadour* and *trouvère* songs—hence there is no harmony
	Medieval polyphony (Mass, motet, and chanson) has dissonant phrases ending with open, hollow-sounding chords
Rhythm:	Gregorian chant as well as *troubadour* and *trouvère* songs sung mainly in notes of equal value without clearly marked rhythms; medieval polyphony is composed mostly in triple meter and uses repeating rhythmic patterns
Color:	Mainly vocal sounds (choir or soloists); little instrumental music survives
Texture:	Mostly monophonic—Gregorian chant as well as *troubadour* and *trouvère* songs are monophonic melodies
	Medieval polyphony (two, three, or four independent lines) is mainly contrapuntal
Form:	Strophic form of *troubadour* and *trouvère* songs; ternary form of the Kyrie; rondo form of the French *rondeau*

Renaissance: 1475–1600

Melody: Mainly stepwise motion within a moderately narrow range; still mainly diatonic, but some intense chromaticism found in madrigals from end of period

Harmony: More careful use of dissonance than in the Middle Ages as the triad, a consonant chord, becomes the basic building block of harmony

Rhythm: Duple meter is now as common as triple meter; rhythm in sacred vocal music (Mass and motet) is relaxed and without strong downbeats; rhythm in secular vocal music (chanson and madrigal) and in instrumental dances is usually lively and catchy, with frequent use of syncopation

Color: Although more music for instruments alone has survived, the predominant sound remains that of unaccompanied vocal music, whether for soloists or for choir

Texture: Contrapuntal, polyphonic texture for four or five vocal lines is heard throughout Mass, motet, and madrigal, though occasional passages of chordal homophonic texture are inserted for variety

Form: Strict musical forms are not often used; most Masses, motets, madrigals, chansons, and instrumental dances are through-composed—have no musical repetitions and hence no standard formal plan

Representative composers: Desprez, Palestrina, Byrd, Lasso, Weelkes, Dowland

Principal genres: sacred Mass and motet, secular chanson and madrigal, instrumental dance

Early Baroque: 1600–1710

Melody: Less stepwise movement, larger leaps, wider range, and more chromaticism reflect influence of virtuosic solo singing; melodic patterns idiomatic to particular musical instruments emerge; introduction of melodic sequence

Harmony: Stable, diatonic chords played by *basso continuo* support melody; clearly defined chord progressions begin to develop; tonality reduced to major and minor keys

Rhythm: Relaxed, flexible rhythms of the Renaissance transformed into regularly repeating, driving rhythms

Color: Musical timbre becomes enormously varied as traditional instruments are perfected (e.g., harpsichord, violin, and oboe) and new combinations of voices and instruments are explored; symphony orchestra begins to take shape; sudden shifts in dynamics (terraced dynamics) reflect dramatic quality of Baroque music

Texture: Chordal, homophonic texture predominates; top and bottom lines are the strongest as *basso continuo* creates a powerful bass to support the melody above

Form: Arias and instrumental works often make use of *basso ostinato* procedure; ritornello form emerges in the concerto grosso; binary form regulates most movements of the sonata and orchestral suite

Representative composers: Gabrieli, Monteverdi, Purcell, Corelli, Vivaldi

Principal genres: polychoral motet, cantata, opera, sonata, concerto grosso, solo concerto, orchestral suite

Late Baroque: 1710–1750

Representative composers: Bach, Handel, Telemann, Vivaldi

Principal genres: cantata, opera, oratorio, sonata, orchestral suite, concerto grosso, prelude and fugue

Melody:	Grows longer, more expansive, and more asymmetrical; idiomatic instrumental style influences vocal melodies
Harmony:	Functional chord progressions govern harmonic movement—harmony moves purposefully from one chord to the next; *basso continuo* continues to provide strong bass
Rhythm:	Exciting, driving, energized rhythms propel music forward with vigor; "walking" bass creates feeling of rhythmic regularity
Color:	Instruments reign supreme; instrumental sounds, especially of violin, harpsichord, and organ, set musical tone for the era; one tone color used throughout a movement or large section of movement
Texture:	Homophonic texture remains important, but polyphonic texture reemerges because of growing importance of the contrapuntal fugue
Form:	Binary form in sonatas and orchestral suites; *da capo* aria (ternary) form in arias; fugal procedure used in fugue

Classical: 1750–1820

Representative composers: Mozart, Haydn, Beethoven

Principal genres: symphony, sonata, string quartet, solo concerto, opera

Melody:	Short, balanced phrases create tuneful melodies; melody more influenced by vocal than instrumental style; frequent cadences produce light, airy feeling
Harmony:	The rate at which chords change (harmonic rhythm) varies dramatically, creating a dynamic flux and flow; simple chordal harmonies made more active by "Alberti" bass
Rhythm:	Departs from regular, driving patterns of Baroque era to become more stop and go; greater rhythmic variety within a single movement
Color:	Orchestra grows larger; woodwind section of two flutes, oboes, clarinets, and bassoons becomes typical; piano replaces harpsichord as principal keyboard instrument
Texture:	Mostly homophonic; thin bass and middle range, hence light and transparent; passages in contrapuntal style appear sparingly and mainly for contrast
Form:	A few standard forms regulate much of Classical music: sonata–allegro, theme and variations, rondo, ternary (for minuets and trios), and double exposition (for solo concerto)

Representative composers: Beethoven, Schubert, Berlioz, Mendelssohn, Robert Schumann, Clara Schumann, Chopin, Liszt, Verdi, Wagner, Brahms, Dvořák, Tchaikovsky, Musorgsky, Mahler

Romantic: 1820–1900

Melody:	Long, singable lines with powerful climaxes and chromatic inflections for expressiveness

Harmony: Greater use of chromaticism makes the harmony richer and more colorful; sudden shifts to remote chords for expressive purposes; more dissonance to convey feeling of anxiety and longing

Rhythm: Rhythms are flexible, often languid, and therefore meter is sometimes not clearly articulated

Color: The orchestra becomes enormous, reaching upward of one hundred performers: trombone, tuba, contrabassoon, piccolo, and English horn added to the ensemble; experiments with new playing techniques for special effects; dynamics vary widely to create different levels of expression; piano becomes larger and more powerful

Texture: Predominantly homophonic but dense and rich because of larger orchestra; sustaining pedal on the piano also adds to density

Form: No new forms created, rather traditional forms (strophic, sonata-allegro, and theme and variations, for example) used and extended in length; traditional forms also applied to new genres such as *Lied*, symphonic poem, and orchestral song

Principal genres: symphony, program symphony, symphonic poem, concert overture, opera, *Lied*, orchestral song, solo concerto, character piece for piano, ballet music

Impressionist: 1880–1920

Melody: Varies from short dabs of sound to long, free-flowing lines; chromatic scale, whole-tone scale, and pentatonic scale often replace usual major and minor scales

Harmony: Primarily homophonic; triad is extended to form seventh chords and ninth chords, and these frequently move in parallel motion

Rhythm: Usually free and flexible with irregular accents, making it sometimes difficult to determine the meter; rhythmic ostinatos used to give feeling of stasis rather than movement

Color: More emphasis on woodwinds and brass and less on the violins as primary carriers of melody; more soloistic writing to show that the color of the instrument is as important as the melody line it plays

Texture: Can vary from thin and airy to heavy and dense; sustaining pedal of the piano often used to create a wash of sound

Form: Traditional forms involving clear-cut repetitions rarely used; composers try to develop a form unique and particular to each new musical work

Representative composers: Debussy, Ravel, Fauré

Principal genres: symphonic poem, string quartet, orchestral song, opera, character piece for piano

Twentieth Century: 1900–present

Melody: Wide-ranging disjunct lines, often chromatic and dissonant, angularity accentuated by use of octave displacement

Harmony: Highly dissonant; dissonance no longer must move to consonance but may move to another dissonance

Representative composers: Stravinsky, Schoenberg, Berg, Webern, Bartók, Varèse, Ives, Cage, Prokofiev, Copland, Zwilich, Adams

Principal genres: symphony, solo concerto, string quartet, opera, ballet music, electronic music, chance music

Rhythm: Vigorous, energetic rhythms; conflicting simultaneous meters (poly-meters) and rhythms (polyrhythms) make for temporal complexity

Color: Color becomes an agent of form and beauty in and by itself; composers seek new sounds from traditional, acoustical instruments, from electronic instruments and computers, and from noises in the environment

Texture: As varied and individual as the men and women composing music

Form: A range of extremes: sonata–allegro, rondo, theme and variations benefit from a Neo-classical revival; twelve-tone procedure allows for an almost mathematical formal control; yet chance music permits random happenings and noises from the environment to shape a musical work

MEDIEVAL MUSIC

4

Historians use the term "Middle Ages" as a catchall phrase to refer to the thousand years of history between the fall of the Roman Empire (late 400s) and the age of reawakening and discovery, exemplified by the voyages of Christopher Columbus (late 1400s). It was a period of triumphs and tragedies, of soaring cathedrals and murderous plagues, of sublime spirituality and abject poverty, of knightly chivalry and barbarous warfare. Seen from our modern perspective, the medieval period appears as a vast chronological expanse whose bleak vista is only occasionally broken by the beauty of its churches, paintings, poems, and music.

MUSIC IN THE MONASTERY

There were many kinds of music in the Middle Ages: songs for the knights as they rode into battle, songs for the men in the fields and the women around the hearth, songs and dances for the nobles in their castles, and chants for the priests as they celebrated the Christian service in the monasteries and cathedrals. Unfortunately, most of this music, and virtually all of it emanating from the common folk, is now lost because it was never written down. Only the music of the Church is preserved in any significant amount, because at that time only the men of the Church, and to a lesser degree the nuns, were educated. Even the nobility was more or less illiterate. The reading and copying of texts was the private preserve of the rural monasteries and, somewhat later, the urban cathedrals. The monks were encouraged to read and write as a means of becoming more familiar with the scriptures, and it was they who devised a system to notate and copy music. In this way, the music of the Church could be spread to other monastic communities and taught to succeeding generations of novices.

Life was rigorous in a medieval monastery. The founder of the principal monastic order, St. Benedict (died ca. 547), prescribed a code of conduct, or rule, for his followers. The Benedictines rose at about four o'clock in the morning for the night office (matins), at which they sang psalms and read scripture. After a break "for the necessities of nature" the brethren returned at daybreak to sing another service in praise of the Lord. Thereafter, the monks dispersed to farm and otherwise attend to their lands, reuniting again at seven other times during the day to sing and to pray, and to eat two communal meals. The high point of these services was the Mass, celebrated about nine o'clock in the morning, which, through the ritual act of communion (see page 75), commemorated Christ's sacrifice.

GREGORIAN CHANT

The music sung daily at the eight monastic hours of prayer and at Mass was what we today call Gregorian chant, named in honor of Pope Gregory the Great (540?–604). Ironically, Gregory wrote little, if any, of this music. Being more a church administrator than musician, he merely decreed that certain chants should be sung on certain days of the liturgical year. Melodies for the Christian service had, of course, existed since the time of the apostles, some taken over directly from the Jewish Temple. What we now call **Gregorian chant** (also called **plainsong**) is really a large body of unaccompanied vocal music, setting Latin texts, composed for the Western Church over the course of fifteen centuries, from the time of the earliest Fathers to the Council of Trent (1545–1563), which brought sweeping reforms to the Church.

chant composed during fifteen centuries

Gregorian chant is like no other music. It has a timeless, otherworldly quality that arises, no doubt, because Gregorian chant has neither meter nor regular rhythms. True, some notes are longer or shorter than others, but they do not recur in obvious patterns that would allow us to clap our hands or tap our feet. This is music intended to encourage pious reflection, not cavorting. It is free of tension and drama. All voices sing together in unison*. Thus all Gregorian chant is considered monophony*, or music for one line. There is no instrumental accompaniment, nor, as a rule, are men's and women's voices mixed when performing chant. Finally, Gregorian chant does not use time as a dimension in which to set up contrasts. Any contrast that does occur is of the mildest sort. Sometimes a soloist will alternate with a full choir. Occasionally, a passage of **syllabic singing** (only one or two notes for each syllable of text) will give way to **melismatic singing** (many notes sung to just one syllable), as in Ex. 4–1, from Hildegard of Bingen's *O Greenest Branch*.

all chant is monophonic music

EXAMPLE 4–1

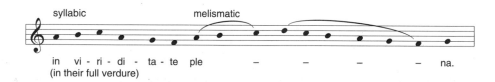

syllabic   melismatic

in vi - ri - di - ta - te ple   —   —   —   — na.
(in their full verdure)

the peace and serenity of chant

The overall effect of Gregorian chant is thus one of endless peace and serenity. Through chant, the receptive listener can gradually disengage from the anxieties and tensions of the present world.

THE GREGORIAN CHANT OF HILDEGARD OF BINGEN (1098–1171)
We know the names of only a few of the composers of Gregorian chant. And what we know of their lives suggests that they thought of themselves not so much as creators or composers, but as conduits for the voice of God—vessels through which the divine message might be brought to those here on earth (Fig.

4–1). One of the most remarkable contributors to the repertoire of Gregorian chant was Abbess Hildegard of Bingen (1098–1171), from whose pen we have received seventy-seven chants. Hildegard was born of noble parents and raised by a group of nuns attached to a Benedictine monastery situated a few miles west of the Rhine River near Mainz, Germany. In the course of time, she manifested her extraordinary intellect and imagination as a playwright, poet, musician, naturalist, pharmacologist, and visionary. During intense religious experiences, she saw images such as the breath of Satan in the guise of a serpent, the fiery descent of the Holy Spirit, and the blood of Christ streaming in the heavens. These images she transferred to poetry, which was set to music as liturgical chant—Gregorian chant. Her song to the Virgin Mary, *O viridissima virga* (*O Greenest Branch*, Ex. 4–2), vividly depicts Mary as the most verdant branch of the tree of Jesse through whom the heat of the sun radiates like the aroma of balm. The joyful Mary brings new life to all flora and fauna of the earth.

Hildegard's *O Greenest Branch* possesses many qualities typical of Gregorian chant. It gravitates around a tonal center—here, the pitch G. Notice in the first stanza (Ex. 4–2) how the music starts on G, works up a fifth to the pitch D and then down an octave to the D below, finally returning to the initial G. Notice also how *O Greenest Branch* is a predominantly stepwise melody, one without large leaps. It also avoids chromatic* twists—added sharps and flats—that might make the chant more difficult to perform. This was, after all, choral music to be sung by the full community of monks or nuns, so it had to be simple and direct. In the case of *O Greenest Branch*, we have a chant intended to be sung at Mass. (It is a Sequentia, the sixth musical portion of the Mass—see page 75.) Finally, *O Greenest Branch* was conceived without rhythm or meter. The notes are generally of one basic value, something close to our eighth note in length. The unaccompanied, monophonic line and the absence of rhythmic drive allow a restful, contemplative mood to develop. The music is meant to float unfettered as it bears the transcendent spirit aloft.

Hildegard of Bingen

FIGURE 4–1
A twelfth-century illumination depicting Hildegard of Bingen receiving divine inspiration, perhaps a vision or a chant, directly from the heavens. To the right a monk peeks in on her in amazement.

EXAMPLE 4–2: Hildegard of Bingen, *O Greenest Branch*

LISTENING GUIDE

Hildegard of Bingen
Gregorian chant, *O Greenest Branch* (ca. 1150)

6CD 1/2; 6Tape 1A
3CD 2/1; 3Tape 2A

Stanza 1

0:00   O viridissima virga, ave
quae in ventoso flabro sciscitationis
sanctorum prodisti.

Hail, o greenest branch
who sprang forth in the airy breeze
of the prayers of the saints.

Continued on next page

Chant at the Top of the Charts

In recent years, Gregorian chant has become all the rage, adored by lovers of classical and popular music alike. The excitement began in 1994 with the release, appropriately enough by Angel Records, of the CD "Chant," which sold one million copies within the first two months of its appearance. Other recordings have followed suit, including "Vision," a reworking (with saxophones!) of seventeen Gregorian chants by Hildegard of Bingen. The new-found popularity of chant, our oldest-known music, is due, ironically, to the stylistic similarity it bears to New Age music. Both are "non-confrontational," in that smooth, uniform, rhythmically fluid sounds predominate. Perhaps Hildegard and her sister clerics would be surprised to see her religious songs dramatized as music videos on MTV. On the other hand, a

medieval visionary who had already seen "the breath of Satan in the guise of the serpent" might not find much of surprise in contemporary music videos.

0:27	Cum venit tempus, quod tu floruisti, in ramis tuis, ave, ave sit tibi, quia calor solis in te sudavit sicut odor balsami.	**Stanza 2** So the time has come that you flourished in your boughs, hail, hail to you, because the heat of the sun radiated in you like the aroma of balm.
1:01	Nam in te floruit pulcher flos qui odorem dedit omnibus aromatibus quae arida erant.	**Stanza 3** For in you bloomed the beautiful flower which scented all parched perfumes.
1:28	Et illa apparuerunt omnia in viriditate plena.	**Stanza 4** And all things have been manifested in their full verdure.
1:46	Unde celi dederunt rorem super gramen et omnis terra leta facta est, quoniam viscera ipsius frumentum protulerunt et quoniam volucres celi nidos in ipsa habuerunt.	**Stanza 5** Whence the skies set down dew on the pasture, and all the earth was made more joyful because her womb produced grain, and because the birds of Heaven built their nests in her.
2:27	Deinde facta est esca hominibus et gaudium magnum epulantium; inde, o suavis virgo, in te non deficit ullum gaudium.	**Stanza 6** Then the harvest was made ready for Man, and a great rejoicing of banqueters, because in you, o sweet Virgin, no joy is lacking.
2:59	Hec omnia Eva contempsit. Nunc autem laus sit altissimo.	**Stanza 7** All these things Eve rejected. Now let there be praise to you in the Highest.

(Listening Exercise 12)

MUSIC IN THE CATHEDRAL

If the monastery was primarily a rural establishment, one of solitude and spiritual contemplation, the cathedral was an urban institution. Every cathedral served as the "home church" of a bishop, the spiritual leader of the people, and only in a city could a bishop minister effectively to a flock of any size. During the twelfth and thirteenth centuries, the population of the urban centers of Europe—Milan, Paris, and London, among others—grew significantly, owing to a healthy revival of trade and commerce. Much of the commercial wealth that flowed to the cities was channeled toward the construction of splendid new churches that served not only as houses of worship but also as civic auditoriums. So substantial was this building campaign that the period 1150–1350 is often called "the Age of the Cathedrals." In these years, the great urban cathedrals of England, France, Italy, and Germany rose above the city skyline; many of them are still visible today. Most were constructed in what we call the Gothic style, with pointed arches, high ceiling vaults, supporting buttresses, and richly colored stained glass.

Gothic architecture began in France and radiated in all directions to foreign lands, even to the Christian-held territories of the Near East. In a similar way, France was the wellspring of other intellectual and artistic developments at this time. Paris, which by the end of the thirteenth century counted eighty thousand inhabitants, had become the leading university town in Europe for the study of the arts and theology. Young clerical scholars from distant countries flocked to the Parisian schools, and when they returned to their native lands they took with them the teachings of philosophers like Peter Abelard (1079–1142) and Thomas Aquinas (1225?–1274) and also the music they had heard at the cathedral of Notre Dame (Our Lady) of Paris (Fig. 4–2).

Paris, an intellectual center

Notre Dame of Paris

Notre Dame of Paris was begun in the 1160s, yet was not completed until more than a hundred years later. Throughout this period the cathedral was blessed with a succession of churchmen who were not only theologians and philosophers but poets and musicians as well. Foremost among these were Master Leoninus (fl. 1169–1201) and Master Perotinus, called the Great (fl. 1198–1236). Leoninus wrote a great book of religious music (*Magnus liber organi*) to adorn the Gregorian chant sung at Notre Dame on high feasts. Perotinus revised the book of Leoninus and also composed many additional pieces of his own.

What is new about this Gothic church music is that it is written in polyphony* (two or more voices, or lines, sounding simultaneously) and not merely monophonic (one-voice) Gregorian chant. In truth, earlier church musicians had attempted to enhance the sound of the plainsong of the Church by adding another voice to it, but these efforts often required the new voice to move in exact parallel motion, usually at the interval of a fourth, a fifth, or an octave, with the preexisting chant. Leoninus, however, seized the opportunity to create an autonomous second voice, one that did not merely duplicate and amplify the plainsong but that complemented and graced it. Indeed, the added voice became the center of attention itself. In this musical development, we see an early instance of an artistic spirit breaking free of the constraints of the ancient authority of the Church.

LEONINUS: ORGANUM *VIDERUNT OMNES*

The expressive freedom Leoninus imparted to the new voice can be seen in his setting of the Gregorian chant *Viderunt omnes* for Mass on Christmas Day. By adding his own musical line above the chant, Leoninus created a two-voice

FIGURE 4–2

The cathedral of Notre Dame of Paris, begun ca. 1160, was one of the first to be built in the new Gothic style of architecture.

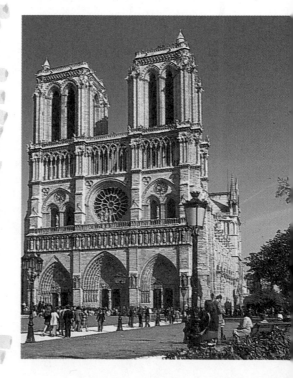

FIGURE 4–3

A thirteenth-century manuscript preserving Leoninus's organum for Christmas, *Viderunt omnes*. Leoninus's newly created voice is on each of the upper four-line staffs, while the slower-moving Gregorian chant, with the text below, is on each of the lower staffs.

organum, the name given to early church polyphony. The old chant is strung out in the lower voice and Leoninus's newly created line is on top. Soloists were assigned to the organum. Yet they sang in this new polyphonic style only for the first two words of the chant, "Viderunt omnes," which are greatly extended because of the addition of the new voice. Thereafter, the full clerical choir entered to continue and complete the remaining music in monophonic Gregorian chant. Try listening to this piece twice, first as it is given in the nearby Listening Guide, which shows the Gregorian chant in full below and a graphic indication of Leoninus's added part above. Then listen again, now trying to follow both lines of the organum as they appear in an original thirteenth-century manuscript from Paris (Fig. 4–3). As you can see in the manuscript, Leoninus's newly created upper voice undulates and even cascades in a virtuosic way as the lower voice holds the chant in long notes. Only at the beginning of the word "omnes" is any sort of rhythmic precision introduced. At this time medieval musical notation could indicate pitches accurately, but was only beginning to deal with matters of rhythm. What Leoninus has fashioned here is a rather free, rhapsodic hymn in praise of the Christ child. Imagine how these new sounds struck the ear of the medieval citizen of Paris as they rebounded around the bare stone walls of the vast, newly constructed cathedral of Notre Dame.

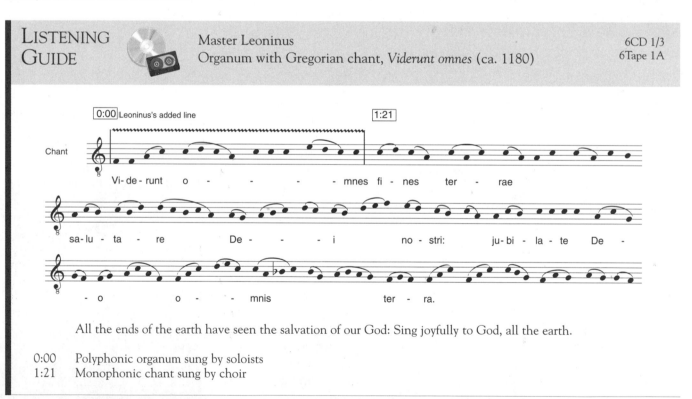

LISTENING GUIDE

Master Leoninus
Organum with Gregorian chant, *Viderunt omnes* (ca. 1180)

6CD 1/3
6Tape 1A

0:00 Leoninus's added line   1:21

Chant

Vi- de- runt o- - - - mnes fi- nes ter- rae

sa- lu- ta- re De- - i no- stri: ju- bi- la- te De-

- o o- - mnis ter- ra.

All the ends of the earth have seen the salvation of our God: Sing joyfully to God, all the earth.

0:00 Polyphonic organum sung by soloists
1:21 Monophonic chant sung by choir

Notre Dame of Rheims

Notre Dame of Paris was not the only important cathedral devoted to Our Lady in northern Europe. The city of Rheims, one hundred miles east of Paris in the Champagne region, was graced with a monument equally large and impressive (Fig. 4–4). In the fourteenth century it, too, benefited from the service of a poetically and musically talented churchman, Guillaume de Machaut (1300?–1377).

Musical Portions of the Mass

PROPER OF THE MASS	ORDINARY OF THE MASS
1. Introit (an introductory chant for the entry of the celebrating clergy)	
	2. Kyrie (a petition for mercy)
	3. Gloria (a hymn of praise to the Lord)
4. Gradual (a reflective chant)	
5. Alleluia or Tract (a chant of thanksgiving or penance)	
6. Sequentia (a chant commenting on the text of the Alleluia)	
	7. Credo (a profession of faith)
8. Offertory (a chant for the offering)	
	9. Sanctus (an acclamation to the Lord)
	10. Agnus Dei (a petition for mercy and eternal peace)
11. Communion (a chant for communion)	

Judging by his nearly 150 surviving works, Machaut was the most important composer of the fourteenth century. And he was equally esteemed as a narrative and lyric poet. Today, historians of literature place him on a pedestal with his slightly younger English counterpart, Geoffrey Chaucer (1340?–1400), author of the *Canterbury Tales*.

MACHAUT: *MASS OF OUR LADY*

Machaut's *Messe de Nostre Dame (Mass of Our Lady)* is deservedly the best-known work in the entire repertoire of medieval music. It is impressive for its length and innovative in the way music is applied to the texts of the **Mass**—the central and most important service of the Roman Catholic Church. Before Machaut's time, composers writing polyphony for the Mass had set only one or two sections of what is called the **Proper of the Mass** (chants whose texts changed to suit the feast day in question). Leoninus's *Viderunt omnes*, for example, is a setting of the Gradual (see below) of the Proper of the Mass for Christmas Day. Machaut, on the other hand, chose to set all of the chants of the **Ordinary of the Mass** (chants with unvarying texts that were sung virtually every day), and he united, or linked, these together by placing a distinctive musical motive, a descending scale, in each of the five movements. Setting the Ordinary of the Mass had the obvious practical advantage that the composition could be heard more than on just one feast day of the church year. Machaut's *Mass of Our Lady*, for example, could be sung any time a Mass in honor of the Virgin Mary was celebrated. Nearby are listed the musical portions of the Mass and the order in which they are sung.

Although Machaut's innovation—creating a unified setting of the Ordinary of the Mass—was not embraced immediately by all composers in all regions, by the early fifteenth century his idea had come to be adopted universally in the West. Henceforth, to write a polyphonic Mass for the Church meant that a composer would set the five texts of the Ordinary (Kyrie, Gloria, Credo, Sanctus, and Agnus Dei) and find some way to bind or shape them musically into an integrated unit. This is true not only for later masters like Bach, Mozart, Beethoven, and Schubert, but also for more modern composers like Igor Stravinsky, whose Mass of 1948, by his own admission, owes much to the model of Machaut.

FIGURE 4–4

Interior of the cathedral of Rheims looking east to west. The high, ribbed vaults and pointed arches give this Gothic cathedral a feeling of great upward movement.

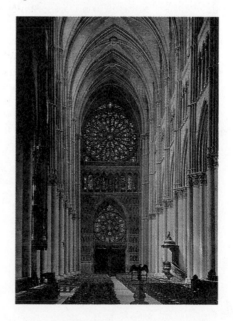

The *Kyrie* of Machaut's *Mass of Our Lady* is a threefold petition for mercy (*Kyrie eleison* means "Lord have mercy upon us"). As in the previous example by Leoninus, it is built on a preexisting Gregorian chant that is held in longer notes than the surrounding material. Because the men who sang the chant sustained it, they came to be called the "tenors" (from the Latin *tenere*, "to hold"). Around them Machaut added not one new line but three, thereby creating four-voice polyphony. The two voices added above the tenor came to be called the *superius* and the *contratenor altus*, whence we get our terms "soprano" and "alto." The voice added below the tenor was called the *contratenor bassus*, whence our term "bass" (for more on the four standard voice parts, see page 41). By writing for four voices and spreading these over a range of two and a half octaves, Machaut was able to create truly sonorous choral polyphony. In the *Kyrie* of his Mass, Machaut intended his four-voice polyphony to alternate with the sections of monophonic Gregorian chant.

When you listen to Machaut's *Kyrie* for the first time, you will be struck by its dark, dissonant sound. The dark quality is present because only male voices are employed here, and hence the range is rather low. Only men and boys were allowed to sing in medieval cathedrals. Sacred singing by women was confined to nunneries (for more on this point, see pages 77 and 93). As to the dissonant, biting sound, it is caused by the fact that Machaut makes use of many unusual dissonances, ones later forbidden in Western polypohonic music by music theorists. In stark contrast to these dissonances, each section of polyphony ends with an open, somewhat hollow-sounding consonant chord. These chords use only the intervals of a fifth and an octave. Such open, hollow final chords sound especially rich in buildings with very resonant, or "lively," acoustics of the sort universally found in medieval cathedrals.

MUSIC AT THE COURT

Machaut wrote music for the cathedral of Rheims, but he composed for the court as well. At various times in his career, he was employed by powerful nobles, such as the king of Bohemia, the king of Navarre, and the duke of Berry. It may seem strange that a man of the cloth was active in affairs at court, but in the Middle Ages learned churchmen were much in demand for their ability to read and write. And because of their skill with letters and music learned in the church, clerics were inevitably drawn to the poetry and music of the courtly song. Indeed, most of the polyphonic love songs emanating from the court in the late Middle Ages were written by ordained priests.

The court first emerged as a center for the patronage of the arts during the years 1150–1400. The fourteenth century in particular witnessed a general decline in the authority of the Church, epitomized by the "Babylonian captivity" (1309–1377), during which the popes, driven from Rome, lived as exiles in France. Kings, dukes, counts, and lesser nobles now assumed responsibility for the defense of the land as well as for affairs of commerce and justice. The aristocratic court became a small city-state, yet one continually on the move within the lord's lands, from town to town or château to château. To enhance the ruler's prestige and show that he or she was a person of refinement and sensibility, the noble often engaged bands of trumpeters to herald an arrival, instrumentalists to provide dance music for the festivals of the court, and singers and poets to create lyric verse.

growing importance of the court

The first composer-poets to appear at court in any number in the West were the musicians who graced the castles of southern France and northern Spain and Italy in the late twelfth and thirteenth centuries. They were called **troubadours** because they were thought to be "finders" or "inventors" of words and melodies (*trobar* means "to find" in the medieval French of southern France). Their art was devoted mainly to the creation of songs of love that extolled the courtly ideals of faith and devotion, whether to the ideal lady, to the just seigneur, or to the Christian cause in the Moslem East. Their songs were not in the Latin of the Church, but in the vernacular tongue: medieval Italian, Catalan, and Provençal (medieval French of the South). The origins of the *troubadours* were equally varied. Some were sons of bakers and drapers, others were members of the nobility, many were clerics living outside the church, and not a few were women.

the troubadours

In the Middle Ages, and later during the Renaissance (1475–1600), women were not allowed to sing in church, except in convents, owing to the early injunction of the Apostle Paul ("A woman must be silent in the church"). But at court, women often appeared as reciters of poetry, singers, and performers on the so-called *bas* (soft) instruments like the harp, lute, rebec (medieval fiddle), and flute (Fig. 4–6). Women *troubadours* were not merely performers, but creators in their own right. One such composer was the Countess of Dia (Fig. 4–7), about whom we know virtually nothing except that she was a member of the minor nobility. Her song *A chantar m'er* (*I Must Sing*) laments her failure in love,

women troubadours

FIGURES 4–6 AND 4–7
(left) A thirteenth-century Spanish miniature showing a medieval fiddle (the rebec) on the left and a lute on the right. (right) The Countess of Dia as depicted in a manuscript of *troubadour* and *trouvère* poetry.

despite her self-proclaimed charms. It is composed of five strophes, or stanzas, each with seven lines of text and seven musical phrases. The seven-phrase melody, which owes much to the music of the Church in its stepwise movement and strong tonal feeling, displays a clear musical form, **ABABCDB** (the use of letters to indicate musical form is explained on page 55). Also in common with the chant of the Church, this *troubadour* song, as true of most, has no clearly articulated meter and rhythm, but is sung in notes of more or less equal length.

LISTENING GUIDE   Countess of Dia   6CD 1/5
                                       Troubadour song, *I Must Sing* (ca. 1200)   6Tape 1A

0:00   Improvised introduction played on a medieval fiddle
0:26   Solo voice enters and sings first of five strophes

(I must sing of that which I'd rather not,
So vexed am I by him to whom I am a friend,
Because I love him more than anything that be,
But with him kindness and courtliness get me nowhere:
Neither my beauty, nor my worth, nor my wits.
In this way am I thwarted and betrayed,
Just as I would be if I were ugly.)

Gradually, the musical traditions created by the *troubadours* were carried to the north of France, where such composer-performers came to be called **trouvères,** and even to Germany, where they were called **Minnesingers.** Around 1300, some of the *trouvères* began to mix the traditions of the *troubadours* with the learned vocal polyphony coming from the Church. Soon churchmen like Guillaume de Machaut (see earlier) adopted the musical forms and poetic style of the *trouvères* to fashion a new genre of music, the polyphonic **chanson** (French for "song"). The chanson is simply a love song, normally in French, for two, three, or four voices, which usually follows a set poetic and musical form. At its best, the chanson is a small jewel of poignant lyricism.

During the fifteenth century, Gilles Binchois (1400?–1460) and Guillaume Dufay (1400?–1474) excelled at writing chansons (Fig. 4–8). Both men were ordained priests, yet both moved easily between ecclesiastical and courtly circles in northern France. Dufay's *Craindre vous vueil (I Wish to Honor You)* is a lovely three-voice chanson with the structure of a **rondeau**—a musical and textual form with a recurring refrain like the rondo* (see page 58). All three voices may be sung, or the lower two may be played on accompanying instruments like the lute or rebec (medieval fiddle). Notice that the composer, who undoubtedly was the author of the text, has linked himself amorously to a certain woman named "Cateline" by means of an acrostic: The first letters of each line spell out "Cateline-Dufay" (*i, j,* and *y* being interchangeable in the Middle Ages, as well as *u* and *v*). A rather daring act for a priest!

EXAMPLE 4–3: Guillaume Dufay: Chanson, *I Wish to Honor You*[†] (ca. 1430)

[†] Recorded by the Medieval Ensemble of London on *Guillaume Dufay: Complete Secular Music*, L'Oiseau-lyre 237D 3.

Craindre vous vueil, douce dame de pris,
Amer, doubter, louer en fais, en dis,
Tout mon vivant, en quelque lieu que soye.   **refrain**
Et vous donner, m'amour, ma seule joye,
Le cuer de moy tant que je seray vis.

Iamais ne suy annuieux ne pensis
Ne douleureux, quant je voy vo clair vis
Et vo maintieng en alant par la voie.

Craindre . . .   (repeat **refrain**)

De vous amer cel m'est un paradis,
Vëu les biens qui sont en vous compris;
Faire le doy quoy qu'avenir en doye.
A vous me rens, lÿes meiux que de soye,
Ioieusement, en bon espoir toudis.

Craindre . . .   (repeat **refrain**)

FIGURE 4–8

Guillaume Dufay and Gilles Binchois. Dufay, who spent most of his life employed at various churches, stands next to an organ to symbolize his role as a church musician, while Binchois holds a secular harp to suggest his position as a musician at the worldly court of Burgundy.

* * * * * *

(I wish to honor you, sweet worthy lady,
To love, esteem, and praise you in word and deed,
All my life, no matter where I may be.   **refrain**
And to give you, my love, my only joy,
My heart as long as I shall live.

I am never anxious or melancholy,
Or sad when I see your bright face,
And I will stand by you through life.

I wish to honor . . .   (repeat **refrain**)

To love you is paradise for me
Such are your charms.
I must do so, no matter what the future brings.
To render myself to you, in a bond tighter than silk
Joyfully, in bliss forever.

I wish to honor . . .)   (repeat **refrain**)

At various times, both Guillaume Dufay and his colleague Gilles Binchois were employed at the court of a French nobleman, Philip the Good, duke of Burgundy (ruled 1419–1467). Owing to a succession of marriages and territorial conquests in France, Germany, and the Low Countries, the dukes of Burgundy had become the most powerful rulers in Europe and their ostentatious court the envy of all the West. Here fashions, including conical headdress for women and long, pointy-toed shoes for men, attained bizarre proportions (Fig. 4–9). Equally fanciful were the evening entertainments of the court. At one banquet in Lille, in *the court of Burgundy* 1454, twenty-eight persons "playing on diverse instruments" were placed in a round tower, and a costumed stag with a boy on its horns sang a two-voice love song (*I've Never Seen the Likes of You*) variously attributed to Dufay or Binchois. Dancing was an inevitable part of such courtly displays, and for this a standard band of two or three **shawms** (ancestor of the oboe), a **sackbut** (parent of the trombone), and sometimes a drum provided the music. The sackbut played the dance tune in long notes while the shawms or other instruments wove ornamental lines, much like a contemporary jazz quartet in which a piano and saxophone improvise above the fundamental bass notes provided by the double bass or the guitar. The late fifteenth-century tune entitled *La Spagna (The Spanish Tune)* is typical of the dance melodies played at the court of Burgundy during the waning years of the Middle Ages.

LISTENING GUIDE   Anonymous dance tune   6CD 1/6
                                              The Spanish Tune (ca. 1470)   6Tape 1A
                                              Two versions

0:00   Version 1: tune played by sackbut; alto shawm adds counterpoint against it
1:36   Version 2: tune played by sackbut; soprano and tenor shawms add counterpoint
        against it, somewhat obscuring the tune

(Listening Exercise 13 asks you to focus in greater detail on the individual instruments.)

FIGURES 4–9 AND 4–10

(left) Dance scene at a wedding at a French court in the mid-fifteenth century. The musicians, who play shawms and a sackbut, are placed on high in a balcony. (right) A later scene, ca. 1600, showing musicians in a procession as painted by Denis van Alsloot. The instruments are, from left to right, a cornetto, two shawms, and a sackbut.

LISTENING EXERCISES

12	Hildegard of Bingen Gregorian chant, *O Greenest Branch* (ca. 1150)	6CD 1/2; 6Tape 1A 3CD 2/1; 3Tape 2A

O Greenest Branch was intended to be sung as part of the Mass by male or female clerics, alternating a soloist with a full choir. First listen to this chant to determine which stanzas are sung by a soloist and which by a choir. Next to each stanza, write "soloist" or "choir," as appropriate.

Stanza 1 _____   Stanza 5 _____

Stanza 2 _____   Stanza 6 _____

Stanza 3 _____   Stanza 7 _____

Stanza 4 _____

Now go on to answer the following, more general, questions:

1. Does an organ accompany the female voices on this recording? _____
2. How would you describe the musical texture of this chant?
   a. monophonic   b. polyphonic   c. homophonic
3. Melismatic singing occurs in this chant
   a. more at the beginning of each stanza than at the end.
   b. more at the end of each stanza than at the beginning.

13 Anonymous dance tune   6CD 1/6
    The Spanish Tune (ca. 1470)   6Tape 1A

The Spanish Tune was a popular dance melody that first appears during the late Middle Ages and survives in more than forty different arrangements. Sometimes it is set for two instruments, sometimes for three, and occasionally for just a solo instrument like the lute. The two versions heard here make use of the shawm (predecessor of the oboe) and sackbut (ancestor of our modern trombone). Most of the following questions require you to distinguish the distinctly different sounds of these two medieval instruments.

Version 1 (0:00–1:33)

1. Which instrument is playing a higher range, the shawm or the sackbut?
   _____

2. Which instrument is playing more rapidly moving pitches, the shawm or the sackbut? _____

3. Are the pitches played by the sackbut always of the same duration?
   _____

4. At 1:13–1:26 what does the sackbut play?
   a. an ascending scale
   b. a descending scale
   c. an ascending arpeggio

5. In the very last chord of the dance, which statement correctly describes the disposition of the instruments?
   a. The shawm is an octave higher than the sackbut.
   b. The sackbut is an octave higher than the shawm.

Version 2 (1:36–2:29)

6. How many instruments are playing? _____

7. Which instrument is playing the highest part, a shawm or a sackbut?
   _____

8. Are the pitches played by the sackbut always of the same duration?
   _____

9. Is there a drum playing in this dance? _____

10. What is the meter of this dance, duple or triple? _____

KEY WORDS

chanson	Ordinary of the Mass	sackbut
Gregorian chant	organum	shawm
Mass	plainsong	syllabic singing
melismatic singing	Proper of the Mass	*troubadour*
Minnesinger	*rondeau*	*trouvère*

For a checklist of musical styles of the medieval period, see page 64.

RENAISSANCE

5

"**R**enaissance" means rebirth or reawakening. As a historical designation, the term was first used in the nineteenth century to characterize a great flowering of intellectual and artistic activity that occurred first in Italy and then in France, Germany, England, and the Low Countries during the years 1350–1600. In music the term is more narrowly applied to musical developments in those countries between the years 1475 and 1600. Although the Renaissance did not represent a radical split with an earlier period of darkness and ignorance, as has sometimes been assumed, it was, nonetheless, a time in which new ideas and new attitudes sprang forth and flourished in a hospitable Italian climate. As the Florentine philosopher Marsilio Ficino said in the eventful year 1492:

> If then we are to call any age golden, it is beyond doubt that age which brings forth golden talents in different places. That such is true of this our age he who wishes to consider the illustrious discoveries of this century will hardly doubt. For this century, like a golden age, has restored to light the liberal arts, which were almost extinct: grammar, poetry, rhetoric, painting, sculpture, architecture, and music, the ancient singing of songs to the Orphic lyre.

The restoration of the philosophy, literature, and art of ancient Greece and Rome could take place, particularly in Italy, because many classical texts still survived and the ruins of the mighty Roman colonnades and arches were everywhere to be seen. But for musicians in Italy and elsewhere, the process of reviving things classical—singing songs to the Orphic lyre—was less obvious and immediate, for almost no music from classical antiquity survived for them to imitate, and what little there was could not be deciphered. Hence, for musicians, rebirth meant not copying earlier musical styles but adopting the attitudes about music that the ancients had possessed. This was done, in part, by writing books about music—on melody, harmony, counterpoint, and rhythm—in which the author adopted the format and vocabulary of the ancient authors.

The ancient Greek writers, especially Homer and Plato, had spoken of the great emotional power of music. Their stories told how music had calmed the agitated spirit, made brave the warrior, and even induced the wanton wife to chastity. The musicians of the Renaissance eagerly embraced this notion that music could sway the emotions, even the behavior, of the listener. To heighten the

FIGURES 5–1 AND 5–2

(left) The expressive grief of the Virgin and St. John mark this portion of an altarpiece painted by Mathias Grünewald in 1510–1515. (right) Virgin and Child with St. Anne by Leonardo da Vinci (1509–1510). Notice the human expression and near-complete absence of traditional religious symbolism, as well as the highly formalistic composition of the painting—the figures form successively larger triangles.

FIGURE 5–3

Michelangelo's giant statue of David (1501–1504) expresses the heroic nobility of man in a near perfect form. Like da Vinci, Michelangelo made a careful study of human anatomy.

emotional intensity of music, they selected a mode (major, minor, or one of several others then in use) and a musical style that would amply suit the meaning of the text they wished to set. A hymn would be set in one style, a lament in another, a love song in yet a third. The belief in the persuasive power of music and the capacity of music to reinforce the meaning of the text were two primary articles of faith held by musicians of the Renaissance. When transformed into real compositions, these beliefs produced pieces in a great variety of musical styles and a wide range of moods. In this way music mirrored the visual arts of the Renaissance, which now likewise allowed for a great range of emotional expression. Compare, for example, the serene and abstract quality of the medieval statue from the cathedral of Rheims (page 76, Fig. 4–5) with the intense expressiveness of the Renaissance figures in the altarpiece from the parish church at Issenheim (Fig. 5–1), or with the warm human glow of Mary, St. Anne, and the Christ child as painted by Leonardo da Vinci (Fig. 5–2).

Attending the rebirth of the arts and letters of classical antiquity was a renewed interest in humankind itself. We have come to call this enthusiastic self-interest humanism. Simply said, **humanism** is the belief that people have the capacity to shape their world, to create many things good and beautiful; that they are something more than a mere conduit for gifts descending from heaven. Even the human form, in all its physical fullness, has aesthetic value (Fig. 5–3). This attitude, with its emphasis on self-esteem and human worth, differs markedly from the prevailing view in the Middle Ages, when the individual was seen as a covered, almost faceless object in a great, divine pageant. The culture of the Middle Ages was fostered by the Church; it emphasized the group and contemplation of the almighty within a cloistered setting. The culture of the Renaissance, on the other hand, with its focus on personal achievement, looked outward and indulged its passion for travel, adventure, and discovery.

New meaning and value were given to what artists produced in the Renaissance, as well as to the artists themselves. By the end of the fifteenth century, the system of the medieval guilds, which regulated the type of work an artist might accept, began to break down. Now an artist might take any commission he wished. He became the intimate friend of leading citizens, and his idiosyncracies were tolerated. No longer was he merely a craftsman who manipulated materials; he was a discoverer, an inventor, a thinker, a visionary. Consequently, the work of art itself came to be viewed as a visible record of the artist's creative mind.

This new attitude about art and about the artist affected the way in which society viewed the composer and the way in which the listener appreciated the composer's work. In the Middle Ages most compositions were preserved anonymously in manuscripts, but, from the fifteenth century on, the name of the creator was usually placed at the head of each piece. One composer even went so far as to insert his own name in a setting of a liturgical text in honor of the Virgin, a novel act of self-aggrandizement. (In a similar way the artists Raphael, Botticelli, and Michelangelo painted their own faces into various religious frescoes they created.) Composers also gained an increased awareness of the monetary value of their art. This can be seen not only in the high salaries they commanded at court, but also in the astute way in which they played one patron off against another to gain additional economic benefits.

new value given the work of art

One reason for this new estimation of music was that it was now viewed as a fine art rather than a science. During the Middle Ages music had been grouped along with geometry, astronomy, and arithmetic as one of four core sciences, because, like these other disciplines, it could be precisely measured (as the interval of a fifth can be measured as the result of two simultaneously sounding strings with a ratio of 3 to 2). Now music left the sciences to join poetry, literature, drama, and painting among the expressive, less rational fine arts. No longer was music the subject of abstract speculation and endless theorizing. No longer was it created by humble craftsmen working only for the greater glory of God. Music in the Renaissance was composed by proud artists whose aim was to give pleasure

music becomes a fine art

FIGURE 5–4

Apollo among the Muses, painted by Raphael for the papal apartments in 1509–1511. "Music," in the form of the god Apollo, plays a fiddle, surrounded by personifications of other fine arts: song, dance, poetry, and drama. Earlier, in the Middle Ages, music had been classified as a science, along with geometry, arithmetic, and astronomy.

to listening men and women. Their music was judged good or bad only to the degree that it pleased fellow human beings. Music, like the other arts, could now be freely evaluated in the secular world for its quality, and the composers ranked according to their greatness. The process of artistic judgment, appreciation, and criticism enters Western thought for the first time in the humanistic Renaissance.

FIGURE 5–5

The only surviving portrait of Josquin Desprez.

Josquin, the Michelangelo of music

JOSQUIN DESPREZ (CA. 1440–1521) AND THE RENAISSANCE MOTET

Josquin Desprez was one of the greatest composers of the Renaissance or, indeed, of any age (Fig. 5–5). He was born somewhere near the present border between France and Belgium about 1440, and died in the same region in 1521. Yet, like so many musicians of northern France, he was attracted to Italy for reasons of professional and monetary gain. Between 1459 and 1504 he worked successively as a singer at the cathedral of Milan, in the chapel of a cardinal in Rome, in the Sistine Chapel of the pope, and finally in the chapel of the duke of Ferrara. Several contemporary accounts, as well as his frequent movement from one employer to another, suggest that he possessed a temperamental, egotistical spirit typical of many artists of the Renaissance: He composed only when he, not his patron, wished; he demanded a salary twice that of composers only slightly less gifted; and he would break into a rage when singers tried to tamper with the notes he had written. One exasperated patron, the duke of Milan, threatened to throw him in jail unless he stopped working on pieces for outside clients. Yet Josquin's contemporaries and immediate successors recognized his genius. Castiglione (*The Book of the Courtier*, 1528) and Rabelais (*Pantagruel*, 1535) praised him. He was the favorite of Martin Luther, who said, "Josquin is master of the notes, which must express what he desires; other composers can do only what the notes dictate." Florentine humanist Cosimo Bartoli compared him to the great Michelangelo (1475–1564), who decorated the ceiling of the chapel where Josquin had once sung (Fig. 5–9):

> Josquin may be said to have been a prodigy of nature, as our Michelangelo Buonarroti has been in architecture, painting, and sculpture; for, as there has not thus far been anybody who in his compositions approaches Josquin, so Michelangelo, among all those who have been active in these his arts, is still alone and without a peer; both one and the other have opened the eyes of all those who delight in these arts or are to delight in them in the future.

the motet

Josquin wrote more than twenty settings of the Ordinary of the Mass and a large number of French chansons (see pages 75–79). But he especially excelled in the genre of the motet. Composers had written motets in different forms and musical styles since the thirteenth century and continued to do so into the nineteenth. The **motet** in the Renaissance can be defined as a composition for a choir, setting a Latin text on a sacred subject, and intended to be sung in a church or chapel or at home in private devotion. Most motets in the Renaissance, as well as most Masses for the church, were sung **a cappella** (literally, "in the chapel"), meaning that they were performed by voices alone, without any instrumental accompaniment. (Instruments other than the organ were generally not allowed in churches during the Middle Ages and the Renaissance.) This, in part, accounts for the often serene quality of the sound of Renaissance sacred music. Indeed, the Renaissance has been called "the golden age of *a cappella* singing."

a cappella *singing*

Josquin's motet *Ave Maria* was written about 1475 when the composer was in Milan in the service of the duke of Milan. It was composed in honor of the Virgin Mary, and employs the standard four voice parts: soprano, alto, tenor, and bass. As the motet unfolds, the listener hears the voices enter in succession with the same musical motive. This process is called **imitation,** a procedure whereby one or more voices duplicate in turn the notes of a melody:

imitation

EXAMPLE 5–1

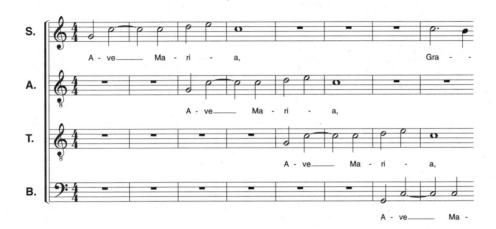

Josquin will also sometimes have one pair of voices imitate another, the tenor and bass, for example, imitating what the alto and soprano have just sung:

EXAMPLE 5–2

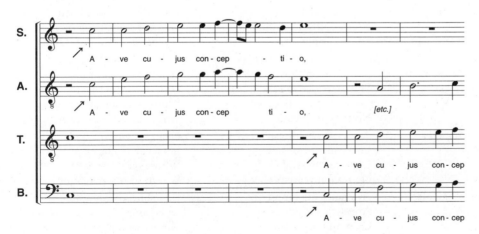

In imitative writing the voices all have a chance to present equally the melodic material and thus are all of equal importance. Moreover, because the voices all enter independently, imitative writing invariably produces counterpoint*— independent voices working with and against one another in a harmonious fashion. In Josquin's *Ave Maria*, sections in imitative counterpoint (polyphony*) alternate with passages of chordal writing (homophony*) in order to achieve musical variety. Josquin and his contemporaries favored imitative writing because the quality of balance and proportion that could be achieved by four equal voices was harmonious with the notion of balance and symmetry much prized in the visual arts during the Renaissance (see Fig. 5–2).

As to the overall structure of Josquin's *Ave Maria*, it is organized in something akin to the way a humanistic orator would construct a persuasive speech or address. It begins with an introductory salutation to the Virgin sung in imitation. Thereafter, a key word, "Ave" ("Hail"), sparks a series of salutes to the Virgin, each making reference to one of her principal feast days during the church year (Conception, Nativity, Annunciation, Purification, and Assumption). At the end of this series of hails comes a final exclamation, "O mother of God, be mindful of me. Amen." These last words are set in a striking succession of imposing chords, with each syllable of text getting its own chord. The chordal, homophonic treatment allows this final sentence to stand out with absolute clarity. In this way is fulfilled the humanistic ideal that text and music work together to persuade and move the listener, in this case toward greater devotion to the Virgin Mary.

LISTENING GUIDE	Josquin Desprez Motet, *Ave Maria* (ca. 1475)	6CD 1/7; 6Tape 1A 3CD 2/2; 3Tape 2A

0:00	All four voices present each two-word phrase in turn	Ave Maria, gratia plena, Dominus tecum, virgo serena.	Hail Mary, full of grace. The Lord be with you, serene Virgin.
0:46	Soprano and alto are imitated by tenor and bass; then all four voices work to a peak on "laetitia" ("joy")	Ave cujus conceptio, Solemni plena gaudio, Coelestia, terrestria, Nova replet laetitia.	Hail to you whose conception, With solemn rejoicing, Fills heaven and earth With new joy.
1:20	Imitation in pairs; soprano and alto answered by tenor and bass	Ave cujus nativitas Nostra fuit solemnitas, Ut lucifer lux oriens, Verum solem praeveniens.	Hail to you whose birth Was to be our solemnity, As the rising morning star Anticipates the true sun.
1:58	More imitation by pairs of voices; soprano and alto followed by tenor and bass	Ave pia humilitas, Sine viro foecunditas, Cujus annuntiatio, Nostra fuit salvatio.	Hail pious humility, Fruitful without man, Whose annunciation Was to be our salvation.
2:26	Chordal writing (no imitation); meter changes from duple to triple	Ave vera virginitas, Immaculata castitas, Cujus purificatio Nostra fuit purgatio.	Hail true virginity, Immaculate chastity, Whose purification Was to be our purgation.
3:03	Return to duple meter; soprano and alto imitated by tenor and bass	Ave praeclara omnibus Angelicis virtutibus, Cujus fuit assumptio Nostra glorificatio.	Hail shining example Of all angelic virtues, Whose assumption Was to be our glorification.
3:58	Strict chordal writing; clear presentation of the text	O Mater Dei, Memento mei. Amen.	Oh Mother of God, Be mindful of me. Amen.

(Listening Exercise 14)

POPULAR MUSIC IN THE RENAISSANCE: THE MADRIGAL

The chordal section that catches the listener's attention at the end of Josquin's *Ave Maria* is both distinctive and new. Yet chordal writing during the Renaissance first rose to prominence not in the Masses and motets of the church, but in the secular, more popular music of the middle class. The appearance of a middle class—and a musical repertoire for it—was an important social phenomenon of the sixteenth century. Whereas medieval society had been structured in a two-tier hierarchy with the clergy and aristocracy on top and the vast mass of common laborers at the bottom, now in the sixteenth century a third class arose. It was made up of tradesmen, merchants, bankers, lawyers, physicians, and civil servants. This "third estate" was concentrated in the cities and constituted a small but growing percentage of the population. Naturally, the urban middle class had different, more popular musical tastes than did the churchmen and the nobles.

rise of the middle class

Of course, there had always been popular music for the less exalted members of society. Yet we know much less about its history than we do of the music of the church and the aristocratic court. The reason for this is simple: Popular music usually was not written down and only rarely survived in written form. It was most often improvised on the spot, created on the spur of the moment by musicians who had learned their art orally from master teachers rather than by studying written manuscripts. Like jazz artists, blues singers, and rock musicians of today, they performed without benefit of written musical notation. Music manuscripts in the Middle Ages had been copied laboriously by hand, making them expensive. Written music was traditionally the private preserve of a wealthy, educated elite.

All of this changed, however, with Johann Gutenberg's invention of printing via moveable type around 1460. Printing revolutionized the world of information in the late fifteenth century no less than the computer has during the late twentieth century. Hundreds of copies could be quickly produced once the type of a book had been set. By 1500, thirty thousand individual works had been published, most out of printing shops in Venice and Rome. The first printed book of music appeared in Venice in 1501, and to this important event can be traced the origins of the "music business" of today. Mass production drastically reduced the cost of the individual book, putting notated music within the reach of the banker, merchant, and shopkeeper as well as bishop and prince. What is more, the new consumers lured to the market by a lower-cost product wanted a more immediately accessible sort of entertainment. They wanted music they could learn to sing and play in their homes—music in a simpler, more chordal, more tuneful style. Henceforth public taste shaped musical style, at least the style of music sold commercially for recreation and entertainment.

music printing

About 1530 a new genre of music, the madrigal, arose in Italy as a direct result of this demand for a new, more popular kind of music. The **madrigal** was a piece for several solo voices (usually four or five) that set a poem, most often about love, written in some vernacular (non-Latin) tongue. At times imitative and contrapuntal, at other times chordal and homophonic, the music of the madrigal seeks to mirror the meaning of the poetry at any given moment. What mat-

the madrigal

FIGURE 5–6

Queen Elizabeth I of England (1533–1603) painted by an anonymous artist.

the English madrigal

FIGURE 5–7

Singers of a four-part madrigal during the middle of the sixteenth century. Women were very much a part of this secular, nonreligious music-making.

tional range of a madrigal might move from the airy heights of a starry night to the depths of a lover's despair.

Nowhere in all of music does sound so artfully depict, even mimic, text as in the sixteenth-century madrigal. Each individual phrase, sometimes each word of an extravagant text, will receive its own musical painting. Thus, when the madrigal text says "chase after" or "follow quickly," the music becomes fast and one voice chases after another in musical imitation. Should the text say "arise, awake" or "clouds in showers descending," the music will ascend or descend. For words such as "pain," "anguish," "death," and "cruel fate," invariably the madrigal composer will employ a twisting chromatic* scale or a biting dissonance*. The practice of depicting the text in music, be it subtly, overtly, or even jokingly as a musical pun, is called **word painting**. Word painting became all the rage with madrigal composers in Italy and England. Even today such musical clichés as sighs and dissonances for "harsh" words are called **madrigalisms**.

The madrigal was born in Italy, but popular favor soon carried it over the Alps to Germany, Denmark, the Low Countries, and England. The first madrigals to be printed in England appeared in a publication of 1588 called *Musica transalpina* (*Music from across the Alps*), a collection of more than fifty madrigals, mainly by Italian composers, with the texts translated into English. Soon English composers—all contemporaries of William Shakespeare (1564–1616)—were writing their own madrigals to new English poems. One of the best of the English madrigalists was Thomas Weelkes (1576–1623), an organist who spent most of his career in rural Chichester but ended his days in London, an honorary Gentleman of the Royal Chapel.

In 1601 Weelkes and twenty-three other English composers each contributed a madrigal to a collection entitled *The Triumphs of Oriana*, an album of music compiled in honor of the Virgin Queen Elizabeth (1533–1603). (Oriana, a legendary British princess and maiden, was widely used as the poetic nickname of Queen Elizabeth.) Thomas Weelks's contribution to *The Triumphs of Oriana* was the six-voice madrigal *As Vesta Was from Latmos Hill Descending*. Its text, likely fashioned by Weelkes himself, is a rather confused mixture of images from classical mythology: The Roman goddess Vesta, descending the Greek mountain of Latmos, spies Oriana (Elizabeth) ascending the hill; the nymphs and shepherds of the goddess Diana desert their mistress to sing the praises of Oriana. The virtue of this verse is that it provides frequent opportunity for word painting in music. The music descends, ascends, runs, mingles imitatively, and offers "mirthful tunes" to the maiden Queen as the text commands. Would the mirror on the wall have deemed the Queen "the fairest of them all" (see Fig 5–6)? Perhaps not. Yet Weelkes saw fit to end his madrigal with imitative cries of "Long live fair Oriana"—an exceptional example of art doing duty as political flattery in Elizabethan England.

The madrigal was a truly social art, one for both men and women (Fig. 5–7). It was meant to be sung, usually with just one singer on a part, though a lute or a harpsichord might sometimes provide a background accompaniment. Most madrigals were not difficult to perform, for above all else they were intended to provide recreation for cultivated amateurs. Skill in singing such pieces was thought to be a necessary social grace for members of the upwardly mobile middle class—just as playing the piano would become in the nineteenth century. And it was meant to be fun for the performer! Vocal lines were written within a comfortable range, melodies were often triadic, rhythms were catchy, and musical puns plentiful. More than a thousand collections of madrigals, each containing approximately twenty pieces, were printed in Europe before 1620. The pleasure the madrigal gave performers accounts for its widespread popularity in the Renaissance as well as the existence of madrigal groups and societies even today.

LISTENING GUIDE	Thomas Weelkes Madrigal, *As Vesta Was from Latmos Hill Descending* (1601)	6CD 1/8; 6Tape 1A 3CD 2/3; 3Tape 2A

0:00	As Vesta was from Latmos hill descending, [Opening homophonic chords give way to falling pitches on "descending"]
0:13	She spied a maiden Queen the same ascending, [Imitation falls, then rises on the word "ascending"]
0:36	Attended on by all the shepherds' swain; [Repeating-note motive suggests simple, country swains]
0:52	To whom Diana's darlings came running down amain, [All voices come "running down amain"]
1:17	First two by two, then three by three together, [Two voices exemplify "two by two," then three "three by three"]
1:28	Leaving their goddess all alone, hasted thither; [Solo voice highlights "all alone"]
1:41	And mingling with the shepherds of her train, [Imitative entries suggest "mingling"]
1:48	With mirthful tunes her presence did entertain. [Light, rapid singing produces "mirthful tunes"]
2:03	Then sang the shepherds and nymphs of Diana: [Stark chords announce the final acclamation:]
2:15	Long live fair Oriana. [Long life to the Queen is declaimed endlessly]

(Listening Exercise 15)

THE COUNTER-REFORMATION AND PALESTRINA (1525–1594)

On October 31, 1517, an obscure Augustinian monk named Martin Luther nailed his ninety-five theses to the door of the castle church at Wittenberg, Germany, the first defiant act in what was to become the Protestant Reformation. Luther and his fellow reformers sought to bring an end to the persistent corruption within the Roman Catholic Church: the increased opulence and worldliness of the papacy, the selling of indulgences (spiritual grace in exchange for money), and the abuse of power in church appointments (one pope rewarded the fifteen-year-old keeper of his pet monkey by making him a cardinal). By the time the Protestant Reformation had run its course, most of Germany, Switzerland, the Low Countries, and all of England, as well as parts of France, Austria, Bohemia, Poland, and Hungary, had gone over to the Protestant cause. The established Roman Catholic Church was shaken to its very foundations.

church reform

In response to this religious challenge and its attendant social and economic upheaval, the Church of Rome began to clean its own house. The cleansing applied not only to matters of spirituality and church administration, but to art, liturgy, and music as well. Nudity in religious paintings, musical instruments within the church, secular tunes in the midst of polyphonic Masses, and married church singers were now deemed inappropriate to a truly pious environment.

the Council of Trent

The movement that fostered this counter reform and a more conservative and austere art within the established Church is called the **Counter-Reformation.** Its spirit was institutionalized in the **Council of Trent** (1545–1563), a congress of bishops and cardinals held at the small town of Trent in the Italian Alps. Although the assembled prelates debated many aspects of reform within the Church of Rome, the liturgy and its music occupied much of their time. What bothered the Catholic reformers most about the church music of the day was that the incessant entry of voices in musical imitation caused an overlapping of lines that obscured the text—excessively dense counterpoint was burying the sacred word of the Lord. As one well-placed bishop said derisively:

> In our times they [composers] have put all their industry and effort into the writing of imitative passages, so that while one voice says "Sanctus," another says "Sabaoth," still another says "Gloria tua," with howling, bellowing, and stammering, so that they more nearly resemble cats in January than flowers in May.

FIGURE 5–8

A portrait of Giovanni Palestrina. Palestrina was the first important composer of the Church to have been a layman rather than a member of the clergy.

Initially, the assembled prelates considered banning music altogether from the service or limiting it to just the old, monophonic Gregorian chant. But the timely appearance of a few sacred compositions by Giovanni Pierluigi da Palestrina (1525–1594), among them his *Mass for Pope Marcellus* (1562), demonstrated to the council representatives that sacred polyphony for four, five, or six voices could still be written in a clear, dignified manner. For his role in maintaining a place for composed polyphony within the established Church, Palestrina came to be called "the savior of church music."

Palestrina was born in the small town of that name outside Rome, and spent almost his entire professional life as a singer and composer at various churches in and around the Vatican: St. Peter's Basilica, St. John Lateran, St. Mary Major, and the **Sistine Chapel** (Fig. 5–9), the pope's private chapel within his Vatican apartments. Although Paul IV, one of the more zealous of the reforming popes, dismissed him from the Sistine Chapel in 1555 because he was a married layman not conforming to the rule of celibacy, Palestrina returned to papal employment at St. Peter's in 1571, holding the titles *maestro di cappella* (master of the chapel) and ultimately *maestro compositore* (master composer).

The *Sanctus* of Palestrina's *Missa Aeterna Christi munera* (*Mass: Eternal Gifts of Christ*) epitomizes the musical spirit of the Counter-Reformation that then radiated from Rome. (Remember, a *Sanctus* is the fourth of five parts of the Ordinary of the Mass* that composers traditionally set to music.) Palestrina's *Sanctus* unfolds slowly and deliberately with long notes gradually giving way to shorter, faster-moving ones, but without catchy rhythms or a strong beat. As is true for Gregorian chant*, the melodic lines move mainly in stepwise fashion, avoiding

Male Choirs

Notice on our recording of Palestrina's *Sanctus* that the soprano part is performed by men singing in head voice, or what is called **falsetto voice.** This is a historically authentic manner of performance. Following an early decree of the Apostle Paul, women in the Middle Ages and Renaissance were not allowed to sing in the Roman Church, except in convents. Similarly, women were not allowed to appear in public in theatrical productions, tragic or comic, in territories under strict church control. Their participation in musical activities was limited to secular music-making at court and at home, singing madrigals, for example, in a more domestic environment. Thus, polyphonic church choirs in the Renaissance were exclusively male, the soprano part being performed by either choirboys or by adult men singing in *falsetto*. Beginning in 1565, however, **castratos** (castrated males) were introduced into the papal chapel, mainly as a money-saving measure. A single castrato could produce as much volume as two falsettists or three or four boys. Castrati were renowned for their power and their great lung capacity, which allowed them to execute unusually long phrases in a single breath. Surprisingly, castrati sopranos remained a hallmark of the papal chapel until 1903, when they were officially banned by Pope Pius X.

All-male choir with choirboys for the soprano part as depicted in a sixteenth-century Italian fresco.

large leaps and chromatic turns. The sober mood is created in part by the careful use of imitative counterpoint. Each phrase of text is assigned its own motive*, which appears, in turn, in each voice. A motive used in this fashion is called a **point of imitation.** Palestrina's *Sanctus* has four points of imitation (see examples in the following Listening Guide). The first enters in the order soprano, alto,

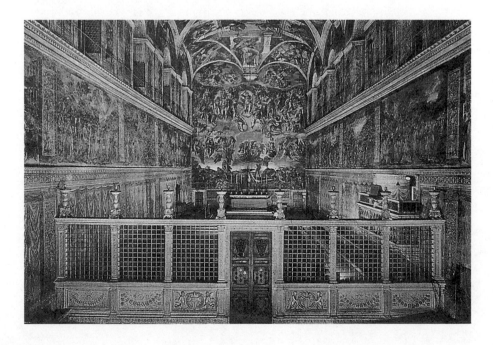

FIGURE 5–9

Interior of the Sistine Chapel. The high altar and Michelangelo's "Last Judgment" are at the far end, the balcony for the singers at the lower right.

successive points of imitation

tenor, bass, and the music works to a cadence*. While the soprano and bass conclude the cadence, the alto and tenor begin the second point of imitation. Soon this section cadences in the soprano and alto as the bass and tenor enter with the third point. Palestrina was a master of sewing a cadence to the beginning of a new point of imitation. The listener experiences not only a sense of satisfaction on arrival at the cadence, but also a feeling of ongoing progress as the new point pushes forward. As you listen to the *Sanctus*, follow the diagram in the Listening Guide and see if you can hear when the voices are cadencing and when a new point of imitation begins.

Palestrina's serene music best captures the restrained, sober spirit of the Counter-Reformation, embodying all that Roman authority thought proper church music should be. After his death in 1594, the legend of Palestrina, "savior of church music," continued to grow. Later composers, such as Bach (*Mass in B minor*, 1733) and Mozart (*Requiem Mass*, 1791) incorporated elements of Palestrina's style into their sacred compositions. Even in our universities today, courses in counterpoint for advanced music students usually include some practice in composing in the pure, contrapuntally correct style of Palestrina. Thus the spirit of the Counter-Reformation, distilled into a set of contrapuntal rules, continued to influence musicians long after the Renaissance had come to an end.

LISTENING EXERCISES

14 Josquin Desprez
Motet, *Ave Maria* (ca. 1475)

6CD 1/7; 6Tape 1A
3CD 2/2; 3Tape 2A

Ave Maria by Josquin Desprez is a fine example of a motet using imitative counterpoint, a texture that dominated the musical style of sacred motets and Masses during the Renaissance. As you work through this exercise, you will become more familiar with how the voices unfold in this imitative, polyphonic texture.

1. (0:00) What is the order in which the voices enter?
   a. bass, tenor, alto, soprano
   b. soprano, bass, tenor, alto
   c. soprano, alto, tenor, bass
2. (1:05–1:14) What is the general direction of the music during the phrase "Coelestia, terrestria" ("heaven and earth")?
   a. rises from "heaven" to "earth"
   b. falls from "heaven" to "earth"
3. (1:18) Which voice sings the final "laetitia"?
   a. soprano   b. male alto   c. bass
4. (2:26) The meter has changed here. Which is correct?
   a. It has changed from duple to triple.
   b. It has changed from triple to duple.
5. (2:57) Which voice ends this section (on the word "purgatio")?
   a. bass   b. male alto   c. soprano
6. (3:58) Is this final, chordal section written in homophony or polyphony (counterpoint)? _____
7. (4:23) On the last word ("Amen"), do the voices change pitches on the two syllables ("A" and "men"), or do they repeat their pitches?

   _____
8. Which is true throughout this motet?
   a. In the imitative sections the soprano and alto always enter before the tenor and bass.
   b. In the imitative sections the tenor and bass always enter before the soprano and alto.
9. Are there any instruments accompanying the voices in this performance?

   _____
10. What do we call the style of performance referred to in Question 9?

    _____

15 Thomas Weelkes
Madrigal
As Vesta Was from Latmos Hill Descending (1601)

6CD 1/8; 6Tape 1A
3CD 2/3; 3Tape 2A

So striking is the depiction of the text through music in the madrigal of the Renaissance that these instances of musical word painting are called "madrigalisms." To be sure that you are hearing this close correlation between text and music, this exercise begins by asking you to indicate the moment at which five very clear instances of word painting start.

	Text	*Time*	*Word Painting in music*
Example	"descending"	0:06	musical line descends
1.	"ascending"	_____	musical line ascends
2.	"running"	_____	rapid entries, fast notes
3.	"two by two"	_____	only two voices are heard
4.	"three by three"	_____	three voices heard
5.	"all alone"	_____	solo voice

6. What is the texture of the music at the words "all alone?"
   a. monophony   c. imitative polyphony
   b. homophony   d. non-imitative polyphony

7. What is the texture of the music at the words "Then sang the shepherds" (2:03–2:10)?
   a. monophony   c. imitative polyphony
   b. homophony   d. non-imitative polyphony

8. What is the texture of the music at the words "Long live fair Oriana" (2:15–3:09)?
   a. monophony   c. imitative polyphony
   b. homophony   d. non-imitative polyphony

9. When the bass finally enters with a presentation of "Long live fair Oriana" (2:20–2:45) are his notes moving faster or slower than the previous entries?

   _____

10. Which statement correctly describes the forces used in the performance of this madrigal?
    a. There is only one voice on each part.
    b. There are two voices singing each part.
    c. There is one voice and one instrument on each part.

KEY WORDS

a cappella	humanism	point of imitation
castrato	imitation	Sistine Chapel
Council of Trent	madrigal	word painting
Counter-reformation	madrigalism	
falsetto voice	motet	

For a checklist of musical style in the Renaissance, see page 65.

EARLY BAROQUE MUSIC

6

It is a fact of historical evolution that the fruits of any cultural period have grown from seeds sown in the preceding epoch. So it is with the Baroque era that certain qualities in the music of the late Renaissance were cultivated to the exclusion of all others. These aspects of musical style developed to the point that the art they embodied was fundamentally different from that of the preceding epoch, and soon this new art was given a new name.

"Baroque" is the term used to describe the art, architecture, dance, and music of the period 1600–1750. It is taken from the Portuguese word *barroco*, meaning a pearl of irregular shape then used in jewelry and fine decoration. During the eighteenth century the term "Baroque" was applied by various observers to indicate a rough, bold instrumental sound in music and excessive ornamentation in the visual arts. To the philosopher Jean-Jacques Rousseau (1712–1778), "A baroque music is that in which the harmony is confused, charged with modulations and dissonances, the melody is harsh and little natural, the intonation difficult, and the movement constrained." Thus, originally, "Baroque" had a pejorative meaning. It signified distortion, excess, and extravagance. Only during the twentieth century, with a new-found appreciation of the painting of Peter Paul Rubens (1577–1640), the sculpture of Gian Lorenzo Bernini (1598–1680), and the music of Johann Sebastian Bach (1685–1750), among others, has the term "Baroque" come to assume a positive meaning in Western cultural history.

Baroque art and architecture have several distinctive characteristics. These qualities are observable in the music of the period as well. What strikes us most when we encounter a monument of Baroque planning, such as the basilica of St. Peter in Rome or the palace of Versailles outside of Paris, is that everything is constructed on a massive scale. The plazas, gardens, fountains, colonnades, and buildings are all of the grandest design. Similarly, human forms, as presented in the painting and sculpture of the time, are larger than life. Look at the ninety-foot-high baldachin inside St. Peter's and imagine how it dwarfs the priest at the altar below (Fig. 6–1). The nearby statue of St. Helena with Cross is almost twenty feet tall. Outside the basilica a circle of colonnades forms a courtyard large enough to encompass several football fields (Fig. 6–2). Or consider the French king's palace of Versailles, constructed during the reign of Louis XIV

FIGURES 6–1 AND 6–2

(left) Bernini's baldachin in St. Peter's, Rome. Standing more than ninety feet high, this canopy above the high altar is marked by twisted columns and curving shapes, color, and movement, all typical of Baroque art. (right) St. Peter's Square, designed by Bernini in the mid-seventeenth century, here shown in a drawing by G. B. Piranesi (ca. 1720–1778).

FIGURE 6–3

The chapel of the palace of Versailles (1699–1710) exalts the power of the French monarch as much as it does the Lord. Note the organ in the background.

(1643–1715), so monumental in scope that it formed a small independent city, home to several thousand court functionaries (Fig. 6-3).

The music composed for performance in such vast expanses was also grandiose. Instrumental groups approaching the size of the modern orchestra came into being, and choral works for twenty-four, forty-eight, and even fifty-three separate vocal parts were written. Mostly intended for spacious churches, these compositions for multiple choruses with instrumental accompaniment have come to epitomize the grand or colossal Baroque.

Once the exteriors of these large Baroque palaces and churches were built, the artists of the time went to the opposite extreme, filling the long lines with an overabundance of small, decorative details. It is as if monumental space had created a vacuum into which the artist rushed with a certain nervous energy. The large painting entitled *Rape of the Sabine Women* by Nicolas Poussin (1594–1665), for example, has the spatial proportions of colossal Baroque art, anchored by the towering figure of Romulus on the left and massive Roman columns in the center; yet it has energy, power, and movement, mainly because of the great number of participants in the drama, the positioning of the figures, and the detail with which they are drawn (Fig. 6–4). The painting is at once spacious and cluttered. When filling the interior of a church the sculptor or carver employed decorative scrolls, floral capitals, and multiple layers of adornment to complete and add warmth to a large expanse (Fig. 6–5).

Similarly, when expressed in the music of the Baroque era, this love of busy detail within large-scale compositions took the form of vigorous, pulsating rhythms with strong, regular beats and many smaller subdivisions. It also was expressed by the use of musical ornaments, whether for instruments such as the violin or harpsichord (see page 103) or for voice. Notice, in Fig. 6–6, the abundance of ornaments and figural patterns in just a few bars of music for violin by Arcangelo Corelli (1653–1713). Such ornaments were equally popular with the singers of the early Baroque era, when the cult of the vocal virtuoso first began to emerge.

We observed in the music of the Renaissance (1475–1600) a growing awareness of the capacity of this art to sway, or affect, the emotions. This belief in the powers of music to move the listener intensified in the Baroque period. Musical moods now came to be called the "affections," and it was the task of the composer to fashion a musical language that could vividly express many and varied affections. Composers of early Baroque opera, in particular, aimed to convey impassioned speech through music.

Painters and sculptors, too, sought to increase emotional expression, which they did by means of exaggeration and distortion. The new emotionalism in Baroque art can easily be seen by comparing the *David* of Gian Lorenzo Bernini (1598–1680), with its fierce visage and twisted body (Fig. 6–7), with Michelangelo's serenely balanced treatment of the same subject done about a hundred years earlier (see page 85). Moreover, the spirit of the Baroque age required of both artist and composer that the emotional "units" they created be large, or

FIGURES 6–4 AND 6–5

(left) Nicolas Poussin, *Rape of the Sabine Women* (1647). The painter said of this work that "it is violent and furious, very severe and calculated to produce amazement." (right) Church of the monastery of St. Florian, Austria (1686–1708). The powerful pillars and arches provide a strong structural framework, while the painted ceiling and heavily foliated capitals provide decoration and warmth.

FIGURE 6–6

Corelli's sonata for violin and *basso continuo*, Opus 5, No. 1. The continuo provides the structural support, while the violin adds elaborate decoration above.

FIGURE 6–7

Gian Lorenzo Bernini's *David* (1623) displays a vitality and restless energy of the sort that can be heard in the music of the Baroque era.

long-lasting, and clearly defined. Baroque music does not change hurriedly from one mood to another as was the practice, for example, in the Renaissance madrigal where the musical feeling changed to reflect the meaning of each new phrase or word (see page 90). Instead, in the newer Baroque style each piece or each large section of a piece carried a single mood or affection throughout—joy, jealousy, resignation, agony, triumph, and others. What is perhaps unique about Baroque music and Baroque art in general is not only its intense expression but also the clear-cut way in which one emotion, color, or spatial unit is kept separate and distinct from the next.

CHARACTERISTICS OF BAROQUE MUSIC

The hundred and fifty years encompassed by the Baroque era (1600–1750) witnessed significant changes in musical style, from the straightforward homophony of Giovanni Gabrieli (ca. 1557–1612) to the complex polyphony of Johann Sebastian Bach (1685–1750). It also saw the introduction of many new musical forms and genres, which we discuss later in this chapter and the next: the sonata, suite, concerto, cantata, opera, oratorio, and fugue. Yet despite such stylistic evolution and formal innovation, there was one musical element that remained constant throughout the Baroque—the *basso continuo*, or "thorough bass," as it was called in seventeenth-century England.

The Basso Continuo

The **basso continuo** was a small ensemble of at least two instrumentalists who provided a foundation for the melody or melodies above. One performer played an instrument that could produce chords, usually the organ or harpsichord, but sometimes even a large lute. The other played a low-sounding instrument, like the cello, the cellolike *viola da gamba* (Fig. 6–8) or the bassoon, which played the bass line. By having the harpsichord, for example, generate the basic chords of

FIGURE 6–8

Basso continuo and violin. This continuo consists of a harpsichord and a large string instrument, the **viola da gamba,** or **bass viol,** as it was called in England. The viol had six strings and produced a slightly darker, less brilliant sound than members of the violin family. The gambist playing here is Eva Linfield.

the piece, a composition acquired a solid harmonic foundation. At the same time, the bass instrument always doubled the lowest note played by the left hand of the harpsichordist, thereby giving the bass line new and greater power.

The additional weight that the *basso continuo* lent to the bass reflected the fact that the music of the early Baroque period had assumed a new structure. In the Mass and motet of the Renaissance, the voices spin out a web of imitative counterpoint, and the character and importance of each of the lines is equal:

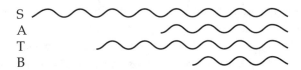

In early Baroque music, however, the voices are no longer equal. Rather, there is a polarity of force directed toward the top and bottom:

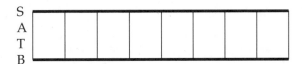

The soprano carries the melody; the bass provides a strong harmonic support. In between, the middle voices often do little more than fill out the texture. If Renaissance music is conceived polyphonically and horizontally, line by line, that of the early Baroque period is organized homophonically and vertically, chord by chord. The *basso continuo* helps establish a strong bass and ensures that the fundamentally chordal structure of the music holds tight.

The sound of the *basso continuo* (or simply continuo in English) pervaded almost all Baroque music. When a solo violinist or flutist played a sonata, or when a singer performed a recitative or aria (see page 108), the continuo was there; thus, three performers were involved, a principal and an accompanying cast of two (Fig. 6–8). As we shall see, the continuo also held together soloists and orchestra in the Baroque concerto, just as it unified multiple choirs in polychoral motets for the church. For church music it was the organ—the traditional instrument of the church—that played the keyboard continuo, while in virtually all other music that chord-supplying function was provided by the harpsichord. Indeed, it is the continual tinkling of the harpsichord, in step with the bass sounds of a cello, *viola da gamba*, or bassoon, that signals to the listener that the music being played comes from the Baroque era.

universal use of the basso continuo

Treatment of Musical Elements

Baroque music, as we have seen, is marked by spaciousness and grandeur, by the desire to create a powerful, unified mood within each work or large section of a work, and by its chordal framework and strong bass line, both generated by the *basso continuo*. These are qualities to be heard in all Baroque music. But there are others as well that appear as distinctive treatments of familiar musical elements. (In the next chapter we see how the stylistic traits of early Baroque music were modified and extended by Bach and Handel in the late Baroque period.)

MELODY. In the Renaissance, melody was more or less all of one type. It was a direct, uncomplicated line that could be either sung by the voice or played on an instrument, according to the wishes of the performer. Now in early Baroque music, beginning about 1600, two different melodic styles begin to develop: a dramatic, virtuosic style in singing and, by contrast, a more mechanical, repetitious style in instrumental music. Despite the increasing virtuosity of vocal music, attention is no longer focused exclusively on the voice. Throughout the Baroque era there is a new emphasis on writing melodies specifically for instruments such as the harpsichord and violin, melodies that were idiomatic (well-suited) to the technical demands of these instruments.

melodic sequence

Early in the Baroque period a new melodic technique called sequence was applied to melody. A **melodic sequence** is the repetition of a musical motive at successively higher or lower degrees of the scale. Example 6–1 shows a sequence, indeed an exceptionally long sequence, from the music of the early Baroque composer Claudio Monteverdi (1567–1643). Notice how the initial motive is repeated seven times, each time one step lower than before.

EXAMPLE 6–1

The melodic sequence first appears extensively in the music of the Baroque era and continues to be a standard melodic device into the twentieth century.

HARMONY. Baroque harmonies are chordally conceived and tightly bound to the *basso continuo*. As the seventeenth century progresses, harmonies unfold more and more in familiar patterns as standard harmonic progressions—chord progressions*—begin to emerge. The shortest and most frequent of these is the V–I (dominant–tonic) cadence (see page 32). The advent of standard harmonic progressions like the V–I cadence gives added direction and cohesion to the music.

chord progressions

major and minor keys

Attending this development is the growing importance—and eventual total domination—of the major and minor system of keys. These two scale patterns, major and minor, replaced the dozen or so scales (or "modes," as they were called) used during the Renaissance and before. Moreover, as music was reduced to just two qualities of sound, the listener could more easily distinguish one from the other. Composers could play minor off against major, or vice versa, to create the emotional effects so important in Baroque music.

RHYTHM. Rhythm in Baroque music is characterized by uniformity. Just as a single mood, or affect, is carried from the beginning to the end of a piece, so the rhythmic patterns heard at the beginning will surface again and again, right to the end. This tendency toward rhythmic uniformity and rhythmic drive becomes more and more pronounced as the Baroque era proceeds.

DYNAMICS. Baroque music, like Baroque art, is organized in units of distinctly different, yet independent, moods and colors. Dynamics do not change gradu-

The Harpsichord

The **harpsichord** has been called the workhorse of the Baroque era because it served both as the main instrument for accompaniment and as a solo instrument in its own right (see Figs. 3–14 and 6–8). In this sense the harpsichord functioned much like the piano would later in the Classical and Romantic periods, as an accompanying and a solo instrument. The sound of the harpsichord is produced by depressing a key that pushes up a quill or (nowadays) a plastic "pick" to pluck a taut wire string. This abrupt plucking of wire is what creates the tinkling sound of the instrument. Unlike the piano, in which a complicated mechanism permits different levels of finger pressure to achieve a wide range of dynamics, the harpsichord cannot produce a louder or softer sound, because the plucking mechanism transmits a constant level of force to the string. There are, therefore, no subtle gradations of sound on the harpsichord. When greater volume is needed, an additional full set of strings is brought into play to double the sound, and all the music thereafter will be loud until this set of strings is disengaged. Thus, the harpsichord typifies the way in which sound was produced in the Baroque period. There are no gradual swells and decreases, but only abrupt changes in the amount or volume of sound. The harpsichord was invented in the late Middle Ages, reached the peak of its popularity in the Baroque era, and went out of fashion in the time of Mozart (1756–1791), replaced by the more flexible, responsive, and potentially powerful piano.

ally from one section or piece to the next. Rather, a single dynamic range, whether loud or soft, will hold fast until abruptly replaced by another. This phenomenon of shifting the volume of sound suddenly and dramatically from one level to another is called **terraced dynamics.** Changing dynamics in this fashion, especially when combined with equally abrupt changes in orchestration and shifts to major or minor tonality, helps create the clearly sectionalized sound of Baroque music.

terraced dynamics

The Rise of Instrumental Music

Composers of the early Baroque period were the first to think of instrumental music as different from vocal music. As we have said, musical lines in the Renaissance were assigned indiscriminately to any voice or any instrument. Baroque composers not only started to differentiate between a vocal style of writing and an instrumental one, but they also began to assign specific musical lines to specific instruments, according to their natural strengths and weaknesses. The brasses, for example, were often given short figures with dotted rhythms, which maximized their capacity for sharp attacks. They would not, however, be asked to run up and down a full-octave scale, because of the difficulties in pitch they would encounter. Fast scales were most often given over to the more agile violins. Thus here in the early Baroque era, the practice of writing idiomatically for the instruments first appears. The first composer to conceive of musical lines in terms of particular instruments was Giovanni Gabrieli (ca. 1557–1611), who spent his entire career in Venice.

idiomatic writing for instruments

THE VENETIAN POLYCHORAL MOTET

Venice, the Queen of the Seas, was—and remains—a city of canals, arching bridges, and colorful palaces. Reaching its zenith of commercial and economic

FIGURE 6–9

A map of present-day Italy showing Mantua, Venice, Florence, and Rome, each an important city for the cultivation of music during the early Baroque period.

FIGURE 6–10

Piazza San Marco painted by Gentile Bellini (ca. 1429–1507). St. Mark's was the focal point of all religious and civic activities in Venice.

importance in the fifteenth century, it owed its success partly to its truly republican form of government and partly to its strategic location at the head of the Adriatic Sea, which made it a natural center of trade (Fig. 6–9). By 1581 its population had reached ninety thousand. The focus of civic and spiritual life in Venice was the palace of the doge (or mayor) and the adjoining basilica of St. Mark, with its spacious piazza in front (Fig. 6–10). St. Mark's, which preserves the remains of the Apostle Mark beneath the high altar, has an architectural plan unique among the major churches of the West. It is built in the form of an equal-sided Greek cross, probably because for centuries Venice was under the political and artistic domination of the Byzantine Empire.

Beginning in the mid-sixteenth century, musicians exploited the unusual architectural plan of St. Mark's by composing motets for it for two or more choirs. At first these separate ensembles were placed in the two singers' galleries on opposite sides of the main aisle (Fig. 6–11). Later they were also stationed in the other elevated galleries that adjoined the central dome. By situating groups of musicians in these separate, elevated lofts—or loggias, as they are called—composers were able to create new sonic effects that astonished the listeners seated or standing below. To a visitor to St. Mark's in the early seventeenth century, the novelty of the musical environment must have been as striking as the twentieth-century change from monophonic to quadrophonic surround sound.

Giovanni Gabrieli (ca. 1557–1612)

The composer who made the most of the opportunities afforded by the architecture of St. Mark's was Giovanni Gabrieli, a native of Venice. Gabrieli wrote little secular music and few Masses for the church. Most of his creative energy was devoted to the composition of ceremonial motets for the semireligious occasions

of state that took place beneath the domes of St. Mark's. One such piece is his polychoral motet *In ecclesiis* (*In the Churches*), written for three choirs. Gabrieli's first musical group consists of a quartet of vocal soloists; the second is a vocal chorus; and the third is an ensemble of six instruments: a violin, two trombones, and three cornettos (see page 81, Fig. 4–10). Accompanying all three groups is the *basso continuo*, here supplied by an organ.

Not only was Gabrieli the first composer to prescribe specific instruments, he was also one of the first to indicate in the score a dynamic level at which the music was to be played, either *piano* (soft) or *forte* (loud). The volume of sound was changed not gradually but suddenly, being added or subtracted in blocks, as is typical of Baroque music. As you listen to the motet *In the Churches*, notice how exuberant and virtuosic the vocal writing of the soloists (Choir 1) has become and how this unit of music differs in style from the block created by the instruments (Choir 3). Notice also that the chorus (Choir 2) regularly inserts a refrain on the word "Alleluja." This serves as a solid counterweight to keep the extravagant lines of the solo singers in balance. Energetic expression within solidly constructed formal units is a hallmark of Baroque art.

FIGURE 6–11

Interior of the basilica of St. Mark, with a view of the upper galleries, where musicians sometimes performed polychoral motets.

LISTENING GUIDE

Giovanni Gabrieli
Motet, *In the Churches* (1612)

6CD 1/10
6Tape 1B

Time	Description	Latin	English
0:00	Soprano soloist of Choir 1 plus organ *basso continuo*	In ecclesiis, benedicite Domino	In the churches, bless the Lord
0:16	Choir 2 and soprano echo, rising rapid notes on third and final time	Alleluja	
0:31	Bass soloist of Choir 1 plus continuo; peaks on "anima mea" ("my soul")	In omni loco dominationis, benedic anima mea Dominum	In every holy place, may my soul bless the Lord
1:09	Choir 2 and bass echo	Alleluja	
1:21	An instrumental interlude; begins solemnly but changes to lively dotted rhythms, ends with descending melodic sequence	Choir 3	
1:53	Tenor and alto of Choir 1 sing duet accompanied by the instrumental ensemble and continuo	In Deo salutari meo, et gloria mea	In God is my salvation and my glory
2:35	Duet continues; notes become more rapid and rise in a melodic sequence	Deus, auxilium meum et spes mea in Deo est	Lord, my help and my hope is in God
3:20	Choir 2 with alto and tenor echos	Alleluja	
3:35	Soprano and bass duet with imitation and echos	Deus noster, te invocamus, te laudamus, te adoramus	Our Lord, we call to you, we praise you, we adore you
4:17	Duet continues; change to lively triple meter on "vivifica nos" ("revivify us")	Libera nos, salva nos, vivifica nos	Deliver us, save us, revivify us
4:46	Choir 2 with soprano and bass echo	Alleluja	
5:03	Rich-sounding chords for all three choirs on "Deus," followed by long notes in the bass	Deus, adjutor noster in aeternum (repeated)	Lord, our judge forever
6:25	Choirs 2 and 3 with echoes by Choir 1 (soloists); third statement of "Alleluja" repeated; strong final cadence added	Alleluja	

(Listening Exercise 16)

The contrast between Gabrieli's instrumentally supported motet of the early Baroque and Palestrina's *a cappella* (unaccompanied) *Sanctus* of the Renaissance (see page 92) could not be more striking. Palestrina's work is serene, otherworldly, and uniform from beginning to end. Gabrieli's motet, on the other hand, displays dramatic changes of texture, dynamics, and musical color, all for bold effects, as it moves from large section to section. A prominent place is now given to a colorful instrumental ensemble (Choir 3). *In the Churches* sounds exuberant, brash, even prideful, like the city of Venice itself.

EARLY BAROQUE OPERA

Given the popularity of opera today—and the fact that there had been opera in China and Japan since the thirteenth century—it is surprising that this genre of music emerged comparatively late in the history of Western European culture. Not until around 1600 did opera appear, and its native soil was Italy.

Opera literally means "work": The word was first employed in the Italian phrase *opera drammatica in musica* (a dramatic work set to music). In opera, then, the lines of the actors and actresses are not merely spoken, but sung. In this way music is used to heighten the emotional intensity of the action that unfolds on the stage. Rejecting the notion that the emotions of an individual could be best expressed by a group of singers, opera stressed solo singing at the expense of the polyphonic choir. Choral singing might be a useful way to convey abstract religious thought in a Mass or motet. But to communicate raw human emotion, solo singing allowed the individual more freedom to express his or her feelings in a direct, personal way. Tying together a succession of solo songs and recitations so as to create a large-scale musical drama satisfied the Baroque desire for grandiose form as well as the Baroque need for intense, even exaggerated, personal expression.

new emphasis on solo singing

The northern Italian city-states of Florence, Mantua, and Venice possessed the most progressive musical thinkers in the early Baroque era. Their efforts to create a new dramatic style was harmonious with, and indeed a continuation of, the aim of the humanists of the late Renaissance. The collective goal was to rediscover the power and intensity of the music of ancient Greece. Florence, in particular, was home to several musically gifted intellectuals, including Vincenzo Galilei (1533–1591), the father of the famous astronomer Galileo Galilei (1564–1642), who urged that in dramatic music renewed importance be given to the meaning of the individual word through the choice of an appropriate supporting harmony. In this way, these musicians theorized, a new dramatic style could be created, one that would emulate the musically accompanied drama of the Greeks. From these developments emerged the first full-fledged opera, Claudio Monteverdi's *Orfeo*.

humanists urged new attention to the word

Claudio Monteverdi (1567–1643)

Claudio Monteverdi was a musical genius who could manifest his enormous talents equally well in a madrigal, a motet, or an opera. He was born in the northern Italian town of Cremona in 1567 and moved to the larger city of Mantua (see Fig. 6–9) about 1590 to serve Duke Vincenzo Gonzaga as a singer and as a player of string instruments. In 1601 he was appointed director of music, and in this capacity composed two operas for the court, *Orfeo* (1607) and *Arianna* (1608).

FIGURES 6–12 AND 6–13

(left) Portrait of Claudio Monteverdi by Bernardo Strozzi (1581–1628). (right) Adriana Basile (ca. 1580–ca. 1640), one of the first "stars" of the operatic stage. Monteverdi may have had her contralto (low alto) voice in mind when he composed the part of Orfeo, but at the first performance in 1607 the role was sung by a tenor.

But the duke failed to pay Monteverdi what he had promised. "I have never in my life suffered greater humiliation of the spirit than when I had to go and beg the treasurer for what was mine," said the composer some years later. Thus disenchanted with Mantua, Monteverdi accepted the much-coveted position of *maestro di cappella* at St. Mark's in Venice, which fell vacant on the death of Giovanni Gabrieli in 1612. Although called to Venice ostensibly to write church music, Monteverdi nevertheless continued to compose opera as well. Among his important later works in this genre are *The Return of Ulysses* (1640) and *The Coronation of Poppea* (1642). He died in Venice in 1643 after thirty years of faithful service.

Monteverdi's first operatic masterpiece—indeed the first important opera in the history of Western music—is his *Orfeo*. As is appropriate for a work intending to emulate the style of the ancient Greeks, the **libretto** (text of the drama) of *Orfeo* is drawn from classical Greek mythology. Our hero is Orfeo (Orpheus), the son of Apollo, the Greek God of the sun and of music. Orfeo finds terrestrial love in the form of beautiful Euridice, but on their wedding day she is fatally bitten by a serpent and carried off to Hades (the realm of the dead). Orfeo mourns her death and vows to descend into the Underworld to rescue her and restore his love to earthly life. This he nearly accomplishes by exploiting his divine musical powers, for Orfeo can make trees sway, calm savage beasts, and even overcome the demonic forces of Hades with the beauty of his song. The theme of *Orfeo*, then, is the divine power of music.

Monteverdi's Orfeo

To convey a feeling of heightened passions, Monteverdi and other composers of early opera developed a new, more expressive and flexible style of solo singing for the stage called **stile rappresentativo** ("the representational style"). Sometimes requiring rapid declamation on a single pitch, and at other times wide-ranging vocal flourishes, *stile rappresentativo* permitted the singer to move almost imperceptibly from one mood to another. Monteverdi himself said: "I am aware that contrasts are what stir our souls, and that such stirring is the aim of all good music." In the hands of Monteverdi and later composers, *stile rappresentativo* would soon be transformed into two different and contrasting types of vocal writing, recitative and aria.

stile rappresentativo

recitative   **Recitative,** from the Italian word *recitativo* ("something recited"), is musically heightened speech. In opera recitative is usually used to tell the audience what has happened. Because recitative attempts to mirror the natural stresses of oral delivery, it is often made up of rapidly repeating notes followed by one or two long notes at the ends of phrases, as in the following recitative from Act II of *Orfeo.*

EXAMPLE 6–2

Al'a-ma - ra no-vel-la Ras-sem-bra l'in-fe-li - ce un mu-to sas-so
(At the bitter news the unhappy one resembled a mute stone)

Recitative in Baroque opera is accompanied only by the *basso continuo* playing simple chords. Such a sparsely accompanied recitative is called **secco recitative,** from the Italian for "dry." (By the nineteenth century, recitative will be accompanied by the full orchestra and will be called *accompagnato*.) A good example of *secco* recitative can be heard at the beginning of the vocal excerpt from Act II of *Orfeo* discussed later in the Listening Guide.

aria   If a recitative relates action, an aria expresses feeling. An **aria,** Italian for "song" or "ayre," is more passionate, more expansive, and more tuneful than a recitative. It also tends to have a clear meter and more regular rhythms. Finally, arias are usually sung with a less rapid-fire delivery and more in the way of vocal melisma* (one vowel luxuriously spread out over many notes) as can be seen, for example, in Orfeo's aria "Powerful spirit."

EXAMPLE 6–3

Pos - sen - te   Spir - to

e for-mi- da - bil   Nu - me
(Powerful spirit and formidable god)

Similarly, while the text of a recitative is normally written in blank verse, that of an aria is usually composed in rhyming lines organized in stanzas (strophes). The text of Orfeo's aria "Powerful spirit" consists of five three-line stanzas, each with a rhyme scheme "a-b-a." Moreover, the music for each stanza starts and ends in the same key (G minor). Tonally and textually, then, an aria constitutes a self-contained, independent musical unit. Operatic arias are nearly always accompanied not merely by the *basso continuo,* but also by part or all of the orchestra. Monteverdi gives special prominence to the violins and the cornettos in "Powerful spirit" to show how music can charm and delight even the guardians of Hades.

          Recitative and aria are the two main structural units and styles of singing in Baroque opera and in opera in general. In addition, there is a third structural unit
arioso   called the arioso. An **arioso** is a passage of vocal music sung in a manner halfway between aria and recitative. Its style is actually more faithful to the original concept of *stile rappresentativo* than either aria or recitative. An arioso is more

FIGURE 6–14
The beginning of the third act of Monteverdi's *Orfeo* (1607), from the original print of the opera. The vocal part of Orfeo is on the staff above, the bass line of the *basso continuo* is below.

declamatory than an aria but has fewer quickly repeating notes than a recitative. The lament that Orfeo sings on learning of the death of Euridice, "Thou art dead," is a classic example of an arioso and *stile rappresentativo* singing as well.

Like all operas, *Orfeo* begins with an introductory piece for instruments alone, here called a toccata. The term **toccata** (literally "a touched thing") refers to an instrumental piece, for keyboard or other instruments, requiring great technical dexterity of the performers. It is, in other words, an instrumental showpiece. Here the trumpet races up and down the scale while many of the lower parts rapidly articulate repeating pitches. Monteverdi instructs that the toccata be sounded three times. Brief though it may be, this toccata is sufficiently long to suggest the richness and variety of instrumental sounds available to a composer in the early Baroque period. Its theatrical function, of course, is to call the audience to attention, to signal that the action is about to begin.

LISTENING GUIDE	Claudio Monteverdi *Orfeo* (1607) Toccata	6CD 1/11 6Tape 1B

0:00	Trumpet highlights highest part
0:28	Repeat of toccata
0:54	Repeat of toccata

Although Monteverdi divided his *Orfeo* into five short acts, this two-hour opera was originally performed at Mantua without intermission. The first dramatic high point occurs midway through Act II, when the hero learns that his new bride, Euridice, has been claimed by the Underworld. In a heartfelt arioso, "Thou art dead," Orfeo laments his loss and vows to enter Hades to reclaim his treasure. Listen especially to the poignant conclusion in which Orfeo, by means of an ascending chromatic vocal line, bids farewell to earth, sky, and sun, and thus begins his journey to the land of the dead.

LISTENING GUIDE

Claudio Monteverdi
Orfeo (1607)
Act II, Recitative, "At the bitter news," and Arioso, "Thou art dead"

6CD 1/12
6Tape 1B

Characters: Orfeo and two shepherds
Situation: The shepherds relate that, on the news of the death of Euridice, Orfeo fell into a stunned silence. He soon regains his powers of expression, laments her loss, and vows to reclaim her.

Recitative   **Shepherd I**

0:00	*Secco* recitative (accompanied by *basso continuo* of bass lute)	A l'amara novella Rassembra l'infelice un muto sasso Che per troppo dolor no può dolersi.	At the bitter news the unhappy one resembles a mute stone who is too sad to express sadness.

Recitative   **Shepherd II**

0:16	*Secco* recitative (accompanied by *basso continuo* of harpsichord, bass viol, and bass lute)	Ahi, ben avrebbe un cor di tigre o d'orsa Chi non sentisse del tuo mal pietade, Privo d'ogni tuo ben, misero amante.	Ah, he must surely have a heart of a tiger or a bear, who did not pity thy misfortune, having lost all, unfortunate lover.

Arioso   **Orfeo**

0:44	*Basso continuo* of organ and a bass lute	Tu se' morta, mia vita, ed io respiro? Tu se' da me partita Per mai più non tornare, ed io rimango?	Thou art dead, my life, but I still breathe? Thou hast left me, never to return and yet I remain?
1:44	Mention of descent into hell accompanied by fall in vocal line	No, che se i versi alcuna cosa ponno, N'andrò sicuro a'più, profundi abissi E, intenerito il cor del re de l'ombre,	No, if my verses possess my power, I will go undaunted into the deep abyss. And, having softened the heart of the king of Hades,
2:03	Vision of Euridice climbing to heaven causes flourish in high register	Meco trarrotti a reveder le stelle; O, se ciò negherammi empio destino, Rimarrò teco in compagnia di morte.	will transport thee to again see the stars. And, if cruel destiny works against me, I will remain with thee in the company of death.
2:32	Growing conviction portrayed by chromatic ascent in vocal line	Addio terra, addio, cielo e sole, addio.	Farewell earth, farewell heaven and sun, farewell!

Having descended to the shores of Hades, Orfeo now invokes all his musical powers to gain entry. In the aria "Powerful spirit," he addresses Charon, the spirit who controls access to the kingdom of the dead. Orfeo's elaborate, florid vocal style and the exotic instrumental sounds he creates soon disarm the frightful guard.

LISTENING GUIDE

Claudio Monteverdi
Orfeo (1607)
Act V, Aria, "Powerful spirit" (strophes 1 and 2 only)

6CD 1/13
6Tape 1B

Characters: Orfeo and Charon
Situation: Orfeo pleads through his music that Charon grant passage into Hades

Aria (strophe 1)   **Orfeo**

0:00	Florid singing, joined by violin flourishes, above a *basso continuo*	Possente spirto e formidabil nume, Senza cui far passagio a l'altra riva Alma da corpo sciolta in van presume	Powerful spirit and formidable god, without whom no soul, deprived of body, may presume to pass to Hades's shore.
1:35	Instrumental postlude played by *basso continuo* and two solo violins		

Aria (strophe 2)   **Orfeo**

1:57	Florid singing continues, joined now by cornettos, above a *basso continuo*	Non viv'io, no, che poi di vita è priva Mia cara sposa, il cor non è più meco, E senza cor com'esser può ch'io viva?	I live no longer, since now my dear spouse is deprived of life, I have no heart within me, and without a heart how can I still be alive?
3:07	Instrumental postlude played by *basso continuo* and two solo cornettos		

In the original Greek myth, the lord of Hades, Pluto, releases Euridice to Orfeo with one condition: He is to have faith in her devotion and not to look back to see if she follows him back to earth. When Orfeo yields to the temptation to embrace his beloved, she is reclaimed by Pluto forevermore. In his opera *Orfeo*, Monteverdi altered this tragic conclusion: Apollo now transforms Orfeo into a constellation, which radiates eternal spiritual harmony with the beloved Euridice. In so doing, Monteverdi established what was to become a convention for seventeeth- and eighteenth-century opera, the happy ending.

Henry Purcell (1659–1695)

An equally famous example of Baroque opera is *Dido and Aeneas*, by Henry Purcell. Purcell, arguably the finest of all English composers, was appointed organist at London's great Westminster Abbey in 1679 and was elevated to organist of the king's Chapel Royal in 1682. His *Dido and Aeneas*, believed by most authorities to have been composed in 1689, was among the first operas written in the English language. Yet it was apparently created not for the king's court, but for a private girls' boarding school in the London suburb of Chelsea. The students evidently served as the singers of the chorus, while professionals from London sang the principal roles. The libretto of the opera, one appropriate for a school curriculum steeped in classical Latin, is drawn from Virgil's *Aeneid*. The Trojan hero Aeneas, fleeing his conquered homeland, sails west to found the city of Rome, but is blown off course and onto the shores of Carthage, where the widowed Dido rules as queen. No sooner does the proud queen surrender herself to the soldier of fortune than the gods command him to depart for Italy and fulfill his divine destiny—to found the city of Rome. Betrayed and alone, Dido vents her feelings in an exceptionally beautiful aria, "When I am laid in earth," and then expires of a broken heart.

Dido's aria is introduced by a brief bit of recitative, "Thy hand, Belinda." As recitative goes, this is one of the more expressive examples of what is at heart a declamatory, businesslike style. In the stepwise scale that descends an octave, one can feel the resignation of the abandoned Dido as she slumps into the arms of her servant Belinda:

FIGURE 6–15

Henry Purcell by an anonymous painter.

Purcell's Dido and Aeneas

EXAMPLE 6–4

Thy hand, Be-lin-da! Dark - - ness shades me; on thy bo-som let me rest. More I would, but Death in-vades me: Death is now a wel-come guest.

The aria that follows is constructed of two beautifully shaped musical phrases that carry the following two lines of text:

"When I am laid in earth, may my wrongs create
no trouble in thy breast.
Remember me, but ah! forget my fate."

Each of the lines is repeated, as are many individual words and pairs of words within them. Repetition of text is typical of an aria but not a recitative. It is one means by which the composer depicts emotion—the heroine can vocalize but cannot clearly articulate her feelings in complete sentences. The listener cares less about the syntax and more that the text and music together are emotionally charged. No fewer than six times does Dido plead with Belinda, and with us, to remember her. And, indeed, we do remember, for this plaintive aria is one of the most moving in all of opera.

Purcell constructs his aria "When I am laid in earth" on a *basso ostinato*. The term **basso ostinato** is an extension of the Italian word *ostinato* (meaning "obstinate," "stubborn," or "pig-headed") and refers to the fact that a phrase in the bass, whether just a few notes or several measures, repeats over and over. English composers of the seventeenth century called the *basso ostinato* the **ground bass** because the repeating bass provided a solid foundation on which an entire composition could be built, or grounded. The repeated bass pattern may be only a few notes or several measures in length. *Basso ostinato* is a common feature of Baroque music, often used to symbolize grief.

The ostinato, or ground bass, Purcell composed for Dido's lament is five measures long and is heard eleven times. It consists of two sections (see the Listening Guide): a chromatic descent over the interval of a fourth (G, F♯, F, E, E♭, D) and a two-measure cadence returning to the tonic G (B♭, C, D, G). The aria begins with one statement of this ostinato pattern played by low string instruments alone. When Dido enters she sings her phrase "When I am laid in earth, may my wrongs create no trouble in thy breast" above two statements of the ostinato. This music and text together are then repeated. The second and last phrase, "Remember me, but ah! forget my fate," is also stated and then repeated. At the end of the repeat of this final line, the singer breaks off, as if unable to articulate further her grief. But the strings press on, carrying Dido's highly charged emotion across two final statements of the ostinato.

basso ostinato (*ground bass*)

FIGURE 6–16

Rehearsal of an Opera (ca. 1709) by Marco Ricci. A female lead rehearses for an opera in London. The small orchestra (left) includes a *basso continuo* of harpsichord and cello.

LISTENING GUIDE	Henry Purcell *Dido and Aeneas* (1689) Aria, "When I am laid in earth"	6CD 1/14; 6Tape 1B 3CD 2/4; 3Tape 2A

Characters: Dido, queen of Carthage; Belinda, her servant
Situation: Having been deserted by her lover, Aeneas, Dido sings
  farewell to Belinda (and to all) before dying of a broken heart.

BRIEF RECITATIVE

0:00   Continuo played by harpsichord and cello   Thy hand, Belinda! Darkness shades me; on thy bosom let me rest. More I would—but Death invades me: Death is now a welcome guest.

ARIA

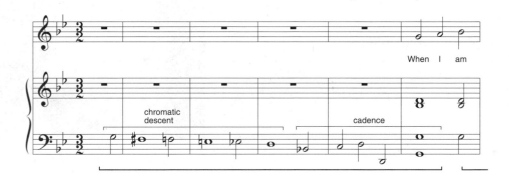

0:55	*basso ostinato* alone in cellos and double basses	When I am laid in earth, may my wrongs create no trouble in thy breast. Remember me, but ah! forget my fate.
1:13	*basso ostinato* with voice and strings	
1:35	*basso ostinato* repeats beneath voice	
1:59	*basso ostinato* repeats beneath voice	
2:20	*basso ostinato* repeats beneath voice	
2:45	*basso ostinato* repeats beneath voice	
3:07	*basso ostinato* repeats beneath voice	
3:30	*basso ostinato* repeats beneath voice	
3:52	*basso ostinato* repeats beneath voice	
4:19	*basso ostinato* alone with strings	
4:40	*basso ostinato* alone with strings	

(Listening Exercise 17)

Elton John and *Basso Ostinato*

For an up-to-date example of ostinato bass, we can look at a modern aria-lament by a more recent English composer, Elton John. Although not built exclusively on an ostinato figure, John's song *Sorry Seems to Be the Hardest Word* (*Live in Australia*, MCA2-8022) nonetheless has one striking affinity to the aria by Purcell—it, too, makes use of a *basso ostinato*, incorporating a chromatically descending fourth as a way of setting a very, very sad text. The ostinato pattern begins on G, with a chromatically descending fourth followed by a one-measure cadence.

It's sad (so sad), it' a sad, sad situation
Bass
G   F♯   F   E
                              And it's getting more and more absurd
                       E♭   D   F♯GAD
                                                          (cadence)

This *basso ostinato*, and a slightly varied form of it, is then repeated several times for this and other lines of text. Compare Elton John's bass line with Purcell's *basso ostinato* (see page 113) and note that both laments are set in the key of G minor. Was the pop artist, who studied at the Royal College of Music in London, inspired by the famous aria of his well-coiffured countryman (see Fig. 6–15)?

Elton John

The Rise of Instrumental Music: Sonata and Concerto Grosso

The Baroque period, as we have seen, was one in which instrumental music—music without text—rose to new prominence. Indeed, during the seventeenth century, instrumental music came to rival and ultimately surpass vocal music in importance. Idiomatic instrumental music—music written specifically to exploit the technical strengths of a particular instrument—came to be cultivated by most composers. These creators likewise demanded virtuosity—the ability to play technically demanding passages rapidly and surely—of the performer. Many of the most renowned composers of the Baroque era, including Corelli (1653–1713), Vivaldi (1678–1741), and Bach (1685–1750), were themselves virtuosos on a particular instrument. Naturally, their passion for instrumental music led to the creation of new musical forms, like the fugue (see page 136), and new musical genres, such as the sonata and concerto.

The Baroque Sonata

A **sonata** is a type of chamber music to be played on an instrument. The term was first used in Venice around 1600 to indicate a composition intended specifically to be played or sounded, as opposed to one that was to be sung. Hence, a sonata is "something sounded" in distinction to a cantata (see page 128), which is "something sung."

Usually, a sonata consisted of a collection of short pieces, each of which is called a **movement.** In the Baroque era these collections of movements were of two types. One, called the **sonata da camera** (chamber sonata), was made up of a series of dancelike movements that had the name and character of a particular dance. A typical chamber sonata might consist of an allemand, sarabande, gavotte, and gigue—all dances. The second type of sonata was called the **sonata da chiesa** (church sonata), and its movements were designated only by a tempo marking such as *grave, vivace, adagio,* or *allegro* (grave, fast and lively, slow, fast)— it was thought inappropriate to have the movements of a piece destined for the church associated with secular dances. Indeed, as the names *sonata da camera* and *sonata da chiesa* indicate, the church sonata was intended to provide background music for religious services, while the chamber sonata, with its links to the dance, was usually heard at court or in the private homes of the well-to-do.

chamber sonata

church sonata

A sonata might be written for a solo keyboard instrument like the harpsichord. Or it might be composed for a solo melody instrument like the violin, in which case three performers would be involved—the violinist and two persons playing the continuo (Fig. 6–8). But whether for solo keyboard or solo melody instrument plus continuo, the work was called a **solo sonata.** Similarly, many Baroque sonatas were written for two melody instruments, two violins or violin and oboe, for example, plus continuo. Such a force was called a **trio sonata** because the composer wrote only three musical lines, even though four performers were involved—two soloists and two players on the *basso continuo*.

trio sonata

Arcangelo Corelli (1653–1713)

The composer-virtuoso who made the Baroque solo and trio sonata internationally popular was Arcangelo Corelli. Corelli was born in 1653 near Bologna, Italy, then an important center for violin instruction and performance. By 1675 he had moved to Rome, where he remained for the duration of his life as a teacher, composer, and performer on the violin. Although Corelli's musical output was small, consisting only of five sets of sonatas and one of concertos, his works were widely admired. Such diverse composers as Johann Sebastian Bach in Leipzig, François Couperin (1668–1733) in Paris, and Henry Purcell in London either borrowed his melodies directly or more generally studied and absorbed his style.

The most remarkable aspect of Corelli's music is its harmony. It sounds modern to our ears. That is to say, we have heard so much classical and popular music that we have come to possess an almost subconscious sense of how a succession of chords, or harmonic progression, should sound. Corelli was the first in a long line of composers to establish that harmonic norm. He was the first to write fully functional harmony; in other words, in his sonatas each chord has a specific function or role in the succession of chords. Not only does the individual chord constitute an important sound in itself, but it also prepares or leads toward the next, thereby helping to form a tightly linked chain of chords. They sound purposeful, well directed. The most basic link in the chain is the V–I (dominant–tonic) cadence (see page 32). In addition, Corelli will often construct a bass line that moves upward chromatically by half step. This chromatic, stepwise motion pulls up and into the next higher note, increasing the sense of direction and cohesiveness we feel in Corelli's music. This strong feeling of functional harmony can be heard equally well in the music of Corelli's younger contemporary, Antonio Vivaldi.

FIGURE 6–17

Arcangelo Corelli looks placid enough in this late seventeenth-century portrait. But when playing the violin, according to a contemporary, "his eyes turn red as fire, his face becomes distorted, and his eyeballs roll as if in agony."

The Baroque Concerto

Abrupt contrast within a unity of mood—this is a hallmark of Baroque music, just as striking change between the zones of light and darkness often characterizes a Baroque painting (see, for example, Fig. 6–20). This aesthetic doctrine of sectional contrast within overall unity can be heard most vividly in the Baroque concerto.

A **concerto** (from the Latin *concertare*, "to strive together") is a musical composition marked by a friendly contest or competition between a soloist and an orchestra. When only one soloist confronts the orchestra, the work is a **solo concerto.** When more than one is present and they function as a unit, the piece is a **concerto grosso.** The soloists in a concerto grosso constitute a subgroup called the **concertino** ("little concert"), and the full orchestra is called the **tutti** ("all" or "everybody"). A typical concerto grosso had a concertino of two or four violins and continuo. The soloists were not highly paid masters imported from afar, but rather the regular first-chair players who, when they were not serving as soloists, joined with the tutti to play the orchestral string parts. The contrast in sound between the heavy tutti and the lighter, more virtuosic concertino is the most distinctive feature of the concerto grosso.

concerto grosso

As written by Vivaldi, Bach, and Handel, the solo concerto and the concerto grosso usually had three movements: fast, slow, fast. The serious first movement is composed in a carefully worked-out structure called ritornello form (see page 118); the second movement is invariably more lyrical and tender; while the third movement, though usually using ritornello form, tends to be lighter, more dance-like, sometimes even rustic in mood. Both the solo concerto and the concerto grosso originated in Italy toward the end of the seventeenth century. Solo concertos for violin, flute, recorder, oboe, trumpet, and harpsichord were especially popular. The vogue of the concerto grosso peaked about 1730 and then all but came to an end about the time of the death of Bach (1750). But the solo concerto continued to be cultivated during the Classical and Romantic periods, becoming increasingly a showcase in which a single soloist could display his or her technical mastery of an instrument.

Antonio Vivaldi (1678–1741)

No composer was more influential, and certainly none more prolific, in the creation of the Baroque concerto than Antonio Vivaldi. Vivaldi, like Gabrieli, a native of Venice, was the son of a barber and part-time musician at the church of St. Mark (Figs. 6–10 and 6–11). Surprisingly, it was not unusual in the seventeenth and eighteenth centuries for barbers to be semiprofessional musicians, since their shops were frequently supplied with musical instruments with which waiting customers could amuse themselves. Young Vivaldi's proximity to St. Mark's naturally brought him into contact with the clergy. Although he became a skilled performer on the violin, he also entered Holy Orders, ultimately becoming a priest. Vivaldi's life, however, was by no means confined to the realm of the spirit: He concertized on the violin throughout Europe; he wrote and produced nearly fifty operas, which brought him a great deal of money; and for fifteen years he lived with a French soprano. The worldly pursuits of *il prete rosso* (the red-haired priest) eventually got him into trouble with the authorities of the Roman Church, and in 1737 Vivaldi was forbidden to practice his musical artistry in papally controlled lands. This ban affected his income as well as his creativity:

FIGURE 6–18

Portrait of a violinist and composer believed by some to be the musician Antonio Vivaldi.

The Baroque Violin

The most important string instrument in the Baroque period was the violin. During the seventeenth century the violin, along with its larger cousins, the viola and cello, came to form the core of the orchestra. Before that time it had been the poor man's string instrument, used mainly for playing dances in taverns. But the violin had two special virtues: First, it produced a more powerful, penetrating sound than had the earlier viol (Fig. 6–8); and second, it was more versatile and expressive. Of all the instruments, the violin comes closest to the sound of the human voice in its agility, flexibility, and expressiveness. It can play a gentle lullaby with great tenderness, just as it can a loud fanfare with splendor. By 1650 the violin had become the instrument of preference for the opera, the solo and trio sonata, and the concerto.

As the violin's popularity increased, so did the number of makers producing the instrument. The earliest of these were centered in northern Italy in small towns such as Cremona and Brescia (both near the Italian Alps). The most gifted of the Cremonese craftsmen was **Antonio Stradivari** (1644–1737), in whose hands the violin assumed its definitive form. Stradivari produced more than a thousand instruments in his lifetime, including violas, cellos, lutes, and guitars, and about 650 of his violins have survived. They not only exhibit the highest quality of materials—including a miraculous varnish made according to a now-lost formula—

but also reflect years of practice and experimentation. In fact, Stradivari was still making violins in his last year, at the age of ninety-two. So rich and singing is the tone of a Stradivari violin that for two centuries most of the world's great artists have preferred this instrument. Unfortunately, in recent times the Stradivari has become the darling of commercial auction houses, one selling recently at Sotheby's in London for $1.76 million. Needless to say, such prices put the Stradivari well beyond the means of all but a very few performing musicians.

Front of a Stradivari violin photographed in ultraviolet light.

He died poor and obscure in 1741 in Vienna, where he had gone in search of a post at the imperial court.

From 1703 until 1740 Vivaldi worked in Venice at the *Ospedale della Pietà* (Hospice of Mercy), first as a violinist and music teacher and then as its musical director. The Hospice of Mercy was an orphanage for the care and education of young women. It was one of four such charitable institutions in Venice that accepted abandoned, mostly illegitimate girls, who, as several reports state, "otherwise would have been thrown in the canals." By 1700 Vivaldi's Hospice of Mercy offered a rigorous musical education to four hundred such foundlings. The performers were grouped into orchestras, some of which were among the finest ensembles in Europe. Each Sunday afternoon, and on feast days as well, the girls offered public performances for the well-to-do of Venice (Fig. 6–19). Also attending these concerts were foreign visitors—Venice was already a tourist city—among them a French diplomat, who wrote in 1739:

music in Venetian orphanages

These girls are educated at the expense of the state, and they are trained solely with the purpose of excelling in music. That is why they sing like angels and play violin, flute, organ, oboe, cello, and bassoon; in short, no instrument is so big as to frighten them. They are kept like nuns in a convent. All they do is perform concerts, always in groups of about forty girls. I swear to you that there is nothing as pleasant as seeing a young and pretty nun, dressed in white, with a little pomegranate bouquet over her ears, conducting the orchestra with all the gracefulness and incredible precision one can imagine.

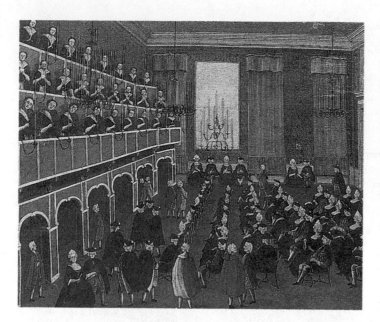

FIGURES 6–19 AND 6–20

(left) A public concert by young women at the Venetian Hospice of Mercy, where Vivaldi served as a teacher and then director. Note how the performers are placed in special galleries to the left. (right) Musicians of Prince Ferdinando de Medici. The prince was a fine amateur keyboard player himself and an important patron of Vivaldi.

VIOLIN CONCERTO IN E MAJOR, OPUS 8, NO. 1, "THE SPRING" (EARLY 1700s)

During the early 1700s Vivaldi composed literally hundreds of solo concertos for the all-female orchestras of the Hospice of Mercy in Venice. In 1725 he gathered twelve of the more colorful of these together and published them under the title "Opus 8." (Composers frequently use **opus,** the Latin noun meaning "work," to enumerate and identify their compositions at the time of publication; this set of concertos was thus Vivaldi's eighth published work.) In addition, he called the first four of these solo concertos **The Seasons.** What Vivaldi meant by this was that each of the four concertos in turn represents the feelings, sounds, and sights of one of the four seasons of the year, beginning with spring. So that there be no ambiguity as to what sensations and events the music represents at any given moment, Vivaldi wrote precise verbal descriptions above the notes of the players, specifying at one point that the violins are to sound "like barking dogs."

"The Spring" Concerto for solo violin and small orchestra is Vivaldi's most popular work. As is usually the case in the three-movement solo concerto, the *ritornello form* fast first movement is composed in **ritornello** form. The Italian word *ritornello* means "return" or "refrain." In ritornello form, all or part of one main theme—the ritornello—returns again and again, invariably played by the tutti, or full orchestra. Between the tutti's statements of the ritornello, the soloist inserts fragments and extensions of this ritornello theme in virtuosic fashion.

The jaunty ritornello theme of the first movement of "The Spring" Concerto has two complementary parts, the second of which returns more often than the first. Between appearances of the ritornello, Vivaldi inserts the music that represents his feelings about spring. He creates the songbirds of May by asking the violins to play rapidly and staccato* in a high register. Similarly, he depicts the sudden arrival of thunder and lightning by means of a tremolo* and shooting scales, then returns to the cheerful song of the birds. Thereafter, in the slow second movement, a vision of a flower-strewn meadow is conveyed by an expansive, tender melody in the violin. Finally, during the fast finale, a sustained droning in the lower strings invokes "the festive sounds of country bagpipes." "The Spring"

Concerto is thus an early example of program music, a type of descriptive instrumental writing that would flourish during the later Romantic period (see page 243). The full text of Vivaldi's "program" for the first movement of "The Spring" Concerto is given in the Listening Guide.

| LISTENING GUIDE | Antonio Vivaldi
Violin Concerto in E major, Opus 8, No. 1 ("The Spring"; early 1700s) First movement, *Allegro* (fast) | 6CD 1/15; 6Tape 1B
3CD 2/5; 3Tape 2A |

0:00	Ritornello part 1 played by tutti	
0:07	Ritornello part 1 repeated by tutti *pianissimo*	
0:14	Ritornello part 2 played by tutti	
0:22	Ritornello part 2 repeated by tutti *pianissimo*	
0:30	Solo violin (aided by two violins from tutti) chirp on high	"Spring with all its festiveness has arrived And the birds salute it with happy song"
1:05	Ritornello part 2 played by tutti	
1:13	Tutti softly plays running sixteenth notes	"And the brooks, kissed by the breezes, Meanwhile flow with sweet murmurings"
1:36	Ritornello part 2 played by tutti	
1:45	Tutti plays tremolo and violins shoot up the scale	"Dark clouds cover the sky Announced by bolts of lightning and thunder"
1:51	Solo violin plays agitated, broken triads while tutti continues with tremolos below	
2:11	Ritornello part 2 played by tutti	
2:19	Solo violin chirps on high, adding an ascending chromatic scale and trill	"But when all has returned to quiet The birds commence to sing once again their enchanted song"
2:37	Ritornello part 1, slightly varied, played by tutti	
2:48	Solo violin plays rising sixteenth notes	
3:03	Ritornello part 2 played by tutti	

(Listening Exercise 18)

Vivaldi's more than 450 concertos were widely admired in the early eighteenth century, but within a few years of his death he was largely forgotten, a victim of rapidly changing musical tastes. Not until the revival of Baroque music in the 1950s were his scores resurrected from obscure libraries and dusty archives. Now his music is loved for its freshness and vigor, its exuberance and daring. Today it can be heard as background music at shopping malls, in television commercials, and in film scores. More than 150 professional recordings have been made of *The Seasons* alone. If nothing else, Vivaldi's life and posthumous reputation suggest the fickleness of fame, fortune, and public favor!

Vivaldi's posthumous reputation

LISTENING EXERCISES

16   Giovanni Gabrieli   6CD 1/10
         Motet, *In the Churches* (1612)   6Tape 1B

The text of this motet is given below. First listen to the motet following the text, then answer the questions that follow:

In ecclesiis, benedicite Domino Alleluja	In the churches, bless the Lord
In omni loco dominationis, benedic anima mea Dominum Alleluja	In every holy place, may my soul bless the Lord
In Deo salutari meo, et gloria mea Deus, auxilium meum et spes mea in Deo est Alleluja	In God is my salvation and my glory Lord, my help and my hope is in God
Deus noster, te invocamus, te laudamus, te adoramus Libera nos, salva nos, vivifica nos Alleluja	Our Lord, we call to you, we praise you, we adore you Deliver us, save us, revivify us
Deus, adjutor noster in aeternum Alleluja	Lord, our judge forever

1. (0:08 and 0:13) At the repeat of the words "benedicite Domino," the sopra-no repeats the music:
   a. on a higher pitch   b. on the same pitch   c. at a lower pitch
2. (0:16–0:30) Is this "Alleluja" (and, indeed, all statements of the "Alleluja") in duple or triple meter? _____
3. (0:31–0:59) In this bass solo the words "In omni loco," "dominationis," and "benedic" are each *repeated*:
   a. once   b. twice   c. three times
4. (1:43–1:52) What melodic device is used at the end of this instrumental passage?
   a. sequence   b. pizzicato   c. pedal point
5. (1:53–3:20) Do you ever hear more than two voices singing in this section?
   _____
6. (3:35) What happens at the beginning of this section ("Deus, te invocamus")?
   a. soprano sings first and bass answers
   b. bass sings first and soprano answers
7. (4:46) Is the instrumental choir playing during this "Alleluja"?
   _____
8. (5:03–5:14) Do the instruments accompany the singers on the important word "Deus"? _____
9. (6:58) Is the final chord major or minor (does it sound bright or dark and gloomy)? _____
10. Finally, is *In the Churches* an example of an *a cappella* motet?
    _____

17 Henry Purcell   6CD 1/14; 6Tape 1B
     Recitative, "Thy hand, Belinda" and aria,   3CD 2/4; 3Tape 2A
     "When I am laid in earth" from *Dido and Aeneas* (1689)

Your selection begins with about a minute of recitative (see page 111). Notice
how Dido's deflated spirits are reflected in the music: She gradually sinks down
from the C above middle C to middle C itself, touching the chromatic notes of
the scale along the way. Begin, however, with the aria that follows, "When I am
laid in earth." The opening is easy to recognize because it starts with a chromatically descending ostinato bass.

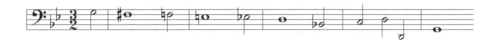

First draw a line beneath the text to show where each statement of the *basso
ostinato* begins and ends. Then number all the lines (1–11). The lines and numbers for the opening continuo statement and the final two statements are provided for you, as is the first statement beneath the text. The repetitions in the
text are included to facilitate your efforts.

1 _____ 2 <u>When I am laid (am laid) in earth, may my wrongs</u>
<u>create</u> no trouble (no trouble) in thy breast. (When I am laid, am laid
in earth, may my wrongs create no trouble, no trouble in thy breast.)
Remember me (remember me), but ah! forget my fate. (Remember me, but
ah! forget my fate. Remember me, remember me, but ah! forget my fate.
Remember me, but ah! forget my fate.) 10 _____
11 _____

Now answer the following questions:

1. Is the recitative "Thy hand, Belinda" an example of *secco* recitative (accompanied only by *basso continuo*) or *accompagnato* recitative (accompanied by
   full orchestra)? _____

2. In the aria "When I am laid in earth," is the mode major or minor?
   _____

3. Is the meter of the aria duple or triple? _____

4. Listen once again to the end of the aria, to the last two statements of the
   ground bass after Dido has fallen silent. The strings play with the continuo
   but without the voice. Compare this to the first statement of the ostinato at
   the very beginning of the aria. In what way is the texture thicker now than at
   the beginning? _____

5. In the final two statements of the ground bass (10–11), what is the general
   direction of the melody?
   a. up by step
   b. up by leaps
   c. down by step
   d. down by leaps

18 Antonio Vivaldi
Violin Concerto in E major, Opus 8, No. 1
("The Spring"; early 1700s)

6CD 1/15; 6Tape 1B
3CD 2/5; 3Tape 2A

Listen once again to the opening movement of Vivaldi's "The Spring" Concerto, and answer the following questions regarding instrumentation, rhythm, meter, tonality, and structure.

1. Do you hear any woodwinds, brass, or percussion playing in Vivaldi's orchestra in this concerto? _____

2. Is the harpsichord or the organ used as the keyboard instrument in the *basso continuo*? _____

3. How would you describe the rhythms of this movement?
   a. energetic with regularly repeating patterns
   b. languid with no clear sense of a downbeat

4. Is the meter duple or triple? _____

5. How would you describe the activity of the bass during the opening presentation of the ritornello theme (0:00–0:29)?
   a. moves slowly and continually up the scale
   b. moves up the scale and then repeats one pitch
   c. repeats one pitch and moves only at the end of each phrase

6. (0:30–1:05) Does the *basso continuo* play during the first solo section? _____

7. (1:05–1:12) Does the *basso continuo* play during the return of the ritornello theme? _____

8. (2:11–2:18) Is this reappearance of the ritornello theme in major or minor? _____

9. (2:19–2:29) How many statements of a chromatically rising scale do you hear the violins play in this solo section? _____

10. (3:11–3:23) At the very end of the movement one of the two parts of the ritornello theme is repeated quietly (*piano*). Is it part 1 or part 2 that is heard *piano*? _____

KEY WORDS

Antonio Stradivari	melodic sequence	*sonata da camera*
aria	movement	*sonata da chiesa*
arioso	opera	*stile rappresentativo*
basso continuo	opus	terraced dynamics
basso ostinato (ground bass)	recitative	toccata
concertino	ritornello	trio sonata
concerto grosso	*The Seasons*	tutti
harpsichord	*secco* recitative	*viola da gamba* (bass viol)
libretto	solo concerto	
	solo sonata	

For a checklist of musical style in the early Baroque period, see page 65.

Late Baroque Music: Bach and Handel

7

The music of the late Baroque era (1710–1750), represented by the two great figures Johann Sebastian Bach and George Frideric Handel, stands as a high-water mark in Western musical culture. In this period were created such masterpieces as Bach's cantata *Awake, a Voice Is Calling* and Handel's *Messiah*. These are large, grandiose works distinguished, at various moments, by great dramatic power, broad gestures, complex counterpoint, and opulent instrumental color. At the same time they convey to the listener a sense of technical mastery—that Bach and Handel could compose with grace and skill in a variety of musical forms, techniques, and styles—building on the innovations of previous Baroque composers.

Earlier in the Baroque era, in the early 1600s, the desire for passionate expression had led to far-reaching stylistic innovations, such as the *basso continuo** and the recitative*. Claudio Monteverdi (1567–1643) helped create an entirely new category of music, namely, opera*. Other new genres—the sonata*, the solo concerto*, and the concerto grosso*—emerged during the second half of the seventeenth century. But the opera, the sonata, and the concerto of the early Baroque era show all the signs of an art in its adolescence. They possess a certain awkwardness and instability, no matter how exciting, vital, and brash they may sound.

The late Baroque, by contrast, is not a period of musical innovation, but one of perfection. Bach and his contemporaries did not, in the main, invent new forms, styles, techniques, or genres, but rather gave greater weight, length, and polish to those established by their musical forebears. Arcangelo Corelli (1653–1713), for example, had introduced functional harmony in his sonatas, but Bach and Handel smoothed away the occasional jarring chord and made the harmony work so as to expand small musical units into larger, more compelling works of art. Bach and Handel approached the craft of composition with unbounded self-confidence. Their music has a sense of rightness, solidity, and maturity about it. Each time we choose to listen to one of their compositions, we offer further witness to their success in bringing a hundred years of musical development to a glorious culmination.

THE THEATRICAL QUALITY OF BAROQUE ART

A striking feature of much Baroque art is its theatrical quality. Drama in the arts is created by conflict, by forces that move in opposition, and yet, at the same time, are so positioned as to project a satisfying wholeness. In late Baroque music the competing musical units are generally lengthy and unchanging in mood. Large, clearly defined blocks of sound are placed in opposition.

By the early 1700s, Bach and Handel could make music theatrical by drawing on many opposing styles, textures, colors, and performing groups. For example, a chorus could be set against instruments, a soloist against a full orchestra, an aria against a recitative, and a homophonic passage against a polyphonic one. Nonetheless, these large-scale forces compete within boundaries carefully defined by musical form. In Handel's *Messiah,* for example, ternary form* controls the flow of several arias, whereas strict fugal procedure regulates parts of the "Hallelujah" chorus. This same theatrical equilibrium is apparent in the visual arts of the late Baroque, as can be seen, for example, in Giambattista Tiepolo's *The Triumph of Nobility and Virtue over Ignorance* (Fig. 7–1). Here, two large-scale units contrast in position (high and low) and color (white and black). Yet the artist creates a grand spatial harmony because the two units have approximately the same mass and because intersecting diagonal lines within each unit pull with equal force. There is energy, movement, spectacle, and grandeur—theatricality—yet there is formal control. These are important qualities of late Baroque art, widely expressed in music as well as painting.

ASPECTS OF LATE BAROQUE MUSICAL STYLE

Treatment of Musical Elements

During the years 1710–1750, Bach, Handel, and their contemporaries continued to develop the distinctive elements of musical style that appeared in the early Baroque era (see pages 100–103), now amplifying and extending them. In brief, melodies became longer, rhythms more driving, harmonies more purposeful, and textures more contrapuntal.

MELODY. Melody in late Baroque music is governed by the principle of continuing development. An initial motive or theme is set forth and then continually expanded, or spun out, over an ever-lengthening line. Such a melody tends to be long and ornate. Often the notes are propelled forward by melodic sequence*, the repetition of a motive or phrase on successively higher or lower degrees of the scale. Sequence helps the melody fly higher and farther and postpones the time when it must arrive at a cadence, as is the case in this example from Handel's *Messiah:*

EXAMPLE 7–1

ex - alt - ed,

FIGURE 7–1

The Triumph of Nobility and Virtue over Ignorance (ca. 1740) by Giambattista Tiepolo (1692–1770) offers a splendid example of late Baroque theatricality, with its grand gestures, vivid colors, and distinctly separate, yet balanced, zones of action.

The exuberant quality of late Baroque melody, however, makes it more impressive than memorable; that is, it is hard to sing or hum, even after repeated hearings. This is due, in part, to the fact that the phrases are frequently not short, narrow, and symmetrical, but rather long, expansive, and irregular. They are also often instrumental in nature, meaning that melodic patterns that can easily be played on instruments are frequently transferred to the voice, where they can be difficult to sing. Bach, for example, often wrote difficult vocal lines that are instrumental in character.

RHYTHM. Rhythm is the most distinctive and exciting element of late Baroque music. If a concerto by Bach or Handel seems to chug along with an irrepressible optimism and vitality, it is because of the almost unstoppable quality of the rhythm. A piece will begin with one prominent rhythmic idea, and it or a complementary one will continue energetically to the very end of the movement. In this context, meter is firmly established by regular accents and a steady beat. Indeed, meter is more easily recognized in late Baroque music than in the music of any other period. Usually, one or two prominent instruments, often those assigned the bass line, play a regular rhythmic pattern that sets a strong beat. This clear, regular beat, in turn, makes the meter immediately audible. The strong beat and powerful bass are elements of late Baroque music that make it appealing to modern listeners. In these it has a certain affinity to contemporary rock and jazz.

driving rhythms

HARMONY. The pull of forceful chord progressions and the use of only major and minor keys were qualities of harmony found earlier, in the music of Corelli (see page 115). They continue to be embodied in the music of the late Baroque era. So, too, does the *basso continuo* (see page 100), that small ensemble of usually keyboard and a bass instrument that gives added weight to the bass and generates chords, thereby providing the harmonic support for the melody above. What chords the keyboard player is to construct are suggested to him or her by means of a **figured bass**—a numerical shorthand placed in the music that tells the player which unwritten notes to fill in above the written bass note. (Figured bass is similar in intent to the numerical code found in "fake books" used by modern jazz pianists that indicates which chords to play beneath the written melody.)

figured bass

EXAMPLE 7–2A AND 7–2B

What is new in the harmony of the late Baroque is the regularity with which it moves. Specifically, chords appear at regular intervals and produce a constant rate of harmonic change. Chord changes may occur every beat, every other beat, or just once in each measure, but usually the rate of change is stable. Regular harmonic change and repetitious rhythms are what give the music of this period its sense of relentless, unstoppable movement.

regular chord changes

TEXTURE: THE RETURN OF COUNTERPOINT. We have seen that imitative counterpoint with independent polyphonic lines dominated the church music of the Renaissance and that, partly as a reaction to this, composers of the early Baroque era began to avoid counterpoint. In the late Baroque period, however, they returned to contrapuntal writing, in part to add richness to the middle range of what was otherwise a top–bottom (soprano–bass) dominated texture. German composers were particularly fond of counterpoint, perhaps because of their traditional love of the organ, an instrument with several keyboards and thus well suited to playing many musical lines at once. The gradual reintegration of counterpoint into the fabric of Baroque music culminates in the rigorously countrapuntal vocal and instrumental music of Bach.

The Late Baroque Orchestra

During the seventeenth century, changes occurred in the makeup of the orchestra. The trumpet, which had formerly been used alone (or with drums) as a purely ceremonial or military instrument, was now welcomed into the ensemble for its bright sound, while the older, duller wooden cornetto (see page 81) quickly disappeared. At the same time the horn left the hunting field and watchtower and took a place in the orchestra. Similarly, the oboe, usually appearing in pairs, was admitted as the principal woodwind instrument because of its penetrating sound, though it might be replaced by one or two flutes, especially if no trumpets or horns were present. Members of the violin family replaced those of the viol (see page 100), whose "still music," as Shakespeare called it, was thought too del

icate, and other soft, plucked instruments from the Renaissance, like the lute, were sent packing. The core of the orchestra was now provided by the violins, violas, cellos, and double basses (which doubled the cello line an octave below). They were supported, still, by a continuo group of harpsichord (or organ in church) and cello, perhaps with a double bass playing as well. The bassoon joined the continuo group in this period to give even more strength to the bass line (see Fig. 7–2).

Many concerti grossi*, opera overtures (see page 139), and dance suites (see pages 139–140) of the late Baroque period were written for an orchestra of just string instruments and continuo. Pieces for especially festive occasions, however, would normally include a greater number of instruments for greater brilliancy. Yet never were all available instruments heard at once, even in the largest orchestral scores. If there were trumpets, there were usually no horns; if there were oboes, there were no flutes, and vice versa. Hence, by modern standards the late Baroque orchestra was at best a mid-size group. Rarely did it include more than thirty-five players, about twenty of whom belonged to the nucleus of strings.

JOHANN SEBASTIAN BACH (1685–1750)

In the creations of Johann Sebastian Bach, the music of the Baroque reaches its greatest glory. Bach was born to a musical dynasty, though one originally of common standing. For nearly two hundred years members of the Bach family served as musicians in small towns in Thuringia, a province in central Germany. Johann Sebastian was merely the most talented of the ubiquitous musical Bachs, though he himself had four sons who achieved international fame. Although he received an excellent formal education in the humanities, as a musician Bach was largely self-taught. To learn his craft he studied, copied, and arranged the compositions of Corelli, Vivaldi, Pachelbel, and even Palestrina. He also learned to play the organ, in part by emulating others, once traveling two hundred miles on foot to hear a great performer. By the time of his maturity he had become the most renowned virtuoso of the organ in Germany, and his improvisations on that instrument became legendary.

Bach's first position of importance was in the town of Weimar, Germany, where he served as organist to the court beginning in 1708. It was here that he

FIGURE 7–2

Detail of an orchestra playing for a Baroque opera. From left to right are a bassoon, two French horns, a cello, a double bass, a harpsichord, and then violins, violas, and oboes.

FIGURE 7–3

Portrait of Johann Sebastian Bach painted by Elias Gottlob Haussmann in 1748.

Leipzig, St. Thomas's Church (center) and choir school (left) from an engraving of 1723, the year in which Bach moved to the city.

wrote many of his finest works for organ, including the G minor fugue discussed later (see page 136). In 1717 Bach accepted a better position at a court in Cöthen, Germany. However, his employer in Weimar, Duke Wilhelm Ernst of Saxe-Weimar, was displeased that his organist had "jumped ship," and summarily had Bach arrested and jailed. (Composers before the era of Beethoven were little more than indentured servants who needed to obtain a release from one employer before they could enter the service of another.) After languishing in prison for some months, Bach was released to take up his duties in Cöthen, where he served as conductor of a small court orchestra. In 1723 Bach moved yet again, this time to assume the coveted position of cantor of St. Thomas's Church and choir school in Leipzig, Germany (Fig. 7–4), a post he retained until his death in 1750. He seems to have been attracted to Leipzig, then a city of about thirty thousand inhabitants, because of the excellent schools and university in which his sons might enroll.

Although prestigious, the post of cantor of the Lutheran church of St. Thomas was not an easy one. As an employee of the town council of Leipzig, Bach was charged with superintending the liturgical music of the four principal churches of that city. He also played organ for all funerals, composed any music needed for ceremonies at the university, and taught Latin grammar to the boys at the choir school of St. Thomas. But by far the most burdensome part of his job as cantor was to provide new music for the church each Sunday and religious holiday, a total of about sixty days a year. In so doing, Bach brought an important genre of religious music, the cantata, to the highest point of its development.

The Cantata

Like the opera, the sonata, and the concerto, the **cantata** was a genre of music that arose in Italy in the seventeenth century. Originally, a cantata ("something sung") was simply a sung aria, as opposed to the sonata, which was a piece played or sounded on instruments. Gradually, the cantata was expanded to several movements, including one or more arias, ariosos, and recitatives, all with instrumental accompaniment. As was true of the sonata, the cantata was heard by audiences in both the aristocratic salon and the church. Secular chamber cantatas on themes of love, morality, and politics were favored by the Italians, while the Germans preferred religious subjects. Composers like Bach and Georg Philipp Telemann (1681–1767) made the German church cantata the musical centerpiece of the German Protestant service, and their works include music for chorus as well as solo arias and recitatives.

the German church cantata

cantata expands on theme of Gospel

In Bach's time St. Thomas's Church celebrated a Sunday Mass, as prescribed by Martin Luther (1483–1546) nearly two centuries earlier. The service began at seven o'clock in the morning and lasted nearly four hours. The musical high point was the cantata. It came after the reading of the Gospel and provided a commentary on the Gospel text, allowing the congregation to meditate on the word of the Lord. The preacher then delivered an hour-long sermon, which also expounded on the scriptural theme of the day. Bach wrote almost three hundred cantatas for the citizens of Leipzig (five annual cycles), though only about two-thirds of these survive. His musical forces consisted of singers from the St. Thomas choir school and instrumentalists from the university and town. The ensemble was placed in a choir loft above the west door (Fig. 7–8), and Bach himself conducted the group, beating time with a roll of paper.

AWAKE, A VOICE IS CALLING (1731)

Bach was a devoted husband, a loving father to twenty children, and a respected burgher of Leipzig. Yet above all he was a religious man who composed not for self-expression, but for the greater glory of God. His cantata *Awake, a Voice Is Calling* reveals his abiding faith in the religious traditions of his German Lutheran community. It was written in 1731 for a service on a Sunday immediately before the beginning of Advent (four Sundays before Christmas). The text of the cantata announces the coming of a bridegroom toward his hopeful bride. Christ is the groom. A group of Wise Virgins, whose story is recounted in the Gospel of St. Matthew (25:1–13), symbolizes the bride. It is this Gospel of Matthew that was read to the congregation at St. Thomas's Church immediately before Bach's cantata was performed.

> Then shall the kingdom of heaven be likened unto ten virgins, which took their lamps, and went forth to meet the bridegroom. And five of them were wise, and five were foolish. They that were foolish took their lamps, but took no oil with them. . . . And at midnight there was a cry made, Behold, the bridegroom cometh; go ye out to meet him. Then all those virgins arose, and trimmed their lamps. And the foolish said unto the wise. Give us of your oil; for our lamps are gone out. But the wise answered, saying, Not so; lest there be not enough for us and you: but go ye rather to them that sell, and buy for yourselves. And while they went to buy, the bridegroom came; and they that were ready went in with him to the marriage: and the door was shut . . . . Watch therefore, for ye know neither the day nor the hour wherein the Son of man cometh.

The message of both Matthew's Gospel and Bach's cantata was for all good Lutherans of Leipzig to awake and purify their hearts to receive the spirit of the coming Christ.

The cantata *Awake, a Voice Is Calling* is made up of a succession of seven independent movements. Those for chorus provide a structural framework, coming at the beginning, the middle, and the end. They make use of the three stanzas of text of a sixteenth-century Lutheran hymn, *Awake, a Voice Is Calling*, from which this cantata derives its name. The text of the recitatives and arias is a patchwork of biblical quotations cobbled together by a contemporary of Bach's. Thus the chorus sings the verses of the traditional hymn while the soloists present the biblical excerpts in the recitatives and arias. Notice how the structure of the cantata creates a formal symmetry: recitative–aria pairs surround the central choral movement, and are preceded and followed in turn by a chorus.

FIGURE 7–5

Looking toward the altar in the interior of St. Thomas's Church, Leipzig, as it was in the mid-nineteenth century.

			Movement:			
1	2	3	4	5	6	7
Chorus	Recitative	Aria (duet)	Chorus	Recitative	Aria (duet)	Chorus
1st stanza			2nd stanza			3rd stanza

Awake, a Voice Is Calling is a chorale cantata, meaning that the work is built around a chorale. A chorale is a well-known spiritual melody or religious folksong of the German Protestant (Lutheran) church, what other denominations would simply call a hymn. In this case the chorale had been written in 1597 and had been widely used in the Lutheran church before Bach took it up. The structure of *Awake, a Voice Is Calling* is typical of chorale melodies (see upcoming Listening Guide). It begins with three phrases that emphasize, in turn, the tonic,

the chorale cantata

the dominant, and again the tonic of the key E♭ major. These are stated and repeated. Thereafter come four shorter phrases that allow for tonal contrast. Finally, a concluding phrase, which is nothing other than a repeat of phrase three, rounds off the melody. The form of this chorale is thus **AAB,** with both **A** and **B** ending with phrase three.

Of the seven movements of the cantata *Awake, a Voice Is Calling,* the most remarkable is the first, a gigantic choral fantasy that displays a polyphonic mastery exceptional even for Bach. Here Bach creates a multidimensional spectacle surrounding the coming of Christ. First the orchestra announces Christ's arrival by means of a three-part ritornello* that conveys a sense of growing anticipation. Part **a,** with its dotted rhythm, suggests a steady march; part **b,** with its strong downbeat and then syncopations, imparts a tugging urgency; part **c,** with its rapid sixteenth notes, implies an unrestrained race toward the object of desire. Now the chorale melody enters, high in the sopranos, the voice of tradition, perhaps the voice of God. In long, steady notes placed squarely on downbeats it calls the people to prepare themselves to receive God's Son. Beneath this the voices of the people—the altos, tenors, and basses—scurry in rapid counterpoint, excited by the call to meet their savior. Lowest of all is the bass of the *basso continuo.* It plods along, sometimes in a dotted pattern, sometimes in rapid eighth notes, but mostly in regularly recurring quarter notes falling on the beat. In sum, the opening movement of *Awake, a Voice Is Calling* is the musical equivalent of a great religious painting in which the canvas is energized by several superimposed levels of activity (see Fig. 7–6). The enormous complexity of a movement such as this shows why musicians, then and now, view Bach as the greatest contrapuntalist who ever lived.

FIGURE 7–6

Tiepolo's *Vision of St. Clement* projects three distinct levels of activity: the Trinity on high, two angels in the middle, and Pope Clement I, Christ's vicar on earth, at the bottom.

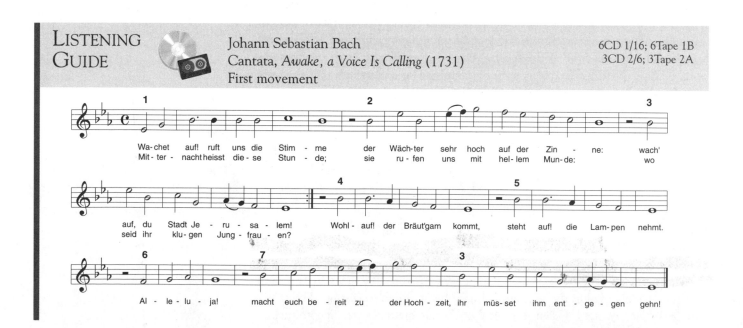

LISTENING GUIDE

Johann Sebastian Bach
Cantata, *Awake, a Voice Is Calling* (1731)
First movement

6CD 1/16; 6Tape 1B
3CD 2/6; 3Tape 2A

A section of chorale tune
0:00   Ritornello parts   a

b

c

(Chorale phrases sung by sopranos accompanied by a horn, the instrument of the watchmen)

0:33	Chorale phrase 1	Wachet auf, ruft uns die Stimme	Awake, a voice is calling
0:52	Ritornello part **a**		
0:58	Chorale phrase 2	Der Wächter sehr hoch auf der Zinne	From the watchmen from high in the tower
1:17	Ritornello part **b**		
1:28	Chorale phrase 3	Wach auf, du Stadt Jerusalem!	Awake, Jerusalem!

* *

Repeat of **A** section of chorale tune (0:00–1:49) with new text as required by repeat in chorale tune

1:50	Ritornello parts **a, b,** and **c**		
2:22	Chorale phrase 1	Mitternacht heisst diese Stunde	Midnight is the hour
2:41	Ritornello part **a**		
2:48	Chorale phrase 2	Sie rufen uns mit hellem Munde	They call us with a clarion voice
3:07	Ritornello part **b**		
3:18	Chorale phrase 3	Wo seid ihr klugen Jungfrauen?	Where are the Wise Virgins?

* *

B section of chorale tune

3:40	Variation of ritornello parts **a, b,** and **c** leads to new keys		
4:05	Chorale phrase 4	Wohl auf, der Bräutgam kommt	Get up, the Bridegroom comes
4:19	Ritornello part **a**		
4:27	Chorale phrase 5	Steht auf, die Lampen nehmt	Stand up and take your lamps
4:44	Altos, tenors, and basses enjoy extended imitative fantasy on "Alleluja"		
5:18	Chorale phrase 6	Alleluja	Alleluia
5:30	Ritornello part **b**		
5:40	Chorale phrase 7	Macht euch bereit	Prepare yourselves
5:50	Ritornello part **c**		
5:57	Chorale phrase 8	Zu der Hochzeit	For the wedding
6:11	Ritornello part **a**		
6:17	Chorale phrase 3	Ihr müsset ihm entgegen gehn!	You must go forth to meet him!
6:38	Ritornello parts **a, b,** and **c**		

(Listening Exercise 19)

Movement 2: Recitative in which the Evangelist (the narrator) invites the daughters of Zion to the wedding feast; no use of chorale tune. In Bach's religious vocal music the Evangelist is invariably sung by a tenor.

Movement 3: Aria (duet) between the Soul (soprano) and Jesus (bass); no use of chorale tune. It is traditional in German sacred music of the Baroque era to assign the role of Christ to a bass.

Movement 4: For this meeting of Christ and the daughters of Zion (true believers), the chorale tune, now carrying stanza two of the text, serves as a unifying force. Bach again constructs a musical tapestry for chorus and orchestra, but a less complex one than the first movement. Here we hear only two central motifs: the chorale melody sung by all the tenors—they are the watchmen calling Jerusalem (Leipzig) to awake; and the exquisitely beautiful, lilting melody played by all violins and violas in unison—their togetherness symbolizes the unifying love of Christ for His people. This unison line is a perfect example of a lengthy, ever-expanding Baroque melody and one of the most memorable of the entire era. Beneath it we hear the measured tread of the ever-present *basso continuo*, here again playing regularly recurring quarter notes on the beat. A bass that moves at a moderate, steady pace, mostly in equal note values and often stepwise up or down the scale, is called a **walking bass**. The walking bass in this movement

walking bass

enhances the meaning of the text, underscoring the steady approach of the Lord.

LISTENING GUIDE

Johann Sebastian Bach
Awake, a Voice Is Calling
Fourth movement

6CD 1/17
6Tape 1B

0:00	Violins and violas play flowing melody above walking bass		
(Chorale phrases sung by the tenors)			
0:43	Chorale phrases 1, 2, and 3	Zion hört die Wächter singen,	Zion hears the watchmen singing
		Das Herz tut ihr vor Freuden springen,	Her heart fills with joy
		Sie wachet und steht eilend auf.	She awakes and quickly rises.
1:12	Flowing string melody repeated		
1:55	Chorale phrases 1, 2, and 3 repeated	Ihr Freund kommt vom Himmel prächtig,	Her splendid friend arrives from Heaven
		Von Gnaden stark, von Wahrheit mächtig,	Mighty in grace, strong in truth
2:24	Flowing string melody repeated	Ihr Licht wird hell, ihr Stern geht auf.	Her light grows bright, her star arises.
2:51	Chorale phrases 4, 5, and 6	Nun komm, du werte Kron,	Now come, you worthy crown
		Herr Jesu, Gottes Sohn!	Lord, Jesus, Son of God
		Hosanna!	Hosanna!
3:09	String melody continues in minor		
3:33	Chorale phrases 7 and 3	Wir folgen all	We will follow all
		Zum Freudensaal	to the banquet hall
		Und halten mit das Abendmahl.	And share in the Lord's supper.
4:00	String melody concludes movement		

Movement 5: Recitative for Christ (bass); no use of chorale tune. Christ invites the anguished Soul to find comfort in Him.

Movement 6: Aria (duet) for bass and soprano; no use of chorale tune. This is a strict *da capo* aria (see page 144) in which Christ and the Soul sing of their mutual love.

Movement 7: Bach's cantatas usually end with a simple four-voice homophonic setting of the last stanza of the chorale. He always places the chorale tune in the soprano part, harmonizing and supporting it with the other three voices below. The instruments of the orchestra double the four vocal parts. But more important, the members of the congregation join in the singing of the chorale melody. At that moment all of the spiritual energy of Leipzig was concentrated into this one emphatic declaration of belief. The coming Christ reveals to all believers a vision of life in the celestial kingdom.

| LISTENING GUIDE |  | Johann Sebastian Bach *Awake, a Voice Is Calling* Seventh and last movement | 6CD 1/18 6Tape 1B |

0:00	Gloria sei dir gesungen	May Glory be sung to you
	Mit Menschen und englischen Zungen	With the tongues of man and the angels
	Mit Harfen und mit Zimbeln schon.	And harps and cymbals too.
0:38	Von zwölf Perlen sind die Pforten,	The gates are of twelve pearls,
	An deiner Stadt, wir sind Konsorten	In your city we are consorts
	Der Engel hoch um deiner Thron.	Of the angels high above your throne.
1:16	Kein Aug hat je gespürt,	No eye has ever seen,
	Kein Ohr hat je gehört	No ear has ever heard
	Solche Freude.	Such joy.
	Des sind wir froh,	Let us therefore rejoice,
	Io, io!	Io, io!
	Ewig in dulci jubilo.	Eternally in sweet jubilation.

An orchestra and a small chorus perform in a German coffeehouse in the mid-eighteenth century. The *basso continuo* (foreground) is comprised of harpsichord, cello, and bassoon.

Bach's Orchestral Music

In 1729 Bach became director of the Collegium Musicum of Leipzig, in addition to being cantor of St. Thomas's Church. The Collegium was an organization of university students and town musicians who voluntarily came together to give weekly concerts in a local coffeehouse (one run by a certain Herr Zimmerman), where the patrons sipped beer and puffed long pipes (Fig. 7–7). By means of such societies, middle-class musical culture flourished in the eighteenth century. (The Collegium has persisted in European and American universities down to the present day, though now it exists mainly to promote "early music"—the music of Bach's time and before.) Bach's association with the Collegium of Leipzig gave him the opportunity to perform secular music, most of it instrumental. Over a period of twenty-five years, from about 1705 until 1730, Bach had written an impressive array of instrumental music that the Collegium might now perform: four suites (see page 139), more than a dozen solo concertos (some of which were arrangements of works by other composers), and six concertos of the concerto grosso type. This latter set has come to be called the Brandenburg Concertos.

THE BRANDENBURG CONCERTOS (1715–1721)

Early in his career, in 1721, Bach gathered together a half dozen of his best concertos and sent them to Margrave Christian Ludwig of Brandenburg, whose court was in the Prussian capital of Berlin. Undoubtedly, Bach was angling (unsuccessfully) for a job in the politically more important city of Berlin, and hoped that this display of skillful writing in the genre of concerto grosso would impress his prospective employer. The concerto grosso, as we have seen (page 116), is a

the concerto grosso

three-movement work involving a musical give-and-take between a full orchestra (tutti) and a much smaller group of soloists (concertino), consisting usually of just two or three violins and continuo. In the first movement, the tutti normally plays a recurring musical theme, called the ritornello. The soloists in the concertino play along with the tutti; but when the ritornello stops, they go on to present their own musical material in a flashy, sometimes dazzling show of technical skill.

Bach's Brandenburg Concertos are unusual in that they feature not merely two or three violins in the concertino, but a highly varied collection of solo instruments. In Concerto No. 5, for example, the concertino is made up of harpsichord, violin, and flute, while in Concerto No. 2 the solo group consists of violin, oboe, recorder*, and high-pitched trumpet.

Bach's aim in the Brandenburg Concertos was evidently to show his ability to write challenging music for any and all instruments. A listener cannot fail to be impressed by the brilliant writing for the trumpet in Concerto No. 2, for example. Bach would have called on one of the town's *Stadtpfeifer* (city pipers), a special guild of virtuosic brass players employed for civic events, to execute this difficult trumpet part. Today this brilliant style of playing in the high range of the trumpet, called **clarino playing,** is virtually a lost art. The sound of the trumpet is so distinctive in Concerto No. 2 that whenever it plays, whether as a member of the tutti or as a soloist in the concertino, it dominates the texture.

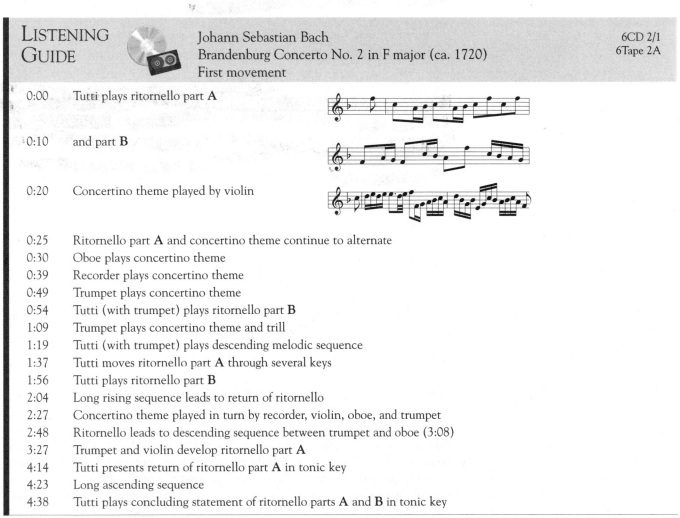

LISTENING GUIDE

Johann Sebastian Bach
Brandenburg Concerto No. 2 in F major (ca. 1720)
First movement

6CD 2/1
6Tape 2A

0:00	Tutti plays ritornello part **A**
0:10	and part **B**
0:20	Concertino theme played by violin
0:25	Ritornello part **A** and concertino theme continue to alternate
0:30	Oboe plays concertino theme
0:39	Recorder plays concertino theme
0:49	Trumpet plays concertino theme
0:54	Tutti (with trumpet) plays ritornello part **B**
1:09	Trumpet plays concertino theme and trill
1:19	Tutti (with trumpet) plays descending melodic sequence
1:37	Tutti moves ritornello part **A** through several keys
1:56	Tutti plays ritornello part **B**
2:04	Long rising sequence leads to return of ritornello
2:27	Concertino theme played in turn by recorder, violin, oboe, and trumpet
2:48	Ritornello leads to descending sequence between trumpet and oboe (3:08)
3:27	Trumpet and violin develop ritornello part **A**
4:14	Tutti presents return of ritornello part **A** in tonic key
4:23	Long ascending sequence
4:38	Tutti plays concluding statement of ritornello parts **A** and **B** in tonic key

The trumpeter gets a welcome rest in the slow second movement of Brandenburg Concerto No. 2. Now the other members of the concertino (recorder, violin, and oboe) create a wholly different mood as they weave in and out with soft, tender threads of melody. The high-flying trumpet returns in the third and final movement. This fast finale is dominated by fugal writing, a style in which Bach excelled above all other composers.

Fugue

Bach was the master of counterpoint, and it is his love of contrapuntal writing that gives his music unparalleled substance and complexity. A fugue is a contrapuntal form and procedure that flourished during the late Baroque era. The word "fugue" itself comes from the Latin *fuga,* meaning "flight." Within a fugue one voice presents a theme and then "flies away" as another voice enters with the same theme. The theme in a fugue is called the **subject.** At the outset each voice presents the subject in turn, and this successive presentation is called the **exposition** of the fugue. As the voices enter, they do not imitate or pursue each other exactly—this would produce a canon* (see page 52). Rather, passages of exact imitation are interrupted by sections of free writing in which the voices more or less go their own ways. These freer sections, where the subject is not heard in its entirety, are called **episodes.** Episodes and further presentations of the subject alternate throughout the remainder of the fugue.

subject, exposition, episode

Fugues have been written for two to as many as thirty-two voices, but usually the norm is three, four, or five. These may be actual voices in a chorus or choir, or they may be simply lines or parts played by a group of instruments, or even by a solo instrument like the piano, organ, or guitar, which has the capacity to play several "voices" simultaneously. Thus, a formal definition of a **fugue** might be as follows: a composition for three, four, or five parts played or sung by voices or instruments, which begins with a presentation of a subject in imitation in each part (exposition), continues with modulating passages of free counterpoint (episodes) and further appearances of the subject, and ends with a strong affirmation of the tonic key. Fortunately, the fugue is easier to hear than to describe: The unfolding and recurrence of one subject makes it easy to follow.

ORGAN FUGUE IN G MINOR (CA. 1710)

Bach has left us nearly one hundred keyboard fugues, about a third of these for organ. The organ was Bach's favorite instrument, and in his day he was known more as a performer and improviser on it than as a composer. Bach's G minor organ fugue was composed rather early in his career, sometime between 1708 and 1717. It is written for four voices, which we will refer to as soprano, alto, tenor, and bass, and it begins with the subject appearing first in the soprano:

EXAMPLE 7–3

As fugue subjects go, this is a rather long one, but it is typical of the way Baroque composers liked to "spin out" their melodies. It sounds very solid in tonality. That's because the subject is built clearly around the notes of the G minor triad (G, B♭, D), not only in the first measure but on the strong beats of the final measures as well. The subject also conveys a sense of gathering momentum. It starts moderately with quarter notes, and then seems to gain speed as eighth notes and finally sixteenth notes are introduced. This, too, is typical of fugue subjects. After the soprano gives forth the subject, it is then presented, in turn, by the alto, the tenor, and the bass. The voices need not appear in any particular order; here Bach just decided to have them enter in succession from top to bottom.

Once Bach has each voice present the subject and join the polyphonic complex, his exposition is at an end. Now a short passage of free counterpoint follows—the first episode—which makes use of just bits and pieces of the subject. Then the subject returns, but in a highly unusual way: It begins in the tenor, but continues and ends in the soprano (see † in the following Listening Guide). Thereafter, Bach's G minor fugue unfolds in the usual alternation of episodes and statements of the subject. The episodes sound unsettled and convey a sense of movement. They modulate from one key to another. The subject, on the other hand, doesn't modulate. It is *in* a key, here the tonic, G minor, or the dominant, D minor, or some other closely related key. This tension between unsettled music (the episode) and stationary music (the subject) is what creates the exciting, dynamic quality of the fugue. Ultimately, Bach modulates back to the tonic key, G minor, for one final statement of the subject in the bass, and the fugue is ended. Note that, although this fugue is in a minor key, Bach puts the final chord in major. This is common in Baroque music, composers preferring the brighter, perhaps more conclusive, sound of major in the final chord.

To hear this and other fugues, then, the listener is encouraged to proceed in the following manner: Follow the unfolding of the subject as it appears in rapid succession in each voice in the exposition; identify the episodic material as dis-

FIGURE 7–8

The organ presently in the choir loft of St. Thomas's Church, Leipzig. It was from this loft that Bach played and conducted.

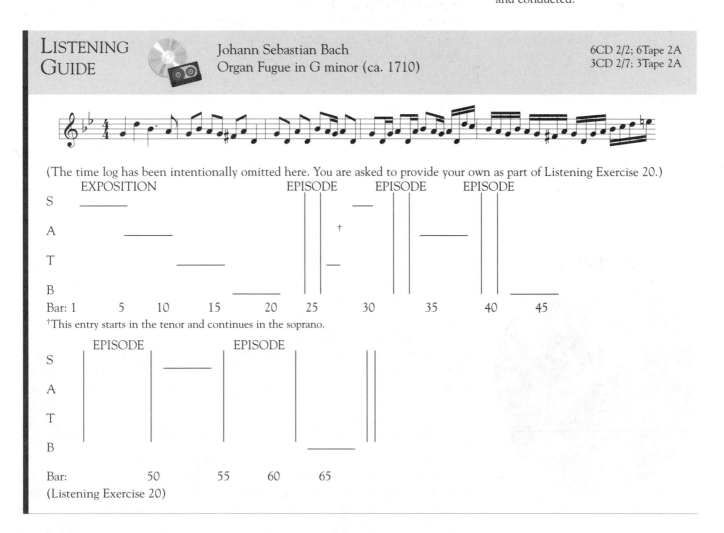

LISTENING GUIDE

Johann Sebastian Bach
Organ Fugue in G minor (ca. 1710)

6CD 2/2; 6Tape 2A
3CD 2/7; 3Tape 2A

(The time log has been intentionally omitted here. You are asked to provide your own as part of Listening Exercise 20.)

†This entry starts in the tenor and continues in the soprano.

(Listening Exercise 20)

tinct from the subject (sense that the subject is no longer present and that the music is changing key); listen for the subsequent alternation between episodes and further appearances of the subject, and, finally, recognize that the home key has been reached when the subject enters in strong fashion for the last time.

Perhaps the best-known collection of fugues by Bach is *The Well-Tempered Clavier* (1720–1742), "clavier" simply being Bach's word for keyboard. It consists of two sets of twenty-four preludes and fugues. The prelude is a short improvisatory-like piece that sets a mood and serves as a technical warm-up for the player before the fugue. In both sets of twenty-four there is one prelude and fugue in each of the major and minor keys: the first pair in C major, the next in C minor, the next in C♯ major, then C♯ minor, and so on. Through this arrangement Bach showed that it was possible to write a piece—in this case a prelude and fugue—in every key, something that had not been done in a systematic fashion up to that time.

The Well-Tempered Clavier

Such rigorous, systematic music was not always popular in the eighteenth century. Indeed, Bach was not fully appreciated by the citizens of Leipzig or the music critics of the time. With his heavy reliance on traditional chorale tunes and on dense counterpoint, they found his style to be old-fashioned and rigid, even pedantic. By the 1730s new musical currents were in the air. The public wanted singable melodies, lighter textures, and simple phrasing. Although Bach's sons adjusted to the tastes of the day, "the old Wig," as one of them irreverently called him, did so only sporadically. When Bach died in 1750 he was soon forgotten, and mention of the name "Bach" shortly thereafter conjured up the image of one or the other of his fashionable sons, not the great polyphonic master. Yet a small group of musicians, including Mozart, Beethoven, Schumann, and Mendelssohn, kept the knowledge of his extraordinary music alive. When Mendelssohn performed Bach's *St. Matthew Passion* (an oratorio*) in 1829 on the centenary of its first performance, a "Bach revival" was under way. From that time on, the listening public has never ceased to admire Bach's music for its stylistic integrity, grand design, and superhuman craftsmanship.

Bach and posterity

FIGURE 7–9

Portrait of George Frideric Handel painted by Balthasar Denner ca. 1727.

GEORGE FRIDERIC HANDEL (1685–1759)

The careers of Bach and Handel could hardly have been more different. While Bach spent his life confined to towns in central Germany, his cosmopolitan countryman Handel traveled the world—from Rome, to Venice, to Hamburg, to Amsterdam, to London, to Dublin. If Bach was most at home conducting chorale cantatas and playing organ fugues from the church choir loft, Handel was a man of the public theater, a denizen of the orchestra pit, by training and temperament a composer of opera. And if Bach fell into virtual obscurity at the end of his life, retreating into a world of esoteric counterpoint, Handel's stature only grew larger on the international stage. He became the most famous composer in Europe and a treasured national institution in England.

George Frideric Handel (as he styled himself after becoming a naturalized English citizen) was born in the town of Halle, Germany, in 1685, and died in London in 1759. Although his father had decreed a program of study in law, the young Handel managed to cultivate his intense interest in music, sometimes secretly by candlelight. At the age of eighteen he got his first taste of opera in the city of Hamburg, where he had gone to take a job as violinist in the public opera theater. But since the musical world around 1700 was dominated by things Italian, he, too, set off for Italy to learn his trade and broaden his horizons. He moved between Florence and Venice, for which cities he wrote operas, and Rome, where he composed mainly secular cantatas. In 1710 Handel returned to North Germany to accept the post of chapel master to the elector of Hanover, but on the condition that he be given an immediate leave of absence to visit London. Although he made one additional voyage back to his employer in Hanover in 1711 and many subsequent visits to the Continent, Handel conveniently forgot about his obligation to the Hanoverian court. London became the site of his musical activity and the place where he won fame and fortune.

After four years in Italy, London must have seemed a cultural backwater to Handel. Many of the streets were unpaved, the buildings were black with the soot of coal fires, and there was none of the art and architecture that graced Venice, Florence, or Rome. But there was opportunity. Handel soon found employment in the homes of the aristocracy and became the music tutor to the English royal family. As fate would have it, his continental employer, the elector of Hanover, became King George I of England in 1714, when the Hanoverians acceded to the throne on the extinction of the Stuart line. Fortunately for Handel, the new king bore his truant musician no grudge, and he was called on frequently to compose festival music to entertain the court or mark its progress. For these events Handel produced such works as *Water Music* (1717), *Music for the Royal Fireworks* (1749), and *Coronation Service* (1727), parts of which have been used at the coronation of every English monarch since its first hearing.

Handel in London

Handel and the Orchestral Dance Suite

WATER MUSIC (1717)

Aside from *Messiah*, Handel's most beloved composition is his *Water Music*. Handel's *Water Music* belongs to a genre of composition called a dance suite, a term derived from the French word *suite* (a succession of pieces). The dance suite is a collection of dances, usually varying from four to seven, all in one key and for one group of instruments, be it full orchestra, trio, or solo. *Water Music*, in fact, is a collection of three suites for orchestra that were performed one after the other. The listeners did not dance the music of Handel's suites. These were stylized, abstract dances. But it was the job of the composer to bring each one to life, to make it recognizable to the audience by incorporating the salient elements of rhythm and style of each particular dance.

the dance suite

Most Baroque dance suites begin with an overture, usually a **French overture,** so called because this style of overture was first created at the French royal court by Jean Baptiste Lully (1632–1687), the favored composer of King Louis XIV. (The French overture consists of two sections, the first slow, in duple meter, with dotted rhythms, and the second fast and light with imitative counterpoint.) After the overture comes the succession of dances. Among the dances that Handel popularized in his orchestral suites are the following.

FIGURE 7–10

The Prince of Wales (the future King George III) and his sisters, painted in 1733 by Philip Mercier. The Prince plays the cello and Princess Anne the harpsichord. Handel was the music tutor to the English royal family.

Water Music *heard on the River Thames*

Allemande: A stately dance in $\frac{4}{4}$ meter with gracefully interweaving lines.

Courante: A lively dance in $\frac{6}{4}$ with an upbeat* and frequent changes of metrical accent.

Saraband: A slow, elegant dance in $\frac{3}{4}$ with a strong accent on the second beat.

Minuet: A moderate dance in $\frac{3}{4}$ usually followed by another, shorter dance in the same style called the *trio* (see page 168).

Hornpipe: An energetic dance, derived from the country jig, in either $\frac{3}{2}$ or $\frac{2}{4}$ time.

Gigue: A fast dance in $\frac{6}{8}$ or $\frac{12}{8}$ with a constant eighth-note pulse that produces a galloplike effect.

But no matter what the rhythm or style of the dance, the form of each dance movement in the Baroque era was invariably the same: binary form* (see page 57). Binary form, of course, is a musical form with only two sections, **A** and **B,** each of which may be repeated. Normally **A** takes the movement from tonic to dominant, while **B** brings it back home to the tonic. Some dance movements are followed by a second, complementary dance, as the minuet is followed by a trio. In such cases the first dance should be repeated after the second.

Handel composed his *Water Music* during the summer of 1717 to please his patron, King George I, who was trying, in turn, to please his subjects. The German-born George I, the first of those stalwart Hanoverian monarchs who have sat on the throne of Great Britain up to the present day, was not universally loved. He refused to speak a word of English, preferring his native German. He fought with his son, the Prince of Wales, and banned him from court. His subjects thought the king dimwitted, "an honest blockhead," as one contemporary said.

To counter the growing unpopularity of the royal family, the king's ministers urged a program of public entertainments, including an evening of diversion on the River Thames for the lords of Parliament and the lesser people of London. Thus on July 17, 1717, the King and his court left London, accompanied by a small navy of boats, and progressed up the Thames to the strains of Handel's orchestral music. An eyewitness describes in detail this nautical parade:

> About eight in the evening the King repaired to his barge, into which were admitted the Duchess of Bolton, Countess Godolphin, Madam de Kilmansech, Mrs. Were and the Earl of Orkney, the Gentleman of the Bedchamber in Waiting. Next to the King's barge was that of the musicians, about 50 in number, who played on all kinds of instruments, to wit trumpets, horns, hautboys [oboes], bassoons, German flutes, French flutes [recorders], violins and basses; but there were no singers. The music had been composed specially by the famous Handel, a native of Halle [Germany], and His Majesty's principal Court Composer. His Majesty so greatly approved of the music that he caused it to be repeated three times in all, although each performance lasted an hour—namely twice before and once after supper. The evening weather was all that could be desired for the festivity, the number of barges and above all of boats filled with people desirous of hearing the music was beyond counting.

So broad are Handel's musical gestures and so brilliant his orchestral effects that even the "blockhead" king was enchanted by the fifty musicians playing *Water Music* on the neighboring barge. What makes the dance movements of *Water Music* so easy to comprehend is their formal clarity. Notice in the Minuet how Handel asks the French horns and trumpets first to announce both the **A** and **B** sections before passing this material on to the woodwinds and then to the full orchestra.

FIGURE 7–11

This view of London and the Thames River by Canaletto (1697–1768) captures vividly the setting for Handel's *Water Music*.

LISTENING GUIDE

George Frideric Handel
Water Music (1717)
Minuet and Trio

Intro CD (32)—Tape (A)

Minuet (triple meter, major key)
0:00   Horns introduce part **A**

0:12   Trumpets introduce part **B**

0:29   Winds and continuo play **A**
0:42   Full orchestra repeats **A**
0:55   Winds and continuo play **B**
1:08   Full orchestra repeats **B**

Trio (triple meter, minor key)
1:28   Strings and continuo play part **C**
1:43   Strings and continuo play part **D**

Minuet
2:19   Full orchestra plays **A**
2:31   Full orchestra plays **B**

The jaunty triple-meter Hornpipe is very brief, the complete dance requiring only forty seconds. For such a short piece to have an effect, Handel directed that it be played three times, first by strings and continuo, then by woodwinds and continuo, and finally by both strings and woodwinds together, along with continuo. The Minuet and the Hornpipe are just two of the twenty dances that make up Handel's *Water Music*.

LISTENING GUIDE

George Frideric Handel
Water Music
Hornpipe

Intro CD (33)—Tape (A)

(triple meter, major key)
0:00   Strings and continuo play part **A**

0:18   Sudden *piano* signals beginning of part **B**

(Hornpipe is repeated with new orchestration)
0:41   Woodwinds, drum, and continuo play part **A**
0:58   Woodwinds, drum, and continuo play part **B**

(Hornpipe is repeated with new orchestration)
1:19   Strings, woodwinds, drum, and continuo play part **A**
1:37   Sudden *piano* signals beginning of part **B**

Handel and the Oratorio

Handel moved to London in 1710, not for the chance to entertain the royal family, and certainly not for the climate or cuisine, but for the potentially lucrative opportunity to compose opera. With the rare exception of a work such as Purcell's *Dido and Aeneas* (see page 111), there was no English opera at this time. Instead, spoken plays with occasional musical interludes dominated the London stage. Handel intended to fill this void by importing Italian opera, which was then enormously popular on the Continent. Guaranteed a healthy share of the profits from the operas he produced, Handel rented the theater, composed the music, engaged high-paid soloists from Italy, led the rehearsals, and conducted the finished product from the harpsichord in the orchestral pit. From 1710 until 1728 he had great artistic and financial success, producing some two dozen examples of Italian *opera seria* (literally, serious, as opposed to comic, opera). Foremost among these was *Giulio Cesare* (*Julius Caesar*; 1724), a recasting of the story of Caesar's conquest of the army of Egypt and its queen, Cleopatra. But in 1728 the opera company Handel had founded, called the Royal Academy of Music, went bankrupt, a victim of the exorbitant fees paid the star singers and competition from other, upstart operatic companies. Handel continued to write opera into the 1730s, but he increasingly turned his attention to a musical genre similar in construction to opera, oratorio.

Handel as composer of Italian opera seria

An oratorio is literally "something sung in an oratory," an oratory being a hall or chapel used specifically for religious devotion as expressed in prayer and music. Thus, the oratorio as it first appeared in seventeenth-century Italy was an extended musical setting of a sacred text intended for the spiritual edification of the faithful and performed in a special hall or chapel. By the time it reached Handel's hands, however, the oratorio had become in most ways nothing but an opera with a religious subject.

Handel turns to oratorio

Both Baroque oratorio and opera begin with an overture, are divided into acts, and are composed primarily of recitatives and arias. But there are a few important differences, aside from the obvious fact that oratorio treats a religious subject. Oratorio, being a quasi-religious genre, is performed in a church, a theater, or a concert hall, but makes no use of staging and costumes. Because the subject matter is almost always sacred, there is more of an opportunity for moralizing, a dramatic function best performed by a chorus. Thus the chorus assumes greater importance in an oratorio. It sometimes serves as a narrator, but more often functions, like the chorus in ancient Greek drama, as the voice of the people commenting on the action that has transpired. Add to these the fact that oratorio in England is sung in English (not Italian), and its potential impact on a large segment of English society becomes obvious.

oratorio and opera compared

By the 1730s oratorio appeared to Handel as an attractive alternative to the increasingly unprofitable opera in London. He could do away with the irascible and expensive castrati and prima donnas. He no longer had to pay for elaborate sets and costumes. He could draw on the ancient English love of choral music, a tradition that extended well back into the Middle Ages. And he could exploit a new, untapped market—the faithful of the Puritan, Methodist, and growing evangelical sects in England who had viewed the pleasures of operatic theater with distrust and even contempt.

advantages of oratorio

MESSIAH (1741)

Beginning in 1732 and continuing over a twenty-year period, Handel wrote upward of twenty oratorios. The most famous of these is his *Messiah*, composed in the astonishingly short period of three and a half weeks during the summer of 1741. It was first performed in Dublin, Ireland, the following April as part of a charity benefit, with Handel conducting. Having heard the dress rehearsal, the local press waxed enthusiastic about the new oratorio, saying that it "far surpasses anything of that Nature, which has been performed in this or any other Kingdom." Such a large crowd was expected for the work of the famous Handel that ladies were urged not to wear hoopskirts, "as it will greatly encrease the Charity, by making Room for more company."

premiere in Dublin

Buoyed by his artistic and financial success in Dublin, Handel took *Messiah* back to London, made minor alterations, and performed it in Covent Garden Theater. In 1750 he again offered *Messiah*, this time in the chapel of the Foundling Hospital for orphans in London (Fig. 7–12), and again there was much popular acclaim for Handel as well as profit for charity. This was the first time one of his oratorios was sung in a religious setting rather than a theater or a concert hall. The annual repetition of *Messiah* in the Foundling Hospital chapel during Handel's lifetime and long after did much to convince the public that his oratorios were essentially religious music to be performed in church.

early performances

FIGURE 7–12

The chapel of the Foundling Hospital, London, where *Messiah* was performed annually for the benefit of the orphans.

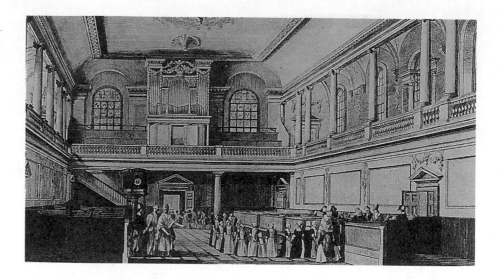

story of Messiah

In a general way, *Messiah* tells the story of the life of Christ. It is divided into three parts (instead of three acts): (I) the prophecy of His coming and His Incarnation; (II) His Passion and Resurrection, and the triumph of the Gospel; and (III) reflections on the Christian victory over death. In *Messiah* dramatic confrontation is replaced by a mood of lyrical meditation and, ultimately, exaltation. The music consists of fifty-three numbers: Nineteen are for chorus, sixteen are solo arias, sixteen are recitatives, and two are purely instrumental pieces.

There are many beautiful and stirring arias in *Messiah*, including "Every valley shall be exalted," "O thou that tellest good tidings to Zion," and "Rejoice greatly, o daughter of Zion." Significantly, "Rejoice greatly, o daughter of Zion" is on the same topic as Bach's cantata, *Awake, a Voice Is Calling* (see page 129): It tells of the joy felt by all true believers, here personified by the daughter of Zion, at the coming of the Messiah.

da capo *aria*

Handel composed "Rejoice greatly, o daughter of Zion" in the form of a modified *da capo* aria. A da capo aria has two musical sections, **A** and **B,** with the second usually having a different key and mood. When the singer reaches the end of part **B,** he or she is instructed by the words "da capo" to "take it from the top" and thus repeat **A,** note for note. What results is **ABA,** another example of ternary form* in music. Composers such as Handel and Bach sometimes change **A** when it returns so as to achieve variety. A modified *da capo* aria (**ABA′**) is thus created. When such a modification is effected, it usually allows the soloist to build to a final climax of vocal virtuosity. At the end of "Rejoice greatly, o daughter of Zion," for example, what was a relatively easy passage of simple stepwise motion at the end of **A** is transformed into a more difficult, and dramatic, series of leaps of octaves and sevenths in **A′.**

EXAMPLE 7–4

be- hold, thy   King   cometh   un - to   thee   be-hold, thy King comethun- to thee, be-hold, thy King

Examples of *da capo* form and modified *da capo* form abound in arias in both oratorio and opera of the late Baroque era. Indeed, the line of distinction between these two Baroque musical genres, between the sacred oratorio and the profane opera, was a thin one. Although the text of "Rejoice greatly, o daughter of Zion" comes from scriptures (Zechariah 9:9–10), the flamboyant style of singing has its origins in the more worldly opera house.

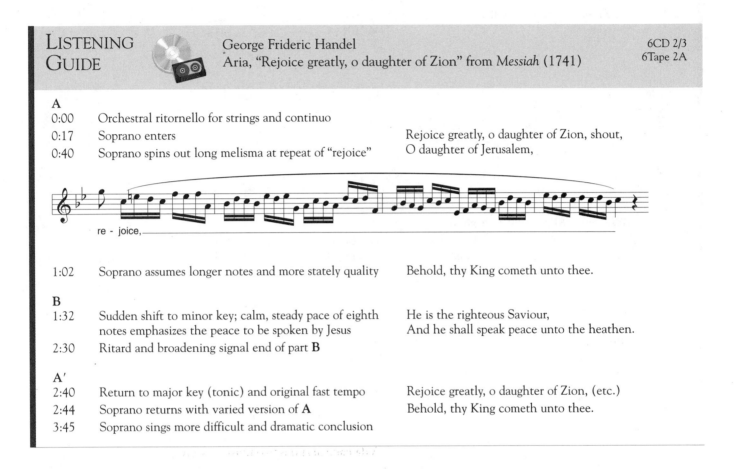

LISTENING GUIDE

George Frideric Handel
Aria, "Rejoice greatly, o daughter of Zion" from *Messiah* (1741)

6CD 2/3
6Tape 2A

A

0:00	Orchestral ritornello for strings and continuo	
0:17	Soprano enters	Rejoice greatly, o daughter of Zion, shout,
0:40	Soprano spins out long melisma at repeat of "rejoice"	O daughter of Jerusalem,

re - joice,

1:02	Soprano assumes longer notes and more stately quality	Behold, thy King cometh unto thee.

B

1:32	Sudden shift to minor key; calm, steady pace of eighth notes emphasizes the peace to be spoken by Jesus	He is the righteous Saviour, And he shall speak peace unto the heathen.
2:30	Ritard and broadening signal end of part **B**	

A'

2:40	Return to major key (tonic) and original fast tempo	Rejoice greatly, o daughter of Zion, (etc.)
2:44	Soprano returns with varied version of **A**	Behold, thy King cometh unto thee.
3:45	Soprano sings more difficult and dramatic conclusion	

Despite the bravura quality of the arias, the true glory of *Messiah* is to be found in its choruses. Handel was arguably the finest composer for chorus who ever lived. As a world traveler with an unsurpassed ear, he had absorbed the German tradition of the fugue and the Lutheran chorale; he knew the Venetian polychoral style of Gabrieli (see page 104) and the powerful English church anthems* (extended motets) of Henry Purcell; and, of course, he had a flair for the dramatic, gained from a lifetime in the theater.

Handel's choruses

Nowhere is Handel's choral mastery more evident than in the justly famous "Hallelujah" chorus that concludes Part II of *Messiah*. Here a variety of choral styles are displayed in quick succession: chordal, unison, chorale, fugal, and fugal and chordal together. As we have seen (page 124), contrast of styles, textures, and colors creates the theatrical quality of Baroque art. So moved was King George II when he first heard these great opening chords, as the story goes, that he rose to his feet in admiration, thereby establishing the tradition of the audience standing for the "Hallelujah" chorus—for no one sat while the king stood. Indeed, this movement would serve well as a royal coronation march, though in *Messiah*, of course, it is Christ the King who is being crowned.

LISTENING GUIDE

George Frideric Handel
"Hallelujah" chorus from *Messiah* (1741)

Intro CD (39)—Tape (B)
6CD 2/4; 6Tape 2A

0:00	Brief string introduction
0:06	Chorus enters with two salient motives:

0:16	Five more chordal exclamations of the "Hallelujah" motive, but at a higher pitch level
0:25	Chorus sings new theme in unison answered by chordal cries of "Hallelujah"

0:35	Music repeated but at a lower pitch	
0:47	Fuguelike imitation begins with subject	"For the Lord God omnipotent reigneth"
1:13	Quiet and then loud; set in chorale style	"The kingdom of this world is become the Kingdom of our Lord . . ."
1:31	New fuguelike section begins with entry in bass	

1:53	Altos and then sopranos begin long ascent in long notes	"King of Kings and Lord of Lords"
2:33	Basses and sopranos reenter with	"And he shall reign for ever and ever"
2:44	Tenors and basses sing in long notes	"King of Kings and Lord of Lords"
3:00	Incessant major tonic chord	"King of Kings"
3:26	Broad final cadence	"Hallelujah"

(Listening Exercise 21)

The "Hallelujah" chorus is a strikingly effective work mainly because the large choral force creates a sense of heavenly power and strength. In fact, however, Handel's chorus for the original Dublin *Messiah* was much smaller than those used today. It included no more than four singers on the alto, tenor, and bass parts and six choirboys singing the soprano. The orchestra was equally slight. For the Foundling Hospital performances of the 1750s, however, the orchestra grew to thirty-eight players. Then, in the course of the next hundred years, the chorus progressively swelled to as many as four thousand with a balancing orchestra of five hundred in what were billed as "Festivals of the People" in honor of Handel (Fig. 7–13).

Handel's fame grows   And just as there was a continual increase in the performing forces for his *Messiah,* so too Handel's fortune and reputation grew. Toward the end of his life he owned a squire's house in the center of London, bought paintings, including a large and "indeed excellent" Rembrandt, and, on his death, left an enormous estate of nearly twenty thousand pounds, as the newspapers of the day were quick

to report. More than three thousand persons attended his funeral in Westminster Abbey on April 20, 1759, and a sculpture of the composer holding an aria from *Messiah* was erected above his grave and is still visible today (Fig. 7–14). As a memento of Handel's music, *Messiah* was an apt choice, for it is still performed each year at Christmas by countless amateur and professional groups throughout the world.

FIGURES 7–13 AND 7–14

(left) An enormous orchestra, and even larger chorus, performing an oratorio of Handel's at the Great Handel Festival, London, 1859.
(right) Handel's funeral monument at Westminster Abbey. The composer holds the aria "I know that my Redeemer liveth" from *Messiah*.

LISTENING EXERCISES

19 Johann Sebastian Bach
Cantata, *Awake, a Voice Is Calling* (1731)
First movement

6CD 1/16; 6Tape 1B
3CD 2/6; 3Tape 2A

The purpose of this listening exercise is to have you learn to recognize a chorale tune and to differentiate it from the surrounding musical texture. First, read through the questions. Then listen to the entire first movement following the Listening Guide on page 130. This will give you an overall sense of the relationship of the chorale to the other voices and to the instruments. If some of these questions seem complex, so is Bach's writing in this impressive choral fantasy!

1. Throughout the course of this movement, does the soprano part do anything other than sing the chorale tune in long note values? _____ If so, what? _____
2. Which part is moving the fastest in this complex musical texture?
   a. the soprano part with the chorale tune
   b. violins
   c. the bass line played by cellos and double basses
3. Which part is moving the slowest in this texture?
   a. the soprano part with the chorale tune
   b. violins
   c. the bass line played by cellos and double basses

4. (0:33–0:51) The sopranos enter with the first phrase of the chorale melody. Do the other voices (altos, tenors, and basses) enter before or after them? _____

5. (0:33–0:51) While the sopranos sing on high, what are the cellos and double basses playing?
   a. a dotted note pattern
   b. slow equal notes
   c. fast running notes

6. (0:58–1:16) The second phrase of the chorale tune now is heard in the soprano part while the lower voices enter in ascending lines of counterpoint against it. What do the cellos and double basses do at 1:08 in response to this rising counterpoint?
   a. They join in the counterpoint, rising rapidly as had the voices.
   b. They continue on with the dotted note pattern.
   c. They continue on with the slow equal notes.

7. (1:28–1:49) Here the sopranos sing the third phrase of the chorale. Do the other voices, which have been singing counterpoint against the sopranos, disappear in this section? _____

8. (1:50–3:39) Now the previous music (0:00–1:49) is repeated with new text. Are the roles of the various parts still the same in the repeat? (Do sopranos still carry the chorale; altos, tenors, and basses provide a counterpoint; violins play a ritornello; and cellos and basses set a harmonic foundation?) _____

9. (4:44–5:27) Here on the word "Allelujah" the altos, tenors, and then basses enter joyfully and in succession. What musical texture do they create?
   a. imitative polyphony
   b. nonimitative polyphony
   c. chordal homophony

10. Now go on to listen to the opening (0:00–0:47) of the famous "Hallelujah" chorus of Handel's *Messiah* (Intro CD (39)—Tape (B); 6CD 2/4; 6Tape 2A). In what ways is Handel's writing for chorus different from Bach's as exhibited in this first movement of his cantata? Specifically, circle each of the following statements that is correct.
    a. Handel has the voices, not the instruments, begin his chorus.
    b. Handel makes no use of a chorale tune in long notes in the soprano.
    c. Handel has no instrumental ritornello that is different in mood and style from the choral parts.
    d. Handel has his chorus sing the first word, "Hallelujah," in clear, chordal homophony.

| 20 | Johann Sebastian Bach | 6CD 2/2; 6Tape 2A |
| | Organ Fugue in G minor (ca. 1710) | 3CD 2/7; 3Tape 2A |

The following diagram is essentially the same as that found on page 137. It charts the flow of the music as Bach's Organ Fugue in G minor unfolds from the straightforward exposition, through the increasingly lengthy episodes, to the final statement of the subject in the bass. For this exercise, you are asked to make your own time log, or listening guide, for the nine entries of the subject. Above the blank line that shows each subject entry (_____), write in the time at which the subject appears. The first, of course, will be "S0:00." You don't have to indicate times during the episodes, but see if you can sense that modulations are occurring.

†This entry starts in the tenor and continues in the soprano.

---

21 George Frideric Handel
"Hallelujah" chorus from *Messiah* (1741)

Intro CD (39)—Tape (B)
6CD 2/4; 6Tape 2A

1. How many musical lines are prominent during the instrumental introduction?
   a. one: basses (cellos and double basses)
   b. two: violins and basses (cellos and double basses)
   c. three: oboes, violins, and basses (cellos and double basses)
2. What musical texture does Handel create as the chorus first sings "Hallelujah"?
   a. homophony   b. polyphony   c. monophony
3. (0:25–0:31; "For the Lord God omnipotent reigneth") As the chorus sings in unison, do the violins double (play the same line as) the voices?

_____

4. Unison singing and playing creates what kind of texture?

_____

5. (0:47–1:12; "For the Lord God omnipotent reigneth") Now we have a passage of imitative, fuguelike writing in which a subject is presented in succession in the voices. In what order do the voices enter with this subject?
   a. soprano, alto, male voices
   b. alto, male voices, soprano
   c. soprano, male voices, alto

6. (1:32–1:52; "And he shall reign for ever and ever") Again, Handel offers another passage of fugal writing, with a new subject. In what order do the voices enter?
   a. bass, alto, tenor, soprano
   b. bass, tenor, soprano, alto
   c. bass, tenor, alto, soprano
   d. bass, soprano, alto, tenor

7. (2:06–2:30) What are the sopranos doing here?
   a. rising by step
   b. rising by leap
   c. rising in an arpeggio

8. (beginning at 2:52) Which brass instrument reinforces and ornaments the soprano line from here to the end? _____

9. (3:22–3:24) In a brilliant stroke Handel sets off and highlights the final statement of "Hallelujah" (and the final cadence) in which of the following ways?
   a. precedes it by a "pregnant pause," a long rest
   b. anticipates the "Hallelujah" with an entry in the bass

10. What is it that creates the drama and grandeur in this choral movement?
    a. the skillful use of a variety of textures and styles
    b. a very clear setting of the English text (music reflecting the natural stresses in the words)
    c. the concentration of all voices and instruments on a few, simple musical gestures
    d. all of the above

KEY WORDS

cantata	exposition	prelude
chorale	figured bass	subject
clarino playing	French overture	*The Well-Tempered*
da capo aria	fugue	*Clavier*
dance suite	*opera seria*	walking bass
episode	oratorio	

For a checklist of musical style of the late Baroque period, see page 66.

CLASSICAL IDEALS: THE WORLD OF HAYDN AND MOZART

8

"Classical" as a musical term has two separate, though related, meanings. We use the word "classical" to signify the "serious" or "art" music of the West as distinguished from folk music, popular music, jazz, and the traditional music of various ethnic cultures. We call this music "classical" because there is something about the excellence of its form and style that makes it enduring, just as a finely crafted watch or a vintage automobile may be said to be a "classic" because it has a timeless beauty. Yet in the same breath we may refer to "Classical" music (now with a capital C), and by this we mean the music of a specific historical period, 1750–1820, a period of the great works of Haydn and Mozart and the early masterpieces of Beethoven. The creations of these artists have become so identified in the public mind with musical proportion, balance, and formal correctness—with standards of musical excellence—that this comparatively brief period has given its name to all music of lasting aesthetic worth.

"Classical" derives from the Latin *classicus*, meaning "something of the first rank or highest quality." To the men and women of the eighteenth century, no art, architecture, philosophy, or political institutions were more admirable, virtuous, and worthy of emulation than those of ancient Greece and Rome. Other periods in Western history also have been inspired by classical antiquity—the Renaissance heavily, the early Baroque less so, and our own century to some degree—but no period more than the eighteenth century. This was the time of the discovery of the ruins of Pompeii (1748), of the publication of Winkelmann's *History of Ancient Art* (1764) and Gibbon's *Decline and Fall of the Roman Empire* (1788).

It was also the period in which young English aristocrats made the "grand tour" of Italy and carted back to their country estates Roman statues, columns, and parts of entire villas. Classical architecture, with its formal control of space, geometric shapes, balance, and symmetrical design, became the only style thought worthy for domestic and state buildings of consequence. European palaces, opera houses, episcopal residences, and country homes all made use of it. Thomas Jefferson also traveled to Italy in these years while American ambassador to France, and later was instrumental in establishing Classical design in this country. Our nation's capitol, many state capitols, and countless other governmental and university buildings abound with the well-proportioned columns, porticos, and rotundas of the Classical style.

FIGURES 8–1 AND 8–2

FIGURES 8–1 AND 8–2

(left) The fourth-century Pantheon in Rome. (right) The Library of the University of Virginia, designed by Thomas Jefferson in the late eighteenth century. Jefferson had visited Rome and studied the ancient ruins while ambassador to France (1784–1789). The portico, with columns and triangular pediment, and the central rotunda are all elements of Classical style in architecture.

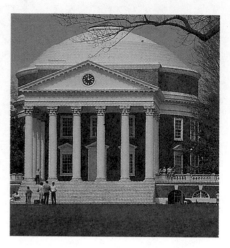

FIGURE 8–3

Thomas Jefferson, by the French sculptor Houdon, 1789.

THE ENLIGHTENMENT

The Classical era in music, art, and architecture coincides with the period in philosophy and letters called the Enlightenment. During the Enlightenment, also referred to as the Age of Reason, thinkers gave free rein to the pursuit of truth and the discovery of natural laws. This is the era that saw the rise of a natural religion called Deism, the belief that a Creator made the world, set it in motion, and has left it alone ever since. This is also the age of such scientific advances as the discovery of electricity and the invention of the steam engine. The first *Encyclopedia Britannica* appeared in 1771 and the French *Encyclopédie* between 1751 and 1772, a twenty-four volume set whose authors discarded traditional religious convictions and superstitions in favor of more rational scientific, philosophical, and political beliefs. In France the encyclopedists Voltaire (1694–1778), Rousseau (1712–1778), and Diderot (1713–1784) espoused the principles of social justice, equality, religious tolerance, and freedom of speech. These Enlightenment ideals subsequently became fundamental to all democratic governments and were enshrined in our American constitution.

Needless to say, the notion that all persons are created equal and should enjoy full political freedom put the thinkers of the Enlightenment on a collision course with the defenders of the existing social order. The old political structure had been built on the mysteries of the church, the privileges of the nobility, and the divine right of kings. Voltaire attacked the habits and prerogatives of both clergy and aristocracy, and championed middle-class virtues: honesty, common sense, and hard work. The extravagant gestures, sword, and wig of the frivolous courtier were an easy target for his pen. A more natural appearance, one appropriate to a tradesman, merchant, or manufacturer, now became the paradigm.

Spurred on by economic self-interest and the principles of the philosophers, an increasingly numerous and self-confident middle class in France and America rebelled against the monarchy and its supporters. The Age of Reason gave way to a newer Age of Revolution.

MUSIC AND SOCIAL CHANGE: COMIC OPERA

Music was affected by these profound social changes, and in some ways it helped to precipitate them. A new form of opera, comic opera, proved to be a powerful vehicle for social reform. Opera in the Baroque period had been dominated by *opera seria** (see page 142). It was beautiful, grandiose, somewhat stiff, and expensive to mount. Portraying the deeds of mythological heros, gods and goddesses, and historical emperors and kings, it was the quintessential opera of the aristocracy. By contrast, the new **comic opera,** called **opera buffa** in Italy, was the opera of the middle class. It made use of everyday characters and situations; it employed spoken dialogues and simple songs in place of recitatives and *da capo** arias; and it was liberally spiced with sight gags, slapstick comedy, and bawdy humor. The librettos, such as they were, either poked fun at the nobility for its pomposity and incompetence or criticized it for being heartless.

Like seditious pamphlets, comic operas appeared in every country; among them were John Gay's *The Beggar's Opera* (1728) in England, Giovanni Pergolesi's *La serva padrona* (*The Maid Made Master*, 1733) in Italy, and Jean-Jacques Rousseau's *Le devin du village* (*The Village Soothsayer*, 1752) in France. And composers of greater stature were seduced by the charms of this middle-class entertainment. Mozart, who was treated poorly by the nobility throughout his short life, set one libretto in which a barber outsmarts a count and holds him up to public ridicule, *Le nozze di Figaro* (*The Marriage of Figaro*, 1786) (Fig. 8–4), and another, *Don Giovanni* (1787), in which the villain is a leading nobleman of the town. The play that served as the basis for Mozart's *Figaro* was banned by the authorities when it first appeared in Paris. By the time of the French Revolution (1789), comic opera, a rebellious upstart, had nearly driven the established *opera seria* off the eighteenth-century stage.

PUBLIC CONCERTS

The social changes of the eighteenth century, in turn, affected who it was that listened to music. In an earlier day a citizen might only hear sacred vocal music in a church or a bit of instrumental music at court, if he or she happened to be lucky enough to be an invited guest. But by mid-century the bookkeeper, physician, cloth merchant, and customs agent collectively had enough disposable income to organize and patronize their own concerts. In Leipzig, for example, the merchants got together to form the *Gewandhaus* ("Clothiers' House") concerts, which were held in the great hall of that guild; this *Gewandhaus* orchestra is still active today. Entrepreneurs in London offered concerts in the Vauxhall Gardens, where music could be heard inside in the orchestra room and outside as well (Fig. 8–5).

FIGURE 8–4

"Cherubino is discovered by the Count," an illustration from a 1785 edition of Pierre Beaumarchais's play *The Marriage of Figaro*. It was on this play that Mozart based his opera of the same name.

FIGURE 8–5

A public concert in the Vauxhall Gardens, London. A singer (right) performs from the balcony, with an accompanying orchestra (left) behind her.

In Paris, then a city of 500,000, one could attend, as a citizen of the day said, "the best concerts every day with complete freedom." The most successful Parisian concert series was the *Concert spirituel*, which was advertised to the public by means of flyers or handbills distributed in the streets. To make its offerings accessible to a broad stratum of society, it also instituted a two-tiered system of prices (four livres for boxes and two livres for the pit). Thus we can trace to the middle of the eighteenth century the tradition of middle-class citizens attending public performances in return for an admission fee. The institution of "concerts" as we know them and the development of a broadly based listening audience date from this time.

FIGURE 8–6

Mozart's piano, preserved in the house of his birth in Salzburg. The keyboard spans only five octaves, typical for the late eighteenth-century piano.

THE ADVENT OF THE PIANO

The newly affluent middle class wished not only to listen to music but to play it as well. Most of this music making was centered in the home and around an instrument that first entered public consciousness in the Classical period: the piano. Invented in Italy about 1700, the piano gradually replaced the harpsichord as the keyboard instrument of preference (Fig. 8–6). And with good reason, for the piano could play at more than one dynamic level (hence the original name pianoforte, "soft-loud"). Compared with the harpsichord, the piano could generate music that was more dramatic—because of the possibility of sudden contrast—and at the same time more subtle—because of the way phrases could be graded and shaped by increasing or diminishing the volume of successive notes.

women play the piano

Those who played this new domestic instrument were mostly amateurs, and the great majority of these were women. Young ladies were encouraged to show skill on the piano as a means of demonstrating their refinement. This social requirement, in turn, encouraged a simpler, more homophonic keyboard style, one that would presumably not tax the technical limitations of the female performer. The spirit of democracy may have been in the air, but this was still very much a sexist age. It was assumed that ladies would not wish, as one publication said, "to bother their pretty little heads with counterpoint and harmony," but would be content with a tuneful melody and a few rudimentary chords to flesh it out. Collections such as *Keyboard Pieces for Ladies* (1768) were directed at these new musical consumers.

CLASSICAL SIMPLICITY AND BALANCE

Painting of the late eighteenth century is often called Neoclassical, because it draws heavily on the themes and styles of classical antiquity. Many of the major artists of the day—among them American Benjamin West (1738–1820), Frenchman Jacques-Louis David (1748–1825) (Fig. 8–7), and Englishwoman Angelica Kauffman (1741–1807)—traveled to Rome between 1760 and 1790 to study the architecture, mosaics, and sculpture that remained in the Roman forum

FIGURE 8–7

Immobile figures and simple yet grand gestures create a sense of "noble simplicity and calm grandeur" in Jacques-Louis David's *The Death of Socrates* (1787).

and elsewhere around the city. They incorporated in their works not only the style and ornament of Roman dress, but also the clarity, simplicity, and formal balance inherent in ancient classical design.

Angelica Kauffman's painting *The Artist [Angelica Kauffman] in the Character of Design Listening to the Inspiration of Poetry* (Fig. 8–8) shows a pair of balanced figures in Roman costume, Design on the left and Poetry on the right. Poetry is crowned with the laurel wreath of the Roman poet laureate. In addition, each figure holds a symbol of her art, Design a drawing board and Poetry a lyre. To their left are a pair of Greek columns, which similarly invoke a feeling of antiquity and at the same time balance the female pair. Nowhere to be seen are secondary figures who might clamor for the viewer's attention. Our eyes focus solely on Design and Poetry. The simplicity, balance, and static quality of the painting creates a feeling of calm, serenity, and repose.

These same features are to be found in the aria "Voi che sapete" ("You ladies who know") from Mozart's comic opera *The Marriage of Figaro* (1786). Here our ears concentrate exclusively on the melody. It consists of a succession of short phrases, amost all of them four measures in length. The opening provides a very clear example of a couplet of four-bar phrases arranged as an antecedent–consequent* pair. Subsequent phrases are also usually grouped in pairs. The simple chordal harmony (spaced out beneath as arpeggios*) supports, but in no way competes with, the lyrical top line. Toward the end, the opening phrase returns to round off the whole. The text is a succession of couplets, one pair for each stanza. All is clarity, balance, and simplicity. Yet somehow, from the simplest of materials, the genius of Mozart creates a musical object of sublime beauty. The aria "You ladies who know" embodies classical perfection.

FIGURE 8–8

Angelica Kauffman's *The Artist in the Character of Design Listening to the Inspiration of Poetry* (1782).

LISTENING GUIDE

Wolfgang Amadeus Mozart
Aria, "You ladies who know"
from the comic opera *The Marriage of Figaro* (1786)

6CD 2/6
6Tape 2A

Characters: Cherubino, an infatuated youth, and Suzanna, the older, wiser betrothed of Figaro. [Because Cherubino is a young adolescent, Mozart wrote the part for a high (soprano) voice. It is traditionally sung by a woman dressed as a boy.]
Situation: Cherubino (a soprano), sings to Suzanna of the pains and pleasures of love.

Time	Description	Italian	English
0:00	Orchestral introduction with antecedent–consequent phrases		
0:17	Voice enters with the antecedent phrase, inserts a new four-bar phrase, and then moves on to the consequent phrase	Voi che sapete che cosa è amor, donne, vedete s'io l'ho nel cor.	You ladies who know the nature of love, see if I have it within my heart.
0:42	A succession of paired phrases	Quello ch'io provo vi ridirò; è per me nuovo, capir non so. Sento un affetto pien di desir,	What I experience I will explain; it's so new to me I don't understand it. I have a feeling full of desire,
1:08	Charming major on "delightful" turns to anguished minor on "tormenting"	ch'ora è diletto, ch'ora è martir. Gelo, e poi sento l'alma avvampar, e in un momento torno a gelar. Ricero un bene fuori di me, non so chi'l tiene, non so cos'è.	sometimes delightful, sometimes tormenting. At first I freeze, and then my spirit burns, and then in a moment I turn to ice. I seek a treasure outside myself, I don't know who holds it, I don't even know what it is.
1:50	Rising repetitions insistently suggest "sighing and groaning"	Sospiro e gemo senza voler, palpito e tremo senza saper. Non trovo pace notte, nè dì ma pur mi piace languir così.	I sigh and groan without wanting to, I shake and tremble and know not why. I find no peace night or day, yet it only pleases me to languish so.
2:10	Peace is restored with return of opening phrase	Voi che sapete che cosa è amor, donne, vedete s'io l'ho nel cor.	You ladies who know the nature of love, see if I have it within my heart.

Vienna: A City of Music

During the second half of the eighteenth century, Vienna rose to prominence as a place hospitable to the growth of music in the new Classical style. Indeed, Vienna became so important as a center of musical composition that the late eighteenth century is often called the age of the Viennese Classical style. The city owed its importance to a fortuitous location. As the capital city of the old Holy Roman Empire, Vienna was the administrative center for portions of modern-day Germany, Croatia, Bosnia, Serbia, Slovakia, The Czech Republic, Hungary, and Italy, in addition to all of Austria, and thus was a cultural crossroads for Central

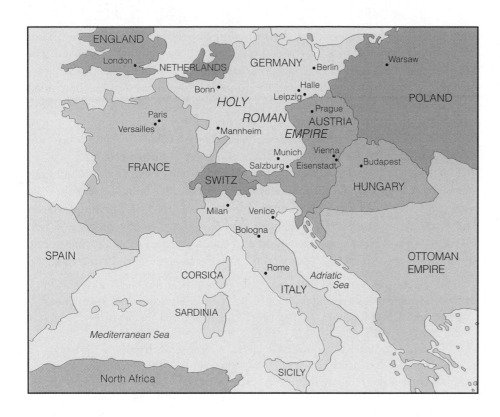

Europe (see Fig. 8–9). Musicians such as Christoph Gluck (1714–1787) from Bohemia (The Czech Republic), Antonio Salieri (1750–1825) from northern Italy, Franz Joseph Haydn (1732–1809) from Rohrau in lower Austria, Wolfgang Amadeus Mozart (1756–1791) from Salzburg in upper Austria, and Ludwig van Beethoven (1770–1827) from the German Rhineland gravitated toward Vienna for its rich musical life. There were theaters for German and Italian opera, concerts in the streets on fine summer nights, and ballroom dances where as many as four thousand persons might sway to a minuet, a contradance, or even a waltz by Mozart or Beethoven. In a city of nearly 200,000 inhabitants (the fourth largest in Europe behind London, Paris, and Naples), there were estimated to be 300 piano teachers. "There cannot be many cities in which musical amateurism is as widespread as it is here. Everybody plays, everybody takes music lessons," reported a journal of the day. And the musical allure of Vienna continued into the nineteenth century. In addition to native-born Franz Schubert (1797–1828), outsiders such as Anton Bruckner (1824–1896), Johannes Brahms (1833–1897), and Gustav Mahler (1860–1911) spent many of their most productive years there. Even today Vienna remains the capital of a nation (Austria) that spends nearly as much money on its state opera as it does on national defense.

"everybody takes music lessons"

FRANZ JOSEPH HAYDN (1732–1809)

Thus, it was only natural that Franz Joseph Haydn, the son of a wheelwright from Rohrau in lower (eastern) Austria, should be sent to the capital to nurture his obvious musical talent. Haydn was born in 1732, and by the age of eight his pleasing voice had caught the attention of local church authorities. Soon he was

FIGURE 8–10

A portrait of Franz Joseph Haydn painted in 1791, when the composer was in London.

composing before the time of copyright

Haydn in London

singing among the choirboys at the cathedral of St. Stephen in Vienna. After nearly ten years of service his voice broke and he was abruptly dismissed. For most of the 1750s Haydn eked out a meager living as a free-lance musician—"miserable breadwinning" he called it: He gave keyboard lessons, accompanied singers, and sang or played violin or organ at three churches each Sunday, moving quickly from one to the next. All the while he studied musical composition. By 1761 he had progressed to the point where he was able to obtain a position as composer and leader of the orchestra at the court of Prince Esterházy.

The Esterházy were a noble Hungarian family with extensive landholdings southeast of Vienna and a passionate interest in music. As did many wealthy aristocrats of the time, Prince Nikolaus Esterházy (1714–1790) maintained an orchestra, a chapel for singing religious music, and a theater for opera. When Haydn was first engaged he was required to sign a contract of employment, one that suggests the subservient place of the composer in eighteenth-century society:

> [He] and all the musicians shall appear in uniform, and the said Joseph Haydn shall take care that he and all the members of the orchestra follow the instructions given, and appear in white stocking, white linen, powdered, and with either a pigtail or a tiewig. . . .
>
> The said [Haydn] shall be under obligation to compose such music as his Serene Highness may command, and neither to communicate such compositions to any other person, nor to allow them to be copied, but he shall retain them for the absolute use of his Highness, and not compose for any other person without the knowledge and permission of his Highness.

Thus, not only did Haydn lead the life of a liveried servant at court, dressing like the other domestics, but he also was prohibited from circulating his music without the express permission of his patron. But Nikolaus Esterházy was a benign ruler, and Haydn's symphonies, quartets, and sonatas came to be known not only in Vienna but in foreign capitals as well. In the 1770s they surfaced in Amsterdam, London, and Paris in "pirated" editions. Since there was no international copyright in those years, a publisher might simply print a work from a copyist's score without the composer's knowledge or consent. When Haydn signed another contract with Prince Nikolaus in 1779, there was no such "exclusive use" provision, and he began to sell his works to various publishers, sometimes consigning the same piece to two or three at the same time!

For a period of nearly thirty years Haydn served Nikolaus Esterházy, writing symphonies and divertimentos* for evening entertainment, operas for the court theater (see Fig. 10–3), and string trios in which the prince himself might participate. When Nikolaus died in 1790, the Esterházy orchestra was dismissed in favor of a smaller, military band. Haydn retained his title as court composer as well as his full salary, but he was now free to travel as he wished. After settling briefly in Vienna, he journeyed to London where he had been engaged at a substantial fee to compose and conduct. From this commission resulted the twelve London symphonies, which were first performed in the Hanover Square Rooms (see Fig. 9–8), a large public concert hall built in part with capital supplied by Johann Christian Bach, old Bach's youngest son. Haydn stayed in London during 1791–1792 and returned again for the concert season 1794–1795. He was presented to the king and queen, received the honorary degree of doctor of music at Oxford, and was generally accorded the status of a visiting celebrity, as a letter written within a fortnight of his arrival attests:

FIGURE 8–11

A public performance of Haydn's oratorio *The Creation* given at the university in Vienna in 1808 to mark the composer's seventy-sixth birthday. Haydn is seated at the lower center. The orchestra, which can be seen on the podium at the rear, is being conducted by Antonio Salieri.

Everyone wants to know me. I had to dine out six times up to now, and if I wanted, I could have an invitation every day; but first I must consider my health and second my work. Except for the nobility, I admit no callers 'til 2 o'clock in the afternoon.

After Haydn returned home to Vienna for good in the summer of 1795, he wrote mainly Masses for chorus and orchestra and two oratorios, *The Creation* (1798) and *The Seasons* (1801)—it seems that he had been deeply impressed by the performances of Handel's oratorios he had heard while in England. His last public appearance was in 1808 for a performance of *The Creation* given in his honor in the festival hall of the university and conducted by court chapel master Antonio Salieri (Fig. 8–11). He died the following spring, on May 31, 1809, just two weeks after the besieging armies of Napoleon had conquered Vienna.

Haydn's long life, commitment to duty, and unflagging industry resulted in an impressive number of musical compositions: 104 symphonies, about 70 string quartets, nearly a dozen operas, 52 piano sonatas, 15 Masses, and 2 oratorios. He began composing before the death of Bach (1750) and did not put down his pen until about the time Beethoven set to work on his Fifth Symphony (1808). Thus, Haydn not only witnessed but, more than any other composer, helped to create the mature Classical style.

Haydn's accomplishments

Despite his accomplishments, he did not rebel against the modest station assigned to him in traditional eighteenth-century society: "I have associated with emperors, kings, and many great people," he said, "and I have heard many flattering things from them, but I would not live in familiar relations with such persons; I prefer to be close to people of my own standing." And though keenly aware of his own musical gifts, he was quick to recognize talent in others, especially Mozart: "Friends often flatter me that I have some genius, but he [Mozart] stood far above me."

WOLFGANG AMADEUS MOZART (1756–1791)

Indeed, Wolfgang Amadeus Mozart may be the greatest musical genius the world has ever known. Mendelssohn (1809–1847) and Schubert (1797–1828) were

FIGURE 8–12

An unfinished portrait of Mozart executed by his brother-in-law Joseph Lange during 1789–1790.

perhaps his equals as youthful composers. But who, except possibly Bach, can match the diversity, breadth of expression, and perfect formal control present in the best works of Mozart?

The stories of Mozart's prodigious musical talent are many. As a child he could identify the notes played in any chord, judge the pitch of an instrument within an eighth of a tone, or pick out a wrong note in a musical score while crawling on his back across a table. As a youth he heard a motet sung in the Sistine Chapel in Rome, went to his room, and wrote it down by memory, note for note. He frequently copied one of his finished compositions onto a score while working out a new piece in his head. Little wonder that the great German poet Goethe (1749–1832), who had heard Mozart play as a child, referred to him as "the human incarnation of a divine force of creation."

Mozart was born in Salzburg, Austria, in 1756. His father, Leopold, was a violinist in the orchestra of the archbishop of Salzburg, and his older sister, Nannerl, was also a talented performer (Fig. 8–13). Leopold was quick to recognize the musical gifts of his son, who by the age of six was playing the piano, violin, and organ as well as composing. The Mozart family coached off to Vienna, where the children displayed their musical wares before Empress Maria Theresa (1717–1780). They then embarked on a three-year tour of Northern Europe that included extended stops in Munich, Brussels, Paris, London, Amsterdam, and Geneva. In London, Wolfgang sat on the knee of Johann Christian Bach (1735–1782) and improvised a fugue. And here, at the age of eight, he heard his first two symphonies performed. Eventually, the Mozarts made their way back to Salzburg. But in 1768 they were off again to Vienna, where the now twelve-year-old Wolfgang staged a production of his first opera, *Bastien und Bastienne,* in the home of the famous Dr. Franz Anton Mesmer (1733–1815), the inventor of the theory of animal magnetism (hence, "to mesmerize"). The next year father and son visited the major cities of Italy, including Rome, where the pope dubbed Wolfgang a Knight of the Golden Spur. Although the aim of this globe-trotting was to acquire fame and fortune, the result was that Mozart, unlike Haydn, was exposed at an early age to a wealth of musical styles—French Baroque, English

FIGURES 8–13 AND 8–14

(left) Young Mozart at the keyboard, with his sister, Nannerl, and his father, Leopold, painted in Paris, 1763–1764, during their three-year tour of Europe. (right) Archbishop Colloredo, the unsympathetic patron of both Wolfgang Mozart and his father Leopold.

Mozart and *Amadeus*

Perhaps you have seen the extraordinary film *Amadeus* (1985) by Milos Forman, based on a play by Peter Schaffer, and wondered if the Mozart portrayed there bore any relation to the real Mozart. The answer is, in a few ways, yes; in most ways, no. To be sure, Mozart's lifestyle was somewhat chaotic, he had expensive tastes, and he was often downright silly in his behavior. Yet there is no hint of drunkenness in the contemporary documents; he had an excellent, if erratic income; and his childish behavior, according to his brother-in-law Joseph Lange, was the way in which he released excess tension built up during concentrated periods of creative activity. Mozart did not die poor. Indeed, his income from two major operas in 1791 and the famous Requiem Mass made his last year one of his most lucrative. Nor was he abandoned to suffer a pauper's funeral. He received the same sort of burial (placed in a common grave) as eighty-five percent of the upper-middle-class in Vienna at that time. Nor, finally, was Mozart poisoned by his principal rival in Vienna, the composer Antonio Salieri (1750–1825). Salieri, court composer to Emperor Joseph II and his two successors, was a universally respected, if not supremely gifted, musician who later went on to become, at various times,

the teacher of Beethoven, Schubert, Liszt, and even one of Mozart's two sons. As court composer to his imperial majesty, Salieri had little to fear from Mozart, no matter how enormous the latter's genius.

A scene from Amadeus.

choral, German polyphonic, and Italian vocal. His extraordinarily keen ear absorbed them all, and ultimately they increased the breadth and substance of his music.

A period of relative stability followed: For much of the 1770s Mozart resided in Salzburg, where, like his father, he had been taken on as a violinist and composer to the archbishop. Unfortunately, the reigning archbishop, Colloredo (Fig. 8–14), was a stern, somewhat miserly man who had little sympathy for Mozart, genius or not. As was the custom since medieval times, this prince of the Church, whom Mozart refers to in his letters as "the Archboobie," was as much a political figure as a spiritual leader. Mozart was given a place in the orchestra, a small salary, and his board. Like the musicians at the court of Esterházy, those at Salzburg ate with the cooks and valets. For a Knight of the Golden Spur who had played for kings and queens across Europe, this was humble fare indeed, and Mozart chafed under this system of aristocratic patronage. After several unpleasant scenes in the spring of 1781, the twenty-five-year-old composer cut himself free of the archbishop and determined to make a living as an independent musician in Vienna.

Mozart chose Vienna partly because of the city's rich musical life and partly because it was a comfortable distance from his overbearing father. In a letter to his sister written in the spring of 1782, Wolfgang spells out his daily regimen in the Austrian capital.

> My hair is always done by six o'clock in the morning and by seven I am fully dressed. I then compose until nine. From nine to one I give lessons. Then I lunch,

FIGURE 8–15

Antonio Salieri (1750–1825). History has unfairly portrayed him as Mozart's nemesis.

FIGURE 8–16

St. Stephen's Cathedral, Vienna, where Mozart was married in 1782 and where his funeral was held in 1791.

unless I am invited to some house where they lunch at two or even three o'clock. . . . I can never work before five or six o'clock in the evening, and even then I am often prevented by a concert. If I am not prevented, I compose until nine. Then I go to my dear Constanze.

Against the advice of his father, Wolfgang married his "dear Constanze" (Weber) in the summer of 1782. But, alas, she was as romantic and impractical as he, though less given to streaks of hard work. In addition to his composing, teaching, and performing, Mozart now found time to study the music of Bach and Handel, play chamber music with his friend Joseph Haydn, and join the Freemasons. Although still very much a practicing Catholic, he was attracted to this fraternity of the Enlightenment because of its belief in tolerance and universal brotherhood. His opera *Die Zauberflöte* (*The Magic Flute*, 1791) is viewed by many as a hymn in praise of masonic ideals.

The years 1785–1787 witnessed the peak of Mozart's success and the creation of many of his greatest works. He had a full complement of pupils, played several concerts a week, and enjoyed lucrative commissions as a composer. Piano concertos, string quartets, and symphonies flowed from his pen, as well as his two greatest Italian operas, *The Marriage of Figaro* and *Don Giovanni*. But *Don Giovanni*, a huge success when first performed in Prague in 1787, was little appreciated when mounted in Vienna in the spring of 1788. "The opera is divine, perhaps even more beautiful than *Figaro*," declared Emperor Joseph II, "but no food for the teeth of my Viennese." Mozart's music was no longer in vogue. His pupils began to dwindle and the elite failed to subscribe to his concerts. His style was thought to be too dense, too intense, too dissonant. One publisher warned him: "Write in a more popular style or else I cannot print or pay for more of your music."

Mozart's last year

Although now in declining health, Mozart was still capable of creating the greatest sort of masterpieces. In his last year (1791) he composed a superb clarinet concerto and the German comic opera *The Magic Flute*, and began work on a Requiem Mass, one he was never to finish. Mozart died on December 5, 1791, at the age of thirty-five. The precise reason for his death has never been determined, though kidney failure made worse by needless bloodletting was the most likely cause. No single event in the history of music was more tragic than the premature loss of Mozart. What he would have given to the world had he enjoyed the long life of a Bach or a Haydn!

CLASSICAL STYLE IN MUSIC

Even for a music lover of many years' experience, it is sometimes difficult to distinguish the sound of Haydn from that of Mozart or, similarly, to differentiate late Haydn or Mozart from early Beethoven. This easy confusion points up the fact that music in the Classical period is more homogeneous in style than in any other period in the history of music—pieces in the same genre but by different composers tend to sound like one another. Clearly, there was then a consensus of opinion among creative musicians as to what music was supposed to sound like, an ideal tacitly agreed to, not only by Haydn, Mozart, and Beethoven in Vienna, but also by lesser composers working in Milan, Paris, London, and elsewhere. The Viennese Classical style embodied universal principles in an age that greatly valued universal ideals.

Much has been written about the Classical style in music: its quiet grace, noble simplicity, purity, and serenity. It is certainly "classical" in the sense that extreme emphasis is placed on formal clarity, order, and balance. Compared with the relentless, grandiose, sometimes pompous sound of the Baroque, Classical music is lighter in tone, more natural, yet less predictable. It is even capable of humor and surprise, as when Mozart again and again leads up to, but carefully avoids, a cadence, or when Haydn explodes with a thunderous chord in the midst of a sea of quiet. But what is it in precise musical terms that creates this feeling of levity and grace, of clarity and balance, in Classical music?

MELODY. Perhaps the first thing that strikes the listener about the music of Haydn or Mozart is that the theme is often tuneful, catchy, even singable. Not only are melodies simple and short but also the phrases tend to be organized in antecedent–consequent*, or question–answer, pairs. The melody usually progresses by playing out these short phrases in symmetrical groups of two, three, four, eight, twelve, or sixteen bars. The brevity of the phrase and frequent cadences allow for ample light and air to penetrate the melodic line.

Classical balance and symmetry

Following is the theme from the second movement of Mozart's Piano Concerto in C major (1785). It is composed of two three-bar phrases—an antecedent and a consequent phrase. The melody is light and airy, yet perfectly balanced. It is also singable and quite memorable—indeed, it has been turned into a popular movie theme (the "love song" from *Elvira Madigan*). Compare this with the long, asymmetrical melodies of the Baroque that were often instrumental in character (see page 124).

EXAMPLE 8–1

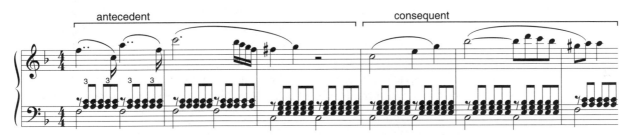

HARMONY. After about 1750 all music assumed a more homophonic, less polyphonic character. The new tuneful melody was supported by a simple harmony. In the preceding example only two chords, tonic and dominant, support Mozart's lovely melody. The bass still generates the harmony, but it does not always move in the regular, constant fashion typified by the Baroque walking bass*. Rather, the bass might sit on the bottom of one chord for several beats, even several measures, then move rapidly, and then stop again. Thus, the rate at which chords change—the harmonic rhythm as it is called—is much more fluid and flexible with Classical composers.

flexible harmonic rhythm

To avoid a feeling of inactivity when the harmony is static, Classical composers invented new accompanying patterns. Sometimes, as in Ex. 8–1, they simply repeat the accompanying chord in a uniform triplet rhythm. More common is the pattern called the **Alberti bass,** named after the minor Italian keyboard composer Domenico Alberti (1710–1740) who popularized this figure. Instead of playing the pitches of a chord all together, the performer spreads them out to provide a continual stream of sound. Mozart used an Alberti bass at the beginning of his famous C major piano sonata (1788):

EXAMPLE 8–2

Alberti bass

The Alberti pattern serves essentially the same function as the modern "boogie-woogie" bass. It provides a feeling of harmonic activity for those moments when, in fact, the harmony is stationary.

RHYTHM. Rhythm, too, is more flexible in the hands of Haydn and Mozart. It animates the stop-and-go character of their melodies and harmonies. Rapid motion may be followed by repose and then further quick movement, but there is little of the driving, perpetual motion of Baroque musical rhythm.

light, homophonic textures

TEXTURE. Musical texture was also transformed in the latter half of the eighteenth century, mainly because composers began to concentrate less on writing dense counterpoint than on creating charming melodies. No longer are independent polyphonic lines superimposed, layer upon layer, as in a fugue of Bach or a polyphonic chorus of Handel. The lessening of counterpoint, then, made for a lighter, more transparent sound, especially in the middle range of the texture. Mozart, after a study of Bach and Handel in the early 1780s, infused his symphonies, quartets, and concertos with greater polyphonic content, but this seems to have caused the pleasure-loving Viennese to think his music too dense!

The Classical Orchestra

The development of the orchestra during the Classical period is discussed in connection with the creation of the Classical symphony in Chapter 10 (page 187). For the moment, suffice it to say that during the late eighteenth century the orchestra grows in size as a direct response to the larger audience that crowded into the new public concert halls. The strings still constitute the core of the orchestra, but the woodwinds—oboes, flutes, bassoons, and the new clarinets—gain increased autonomy. They no longer merely double or echo the violins and the bass line as they had during the Baroque era. Henceforth, they enter and depart, seemingly at will, now to play a theme as a solo, now to thicken momentarily the musical texture or to add a dash of instrumental color.

The Dramatic Quality of Classical Music

What is perhaps most revolutionary in the music of Haydn, Mozart, and their younger contemporary, Beethoven, is its capacity for rapid change and endless fluctuation. Recall that in earlier times a work by Purcell, Corelli, Vivaldi, or

Bach would establish one "affect," or mood, to be rigidly maintained from beginning to end—the rhythm, melody, and harmony all progressing in a continuous,
uninterrupted flow. Such a uniform approach to expression is part of the "single-
mindedness" of Baroque art. Now, with Haydn, Mozart, and the young
Beethoven, the mood or character of a piece may change radically within a few   *frequent changes in mood*
short phrases. An energetic theme in rapid notes may be followed by a second
one that is slow, lyrical, and tender. Similarly, textures may change quickly from
light and airy to dense and more contrapuntal so as to create tension and excite-
ment. For the first time composers began to call for crescendos and diminuendos,   *crescendos and diminuendos*
a gradual increase or lessening of the dynamic level, so that the volume of sound
might continually fluctuate. When skilled orchestras made use of this technique,
audiences were fascinated and rose to their feet. Keyboard players, too, now took
up the crescendo and diminuendo, assuming that the new multidynamic piano
was at hand in place of the old, less flexible harpsichord. These rapid changes in
mood, texture, color, and dynamics give to Classical music a new sense of
urgency and drama. The listener feels a constant flux and flow, not unlike the
continual swings of mood we all experience.

Classical Forms

How did composers of the Classical period reconcile their desire to express
changing moods, colors, and textures with the Classical principles of grace, order,
and balance? They did so, in a word, by means of form. All of the elements of
expression—themes, harmonic relationships, colors, textures, dynamics—are   *form controls the unfolding of musical*
precisely positioned within the boundaries of strict musical form. Limits are set   *events*
as to where the changing or conflicting elements may be placed, how intense
they may be, and how long they may last. By placing the musical events, or sections, in a carefully regulated order, grace, balance, and proportion are achieved.
As one critic observed in 1777: "A knowledge of the proper ordering of sections
is essential to any friend of music who wishes to be a conoisseur and who desires
to derive pleasure from the workings of this art." Indeed, so important is form in
Classical music that the subject requires a chapter unto itself.

KEY WORDS

Alberti bass	Nikolaus Esterházy	*The Magic Flute*
Antonio Salieri	*opera buffa*	*The Marriage of Figaro*
comic opera	*pianoforte*	
London symphonies	Salzburg	

A checklist of musical style in the Classical era is given on page 66.

9

CLASSICAL FORMS

To understand and appreciate Classical music, it is especially important to understand musical form. For in the Classical period, more so than any other, a small number of forms—ternary, sonata–allegro, rondo, and theme and variations—regulated nearly all music. Indeed, there are few compositions written during the years 1750–1820 that are not shaped according to one of these. At the same time, it is important to realize that none of these forms was unique to the Classical period. Ternary form can be found in the earliest examples of Gregorian chant* as well as in all *da capo** arias of the Baroque era (1600–1750). The rondo had its origins in the popular dances and songs of the Middle Ages, though its repetitive structure has made it attractive to such diverse musicians as Mozart, Beethoven, Elton John, and Sting. And theme and variations, as both a musical and a literary process, is at once ancient and eternal. Only sonata–allegro form actually came into being in the Classical period. It dominated musical structure during the time of Mozart and Haydn, but it also remained a potent force in the works of most composers of the Romantic era (1820–1900) and in the creations of some twentieth-century musicians as well. Thus, the forms discussed in this chapter should be thought of not as belonging to the Classical period alone, but in the broader meaning of the term "classical." With the single exception of the more recent sonata–allegro form, they are all timeless and universal.

TERNARY FORM

Ternary structure (**ABA**) is a form often encountered in the history of music. Yet the simple principle of presentation, contrast, and return was especially favored by Classical composers for its simplicity and directness. Everyone is familiar with the tune *Twinkle, Twinkle, Little Star* (also the tune of *Bah, Bah, Black Sheep,* and *A, B, C, D, E, F, G*). Less well known is the fact that it began life as a French folk song, *Ah, vous dirai-je, Maman* (*Ah, Let Me Tell You, Mama*). Wolfgang Amadeus Mozart (1756–1791) came to know the melody when he toured France as a youth, and he wrote it down in a keyboard version. Here is his setting of it:

FIGURE 9–1
A ball at the Redoutensaal in the emperor's palace in Vienna ca. 1800. Mozart, Haydn, and, later, Beethoven composed minuets and "German dances" for officially sponsored events there. The orchestra can be seen in the gallery at the left.

EXAMPLE 9-1

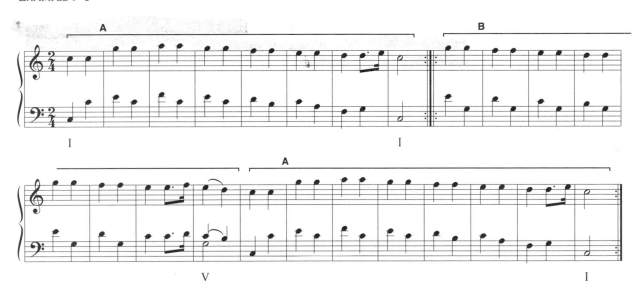

Notice that both units (**A** and **BA**) are repeated. Observe also that **A** is in the tonic, **B** emphasizes a contrasting key (here the dominant), and the returning **A** is again in the tonic. If a piece in ternary form is in a minor key, the contrasting **B** section will usually be in what is called the **relative major.**[†] Needless to say, most pieces in ternary form are more complex than *Twinkle, Twinkle*. Most have more contrast of melody, key, and/or mood between the **B** section and the surrounding units of **A.**

[†] Relative keys are keys that share the same key signature, E♭ major and C minor (both with three flats), for example.

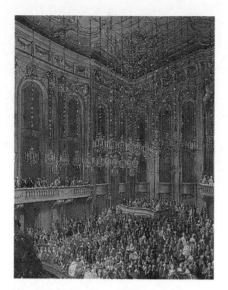

FIGURE 9–2

The Redoutensaal was also used for the production of opera. Here the audience, which included the six-year-old Mozart, is assembled for a production of an *opera seria* in 1762.

Mozart's A Little Night Music

Minuet and Trio

The most common use of ternary form in the Classical period is found in the minuet and trio. Strictly speaking, the **minuet** is not a form, but rather a genre of dance implying an elegant musical style, stately tempo, and constant triple meter. It first appeared at the French royal court early in the reign of King Louis XIV (1643–1715). Most minuets in the Baroque era were in binary form*. But by 1770 the minuet was usually composed in ternary form and grouped with a second minuet possessing a much lighter texture. Because this second minuet had originally been played by only three instruments, it was called the **trio,** a name that persisted into the nineteenth century, no matter how many instrumental lines were required in this second minuet. Once the trio was finished, convention dictated that there be a return to the first minuet, now performed without repeats. Since the trio also was composed in ternary form, an **ABA** pattern was heard three times in succession. (In the following, the **ABA** structure of the trio is represented by **CDC,** to distinguish it from the minuet.) And, since the trio was different from the surrounding minuet, the entire movement minuet–trio–minuet formed an **ABA** arrangement.

A (minuet)	**B** (trio)	**A** (minuet)
‖: **A** :‖: **BA** :‖	‖: **C** :‖: **DC** :‖	**ABA**

Mozart's *Eine kleine Nachtmusik (A Little Night Music)*, written in the summer of 1787, is among his most popular works. It is a **serenade,** a light, multi-movement piece for strings alone or small orchestra, one intended for public entertainment and often performed outdoors. Although we do not know the precise occasion for which Mozart composed it, we might well imagine *A Little Night Music* providing the musical backdrop for a torch-lit party in a formal Viennese garden. The *Menuetto* appears as the third of four movements in this serenade, and is a model of grace and concision.

EXAMPLE 9-2

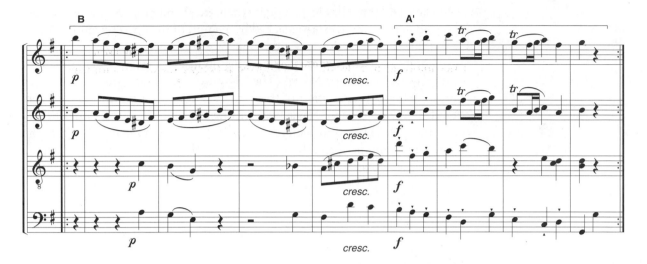

As you can see, the **B** section is only four measures long, and the return to **A** does not reproduce the full eight bars of the original but only the last four—thus, this pattern might be viewed as **ABA'**. In the trio that follows, a lighter texture is created as the first violin plays a solo melody quietly above a soft accompaniment in the lower strings. The **D** section of the trio is distinguished by a *forte* stepwise run up and down the scale, and then the quiet melody of **C** returns to complete the ternary form. Finally, the minuet appears once again, but now without repeats.

LISTENING GUIDE	Wolfgang Amadeus Mozart Serenade, *A Little Night Music* (1787) Third movement, Minuet and Trio	6CD 2/8 6Tape 2A

MINUET

		Form	Number of bars
0:00	Strong violin melody with active bass	A	8
0:10	Repeat of **A**		
0:20	Softer violin scales	B	4
0:26	Return of violin melody	A'	4
0:30	Repeat of **B** and **A'**		

TRIO

0:41	Soft, stepwise melody in violins	C	8
0:52	Repeat of **C**		
1:03	Louder violins	D	4
1:09	Return of soft stepwise melody	C	8
1:20	Repeat of **D** and **C**		

MINUET

1:37	Return of **A**	A	8
1:48	Return of **B**	B	4
1:54	Return of violin melody **A'**	A'	4

We have said that Classical music is symmetrical and proportional. Note here how both minuet and trio are balanced by a return of the opening music (**A** and **C**) and how all the sections are either four or eight bars in length.

If Mozart's *Menuetto* represents the minuet in its most succinct form, the minuet of Haydn's Symphony No. 94 (The "Surprise" Symphony) offers a more typically symphonic presentation of this ternary design. The form is considerably extended, in part because Haydn was writing for a full orchestra rather than a small string ensemble as in Mozart's serenade. (It is axiomatic in music that the larger the performing force, the more extended the musical form.) But keeping the model of Mozart's simple ternary minuet in our ears, we can easily follow Haydn's more expansive formal plan.

LISTENING GUIDE	Franz Joseph Haydn Symphony No. 94, The "Surprise" Symphony (1791) Third movement, Minuet and Trio	6CD 2/10 6Tape 2B

MINUET [ ] = repeats			*Form*
0:00		Rollicking dance in triple meter begins	**A**
0:19		Repeat of **A**	
0:40	[1:33]	Imitation and lighter texture	**B**
0:50	[1:43]	Strong harmonic movement	
0:58	[1:51]	Bass sits on dominant note	
1:05	[1:59]	Return of **A**	**A′**
1:13	[2:07]	Pause on dominant chord	
1:23	[2:17]	Gentle rocking over tonic pedal point	
TRIO			
2:27		Light descending scales for violins and bassoon	**C**
2:37		Repeat of **C**	
2:46	[3:08]	Two-voice counterpoint for 1st and 2nd violins	**D**
2:58	[3:21]	Bassoon reentry signals return of **C**	**C**
MINUET			
3:30		Return to minuet	**A**
3:51		Return of **B**	**B**
4:16		Return of **A**	**A′**

SONATA–ALLEGRO FORM

Sonata–allegro form is at once the most complex and most satisfying of musical forms. It is also the only form to originate during the Classical period (1750–1820). We must keep in mind, however, the distinction between the general term "sonata" and the more specific term "sonata–allegro form"—that is, between the multimovement composition called the sonata and the single-movement form called sonata–allegro.

Recall that in the Baroque period a multimovement work was often called a sonata, either a solo sonata or a trio sonata. These consisted of a succession of binary-form movements that often proceeded slow–fast–slow–fast (see page 115). By the early Classical period, however, the usual arrangement of movements for a sonata had become fast–slow–minuet–fast, or occasionally just fast–slow–fast. When played by a solo instrument like the piano, this group of movements is called a solo sonata. When this same sort of three- or four-movement composition is written for string quartet or quintet, it is called simply a string quartet or quintet. And when intended for a full symphonic orchestra, it is called a symphony.

Yet no matter what the performing force, the form of each of these movements can be one of several different types. As we have seen, if there are four movements the third is usually a minuet with trio. The second and fourth movements might be, for example, in rondo form or theme and variations form (both discussed later in the chapter). The fast first movement, however, is almost invariably written in what is called sonata–allegro form. Thus, the term "sonata–allegro" derives from the fact that sonata–allegro form was usually applied to the fast (allegro) first movement. Slow second movements and fast finales sometimes make use of sonata–allegro form as well. To show at least two typical arrangements, here are the movements and forms of Mozart's *A Little Night Music* and Haydn's Symphony No. 94:

In this painting, the six-year-old Mozart is dressed in the court costume given him by Empress Maria Theresa in 1762.

Mozart, *A Little Night Music* (1787)

Fast	Slow	Minuet and Trio	Fast
(sonato–allegro)	(rondo)	(ternary)	(rondo)

Haydn, Symphony No. 94 (1791)

Fast	Slow	Minuet and Trio	Fast
(sonata–allegro)	(theme and variations)	(ternary)	(sonata–allegro)

Sonata–allegro form came into being around 1750 as a means of incorporating more drama and conflict into a single movement of music. Like a great play, sonato–allegro form has the potential for dramatic presentation, conflict, and resolution. That sonata–allegro form would continue to serve composers into the Romantic period and beyond attests to its compelling logic and great flexibility. It gave composers a formal backdrop on which a musical drama could play out in any number of individual ways.

The Shape of Sonata-Allegro Form

To get a sense of what might happen in a typical first movement of a sonata, string quartet, symphony, or serenade, look at the following diagram. As with all models of this sort, this one is an ideal, an abstraction of what commonly occurs in sonata–allegro form. It is not a blueprint for any composition. Composers have exhibited countless individual solutions to the task of writing in this and every other form. Yet such a model can be of great use to the listener because it gives a clear picture of what we might expect to hear. Ultimately, once we have embraced the form and are familiar with its workings, we will take as much delight in having our musical expectations foiled or delayed as in having them fulfilled.

SONATA-ALLEGRO FORM

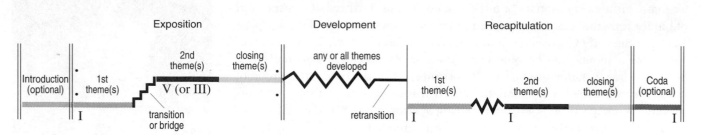

In its broad outline, sonata–allegro form looks much like ternary form. It consists of an **ABA** plan, with the **B** section providing contrast in mood, key, and thematic treatment. The initial **A** in sonata–allegro form is called the exposition, the **B** the development, and the return to **A** the recapitulation. In the early Classical period the exposition (**A**) and the development and recapitulation (**BA**) were each repeated, as in ternary form. But Haydn and Mozart eventually dropped the repeat of the development and recapitulation, and composers of the Romantic period gradually dispensed with the repeat of the exposition. Let's take each of these sections in turn and see what we are likely to hear.

presentation   EXPOSITION. The purpose of the **exposition** is to present, or expose, the main thematic material of the movement, just as the exposition of a fugue exposes the subject.

First theme: The exposition begins with a first theme, or group of themes, and can be anywhere from four to forty measures or more in length. If not easily singable, the first theme is at least distinctive, memorable enough so that later returns and references to it will be recognized and enjoyed by the listener.

Transition: The aim of the **transition,** or **bridge** as it is sometimes called, is to carry the music from the tonic to the dominant (from tonic to relative major if the movement is in a minor key) and prepare for the arrival of the second theme. The transition is usually made up of rapidly moving figural patterns—running scales, arpeggios*, and the like—which are frequently put forth as melodic sequences*. In order to effect the I–V modulation, the bass becomes active and generates quick chord changes. This lively harmonic movement may subside if the transition ends with a solid cadence.

Second theme: Not only does a new melody usually appear at this point, but it enters in the fresh context of a new key, the dominant or, less frequently, the relative major. The second theme often contrasts in mood with the first: If the first is rapid and assertive, the second may be more languid and lyrical. Because a clear-cut theme holds center stage here, the accompanying harmonic material is stable, not modulatory. The listener's attention is focused on melody, not on harmonic movement.

Closing theme: The second theme usually gives way to a closing theme, one that is normally light and carefree in style. It often ends in a harmonically simple way, merely rocking back and forth between dominant and tonic chords. The static

FIGURE 9–4

The autograph manuscript of *A Little Night Music* (1787). Mozart was composing here with a score of four staffs: First and second violins are on the top two staffs, violas on staff three, and cellos and double basses on four. One can sense with what extraordinary speed, yet accuracy, Mozart could set music on paper.

harmony and repeated full cadences* signal the conclusion of the exposition. The piece has stopped moving forward, and therefore the exposition is at an end. Tradition requires that the exposition now be repeated note for note.

DEVELOPMENT. As the name indicates, the development is a section in which there is a further working out, or developing, of the thematic material presented in the exposition. Both the first and the second theme may be manipulated, and occasionally even the closing theme is exploited as well. A theme may be elaborated on and expanded, or, just as often, it may be taken apart, reduced to just a few notes to be tossed around from instrument to instrument. One typical technique is for the composer to show the contrapuntal possibilities lurking within a theme by using it as the subject of a brief fugue*. (A fugue within a movement of a sonata is called a **fugato**.) Like the transition, the development tends to have unstable harmonies. The use of both melodic and harmonic sequence is plentiful, and this encourages rapid modulation from one key, or tonal center, to another. Only toward the end of the development, in the area called the **retransition,** does tonal stability return, often in the form of a pedal point* on the dominant note. The retransition helps prepare the ear for the return of the tonic key and the restatement of the first theme.

confrontation

RECAPITULATION. After the dramatic disruptions of the development, the listener greets the return of the first theme and the tonic key of the exposition with welcome relief. Though the **recapitulation** is not an exact, note-for-note repetition of the exposition, it nonetheless presents the same musical events in the same order, reaffirming the logic and integrity of the original. The only change that regularly occurs in this restatement is the rewriting of the transition, or bridge. Because the movement must end in the tonic, the bridge must not modulate to the dominant (or relative major) as before but stay at home in the tonic key. Thus, the recapitulation imparts to the listener not only a feeling of

resolution

return to familiar surroundings but also an increased sense of harmonic stability, as all themes are now heard in the tonic key.

The following two elements are optional to sonata–allegro form.

optional elements

INTRODUCTION. About half the mature symphonies of Haydn and Mozart have brief introductions before the exposition begins. These are, without exception, slow and stately and usually filled with ominous or puzzling chords designed to set the listener wondering what sort of musical excursion he or she is about to undertake. That the introduction is not part of the exposition is shown by the fact that it is never repeated.

CODA. As the name **coda** (Italian for "tail") indicates, this is a section added to the end of the sonata–allegro movement. It may be just a few bars long, as is most often the case with Mozart, or it may, in the hands of Beethoven, for example, expand into an independent section, one equal in size to the development. The melodic material is usually no more than a short motive extracted from the first theme or sometimes from the closing theme, or it may be a newly created motive. But whatever the source, normally this motive is sounded again and again in conjunction with repeating dominant–tonic chords, or merely the tonic chord alone played over and over, all intended to create a grand effect and announce to the listener that the movement is at an end. Again, thematic repetition at the same pitch level and static harmony are two ways a composer can signal the end of a section or the end of a piece. The more of this that goes on, the greater the feeling of conclusion.

Hearing Sonata–Allegro Form

the challenge of sonata-allegro form

Given its central place in the music of Mozart and Haydn, and later in Beethoven, Schubert, Brahms, and Mahler, among others, sonata–allegro is perhaps the most important of all musical forms. But it is also the most complex and the most difficult for the listener to follow. A sonata–allegro movement tends to be long, lasting anywhere from a minimum of four minutes in a simple piece of the Classical period to twenty minutes or more in a full-blown movement of the Romantic era. Moreover, it embodies many kinds of musical events and many styles of writing—thematic and transitional, for example. And finally, sonata–allegro form does not merely involve one theme but incorporates several, and all of these have to be remembered and their development followed.

How does one get the better of this musical beast? First of all, be sure you have the model of sonata–allegro form clearly in mind. This will help you know what to expect, what you are likely to hear. Next, sharpen your ability to grasp and remember melodies, or at least the beginnings of melodies. If necessary, return to Chapter 2 and practice some melodic graphing. And finally, think carefully about the four principal styles of writing found in sonata–allegro form. Each has

four styles of music in sonata-allegro form

its own distinct character. A thematic section has clearly recognizable themes or melodies, sometimes even singable tunes. The transition is full of melodic movement, sequences, and rapid chord changes. The development is also disjunct, agitated, contrapuntal, and harmonically active, but it makes use of a recognizable theme, albeit extended or cut up into small pieces. And a concluding passage, whether at the end of the exposition, in the retransition at the end of the development, or in the coda at the end of the movement, tends to repeat motives or cadential phrases over and over above a static harmony. Much of your success in hearing sonata–allegro form will come from your ability to differentiate thematic, transitional, developmental, and concluding sections. With this by way of preparation, let's listen to a movement in sonata–allegro form.

For this we once again turn to the familiar sound of Mozart's *A Little Night Music*. The first movement (*Allegro*) of this four-movement serenade offers a concise, graceful example of sonata–allegro principle. Yet even a straightforward sonata–allegro-form movement such as this requires the listener's full attention. The following Listening Guide is not typical of this book. It is unusually lengthy so as to lead you through the difficult process of hearing sonata–allegro form. First read the description in the center column, then listen to the music, stopping where indicated to rehear each of the principal sections of the form.

LISTENING GUIDE	Wolfgang Amadeus Mozart *A Little Night Music* (1787) First movement, *Allegro* (fast)	6CD 2/7; 6Tape 2A 3CD 2/9; 3Tape 2A

FIRST THEME GROUP [ ] = repeats

0:00 [1:37] The movement opens aggressively with a leaping, fanfarelike motive. It then moves on to a more confined, pressing melody with sixteenth notes agitating beneath, and ends with a relaxed, stepwise descent down the G major scale, which is repeated with light ornamentation.

STOP: LISTEN TO THE FIRST THEME GROUP AGAIN

TRANSITION

0:30 [2:08] This starts with two quick turns and then races up the scale in repeating sixteenth notes. The bass is at first static, but when it finally moves it does so with great urgency, pushing the modulation along until a cadence. The stage is then cleared by a brief pause, allowing the listener an "unobstructed view" of the new theme that is about to enter.

0:30 Rapid scales
0:40 Bass moves
0:45 Cadence and pause

STOP: LISTEN TO THE TRANSITION AGAIN

SECOND THEME

0:48 [2:26] With its *piano* dynamic level and separating rests, the second theme sounds soft and delicate. It is soon overtaken by a light, somewhat humorous closing theme.

STOP: LISTEN TO THE SECOND THEME AGAIN

(Continued on next page)

CLOSING THEME

1:01   [2:39]   The light quality of this melody is produced by its repeating note and the simple rocking of dominant-to-tonic harmony below. Toward the end of it more substance is added when the music turns *forte*, and good counterpoint is inserted in the bass. The bass closing theme is then repeated, and a few cadential chords are tacked on to bring the exposition to an end.

1:09 Loud; more counterpoint in
1:14 Closing theme repeated
1:33 Cadential chords

STOP: LISTEN TO THE CLOSING SECTION AGAIN

1:37   The exposition is now repeated.

DEVELOPMENT

3:15   Just about anything can happen in a development, so the listener had best be on guard. Mozart begins with the fanfarelike first theme again in unison, as if this were yet another statement of the exposition! But abruptly the theme is altered and the tonal center slides up to a new key. Now the closing theme is heard, but soon it, too, begins to slide tonally, down through several keys that sound increasingly remote and bizarre. From this arises a unison scale (all parts move up stepwise together) in a dark-sounding minor key. The dominant note is held, first on top in the violins and then in the bass. This begins the retransition. The mode changes from dark minor to bright major, and the first theme returns with force in the tonic key, signaling the beginning of the recapitulation.

3:15 First theme developed
3:20 Quick modulation
3:25 Closing theme developed
3:32 More modulations
3:41 Rising scale in unison
3:48 Held note (dominant) in violins and then bass

STOP: LISTEN TO THE DEVELOPMENT AGAIN

RECAPITULATION

3:52   It is this "double return" of both the tonic key and the first theme that makes the arrival of this and all recapitulations so satisfying. We expect the recapitulation to more or less duplicate the exposition, and this one holds true to form. The only change comes, as usual, in the transition, or bridge, where the modulation to the dominant is simply omitted—there's no need to modulate to the dominant since tradition demands that the second theme and the closing theme appear in the tonic.

3:52 Loud return of first theme
4:23 Transition much abbreviated
4:38 Second theme
4:51 Closing theme
5:05 Closing theme repeated
5:23 Cadential chords

CODA

5:26   After the cadential chords that ended the exposition are heard again, a brief coda begins. It makes use of a fanfare motive that strongly resembles that of the opening theme, but this one is supported below by a pounding tonic chord that drives home the feeling that the movement has come to an appropriate end.

What we have just heard is an example of sonata–allegro form in miniature. Rarely has this design been produced in less time, or space, and almost never as artfully. But sonata–allegro is a dynamic, flexible form, one that can serve equally well as an appropriate vessel for a large symphonic movement, a dramatic overture to an opera, or a Romantic tone poem*. We will meet it again in several later compositions. Listening Exercise 22 presents another, even more dramatic, unfolding of sonata–allegro form: the overture to Mozart's tragic-comic opera *Don Giovanni*.

THEME AND VARIATIONS

After the complexity of sonata–allegro form, a movement in theme and variations form seems relatively simple and straightforward. This is partly because just one theme is used and that theme is subjected to only one sort of compositional treatment: variation. For theme and variations to be effective, the theme itself must be easy to grasp and clearly stated at the outset. As the Enlightenment philosopher Jean-Jacques Rousseau said in his *Dictionnaire de musique* (1768): "Through all the embroidery, one must always be able to recognize the essence of the melody."

To that end composers of the Classical period and beyond often chose themes that were already well-known to the listener: folk songs, popular tunes, and favorite arias and marches from successful operas, for example. Patriotic songs have always seemed especially apt for musical variation. Those so treated include *God Preserve Franz the Emperor* (Haydn), *God Save the King* (Beethoven), *Rule Britannia* (Beethoven), and later *Yankee Doodle* (Vieuxtemps) and *America* (Ives). Such tunes are popular, in part, because they are simple, and this, too, is an advantage for the composer. Melodies that are spare and uncluttered can more easily be dressed in new musical clothing. The essence of theme and variations, then, is to present a simple, direct melody and restate it again and again, each time musically varying or disguising the theme in some novel fashion.

How is variation of a theme brought about? It is done one of two ways: either by merely ornamenting the theme, overlaying it with figural patterns, or, what produces a more radical transformation, by altering its shape—changing its rhythmic, harmonic, or melodic profile in some way. In the two examples that follow, one by Mozart and one by Haydn, the specific techniques of ornamentation and alteration of a melody will become apparent. You will be challenged to retain a familiar tune in your ear as the composer embellishes or transforms it.

In the Classical period it was common for a composer-pianist to improvise in concert a set of variations on a well-known tune, perhaps one called out from the audience. Contemporary reports tell us that Mozart was especially skilled in this art of spontaneous variation. In 1778 he published, as was mentioned earlier, a set of such improvised variations built on the French folk song *Ah, vous dirai-je, Maman*, which we know as *Twinkle, Twinkle, Little Star*. With a tune as well known as this, it is easy to follow the melody as it is subjected increasingly to ornamentation and transformation in the course of twelve variations. (Only the first eight bars of the theme are given here; for the complete melody, see page 167; the music can be heard on 6CD 2/11 and 6Tape 2B.)

FIGURE 9–5

A portrait of the young Mozart at the keyboard painted during his first trip to Italy, in 1770.

Mozart's variations on Twinkle, Twinkle

EXAMPLE 9–3a: *Twinkle, Twinkle, Little Star*, Basic Theme

FIGURE 9–6

Emperor Joseph II with two of his sisters. Mozart made a point of meeting the musically knowledgeable emperor in 1781. The score on the piano is by Mozart's rival at court, Antonio Salieri.

Variation 1 ornaments the theme and almost buries it beneath an avalanche of sixteenth notes. Would you know that *Twinkle, Twinkle* lurks herein (see the asterisks) if you did not have the tune securely in your ear?

EXAMPLE 9–3b: Variation 1

In variation 2 the rushing sixteenth notes are transferred to the bass, so that the theme surfaces again rather clearly in the upper voice.

EXAMPLE 9–3c: Variation 2

In variation 3, triplets appear in the right hand, and only the general contour of the melody is audible. Thus, the melody here is transformed.

EXAMPLE 9–3d: Variation 3

After the same technique has been applied to the bass (variation 4), a thematic alteration again occurs in variation 5. Here the rhythm of the melody is "jazzed up" by placing part of it off the beat, in syncopated fashion.

EXAMPLE 9–3e: Variation 5

FIGURE 9–7

The Hanover Square Rooms in London, the hall in which Haydn's "Surprise" Symphony was first performed, in 1792.

Of the remaining seven variations, some change the tune to minor, others add Bach-like counterpoint against it, while the final variation presents this duple-meter folk tune reworked into a triple-meter waltz! Yet throughout all of Mozart's magical embroidery, the theme remains clearly audible, so well ingrained is *Twinkle, Twinkle* in our musical memory.

*   *   *   *   *

Joseph Haydn (1732–1809) was the first composer to take theme and variations form and use it for a movement inside a symphony. His Symphony No. 94 (The "Surprise" Symphony) has been his most celebrated composition ever since it was first performed in London early in 1792.

We have already discussed the third movement, the minuet (see page 170). But the work owes its popularity, and its nickname, to the slow second movement *(Andante)*, written in theme and variations form. The famous opening theme possesses both simplicity and immediate appeal. Notice how the beginning is shaped by laying out in succession the notes of a tonic triad (I) and a dominant chord (V) in C major. The chordal implications of the tune account for its folk-song–like quality and make it easy to remember during the variations that follow (see the first example in the Listening Guide). These first eight bars (**A**) are stated and then repeated quietly. And just when all is ending peacefully, the full orchestra comes crashing in with a *fortissimo* chord, as if to shock the drowsy listener back to attention. What better way to show off the latent dynamic power of the large Classical orchestra? The surprise *fortissimo* chord is a dominant chord that leads into the **B** section of the theme (second example in the Listening Guide), another eight-bar phrase, which is also repeated but with added flute and oboe accompaniment. With the simple yet highly attractive binary theme now in place, Haydn proceeds to compose four variations on it, adding then a superb coda at the end.

FIGURE 9–8

A portrait of Joseph Haydn at work. His left hand is trying an idea at the keyboard while his right is ready to write it down. Haydn said about his compositional process: "I sat down at the keyboard and began to improvise. Once I had seized upon an idea, my whole effort was to develop and sustain it."

LISTENING
GUIDE

Joseph Haydn
Symphony No. 94, The "Surprise" Symphony (1791)
Second movement, *Andante* (moving)

6CD 2/9
6Tape 2A

THEME

0:00   First part (**A**) of the theme
0:16   **A** repeated softly, then *fortissimo* chord

0:33   Second part (**B**) of the theme
0:49   **B** repeated with flute and oboe added

VARIATION 1

1:06   Loud chord, then **A** ornamented above by first violins and flutes
1:22   **A** repeated
1:39   **B** with ornamentation continuing above in violins and flutes
1:55   **B** repeated

VARIATION 2

2:11   **A** played loud and in minor key, shift (2:19) to rich major chord
2:27   **A** repeated
        (Variation of **B** omitted)
2:43   Full orchestra develops **A** in minor key
3:11   First violins alone, playing in unison

VARIATION 3

3:20   **A** ornamented rapidly by oboe
3:34   **A** repeated; melody in strings with oboe and flute ornamenting above
3:50   **B** now in strings with oboe and flute ornamenting above
4:05   **B** repeated

VARIATION 4

4:23   **A** loud, in full orchestra, with violins playing running scales
4:38   **A** repeated with theme rhythmically varied
4:55   **B** varied further by the violins
5:11   **B** repeated loudly by full orchestra
5:27   Transition to coda, pause (5:35)

CODA

5:40   Reminiscences of theme in its original form

After listening to this movement by Haydn, you can now understand that hearing theme and variations form requires listening to discrete units of music. Each block (variation) is marked by some new treatment of the theme. In the Classical period all the units are usually the same size, that is, the same number of measures. The variations become progressively more complicated as more ornamentation and transformation are applied. The addition of a coda after the last variation gives extra weight to the end, so that the listener feels the set of variations has reached an appropriate conclusion. If such extra bars were not appended, the audience would be left hanging, expecting yet another variation to begin.

Rondo Form

Rondo form is an ancient musical structure in which a refrain continually alternates with contrasting material. We have previously seen this formal plan at work in the music of the Middle Ages (see page 79) and of the Baroque era (see pages 58 and 118). During the Classical period composers like Haydn and Mozart took the principle of rondo form and expanded and enlivened it. Not only were simple designs like **ABABA** and **ABACA** used, but sometimes more complex arrangements as well, such as **ABACABA** and **ABACADA.** What is more, they borrowed a style of writing found in sonata–allegro form. The more expansive and dramatic musical treatment of the transitions and development sections of sonata–allegro form was brought into the rondo. The rondo of the Classical period, therefore, is not merely a collection of short sections linked back to back, as is usually true of the Baroque rondo (see page 58), but an elastic, flexible form in which the recurring theme and the subordinate ideas develop and expand to new proportions. The subordinate ideas may be themes in their own right (lettered **B, C,** and **D**), or they may simply be digressions (**X**) away from the periodic refrain. Haydn uses the latter approach—refrain–digression—in the last movement of his Symphony No. 88 (1789). Here the theme (refrain) is a carefree tune in bright G major, and, though lengthy, it has a clear ternary (**aba'**) shape to it. You can remember the beginning more easily if you hear it as a descending triad (D, B, G) with each note quickly repeated.

an ancient form expanded and enlivened

LISTENING GUIDE

Joseph Haydn
Symphony No. 88 (1789)
Fourth movement, *Allegro con spirito* (fast with spirit)

6CD 2/12; 6Tape 2B
3CD 2/11; 3Tape 2B

(Continued on next page)

A Rondo By Sting

While the rondo may have enjoyed its greatest favor in the sphere of art music during the Baroque and Classical periods, it has continued to live on in the realm of folk and popular song, undoubtedly because the refrain–digression pattern has such universal appeal. Traditional ballads such as *Tom Dooley* make use of it, and so do more recent pop songs by artists such as Arlo Guthrie in *City of New Orleans*. Sting's *Every Breath You Take* produces a rondo pattern (**ABACABA**) that in its symmetrical, indeed palindromic, shape would do any Classical composer proud:

Sting (Gordon Sumner)

Every breath you take	Every single day	
Every move you make	Every word you say	
Every bond you break	Every game you play	**A**
Every step you take	Every night you stay	
I'll be watching you.	I'll be watching you.	

O can't you see, you belong to me
How my poor heart aches, with every step you take.　**B**

Every move you make
Every vow you break
Every smile you fake　　　　　　　　　　　　　　**A**
Every claim you stake
I'll be watching you.

Since you've gone I've been lost without a trace
I dream at night I can only see your face
I look around but it's you I can't replace　　　　　**C**
I feel so cold and I long for your embrace
I keep crying baby please.

Instrumental interlude (no text) to **A** music,　　**A**

O can't you see, you belong to me . . . (etc.)　　　**B**
Every move you make . . . (etc.)　　　　　　　　　**A**

Coda (fade out)

(Available on A & M Records CD 75021 3902 2)

			Rondo form
0:00	Statement of **a**	⎫	
0:06	Repeat of **a**	⎪	
0:12	Beginning of **b**	⎬ ternary form	**A** (refrain)
0:26	Statement of **a′**	⎪ with repeats	
0:34	Repeat of **b** and **a′**	⎭	
0:54	Scales and rapid movement		
1:11	Hint of **a** and turn to minor		**X** (digression)
1:23	More scales and active bass		
1:39	**a** and **b** but without concluding **a′** and without repeats		**A**
2:00	Development of turn motive		
2:36	Texture thins out to just two repeating notes		**X**
2:43	Return of **aba′** but without repeats		**A**
3:09	Chords signal beginning of coda; then running scales and final cadential chords		**Coda**

(Listening Exercise 23)

The general mood of this movement by Haydn is typical of the lively rondo, which tends to be lighter and more jovial in spirit than does a movement in sonata–allegro form. Classical composers most often used rondo form as the final movement (finale) of a sonata, quartet, or symphony. The tuneful refrain and easily grasped digressions produce a light-hearted ending intended to leave the audience, if not euphoric, at least in a pleasant state of mind.

FORM, MOOD, AND THE LISTENER'S EXPECTATIONS

The audience of the late eighteenth century brought to the concert hall certain expectations, not only about the structure, but also about the mood of the music that was to be performed. Listeners had a notion of what the form, tempo, and general character would be of each movement of a sonata, quartet, or symphony. For the Classical period we might summarize these as follows:

Movement:	1	2	3	4
Tempo:	Fast	Slow	Lively	Fast
Form:	Sonata–allegro	Large ternary, theme and variations, or rondo	Minuet and trio in ternary form	Sonata–allegro, theme and variations, or rondo
Mood:	Serious and substantive despite fast tempo	Lyrical and tender	usually light and elegant, sometimes spirited	Bright, light-hearted, sometimes humorous

Ludwig van Beethoven (1770–1827) and later composers of the Romantic period (1820–1900) modified somewhat this conventional format—the third movement, for example, was often treated as a boisterous scherzo (see page 223) rather than as an elegant minuet, and the finale became a more serious, weighty conclusion, with the result that the lighthearted rondo fell out of fashion. Yet the Classical model was well established in the mind of the listener. For unlike previous periods in the history of music, succeeding generations did not forget the music of Haydn, Mozart, and their contemporaries. Their sonatas, quartets, and symphonies enjoyed undiminished favor with the listening public, and the formal designs they created or popularized have remained, with a few exceptions, the norm for the concert hall down to the present day.

lasting influence of the Classical model

LISTENING EXERCISES

22	Wolfgang Amadeus Mozart Overture to the opera *Don Giovanni* (1787)	6CD 3/1 6Tape 3A

As is typical of overtures in the Classical period, the one Mozart wrote to precede his opera *Don Giovanni* (1787) is composed in sonata–allegro form. (The opera itself is discussed at length in the following chapter.) Mozart begins his overture with a slow introduction that incorporates many of the musical motives he will later use within the opera. This ominous beginning is written in D minor, which brightens to D major at the start of the exposition. Since this is an overture and not a symphony, there is no repetition of the exposition.

In the exercise that follows, the sections of the exposition are identified for you so that you become familiar with the main thematic material of this piece. Then, beginning with the development and continuing through the recapitulation and brief coda, you are asked a series of questions that follow the unfolding of sonata form.

0:00   Slow, portentous introduction that makes use of a fateful dotted rhythm, twisting chromaticism, and, finally, writhing scales.

1:56   Exposition begins fast but quietly in major key with first theme in the strings.

2:15   Cadential pattern brings first theme group to a close.

2:20   Transition starts with scalar theme presented in sequence.

2:30   Continues with unstable chords that build tension.

2:35   Transition ends with strong cadence.

2:41   Second theme marked by scalar descent and then "birdlike fluttering" in woodwinds.

3:00   Light closing theme.

3:10   Static, cadential harmony signals end of exposition.

Questions:

1. 3:20   Which theme is used at the beginning of the development?

_____

2. 3:31   This same theme is now heard in the woodwinds in which guise?
                  a. as a cadence
                  b. in overlapping imitation
                  c. as a chorale

3. 3:40   Which theme enters? _____

4. 3:54   Which theme now returns? _____

5. 4:20–4:26   In this section is the harmony active or static? _____ [Listen to the double basses and tim-pani. Are they moving to different pitches (active harmony) or just repeating one note (static harmony)?]

6. 4:27   Now the recapitulation begins. Does it commence as expect-ed, with the first theme? _____

7. 4:49   Does the transition return again at this point? _____

8. 5:08   Do both the descending scale and the "flutter" motive appear as the second theme returns? _____

9. 5:29   Does the closing theme return? _____

10. 5:45   A brief coda begins here. A reminiscence of which theme is heard as the main melodic material? _____

N.B. There are no *forte* cadential chords to produce a "big bang" ending for this overture. Rather, Mozart writes an orchestral fadeout designed to coincide with the raising of the curtain and to lead into the music of the first scene.

---

23   Joseph Haydn   6CD 2/12; 6Tape 2B
Symphony No. 88 (1789)   3CD 2/11; 3Tape 2B
Fourth movement, *Allegro con spirito* (fast with spirit)

The first four questions of this exercise pertain to issues of orchestration; the final six address the form and general feeling of a rondo. Be sure you are famil-iar with the Listening Guide on page 181.

1. (0:00–0:13) Which woodwind instrument plays along with the strings dur-ing the first part (**a**) of the refrain?
   a. flute   b. clarinet   c. bassoon

2. (0:27–0:34 and 0:48–0:54; for both passages the answer is the same) Which two woodwind instruments play the return of the first part (**a′**) of the refrain?
   a. flute and clarinet   b. clarinet and bassoon   c. flute and bassoon

3. (1:39–1:46) Which woodwind instrument plays the refrain here at its first return?
   a. flute   b. clarinet   c. bassoon

4. (2:43–2:50) Which woodwind instruments play the refrain here at its second return?
   a. flute and clarinet   b. clarinet and bassoon   c. flute and bassoon

5. The refrain, or theme **A,** of this rondo is constructed in ternary form (**aba′**). Ternary from is equivalent to which form from the Baroque era?
   a. *da capo* aria form   b. rondo form   c. fugal form

6. Is there a second theme in this movement, one that contrasts with the refrain (**A**)? _____

7. (0:54–1:12 and 2:00–2:23) In this rondo the sections that begin to digress from the refrain are *least* like which functional type of music found in sonata–allegro form?
   a. transitional   b. developmental   c. cadential

8. What is the overall mood of this rondo?
   a. lyrical and hymnlike
   b. serious, even anguished
   c. light and carefree
9. What helps create this mood?
   a. There is much staccato playing throughout.
   b. The movement is mostly in a major key.
   c. The tempo is fast.
   d. There are many short notes that repeat quickly.
   e. all of the above
10. What is the function of the coda in this rondo?
    a. adds cadential material to give feeling of conclusion
    b. allows for one final statement of the refrain

KEY WORDS

coda	minuet	serenade
development	recapitulation	sonata–allegro form
exposition	relative major	transition (bridge)
fugato	retransition	trio

A checklist of musical style in the Classical period is given on page 66.

CLASSICAL GENRES

10

I n music the general term "genre" refers to that special quality of musical style, form, performing medium, and even place of performance that we associate with one class or type of music. The string quartet is a genre of music just as is the country music ballad, the cabaret song, the military march, and even the straight-ahead rock 'n' roll tune. When we choose to hear pieces of one genre or another, we listen with certain expectations as to how these works will sound, how they will progress, and how long they will last. We may even go to a special place, a theater or perhaps a bar, and dress a certain way, depending on the genre of music we will hear.

In the Classical period there were five main genres of secular art music: the symphony, string quartet, sonata, concerto, and opera. Though performed by different forces and usually in different environments, the same sort of audience might attend each. One of these genres, the opera, was taken over from the Baroque era and, though modified by Classical composers, retained its fundamental structure. Two others, the sonata and concerto, had also existed during the Baroque period, but were so changed by Haydn, Mozart, and their contemporaries that they were now tantamount to new genres. And still two others, the symphony and the string quartet, had no immediate ancestors in the Baroque era but were created wholly new during the Classical period.

THE SYMPHONY

It was during the Classical era that the symphony sprang forth to become the preeminent musical genre. That Haydn composed so many (104) and Mozart an even more astonishing number (41), given his short life, shows that the symphony had become, and would remain, the genre through which an aspiring composer might test his mettle and start on the road to international fame.

The symphony traces its origins to the late seventeenth-century Italian opera overture called the **sinfonia** ("a harmonious sounding together"). Around 1700 the typical Italian *sinfonia* was a one-movement instrumental work in three sections, fast–slow–fast. Soon Italian musicians and foreigners alike took the *sinfonia* out of the opera house and expanded it into three separate and distinct move-

FIGURE 10–1

At the right, the Burgtheater, Vienna, where many symphonies, concertos, and operas by Mozart were first heard. The building to the left now serves as the famous Spanish Riding School.

ments. A fourth movement, the minuet, was inserted by composers north of the Alps beginning in the 1740s. Thus, by mid-century the symphony had emerged as an independent genre and assumed its familiar four-movement format, fast–slow–minuet–fast.

The public favor the symphony came to enjoy was tied directly to certain revolutionary social changes that swept Europe during the Enlightenment. Not the least of these, as we have seen, was the impressive growth of public concerts (see page 153). The center of musical life in such cities as London, Paris, and, to a lesser degree, Vienna gradually shifted from the aristocratic court to the newly constructed or refurbished public concert hall. Larger audiences and greater financial gain for the composer could be had at public concerts like those mounted in the Hanover Square Rooms in London (see page 180) or the Burgtheater in Vienna (Figs. 10–1 and 10–2), where commoner and aristocrat met on more-or-less equal footing. Although some members of the nobility, notably the elector at Mannheim and the Esterházy princes, were important patrons of the early symphony, the genre ultimately flourished in an upper-middle-class environment. All but a few of Haydn's last twenty symphonies were composed for public performance in Paris and London, and Mozart apparently wrote no symphonies for a court patron during the last ten years of his life. His G minor symphony was apparently first performed in a casino (see Fig. 10–4)—that's where the people were and that's where the money was to be found. Henceforth, the listening public, and not the aristocratic prince, provided the principal support for the symphony and for the instrumental ensemble that performed it, the symphony orchestra.

Naturally, as the place of performance of the symphony moved from the aristocratic salon to the public auditorium, the size of the audience and the size of the concert hall increased. The orchestra of Haydn's patron, Prince Nikolaus Esterházy, was never larger than twenty-five, and the audience at court was often only the prince and his staff (Fig. 10–3). But when Haydn went to London to appear before the public in 1791, his "London Symphonies" were performed in

FIGURE 10–2

The interior of the Burgtheater, which could accommodate an audience of about seven hundred. Mozart directed four of his operas and performed several of his piano concertos there. Beethoven made his Viennese debut in this theater on March 29, 1795.

FIGURE 10–3

Haydn leading the orchestra at the court of the Esterházy princes during a performance of a comic opera. The composer is seated at the keyboard, surrounded by the cellos. The higher strings and woodwinds are seated at the desk.

the Hanover Square Rooms (see page 180), which accommodated between eight hundred and nine hundred persons. Indeed, for one of his public concerts in the spring of 1792, nearly 1,500 eager patrons crowded in. To fill these larger halls with sound, a larger orchestra was needed. Mozart mentions an orchestra of at least eighty players, including forty violins, ten violas, eight cellos, and ten double basses, for a public concert in the Burgtheater in Vienna in 1781 (Fig. 10–2). And although this ensemble was unusually large, orchestras of fifty or sixty players for public performance were not uncommon in Paris and London by the end of the century.

The heart of the Classical orchestra, as had been true of the earlier Baroque orchestra, was the string section: the ensemble of violins, violas, cellos, and double basses. But not only were there now more instruments in the group, the violin was modestly different as well. To produce a larger, more penetrating tone, metal strings, which could be strung to greater tension, began to replace those of animal gut. The winds were also increased in number so as to be heard in the midst of the large string sound. Now, instead of just one flute or one bassoon, there were usually pairs. And a new woodwind was introduced, the clarinet. Mozart was particularly delighted when he first heard the clarinet used as an orchestral instrument during a visit to the Mannheim court in 1778. "Ah, if only we had clarinets too! You cannot imagine the glorious effect of a symphony with flutes, oboes, and clarinets," he wrote to his father back in provincial Salzburg. Later Beethoven and Schubert would share his love for the rich color of this instrument. By the 1780s, then, the full Classical orchestra consisted of strings, two oboes, two flutes, two clarinets, two bassoons, two horns, and, for especially festive symphonies, two trumpets and timpani.

the Classical orchestra

clarinet added

Mozart: Symphony No. 40 in G Minor (1788)

Mozart's celebrated symphony in G minor requires all of the full instrumental sound and disciplined playing the late eighteenth-century orchestra could muster. This is not a festive composition (hence no trumpets and drums), but rather an intensely brooding work that suggests tragedy and feverish despair. While we might be tempted to associate the minor key and despondent mood with a specific event in Mozart's life, apparently no such causal relationship exists. This was one of three symphonies, his last three, that Mozart produced in the incredibly short span of six weeks during the summer of 1788, and the other two are sunny, optimistic works. Rather than responding to a particular disappointment, it is more likely that Mozart invoked the tragic muse in this G minor symphony by drawing on a lifetime of disappointments and a premonition—as his letters attest—of an early death.

FIRST MOVEMENT (*MOLTO ALLEGRO*)

Exposition: Although Mozart begins his G minor symphony with a textbook example of Classical phrase structure (four-bar antecedent, four-bar consequent phrases), an unusual sense of urgency is created by the repeating, insistent eighth-note figure at the beginning. This urgent motive is immediately grasped by the listener and, indeed, is the most memorable theme of the work.

EXAMPLE 10–1

accelerating harmonic rhythm

What is not so quickly seized, but yet contributes equally to the sense of urgency, is the accelerating rate of harmonic change. At the outset chords are set beneath the melody at an interval of one chord every four measures, then one every two bars, then one every measure, then two chords per measure, and finally four. Thus, the harmony, or harmonic rhythm, is moving sixteen times faster at the end of this section than at the start. This is how Mozart creates the drive and urgency we all feel yet may be unable to explain. After this quickening start, the first theme begins once again, but soon veers off its previous course and into the transition. Transitions are filled with motion, especially running scales, and this one is no exception. What is unusual is that a motive is inserted, one so distinctive we might call it a transition theme (see the example in the following Listening Guide). As if to reciprocate for an extra theme here, Mozart dispenses with one toward the end of the exposition, at the point where we would expect a closing theme to appear. Instead, as closing material he makes use of the persistent motive and rhythm from the beginning of the first theme, and this rather nicely rounds off the exposition. Finally, a single, isolated chord is heard, one that leads back to a repeat of the exposition, or, second time through, launches into the development.

Development: In the development Mozart employs only the first theme (and then only the first four bars), but subjects it to a variety of musical treatments. First he carries it through several distantly related keys, next shapes it into a fugue subject for use in a fugato*, then sets it in descending sequence, and finally inverts it melodically:

becomes

The retransition* is suddenly interrupted by *sforzandi* (loud attacks). But soon a dominant pedal point* is heard in the bassoons, and above it the flute and clarinets begin to cascade down to the tonic note. This use of soloistic woodwinds in the retransition is a hallmark of Mozart's symphonic style.

Recapitulation: As expected, the recapitulation offers the themes in the same order in which they appeared in the exposition. But now the transition theme, which Mozart has left untouched since its initial appearance, receives extended treatment, creating something akin to a second development section as it is pulled through one new key after another, only to end up back in the original tonic minor. When the lyrical second theme finally reappears, it has a more somber, plaintive mood now that it is in minor. Because the repeating figure of the first theme rounds off the recapitulation by way of a closing theme, only the briefest coda is needed to end this passionate, haunting movement.

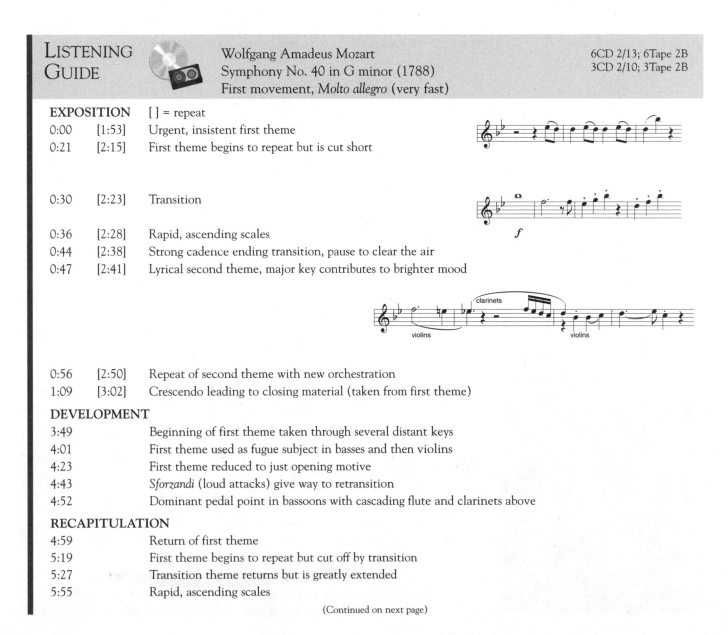

LISTENING GUIDE

Wolfgang Amadeus Mozart
Symphony No. 40 in G minor (1788)
First movement, *Molto allegro* (very fast)

6CD 2/13; 6Tape 2B
3CD 2/10; 3Tape 2B

EXPOSITION   [ ] = repeat
0:00   [1:53]   Urgent, insistent first theme
0:21   [2:15]   First theme begins to repeat but is cut short

0:30   [2:23]   Transition

0:36   [2:28]   Rapid, ascending scales
0:44   [2:38]   Strong cadence ending transition, pause to clear the air
0:47   [2:41]   Lyrical second theme, major key contributes to brighter mood

0:56   [2:50]   Repeat of second theme with new orchestration
1:09   [3:02]   Crescendo leading to closing material (taken from first theme)

DEVELOPMENT
3:49   Beginning of first theme taken through several distant keys
4:01   First theme used as fugue subject in basses and then violins
4:23   First theme reduced to just opening motive
4:43   *Sforzandi* (loud attacks) give way to retransition
4:52   Dominant pedal point in bassoons with cascading flute and clarinets above

RECAPITULATION
4:59   Return of first theme
5:19   First theme begins to repeat but cut off by transition
5:27   Transition theme returns but is greatly extended
5:55   Rapid, ascending scales

(Continued on next page)

6:04	Cadence and pause
6:07	Return of second theme now in (tonic) minor
6:17	Repeat of second theme with new orchestration
6:30	Return of crescendo leading to closing material (taken from first theme)
CODA	
7:11	Begins with rising chromatic scale
7:18	Return of opening motive, then three final chords

(Listening Exercise 24)

FIGURE 10–4

The New Market in Vienna as painted in 1759. The building on the right housed the city casino, and it was here that Mozart's G minor symphony was first performed in 1788. Even today famous musicians, such as Luciano Pavarotti, still perform in casinos—that's where the money is!

SECOND MOVEMENT (*ANDANTE*): After the feverish excitement of the opening movement, the slow, lyrical *Andante* comes as a welcome change of pace. What makes this movement exceptionally beautiful is the extraordinary interplay between the light and dark colors of the woodwinds against the constant tone of the strings. If there is no thematic contrast and confrontation here, there is, nonetheless, heartfelt expression brought about by Mozart's masterful use of orchestral color.

THIRD MOVEMENT (*MINUETTO: ALLEGRETTO*): We expect the aristocratic minuet to provide elegant, graceful dance music. But much to our surprise, Mozart returns to the intense, somber mood of the opening movement. This he does, in part, by choosing to write in the tonic minor key—a rare minuet in minor.

FOURTH MOVEMENT (*ALLEGRO ASSAI*): The finale starts with an ascending rocket that explodes in a rapid, *forte* flourish—and only carefully rehearsed string playing can bring off the brilliant effect of this opening gesture. The contrasting second theme of this sonata–allegro form movement is typically Mozartean in its grace and charm, a proper foil to the explosive opening melody. Midway through the development musical compression takes hold: There is no retransition, only a pregnant pause before the recapitulation; the return dispenses with the repeats built into the first theme; and a coda is omitted. This musical foreshortening at the end produces the same psychological effect experienced at the very beginning of the symphony—a feeling of urgency and acceleration.

THE STRING QUARTET

If the symphony is the ideal genre for the public concert hall and aims to please a large listening public, the string quartet is intended for the private chamber and sometimes for an audience of just the performers themselves. Unlike the symphony, which even in the Classical era might have a dozen violinists joining on the first violin line, the string quartet has only one player per part: one first violinist, one second violinist, one violist, and one cellist (Fig. 10–5). Moreover, there is no conductor. All performers function equally and communicate direct-

FIGURE 10–5

A representation of a string quartet at the end of the eighteenth century. The string quartet was at first an ensemble for playing chamber music in the home. Not until 1804 did a string quartet appear in a public concert in Vienna, and not until 1814 in Paris.

ly among themselves. No wonder the German poet Johann Wolfgang von Goethe (1749–1832) compared the string quartet to a conversation among four intelligent people. Although chamber music can include many modes of performance, ranging from a solo piano or violin to a piano trio, wind quintet, or even a string octet, all employ just one player on a part. Of these chamber media, the string quartet is historically the most important.

chamber music: one player per part

In the Baroque era the favored ensemble for chamber music was the trio sonata*, a group of two melody instruments, usually violins, and a *basso continuo** (including keyboard), which set the harmonies from below. With the emphasis shifting from the bottom-heavy Baroque to the lighter, simpler melodies of the early Classical period, the trio sonata ceded pride of place in the 1750s to the string quartet. The *basso continuo* gradually disappears and a new type of bass line emerges, one played by an agile cello alone. Moreover, the middle of the texture is given greater substance by assigning an active role to the viola, the instrument playing immediately above the cello.

FIGURE 10–6

Title page of six string quartets by Mozart dedicated to Haydn (1785). Mozart offers them to Haydn as "six children," asking Haydn to be their "father, guide, and friend."

Joseph Haydn created this new style of chamber music. In his mature quartets the spectrum of sound from top to bottom is covered evenly by four instruments that participate more or less equally in a give and take of theme and motive. As with most Classical quartets, Haydn's have the usual sequence of four movements, fast–slow–minuet–fast. But in a set he wrote in 1772 Haydn dubbed each minuet a **scherzo** (Italian for "joke"), suggesting the high-spirited style of playing intended for this movement and the string quartet in general.

It was the chance to play string quartets together that gave rise to a lasting friendship between Haydn and Mozart. During the summer of 1784 and winter of 1785, the two men met in Vienna, sometimes at the home of an aristocrat, sometimes in Mozart's own apartments. Haydn played first violin, Mozart viola in their quartet. As a result of this experience, Mozart was inspired to dedicate a set of his best works in this genre to the older master, which he published in 1785 (Fig. 10–6). Yet in this convivial, domestic music-making, Haydn and Mozart

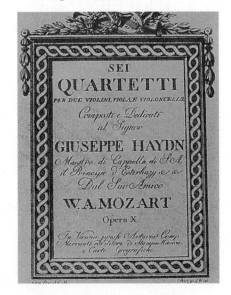

merely joined in the fashion of the day. For whether in Vienna, Paris, or London, aristocrats and members of the well-to-do middle class were encouraged to play quartets with friends as well as to engage professional musicians to entertain their guests. Haydn, Mozart, Beethoven, and young Schubert wrote some of their finest works for these amateur and professional ensembles. Their trios, quartets, and quintets have come to occupy such an important place in the repertoire that Classical chamber music has become almost synonymous with chamber music itself.

Haydn: Opus 76, No. 3, The "Emperor" Quartet (1797)

Haydn's "Emperor" Quartet, written in Vienna during the summer of 1797, is counted among the best works of the string quartet genre. It is known as The "Emperor" because it makes liberal use of *The Emperor's Hymn*, a melody Haydn himself composed the previous January in honor of Emperor Franz II. The invasion of imperial lands by the armies of Napoleon in that year had started a patriotic firestorm in Vienna, and Haydn's tune, set to the text "Gott erhalte Franz den Kaiser" ("God preserve Franz the Emperor"), was all the rage. (It subsequently became, in addition to a Protestant hymn, the Austrian national anthem.) Although the charming minuet makes no use of the emperor's tune, and the opening and closing movements of this quartet only allude to it, the slow second movement uses the majestic melody as the basis of a theme and

equality of instruments

variations set. The theme (see the example in the following Listening Guide) is first presented by the first violin, and harmonized in simple chords. Four variations follow. In these all four instruments are given equal opportunity to hold forth with the tune. Example 10–2 shows how in the Classical string quartet the melodic profile of each of the lines is pretty much the same, a far cry from the melody–walking-bass* polarity that typified the earlier Baroque trio sonata.

EXAMPLE 10–2

active role of the cello

Had Haydn been writing for a symphony orchestra, he could not have composed his bass line in this fashion. For the lowest string instrument in the symphony is the low double bass, which plays an octave below the cello and in that range produces a resonant, yet slightly muddled sound. But the more flexible fingering and singing tone of the cello make it possible for even the lowest instrument of the string quartet to participate as an equal partner. What the quartet gives up by way of depth and richness of sound, it gains in increased motivic interaction and in a more transparent texture.

LISTENING GUIDE

Joseph Haydn
String Quartet, Opus 76, No. 3, The "Emperor" Quartet (1797)
Second movement, *Poco adagio cantabile* (rather slow, songlike)

6CD 2/14; 6Tape 2B
3CD 2/12; 3Tape 2B

THEME

(repeat)

(repeat)

0:00   Theme played slowly in first violin; lower three parts provide chordal accompaniment

VARIATION 1
1:19   Theme in second violin while first violin ornaments above it

VARIATION 2
2:35   Theme in cello while other three instruments provide counterpoint against it

VARIATION 3
4:04   Theme in viola; other three instruments only gradually enter

VARIATION 4
5:31   Theme returns to first violin, but now the accompaniment is more contrapuntal than chordal

(Listening Exercise 25)

THE SONATA

The **sonata** was another important genre of chamber music that flourished during the Classical period. No longer was it a succession of four or five dance movements, as was usually the case during the Baroque era (see page 115). Now the sonata was a work in three movements (fast–slow–fast), each of which might make use of one or another of the forms favored by Classical composers: sonata–allegro, ternary, rondo, or theme and variations.

The sonata came to enjoy great popularity during the Classical period. According to publishers' inventories from the end of the eighteenth century, more sonatas were printed than any other type of music. The explanation for this sudden vogue is tied to the equally sudden favor experienced by the piano. Indeed, the word "sonata" has become so closely associated with the piano that unless otherwise qualified as "violin sonata," "cello sonata," or the like, we usually assume that "sonata" refers to a three-movement work for piano.

the piano sonata

Who played this flood of new sonatas for the piano? Amateur musicians, mostly women, who practiced and performed for polite society in the comfort of their

FIGURE 10–7

A performance of a sonata for piano and cello as depicted in 1775 by Joseph Zophany. This is one of the earliest paintings to show a piano rather than a harpsicord. Here the piano is a square piano of the type then manufactured in London.

own homes. As we have seen (page 154), in Mozart's time the ability to play the piano, to do fancy needlework, and to utter a few selected words of French were thought by male-dominated society all that was necessary to be a cultured young lady. To teach the musical handicraft, instructors were needed. Both Haydn and Mozart served as piano teachers in fashionable circles early in their careers. When Mozart arrived in Vienna in 1781 he took on four pupils, charged them a hefty fee, and wrote some of his best sonatas for the more talented of them. One of these, Josephina Auernhammer, rose above societal expectations for her sex to become a respected composer and public performer in her own right. But the piano sonatas that Mozart, Haydn, and Beethoven composed for their numerous pupils were not intended to be played in the public concert halls. Sonatas were to provide students with material that they might practice to develop technique and that they might play as musical entertainment in the home. Even among the splendid thirty-two piano sonatas that Beethoven composed, only one was ever performed at a public concert in Vienna during his lifetime.

piano sonatas for women

(An example of a Classical piano sonata by Beethoven, his *Pathétique* Sonata, is found on 6CD 3/4, 6Tape 3A, 3CD 2/13, and 3Tape 2B. It is discussed in detail on page 213.)

THE CONCERTO

With the genre of the concerto we leave the salon or private chamber and return once again to the public concert hall. For the Classical concerto is a large-scale, three-movement work for instrumental soloist and orchestra, and thus of the same magnitude as the symphony itself. And while the symphony might provide the greatest musical substance at a concert, more often than not the audience was lured to the hall by the prospect of hearing a virtuoso performer play a concerto. Audiences then as now had a special fascination with personal virtuosity

FIGURE 10–8

King Frederick the Great of Prussia performing a flute concerto at his court in Berlin. C. P. E. Bach, the second son of J. S. Bach, is at the keyboard.

and all the daring and excitement that a stunning technical display might bring. The soloist in such concertos was a single performer whose place in the musical firmament was that of a star. Gone was the Baroque tradition of the concerto grosso*, which pitted an orchestra (*tutti**) against a *group* of soloists (the *concertino**). From now on the concerto was a **solo concerto,** usually for piano, but sometimes for violin, cello, or wind instrument.

solo concerto offers technical display

Development of the solo concerto for piano had begun with the two sons of Johann Sebastian Bach, one living in Berlin, the other in London. The Berlin Bach, Carl Philip Emanuel Bach (1714–1788), was the keyboard player for the flute-playing King Frederick the Great (1712–1786) of Prussia, who drilled his troops during the day and played concertos in the evening (Fig. 10–8). Johann Christian Bach (1735–1782), the London Bach as he was called, experimented with the piano concerto in connection with a series of public concerts he gave both in London and Paris during the 1760s and 1770s. But no one did more to bring the form and style of the piano concerto to maturity than Wolfgang Amadeus Mozart.

Mozart wrote twenty-three piano concertos, more than any other important composer. He did so mainly because his economic livelihood depended on it, especially after he took up residence in Vienna as a freelance musician in 1781. Most of his masterpieces in this genre were composed so that Mozart himself might showcase his talents at public concerts that he alone had organized, for to attract attention in this period a composer not only had to write the music but also had to serve as performer, concert manager, and ticket seller all in one (see Fig. 10–9). It was up to Mozart to rent the hall (see Figs. 10–1 and 10–2), hire the orchestra, solicit an audience, and offer his paying public a collection of his newest creations. A musical journal for March 22, 1783, reports one of Mozart's more successful ventures of this sort:

FIGURE 10–9

One of the few surviving tickets to a concert mounted by Mozart in Vienna.

FIGURE 10–10

Another view of Mozart's piano. Mozart purchased this instrument in Vienna in 1784 and had it transported wherever he played in the city. His Concerto in A major was composed and first performed on this piano.

Today the celebrated Chevalier Mozart gave a musical concert for his own benefit at the Burgtheater in which pieces of his own music, which was already very popular, were performed. The concert was honored by the presence of an extraordinarily large audience and the two new concertos and other fantasies which Mr. Mozart played on the Forte Piano were received with the loudest approval. Our Monarch [Emperor Joseph II], who contrary to his custom honored the entire concert with his presence, joined in the applause of the public so heartily that one can think of no similar example. The proceeds of the concert are estimated at sixteen hundred gulden.

With a take such as this, Mozart could, at least for a time, indulge his expensive tastes.

Mozart: Piano Concerto in A Major (1786)

Mozart composed his Piano Concerto in A major for the concert season of 1786. In it the Classical love of balance is immediately evident, for the piano and orchestra appear in equal measure. Of all the solo instruments, the piano, with its capacity for melody, for speed of execution, and for full sound, is perhaps most up to the task of competing with an orchestra in a spirited give-and-take of musical material. When the orchestra comes forward with a rich full sound or varied instrumental color, the piano can counter with a line of tender expression, a virtuosic run, or a passage of *fortissimo* chords. The constant exchange between orchestra and soloist requires special attention on the part of the listener. As a biographer of Mozart has said: "Listeners who can really appreciate Mozart's piano concertos are the best audience there is."

FIRST MOVEMENT (*ALLEGRO*) As with all of Mozart's concertos, this one is in three movements (there is never a minuet or scherzo in a concerto). And, as is invariably the case, the first movement is written in sonata–allegro form. However, here it is modified to meet the special demands and opportunities of the concerto. What results is **double exposition form,** an extension of sonata–allegro form in which the orchestra plays one exposition and the soloist then plays another. First the orchestra presents the first, second, and closing themes, all in the tonic key. Then the soloist enters and, with orchestral assistance, offers the piano's version of the same material, but now modulating to the dominant before the second theme. After the piano expands the closing theme, part of the first theme group returns, a throwback to the ritornello* principle of the old Baroque concerto grosso.

Then, in this concerto in A, a surprise: Instead of the usual closing chords, Mozart ends this second exposition with a lyrical new melody presented by the strings. This is another feature of the Classical concerto—a melody held back, or saved, for presentation by the soloist at some unexpected moment in the second exposition.

DOUBLE EXPOSITION FORM

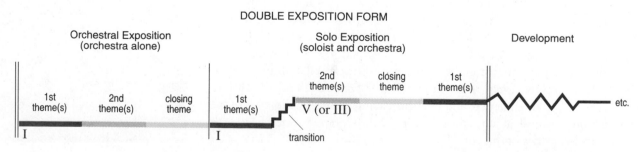

| Orchestral Exposition (orchestra alone) | Solo Exposition (soloist and orchestra) | Development |

The development here is concerned exclusively with exploiting the new theme that had appeared at the end of the second exposition. The recapitulation compresses the two expositions into one, presenting the themes in the same order as before but now all in the tonic key. Finally, toward the end of the movement the orchestra suddenly stops its forward motion and comes to rest on a single chord for several moments. Using this chord as a point of departure, the pianist plunges headlong into a flight of virtuosic fancy called a cadenza. In a **cadenza** the soloist, playing alone, mixes rapid runs, arpeggios, and snippets of previously heard themes into a fantasy-like improvisation. Indeed, Mozart didn't write down this cadenza when he first performed it, but improvised it on the spot, just as in our own century a talented jazz musician might improvise an extended solo. After a minute or so of this virtuosic dazzle, the pianist plays a trill* in the right hand and a V chord in the left to signal the orchestra that it is time for it to reenter the competition. From here to the end the orchestra holds forth, making use of the original closing theme. There is much to follow in the Listening Guide for this movement in double exposition form, but the glorious music of Mozart will amply reward the attentive listener.

virtuosic dazzle in the cadenza

LISTENING GUIDE	Wolfgang Amadeus Mozart Piano Concerto in A major (1786) First movement, *Allegro* (fast)	6CD 2/15 6Tape 2B

EXPOSITION 1 (orchestra)

0:00	Strings present first theme, part **a**
0:16	Woodwinds repeat first theme, part **a**
0:34	Full orchestra presents first theme, part **b**
0:56	Strings present second theme, part **a**
1:12	Woodwinds repeat second theme, part **a**
1:27	Strings present second theme, part **b**
1:32	Strings present closing theme, part **a**
1:57	Woodwinds present closing theme, part **b**

(Continued on next page)

EXPOSITION 2 (piano and orchestra)

2:07	Piano enters with first theme, part **a**
2:35	Orchestra plays first theme, part **b**
3:05	Piano plays second theme, part **a**
3:20	Woodwinds repeat second theme, part **a**
3:36	Piano plays and ornaments second theme, part **b**
3:41	Piano and orchestra in dialogue play closing theme, part **a**
4:15	Piano trill heralds return of first theme, part **b**
4:29	Strings quietly offer lyrical new theme

DEVELOPMENT

4:54	Woodwinds transform the new theme as piano interjects scales and then arpeggios
5:25	Woodwinds offer the new theme in imitative counterpoint
5:37	Pedal point on dominant note in low strings signals beginning of retransition
5:50	Piano takes over dominant pedal point
6:07	Piano flourish above held dominant chord leads to recapitulation

RECAPITULATION

6:17	Orchestra plays first theme, part **a**
6:31	Piano repeats first theme, part **a**
6:45	Orchestra plays first theme, part **b**
6:54	Scales in piano sound beginning of transition
7:13	Piano plays second theme now in tonic, part **a**
7:28	Woodwinds repeat second theme, part **a**
7:43	Piano plays second theme, part **b**
7:48	Piano and orchestra divide closing theme, part **a**
8:15	Piano plays the new theme
8:28	Woodwinds play the new theme while piano offers scales and arpeggios against it
8:54	Trill in piano announces return of first theme, part **b**
9:21	Orchestra stops and holds chord
9:25	Cadenza for piano
10:36	Trills signal reentry of orchestra
10:47	Orchestra plays closing theme, parts **a** and **b**
11:05	Final cadential chords

SECOND MOVEMENT (*ANDANTE*) The essence of this movement rests in Mozart's exquisitely crafted lines and coloristic harmonies. This is the only work the Viennese master ever wrote in the remote key of F♯ minor, and the daring harmonic changes it contains prefigure those of the Romantic era. Musicians who have lived with Mozart's music from childhood to old age continue to be profoundly moved by this extraordinary movement. It is at once sublimely beautiful but distantly remote, its ending as cold and desolate as death itself.

THIRD MOVEMENT (*PRESTO*) The sublime pessimism of the *Andante* is suddenly shattered by a boisterous rondo refrain in the piano. As Mozart was well aware, this movement, not the previous slow one, has the kind of music the fun-loving Viennese would pay to hear. And in this rondo his subscribers got more than their money's worth, for the refrain alone has no fewer than five separate and distinct parts. The feeling that predominates throughout is not so much a tug-of-war between soloist and orchestra but rather a high-spirited race to see which party can finish first the wealth of musical ideas.

PERA

Opera in the Classical period maintained the broad features passed on to it from the Baroque era. It still began with an overture, was divided into two or three acts, and made use of a succession of arias and recitatives along with an occasional choral number. Also, needless to say, it still was performed in a theater, one large enough to accommodate both an orchestra and elaborate stage sets.

Yet while the genre of opera retained its overall shape, it nonetheless underwent important internal changes during the second half of the eighteenth century. Italian comic opera *(opera buffa)*, a powerful voice for social change in the Enlightenment (see page 153), came to dominate the stage and gradually replace the serious opera *(opera seria)* of the Baroque period. The statuelike gods and goddesses, emperors and queens, of the older style have departed, replaced by more natural, realistic characters drawn from everyday life. Gone, too, are the rigid sectional divisions between aria, recitative, and chorus set in place to segregate one emotion from another. Although aria and recitative were still differentiated, in Classical opera they now flow more easily one to another. The mood of the music changes rapidly to reflect the fluctuating emotions of the characters. The new Classical style, marked by fluid changes of mood, is well suited to comic situations that invariably involve a quick give-and-take between characters.

easy flow of comic opera

Comic opera also brought a new element into the opera house, the **vocal ensemble.** While recitatives are still used to narrate action and arias to express emotion, now a variety of emotions can be expressed simultaneously by means of a vocal trio, quartet, or even sextet of soloists. One character might sing of her love, another of his fear, another of her outrage, while a fourth pokes fun at the other three. Vocal ensembles are especially favored at the ends of acts. No longer does the curtain fall after a solo "exit aria" from a famous prima donna (leading lady), but after a vocal ensemble including the principals—another manifestation of the collective spirit, and better dramatic sense, of the late eighteenth century.

the vocal ensemble

The master of Classical opera, and of the vocal ensemble in particular, is Wolfgang Amadeus Mozart. While Haydn wrote more than a dozen operas and conducted others (see Fig. 10–3, page 189), he lacked Mozart's instinct for what would work in the theater and what would not. Nor did he have Mozart's uncanny ability to depict and differentiate characters through music. With its lightning-quick changes in mood and color, and juxtaposition of themes of different character, Mozart's music is inherently theatrical and perfectly suited to the genre of opera.

Mozart wrote Italian *opera seria* of the old Baroque sort as well as German comic opera, which was called *Singspiel*. Like a Broadway musical, a Singspiel is made up of spoken dialogue (instead of recitative) and songs. Mozart's best work of this type is *Die Zauberflöte* (*The Magic Flute*, 1791), more recently popularized in a film version (1975) by the Swedish director Ingmar Bergman. But Mozart also wrote operas more in the tradition of Italian comic opera. These include his masterpieces *Le nozze di Figaro* (*The Marriage of Figaro*, 1786), *Don Giovanni*

Lorenzo da Ponte: Librettist to Mozart

Mozart's principal librettist during the 1780s was Lorenzo da Ponte, whose own life was more unbelievable than the theatrical characters he created. Born in northern Italy of Jewish parents, he received his only formal education in a Catholic seminary. He became a teacher of Italian and Latin literature and then an ordained priest, but was banned from his native Venice for his unreligious thinking and adulterous liaisons. Having made his way to Vienna in 1781, he was introduced to Emperor Joseph II by the imperial court composer Antonio Salieri (see page 161). Da Ponte became the official court librettist ("Poet to the Imperial Theaters"), and both Salieri and Mozart made use of his talents. But when Joseph died in 1790 and Mozart the following year, da Ponte's fortunes in Vienna declined. After passing time with another famous Venetian adventurer, Giovanni Casanova (1725–1798), da Ponte made his way to London, where he opened a bookstore. But he was soon charged with shady financial dealings, so in 1805 da Ponte stole away from London for America, one step ahead of his creditors. After a brief stop in New York, he established himself in Sunbury, Pennsylvania, as a trader, distiller, and occasional gunrunner during the War of 1812. Eventually, he gave this up and returned to New York, becoming the first professor of Italian literature at Columbia University in 1825. The high point of his final years came in May 1826, when he helped bring *Don Giovanni* to the stage in New York, the first opera by Mozart to be performed in America.

Lorenzo da Ponte (1749–1838).

(1787), and *Così fan tutte* (*Thus Do They All*, 1790), all three with text (libretto) by Lorenzo da Ponte.

Mozart: *Don Giovanni* (1787)

Don Giovanni has been called not only Mozart's greatest opera but also the greatest opera ever written. The story tells the tale of a wicked philanderer, a Don Juan, who seduces and murders his way across Europe before being pursued and finally dragged down to hell by the ghost of a man whom he has killed. Since the seducer and mocker of public law and morality is a nobleman, *Don Giovanni* is implicitly critical of the aristocracy, and Mozart and da Ponte danced quickly to stay one step ahead of the imperial censor before production. Mozart's opera was first performed on October 29, 1787, at the Nostitz Theater (Fig. 10–11) in Prague, a city in which his music was especially popular. As fate would have it, the most notorious Don Juan of the eighteenth century, Giovanni Casanova (1725–1798), was in the audience that first night in Prague. It turns out that he had had a small hand in helping his friend da Ponte shape the libretto.

overture

The overture to *Don Giovanni*, as we have seen (Listening Exercise 22), is written in sonata–allegro form. It begins with a slow introduction that incorporates several themes or motives important later in the opera. Just as an author postpones writing a preface until after a book is finished, so a composer saves the overture for the end of the creative process. In this way the overture can not only prefigure important themes in the opera but also characterize the overall tone of the work. Mozart, as was his custom, postponed much of the writing of *Don Giovanni* to the last minute, and the overture was not completed until the night before the premiere, the copyist's ink still wet on the pages as the music was handed to the orchestra.

FIGURE 10–11
A view of the Nostitz, or National Theater, Prague, where *Don Giovanni* was first performed on October 29, 1787. The theater still stands today and has been used for the filming of *Amadeus* (1985) and *Immortal Beloved* (1994).

As the last strains of the overture die away, the curtain rises on the comic figure Leporello, Don Giovanni's faithful, though somewhat reluctant, servant. He has been keeping a nocturnal vigil outside the house of Donna Anna while his master is at work inside. Grumbling as he paces back and forth, Leporello sings about how he would gladly trade places with the fortunate aristocrat ("I would like to play the gentleman"). Immediately, we see Mozart working to establish the musical character of Leporello: He sets this opening song in F major, a traditional key for the pastoral in music, showing that Leporello is a rustic fellow; he gives him a purely diatonic scale, but no fancy chromaticism; and he has him sing quick repeated notes, almost as if he were stuttering. This last technique, called "patter song," is a stock device used to depict low-caste characters in comic opera.

character depiction through music

As Leporello concludes his complaint, the masked Don Giovanni rushes on stage, chased by the virtuous Donna Anna. Here the strings rush up the scale and the music modulates up a fourth (at 1:32) to signify that we are now dealing with the highborn. It seems that the Don has been checked in his advances toward Donna Anna, and the affronted lady wants him captured and unmasked. While the gentleman and lady carry on a musical tug-of-war in long notes above, the cowering Leporello patters away fearfully below. The vocal ensemble makes clear the conflicting emotions of each party.

Now the cast of characters in the ensemble changes as Donna Anna runs to get help and her father enters to challenge Don Giovanni. The listener senses that this bodes ill—there is an ominous tremolo* in the strings, and the music shifts from major to minor (2:50). Our fear is immediately confirmed as the Don, first refusing to duel, draws his sword and attacks the aging Commandant. In the brief exchange of steel, Mozart depicts the rising anxiety by means of ascending chromatic scales and tight, tense chords (3:32). At the very moment Don Giovanni's sword pierces the Commandant, the action stops and the orchestra holds on a painful diminished chord (3:44)—a chord made up of all minor thirds. Mozart then clears the air of discord with a simple texture and accompaniment as Don Giovanni and Leporello gaze in horror on the dying Commandant. The

a duel set to music

listener can feel the Commandant expire, his life sinking away through the slow descent of a chromatic scale (4:52). In its intensity and compression, the opening scene of *Don Giovanni* has no equal outside of Shakespeare's *King Lear*.

LISTENING GUIDE

Wolfgang Amadeus Mozart
Opera, *Don Giovanni* (1787)
Act I, Scene 1

6CD 3/2
6Tape 3A

Characters: Don Giovanni, a rakish lord; Leporello, his servant; Donna Anna, a virtuous noblewoman; the Commandant, her father, a retired military man

ARIA

0:00   The watchful Leporello grumbles as he awaits his master Don Giovanni

Leporello

Notte e giorno faticar,	On the go from morn 'til night
per chi nulla sa gradi,	for one who shows no appreciation,
piova e il vento sopportar,	sustaining wind and rain,
mangiar male e mal dormir.	without proper food or sleep.
Voglio far il gentilumo	I would like to play the gentleman
e non volgio più servir . . .	and no more a servant be . . .

(Leporello continues in this vein)

1:32   Violins rush up the scale and music modulates upward as Don Giovanni and Donna Anna rush in

ENSEMBLE (TRIO)

1:38   Donna Anna tries to hold and unmask Don Giovanni while Leporello cowers on the side

Donna Anna

Non sperar, se non m'uccidi,	Do not hope you can escape
ch'io ti lasci fuggir mai'.	unless you kill me.

Don Giovanni

Donna folle, indarno gridi,	Crazy lady, you scream in vain,
chi son io tu non saprai.	you will never know who I am.

Leporello

Che tumulto, oh ciel, che gridi	What a racket, heavens, what screams,
il padron in nuovi guai.	my master in a new scrape.

Donna Anna

Gente! Servi! Al traditore!	Everyone! Help! Catch the traitor!
Scellerato!	Scoundrel!

Don Giovanni

Taci et trema al mio furore!	Shut up and get out of my way!
Sconsigliata!	Fool!

Leporello

Sta a veder che il malandrino	We will see if this malefactor
mi fara recipitar. . . .	will be the ruin of me. . . .

(The trio continues in this manner with liberal repeats of text and music.)

2:50   String tremolo and shift from major to minor as the Commandant enters

ENSEMBLE (TRIO)

The Commandant comes forward to fight; Don Giovanni first refuses, then duels; Leporello tries to flee

Commandant

Lasciala, indegno!	Let her go, villain!
Battiti meco!	Fight with me!

Don Giovanni

Va! non mi degno	Away, I wouldn't deign
di pugnar teco!	to fight with you!

Commandant

Così pretendi	So you think
da me fuggir!	you can get away thus?

Leporello (aside)

| Potessi almeno | If I could only |
| di qua partir! | get out of here. |

Don Giovanni

| Misero! attendi | You old fool! Get ready then, |
| se vuoi morir! | if you wish to die! |

3:32   Musical duel (running scales and
       tense diminished chords)

3:44   Climax on intense chord (the
       Commandant falls mortally wounded),
       then a pause

ENSEMBLE (TRIO)

3:50   Don Giovanni and Leporello look
       on the dying Commandant; the "ticking"
       sound in the strings freezes time

Commandant

Ah, soccorso! son tradito.	Ah, I'm wounded, betrayed
L'assassino m'ha ferito,	The assassin has run me through,
e dal seno palpitante	and from my heaving breast
sento l'anima partir.	I feel my soul depart.

Don Giovanni

Ah, gia cade il sciagurato,	Ah, already the old fool falls,
affannoso e agonizzante,	gasping and writhing in pain,
gia del seno palpitante	and from his heaving breast
Veggo l'anima partir.	I can see his soul depart.

Leporello

Qual misfatto! qual eccesso!	What a horrible thing, how stupid!
Entro il sen dallo spavento	I can feel within my breast
palpitar il cor mi sento.	my heart pounding from fear.
Io non so che far, che dir.	I don't know what to say or do.

4:52   A slow, chromatic descent as the last
       breath seeps out of the Commandant

When we next meet the unrepentent Don Giovanni, he is in pursuit of the country girl Zerlina. She is the betrothed of another peasant, Masetto, and the two are to be married the next day. Don Giovanni quickly dismisses Masetto and turns his charm on the naive Zerlina. First he tries verbal persuasion carried off in *secco* recitative* (the harpsichord is still used to accompany *secco* recitatives in Classical opera, a vestige of the older Baroque practice). Zerlina, he says, is too lovely for a common swain like Masetto. Her beauty demands a higher state: She will become his wife.

This preliminary discussion in *secco* recitative now gives way to more passionate expression in the form of a charming duet, "Là ci darem la mano" ("Give me your hand, oh fairest"). Don Giovanni begins with a seductive melody (**A**) cast squarely in the Classical mold of two four-bar phrases. Zerlina repeats and extends this, but is still singing alone and untouched. The Don becomes more insistent in a new phrase (**B**), and Zerlina, in turn, becomes flustered, as her quick sixteenth notes reveal. The initial melody (**A**) returns but is now sung together by the two principals, their voices intertwining—musical union accompanies the act of physical touching that occurs on stage. Finally, as if to further affirm this coupling through music, a concluding section (**C**) is added in which the two characters skip off, arm in arm ("Let's go, my treasure"), their voices linked together, mainly in parallel-moving thirds to show unity of feeling and purpose.

FIGURE 10–12

Don Giovanni (Sherrill Milnes) and Zerlina (Teresa Stratas) sing the duet "Là ci darem la mano" from *Don Giovanni*.

LISTENING
GUIDE   Wolfgang Amadeus Mozart   6CD 3/3
                                Opera, *Don Giovanni* (1787)   6Tape 3A
                                Act I, Scene 7

Characters: Don Giovanni and the peasant girl Zerlina
Situation: Don Giovanni tries, and apparently succeeds, in the
seduction of Zerlina.

RECITATIVE   **Don Giovanni**

0:00   Alfin siam liberati, Zerlinetta gentil,   At last, gentle Zerlina,
       da quel sioccone.   we are free of that clown.
       Che ne dite, mio ben,   And say, my love, didn't
       sò far pulito?   I handle it well?

                                        Zerlina

       Signore, è mio marito . . .   Sir, he is my fiance.

                                        Don Giovanni

       Chi? Colui?   Who? Him?
       Vi par che un onest'uomo,   Do you think that an honorable
       un nobil cavalier, qual io mi vanto,   man, a noble cavalier as I
       possa soffrir che quel visetto d'oro,   believe I am, could let such a
       quel viso inzuccherato   golden face, such a sweet
       da un bifolcaccio vil sia strapazzato?   beauty, be profaned by that
                                                     clumsy oaf?

                                        Zerlina

       Ma, signor, io gli diedi   But sir, I have already given
       parola di sposarlo.   my word to marry him.

                                        Don Giovanni

       Tal parola non vale un zero.   Such a promise counts for
       Voi non siete fatta per esser paesana;   nothing. You were not made
       un altra sorte vi procuran quegli   to be a peasant girl, a higher
       occhi bricconcelli, quei labretti si   fate is in store for those
       belli, quelle dituccia candide e   roguish eyes, those beautiful
       odorose, par me toccar giuncata e   lips, those milky, perfumed
       fiutar rose.   hands, so soft to touch,
                                                     scented with roses.

                                        Zerlina

       Ah! . . . Non vorrei . . .   Ah! . . . I do not wish . . .

                                        Don Giovanni

       Che non vorreste?   What don't you wish?

                                        Zerlina

       Alfine ingannata restar.   In the end to be decieved.
       Io sò che raro colle donne voi   I know that rarely with
       altri cavalieri siete onesti e sinceri.   women are you noblemen
                                                     honest and sincere.

                                        Don Giovanni

       Eh, un'impostura della gente plebea!   A vile slander of the low
       La nobiltà ha dipinta negli occhi   classes. Nobility can be
       l'onestà. Orsù, non perdiam tempo;   seen in honest eyes. Now
       in questo istante io ti voglio sponsar.   let's not waste time. I
                                                     will marry you immediately.

                                        Zerlina

       Voi?   You?

Don Giovanni

Certo, io. Quell casinetto è mio.	Certainly I. That villa
Soli saremo, e là, gioiello mio,	over there is mine. We
ci sposeremo.	will be alone, and there, my
	little jewel, we will be married.

ARIA (DUET)

A

1:45   **Don Giovanni**

Là ci darem la mano,	Give me your hand, oh fairest,
là mi dirai di sì.	whisper a gentle "yes."
Vedi, non è lontano:	See, it's not far,
partiam, ben mio, da qui.	let's go, my love.

Zerlina

2:03   Vorrei, e non vorrei,   I'd like to but yet I would not.

mi trema un poco il cor;   My heart will not be still.

felice, è ver, sarei,   Tis true I would be happy,

ma può burlarmi ancor.   yet he may deceive me still.

B   **Don Giovanni**

2:26   Vieni, mio bel diletto!   Come with me, my pretty!

                         Zerlina

Mi fa pietà Masetto!   May Masetto take pity!

                         Don Giovanni

Io cangierò tua sorte!   I will change your fate!

                         Zerlina

Presto, non son più forte.   Quick then, I can no longer resist.

A′

2:51   repeat of first eight lines, but with Don Giovanni's and Zerlina's parts moving closer together

B′

3:14   repeat of next four lines

C

3:42   Change of meter to dancelike 6/8 as the principals skip off together

                                  Together

Andiam, andiam mio bene,	Let's go, let's go, my treasure,
a ristorar le pene	to soothe the pangs
d'un innocente amor!	of innocent love.

Ultimately, in the duet "Give me your hand, oh fairest," Don Giovanni persuades Zerlina to extend her hand and the prospect of a good deal more. The tune, perhaps the most memorable of the opera, became a popular favorite in the nineteenth century. No less so *Don Giovanni*. From the moment of its first performance in Prague, Mozart's tragic-comic opera has enjoyed enormous favor with all who are moved by alluring melodies and passionate drama. *Don Giovanni* is one of those rare instances in the fine arts of a work that has immediate popular appeal, yet is universally judged to be a masterpiece of the highest order.

LISTENING EXERCISES

| 24 | Wolfgang Amadeus Mozart
Symphony No. 40 in G minor (1788)
First movement, *Molto allegro* (very fast) | 6CD 2/13; 6Tape 2B
3CD 2/10; 3Tape 2B |

Mozart's Symphony No. 40 in G minor has been discussed in detail (page 189), as has the development of the symphony orchestra in the Classical period. The following questions focus on the various instruments and instrumental families of the orchestra as they work within the context of sonata–allegro form. This is not a festive symphony, so there are no trumpets and drums. Mozart is writing for French horns, woodwinds, and strings. How does he use these instrumental forces to achieve his musical aims?

0:00–0:20   Beginning of first theme
  1. Which instruments are playing the melody here?
     a. violins   b. violas   c. cellos
  2. At which time do the woodwinds finally enter? _____

0:30–0:45   Transition
  3. Which instruments dominate the transition?
     a. cellos   b. flutes   c. violins

0:47–1:04   Second theme
  4. Which is true?
     a. The strings dominate this second theme area.
     b. The strings and woodwinds participate equally.

1:22–1:32   Echoes of the first theme provide a closing
  5. Which woodwind instrument can be heard playing the main motive of the first theme?
     a. French horn   b. trumpet   c. bassoon

1:53–3:45   Repeat of exposition

3:49–4:28   Development section, first of two parts
  6. Which family of instruments dominates this contrapuntal working out of the first theme?
     a. strings   b. woodwinds   c. brasses

4:52–4:58   Retransition at the end of the development
  7. Which family of instruments dominates this retransition?
     a. strings   b. woodwinds   c. brasses

4:59–5:26   Beginning of recapitulation
8. Which of the following is true?
   a. The orchestration here at the beginning of the recapitulation is mostly
   the same as that at the beginning of the movement (strings followed by
   later woodwind entry).
   b. Mozart has radically changed the orchestration. The woodwinds come in
   first with the theme, and the strings come in later.

5:27–6:05   Transition
9. Which family of instruments dominates this extended transition?
   a. strings   b. woodwinds   c. brasses

6:07–6:25   Second theme

6:48   Echoes of first theme provide a closing
10. Which of the following is true generally about this movement?
   a. The woodwinds never introduce a new theme; they only repeat and elaborate themes presented by the violins as well as add instrumental color.
   b. The woodwinds introduce new themes in this movement just as often as
   the violins; they also add instrumental color.

---

25   Joseph Haydn   6CD 2/14; 6Tape 2B
         Opus 76, No. 3, The "Emperor" Quartet (1797)   3CD 2/12; 3Tape 2B
         Second movement, *Poco adagio cantabile* (rather slow, songlike)

The string quartet is a type of chamber music, and its musical style is different
from that of the symphony. Here we have a quartet by the aging Haydn in
which the slow movement is composed in the form of theme and variations. Go
back and have another look at the melody that constitutes the theme (page
195) and then answer the following questions.

0:00–1:17   Theme
1. Listen to the theme as it is played by the first violin. Is it in a major or a
   minor key? _____
2. Why does this melody sound so secure and firm?
   a. because all the notes are the same length
   b. because each phrase ends on a dominant or a tonic note
   c. because there are many modulations

1:19–2:33   Variation 1
3. The second violin has the theme while the first violin rapidly ornaments
   above. Do the viola and cello (the lowest two instruments) play at all during this variation? _____

2:35–4:02   Variation 2
4. The cello has the theme in this variation. Would you say the instrument is
   playing in the higher or the lower part of its range? (Listen especially to the
   last section of the melody.) _____

4:04–5:29   Variation 3
5. The viola has the melody but is gradually joined by the other instruments.
   Which instrument is the *last* to enter in this variation?
   a. first violin   b. second violin   c. cello

6. Is the style of writing in this variation homophonic (chordal) or polyphonic (contrapuntal)? _____

5:31–6:55   Variation 4

7. The theme now returns to the first violin. When the violin repeats the first phrase of the melody, it does so
   a. an octave higher.   b. an octave lower.   c. at the same pitch level.

8. (6:57) Is there a brief coda added here? _____

9. This ending sounds suddenly darker; why?
   a. because a minor chord is heard
   b. because the tempo gets faster
   c. because the theme now is played on the lowest instrument

10. A general question about this movement: Which of the following is true?
    a. In this set of theme and variations Haydn keeps the theme pretty much intact and changes, or varies, the context in which it appears.
    b. In this set of theme and variations Haydn radically transforms the theme while keeping its context pretty much intact.

KEY WORDS

cadenza	scherzo	string quartet
diminished chord	*sinfonia*	*The Emperor's Hymn*
double exposition form	*Singspiel*	vocal ensemble
Lorenzo da Ponte	solo concerto	
prima donna	sonata	

A checklist of musical style in the Classical period is given on page 66.

THE BRIDGE TO ROMANTICISM: LUDWIG VAN BEETHOVEN

11

No composer is more revered than Ludwig van Beethoven (1770–1827), no music more loved than his. Indeed, when one conjures up the image of a composer of music, most likely it is the figure of Beethoven that comes to mind—the angry, defiant, disheveled Beethoven. Is it not the bust of Beethoven, rather than the elegant Mozart or the stalwart Bach, that sits atop the piano in the comic strip *Peanuts?* Is it not Beethoven who is the namesake of popular canine movies (*Beethoven* and *Beethoven 2nd*) and whose love-life is likewise chronicled on film (*Immortal Beloved*)? Is it not Beethoven who is the butt of all "decomposing" jokes? Such observations are not mere trivialities. The image of Beethoven is deeply ingrained in our popular culture. For many, Beethoven personifies the ideal of "the musician as artist"; for some he is the consummate "artist as hero."

His music, too, enjoys great public favor. Statistics show that Beethoven's symphonies, sonatas, and quartets are performed in concert halls and heard on radio more than those of any other classical composer. His works are tender but powerful, perfectly balanced yet bursting with energy. And just as Beethoven the composer struggled to overcome personal adversity—his growing deafness—so his music imparts a feeling of struggle and ultimate victory. It has a sense of rightness, even morality, about it. It elevates and inspires the listener, and for that reason it has an immediate and universal appeal.

Beethoven's life spanned the last quarter of the eighteenth century and the first quarter of the nineteenth. For the most part his music belongs to the tradition of the Viennese Classical masters. He composed predominantly in the Classical genres of symphony, piano sonata, concerto, string quartet, and opera; and he wrote within the Classical forms of sonata–allegro, rondo, and theme and variations. Yet even in the compositions of his youth, there is unmistakably a new spirit at work in his music, one that foreshadows the musical style of the Romantic period (1820–1900). An intense, lyrical expression is heard in his slow movements, while his allegros abound with striking themes, pounding rhythms, and startling dynamic contrasts. He stays within the bounds of Classical forms, yet he pushes their confines to the breaking point, so great is his urge for personal expression. Though a pupil of Haydn and a lifelong admirer of Mozart, he nonetheless elevated music to new heights of eloquence and dramatic power. For this reason he can rightly be called the prophet of Romantic music.

THE EARLY YEARS (1770–1802)

Like Bach and Mozart before him, Beethoven came from a family of musicians. His father and grandfather were performers at the court of the Elector at Bonn, Germany, a small town on the Rhine River where Beethoven was born on December 17, 1770. Seeing great musical talent in his young son, Beethoven's father, a violent, alcoholic man, forcibly made him practice at the keyboard all hours, day and night. Soon he tried to exploit his son as a child prodigy, a second Mozart, telling the world the diminutive boy was two years younger than he actually was. At the age of seventeen Beethoven was packed off to faraway Vienna to study with Mozart himself. But no sooner had he arrived and played for the master than his mother became seriously ill, and he was forced to return to Bonn. Five years later, in 1792, Beethoven finally went to Vienna for good. As one of his benefactors said, "You are going to Vienna in fulfillment of your long-frustrated wishes . . . you will receive the spirit of Mozart from the hands of Haydn."

Indeed, Mozart had died since Beethoven's last visit, so he now took up the study of musical composition with Haydn. But the aging Haydn and the youthful, impetuous Beethoven were not compatible. So when Haydn set off for his second sojourn in London in 1794 (see page 158), Beethoven began to work with other teachers, including a certain Johann Albrechtsberger (1736–1809), with whom he studied fugue, and the ever-present Antonio Salieri (1750–1825; see page 161), who taught him the Italian vocal style. At the same time Beethoven tried to make himself acceptable to polite society in Vienna: He bought new clothes, located a wigmaker, and found someone who could give him dancing lessons.

Beethoven and the aristocracy

Beethoven's aim was to gain an entrée into the homes of the wealthy of the Austrian capital. And this he soon did, not because of his skill as a composer, and less because of his social graces, but because of his phenomenal talent as a pianist. His playing was louder, more violent, more forceful, yet more expressive than the aristocrats of the salons had ever heard. He possessed an extraordinary technique—even if he did hit occasional wrong notes—and this he put to good use, especially in his fanciful improvisations. As a contemporary witness observed: "He knew how to produce such an impression on every listener that frequently there was not a single dry eye, while many broke out into loud sobs, for there was a certain magic in his expression."

The aristocracy was captivated. One patron put a string quartet at his disposal, another made it possible for Beethoven to experiment with a small orchestra, and all showered him with gifts. He acquired well-to-do pupils; he sold his compositions ("I state my price and they pay," he said with pride in 1801); and he requested and eventually received an annuity from three noblemen so that he could work undisturbed. The text of this arrangement includes the following lines:

> It is recognized that only a person who is as free as possible from all cares can consecrate himself to his craft. He can only produce these great and sublime works which ennoble Art if they form his sole pursuit, to the exclusion of all unnecessary obligations. The undersigned have therefore taken the decision to ensure that Herr Ludwig van Beethoven's situation shall not be embarrassed by his most necessary requirements, nor shall his powerful genius be hampered.

What a contrast between Beethoven's contract and the one signed by Haydn four decades earlier! Music is no longer merely a craft and the composer a servant. It is now an exalted Art, and the great creator a Genius who must be protected and nurtured—this is a new notion of the value of music, one of the Romantic age. And Beethoven did his best to encourage a belief in the exalted mission of the composer as artist. He would not stand at the beck and call of a master. When one patron demanded that he play for a visiting French general, Beethoven stormed out of the salon and responded by letter: "Prince, what you are, you are through the accident of birth. What I am, I am through my own efforts. There have been many princes and there will be thousands more. But there is only one Beethoven!"

Piano Sonata, Opus 13, The *Pathétique* Sonata (1799)

The bold originality in Beethoven's music can be seen in one of his most celebrated compositions, the *Pathétique* Sonata. A sonata*, as we have seen, is a multimovement work for solo instrument or an instrument with keyboard accompaniment. That Beethoven himself supplied the title *Pathétique* for this solo piano sonata suggests the passion and pathos he felt within this work. It has more drama and intensity, and requires more technical skill of the pianist, than any piano sonata of Mozart or Haydn. Beethoven himself frequently performed the *Pathétique* in the homes and palaces of the Viennese aristocracy.

FIRST MOVEMENT: Contemporaries recount how Beethoven the pianist played with "superhuman" speed and force, and how he banged so hard on one occasion that he broke six strings. The crashing C minor chord that opens the *Pathétique* Sonata suggests Beethoven's sometimes violent approach to the instrument. After this startling opening gesture, Beethoven the dramatist continues by juxtaposing music of wildly differing moods: the *sforzando* chord is immediately followed by quiet lyricism, only to be interrupted by another chordal thunderbolt. This slow introduction probably is a written-out version of the sort of improvisation at the piano that gained Beethoven great fame in Vienna. The introduction leads to a racing first theme that rises impetuously in the right hand. The sense of anxiety the listener feels is amplified by the bass, where the left hand of the pianist plays broken octaves (the alternation of two tones an octave apart) reminiscent of the rumble of distant thunder.

FIGURE 11–2

Beethoven's study in the last year of his life (1827). The piano was given him by the English maker Broadwood in 1818. The tower of St. Stephen's cathedral can be seen in the background (see Fig. 8–16).

dramatic introduction

EXAMPLE 11–1

Thereafter the movement plays out as a struggle of the impetuous, racing themes pitted against the sound of the stormy introduction, which is reintroduced at regular intervals. There is much passion and intensity here, yet there is also Classical formal control: The crashing chords come back at the beginning of both the development and the coda in this sonata–allegro form movement. Thus the chords simultaneously set the formal boundaries and prevent the racing themes from flying out of control.

LISTENING GUIDE

Ludwig van Beethoven
Piano Sonata, Opus 13, The *Pathétique* Sonata (1799)

6CD 3/4; 6Tape 3A
3CD 2/13; 3Tape 2B

First movement, *Grave; Allegro di molto e con brio* (grave; very fast and with gusto)

INTRODUCTION

0:00	Crashing chords alternate with softer, more lyrical chords
0:46	Softer chords continually cut off by crashing chords below
1:10	Melody builds to a climax and then rapid descent

EXPOSITION [ ] = repeats

1:41 [3:14]	Rising agitated melody in right hand against broken octaves in left (first theme)

1:59 [3:34]	Transition with modulation to new key, thinner texture
2:11 [3:44]	Bass, followed by treble, initiates a "call and response" (second theme)

2:39 [4:12]	Right and left hands race in opposite directions (closing theme, part 1)
2:58 [4:31]	Rapid scales in right hand above simple chords in left (closing theme, part 2)
3:04 [4:37]	Reminiscence of first theme
[3:14–4:47]	Repeat of exposition

DEVELOPMENT

4:48	Crashing chords and softer chords from introduction
5:32	First theme extended and varied
6:09	Rapid twisting descent played by right hand leads to

RECAPITULATION

6:15	Rising agitated melody in right hand (first theme)
6:25	Transition
6:35	Call and response between bass and treble (second theme)
6:59	Hands move rapidly in opposite directions (closing theme, part 1)
7:18	Scale runs in right hand (closing theme, part 2)
7:24	Reminiscence of first theme

CODA

7:35	Recall of chords from the introduction
8:14	Reminiscence of first theme leads to a drive to the final cadence

(Listening Exercise 26)

SECOND MOVEMENT: Eyewitnesses who heard Beethoven at the piano remarked on the "legato" quality of his playing, and contrasted it with Mozart's lighter, more staccato style. Beethoven himself said in 1796 that "one can sing on the piano, so long as one has feeling." We can hear Beethoven sing through the legato melodic line that dominates the slow second movement of the *Pathétique* Sonata. Indeed, the expression mark he gave to the movement is *cantabile* ("songful"). The mood here is of a slow, elegiac hymn. The lyrical line of this *Adagio* would set the tone for many other long, lyrical themes later in the nineteenth century.[†] Here in early Beethoven we already find the essence of Romantic melody.

[†]Pop star Billy Joel, who was trained as a classical pianist, borrowed this theme for the chorus of his song "This Night" on the album *Innocent Man*.

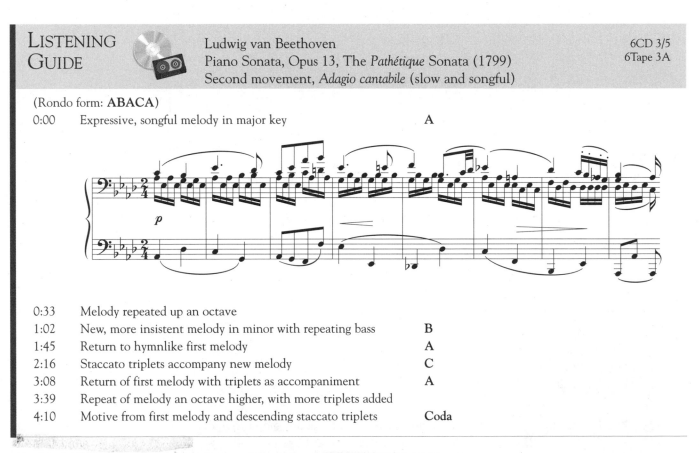

LISTENING GUIDE

Ludwig van Beethoven
Piano Sonata, Opus 13, The *Pathétique* Sonata (1799)
Second movement, *Adagio cantabile* (slow and songful)

6CD 3/5
6Tape 3A

(Rondo form: **ABACA**)

0:00	Expressive, songful melody in major key	**A**

0:33	Melody repeated up an octave	
1:02	New, more insistent melody in minor with repeating bass	**B**
1:45	Return to hymnlike first melody	**A**
2:16	Staccato triplets accompany new melody	**C**
3:08	Return of first melody with triplets as accompaniment	**A**
3:39	Repeat of melody an octave higher, with more triplets added	
4:10	Motive from first melody and descending staccato triplets	**Coda**

THIRD MOVEMENT: A comparison of the second and third movements of the *Pathétique* Sonata will show that musical form does not determine musical mood. Although both the *Adagio* and the fast finale are in rondo form, the first is a lyrical hymn and the latter a passionate, but slightly comical, chase. The finale has hints of the crashing chords and stark contrasts of the first movement, but the earlier violence and impetuosity have been softened into a mood of impassioned playfulness.

Beethoven cut a strange, eccentric figure as he wandered the streets of Vienna, sometimes humming, sometimes mumbling, and sometimes jotting on music paper (Fig. 11–3). Adding to the difficulties from his somewhat unstable personality was the fact that he was gradually going deaf—a serious handicap for any

Beethoven's Confession: The Heiligenstadt Testament

Beethoven was a physically powerful, proud, egotistical man who suffered no fools and had few doubts about his own worth as a musician. The loss of his hearing, which began in 1798, was a near fatal blow. It not only jeopardized his profession but also caused him to withdraw increasingly from society, creating the image of Beethoven the loner, the outcast, the misanthrope. The Heiligenstadt Testament is a lengthy, public letter that Beethoven, having finally decided against suicide, wrote in the fall of 1802. It is a remarkable document—part plea for understanding, part artistic manifesto. The name "Heiligenstadt" derives from the fact that Beethoven penned it in the village of that name, just to the north of Vienna, where he had gone in 1802 for a "cure" for his deafness. Here are a few lines of Beethoven's public declaration:

Oh my fellow men who consider me an unfriendly, hostile, peevish man or even misanthropic, how greatly you wrong me. For you do not know the secret reason why I appear to be so to you. . . . Though endowed with a passionate and lively temperament and even fond of the distractions offered by society, I was soon obliged to withdraw and live in solitude. . . . I could not bring myself to say to people: "Speak up, shout, for I am deaf." Alas, how could I possibly mention the loss *of a sense* which in me should be more perfectly developed than in other people, a sense which at one time I possessed in the greatest perfection, even to a degree few in my profession possess or have ever possessed. . . . But how humiliated I have felt if somebody standing beside me heard the sound of a flute in the distance and *I heard nothing!* Such experiences made me despair. I would have ended my life—it was only *my art* that held me back.

FIGURE 11–3

Beethoven as sketched from behind in 1819. Note that he carries manuscript paper in his left hand so that acquaintances can write out their part of conversations with the totally deaf composer. Beethoven also carried paper on which to notate musical ideas that he transferred to his sketchbook when he returned home.

person, but a tragic condition for a musician. The symptoms first manifested themselves in the late 1790s, and, quite understandably, the victim suffered considerable anguish and depression. His deafness perhaps least affected his work as a composer—good musicians can hear with an "inner ear" and do not need actual sound. But it caused him to retreat from society even more, and it all but ended his career as a performer, since he could no longer gauge how hard to press the piano keys. By late 1802 Beethoven recognized that he would suffer a gradual, though ultimately total, loss of hearing. Yet he emerged from his period of depression with a renewed conviction to do great things. His music had sustained him: "I would have ended my life—it was only *my art* that held me back," he said. He would now "seize Fate by the throat."

THE "HEROIC" PERIOD (1803–1813)

It was in this resurgent, defiant mood that Beethoven entered what we call his "heroic" period of composition (1803–1813). His works became longer, more assertive, full of broad themes and grand gestures. A watershed is his "Eroica" Symphony (Symphony No. 3, 1803). It is forty-five minutes long, about twice the length of the average symphony of Haydn or Mozart. Themes and motives are endlessly manipulated, crescendos gradually swell over long spans of time, and repeating syncopations are played *sforzando* (with a loud attack) to create a novel, almost shocking, rhythmic effect. Unprecedented in a symphony is the slow second movement, entitled *Marcia funèbre (Funeral March)*. It is composed in the style of many funeral marches created in Paris in those years to honor the fallen heroes of the French Republic. Although Austria was at war almost continually with France early in the nineteenth century, Beethoven was much taken with the enemy's revolutionary call for liberty, equality, and fraternity. Napoleon Bonaparte became his hero, and the composer entitled this, his third symphony,

Bonaparte. But when Napoleon declared himself emperor, Beethoven flew into a rage and ripped the title page in two saying, "Now he, too, will trample on all the rights of man and indulge only his ambition." When the work was published, Napoleon's name had been removed in favor of the more general title, "Heroic" Symphony.

Beethoven wrote nine symphonies in all, six of them in his "heroic" period. Although few in number compared with earlier Classical composers, Beethoven's symphonies nonetheless set the standard for the genre of the symphony for the remainder of the nineteenth century. Noteworthy, in addition to the "Eroica" (Third), are the famous Fifth Symphony, the Sixth (called the "Pastoral" because it tries to evoke the ambiance of the Austrian countryside), the Seventh, and the monumental Ninth. In these Beethoven introduces new orchestral colors by bringing new instruments into the symphony orchestra: the trombone (Symphony Nos. 5, 6, and 9), the contrabassoon (Symphony Nos. 5 and 9), the piccolo (Symphony Nos. 5, 6, and 9), and even the human voice (Symphony No. 9). He also changes the nature of the four principal movements of the symphony: The first movement becomes even larger as the development section and the coda are expanded; the slow movement assumes a solemn, hymnlike, sometimes tragic quality; the third movement loses the dance character of the minuet and becomes a faster, driving scherzo* (see page 193); and the finale, which had previously been marked by lightness and gaiety, takes on a weightier, often triumphant tone, one sufficient to balance the general seriousness of the opening movement.

Symphony No. 5 in C Minor (1808)

The four movements of Beethoven's well-known Symphony No. 5 have these characteristics and something more. The movements work together in a new way to convey a sense of psychological progression. An imaginative listener might feel the following sequence of events: (1) a fateful encounter with elemental forces, (2) a period of quiet soul-searching, followed by (3) a further wrestling with the elements, and, finally, (4) a triumphant victory over the forces of Fate. Beethoven himself is said to have remarked with regard to the famous opening motive of the symphony: "There Fate knocks at the door!"

The rhythm of the opening—perhaps the best-known moment in all of classical music—animates the entire symphony. Not only does it dominate the opening *Allegro* but it reappears in varied form in the three later movements as well, binding the symphony into a unified whole.

FIGURE 11–4

As a young officer, Napoleon Bonaparte seized control of the government of France in 1799 and established a new form of Republic. When Napoleon elevated himself to emperor in 1804, Beethoven changed the title of his Symphony No. 3 from "Bonaparte" to "Eroica." The portrait by Jacques-Louis David shows the newly crowned Napoleon in full imperial regalia. Liberator had become oppressor.

EXAMPLE 11–2

FIGURE 11–5

Interior of the Theater an der Wien, Vienna, where Beethoven's Symphony No. 5 received its premiere on December 22, 1808. During this first performance the orchestra frequently halted because of the difficulties in playing Beethoven's radically new music.

FIRST MOVEMENT: At the very outset the listener is jolted to attention, forced to sit up and take notice by a sudden explosion of sound. And what an odd beginning to a symphony—a blast of three short notes and a long one, followed by the same three shorts and a long, all now a step lower. The movement can't quite get going. It starts and stops, then seems to lurch forward and gather momentum. And where is the theme or melody? This three-shorts-and-a-long pattern is more a motive or musical cell than a melody. Yet it is striking by virtue of its power and compactness. As the movement unfolds, the actual pitches of the motive prove to be of secondary importance. Beethoven is obsessed here with rhythm. He wants to demonstrate the enormous latent force that lurks within even the simplest rhythmic cell just waiting to be unleashed by a composer who understands the secrets of rhythmic energy.

To control the sometimes violent forces that will emerge, the musical processes unfold within the traditional confines of sonata–allegro form. The basic four-note motive provides all the musical material for the first theme area:

EXAMPLE 11–3

There is a brief transition played by a solo French horn. It is only six notes long and is formed simply by adding two notes to the end of the basic four-note motive. As expected, the transition moves the tonality from the tonic (C minor) to the relative major* (E♭ major):

EXAMPLE 11–4

The second theme seems to offer a moment of escape from the rush of the motive, but even here the pattern of three shorts and a long is heard underneath in the low strings:

EXAMPLE 11–5

The closing theme, too, is none other than the motive once again, now presented in a somewhat different guise:

EXAMPLE 11–6

With the development, the opening motive returns and assumes all, if not more than all, of the force it had at the beginning. It soon takes on different melodic forms, as it is tossed back and forth between instruments, though the rhythmic shape remains constant:

EXAMPLE 11–7

Following a rhythmic climax and a brief imitative passage, Beethoven reduces the six-note motive of the transition down to merely two notes, and then just one, and he passes these around *pianissimo* between the strings and the winds:

EXAMPLE 11–8

Beethoven was a master of the process of musical fragmentation—stripping away all extraneous material to get to the core of a musical idea. Here in this mysterious *pianissimo* passage he holds up the irreducible minimum of his motive: a single note. In the midst of this quiet, the original four-note motive tries to reassert itself *fortissimo,* yet at first cannot do so. Its explosive force, however, cannot be held back. A thunderous return of the opening chords signals the beginning of the recapitulation.

Although the recapitulation offers a repeat of the events of the exposition, Beethoven has one surprise in store. No sooner has the motive regained its momentum than an oboe interjects a tender, languid, and wholly unexpected solo. Though a deviation from the usual path of sonata–allegro form, this brief oboe cadenza* allows for a momentary release of excess energy. The recapitulation then resumes its expected course.

What is not expected is the enormous coda that follows. It is even longer than the exposition! A new form of the motive appears and it, too, is subjected to development. In fact, what Beethoven does here is write a second development section, so great is his urge to exploit the latent power of this one simple musical idea.

LISTENING GUIDE

Ludwig van Beethoven
Symphony No. 5 in C minor (1808)
First movement, *Allegro con brio* (fast with gusto)

6CD 3/6; 6Tape 3A
3CD 2/14; 3CD 2B

EXPOSITION [ ] = repeats

0:00	[1:23]	Two statements of the motive
0:06	[1:29]	Motive builds momentum in a crescendo working up to climax and three chords, the last of which is held
0:23	[1:46]	Another crescendo begins as motive is piled upon itself in imitative counterpoint
0:40	[2:06]	Loud climax on two chords
0:43	[2:08]	Short transition played by solo horn
0:45	[2:09]	Quiet second theme in new major key (relative major)
0:58	[2:22]	Crescendo
1:04	[2:27]	Loud string passage prepares arrival of closing theme
1:13	[2:36]	Closing theme
[1:23–2:44]		Repeat of exposition

DEVELOPMENT

2:46   Motive played *fortissimo* by horn and strings and then
        passed back and forth between woodwinds and strings

3:07   Another crescendo or "Beethovenian swell"

3:13   Rhythmic climax in which motive is pounded incessantly

3:20   Short passage of imitative counterpoint using transition motive

3:30   Two notes of transition motive passed back and forth

3:40   One note passed back and forth between winds and strings; gets quiet

3:50   Basic four-note motive tries to reassert itself loudly

3:54   More *pianissimo* one-note alternation between winds and strings

3:58   Motive reenters insistently

RECAPITULATION

4:04   Return of motive

4:10   Motive gathers momentum and cadences with three chords

4:20   Unexpected oboe solo

4:36   Motive returns and moves hurriedly to a climax

4:56   Transition now played by bassoon instead of horn

4:59   Quiet second theme with timpani now playing rhythm of motive

5:15   Crescendo leading to closing theme

5:23   Closing theme

CODA

5:40   Motive pounded *fortissimo* on one note, then again a step higher

5:53   Imitative counterpoint

6:07   Rising quarter notes form new four-note pattern

6:19   New four-note pattern alternates between strings and woodwinds

6:39   Pounding on a single note, then motive as at beginning

6:53   Succession of I–V–I chords brings movement to abrupt end

(Listening Exercise 27)

SECOND MOVEMENT: After the pounding we have been subjected to in the explosive first movement, the calm, noble *Andante* comes as a welcome change of pace. The key is now major (A♭), the mood serene, and the melody expansive—instead of beginning with a four-note motive, the opening theme here runs on for twenty-two measures. The musical form is also a familiar one: theme and variations (see pages 177–180). But this is not the simple, easily audible theme and variations of Haydn. There are, in fact, two themes, and the first one has three parts. Not only do the variations become more complex as the movement progresses, but also, beginning with variation 2, Beethoven shuffles the order in which the themes and parts of themes appear.

a more complex theme and variations

LISTENING GUIDE

Ludwig van Beethoven
Symphony No. 5 in C minor (1808)
Second movement, *Andante con moto* (progressing with movement)

6CD 3/7
6Tape 3B

THEMES

0:00   Violas and cellos play beginning of theme 1

0:24   Woodwinds play middle of theme 1

0:38   Violins play end of theme 1

0:54   Clarinets, bassoons, and violins play theme 2

1:16   Brasses play theme 2 in fanfare style
1:34   Mysterious *pianissimo*

VARIATION 1

2:01   Violas and cellos vary beginning of theme 1 by adding sixteenth notes

2:24   Woodwinds play middle of theme 1
2:34   Strings play end of theme 1
2:53   Clarinets, bassoons, and violins play theme 2
3:14   Brasses return with fanfare (theme 2)
3:32   More of the mysterious *pianissimo*

VARIATION 2

4:00   Violas and cellos overlay beginning of theme 1
          with rapidly moving ornamentation

4:36   Pounding repeated chords with theme below in cellos and basses
4:53   Rising scales lead to a fermata (hold)
5:12   Woodwinds play fragments of beginning of theme 1
5:54   Fanfare (theme 2) now returns in full orchestra
6:43   Woodwinds play beginning of theme 1 detached and in a minor key

VARIATION 3

7:23 Violins play beginning of theme 1 *fortissimo*

7:48 Woodwinds play middle of theme 1

7:58 Strings play end of theme 1

CODA

8:12 Tempo quickens as bassoons play reminiscence of beginning of theme 1

8:28 Violins play reminiscence of theme 2

8:37 Woodwinds play middle of theme 1

8:48 Strings play end of theme 1

9:09 Ends with repetitions of the rhythm of the very first measure of the movement

THIRD MOVEMENT: In the Classical period the third movement of a symphony or quartet was usually a graceful minuet and trio (see page 168). Haydn and his pupil Beethoven wanted to infuse this third movement generally with more life and energy, so they often wrote a faster, more rollicking piece and called it a scherzo, meaning "joke." There is nothing really humorous about the mysterious and sometimes threatening sound of the scherzo of Beethoven's Symphony No. 5, yet it is certainly far removed from the elegant world of the courtly minuet.

The formal plan of Beethoven's scherzo, **ABA′**, is taken over from the ternary form of the minuet, as is the triple meter heard here. The scherzo, **A,** is in the tonic key of C minor, while the trio, **B,** is in C major. This conflict, or juxtaposition, of major and minor, of dark and light, is just one of several confrontations that is resolved in the course of the four-movement symphony.

The scherzo opens with a theme in the cellos and double basses. They creep up from the bottom of their register and pass the musical line on to the higher strings. Suddenly, the horns burst in with a second theme, one built on the short–short–short–long pattern of the first movement—evidently, that fateful motive has not yet been put to rest in Beethoven's mind. For the remainder of the scherzo (**A**), the two contrasting themes vie with each other for pride of place, with theme 2 winning out in the end.

the scherzo

The trio begins true to the spirit of a scherzo—the theme is a comical bustle of sound in the cellos and basses. But the treatment of this theme soon becomes anything but humorous. It is worked out as a brief fugato* as the higher strings, one by one, present the subject (or theme).

the trio

The scherzo does not so much reenter as it does sneak back in, played quietly by the cellos and double basses. And the powerful second theme has become merely a ghost of its former self, tiptoeing around in short, detached notes. Now comes one of Beethoven's greatest strokes of genius. He has decided to link the third and fourth movements by means of a musical bridge. He starts by creating a foreboding, eerie sound. The violins hold a single note as quietly as possible while the timpani beats ominously in the background. A three-note motive grows from the violins and is repeated over and over as a wave of sound begins to swell from the orchestra. With enormous force the wave finally crashes down, and from it emerges the triumphant beginning of the fourth movement—one of the most thrilling moments in all of music.

a bridge to the finale

LISTENING GUIDE		Ludwig van Beethoven Symphony No. 5 in C minor (1808) Third movement, *Allegro* (fast)	6CD 3/8 6Tape 3B

SCHERZO

0:00	Cellos and basses creep in with theme 1 and pass it on to higher strings
0:08	Repeat
0:21	Horns enter with theme 2
0:38	Cellos and basses come back with theme 1
0:52	Crescendo
0:59	Full orchestra again plays theme 2 *fortissimo*
1:18	Development of theme 1
1:41	Ends with theme 2 *fortissimo*, then *piano*

TRIO

1:47	Cellos and basses present subject of fugato
	Violas and bassoons enter with the subject
	Second violins enter with the subject
	First violins enter with the subject
2:01 – 2:22	Repeat of these imitative entries
2:23 – 2:49	Subject enters imitatively again: cellos and basses, violas and bassoons, second violins, first violins, and then flutes are added
2:50 – 3:17	Subject enters imitatively again in the same instruments and the flutes extend it

SCHERZO

3:15	Quiet return of theme 1 in cellos and basses
3:24	Pizzicato (plucked) presentation of theme 1 in cellos accompanied by bassoons
3:36	Ghostlike return of theme 2 in short notes in winds and pizzicato in strings

BRIDGE TO FOURTH MOVEMENT

4:26	Long note held *pianissimo* in strings with timpani beating softly below
4:40	Repeating three-note pattern emerges in the first violins
5:00	Great crescendo leads to fourth movement

FOURTH MOVEMENT: When Beethoven arrived at the finale, he was faced with a nearly impossible task: How to write a conclusion that would lift the tension of the preceding musical events yet provide an appropriate, substantive balance to the weighty first movement. He did so by fashioning a monumental work in sonata–allegro form, the longest movement of the symphony, and by bringing some unusual forces into play. To his orchestra he added three trombones, a con-

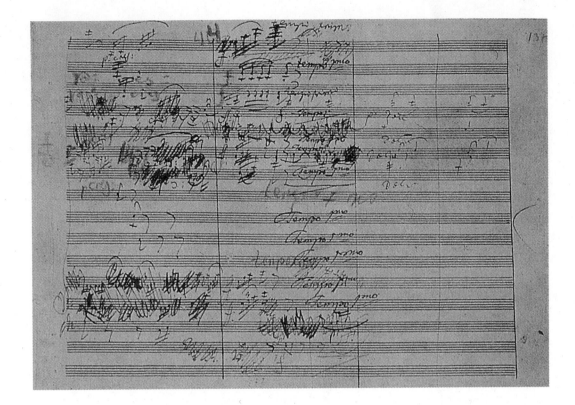

trabassoon (low bassoon), and a piccolo (high flute), the first time any of these instruments had been used in a symphony. He also wrote big, bold, and in most cases, triadic themes, assigning these, often as not, to the powerful brasses. It is these instruments and these themes, along with the final turn from C minor to C major, that cause the finale to project a strong feeling of optimism, a sense that a superhuman will has triumphed over adversity.

Although the finale is a model of sonata–allegro form, the unfolding of the form can be difficult to hear or follow. Beethoven has written a movement without seams. There are no big, obvious cadences that clearly mark off the various sections. The transition moves without pause into the second theme, the exposition into the development, the recapitulation into the coda. We can hardly miss the beginning of the recapitulation, however, because the composer has prepared it in a surprising way. In the retransition (the section that sets up the return of the first theme in the recapitulation), he brings back the ghostlike *pianissimo* scherzo theme of the third movement with its short–short–short–long rhythm. What is a theme from the third movement doing here in the fourth? Obviously, Beethoven wishes to bind tightly movements 3 and 4 as well as evoke again the fateful motive from the beginning of the symphony. Because of this *pianissimo* preparation, the *fortissimo* return of the first theme at the beginning of the recapitulation is unmistakable.

The lengthy coda, too, has its share of surprises, including a change of tempo and a "false ending"—we hear what sound like final chords but instead the piece continues. In fact, there have been so many surprises in this astonishingly original symphony that when Beethoven finally reaches the end, he is compelled to write an exceptionally obvious and repetitious cadence to assure the skeptical listener that this is, in fact, the end.

FIGURE 11–6

Beethoven at work on the second movement of his Symphony No. 5. The many corrections in different-colored inks and red pencil suggest the turmoil and constant evolution involved in Beethoven's creative process.

binding the movements

LISTENING
GUIDE

Ludwig van Beethoven
Symphony No. 5 in C minor (1808)
Fourth movement, *Allegro* (fast)

6CD 3/9
6Tape 3B

EXPOSITION

0:00	Full orchestra with prominent brasses plays first theme	
0:36	Horns play transition theme	
1:04	Strings play second theme	
1:33	Full orchestra plays closing theme	

(Repeat of exposition omitted)

DEVELOPMENT

2:06	Loud string tremolo (fluttering)	
2:11	Strings and woodwinds pass around fragments of second theme in different keys	
2:36	Double basses begin to play countermelody against the second theme	
2:46	Trombones play countermelody	
3:13	Woodwinds and brasses play countermelody above dominant pedal point in cellos and basses	
3:30	Climax and pause on dominant triad	
3:48	Ghostlike theme from the scherzo with four-note rhythm	

RECAPITULATION

4:17	Full orchestra plays first theme *fortissimo*
4:54	Horns bring in transition theme
5:26	Strings play second theme
5:54	Woodwinds play closing theme

CODA

6:26	Violins play second theme
6:37	Brasses and woodwinds play countermelody
6:50	V–I, V–I chords sound like final cadence
6:59	Bassoons, horns, flutes, clarinets, and then piccolo continue with transition theme
7:27	Trill high in piccolo
7:50	Tempo changes to *presto* (very fast)
8:14	Brasses recall first theme but now twice as fast
8:21	V–I, V–I cadence followed by pounding tonic chord

Almost all the qualities we associate with Beethoven's heroic symphonic style are present in his Symphony No. 5. A single theme or short motive is presented and continually elaborated, modified, and developed. It may be fragmented or broken down to just a note or two in the process of development. Small, cell-like units are repeated over and over to build momentum. Long crescendos swell like tidal waves of sound. Climaxes are reached and a rhythmic motive or fragment of a theme is pounded incessantly. In this way, great tension and excitement are created. Extremes of expression, of range, and of mood are accommodated within a single movement. In the quiet string music of the *Andante* (second movement), for example, we are never far from a heroic brass fanfare. Everywhere there is a feeling of raw, elemental power pushed forward by a newly enlarged orchestra. No wonder that during World War II (1939–1945) both sides used the music of this symphony to symbolize "Victory."[†]

Beethoven's symphonic style

THE FINAL YEARS (1814–1827)

By 1814 Beethoven had become totally deaf and had withdrawn almost completely from society. His music, too, took on a more remote, inaccessible quality, placing heavy demands on both performer and audience. In these late works Beethoven requires the listener to connect musical ideas over long spans of time, to follow the variation of a theme when that variation has become quite remote from the original theme itself. Most of these late works are piano sonatas and string quartets—intimate, introspective chamber music. But two pieces, the Mass in D (*Missa solemnis*, 1823) and the Symphony No. 9 (1824), are large-scale compositions for full orchestra and chorus. In these works for larger forces, Beethoven seems again to wish to communicate directly to a broad spectrum of humanity.

Symphony No. 9 (1824)

Beethoven's Symphony No. 9, his last, was the first work in the history of this genre to include a chorus. It is as if the composer's need for expression in his final symphonic work was so great that the instruments of the orchestra alone were no longer sufficient. Something more was necessary: text and voices. And so they enter in the finale of this four-movement work. The text, *An die Freude* (*Ode to Joy*), was written by the German poet Friedrich von Schiller in 1786. It is a hymn, in the spirit of the French Revolution, in honor of universal brotherhood, a theme that had been important to Beethoven since his earliest years. Beethoven set Schiller's text to a melody that has become well known to all of us as his *Ode to Joy*. (In recent times the tune has been popularized in a TV commercial, a movie score, as a Christmas song, and, more appropriately, as an anthem for the United Nations.) Beethoven intentionally constructed a melody that is folk-song-like, even commonplace in shape, a fitting musical companion to a text extolling the commonality of humankind. (For a discussion of the structure of the melody, see page 27 and Listening Exercise 6.)

FIGURE 11–7

A drawing of the deceased Beethoven sketched on the morning of March 28, 1827, the day after the composer's death. It was made by Josef Danhauser, the same artist who painted the group portrait that serves as the cover of this book.

[†]In Morse code, short–short–short–long is the letter "V," as in "Victory."

EXAMPLE 11–8

Ode to Joy

Praise to Joy the God de-scend-ed, Daugh-ter of E-ly-si-um.

Ray of mirth and rap-ture blend-ed, God-dess, to thy shrine wel-come.

By thy ma-gic is u-nit-ed what stern cus-tom part-ed wide. All

man-kind are broth-ers plight-ed where thy gen-tle wings a-bide.

FIGURE 11–8

Beethoven's tombstone in the Central Cemetery in Vienna. Schubert and Brahms are buried only a few feet away.

In the course of this twenty-five-minute finale, the *Ode to Joy* serves as a theme for a magnificent set of variations that marches toward a grandiose climax. Beethoven pushes the voices to sing louder and louder, higher and higher, faster than they can enunciate the text. The instrumentalists, too, are driven by the *presto* tempo to go so quickly they can scarcely play the notes. All performers strain to exceed the limits of their physical abilities, to accomplish the impossible. The sound is not so much beautiful as it is overwhelming, for the chorus and orchestra speak as all humanity. Their message is Beethoven's message: Great art can be achieved by a quest for fulfillment above mortal reach.

The figure of Beethoven towered over all the arts during the nineteenth century. He had shown how personal expression might expand the confines of Classical form with astonishingly powerful results. He had given music "the grand gesture," stunning effects like the crashing introduction of the *Pathétique* Sonata or the gigantic crescendo leading to the finale of the Fifth Symphony. He had shown that pure sound—sound divorced from musical idea—could be glorious in and of itself. At once he had made music both grandiose and intensely lyrical. His works became the standard against which all later composers measured their worth. The cover of this book shows poet, novelist, playwright, performer, and composer all turning in reverence toward the bust of Beethoven. Beethoven, larger than life, gazes down from Olympian heights, a monument to all that is noble and sublime in art.

LISTENING EXERCISES

26	Ludwig van Beethoven Piano Sonata, Opus 13, The *Pathétique* Sonata (1799) First movement, *Grave; Allegro di molto e con brio* (grave; very fast and with gusto)	6CD 3/4; 6Tape 3A 3CD 2/13; 3Tape 2B

This exercise is designed to suggest how drama can be created in music by the use of contrast, pitting loud against soft, high against low, fast against slow, and, in the case of textures, thin against thick.

0:00–1:40 Introduction

1. The introduction creates an unsettled, uncertain feeling in the mind of the listener. What specifically does Beethoven do to create this feeling? (Circle the one answer that is *not* correct.)
   a. contrasts high and low ranges of the piano
   b. puts very loud and very soft sounds in close proximity
   c. contrasts slow chords with racing scales
   d. starts with major chords and moves to minor ones

2. (1:36–1:39) The end of the introduction is marked by a long descent. Which hand of the pianist plays this descent? _____

1:41–3:13 Exposition

3. (1:33–1:53) The descent gives way to the first theme (1:42) and the tempo changes. Which statement is true?
   a. A fast tempo gives way to an even faster one.
   b. A fast tempo gives way to a slower one.
   c. *Grave* (grave) gives way to *allegro con brio* (fast with gusto).

4. (1:59–2:09) A rumbling broken-octave bass had accompanied the agitated first theme (1:41–1:58). Now here in this section of modulation, can these broken octaves still be heard in the bass? _____

5. (2:11–2:38) What about now during the second theme: Are the broken octaves still present? _____

6. (2:39–2:56) Here, in the first part of the closing theme, the right hand drives rapidly to the top range of the piano while the left hand dives deep into the bass. Is this one long, twenty-second passage of music, or two presentations (statement and repeat) of a shorter, ten-second passage? _____

7. (3:07–3:13) The final cadence at the very end of the exposition is marked by a thick texture. How is this created?
   a. The right hand alternates chords in the top and middle ranges while the left plays descending broken octaves.
   b. The left hand alternates chords in the bottom and middle ranges while the right plays ascending broken octaves.

3:14–4:47 Now comes the repeat of the exposition. As you listen, check your answers to questions 4–7.

4:48–6:14 Development

8. (5:15–5:40) The development begins with a return to the chords of the introduction and then proceeds with the first theme. Which statement is true about the tempo in this passage?
   a. The music gets progressively slower, almost stopping, and then suddenly becomes fast.
   b. The music proceeds at a moderate pace and then suddenly becomes fast.
   c. The music accelerates and then becomes progressively slower.

9. (6:09–6:14) Does the left hand (bass) rest during the rapid twisting descent at the end of the development? In other words, is this a solo for the right hand? _____

6:15–7:34 Recapitulation

7:35–8:24 Coda

10. (8:18–8:24) How does this movement end?
    a. with a soft fadeout
    b. with the closing theme
    c. with the crashing chord of the introduction

	Ludwig van Beethoven	6CD 3/6; 6Tape 3A
27	Symphony No. 5 (1808)	3CD 2/14; 3Tape 2B
	First movement, *Allegro con brio* (fast with gusto)	

There is perhaps no more famous single movement in classical music than the first movement of Beethoven's Symphony No. 5. The following questions refer to places that correspond to the major formal divisions of the movement. They are designed to show how Beethoven honored, and sometimes broke with, the usual Classical treatment of sonata–allegro form.

1. (0:00–0:30) Which instruments carry the motive and its immediate repetitions?
   a. strings   b. woodwinds   c. brasses   d. percussion

0:41 French horn plays short transition

2. (0:45–0:51) When the quiet, brief second theme enters it is played three times in succession by three different instruments. In what order do these instruments present the theme?
   a. flute, clarinet, violins
   b. clarinet, violins, flute
   c. violins, clarinet, flute

3. (0:45–0:51) Is this second theme in a major or a minor tonality?

   _____

4. (1:13–1:28) In this passage we have the closing theme and final chords of the exposition, and then the return to the beginning, which commences the repeat of the exposition. What happens to the tonality in this passage from the end of the exposition back to the beginning?
   a. The major tonality shifts back to minor.
   b. The minor tonality shifts back to major.

1:23–2:44 Repeat of the exposition. Check your answers to questions 1–3.

5. (2:46–2:49) When the solo horn announces the beginning of the development, does it do so with the four-note version of the motive or the six-note version used in the transition (see page 220)? _____

6. (3:58–4:08) Here at the end of the development the orchestra insistently repeats the motive, and then the recapitulation begins. What is the dynamic level?
   a. *pianissimo*   b. *piano*   c. *forte*   d. *fortissimo*

7. (4:20–4:36) An oboe suddenly interrupts the recapitulation. Was this lyrical solo heard in the exposition? _____

8. (4:56–5:08) Beethoven reorchestrates and rewrites the transition and second theme in the recapitulation. The brief transition, which was played by

a solo horn in the exposition, is now given over to a solo bassoon. Then the short second theme is played four times and this passage, too, is reorchestrated. Circle the choice that correctly represents the orchestration applied to the four statements of the second theme.

a. violins, flutes, violins, flutes
b. clarinet, violins, flute, clarinet
c. flutes, clarinet, violins, clarinet

9. (4:59–5:08) What is the tonality of the second theme here in the recapitulation, major or minor? _____.

10. Identify at least one way in which Beethoven breaks out of the usual confines of sonata–allegro form in this movement. What does he do that is unusual? _____

KEY WORDS

"Eroica" Symphony   Ode to Joy   Pathétique Sonata
Heiligenstadt Testament

12

THE ROMANTIC SPIRIT (1820–1900)

The mature music of Beethoven, with its powerful crescendos, pounding rhythms, imitations of nature, and larger, more colorful orchestra, announces the arrival of an important change in music in the first decades of the nineteenth century. This is the change from Classicism to Romanticism. It coincides with similar changes in style in the poetry, literature, and painting of the period. In all the arts revolutionary sentiments were in the air: a new desire for liberty, self-expression, bold action, passionate feeling, and a love of nature. And just as the impatient Beethoven finally cast off the wig and powdered hair of the eighteenth century, so now the formal constraints of the old Classical art were thrown aside.

REVOLUTIONARY SENTIMENT AND ROMANTIC CREATIVITY

Romanticism is often defined as a revolt against the Classical adherence to reason, rules, forms, and traditions. Whereas artists of the eighteenth century sought to achieve unity, order, proportion, and a balance of form and content, those of the nineteenth century strove for self-expression, to communicate with passion no matter what sort of imbalance, contradiction, or formal inconsistency might result. If Classical architecture, painting, and music drew its inspiration from the monuments of ancient Greece and Rome, Romantic literature, poetry, painting, and music found creative encouragement in the newly proclaimed liberty of man and in the wonders of nature. The Romantic artist exalted instinctive feelings, human and natural, above all else. These were not the feelings of the masses that Beethoven addressed in his Ninth Symphony, however, but individual, personal, private feelings. Music and her sister arts now withdrew from Beethoven's vision of humanity. They became at the same time more intensely expressive yet highly personal and introspective.

If there was a single feeling or sentiment that pervaded the Romantic era it was love. Indeed, love, or "romance," is at the very heart of the word "Romantic." The loves of Romeo and Juliet and of Tristan and Isolde, for example, captured the imagination of the Romantic century. These were ardent tales in which desire, anguish, longing, and despair were felt far more powerfully than any enjoyment or happiness in love. The endless pursuit of love, the search for the unattainable, became an obsession that when expressed as music, produced the sounds of longing and of yearning heard in so much of Romantic music. Berlioz, Liszt, and Wagner not only wrote about the pursuit of ideal love through their music, but also lived this quest in their personal lives. As art imitates life, so the Romantic composer could not write love-music without being in love.

Yet love was only one of many emotions felt strongly by the Romantics. Despair, revenge, pride, frenzy, and heavenly exaltation were a few of the others they communicated effectively in their music and poetry. Classical music had, in general, exhibited only a narrow range of emotional expression. Romantic music, on the other hand, was marked by wide swings of mood, just as the composers themselves sometimes indulged in wild extremes of behavior. Just how the range of expression was broadened in Romantic music can be seen in the "expression marks" that came into being at this time: *espressivo* (expressively), *dolente* (sadly), *presto furioso* (fast and furiously), *con forza e passione* (with force and passion), *misterioso* (mysteriously), and *maestoso* (majestically). Although these are directives to the performer explaining how a passage is to be played, they also reveal what the composer felt about the music.

Feelings about nature also received unprecedented attention with the Romantics. Nature came to be seen as the source of ultimate truth, of certainty and perfection, a reflection of God and His Eternal Mind. Romantic painters, like J. M. W. Turner (1775–1851) and Caspar David Friedrich (1774–1840), stood in awe of nature's powerful, mysterious forces (see Fig. 12–1). The English Romantic poets John Keats (1795–1821), William Wordsworth (1770–1850), and Lord Byron (1778–1824) communed with her verdant woods, dissolving mists, and tender twilights. Musicians, too, paid homage to nature through sounds that sought to capture her lyrical song, spacious majesty, and destructive fury. Beethoven's "Pastoral" Symphony (Symphony No. 6), with its bird calls and summer storm, was the first of these evocative pieces. Schubert's "Trout" Quintet, Liszt's *Lake of Wallenstadt*, Schumann's "Spring" Symphony, and Strauss's "Alpine" Symphony are just a few of the musical works that continue the tradition.

Associated with this desire to be at one with nature was a passion for travel, what the Germans call a *Wanderlust*. Far-off places and people stirred the imagination of the Romantics. The German composer Felix Mendelssohn (1809–1847) journeyed to Italy, to Scotland, and to the Hebrides Islands to find inspiration for his symphonies and overtures. The English poet Byron sailed to Greece and Turkey and infused his art with a sense of the exotic.

Byron had gone to Greece to help that nation fight for independence from the Turkish Empire. This struggle was symptomatic of the desire of many of Europe's people to throw off the rule of foreign domination or oppressive monarchs. In the 1830s Poland fought (unsuccessfully) for freedom from Russia, Belgium broke free from the Dutch, and Italy, long dominated by the Austrian Empire and Spain, began its difficult march toward liberation and national unity. In 1830, and again in 1848, Paris rebelled against a repressive king. The uprising of 1848 sparked similar revolts in many cities throughout German- and Italian-speaking lands. The composer Hector Berlioz took to the streets of Paris, revolver in hand,

FIGURE 12–1

A *Traveler Looking over a Sea of Fog* (ca. 1818). The themes of isolation, solitude, oblivion, and endless time are explored in this early Romantic painting by Caspar David Friedrich. Friedrich's credo was: "The artist's feeling is his law."

Romantic nature

the Romantic Wanderlust

rebellion and revolt

Lord Byron's *Know You the Land*

George Gordon, Lord Byron, was the epitome of the Romantic hero: dashing, passionate, self-absorbed, idealistic, and guilt ridden (he had had an affair with his half sister). He

A portrait of the English poet Lord Byron in the dress of an Albanian adventurer.

climbed the Swiss Alps, swam the Hellespont (separating Europe from Asia Minor), and died, at age thirty-six, fighting for Greek independence from Turkish rule. His poem *Know You the Land* (from *The Bride of Abydos: A Turkish Tale*) possesses several of the sensibilities dear to the hearts of the Romantics: the colors and sounds of nature, the sights and perfumes of the exotic East, and a hint of forbidden love.

Know you the land of the cedar and vine,
Where the flowers ever blossom, the beams ever shine;
Where the light wings of Zephyr, oppress'd with perfume,
Wax faint o'er the gardens of Gul in her bloom;
Where the citron and olive are fairest of fruit,
And the voice of the nightingale never is mute:
Where the tints of the earth, and the hues of the sky,
In colour though varied, in beauty may vie,
And the purple of Ocean is deepest in dye;
Where the virgins are soft as the roses they twine,
And all, save the spirit of man, is divine?

from Lord Byron's *Know You the Land* (1813)

growing nationalism

during the insurgence of 1830. Richard Wagner led, and then fled, the unsuccessful revolt in Dresden in 1848. Verdi's name was an acronym for the Italian liberation movement (see page 284). Naturally, patriotism and incipient nationalism went hand in hand with revolution. A flood of national anthems, military marches, protest songs, rescue operas, and victory symphonies gave musical voice to popular sentiment during those turbulent times.

Romantic fantasy

Through art the Romantic spirit escaped oppressive reality. Fantasy, imagination, dreams, even nightmares were the stuff of creative inspiration. Composers gave free rein to their musical imagination in countless pieces called "fantasies" and "romances." Writers like the brothers (Jakob and Wilhelm) Grimm wrote fairy tales whose themes expressed the dark side of human nature. Other authors were swept away by the bizarre, the macabre, and the demonic. Johann von Goethe's *Faust* (1808 and 1831), perhaps the most influential work of the nineteenth century, tells the tale of a scholar who sells his soul to the devil, finding beauty in horror and pain. In 1818 Mary Shelley (1797–1851) published her novel *Frankenstein*, and in 1831 Victor Hugo (1802–1885) gave to his readers *The Hunchback of Notre Dame*. In music, as we shall see, magic bullets cursed by the devil (in Weber's *Der Freischütz*, 1821), an evil elfking (in Schubert's *Erlkönig*, 1815), and a witches' black Mass (in Berlioz's *Symphonie fantastique*, 1830) reflect the attraction of the supernatural for the Romantic temperament. To understand all that was good, the artist must know evil as well.

literature and music

As the many parallel developments in music and literature attest, word and sound were never more closely allied than during the nineteenth century. The poets viewed music as the womb from which sprang all true art; tones were capable of expressing emotions and feelings more powerfully, more subtly, more perfectly than could mere words. For their part, composers were as much enraptured by literature as they were by music—Berlioz, Schumann, Liszt, and Wagner were writers of poetry as well as music. They sought to bring external stimuli—poetic and literary themes—into their musical creations as if thereby to double the emotional impact of pure sound. Byron, Goethe, and, above all, Shakespeare struck resonant chords with Romantic composers, who turned the poetry and plays of these writers into overtures, symphonic poems, and operas. Now for the first time Shakespeare became widely read on the Continent, in part because of the publication of an authoritative German translation of his works in 1801. Rare was the Romantic composer who failed to capture in music the spirit of one of the Bard's great plays.

THE MUSICIAN AS ARTIST, MUSIC AS ART

Besides fostering a tight bond between sound and word, the spirit of Romanticism encouraged a new attitude about music as an art. The forceful pens of musician-writers like Berlioz, Schumann, and Wagner persuaded the public that the composer was no longer a mere craftsman but an artist, someone above an ordinary mortal. Bach had been a municipal civil servant, devoted and dutiful, to the town government in Leipzig. Haydn and Mozart served, and were treated, as domestics in the homes of the great lords of Europe. But Beethoven began to break the chains of submission. He was the first to demand, and receive, the respect and admiration due a great creative spirit. Ultimately, Franz Liszt and Richard Wagner, as much through their literary works as through their musical compositions, caused the public to view the artist as a sort of demigod, a prophet able to inspire the audience through the creation of music that was morally uplifting as well as beautiful. They fostered the idea that the artist was a superior being, endowed with exceptional powers of expression. Never was the position of the creative musician loftier than in the mid-nineteenth century.

Just as the musician changed from craftsman to artist in the public mind at this time, so the music he or she produced changed from handicraft to work of art. Classical music had been created for the immediate gratification of patron and audience, with little thought given to its lasting value. With the mature Beethoven and the early Romantics, this attitude began to change. Symphonies, quartets, and piano sonatas sprang to life, not to give immediate pleasure to a listener, but to gratify a deep-seated creative urge within the composer. They became extensions of the artist's personality. These works might not be understood by the creator's contemporaries, as was true of the late piano sonatas of Beethoven and the orchestral works of Hector Berlioz, for example, but they would be understood by posterity, by future generations of listeners. The idea of "art for art's sake"—art free of all functional concerns—was born of the Romantic spirit.

music for future generations

The new exalted position of the composer and his work of art soon brought a more serious tone to the concert hall. Before 1800 people gathered to listen to music more for the opportunity for social interchange than for the chance to enjoy an aesthetic experience. They talked, smoked, drank, ate, played cards, flirted, and wandered about. By the 1830s, however, this had changed. With the revered figure of the Romantic composer-performer now before them, the members of the audience sat in respectful silence. The work of art was surrounded by a sacred aura of devotion and absolute attention (see cover). More was expected

concerts assume a more serious tone

FIGURE 12–2

Witches' Sabbath by Francisco de Goya. Images of the fantastic and demonic were created not only by the early Romantic painters, such as Goya, but by musicians as well. In his *Symphonie fantastique* the composer Hector Berlioz wrote a final movement that he entitled *Witches' Sabbath* (see page 259).

of the listener, partly because symphonies and sonatas were longer and more complex. But the listener, in turn, expected more from the music: not mere entertainment but an emotionally satisfying encounter that would leave the attentive person exhausted yet somehow purified and uplifted by the artistic experience.

Romantic Ideals and Today's Concert Hall

formation of today's concert repertoire

Romanticism has kept its grip on the Western imagination. Belief in the artist as hero, reverence toward the work of art as an object of moral inspiration, and the expectations of silence and even formal dress at a concert—these are all attitudes that developed in the early Romantic period. What is more, the notion that a particular group of pieces should get a repeated hearing gains currency at this time. Prior to 1800 almost all music was disposable music: It was written for the enjoyment of the moment and then was no longer in vogue. But the generation following Beethoven began to see his best symphonies, concertos, and quartets, as well as those of Mozart and Haydn, as worthy of continued performance and preservation. These and the best works of succeeding generations came to constitute a "canon" of music—a body of music possessing attributes of unity, expression, and form that should be continually revisited. Such masterpieces, as they were correctly viewed, came to form the core of today's concert repertoire. Thus what we think about the composer, how we view the work of art, what we can expect to hear at a concert, and even how we behave during the performance are not ideals, with us since time immemorial, but are paradigms created during a special period in history. In many respects, the attitudes about art and music that arose in the early nineteenth century still govern our thinking today.

THE STYLE OF ROMANTIC MUSIC

an expansion of Classical style

The Romantic spirit rebelled against Classical ideals in ways that allow us to generalize these two artistic movements as pairs of opposites: rational against irrational, intellect opposed to heart, conformity versus originality, and the masses in contradistinction to the individual. Yet in purely musical terms, the works of the Romantic composers represent not so much a revolution against Classical ideals as an evolution that goes beyond them. Romantic music is an expansion and amplification of the style created by the Classical masters. The Romantics introduced no new musical forms and only one or two new genres. Instead, Romantic composers took the musical materials received from the hands of Haydn, Mozart, and young Beethoven and made them more intensely expressive, more original, more personal, and, in some cases, more bizarre.

Romantic Melody

The Romantic period witnessed the apotheosis of melody. Melodies become broad, powerful streams of sound intended to sweep the listener away. They go beyond the neat symmetrical units of two plus two, four plus four, inherent in the Classical style. They become longer, rhythmically more flexible, and more irregular in shape. At the same time, Romantic melodies continue a trend that developed in the late eighteenth century in which themes became vocal in conception, more singable. Melodies of Chopin, Tchaikovsky, and Rachmaninoff have been turned into popular songs in our own day. Similarly, today's popular collections of "40 All-Time Favorite Classical Melodies" draw primarily from the symphonies, sonatas, and operas of the Romantic period, simply because these themes are so profoundly expressive. They sigh and lament. They grow and become ecstatic. They start haltingly and then build to a grandiose climax, sublime and triumphant. Example 12–1 is a melody by Hector Berlioz, the principal theme of his *Symphonie fantastique* (1830). Notice that it is long and rhythmically rather free, with many syncopations* that cross the bar lines and obscure the downbeats*. Observe, too, that by means of an ascending melodic sequence* the melody climbs inexorably upward to a lofty climax, from where it relaxes back down to the tonic note.

EXAMPLE 12–1

Colorful Harmony

Part of the emotional intensity of Romantic music is generated by a new, more colorful harmony. Classical music had, in the main, made use of chords built only on the seven notes of the major or minor scale—the so-called diatonic* notes of the scale (see page 27). Romantic composers went farther by constructing chords on the five additional notes within the full twelve-note chromatic scale—the so-called chromatic* notes. This gave more colors to their harmonic palette. It also gave fluency to the sound, as chords and inner voices glide smoothly to notes only a half step away. Using chromatic chords similarly made it easier for the composer to modulate to distant keys, to carry the music tonally away to some far-off, exotic land of six flats or seven sharps.

chromatic harmony

The rich, lush sounds of the Romantics are also created by setting up novel relationships between chords. In the Baroque and Classical periods, harmony often moved along in chord progressions in which the roots of the chords were an interval of a fifth apart. Now chords only a third apart are frequently set in close proximity, and these can require radically different key signatures*—a harmony with four sharps might be followed immediately by one with four flats, for example. The striking sound that results from these unusual relationships is appropriate for music that seeks to express a wider range of feeling.

bold chord progressions

Finally, much of the sound of pain and anguish that we hear in Romantic music comes about because of a greater use of dissonance. Dissonant notes are not only more numerous, but they are held for longer periods of time as well. Since *dissonance longs for consonance*

dissonance always wants to move, or resolve, to consonance, the delay of the resolution produces a feeling of anxiety, longing, and searching, all sentiments appropriate for music that often deals with the subject of love.

All three of these qualities of Romantic harmony—chromaticism, bold chordal relationships, and dissonance–consonance movement—come in quick succession at the end of Franz Liszt's *Liebestraum* (*Love-Dream*, 1850). Neither you nor the author can hear all the music given in Ex. 12–2 simply by looking at it. (To hear it, turn to 6CD 4/5 or 6Tape 4A, band 5, at 3:57.) We can, however, visualize here some of the music's inner workings—first the chromaticism, then the shift from a chord with three sharps to one with four flats, and finally dissonance resolving to consonance. In this way we may begin to understand, when hearing the rich, sensuous sound of Romantic music, how it is created.

EXAMPLE 12–2

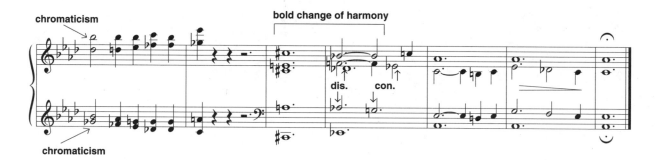

Romantic Tempo: *Rubato*

In keeping with an age that glorified personal freedom and tolerated eccentric behavior, tempo in music was cut loose from the restraints of a regular beat. The watchword here was *rubato* (literally "robbed"), an expression mark for the performer written into the score by the composer. A performer playing tempo **rubato** stole some time here and gave it back there, moving faster or slower so as to effect an intensely personal performance. The free approach to tempo was often reinforced by fluctuating dynamic levels—ritards were done with diminuendos* and accelerations with crescendos*—as a way of explaining, even exaggerating, the flow of the music. Whatever excesses might result, could be excused under license of artistic freedom.

EXPRESSIVE TONE COLORS, GREATER SIZE, GREATER VOLUME

From the listener's perspective, perhaps the most striking aspect of Romantic music is the color and sheer volume of the sound. Sometimes all thematic and harmonic movement stops and nothing but pure sound carries the moment. During the nineteenth century the orchestra became larger and more varied, the piano bigger and more powerful. Composers demanded, and received, musical forces equal to the task of expressing the extremes of emotion, changing moods, and extravagant gestures of the Romantic spirit.

FIGURE 12–3
The Industrial Revolution affected even the production of musical instruments: view of the musical instrument factory of Adolphe Sax (inventor of the saxophone) in Paris in 1848. At the right, a completed baritone saxophone hangs from the ceiling.

The Romantic Orchestra

The Industrial Revolution brought with it mechanical innovations that made the instruments of the symphony orchestra essentially what they are today. The wood of the flute was replaced by silver, and the instrument was supplied with a new fingering mechanism that added to its agility and made it easier to play in tune. Similarly, the trumpet and French horn were provided with valves that improved technical facility and accuracy of pitch in all keys. These brass instruments were now capable of playing intricate, chromatic melodies as well as providing the traditional backdrop of sonic support for the rest of the orchestra. The horn, in particular, became an object of special affection during the Romantic period. Its rich, dark tone and its traditional association with the hunt—and by extension nature—made it the Romantic instrument par excellence. Composers often called on a solo horn when they wished to express something mysterious or distant.

mechanical improvements

importance of the French horn

   Besides improvements to existing instruments, several new instruments were added to the symphony orchestra during the nineteenth century. We have seen how Beethoven brought the piccolo (a high flute), the trombone, and the contrabassoon (a bass bassoon) into the orchestra in his famous Symphony No. 5 (1808). In 1830 Hector Berlioz went even farther, requiring an ophicleide* (an early form of the tuba), an English horn* (a low-pitched oboe), a cornet*, and two harps in his *Symphonie fantastique*. Berlioz, the embodiment of the Romantic spirit, had a typically grandiose notion of what the ideal symphony orchestra should contain. He wanted no fewer than 467 instrumentalists including 120 violins, 40 violas, 45 cellos, 35 double basses, and 30 harps. Needless to say, such a gigantic instrumental force was never assembled, but Berlioz's utopian vision indicates the direction in which Romantic composers were headed. By the second half of the nineteenth century, orchestras with nearly a hundred players were not uncommon. Compare the instruments and their number required for a typical eighteenth-century performance of Mozart's G minor symphony (1788) with

larger orchestras

FIGURE 12–4

Orchestral forces needed for performances of Mozart's Symphony No. 40 (1788) and Wagner's Prelude to *Tristan und Isolde* (1865). Listening Exercise 28 asks you to compare your responses to each of these two orchestral works.

MOZART (1788)	WAGNER (1865)
1 flute	1 piccolo
2 oboes	3 flutes
2 clarinets	2 oboes
2 bassoons	1 English horn
2 French horns	2 clarinets
1st violins (8)†	1 bass clarinet
2nd violins (8)	3 bassoons
violas (4)	4 French horns
cellos (4)	3 trumpets
double basses (3)	3 trombones
	1 tuba
Total: 36	1st violins (18)†
	2nd violins (16)
	violas (12)
	cellos (10)
	double basses (8)
	timpani
	triangle
	cymbals
	harp
	Total: 91

†Number of string players estimated according to standards of the period.

FIGURE 12–5

Silhouette of Karl Maria von Weber conducting with baton, or more correctly a rolled sheet of music, so as to highlight the movement of his hand.

the symphony orchestra called on to play the Prelude (overture) to Richard Wagner's *Tristan und Isolde* (1865) (Fig. 12–4). Our ears today have become so desensitized by constant exposure to electronically amplified sound that we can hardly imagine the overwhelming impact that the newly enlarged orchestra had on listeners in the nineteenth century.

The Conductor

Naturally, someone was needed to coordinate the efforts of the enlarged orchestra. Previously, in the days of Bach and Mozart, the orchestra had been led from within, either by the keyboard player of the *basso continuo** gesturing with his head and hands or by the chief violinist directing with his bow. When Beethoven played and conducted his piano concertos, he did so seated at his instrument. When he led one of his symphonies, especially toward the end of his life, he stood before the orchestra, back to the audience, waving his hands. In 1820 the composer Louis Spohr became the first to use a wooden baton to lead the orchestra and to rehearse the musicians carefully through the problematic spots of his compositions. In the course of the nineteenth century the leader of the orchestra became increasingly a privileged interpreter, sometimes dictator, of the musical score. The modern conductor had arrived.

The Piano

During the nineteenth century the piano became what the computer is today, something of a home entertainment center. Every aspiring household had to have one, as well as the software to make it work. The software then was the piano transcription—a reduction for piano solo of some larger orchestral or operatic work. Thus the symphonies of Beethoven and Berlioz were transcribed for piano, as were the opera overtures of Rossini and entire operas by Bellini and many others. Music lovers in Brussels, Baltimore, or Birmingham might never have the chance to hear a "live" performance of a Beethoven symphony, but they might come to know it at home by means of a piano transcription by Liszt, for example. Before the age of electronically produced sound, the piano transcription was the medium by which the general listening public became familiar with the major works composed for the symphony hall or opera house.

That the piano provided a good two-handed approximation of the symphony orchestra suggests that it, too, grew considerably in size during the early 1800s. Here also the new technology of the Industrial Revolution was decisive. The older, wooden frame was replaced by a cast-iron one that allowed for greater tension on the strings, which, in turn, necessitated thicker strings—all leading to an instrument with greatly increased power. At the same time the hammers were covered with felt, which made the instrument "sing" with a mellow tone, in contrast with the soft "ping" of the older pianos of Mozart's day. The range of the instrument was extended both high and low, expanding from the five-octave piano of the 1790s to a seven-octave instrument by the 1840s. Finally, all pianos became equipped with a **sustaining pedal**, which allowed some strings to continue to sound while others were being struck. The blurred effect that resulted was especially useful when creating a romantic haze, as heard, for example in Liszt's *Liebestraum* (see page 275). In addition, the sustaining pedal made possible special effects on the piano, such as the "three-hand trick" discussed in the next chapter.

Technical Virtuosity

Appropriate for an era that glorified the individual, the nineteenth century was the age of the solo virtuoso. Of course, there had been instrumental virtuosos before—Bach on the organ, Mozart on the piano, to name just two—but now enormous energy was expended by many musicians to raise their performing skills to an unprecedented height. Pianists and violinists in particular practiced long hours just on technical exercises—arpeggios, tremolos, trills, and scales played in thirds, sixths, and octaves—to develop wizardlike hand speed on their instrument. Naturally, some of what they played for the public was lacking in musical substance, tasteless show pieces designed to appeal immediately to the large audiences that packed the ever-larger concert halls. Pianists developed tricks of playing to make it appear they had more hands than two (see Fig. 13–21). Franz Liszt (1811–1886) sometimes played at the keyboard with a lighted cigar between his fingers. The Italian Niccolò Paganini (1782–1840) secretly tuned the four strings of his violin in ways that would allow him to negotiate with ease extraordinarily difficult passages (see Ex. 12–3). If one of his strings broke, he could play with just three; if three broke, he could continue apace with

FIGURE 12–6

The grand piano made by C. Bechstein (Berlin, 1864) at which Richard Wagner finished the opera *Tristan und Isolde* (1865), now preserved in the Yale University Collection of Musical Instruments. It is a vastly larger and more powerful instrument than Mozart had at his disposal (see page 154).

wizards of the piano or violin

(left) Niccolò Paganini. (right) *Paganini and the Witches*, a lithograph by an unknown artist. Paganini's extraordinary powers on the violin led some to believe he was in league with the devil. The fourth string of his violin was said to be made of the intestine of his mistress, whom he had murdered with his own hands. None of this was true, and Paganini undertook several libel suits to disprove it.

just one. As the composer Debussy later remarked, "The attraction of the virtuoso is like that of the circus performer, there's always the hope that something disastrous will happen." The musical showman had taken center stage. Fortunately, as we shall see, some of these showmen were also gifted composers.

EXAMPLE 12–3: Paganini, Caprice, Opus 1, No. 5

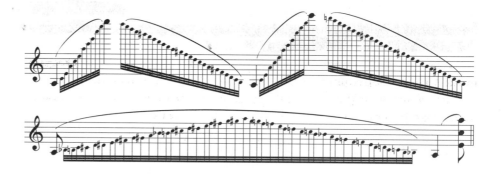

Forms: Monumental and Miniature

The musical forms that had earlier served Haydn and Mozart continued to satisfy the needs of the nineteenth-century composer. Sonata–allegro form, in particular, remained useful because its flexible format could accommodate any number of individual solutions. What developed, then, was not a rush to invent new forms but a trend to extend the existing ones. As composers laid out broad, sweeping melodies, indulged in gigantic crescendos, and reveled in the luxurious sound of the enlarged orchestra, the length of individual movements increased dramatically. Mozart's G minor symphony (1788) lasts about twenty minutes, depending on the tempo of the performance. But Brahm's Symphony No. 1 (1876) takes nearly forty-five minutes, and Mahler's Symphony No. 2 (1894) nearly an hour and a half. Perhaps the longest of all musical works is Richard Wagner's four-opera *Ring* cycle (1853–1876), which continues some seventeen hours during the course of four evenings. In these extended visions the Roman-

colossal symphonies

tic composer seems to be saying along with the poet: "Romanticism is beauty without bounds—the beautiful infinite."

Yet, paradoxically, Romantic composers were fascinated by miniature forms as well. In brief works of a scant minute or two, they tried to capture the essence of one single mood, sentiment, or emotion. Such a miniature was called a **character piece.** It was usually written for the piano and often made use of simple binary (**AB**) or ternary (**ABA**) form. Because the character piece passes by in a twinkling of an eye, it was sometimes given a whimsical title, such as bagatelle (a trifle), humoresque, arabesque, musical moment, caprice, romance, intermezzo, or impromptu. Schubert, Schumann, Chopin, Liszt, Brahms, and Tchaikovsky all enjoyed creating these musical miniatures, perhaps as antidotes to their lengthy symphonies and concertos.

character pieces

NEW GENRES: THE SYMPHONIC POEM AND THE ART SONG

The Classical genres of the symphony, concerto, string quartet, piano sonata, and opera remained fashionable, though somewhat altered in appearance, throughout the nineteenth century. The symphony, as we have seen, now grows in length, embodying the widest possible range of expression, while the concerto becomes increasingly virtuosic, as a heroic soloist does battle against an orchestral mass. In addition, two new genres of music are created during the Romantic century, specifically, the symphonic poem and the art song.

The advent of the symphonic poem (discussed shortly) is tied to the broad development of program music generally in the nineteenth century. **Program music** is a piece of instrumental music, usually for symphony orchestra, that seeks to recreate in sound the events and emotions portrayed in some extramusical source: a story, a play, a historical event, or even a painting. The theory of program music rests on the obvious fact that specific kinds of music can evoke particular feelings and associations. A lyrical melody may recall memories of love, harshly dissonant chords may create a sense of conflict, rapidly flowing notes may produce a vision of a mountain stream, distant trumpet calls may suggest the imminent arrival of a hero. The urge to make music tell a story or play out a theatrical drama is a natural development in the nineteenth century, given the literary tenor of the age.

program music: music inspired by an external source

Some Romantic composers, notably Johannes Brahms (1833–1897) and Anton Bruckner (1824–1896), resisted the allure of program music and continued to write what came to be called **absolute music**—symphonies, sonatas, quartets, and other instrumental music without extramusical or programmatic references. But most composers succumbed to the temptation to make their instrumental works take on an overtly pictorial or narrative character, to depict a scene or recount a story. The programmatic influence crept into established genres like the overture and symphony. It also gave rise to an entirely new genre, the symphonic poem. The principal kinds of nineteenth-century program music can be defined as follows:

absolute music: music without an external reference

Symphonic poem (also called the **tone poem**): A one-movement work for orchestra that gives musical expression to the emotions and events associated with a story, play, political occurrence, personal experience, or encounter with nature. It is usually a lengthy piece composed in any one of several forms including sonata–allegro, theme and variations, and rondo. Examples include Liszt's *Les Préludes* (1854), Modest Musorgsky's *Night on Bald Mountain* (1867), Tchaikovsky's *Romeo and Juliet* (1869), and Richard Strauss's *Don Juan* (1888).

Program symphony: A symphony with the usual three, four, or five movements, but now the individual movements together tell or depict a succession of specific events or scenes drawn from some extramusical work or story. Examples include Berlioz's *Symphonie fantastique* (1830) and Liszt's "Faust" Symphony (1857).

Overture (to an opera or a play): A one-movement work, usually in sonata–allegro form, which foretells in music the essential dramatic events that will follow in an opera or a play. Many overtures, because of unusual color or special effects, became popular with the listening public and came to be performed by themselves. Examples include Rossini's Overture to his opera *William Tell* (1829) and Mendelssohn's Overture to Shakespeare's play *A Midsummer Night's Dream* (1826).

Concert overture: Similar to the overture but *not* designed to precede an opera or play; thus, an independent one-movement work of programmatic content originally intended for the concert hall. Examples include Mendelssohn's *Hebrides Overture* (1830) and Tchaikovsky's *1812 Overture* (1880). In fact, there is little difference between the symphonic poem and the concert overture. Both are one-movement programmatic works intended for the concert hall.

Incidental music: Music to be inserted between the acts or during important scenes of a play to add an extra dimension to the drama. Examples include Mendelssohn's incidental music to Shakespeare's *A Midsummer Night's Dream* (1843) and Edvard Grieg's music to Henrik Ibsen's play *Peer Gynt* (1875).

About 1850 Franz Liszt, a leading advocate of program music, said that an explicit program gave the composer "a means by which to protect the listener against a wrong poetical interpretation and to direct his attention to the poetical idea of the whole." Soon we will hear and discuss three imaginative examples of program music: Berlioz's *Symphonie fantastique* (a program symphony), Mendelssohn's Overture to *A Midsummer Night's Dream* (an overture to a play), and Tchaikovsky's *Romeo and Juliet* (a symphonic poem). You will be able then to judge whether the existence of a program makes the composer's musical poetry easier to follow and increases the enjoyment of listening.

The other new musical genre that flourished in the nineteenth century was the art song. An **art song** is simply a piece for solo voice and piano accompaniment with high artistic aspirations. Of course, there had been songs of artistic merit for voice and accompanying instrument since the Middle Ages. But one of the hallmarks of the Romantic movement, as we have seen, was a quickening interest in literature and especially in poetry. The Romantic poets like Wordsworth, Keats, Shelley, and Byron burst on the English scene in the early 1800s, and they had their counterparts in Germany in the person of the great Goethe and the gifted Heinrich Heine (1797–1856). Literally thousands of odes,

FIGURE 12–9

The nineteenth-century fascination with Shakespeare can be seen in the works of the painter Eugène Delacroix, who recreated scenes from *Romeo and Juliet*, *Hamlet*, and *Macbeth*. Here, Hamlet and Horatio gaze on the skull of the late, lamented Yorick in the famous graveyard scene of *Hamlet*

does a program increase the enjoyment of listening?

the art song

sonnets, stanzas, ballads, and romances poured from their pens and those of lesser talent. Swept up in this new-found enthusiasm for poetry, composers set many of these texts for voice and piano, believing that music could intensify poetic sentiments by expressing things words alone could not. Because the art song was cultivated mainly in German-speaking lands, the genre is also called the **Lied** (plural, **Lieder**), German for "song." The first important composer of the *Lied* was Franz Schubert (1797–1828), and it is to his music and that of the other early Romantics that we now turn.

the Lied

LISTENING EXERCISE

28 Comparing Orchestral Works of the Classical and Romantic Periods

Listen again to the first movement of Mozart's Symphony No. 40 in G minor (1788) (6CD 2/13; 6Tape 2B; 3CD 2/10; 3Tape 2B) and compare it with the Prelude to Richard Wagner's opera *Tristan und Isolde* (1865) (6CD 4/9; 6Tape 4B).

1. Which work has a greater range of dynamic expression (louds and softs)?

   _____

2. Which work uses a larger, more colorful orchestra? _____

3. Which work has a faster tempo, or pace, to it? _____

4. Which work is more sectional? That is, which work has sections that are clearly different in mood, style, and function, one from another?

   _____

5. Which work is introspective in that it continually repeats and turns back on itself? _____

6. Which work is more progressive in that it moves purposefully and without delay from one section to another? _____

7. Does Mozart make use of trumpets? _____ If not, why not? (See page 190.) _____

8. Does Wagner have his brasses introduce and carry the melodies, or merely support and amplify the strings and woodwinds? _____

9. In different ways both Mozart and Wagner wish to express passion in their respective compositions. Describe how the passion, or intensity of feeling, is *different* in the two works.

   _____

   _____

   _____

10. How does each composer create his special sort of passion? In specific terms, describe what each does in his music to make you feel the way you do about his music.

    _____

    _____

    _____

    _____

KEY WORDS

absolute music
art song
character piece
concert overture
incidental music

Lied
overture
piano transcription
program music
program symphony

rubato
sustaining pedal
symphonic poem
tone poem

THE EARLY ROMANTICS

T he decade 1803–1813 was perhaps the most auspicious in the history of music. In this short span of time were born the composers Hector Berlioz (1803), Felix Mendelssohn (1809), Frédéric Chopin (1810), Robert Schumann (1810), Franz Liszt (1811), Giuseppe Verdi (1813), and Richard Wagner (1813). Add to this the shining figure of Franz Schubert (born 1797) and this brilliant galaxy of musical geniuses is complete. We call them Romantics because they were part of, indeed they created, the Romantic movement in music. But with the possible exception of Mendelssohn, they were very unconventional people. Their lives typify all that we have come to associate with the Romantic spirit: self-expression, passion, excess, the love of nature and literature, as well as a certain selfishness, irresponsibility, and even a bit of lunacy. Not only did they create great art, but life, and how they lived it, became an art.

THE ART SONG†

The genre of the art song, or *Lied**, for solo voice and piano became a popular type of musical expression during the early 1800s (see page 244). The enormous outpouring of the Romantic poets was matched by the creative enthusiasm of the Romantic composers, who set hundreds of ballads, odes, and romances to music. Franz Schubert was the greatest of these composers. His special talent was to fashion music that captures both the spirit and the detail of the text, creating a sensitive mood painting in which the voice and accompaniment express every nuance of the poem. Schubert said, "When one has a good poem the music comes easily, melodies just flow, so that composing is a real joy."

Franz Schubert (1797–1828)

Franz Schubert was born in Vienna in 1797. Among the great Viennese masters—Haydn, Mozart, Beethoven, Schubert, Brahms, and Mahler—only he was native-born to the city. Schubert's father was a schoolteacher, and the son, too, was groomed for that profession. Yet the boy's obvious musical talent made it

† The art song is discussed more fully on page 244.

FIGURE 13–1
Franz Schubert.

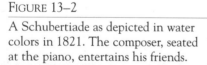

FIGURE 13–2
A Schubertiade as depicted in water colors in 1821. The composer, seated at the piano, entertains his friends.

imperative that he also have music lessons, so his father taught him to play the violin and his older brother, the piano. At the age of eleven Schubert was admitted as a choirboy in the emperor's chapel, and this allowed him to enroll simultaneously in the excellent boarding school associated with the court. Proximity to the royal palace brought young Schubert into contact with Antonio Salieri, erstwhile rival of Mozart and still imperial court composer (see page 161). He began to study composition with Salieri in 1810. Soon Schubert was composing his own musical works at an astonishing rate.

After his voice changed in 1812, young Franz left the court chapel school and enrolled in a teacher's college. He had been spared compulsory military service because he was below the minimum height of five feet and his sight was so poor he was compelled to wear the spectacles now familiar from his portraits (Fig. 13-1). By 1815 he had become a teacher at his father's primary school. But he found teaching demanding and tedious and so, after three unpleasant years, Schubert abandoned this profession to give himself over wholly to music.

"You lucky fellow; I really envy you! You live a life of sweet, precious freedom, can give free rein to your musical genius, can express your thoughts in any way you like." This was Schubert's brother's view of the composer's newfound freedom. But as many Romantics would find, the reality was harsher than the ideal. Aside from some small income he earned from the sale of a few songs, he lacked a means of support. Schubert, unlike Beethoven, kept no company with aristocrats and thus received no patronage from them. Instead, he lived a Bohemian life, helped along by the generosity of his friends, with whom he often lodged when he was broke. His mornings were consumed passionately composing music; his afternoons were passed in cafes discussing literature and politics; and his evenings were often spent playing his songs and dances before friends and admirers.

While Schubert was coming to his artistic maturity, the era of the great aristocratic salon was drawing to an end. Its place, as a focus for artistic expression, was taken by the middle-class parlor or living room. Here in less pretentious surroundings, groups of men and women with a common interest in music, the novel, drama, or poetry would meet to read and hear all that was new in these arts. The gatherings at which Schubert appeared, and at which only his compositions were played, were called **Schubertiades** by his friends. It was in small, purely private assemblies such as these (Fig. 13-2), not in large public concerts, that most of his best songs were first performed.

In 1822 misfortune befell the composer: He contracted syphilis. His lyrical Symphony in B minor of that fateful year was left incomplete (hence the title, the Unfinished Symphony). Yet during the years that remained before his premature death in 1828 he created some of his greatest works: the song cycles *Die schöne Müllerin* (*The Pretty Maid of the Mill*, 1823) and *Winterreise* (*Winter Journey*, 1827), the "Wanderer" Fantasy for piano (1822), and the great C major Symphony (1828). When Beethoven died in 1827, Schubert served as one of the torchbearers at the funeral. The next year, he too was dead, the youngest of the great composers.

In his brief life of thirty-one years, Franz Schubert wrote eight symphonies, fifteen string quartets, twenty-one piano sonatas, seven Masses for chorus and orchestra, and four operas—a sizable *oeuvre* by any standards. Yet in his day Schubert was known almost exclusively as a writer of art songs. Indeed, he composed more than six hundred works of this genre, many of them minor master-

FIGURE 13–3
A contemporary painting of the story of the Erlking, showing the evil king, the father and son, and the king's comely daughters.

pieces. In a few cases, Schubert chose to set several texts together in a series. In so doing he created what is called a **song cycle**—a tightly structured group of individual songs that tell a story or treat a single theme. *The Pretty Maid of the Mill* (twenty songs) and *Winter Journey* (twenty-four songs), both of which relate the sad consequences of unrequited love, are Schubert's two great song cycles.

Schubert's song cycles

ERLKING (1815)

To gain an idea of Schubert's extraordinary musical talent, we need only listen to his song *Erlkönig (Erlking)*, written when he was just seventeen. The text itself is a ballad—a dramatic story told in alternating narrative verse and dialogue—from the pen of the famous poet Goethe. It relates the tale of the evil King of the Elves and his quest for the soul of a young boy, for legend had it that whosoever was touched by the King of the Elves would die. According to the account of one of Schubert's friends, the composer was reading a book of Goethe's poetry, pacing back and forth in his room. Suddenly, he sprang to the piano and, as fast as he could write, set the entire ballad to music. From there Schubert and his friend hastened to the composer's college to play it for a few kindred spirits. In his lifetime *Erlking* became Schubert's best-known song, one of the few that brought him any money.

Goethe's tale

The opening line of the poem sets the frightful nocturnal scene: "Who rides so late through night and wind?" With his feverish son cradled in his arms, a father rides at breakneck speed to an inn to save the child. Schubert captures both the general sense of terror in the scene and the detail of the galloping horse; he creates an accompanying figure in the piano that pounds on relentlessly just as fast as the pianist can make it go:

EXAMPLE 13–1

The specter of death, the Erlking, beckons gently to the boy. He does so in seductively sweet tones, in a melody with the gentle lilt and folksy accompaniment of a popular tune:

EXAMPLE 13–2

(Thou dearest boy, come go with me!)

The frightened boy cries out to his father in an agitated, then chromatic line:

EXAMPLE 13–3

(Dear father, my father, say, did'st thou not hear the Erlking whisper promises in my ear?)

characterization through music

This cry is heard again and again in the course of the song, each time at a successively higher pitch and with increasingly dissonant harmonies. In this way the music mirrors the growing terror of the boy. The father tries to calm him and does so in low tones that are steady, stable, and repetitive. Thus, each of the three characters of the story is portrayed with a specific musical quality. This is musical characterization at its finest: The melody and accompaniment not only support the text but intensify and enrich it as well. Suddenly, the end is reached. The hand of the Erlking has touched his victim. The accompaniment figure is abruptly choked off as the narrator announces with controlled emotion: "But in his arms, his child was dead!"

LISTENING GUIDE

Franz Schubert
Art song, *Erlking* (1818)

6CD 3/10; 6Tape 3B
3CD 2/15; 3Tape 2B

0:00	Introduction by piano accompaniment; pounding triplets in the right hand and an ominous minor motive in the left		

Narrator

0:23		Wer reitet so spät durch Nacht und Wind? Es ist der Vater mit seinem Kind. Er hat den Knaben wohl in dem Arm, er fasst ihn sicher, er hält ihn warm.	Who rides so late through night so wild? A loving father with his child. He clasps his boy close with his arm, He holds him tightly and keeps him warm.

Father

0:56		"Mein Sohn, was birgst du so bang dein Gesicht?"	"My son, what makes you hide your face in fear?"

Son

1:05	With agitated leaps	"Siehst, Vater, du den Erlkönig nicht? Den Erlenkönig mit Kron' und Schweif?"	"Father don't you see the Erlking— the Erlking with crown and shroud?"

Father

1:20	In low, calming tones	"Mein Sohn, es ist ein Nebelstreif."	"My son, it's only some streak of mist."

Erlking

1:30	With a seductive melody	"Du liebes Kind, komm, geh' mit mir! gar schöne Spiele spiel' ich mit dir; manch' bunte Blumen sing an dem Strand, meine Mutter hat manch' gülden Gewand."	"You dear child, come along with me! I'll play some very fine games with you; where varied blossoms sing on meadows fair and my mother has golden garments to wear."

Son

1:55	Tension depicted by tight chromatic movement in voice	"Mein Vater, mein Vater und hörest du nicht, was Erlenkönig mir leise verspricht?"	"My father, my father, do you not hear how the Erlking whispers promises in my ear?"

Father

2:07	In low, steady pitches	"Sei ruhig, bleibe ruhig, mein Kind, in düren Blättern säuselt der Wind."	"Be calm, stay calm, my child, Through wither'd leaves the wind blows wild."

Erlking

2:18	With a happy, lilting tune in major	"Willst, feiner Knabe, du mit mir geh'n? Meine Töchter sollen dich warten schön, meine Töchter führen den nächtlichen Reih'n, und wiegen und tanzen und singen dich ein."	"My handsome young lad, will you come with me? My beauteous daughters wait for you, With them you would join in the dance every night, and they will rock and dance and sing you to sleep."

(Continued on next page)

			Son	
2:36	Same intense chromatic notes as before, but now a step higher; minor key	"Mein Vater, mein Vater und siehst du nicht dort Erlkönigs Töchter am düstern Ort?"	"My Father, my father, don't you see at all the Erlking's daughters over there in the dusk?"	

Father

| 2:48 | Low register, but more leaps (agitation) than before | "Mein Sohn, mein Sohn, ich seh' es genau, es scheinen die alten Weiden so grau." | "My son, my son, the form you there see, is only the aging gray willow tree." |

Erlking

| 3:06 | His music is no longer seductive but now threatening and in minor key | "Ich liebe dich, mich reizt deine schöne Gestalt; und bist du nicht willig, so brauch' ich Gewalt." | "I love you, I'm charmed by your fine appearance; And if you're not willing, I'll seize you by force!" |

Son

| 3:18 | Piercing cries in highest range | "Mein Vater, mein Vater jetzt fasst er mich an! Erlkönig hat mir ein Leids gethan!" | "My father, my father, now he's got me, the Erlking has seized me by his trick." |

Narrator

| 3:32 | With a rising and then falling line | Dem Vater grausets; er reitet geschwind, er hält in den Armen das ächzende Kind. Erreicht den Hof mit Müh und Noth: | The father shudders, he rides headlong, holding the groaning child in his arms. He reaches the inn with toil and dread, |
| | Piano stops, recitative | in seinen Armen das Kind war todt! | but in his arms, his child was dead! |

(Listening Exercise 29)

Tension in Schubert's *Erlking* rises continually from the beginning to the very end. As the story is told, the music, too, unfolds continually without repetition of material, though the cries of the son provide something of a constant refrain. Compositions made up of ever-changing music are called **through-composed**. *Erlking* is thus a through-composed art song. For texts that do not tell a story or project a series of changing moods, however, **strophic form** is often preferred. Here a single poetic mood is maintained from one stanza, or strophe, of the text to the next. Accordingly, the same music is repeated, again and again, for each strophe, as in a hymn or a folk song. Schubert used strophic form, for example, when setting a prayer found in Sir Walter Scott's *The Lady of the Lake*. The result was his immortal *Ave Maria* (1825), a song in which the music for each of three strophes is identical, note for note.

through-composed and strophic forms

THE TROUT (1817)

Schubert's *Die Forelle* (*The Trout*) shows how both the Romantic poet and the musician were attracted to the charms of nature. Picture a fresh mountain stream where a trout darts happily about. Schubert captures this vision with a lively tune and a bubbling accompaniment figure in the piano—whether a spinning wheel, a rippling stream, or a galloping horse, Schubert knew better than anyone how

to create the musical equivalent of such graphic details. The poem is composed
of three eight-line stanzas, each with the rhyme scheme ABABCDCD. The first
sets the scene of the crystal-clear stream, the second introduces a fisherman on
the opposite bank, and the third tells how the invader tricks and catches the
trout. Each strophe is set to the same music, with one exception. At the beginning of the third stanza, where the fisherman tricks the trout by muddying the
stream, the bubbling accompaniment figure is replaced momentarily by a
swirling effect using minor chords. Such a change within the basic strophic form
produces **modified strophic form.** It allows the composer to highlight a particular detail without disturbing the overall structure of strophic form.

modified strophic form

Unlike the dramatic *Erlking* of Goethe, the lyrical text of *The Trout* (by one
Daniel Schubart) is in no way exceptional as a poem. What is remarkable is the
way that Schubert can make even the most ordinary verse into a song of extraordinary beauty.

LISTENING GUIDE	Franz Schubert Art song, *The Trout* (1817)	6CD 3/11 6Tape 3B

0:00   Piano introduces the rippling
accompaniment figure in bright
major key

In ei - nem Bäch - lein hel - le, da schoss in fro - her Eil'

(Continued on next page)

0:07	First strophe	In einem Bächlein helle,	A streamlet clear and sunny
		Da schoss in froher Eil'	With ripples all about,
		Die launische Forelle	Was once the bath for pretty
		Vorüber wie ein Pfeil.	For gentle little trout.
		Ich stand an dem Gestade	On shore I stood observing
		Und sah in süsser Ruh'	With exquisite delight,
		Des muntern Fischleins Bade	The happy little creature
		Im klaren Bächlein zu.	It was a lovely sight.
0:39	Second strophe: exact repeat of music of first strophe	Ein Fischer mit der Rute	A fisher with his angle
		Wohl an dem Ufer stand	Stood on yonder shore
		Und sah's mit kaltem Blute,	Trying to entangle
		Wie sich das Fischlein wand.	The fish from water's floor.
		Solang dem Wasser Helle,	I thought if clear the water
		So dacht ich, nicht gebricht,	Still races all about,
		So fängt er die Forelle	He'd never, never capture
		Mit seiner Angel nicht.	My lovely, little trout.
1:13	Third strophe: minor replaces major; chords replace rippling figure; return to major tonality and rippling figure	Doch endlich ward dem Diebe	Yet the robber had no patience
		Die Zeit zu lang. Er macht	To while away the time
		Das Bächlein tückisch trübe,	He made the brook all muddy
		Und eh' ich es gedacht.	Ere I sensed the crime.
		So zuckte seine Rute,	His line went inward reeling
		Das Fischlein zappelt dran,	My little fish so sweet,
		Und ich mit regem Blute	Then saw I with raging feeling
		Sah die Betrog'ne an.	The cheated and the cheat.

THE "TROUT" QUINTET (1819)

In the summer of 1819, two years after he wrote his song *The Trout*, Schubert decided to vacation in the hills west of Vienna, to enjoy the stunning beauty of the Austrian countryside. There an amateur cellist asked the composer to arrange for string quartet his charming song about a fish. Schubert accepted the challenge but changed the medium of performance. He decided to add a fifth instrument, a piano, to the ensemble (making it a piano quintet) and to replace the usual second violin of the quartet with a double bass. This would give added weight to the bass line and allow the piano to roam with little competition in the upper register. Having selected his instrumental forces, he then composed a five-movement piano quintet, the "Trout" Quintet, perhaps the most lyrical of all works of chamber music.

a theme and six variations

The fourth movement of Schubert's "Trout" Quintet makes prominent use of the lovely tune of the *Lied* and does so in the form of a theme and six variations. The two phrases of the melody (**A** and **B**) are stated and immediately repeated within each variation, though the repeat of **B** extends only to the last four bars (**B′**). Each instrument has its turn to present the melody—the piano does so in variation 1, the viola in variation 2, and the double bass, cello, and violin in variations 3, 5, and 6, respectively. Variations 4 and 5 take us away from the bright tonic key of D major, to D minor and B♭ major, but variation 6 returns us to the tonic major.

Schubert was fond of making use of the melodies of his songs in his instrumental chamber music. The "Trout" Quintet shows that he was not merely a songsmith but could also compose instrumental music with the sort of lyricism, fluidity, and grace that even Mozart might have envied.

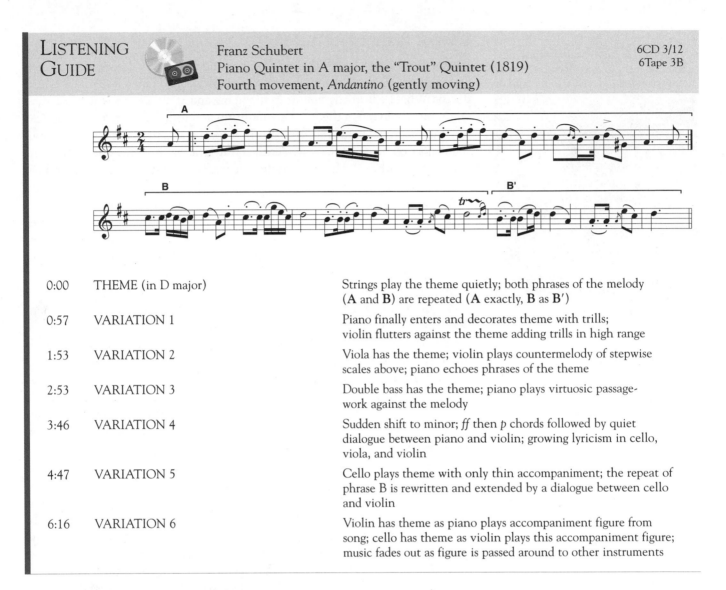

LISTENING
GUIDE

Franz Schubert
Piano Quintet in A major, the "Trout" Quintet (1819)
Fourth movement, *Andantino* (gently moving)

6CD 3/12
6Tape 3B

0:00	THEME (in D major)	Strings play the theme quietly; both phrases of the melody (**A** and **B**) are repeated (**A** exactly, **B** as **B'**)
0:57	VARIATION 1	Piano finally enters and decorates theme with trills; violin flutters against the theme adding trills in high range
1:53	VARIATION 2	Viola has the theme; violin plays countermelody of stepwise scales above; piano echoes phrases of the theme
2:53	VARIATION 3	Double bass has the theme; piano plays virtuosic passage-work against the melody
3:46	VARIATION 4	Sudden shift to minor; *ff* then *p* chords followed by quiet dialogue between piano and violin; growing lyricism in cello, viola, and violin
4:47	VARIATION 5	Cello plays theme with only thin accompaniment; the repeat of phrase B is rewritten and extended by a dialogue between cello and violin
6:16	VARIATION 6	Violin has theme as piano plays accompaniment figure from song; cello has theme as violin plays this accompaniment figure; music fades out as figure is passed around to other instruments

PROGRAM MUSIC†

More than any other period, the nineteenth century was a time in which composers sought and received inspiration from sources outside music. An encounter with nature, the impressions of a voyage, a disappointment in love, a popular legend, or an entire play might provide a story, a scene, or an idea that could be described in music. Of course, music could not actually depict or recreate such extramusical themes. But it could, by using different colors, moods, and sound effects, suggest a particular sequence of happenings and sensations to an attentive listener. To this end composers wrote overtures*, concert overtures*, incidental music*, symphonic poems*, and program symphonies*, which taken together constitute a sizable part of the repertoire of Romantic music. Two of the best composers of this sort of descriptive music were Hector Berlioz and Felix Mendelssohn.

†Nineteenth-century program music is discussed more fully on page 243.

FIGURE 13–4

Hector Berlioz at the age of twenty-nine.

Hector Berlioz (1803–1869)

Hector Berlioz was one of the most original figures in the history of music. He was born in 1803 near the mountain city of Grenoble, France, the son of a local doctor. What he learned of music in the home and at school was scanty: no thorough training in music theory or composition and little exposure to the music of the great masters. Local tutors taught him to play the flute and guitar. Among the major composers of the nineteenth century, he was the only one without fluency at the keyboard. He never studied piano, and could do no more than bang out a few chords.

At the age of seventeen Berlioz was sent off to Paris to study medicine, his father's profession. For two years he pursued a program in the physical sciences, earning a degree in 1821. But Berlioz found the dissecting table gruesome and the allure of the opera house and concert halls irresistible. After a period of soul searching, and the inevitable falling out with his parents over the choice of a career, he vowed to become "no doctor or apothecary but a great composer."

His dismayed father immediately cut off his living stipend, leaving young Berlioz to ponder how he might support himself while studying composition at the Paris Conservatory (the French national school of music). Other composers, finding themselves suddenly on their own, relied on teaching as a means to earn a regular income. Mozart, Haydn, Beethoven, Chopin, and Liszt, for example, all gave piano lessons as young men. But what could Berlioz teach? He had no particular skill on any instrument. So he turned to music criticism, writing reviews and articles for literary journals that poked fun at the French musical establishment. Berlioz was the first composer to earn a livelihood as a music critic, and criticism, not the sale of his music, remained his primary source of income for the remainder of his life.

a music critic

Perhaps it was only natural that Berlioz wrote about music during the years he learned to compose, for literature had a profound impact on his life and art. As a boy his father had taught him to read Virgil's *Aeneid* in the original Latin; later he would use episodes from this classical epic to form the libretto of an opera called *Les Troyens* (*The Trojans*, 1858). As a young man he read Lord Byron's *Childe Harold's Pilgrimage* and Goethe's *Faust*, works that inspired his concerto for viola called *Harold in Italy* (1834) and his dramatic symphony *The Damnation of Faust* (1846). But of all literary influences, none was greater than that of Shakespeare. As we have seen (page 235), Shakespeare burst upon the consciousness of continental Europe for the first time early in the nineteenth century. For Berlioz the experience was shattering: "Shakespeare, coming upon me unawares, struck me like a thunderbolt. The lightning flash of that discovery revealed to me at a stroke the whole heaven of art." Berlioz devoured the English poet's plays and gave musical expression to several. To *The Tempest* and to *King Lear* he wrote concert overtures (see page 244)—independent pieces intended to sum up the spirit of the drama. Berlioz kept a human skull on his desk to remind him of the graveyard scene of *Hamlet* (see Fig. 12–9) and wrote a funeral march (1848) to remember the death of this prince. And he set the main events of *Romeo and Juliet* as a five-movement program symphony, *Roméo et Juliette* (1839), into which a chorus and solo voices intermittently sing Shakespeare's own words.

literature informs his music

In these works inspired by literature, as well as in his religious music, Berlioz called for enormous orchestral and choral forces—hundreds and hundreds of performers. He also experimented with new instruments: the ophicleide (an early

new instruments in the orchestra

form of the tuba), the **English horn** (a low oboe), the harp (an ancient instrument now brought into the symphony orchestra for the first time), the **cornet** (a brass instrument with valves, borrowed from the military band), and even the newly invented saxophone. His approach to musical form was also iconoclastic; he rarely wrote in strict sonata–allegro form or theme and variations, for example. His French compatriots found his compositions "bizarre" and "monstrous" and thought him something of a madman. Increasingly, he crisscrossed Europe to conduct his works before foreigners, who more readily appreciated his unique new sounds. To London, Bonn, Vienna, Prague, Leipzig, and even Moscow he went to introduce such works as *Symphonie fantastique*, *Damnation of Faust*, *Roméo et Juliette*, and *The Trojans*. He died in Paris in 1869, isolated and embittered. The little recognition he received in his native France came "too late," as he said, to help his career or self-esteem.

SYMPHONIE FANTASTIQUE (1830)

Berlioz's most celebrated work, then and now, is his *Symphonie fantastique*, perhaps the single most influential composition of the entire nineteenth century. Its form and orchestration are revolutionary. But what is more, it tells in music a vivid story and, as such, is the first complete program symphony. The story surrounding the creation of the descriptive program of the work is as fascinating as the program itself.

In 1827 a troupe of English actors came to Paris to present Shakespeare's *Hamlet* and *Romeo and Juliet*. Berlioz, of course, had read some of Shakespeare's plays in a French translation, but was eager to see these works performed on stage. Though he understood little English, he was overwhelmed by what he saw. The human insights, touching beauty, and onstage action in Shakespeare's work far surpassed the virtues found in traditional French theater. But not only was Berlioz smitten by Shakespeare, he also fell in love with the leading lady who played Ophelia to Hamlet and Juliet to Romeo, one Harriet Smithson (Fig. 13–6). Like a lovesick adolescent Berlioz swooned at her sight and wrote such violently passionate letters that the frightened starlet refused to meet the student composer. Eventually, his ardor cooled—for a time he even became engaged to someone else. But the experience of an all-consuming love, the despair of rejection, and the vision of darkness and possible death furnished the stimulus—and story line—for an unusually imaginative symphony. (Ultimately, Berlioz did meet and marry Harriet Smithson, and the two lived miserably together ever after.)

Berlioz wrote the *Symphonie fantastique*, not in the usual four movements of a symphony, but in five, an arrangement that may have been inspired by Shakespeare's use of a five-act format. Movements 1 and 5 balance each other in length and substance, as do 2 and 4, leaving the leisurely third movement as the center of the work. But symmetry is not the only element holding the symphony together. Berlioz creates a single melody that reappears as a unifying force, movement after movement, a total of eight times during the symphony. Earlier, Beethoven had experimented with thematic recall and transformation in his fifth and ninth symphonies. But Berlioz takes this technique one step farther by recalling the melody constantly and by associating it with an object, his beloved. The vision of his loved one, and her attending melody, become an obsession. Berlioz called this musical fixation his **idée fixe** ("fixed idea"). As his feelings about the beloved change from movement to movement, so the *idée fixe* is transformed to

FIGURE 13–5

A satirical engraving suggesting the public's impression of Berlioz conducting his vastly enlarged symphony orchestra.

a program symphony

FIGURE 13–6

The actress Harriet Smithson became an obsession for Berlioz and the source of inspiration for his *Symphonie fantastique*. At the time Berlioz wrote this symphony (1830), she was a good deal more famous than he.

reflect these various moods. To make sure that the listener has no doubt as to what these moods are, Berlioz prepared a written program to be read as the music is performed.

First Movement: Reveries, Passions

> Program: A young musician . . . sees for the first time a woman who embodies all the charms of the ideal being he has imagined in his dreams. . . . The subject of the first movement is the passage from this state of melancholy reverie, interrupted by a few moments of joy, to that of delirious passion, with movements of fury, jealousy, and its return to tenderness, tears, and religious consolation.

first vision of the beloved

A slow introduction ("this state of melancholy reverie") prepares the way for the first vision of the beloved, carried forward by the first appearance of the main theme, the *idée fixe*. (The entire melody is given earlier in Ex. 12–1.)

EXAMPLE 13–4

The movement unfolds in sonata–allegro form. The "recapitulation," however, does not so much repeat the *idée fixe* as it does transform the melody to reflect the artist's feelings of sorrow and tenderness.

Second Movement: A Ball

> The artist finds himself . . . in the midst of the tumult of a party.

she appears at a ball

A lilting waltz now begins, but it is interrupted by the unexpected appearance of the *idée fixe*, the rhythm changed to accommodate the triple meter of the waltz. Four harps add a graceful accompaniment when the waltz returns, and, toward the end, there is even a lovely solo for cornet. The sequence of waltz–*idée fixe*–waltz creates, once again, ternary form.

Third Movement: Scene in the Country

> Finding himself one evening in the country, the artist hears in the distance two shepherds piping. . . . He reflects upon his isolation and hopes that soon he will no longer be alone.

loneliness and isolation

The dialogue between the shepherds is presented by an English horn and an oboe, the latter played offstage to give the effect of a distant response. The unexpected appearance of the *idée fixe* in the woodwinds suggests that the artist has hopes of winning his beloved. But has she falsely encouraged him? The shepherd's tune recurs, but the oboe doesn't answer. There is only the lonely call of the English horn and the empty rumble of distant thunder in the timpani.

Fourth Movement: March to the Scaffold

> Having realized that his love goes unrecognized, the artist poisons himself with opium. The dose of the narcotic, too weak to kill him, plunges him into a sleep

accompanied by the most horrible visions. He dreams that he has killed the one he loved, that he is condemned, led to the scaffold, and now witnesses his own execution.

an execution

This drug-induced nightmare centers on the march to the scaffold where the artist is to be executed. The steady beat of the low strings and the muffled bass drum sound the steps of the procession. Near the end the image of the beloved returns in the clarinet, only to be suddenly cut off by a *fortissimo* crash by the full orchestra. The guillotine has fallen.

Fifth Movement: Dream of the Witches' Sabbath

> He sees himself at the witches' sabbath surrounded by a troop of frightful shadows, sorcerers, and monsters of all sorts, gathered for his funeral. Strange noises, groans, bursts of laughter, distant cries echoed by others. The beloved melody returns again, but it has lost its noble, modest character and is now only base, trivial, and grotesque. An outburst of joy at her arrival; she joins in the devilish orgy.

climactic fifth movement

In this monstrous finale Berlioz creates his personal vision of hell. A crowd of witches and other ghouls is summoned to dance around the corpse of the artist on its way to the inferno. Weird sounds are produced by the strings, using mutes, and by the high woodwinds and French horn, playing glissandos*. A piercing clarinet enters with a burlesque parody of the *idée fixe* as Harriet Smithson, now in the frightful garb of a wicked old hag, comes on stage.

a vision of hell

EXAMPLE 13–5

She is greeted by a joyous *fortissimo* outburst by the full assembly as all proceed to dance to the now perverted *idée fixe*. Suddenly, the music becomes ominously quiet and, in one of the most strikingly original moments in all of music, great Gothic church bells are heard. Against this solemn backdrop sounds the burial hymn of the medieval Church, the **Dies irae,** played by ophicleides (tubas) and bassoons.

Dies irae

EXAMPLE 13–6

[Di - es i - rae di - es il - la sol - vet   sae - clum in fa - vil - la]
[Day of anger, day of wrath, on which the ages will be changed to ash]

Not only is the orchestration sensational, the musical symbolism is sacrilegious. Just as he had parodied the melody of the beloved, now Berlioz creates a mockery of one of the most venerable Gregorian chants of the Catholic Church. First the *Dies irae* is played by the horns twice as fast (a process called rhythmic **diminution**). Then the sacred tune is transformed into a jazzed-up dance tune played by a shrill, high clarinet, the entire scene now becoming a blasphemous black Mass (see Fig. 12–2).

a mockery of the Church

EXAMPLE 13–7

a parody of fugue

As the ceremony proceeds, the witches begin to dance. But they do so in an extraordinary way: They enter one by one and create a fugato*, a fugal passage within a symphonic movement. What is a learned fugue doing here in the middle of hell? Presumably because, having just mocked the ancient music of the Catholic Church, Berlioz now decides to ridicule the musical establishment and its strictest form, the academic fugue. But beyond this, the regular entry of more and more voices, or dancing witches, creates the effect of a growing tumult around the corpse of the artist.

EXAMPLE 13–8

col legno technique

A climax is reached as the theme, or subject, of the witches, played in the strings, as well as the *Dies irae* melody, played in the brass and woodwinds, sound together, though in different keys, a bizarre example of **double counterpoint.** Stranger still is the sound that follows, for Berlioz instructs the violins to play **col legno** ("with the wood")—to strike the strings, not with the usual front of the bow, but with the wooden back, creating a noise something akin to the crackling or burning of hellfire.

To the audience that first heard the *Symphonie fantastique* on December 5, 1830, all of this must have seemed incomprehensible: new instruments, novel playing effects, simultaneous melodies in different keys, and a form that is not traditional, like sonata–allegro or rondo, but grows out of the events in a soap-opera–like program. But it all works. Here is a rare example in the history of art in which a creator has not only undertaken to experiment radically but has done so in a way that produces a wholly integrated, unified, and ultimately satisfying work. The separate effects may be revolutionary and momentarily shocking, but they are consistent and logical among themselves when subsumed in the total artistic concept. Had Berlioz never written another note of music, he would be justly famous for this single masterpiece of Romantic invention.

LISTENING GUIDE

Hector Berlioz
Symphonie fantastique (1830)
Fifth movement, Dream of the Witches' Sabbath

6CD 4/1; 6Tape 4A
3CD 3/1; 3Tape 3A

0:00	"Strange noises, groans, bursts of laughter, distant cries" high and low
1:28	Grotesquely transformed *idée fixe* in shrill clarinet
1:36	Joyful, *fortissimo* outburst by full orchestra welcoming the now ugly beloved
1:46	Witches begin to dance to the newly grotesque *idée fixe*; bassoons add raucous counterpoint (1:57)

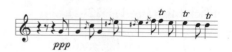

2:39	Sinister transition
2:59	Funeral bells sound
3:26	*Dies irae* heard in tubas and bassoons
3:48	Horns and trombones play *Dies irae* twice as fast (diminution)
3:58	Woodwinds pervert *Dies irae* chant
4:04	Chant melody, its diminution, and its perversion continue
5:04	Introduction to witches' dance; crescendo
5:21	Witches' dance (fugato) begins with four entries of the subject
5:47	Fugal episode
6:06	Three more entries of the subject
6:22	More strange sounds and cries (transition out of fugato)
7:04	Fragments of the *Dies irae*
7:21	Witches' dance (fugue subject) grows to a rapid climax, then *fortissimo* syncopation (7:49)
8:06	Witches' dance and *Dies irae* combined; trumpets now added
8:35	Violins use wooden back of bow to produce a crackling sound
8:56	*Fortissimo* chords
9:13	Fleeting recall of *Dies irae*
9:30	More chords with a striking harmonic shift
9:36	Final cadential fanfare

(Listening Exercise 30)

Felix Mendelssohn (1809–1847)

Berlioz was a child of the Romantic age: He tried suicide at least twice, ran around Italy with a gang of bandits in imitation of Lord Byron, and married an image, an ideal of a woman, with disastrous consequences. Felix Mendelssohn was an altogether different personality, anything but the stereotype of the rebellious, self-absorbed, struggling artist.

Mendelssohn was born in 1809 into a prosperous, indeed wealthy, Jewish family. His father was a banker, and his grandfather, Moses Mendelssohn (1726–1786), was a noted philosopher. At the family home in Berlin young Felix had every advantage: He studied languages, literature, and philosophy with private tutors, as well as painting, dancing, riding, and even gymnastics. In 1816 Mendelssohn's parents had their four children baptized Christians, partly so they might enjoy full legal equality and move freely in all social circles. Indeed, their home became a gathering place for artists and intellectuals of all sorts: the poet Heine, the philosopher Hegel, and the geographer Humboldt (discoverer of the Humboldt current) were all frequent guests. Because Felix had shown extraordinary musical talent, he was not only given piano lessons but also provided with a small orchestra on Sunday afternoons to try out his youthful compositions. At the age of sixteen he composed a masterpiece, his octet for strings. The next year

FIGURE 13–7

Felix Mendelssohn at the age of twenty.

FIGURE 13–8

Exterior of the Gewandhaus in Leipzig, Germany, as depicted by Felix Mendelssohn. In addition to being a musician and composer and speaking four languages fluently, Mendelssohn was a gifted painter, his preferred medium being water color.

(1826) witnessed an equally astonishing work, the Overture to *A Midsummer Night's Dream*. As a composer Mendelssohn was even more precocious than either Mozart or Schubert.

Taking advantage of his privileged station in life, Mendelssohn spent the years 1829–1835 traveling across Europe to discover its natural beauty and to meet the great artists of the day. He walked across most of Switzerland, sketching and painting as he went. He met Goethe in Weimar, Berlioz in Rome, Liszt, Chopin, and the painter Delacroix (see Fig. 13–13) in Paris, and the novelist Sir Walter Scott outside Edinburgh. The itinerant years ended in the spring of 1835 when he was appointed musical director of the Gewandhaus Orchestra in Leipzig, Germany.

Founded in 1781 by the merchants of Leipzig, the **Gewandhaus Orchestra** ("Clothiers' House" Orchestra) played in the guild hall of that trade association (Figs. 13–8 and 13–9). Mendelssohn recruited better players, increased their salaries, established a pension fund for the orchestra, and conducted as a musical interpreter, not just as a mere time-beater. By so doing he soon made the Gewandhaus Orchestra one of the finest in Europe, a position it has continued to hold to the present day.

Leipzig was, of course, the city of Bach. The old contrapuntalist had fallen into nearly complete oblivion after his death there in 1750. But his music was adored by Mendelssohn, who, in 1829, mounted the first performance of Bach's great *St. Matthew Passion* in nearly a hundred years. ("And to think that it should be a Jew who gives back to the world the greatest of Christian works," he said at the time.) While in Leipzig, Mendelssohn continued to program Bach's music as well as the works of other composers of historical interest: Handel, Haydn, and Mozart among them. The idea spread. From this time forward a concert by a symphony orchestra served not only as a forum in which to present new or recent works but also as a museum for the old. Our modern notion that a symphony orchestra exists to preserve a past repertoire, as well as to promote a contemporary art, can be traced to Mendelssohn and his contemporaries. Mendelssohn remained in the post of director of the Gewandhaus Orchestra in Leipzig until his premature death by stroke at the age of thirty-eight.

FIGURE 13–9

A concert in progress, ca. 1840, in the Gewandhaus, the hall where Mendelssohn, Liszt, Berlioz, and Clara and Robert Schumann frequently performed.

Given the fact that Felix Mendelssohn led a revival of the music of the eighteenth-century masters, it is not surprising that his own compositions are the most conservative, the most "classical," of the great Romantic composers. His harmonies are colorful but not revolutionary; his orchestration distinctive but not shocking—a light, dancing string sound is his hallmark; and his use of form is traditional, as seen in his heavy reliance on sonata–allegro form. Never does he indulge in startling outbursts of sound. The classical ideals of unity, grace, and formal balance predominate.

a musical conservative

What makes Mendelssohn a musical Romantic is the fact that nature, travel, and literature provided stimuli for so many of his creations. A trip to Italy in 1830–31 gave rise to his "Italian" Symphony, just as a lengthy sojourn in Scotland a year earlier had planted the seeds for the "Scottish" Symphony. On this same northern voyage he visited the windswept Hebrides Islands and soon captured the spirit of the churning sea and rocky coast in his *Hebrides Overture* (1830). Mendelssohn commented on the difficulty he faced when trying to harness a raging ocean within the confines of sonata–allegro form: "The whole development section smells more of counterpoint than of blubber, gulls, and salted cod."

influence of nature, travel, and literature

As to literary influences, he heard the voices of Goethe and Shakespeare most clearly. To Goethe's *Faust* the composer owed the inspiration for the *Scherzo* of his early Octet (1825) and several later orchestral works. And to Shakespeare, of course, could be traced the genesis of the music for *A Midsummer Night's Dream*.

OVERTURE TO *A MIDSUMMER NIGHT'S DREAM* (1826)

Mendelssohn began to compose, or "to dream *A Midsummer Night's Dream*," as he says, during July 1826, when he was an impressionable youth of seventeen. His aim was to transform the romantic fantasy of Shakespeare's play into an independent concert overture (a piece for the concert hall, not the theater). Some years later, in 1843, he was commissioned by the king of Prussia to create incidental music (music to be heard during an actual performance) for a production of the play planned for Berlin. Among these incidental pieces is his famous *Wedding March*—originally written to accompany the marriage of the characters Theseus and Hippolyta, now traditionally played at weddings as the recessional march.

a concert overture

To enter fully into the enchanted world of Mendelssohn's Overture to *A Midsummer Night's Dream*, we must know something of the play—the program—that inspired it. The drama begins in an imaginary city called Athens, where the ruler, Duke Theseus, is about to marry Hippolyta, queen of the Amazons. Nearby is an enchanted forest ruled by Oberon, king of the elves, and his estranged queen, Titania. Into this magical grove come Lysander and Hermia, another pair of would-be lovers. Then enters a group of common craftsmen, led by the blockheaded Bottom, who have come to prepare for the royal wedding. Finally, the hunting party of Theseus and Hippolyta joins the woodland scene. Confusion reigns as an agent of fairy king Oberon, the spirit Puck, administers a love potion to the wrong parties; fairy queen Titania falls in love with the clownish Bottom, who is made to wear the head of an ass. Eventually, all is set right and the nobles and gentry return to the court of Athens. The events in the enchanted forest had been no more real than a midsummer night's dream.

Shakespeare's play

FIGURE 13–10

Oberon, Titania and Puck with Fairies
Dancing by the English artist and poet
William Blake (1757–1827).

Mendelssohn's Overture closely follows the play. Separate and distinctly different musical colors and styles make the various characters clearly identifiable and the events easy to follow. At the same time, the music unfolds in sonata–allegro form. There is a slow four-chord introduction, a first theme (the dancing fairy music), a transition (royal music of the court of Athens), a second theme (the lovers' music), and a closing theme group (the craftsmen's music and the hunting calls). The fairies dominate the development section and in the coda (or epilogue) have the last word, just as in Shakespeare's play. Mendelssohn's own thoughts best describe the ending: "After everything has been satisfactorily settled and the principal players have joyfully left the stage, the elves follow them, bless the house, and disappear with the dawn. So ends the play, and my overture too."

LISTENING GUIDE

Felix Mendelssohn
Overture to *A Midsummer Night's Dream* (1826)

6CD 4/2
6Tape 4A

Program:		Musical Events:
EXPOSITION		
0:00	Introduction to enchantment	Four sustained chords in the winds (introduction)
0:20	Fairies' music	Rapid, light, staccato notes in violins (first theme)
1:04	Duke Theseus and his court	Full orchestra *fortissimo* (transition)
1:34		Fairies' music mixes into transition
2:08	Lovers' music	Quiet melody in woodwinds and strings grows more passionate (second theme)
3:00	Bottom's music	Raucous motive sounds like braying of a donkey (closing theme, part 1)
3:22	Hunting calls of regal party	Fanfares in brass and woodwinds (closing theme, part 2)
DEVELOPMENT		
3:46	Fairies' music developed	Music of the fairies (first theme) worked out in different keys
4:22	Horn blasts	
4:52	Fairies' music extended	String pizzicato and string tremolo
5:27	Lysander and Hermia sleep	Ritard, soft string sound, music seems to come to a stop
RECAPITULATION		
5:52	Return to enchantment	Four introductory chords return

6:14	Fairies' music	Dancing fairies' music returns (first theme), but transition is eliminated
6:58	Lovers' music	Lyrical melody in woodwinds and strings (second theme) as before
7:47	Bottom's music	Again raucous *fortissimo* music of the ass (closing theme, part 1)
8:52	Hunting party	Fanfares (closing theme, part 2) serve as ending to recapitulation
CODA		
9:16	Epilogue by fairy Puck	Light, quick music of the fairies; toward the end Duke Theseus and the four opening chords are recalled

THE PIANISTS

By the 1840s the piano had evolved into essentially the instrument we know today (see also, page 241). Its thundering power, rapid action, singing tone, and wide range of expression made it the most popular instrument of the Romantic period. No self-respecting middle-class home could be without one. No education was thought complete without lessons at it. Spurred by the extraordinary vogue of the instrument, a host of virtuoso performers set upon the concert halls of Europe with fingers blazing. What they played was often more a display of digital fireworks—rapid octaves, racing chromatic scales, thundering chords—than of musical substance. Happily, however, several of the greatest piano virtuosos of the nineteenth century were also gifted composers. While these artists sometimes wrote songs, symphonies, or concertos, the piano—and piano style—was at the heart of their creative process.

vogue of the piano

Robert Schumann (1810–1856)

In many ways Robert Schumann's life was a failure, indeed a tragedy. Sent to university at Heidelberg to study law, he attended not a single class—he had no more affinity for law than Berlioz had for medicine. With his mother's grudging consent, Schumann moved on to Leipzig to study piano, determined to become a virtuoso. But after two years of lessons with the eminent Friedrich Wieck (1785–1873), all he had to show for his labors was a permanently damaged right hand. His career as a virtuoso now frustrated, composition and music criticism became the focus of his creative energies. During the 1830s he produced a remarkable series of works for solo piano, mostly sonatas, variations, and collections of character pieces*. He also founded and served as editor for the new musical periodical, the *Neue Zeitschrift für Musik (New Journal of Music)*. Schumann became the apostle for new music within the German Romantic movement, championing the works of such "radical" composers as Berlioz, Chopin, Mendelssohn, Liszt, and the young Johannes Brahms.

While studying piano in the Leipzig home of Friedrich Wieck, Schumann met, and soon fell in love with, Wieck's beautiful and talented daughter, Clara. They were married in 1840, over the violent objections of her father. The year of their union was one of feverish creation for Robert; from his pen flowed more than 125

FIGURE 13–11

Robert Schumann.

art songs and character pieces for piano

Lieder, mostly love songs, for voice and piano. These include several now-famous song cycles* such as *Dichterliebe (Poet's Love)* and *Frauenliebe und Leben (Women in Love and Life)*, individual songs of which are the equal in quality to the works of the great Franz Schubert in this genre. Clara now encouraged him to extend himself beyond art songs and character pieces for piano, and into orchestral and chamber music. But in these larger forms he had only mixed success. His piano concerto (1845) and piano quintet (1842) are supreme accomplishments, but his four symphonies are not uniformly compelling. At heart Schumann was a miniaturist whose creativity was inextricably bound to the keyboard. And unlike his idol Beethoven, who composed on sketchbooks as he walked through forest and field, Schumann was unable to generate music except at the piano. Touch and sensation were intrinsic to his creative process.

growing insanity

Life between the Schumanns was marked by symbiotic artistry and personal agony. Husband and wife read poetry together, and each made suggestions on the other's musical compositions. But from his earliest years Robert Schumann had shown himself to be what psychiatrists now call a manic-depressive. He experienced wild swings of mood. Naturally, as with all artists so afflicted, this disease affected his creativity, both for good and for ill. In some years he produced a torrent of music, in others virtually nothing. As time progressed, Schumann's condition grew more extreme. He began to hear voices, both heavenly and hellish, and one morning, pursued by demons within, he jumped off a bridge into the Rhine river. Nearby fishermen pulled him to safety, but from that point on, by his own request, he was confined to an asylum, where he died of self-starvation in 1856. In his final, tragic years, his creative output dwindled to nothing.

Clara Wieck Schumann (1819–1896)

Unlike her husband, Robert, a gifted composer but failed performer, Clara Wieck Schumann was one of the great piano virtuosos of the nineteenth century. A child prodigy, she made her debut at the age of eleven in the Gewandhaus (see Figs. 13–8 and 13–9) in Leipzig, Germany, the city of her birth. She then undertook a concert tour of Europe during which she impressed and befriended Mendelssohn, Berlioz, Chopin, and Liszt. Like these young artists, she too began to compose: a few songs, a number of "romances" for piano, and, at the age of fifteen, a piano concerto.

When she married Robert Schumann in 1840, Clara Wieck was much better known on the international stage than he. Nevertheless, she put aside her own career to play the roles of wife and mother to the eight children she soon bore him (one died in infancy). Her compositions became few and far between, her public performances limited to an occasional tour. But when Robert Schumann was institutionalized in 1854 Clara was compelled by economic necessity again to pursue the concert circuit. There were annual tours to England and more than one to Russia. She continued to concertize until the age of seventy, a legend in her own time. Said the famous London music critic and playwright George Bernard Shaw (1856–1950), "She is an artist of the sort that is the Grail of the critic's quest."

Not only was Clara Schumann a piano virtuoso, she was a gifted composer as well. As a child she had received the kind of exacting education in harmony and counterpoint that was exceptional for her sex. Later, when married to Robert Schumann, she studied the fugues of an earlier musician from Leipzig,

FIGURE 13–12
Clara Schumann.

Where Were the Women?

You may have noticed that female composers are poorly represented in this book. We have seen the works of some, Hildegard of Bingen (page 71) and the Countess of Dia (page 78), for example, and we will meet those of Ellen Taaffe Zwilich later (page 378). But in general, although women have been actively engaged as performers of secular music since the Middle Ages, only rarely, until this century, did they become composers. While the causes of this condition are numerous, one factor stands out above all others: People then had no faith in the capacity, or the propriety, of female creativity. Although a young lady might learn to play the piano in a show of domestic refinement, a woman's function in society was defined as nurturer of children (preferably male) and handmaiden of husband. Fanny Mendelssohn Hensel (1805–1847), the gifted sister of Felix Mendelssohn, was fifteen and considering music as a profession when she received the following directive in a letter from her father: "What you wrote to me about your musical occupations, and in comparison to those of Felix, was rightly thought and expressed. But though music will perhaps become his profession, for you it can and must only be an ornament, never the core of your existence."

With no encouragement to become a creative force outside the home, little wonder that self-doubt arose among women of talent. As Clara Schumann wrote in her diary in 1839: "I once believed that I possessed creative talent, but I have given up this idea; a woman must not desire to compose. There has never yet been one able to do it. Should I expect to be that one?"

Composing a symphony or a string quartet is a complex process requiring years of study in harmony, counterpoint, and instrumentation. Because of discrimination, few women received such formal training in composition. The Paris Conservatory was founded in 1793 but did not admit women into the classes in advanced music theory and composition until almost a century later. (Similarly, women who wished to become painters were barred from anatomy classes, instruction crucial to the figural arts.) Only in those exceptional cases in which a daughter received the same intense musical education as a son, as did Fanny Mendelssohn and Clara Schumann, did a woman have a fighting chance to become a musical creator.

Fanny Mendelssohn

J. S. Bach. The dense textures and intensely chromatic inner parts found throughout Clara's music can be attributed to this rigorous early training and thorough exposure to Bach.

ROMANCE FOR PIANO AND VIOLIN, OPUS 22, NO. 3 (1853)

A romance is a brief instrumental work, usually in a slow tempo, that conveys a single, intensely lyrical mood. It and similar Romantic miniatures are called character pieces* (see page 243). Clara Schumann wrote numerous romances for piano alone. And even in this set of three for piano with violin, it is the pianist who does most of the work, creating a rich chromatic texture, providing the harmony, and sometimes supplying the melody as well. What is of interest in this romance is the composer's unflagging industry and integrity. There are two themes, **a** (heard four times) and **b** (heard twice). Where a lesser composer might have relied on simple repeats, Clara Schumann continually varies the surrounding musical context each time the themes reappear. Here beauty is created through the subtle way in which the two themes continually take on new expressive meaning in an ever-changing sea of harmonic color.

FIGURE 13–13

Clara Schumann in the last years of her life. "Nobly beautiful and poetic" the playwright George Bernard Shaw (1856–1950) called her playing.

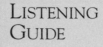

LISTENING GUIDE   Clara Wieck Schumann   6CD 4/3
Romance for Piano and Violin, Opus 22, No. 3 (1853)   6Tape 4A

(Ternary form: **ABA'**)

0:00   Theme **a** in violin; piano plays harmony as rapid arpeggios   A

0:33   Piano briefly joins in return of **a**
0:54   Extension and development of **a**
1:24   Violin plays trills in V–I cadence leading to
1:34   Theme **b** in violin; piano plays harmony as staccato chords   B

1:53   Piano plays theme **b**; violin plays harmony as pizzicato chords
2:11   Extension and development of **b**
2:32   Piano plays **b** while violin adds counterpoint
3:00   Theme **a** in violin; piano plays arpeggios   A'
3:19   Extension and development of **a**
3:55   Piano plays **a** while violin adds counterpoint
4:12   Fragments of **a** and rich harmonies   CODA

(Listening Exercise 31)

FIGURE 13–14

A superbly Romantic portrait of Chopin by Eugène Delacroix. It suggests something of the Romantic notion of an artist as consumed by the fire of genius.

Frédéric Chopin (1810–1849)

In the compositions of Frédéric Chopin, the piano and its music have their most perfect union. This "poet of the piano," as he was called, was born near Warsaw, Poland, of a French father and a Polish mother. The father taught at an elite secondary school for the sons of Polish nobility, and it was there that Frédéric not only gained an excellent general education but acquired aristocratic friends and tastes as well. He then moved on to the newly founded Warsaw Conservatory, where, between 1826 and 1829, he concentrated on the study of piano and composition. It was during this period that he composed his first major work, a brilliant set of variations for piano and orchestra on Mozart's duet "Là ci darem la mano" ("Give me your hand") from *Don Giovanni* (on the duet, see page 205). Warsaw was now thought to be too small, too provincial, for a young man of his musical talents. So in 1830 he departed to seek his fortune in Vienna and Paris. The next year Poland fell to invading Russian troops, and Chopin never returned to his homeland.

born in Warsaw, Poland

After an unsuccessful year in Vienna, the twenty-one-year-old Chopin arrived in Paris in September 1831. His inaugural concerts caught Parisians' fancy, and his imaginative playing soon became the stuff of legends. But Chopin was not cut out for the life of the public virtuoso. He was introverted, physically slight—weighing little more than a hundred pounds—and somewhat sickly. Consequently, he chose to play at private *musicales* (musical evenings) in the homes of the aristocracy and to give lessons for a fee only the very rich, such as the Parisian Rothschilds, could afford. "I have been introduced all around the highest circles," he said within a year of his arrival. "I hobnob with ambassadors, princes, and ministers. I can't imagine what miracle is responsible for all this since I really haven't done anything to bring it about."

moves to Paris

Not only did Chopin become the musical darling of the *haut monde* of Paris, but he also was welcomed into the inner circle of an intellectual and artistic

FIGURE 13–15

Portrait of the novelist Aurore Dude-vant (George Sand) by Eugène Delacroix. Both the painter Delacroix and the composer Chopin often stayed at her summer home in Nohant in the south of France.

works for piano

elite. Among his friends he numbered the poets Heinrich Heine (1797–1856) and Alfred de Musset (1810–1857), the novelists Honoré de Balzac (1799–1850) and Victor Hugo (1802–1885), the composers Liszt and Berlioz, and the Romantic painter Eugène Delacroix (1799–1863).

But Chopin's most intense liaison was with Baroness Aurore Dudevant (1803–1876), a writer who under the pen name of George Sand poured forth a steady stream of Romantic novels roughly akin to our Silhouette Romances. She was also an ardent individualist who often dressed in men's clothing and smoked cigars (see cover and Fig. 13–15). In 1838 she became Chopin's friend, lover, and protector. Many of his best works were composed at Nohant, her residence 150 miles south of Paris where the couple spent their summers. After their relationship ended in 1847, Chopin undertook a taxing concert tour of England and Scotland. While this improved his depleted finances, it weakened his delicate health. He died in Paris of tuberculosis at the age of thirty-nine.

Chopin was something of a rarity as a composer because each and every one of his works is written for the piano alone or features the piano in some way, as in the case of his two piano concertos and twenty art songs (in Polish). His compositional style was perfectly suited for the piano, highlighting the very best qualities of the instrument. Light, rapid passage work is placed in the upper register because the piano can sound quickly with no loss of clarity in its high range. Lovely arialike melodies are assigned to the middle register to exploit the instrument's lyrical, singing tone. Chords are broken into harplike arpeggios and set deep into the bass because the piano can provide a powerful, lush harmony to its own melody. And chromatic scales occur everywhere, taking advantage of the fact that these can be played faster on the piano than on any other instrument.

Chopin applied this idiomatic piano style to many different types of music. He transferred to the piano the spirit of three popular dances of the time: the mazurka and the polonaise (both of Polish origin) and the waltz (originally Viennese, by now everywhere in Europe). He wrote three full-length sonatas, but his large pieces usually have more suggestive names such as "fantasy" or "ballad." His shorter works include twenty-one nocturnes and a set of twenty-four preludes—

FIGURE 13–16

A painting done from memory by the Polish artist Siemiradski shows Chopin playing in the drawing room of Prince Anton Radziwill (seated center), himself a talented amateur musician.

FIGURE 13–17
Delacroix's painting *Liberty Leading the People*, inspired by the Revolution of 1830. The patriotic figure of Liberty carries a rifle in one hand and the French flag in the other. The painter Delacroix was a close personal friend of the composer Chopin.

brief character pieces, one in each of the major and minor keys. Perhaps most remarkable is the set of twenty-four *Etudes*, studies which show that in the hands of a genius mere technical exercises can be transformed into pearls of exquisite beauty.

POLONAISE IN A MAJOR, OPUS 40, NO. 1, THE "MILITARY" POLONAISE (1838)

Chopin's name is closely associated with a genre of dance music called the polonaise. A polonaise (French for "Polish thing") is a slow, stately processional dance in triple meter, without an upbeat but often with an accent on beat two of each 3/4 measure. Originating in Poland, the dance spread to Germany, where polonaises were created by Bach, Handel, and even Beethoven. Like the minuet, the polonaise is followed by a trio* and then a return to the polonaise itself. Because Chopin usually composed both polonaise and trio in ternary form, his works in this genre normally have a strict **aba cdc aba** structure.

the polonaise

Chopin's Polonaise in A major is called the "Military" Polonaise. This name was not bestowed by Chopin himself, but by his contemporaries, who heard in its ♪♫♫♫ rhythm a figure characteristic of a military parade. Chopin composed a dozen polonaises, exciting pieces that enjoyed great popularity throughout Europe in the 1830s, when things Polish were very much in vogue. The Poles were objects of sympathy at this time because of their heroic fight to break free of Russian domination. In November 1830, an insurrection in Warsaw was brutally suppressed. Russia's annexation of Poland in 1832 brought many Polish exiles to Paris. Thus Chopin's "Military Polonaise," as the work of an exiled Polish patriot, suggested to the listener of his day two sentiments that characterized the revolutionary 1830s: nationalism and militarism.

the revolutionary 1830s

LISTENING
GUIDE

Frédéric Chopin
Polonaise in A major, Opus 40, No. 1,
The "Military" Polonaise (1838)

6CD 4/4; 6Tape 4A
3CD 3/2; 3Tape 3A

(Ternary form: **ABA**)

Polonaise **A**

0:00   Bright major chords, snappy military rhythm   a

0:35   Music moves to higher range, hint of minor key   b

0:54   Return to bright chords and snappy rhythm of the beginning   a

(Trio) **B**

1:49   Falling melody in right hand against another martial rhythm in the left   c

3:05   Trills, like drum rolls, deep in the bass   d

3:26   Return of falling melody   c

Polonaise **A**

5:05   Bright major chords, snappy military rhythm   a
5:24   Music moves to higher range, hint of minor key   b
5:44   Return to bright chords, etc.   a

(Listening Exercise 32)

Franz Liszt (1811–1886)

Franz Liszt was born in Hungary of German-speaking parents. His ambitious father moved the family to Vienna in 1822 so that his gifted son might study with the very best teachers. From Vienna it was on to Paris to establish the boy as the latest child prodigy, the newest infant virtuoso. But some years later, when his father died suddenly of typhoid fever, the sixteen-year-old youth was left in Paris more or less on his own. He gave piano lessons, became something of a religious fanatic, and tried to enter a Parisian seminary in hopes of becoming a priest.

But in 1831 Liszt heard the great violin virtuoso Niccolò Paganini (see page 242), and this changed his life. "What a man, what a violin, what an artist! O God, what pain and suffering, what torment in those four strings." Liszt vowed to bring Paganini's technical virtuosity to the piano, and he did. Practicing four to five hours a day—unusual dedication for a prodigy—he taught himself to play on the piano what had never been played before: tremolos, leaps, double trills, glissandos, simultaneous octaves in both hands, all at breathtaking speed. When he returned to the stage for his own concerts, he overwhelmed the audience. He had become the greatest pianist of that era, perhaps of all time.

Then, in 1833, Liszt's life took another unexpected turn. He met the Countess Marie d'Agoult and decided to give up the life of the performing artist in exchange for domestic security. Although she was already married and the mother of two children, she and Liszt eloped, first to Switzerland and then to Italy. Residing in these countries for four years, the couple had three children of their own. (Their youngest daughter would become the wife of Richard Wagner; see Fig. 14–9, page 292.) In Switzerland the natural beauty of the land gave rise to several compositions for solo piano. In Italy a painting by Raphael (1483–1529), a sculpture by Michelangelo (1474–1564), and a reading of the *Divine Comedy* by Dante (1265–1321) inspired other pianistic creations. "Raphael and Michelangelo make Mozart and Beethoven more easy for me to understand," he said at the time. Later he completed and revised these character pieces for the piano in a set called *Années de pèlerinage (Years of Pilgrimage)*.

Beginning in 1839, and continuing until 1847, Liszt once more took to the road as a touring virtuoso. He played more than a thousand concerts: from Ireland to Turkey, from Sweden to Spain, from Portugal to Russia. Everywhere he went the handsome pianist was greeted with the sort of mass hysteria today reserved for rock stars. Audiences of three thousand crowded into the larger halls. Women tried to rip off his silk scarf and white gloves. They fought for a lock of his hair. Lisztomania swept across Europe.

Despite their obvious sensationalism, Liszt's concerts in the 1840s established the format of our modern-day piano recital. He was the first to play entire programs from memory (not reading from music). He was the first to place the piano parallel with the line of the stage so that neither his back nor full face, but rather his extraordinary side profile, was visible to the audience. He was the first to perform on the stage alone—up to that point concerts traditionally had included numerous performers on the program. At first these solo appearances were called "soliloquies," then "recitals," suggesting they were something akin to poetic recitations.

While concertizing in Russia in 1847, Liszt met another married woman who would profoundly change the course of his life—Princess Sayn-Wittgenstein. (He and Marie d'Agoult had separated in 1844.) This new woman persuaded

FIGURE 13–18

Franz Liszt at the age of twenty-four.

FIGURE 13–19

Marie d'Agoult. She was a novelist in her own right, and some of the tracts on music that appeared under Liszt's name were probably penned by her. Like many female writers of the day, including George Sand and George Eliot, she wrote under a masculine *nom de plume*, Daniel Stern.

FIGURE 13-20

Lisztomania. A recital by Liszt in the mid-nineteenth century was likely to create the sort of sensation that a concert by a rock star might generate today. As Liszt modestly said, "Le concert, c'est moi!"

him to give up the life of an itinerant virtuoso and concentrate on composing. Liszt accepted a position at the court of Weimar, Germany, and took up residence with his new mistress. Because a full orchestra was now at his disposal at Weimar, he produced a steady stream of large-scale orchestral works. In 1861 the couple moved to Rome, where it was hoped that the princess would secure a divorce. When this was not forthcoming, Liszt entered the lower Holy Orders of the Roman Church, styled himself "Abbé Liszt," and for a while even lived in the Vatican! But he continued traveling and performing to the very end. He died at the age of seventy-five in Bayreuth, Germany, where he had gone to hear the latest opera of his son-in-law, Richard Wagner.

Liszt's compositions

Liszt wrote a dozen symphonic poems*—one-movement works for orchestra that capture the spirit and sentiments of a preexisting story, literary theme, or poetic idea—as well as two program symphonies* and three piano concertos. He also composed more than sixty religious works, including two oratorios*, almost all dating from his stay in Rome. In his instrumental music Liszt developed the idea of "thematic transformation," in which a single main theme and its offshoots dominate an entire movement or all the movements of a work. In this he was carrying forward Berlioz's use of an *idée fixe* (see page 257).

Liszt the virtuoso

But Liszt was first and foremost a pianist, and it is for his piano music that he is known above all else. If Chopin composed in a way that made the piano sound at its best, Liszt wrote in a style that made him sound best at the piano. He had large hands and unusually long fingers (see Fig. 13–18). He could play a melody in octaves when others could play only the single notes of the line. If others could execute a passage in octaves, Liszt could dash it off in more impressive-sounding tenths. So he wrote daredevil music of this sort. His *Transcendental Etudes* and *Hungarian Rhapsodies* are among the most difficult pieces ever written for piano. Only the most skilled virtuosos attempt them.

FIGURE 13–21
The aged Liszt, still dazzling audiences and destroying pianos, executing what appears to be the "eight-hand trick."

LIEBESTRAUM (LOVE-DREAM) NO. 3 (1850)

During the late 1840s Franz Liszt set to music three Romantic love poems and entitled them *Liebesträume*. In 1850 he returned to these three *Lieder* and arranged them for a piano solo, now calling each one a "nocturne"—a **nocturne,** or night piece, is a slow, introspective type of piano music suggesting moonlit nights, romantic longing, and a certain painful melancholy. The melody of the third *Liebestraum* has remained a favorite down to the present day, having been reworked in this century into more than one popular song and movie theme.

the nocturne

Liszt was a piano virtuoso and showman, and to everything he touched—even a gentle nocturne—he brought pianistic razzle-dazzle. At the beginning of *Liebestraum* he performs the "three-hand trick." The treble and bass make up two musical lines, with the melody, a third line, couched in the middle range. Sometimes played by the thumb of the left hand and sometimes by the thumb of the right, the middle part suggests the presence of a third hand (see first example in the next Listening Guide). Soon the melody returns, and the technical display grows more complex and demanding. Finally, in a third and last statement of the theme, Liszt implies the presence of four hands by creating four very different musical lines: (1) a harmonic bass, (2) an arpeggiated inner voice, (3) a lyrical melody, and (4) a two-chord counterpoint to the melody high in the treble. To bring off this "four-hand trick," the left hand must quickly pass over the right and play in the highest register (see second example in the Listening Guide). In *Liebestraum*, poetry and wizardry unite in an artistry of the highest order.

LISTENING GUIDE

Franz Liszt
Liebestraum No. 3 (1850)

6CD 4/5
6Tape 4A

0:00   Theme, part 1, in middle voice

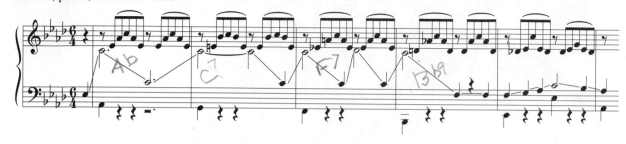

0:42   Theme, part 2, rises upward
1:24   Rapid flourish of thirds and sixths leads to
1:34   Return of theme, now in the high register
2:02   Theme, part 2, played by right hand in octaves
2:45   A whirlwind of seconds, thirds, and arpeggios
3:01   Theme returns in soprano, with left hand crossing over to play chords in the highest range

3:57   Coda: chromatic chords, bold harmonic shift, dissonance resolving to consonance

---

LISTENING EXERCISES

29   Franz Schubert   6CD 3/10; 6Tape 3B
           Art song, *Erlking* (1815)   3CD 2/15; 3Tape 2B

Schubert was a master at bringing to life the essential characters and sentiments of the poetry he set to music. This exercise suggests how he used two very basic musical elements, a shift in mode and a change in the accompaniment, to intensify Goethe's dramatic ballad *Erlking*.

1. (0:00–0:22) Is this opening section, with rapidly repeating notes in the right hand of the accompanist and an ominous motive below in the left, written in a major key or a minor key? _____

2. (1:30–1:52) When the Erlking enters, does he sing in a major key or a minor key? _____

3. (1:30–1:52) Is the ominous motive still heard in the accompaniment in this passage? _____

4. (1:55–2:06) As the son returns to speak, what happens in the piano accompaniment?
   a. Rapidly repeating notes return in the accompanist's right hand and the mode shifts from major to minor.
   b. Rapidly repeating notes return in the accompanist's left hand and the mode shifts from minor to major.

5. (2:18–2:34) For the second appearance of the Erlking, which is true?
   a. Arpeggios replace the rapidly repeating notes in the right hand and the mode is major.
   b. The rapidly repeating notes in the right hand continue and the mode is minor.

6. (3:06–3:17) For the third and final appearance of the Erlking, which is true?
   a. The repeating notes in the right hand continue and the mode changes quickly from major to minor.
   b. The accompaniment pattern changes to arpeggios in the right hand and the mode remains in major throughout.

7. (3:47–3:58) How does Schubert tell us that the galloping horse has arrived at the inn?
   a. The piano accompaniment stops abruptly.
   b. The piano accompaniment gradually ritards and then comes to a stop.

8. (4:06–4:11) How does Schubert emphatically emphasize that the child has died and that there will be no happy ending?
   a. He writes an abrupt V–I cadence in a major key.
   b. He writes an abrupt V–I cadence in a minor key.

9. Excluding the narrator, how many characters are portrayed in Schubert's *Erlking*? _____

10. How many voices actually sing the *Lied**? _____

<table>
<tr><td>30</td><td>Hector Berlioz
Symphonie fantastique (1830)
Fifth movement, Dream of the Witches' Sabbath</td><td>6CD 4/1; 6Tape 4A
3CD 3/1; 3Tape 3A</td></tr>
</table>

Imagine that you were among the audience in Paris on December 5, 1830, when Berlioz's *Symphonie fantastique* was first performed. If you had been a dedicated concertgoer up to that time, you might have heard one or two of the late symphonies of Beethoven. This would have been the extent of your exposure to "radical" new music. How would you have reacted? Of course, it is now impossible to gauge the impact of Berlioz's progressive gestures—our ears have become accustomed to them in the music of other, later composers. The following set of questions asks you to focus on a few special aspects of orchestration and form in this astonishing work. As always, be sure that you have read the discussion of this movement in the text (page 259) and have listened to it at least once following the Listening Guide (page 260).

1. (0:00–0:09) The opening sounds eerie because the high strings are divided into many parts and are playing with a special string technique. What is this technique called?
   a. pizzicato   b. tremolo   c. ostinato

2. (0:19–0:23) Now another string technique is employed by the upper strings. Which is it?
   a. pizzicato   b. tremolo   c. ostinato

3. (1:28–2:16) The *idée fixe*, now transformed, returns in a high clarinet, is cut off, and then begins again. Previously in the symphony Berlioz has cast it sometimes in duple and sometimes in triple meter. Which meter do you feel here?
   a. duple   b. triple

4. (2:39–2:56) The "sinister transition" leading to the introduction of the *Dies irae* chant is a gradual descent. By which family is it mainly carried out?
   a. string   b. woodwind   c. brass

5. (3:48) The French horns now play the *Dies irae* theme twice as fast as before. What is this sort of reduction of note values in music called?
   _____

6. (4:28–4:47) In this passage the *Dies irae* melody continues in the low brasses against a pounding sound produced by the bass drum. Which of the following is true?
   a. The low brasses are playing the melody on the downbeat while the bass drum syncopates against it.
   b. The bass drum is playing on the downbeat while the low brasses syncopate against it.

7. (5:21–5:44) Now the fugato begins. Its structure is made clear, in part, because the composer cuts off the subject each time so as to announce the next entry. He does this by means of a burst of syncopated chords in the brasses. How many times does this occur? _____

8. (7:04–7:18) Which instruments play a reminiscence of the *Dies irae* chant?
   a. bells   b. tubas   c. cellos and double basses

9. (8:06–8:27) Now the *Dies irae* and the witches' dance (fugue subject) are heard simultaneously. How are they orchestrated?
   a. *Dies irae* in violins, witches' dance in trumpets
   b. *Dies irae* in trumpets, witches' dance in violins

10. (8:35–8:48) As the strings produce the crackling sound by playing *col legno* (with the wood of the bow and not the horsehair), a melody is heard in the woodwinds. Which is it?
    a. the *idée fixe*
    b. the *Dies irae* chant
    c. the witches' dance (fugue subject)

31	Clara Wieck Schumann Romance for Piano and Violin, Opus 22, No. 3 (1853)	6CD 4/3 6Tape 4A

Clara Schumann's Romance consists of a lovely melody with two parts (**a** and **b**), played mostly by the violin, and an accompaniment, furnished mainly by the piano. The piano usually plays the accompaniment as arpeggios, but sometimes plays chords. Occasionally, moreover, the roles of the instruments are reversed, with the piano now not only providing the accompaniment but also playing the melody, while the violin either joins in the accompaniment or sets a counterpoint against the melody. Four different ways in which the musical material is allocated to the piano are identified here as A, B, C, and D. Indicate which musical arrangement governs at the important musical moments listed below.

A. piano plays accompaniment only as arpeggios (violin has melody)
B. piano plays accompaniment only as chords (violin has melody)
C. piano plays melody and its own accompaniment as arpeggios
D. piano plays melody and its own accompaniment as chords

0:00 _____	2:32 _____	3:55 _____
1:34 _____	2:47 _____	4:12 _____
1:53 _____	3:00 _____	
2:11 _____	3:34 _____	

---

32 Frédéric Chopin
Polonaise in A major, Opus 40, No. 1,
The "Military" Polonaise (1838)

6CD 4/4; 6Tape 4A
3CD 3/2; 3Tape 3A

As mentioned in the previous discussion of this piece (page 271), the form of Chopin's "Military" Polonaise is unusually rigid for the free-spirited Romantic period: **aba cdc aba.** The explanation for this apparent contradiction is simple: Chopin is recreating a traditional dance as practiced in the more formally rigid eighteenth century. Yet there is more to the form of this polonaise than **aba cdc aba.** Here, as often happens when a composer chooses to write in ternary form, the **a** and then the **ba** sections (and similarly the **c** and the **cd** sections of the trio) are each repeated. Thus the complete form of the work is ‖:a:‖:ba:‖:c:‖:dc:‖ etc. To sharpen your ability to recognize musical repeats, you are first asked in this exercise to indicate the moments at which the repeats commence. To keep things clear, the times for the first statements of each of the sections are provided for you.

A
0:00 **a**
1. _:_ **a** repeated
   0:35 **ba**
2. _:_ **ba** repeated
B
1:49 **c**
3. _:_ **c** repeated
   3:05 **cd**
4. _:_ **cd** repeated
A
5:05 **a**
etc.

5. When the Polonaise (**A**) returns (5:05–6:02), which of the following is true?
   a. **a** and **ba** are each repeated just as before.
   b. **a** and **ba** are played straight through without repeats.

Now answer the following questions.

6. Which of the following is true with regard to the dynamic level of this polonaise?
   a. It is predominately *forte* or *fortissimo* throughout.
   b. It is predominately *piano* or *pianissimo* throughout.

7. Which of the following is true with regard to the tempo?
   a. There are frequent changes in tempo and much use of tempo *rubato*.
   b. The tempo is uniform, indeed strict, throughout.

8. Which is true with regard to the meter?
   a. There is duple meter from beginning to end.
   b. There is triple meter from beginning to end.
   c. Duple and triple meter alternate.

9. Which is true about the texture?
   a. It is homophonic throughout.
   b. It is polyphonic throughout.
   c. It is monophonic throughout.

10. Finally, considering the form, the dynamics, the tempo, the meter, and the texture, would you say Chopin's "Military" Polonaise exhibits a single feeling, or spirit, from beginning to end, or many different feelings?
    a. is emotionally one-dimensional
    b. is emotionally multidimensional

KEY WORDS

col legno	Gewandhaus	polonaise
cornet	Orchestra	recital
Dies irae	Harriet Smithson	romance
diminution	*idée fixe*	Schubertiade
double	Lisztomania	song cycle
counterpoint	modified strophic form	strophic form
English horn	nocturne	through-
George Sand	ophicleide	composed

A checklist of musical style in the Romantic period is given on page 66.

ROMANTIC OPERA

14

T he nineteenth century is often called "the golden age of opera." It is the century of Rossini, Bellini, Donizetti, Verdi, Wagner, Gounod, Bizet, and early Puccini. Even today, two-thirds of the operas produced by the San Francisco Opera Company, the Metropolitan Opera in New York, Covent Garden in London, and La Scala in Milan, for example, are works written during the years 1820–1900.

Italy, of course, is the home of opera. The Italian language, with its evenly spaced, open vowels, is perfectly suited for singing, and the people of Italy seem to have an innate love of melody. The first operas were created, beginning around 1600, for the cities of Florence, Rome, Venice, and Mantua (see page 106). For nearly two centuries Italian opera dominated the international stage. When Handel wrote operas for London in the 1720s, for example, he composed Italian operas, as did Mozart when he created musical theater for the courts of Germany and Austria in the 1770s and 1780s. With the onset of the nineteenth century, however, other peoples, driven by an emerging sense of national pride, developed idiomatic opera in their native tongues. Although Italian opera remained the dominant style, it now had to share the stage, not only with traditional French opera, but with the newer forms of Russian, Czech, and especially German opera as well.

ROMANTIC OPERA IN ITALY

During the early decades of the nineteenth century, the primacy of Italian opera was maintained almost single-handedly by Gioachino Rossini (1792–1868). Surprising as it may seem today, Rossini was the most popular composer of the 1820s, far exceeding in celebrity Beethoven and Schubert. He owed his public favor not only to the charm of his music but also to the fact that the genre of music within which he chose to work—opera—was then the most popular form of public musical entertainment, much more so than the symphony or string quartet, for example. Rossini continued, and indeed brought to a glorious close, the eighteenth-century tradition of comic opera, or *opera buffa* (see page 153). Catchy, oft-repeating melodies, vivacious rhythms, and rollicking crescendos were his trademarks. His best-known comic opera, *The Barber of Seville*, has

FIGURE 14–1

Gioachino Rossini.

never disappeared from the operatic stage since it first appeared in 1816. Even casual music lovers know a little of this enduring work in the form of the "Figaro, Figaro, Figaro" call from the opening aria for the resourceful barber, Figaro. Rossini could also write in a more serious style, as exemplified in his last opera, *William Tell* (1829). This stormy drama, too, has achieved a measure of popular immortality, the overture providing the theme music for the radio and film character of the Lone Ranger.

Italian *Bel Canto* Opera

Whereas German operatic composers would come to emphasize the dramatic power and instrumental color of the orchestra, Italians after Rossini increasingly focused all of their energies on the solo voice and on melody—on the art of beautiful singing, or **bel canto**. The two most gifted of the early creators of this more serious *bel canto* opera were Gaetano Donizetti (1797–1848) and Vincenzo Bellini (1801–1835). In their works there is little orchestral color and almost no counterpoint. The orchestra merely provides a simple harmonic support for the soaring, sometimes divinely beautiful lines of the voice. Look at the opening of the famous aria "Casta diva" from Bellini's *Norma* (1831), in which the heroine sings a prayer to a distant moon goddess. Here the orchestra functions like a giant guitar. Simple chords are fleshed out as arpeggios by the strings while an even simpler bass line is plucked below. All of the musical interest is in the rapturous sound of the human voice. "Opera must make people weep, shudder, die through the singing," Bellini said.

EXAMPLE 14–1

(Chaste goddess, who does bathe in silver light these hallowed, ancient trees)

Not surprisingly, by placing such importance on the solo singer, *bel canto* opera fostered an environment in which was bound to flourish a star system among the cast. Usually, it was the lyric soprano—heroine and "prima donna"—who held the most exalted position in the musical firmament. By the *cult of the diva* 1880s, she would be called a **diva,** which, as in the aria "Casta diva," means "goddess." Indeed, the goddess of the beautiful female voice would rule Italian opera right through the nineteenth century, from the early *bel canto* operas of Donizetti and Bellini through the mature works of Giuseppe Verdi (1813–1901) and Giacomo Puccini (1858–1924).

Giuseppe Verdi (1813–1901)

The name Giuseppe Verdi is virtually synonymous with Italian opera. For six decades, from the time of *Nabucco* in 1842 until *Falstaff* in 1893, he had almost no rival for the affections of the opera-loving public in Italy and elsewhere throughout Europe. Even today the best-loved of the twenty-six operas of Verdi are more readily available—in opera houses, in TV productions, and on videotape—than those of any other composer.

Verdi was born near Busseto in northern Italy in 1813, the son of a tavern keeper. He was apparently no musical prodigy, for at the age of eighteen he was rejected for admission to the Conservatory of Music in Milan because he was already too old and his piano technique faulty. But Verdi stayed on in Milan to study composition. He returned to Busseto in 1835 to serve as the town's bandmaster, and then four years later went back to Milan to earn his livelihood as a composer.

To be a composer in nineteenth-century Italy was to be a composer of opera. Verdi's first, *Oberto,* was produced at the famous La Scala Opera House in Milan (Fig. 14–3) in 1839, and it achieved a modicum of success. But his *Nabucco* of 1842 was a popular triumph, receiving an unprecedented fifty-seven performances at La Scala in that year alone. Through subsequent productions in other theaters, Verdi's name was quickly carried throughout Italy, Europe, and both North and South America. His career was launched.

FIGURE 14–2
Giuseppe Verdi.

FIGURE 14–3
La Scala Opera House about 1830. Verdi's first four and last two operas had their premieres at La Scala, the foremost opera house in Italy.

The text, or libretto*, of *Nabucco*, as well as most of the other operas Verdi composed in the 1840s, concerns the suppression of a people by a cruel foreign power—and by implication the people of Italy by Austria, which then ruled much of the peninsula. Verdi had become a spirited liberal and an Italian patriot. Normally, we do not think of music as expressing political ideas, but opera was such an important part of Italian popular culture that it had the capacity to inspire political revolution. In his libretti Verdi inserted and then set for chorus or solo voice such fiery words as "You may have the universe, so long as I keep Italy" and "Long live Italy! A sacred pact binds all her sons." Partly through such patriotic music and partly by accident, Verdi became a leader in the Risorgimento, the movement for a united Italy free of foreign domination. By handy coincidence, the letters of the composer's last name produced an acronym for **V**ittorio **E**manuele **R**e **d'I**talia (King Victor Emanuel being the people's choice for the throne of a united Kingdom of Italy). Thus, cries of "Viva, Verdi!" echoed throughout Italy in hopes of unification. In 1861, after that goal had been largely achieved, Verdi was elected to the country's first parliament, and later, in 1874, to its senate.

Verdi, a voice for Italian independence

But in the late 1840s the drive for Italian independence was far from complete. Indeed, the liberal Revolution of 1848 failed to oust the Austrians from Milan, and Verdi for a time became disillusioned with politics. He now turned his attention to domestic themes and more personal drama, producing a trio of much-admired operas: *Rigoletto* (1851), *La traviata* (1853), and *Il trovatore* (1853). For most of the early-to-mid-1850s, Verdi lived away from the area of Milan, residing in Paris or traveling throughout Europe to oversee the production of his increasingly numerous works. He called these years of toil and intense productivity "my years as a galley slave."

On his return to his homeland in 1857, the pace of Verdi's opera production slackened. He composed only when the subject was of interest or the fee so substantial he couldn't refuse. *La forza del destino* (*The Force of Destiny*, 1861) was written for St. Petersburg for the enormous commission of 60,000 francs; *Don Carlos* (1867) was composed for Paris for an equally large amount; and *Aïda* (1871), written for Cairo shortly after the opening of the Suez Canal, for the astonishing sum of 150,000 francs. Verdi had become more than a little wealthy, and he retired to his estate in northern Italy to lead the life of a country squire—or so he thought.

FIGURE 14–4

Verdi's long-time mistress and, ultimately, his wife, Giuseppina Strepponi (1815–1897) holding the score of his early opera *Nabucco*.

But like a performer who feels he owes the audience more, or has something more to prove to himself, Verdi returned to the theater for two final encores: *Otello* (1887) and *Falstaff* (1893), both exceptionally well-crafted operas based on dramas of Shakespeare. The latter work was written when the composer was on the threshold of eighty, a feat without parallel in music history or the annals of the dramatic stage. He died peacefully at his country home in 1901, a much-respected national institution.

VERDI'S DRAMATURGY AND MUSICAL STYLE. When the curtain goes up on a Verdi opera, the listener will find elements of dramaturgy—how the drama is put together—and musical style that are unique to this composer. For Giuseppe Verdi conflict was at the root of every emotion, and he expressed conflict, whether personal or national, by juxtaposing self-contained, yet clearly differentiated, units of music. A rousing march, a patriotic chorus, a passionate recitative, and a lyrical aria follow one after the other in quick succession. In each vivid number there is no mistaking which emotion is being communicated to the audience. The composer aims not at musical and dramatic subtlety but rather at immediate effect and direct appeal to the listener's sensibilities. The emotional states of the characters are so clearly drawn, sometimes overdrawn, that the drama comes perilously close to melodrama—excessively sentimental or sensational. But it is never dull. There is action, passion, and intensity. "I would be willing to set even a newspaper, or a letter, to music," he said in 1854, "but in the theater the public will stand for anything except boredom."

each musical number projects a particular emotion

How is this feeling of relentless intensity in a Verdi opera brought about? It is achieved mainly by changing the nature of the recitative and the vocal quality of the aria. Verdi generally continues to use the former to recite or narrate the action and the latter for expression of feeling. But now the old *secco* recitative, with mere keyboard accompaniment, gives way to orchestrally accompanied recitative (**recitativo accompagnato**). This allows the action to flow smoothly from orchestrally accompanied aria to orchestrally accompanied recitative and back without a jarring change of texture. Moreover, Verdi is still very much a composer in the Italian *bel canto* tradition of Bellini and Donizetti. The emphasis throughout remains on the solo aria, on a lyrical, beautiful vocal line. No composer had a greater gift for writing simple, memorable melodies that the audience could whistle on the way out of the theater. Yet Verdi also adds intensity and passion to these arias by pushing the singers to the utmost of their range. The tenor is asked to sing up to the B above middle C, the soprano two octaves and more above middle C. The thrilling moments in which the hero (the tenor) or the heroine (the soprano) go right to the top are literally the high points of any Verdi opera.

accompanied recitative allows action to flow

a composer of bel canto *opera*

LA TRAVIATA (1853)

We may measure the high intensity and passion in Verdi's operas by listening to a portion of his *La traviata* (1853). *La traviata* literally means "The Woman Gone Astray." It tells the story of the sickly Violetta Valery, a courtesan, or "kept woman," who resists and then succumbs to the love of a new suitor, the young Alfredo Germont. For a while the couple retires from Paris to lead a quiet life in the country. But without explanation Violetta deserts Alfredo, in truth so that her former life will not bring disgrace on his respectable family. The hot-tempered Alfredo now publicly insults Violetta, fights a duel with her new "protector," and is banished from France. When the nature of Violetta's sacrifice is revealed, Alfredo rushes back but arrives only a short time before she dies.

Verdi first heard this sentimental tale, one that pits passionate love against middle-class morality, when in Paris during the winter of 1852. There he and his mistress, the singer Giuseppina Strepponi (Fig. 14–4), were captivated by a new play of Alexandre Dumas the younger entitled *The Lady of the Camellias*, now known to English audiences simply as *Camille*. The main character of the drama, Violetta Valery, was modeled after a real-life figure, Marie Duplessis (Fig. 14–5), who had been the mistress of playwright Dumas and, briefly, of composer Franz Liszt as well. Like many in this period, she, too, died young of tuberculosis, at the age of twenty-three. Verdi's compassion toward this heroine probably was

FIGURE 14–5

Marie Duplessis. The end of her brief, scandalous life is the subject of Giuseppe Verdi's opera *La traviata*.

FIGURE 14–6

The great Australian soprano Joan Sutherland singing the role of Violetta and tenor Luciano Pavarotti as Alfredo in Verdi's *La traviata*.

sparked by the fact that his mistress, too, was held in general disrepute at this time, having by then given birth to four illegitimate children.

We join *La traviata* toward the end of the first act. A gala party is in progress in a fashionable Parisian salon, and here the dashing Alfredo has finally managed to cut Violetta away from the crowd to profess to her his love. He does so in the aria "Un dì felice" ("One Happy Day"), which is lovely, yet somber in tone. The seriousness of his intent is underscored by the slow, square, even plodding accompaniment in the orchestra. When Violetta enters she is supported by the same accompaniment, but the mood of the aria is radically changed to one that is light and carefree. Witness how Verdi's direct musical characterization works: Alfredo's slow melody with a hint of minor is replaced by Violetta's flighty sound of high, rapidly moving notes. Eventually, the two join in a duet: he below, somberly proclaiming the mysteries of love; she above, making light of them.

After the duet has come to a cadence, a friend, Gaston, briefly interrupts, singing in accompanied recitative. But soon the voices of Alfredo and Violetta are once more joined. The tempo of the music increases and so does their growing ardor for each other, shown musically by the way the singers rush in breathlessly on successively higher notes. This rapid, final portion of the duet is called a **cabaletta**—the concluding fast section of any two- or three-section aria complex. The cabaletta was an oft-used dramatic device in Italian opera because the increased speed of the music allowed one or both of the singers to race off stage at the end of a scene or act. Here Alfredo kisses Violetta's hand and excitedly departs.

LISTENING GUIDE

Giuseppe Verdi
La traviata (1853)
Act I, Scene 4

6CD 4/6
6Tape 4A

Characters: Alfredo, a young man of good standing; Violetta, a kept woman leading a wanton life in Paris
Situation: A party in a Parisian salon around 1850; Alfredo professes his love to Violetta, who at first rejects him.

Aria

		Alfredo (tenor)	
0:00		Un dì felice, eterea,	One happy day,
		Mi balanaste innante,	you appeared to me.
		E da quel dì tremante	And from this day, trembling,
		Vissi d'ignoto amor.	I have lived in that
		Di quell'amor ch'è palpito	unspoken love, in that love
		Dell'universo intero,	which animates the world,
	Shift to minor	Misterioso, altero,	mysterious, proud, pain
		Croce e delizia al cor.	and delight to the heart.

		Violetta (soprano)	
1:22	Violetta changes aria to lighter mood	Ah, se ciò èver, fugitemi.	If that's true, leave me.
	through faster tempo and shorter notes	Solo amistade io v'offro;	Only friendship I offer you.
		Amar non so, nè soffro	I don't know how to love
		Un cosi eroico amore.	or suffer such a heroic love.
		Io sono franca, ingenua;	I'm being honest and sincere.
		Altra cercar dovete;	You must find another.
		Non arduo troverete	It won't be difficult.
		Dimenticarmi allor.	Just leave me.

(Duet)

		Alfredo	
1:46	Alfredo and Violetta together	Oh amore!	Oh love!
	in rapturous duet	Misterioso, altero,	mysterious, proud, pain
		Croce e delizia al cor.	and delight to the heart.

			Violetta
		Non arduo troverete	It won't be difficult.
		Dimenticarmi allor.	Just leave me.
2:48	Exuberant vocal flourishes for both	"Ah"	"Ah"
			Gaston
Recitative			
3:26	Gaston interrupts	Ebben? che diavol fate?	Well, what the devil's going on?
			Violetta
		Si folleggiava!	Just fooling around.
			Gaston
		Ah, ah, sta ben! restate!	Well then, continue!
Strains of a waltz heard from ballroom			
			Violetta
(Duet)			
3:35	Continues as dialogue	Amor dunque non più.	Well then, no more about love!
		Vi garba il patto?	Is that a promise?
			Alfredo
		Io v'obbedisco. Parto.	I'll obey you. I'm leaving.
			Violetta
		A tal giungeste	So it's come to that already?
		(Si toglie un fiore	(She takes a flower from
		dal seno.)	her bosom.)
		Predete questo fiore.	Take this flower.
			Alfredo
		Perchè?	Why?
			Violetta
		Per riportarlo.	So that you can bring it back.
			Alfredo
		Quando?	When?
			Violetta
		Quando sarà appassito.	When it's withered.
			Alfredo
		O ciel! Domani?	Good god, you mean tomorrow?
			Violetta
		Ebben, domani.	Oh well, tomorrow.
			Alfredo
Cabaletta			
4:01	Tempo increases	Io son, Io son felice!	I'm so happy.
			Violetta
		D'amarmi dite ancora?	Do you still say you love me?
			Alfredo
		Oh! quanto v'amo!	Oh, how much I love you.
		Io son felice.	I'm so happy.
			Violetta
		Partite?	Are you going?
			Alfredo
		Parto.	I'm going.
			Violetta
		Addio.	Adieu.
			Alfredo
		Di più non bramo.	I need nothing more.
		Addio. (esce)	Adieu. (exits)

The musical-dramatic design of the concluding scene of Act I of *La traviata* shows a similar tripartite structure: aria, brief recitative, cabaletta. Violetta is left alone on stage. She reveals, in a slow strophic aria, "Ah, fors'è lui" ("Ah, perhaps he's the one"), that Alfredo may be the lover she has long desired. But then, in an impassioned recitative ("Folly! Folly! What sort of crazy dream is this!"), she jumps to her feet to proclaim that she must always remain free of the entanglements of serious love. This aria, "Sempre libera" ("Always free") is one of the great showpieces for soprano voice. Yet it also helps define through music the character of Violetta—the extraordinary, carefree flourishes on the word "pleasure," for example, reinforce her "enjoy-ourselves-while-we-may" approach to life. This declaration of independence is momentarily broken by the voice of Alfredo, who from outside her window expresses again his feelings about the mysterious powers of love. Violetta brushes these aside and repeats her vow always to be free. Of course, she does not remain emotionally free; she falls fatally in love with Alfredo as Acts II and III reveal. Listen now to the final scene of Act I of Verdi's *La traviata*. You will have the pleasure of hearing two of the greatest voices of the twentieth century, Joan Sutherland (soprano) and Luciano Pavarotti (tenor).

aria-recitative-cabaletta

LISTENING GUIDE

Giuseppe Verdi
La traviata (1853)
Act I, Scene 5

6CD 4/7
6Tape 4B

Characters: Violetta and Alfredo (outside her window)
Situation: Violetta at first believes Alfredo to be the passionate love she has long sought, but then rejects this notion, vowing to remain free.

Aria

First strophe

0:00	Soprano sings first phrase	Ah, fors'è lui che l'anima Solinga ne' tumulti	Ah, perhaps he's the one whom my lonely heart
0:35	First phrase repeated	Godea sovente pingere De' suoi colori occulti.	delighted often to paint with vague, mysterious colors.
0:58	Voice rises up in melodic sequence	Lui, che modesto e vigile All'egre sogli ascese, E nuova febbre accese Destandomi all'amor!	He who, so modest and attentive during my illness, waited and with youthful fervor aroused me again to love!
1:24	Return of Alfredo's major-key refrain from previous aria	A quell'amor ch'è palpito Dell'universo intero, Misterioso altero, Croce e delizia al cor.	To that love which animates the universe, mysterious, proud, pain and delight to the heart.

Second strophe

2:26	Return of first phrase	A me, fanciulla, un candido E trepido desire,	To me, a girl, this was an innocent, anxious desire,
2:53	First phrase repeated	Quest'effigiò dolcissimo Signor dell'avvenire.	this sweet vision, lord of things to come.
3:17	Voice rises up in melodic sequence	Quando ne' cieli il raggio Di sua beltà vedea E tuta me pascea Di quel divino error.	When in the heavens I saw rays of his beauty I fed myself completely on that divine error.
3:44	Return of Alfredo's major-key refrain from previous aria	Sentia che amore è il palpito Dell'universo intero, Misterioso altero, Croce e delizia al cor.	I felt that love which animates the universe, mysterious, proud, pain and delight to the heart.
4:18	Highly ornamental final cadence with lengthy trill		

6CD 4/8; 6Tape 4B; 3CD 3/3; 3Tape 3A

Recitative

0:00	Accompanied by orchestra	**Violetta**	
		Follie! Follie! delirio vano è questo! Povera donna, sola, abbandonata, in questo populoso deserto che appellano Parigi. Che spero or più? Che far degg'io?	**Violetta** Folly! Folly! What sort of crazy dream is this! Poor woman, alone, adandoned in this populated desert that they call Paris. What hope have I? What can I do?
0:49	Flights of vocal fancy as she thinks of pleasure	Gioir! Di voluttà ne' vortici perir! Gioir!	Pleasure! Perish in a whirl of indulgence! Pleasure!
1:05	Introduction to cabaletta		

Cabaletta

1:16		**Violetta** Sempre libera degg'io Folleggiare di gioia in gioia, Vo' che scorra il viver mio Pei sentieri del piacer. Nasca il giorno, o il giorno muoia, Sempre lieta ne' ritrovi, A diletti sempre nuovi Dee volare il mio pensier.	**Violetta** Always free I must remain to reel from pleasure to pleasure, running my life along the paths of joy. From dawn to dusk I'm always happy finding new delights that make my spirit soar.
2:01	Echoes of his previous aria	**Alfredo** Amor è palpito dell'universo, misterioso, altero, croce e delizia al cor.	**Alfredo** Love that animates the world, mysterious, proud, pain and delight to the heart.
2:48	Extravagant flourishes	**Violetta** Follie! Follie! Gioir! Gioir!	**Violetta** Folly! Folly! Pleasure! Pleasure!

Cabaletta returns

3:17	this time even more brilliant in its showy, superficial style	Sempre libera . . .	Always free . . .

(Listening Exercise 33)

ROMANTIC OPERA IN GERMANY

Before 1820, opera was mainly an Italian affair. It was first created in Italy around 1600 and then, during the next two hundred years, was exported to all parts of Europe and eventually to North and South America. But German opera, by comparison, was rather weak and provincial. Before 1820 the only German opera heard outside German-speaking lands was Mozart's *Die Zauberflöte* (*The Magic Flute*, 1791), which owed its widespread appeal to the glories of Mozart's music rather than any fondness for the somewhat primitive conventions of German opera.

What passed as native opera in German-speaking lands went by the name of *Singspiel*. **A Singspiel** ("singing play") is a musical comedy or light musical drama that has, by sheer coincidence, many elements in common with our present-day

FIGURE 14–7
Richard Wagner.

Broadway musical: plenty of topical humor, tuneful solo songs, energetic choral numbers, and spoken dialogue instead of sung recitative. Mozart, in *The Magic Flute* (1791), and Beethoven, in his only opera, *Fidelio* (1805), each wrote a *Singspiel* in which he tried to bring greater seriousness and unity to the genre. A somewhat younger contemporary of Beethoven, Karl Maria von Weber (1786–1826), likewise attempted to develop a tradition of serious German opera distinct from the Italian style. His *Der Freischütz* (1821) makes use of German folk songs, or folklike melodies, as well as a libretto that delights in magic and the supernatural. (Its most memorable moment is the "Wolf Glen" scene at the beginning of the second act during which magical silver bullets are cast in a Satanic ritual.) The German passion for horror subjects and supernatural tales in the Romantic period can be seen in other works, such as Heinrich Marschner's *The Vampire* (1828) and Richard Wagner's *The Flying Dutchman* (1843).

Richard Wagner (1813–1883)

The composer who made the German dream of a truly national opera a reality was the titanic figure Richard Wagner. Wagner was not merely a composer but also a politician, philosopher, propagandist, and bully for his particular vision of dramatic music. For Wagner, opera was the most perfect form of artistic expression and the composer a religious prophet who could reveal a musical kingdom to his congregation, namely, the listening audience. Wagner's music is, indeed, often inspiring. It contains moments of grandeur unmatched by any other composer. His influence on the musical style of other composing musicians at the end of the nineteenth century was enormous. Yet his reception by the musical public at large, then and now, has been divided. Some listeners are immediately converted to adoring Wagnerites at the first sound of the heroic themes and powerful orchestral climaxes. Others are left cold, believing the music long-winded and the operatic plots devoid of real human drama.

a controversial artist

Who was this controversial artist who has stirred such mixed feelings within the musical public for more than a century? Richard Wagner was born into a theatrical family in Leipzig, Germany, in 1813. His first passion was not music but poetry, drama, and the theater. Only in his late teens, when he began to immerse himself in the music of Beethoven, did he begin to consider music as a profession. He made piano transcriptions* of the orchestral music of Beethoven, and took lessons in composition from the cantor of Leipzig's St. Thomas's Church, old Bach's church (see page 128). After a succession of jobs as an opera director in several small German towns, Wagner and his young family moved to Paris in 1839 in hopes of seeing his first opera produced there. Instead of meeting success in Paris, as had Liszt and Chopin before him, Wagner was greeted by thundering indifference. No one could be persuaded to produce his work. Reduced to poverty, he spent a brief sojourn in a Parisian prison for nonpayment of debts.

early years

When Wagner's big break came it was not in Paris but back home in his native Germany, in the city of Dresden. His opera *Rienzi* was given a hearing there in October 1842 and generated such an enthusiastic response that the composer was offered the post of opera director for this important city. During the next six years three additional German Romantic operas by Wagner were given there as

first operas

well: *The Flying Dutchman* (1844), *Tannhäuser* (1845), and *Lohengrin* (1848). In the aftermath of the political revolution that swept much of Europe in 1848, Wagner was forced to flee Dresden, though in truth he took flight as much to avoid his creditors as to escape any repressive government.

Wagner found a safe haven in Switzerland, which was to be his home, on and off, for the next dozen years. Exiled now from the major opera houses in Germany, he began to imagine a complex of music dramas on a vast and unprecedented scale. What he ultimately created was *Der Ring des Nibelungen (The Ring of the Nibelung)*, a set of four operas intended to be performed during the course of four successive evenings. *Das Rheingold*, the first, lasts 2½ hours; *Die Walküre* and *Siegfried* each run nearly 4½; while the finale, *Götterdämmerung (Twilight of the Gods)*, goes on for no less than 5½ hours. The thread of a single story runs from beginning to end. But instead of drawing his theme from a play or a set of historical events, Wagner reached back into Germanic legend for his subject matter. The scene is set in the smoky mists of primeval time, in a land of gods, river nymphs, dwarfs, giants, dragons, and sword-wielding heroes.

the Ring *cycle*

Although the plot of the *Ring* is complex in the extreme, it is best viewed as an allegory exploring the themes of power, greed, lust, honor, and bravery in contemporary nineteenth-century society. Power, for example, is symbolized by the ring belonging to the dwarfish Nibelungs, bravery by the exploits of the hero Siegfried. While these are universal themes, they were harmonious with the growing feeling of German national identity. The German philosopher Friedrich Nietzsche (1844–1900), for a time a friend and confidant of Wagner, modeled his concept of the superhero, or superman, on Wagner's heroic character. In the twentieth century, Adolph Hitler would exploit Wagnerian symbolism to foster the notion of a superior German race, building, for example, a Siegfried Line on the Western Front.

plot of the Ring

Needless to say, publishers and producers were at first reluctant to print or mount the operas of Wagner's *Ring*, given their massive scope and fantastic subject matter. They would, however, pay well for the rights to more traditional works by him. So in the midst of his labors on the *Ring* cycle, the always penurious Wagner interrupted the project for a period of years to create *Tristan und Isolde* (1865) and *Die Meistersinger von Nürnberg (The Mastersingers of Nuremberg*, 1868). But these, too, were long and not easy to produce. The bulky scores piled up on his desk.

In 1864 Wagner was rescued from his plight by King Ludwig II of Bavaria, who paid off his debts, gave him an annual allowance, encouraged him to complete the *Ring* tetralogy, and helped him to build a special theater where his giant operas could be mounted according to the composer's own specifications. This opera house, or Festival Theater as Wagner called it, was constructed at Bayreuth, a small town between Munich and Leipzig. The first "Bayreuth Festival" took place in August 1876 with three successive performances of the entire *Ring* cycle. Wagner's last opera, *Parsifal*, premiered there as well, in 1882. Following Wagner's death the next year, his remains were interred on the grounds of the Wagner villa in Bayreuth. To this day the theater at Bayreuth continues to stage the music dramas of Wagner—and only Wagner. Each summer thousands of opera lovers make the pilgrimage to this theatrical shrine to one of art's most determined, and ruthless, visionaries.

FIGURE 14–8

Bayreuth Festival Theater, an opera house built especially to produce the music dramas of Richard Wagner—and only Wagner.

Wagner's "Music Dramas"

With a few very minor exceptions, Richard Wagner wrote only musical works intended for the theater. He did not call these operas, however, but "music dramas." A **music drama** for Wagner was a musical work for the stage in which all the arts—poetry, music, acting, mime, dance, and scenic design—function as a harmonious ensemble. Such an artistic union Wagner referred to as a **Gesamtkunstwerk** ("total art work"). Thus combined, the unified force of the arts would generate real drama. No longer would the dramatic action grind to a halt in order to spotlight the vocal flourishes of a soloist, as often happened in Italian opera.

the Gesamtkunstwerk

Indeed, Wagner's music drama differs from conventional Italian opera in several important ways. First, it is not made up of distinct and separate numbers—aria, recitative, duet, and the like—but of an almost seamless flow of undifferentiated solo singing and declamation. Second, ensemble singing is almost entirely absent—duets, trios, choruses, and full-cast finales—are rare in the extreme. Finally, the tuneful aria is banished to the wings. Wagner avoids repetition, symmetry, and regular cadences—all things that can make a melody "catchy"—in favor of long-flowing, nonrepetitive, not particularly songlike lines. As the tuneful aria decreases in importance, the role of the orchestra increases.

importance of the orchestra

With Wagner the orchestra is everything. It sounds forth the main musical themes, develops and exploits them, and thereby "plays out" the drama through pure instrumental music. On stage the words and actions of the singers give the audience supplementary clues as to what the musical drama in the orchestra is all about. In the 1850s Wagner drank deeply of the philosophy of Arthur Schopenhauer (1788–1860), who wrote that "music expresses the innermost basis of the world, the essence behind appearances." In music drama what hap-

FIGURE 14–9

Cosima Wagner (daughter of Franz Liszt and Marie d'Agoult), Richard Wagner, and Liszt at Wagner's villa in Bayreuth in 1880. At the right is a young admirer of Wagner, Hans von Wolzogen.

pens on the stage is the appearance; what happens in the orchestra is the reality, the essence of the drama.

We have seen that Wagner was one composer of the Romantic era who greatly expanded the size of the orchestra, using triple woodwinds and an enlarged brass section (see page 240). To be heard above an orchestra of nearly a hundred players requires a large, specially trained voice, the so-called Wagnerian tenor and Wagnerian soprano. Yet during moments of climax even these powerful voices are scarcely audible. Imagine an opera of Verdi in which the voice of the hero or heroine cannot be heard. Impossible! But in a music drama of Wagner, the virtual disappearance of the voice does not matter. By design the singer is ultimately consumed by the greater reality of an all-powerful orchestra. Let us see how the orchestra brings this about in Wagner's music drama *Tristan und Isolde*.

TRISTAN UND ISOLDE (1865)

Wagner began to compose *Tristan und Isolde* during 1857 when living in Switzerland and supported in part by a wealthy patron, Otto Wesendonck. Although still married, the composer began an affair with Wesendonck's wife, Mathilde—so fully did Wagner the man live his life as Wagner the artist that it was impossible for him to create an opera dealing with passionate love without being passionately in love himself. Eventually, his own wife, Minne, caused such a scene that the composer fled to Venice. By 1864 Wagner had made his way to Munich for the first production of the now finished *Tristan*. Having long since forgotten both Mathilde and his wife, he now fell in love with Cosima von Bülow, the wife of the man scheduled to conduct *Tristan*. Cosima was the illegitimate daughter of Franz Liszt and Marie d'Agoult (see Fig. 13–19 and page 273), and she and Wagner soon produced three illegitimate children of their own. The first of these, a daughter born on the first day of rehearsals for *Tristan*, was christened Isolde.

The story of *Tristan und Isolde* comes from an old Arthurian legend. Briefly, it is the tale of the love of a captive Irish princess, Isolde, betrothed to King Mark of Cornwall (England), and of Tristan, the king's trusted knight. Tristan is sent to conduct the reluctant Isolde to her wedding with King Mark. Wishing only for revenge and then death, Isolde asks for a deadly potion, but her devoted servant instead substitutes a love potion, which the unknowing Tristan and Isolde consume. On arrival in Cornwall this passionate, soon adulterous, love is revealed to the court. Despairing of any happy union with Isolde in this world, Tristan allows himself to be mortally wounded in combat and sails off to his native Brittany to die. Isolde pursues him but arrives only in time to have him expire in her arms. Knowing that their union will only be consummated through death, Isolde sings her *Liebestod (Love-Death)*, an ecstatic vision of their love beyond the grave, and then she, too, expires next to her lover's body. This was the sort of all-consuming, sacrificial love so dear to the hearts of Romantic artists.

Wagner begins *Tristan*, not with a rousing, self-contained overture, but with a simple yet beautiful prelude that sets the general tone of the drama and leads directly to the raising of the curtain. The first sound we hear is a plaintive call of the cellos, answered by one in the woodwinds. Each is not so much a lengthy theme as it is a short, pregnant motive. Wagner's disciples called each a **leitmotif**, a brief, distinctive unit of music that is designed to represent a character,

FIGURE 14–10

Original costume designs for the premiere of Wagner's *Tristan und Isolde*, June 1865.

object, or idea and that returns repeatedly in order to facilitate the progress of the drama. We have encountered a representational, or programmatic, theme before in the form of Berlioz's *idée fixe* (see page 257). But Wagner's leitmotifs are much shorter than Berlioz's lengthy melody, and there are many more of them. They are usually not sung but only played in the orchestra. In this way an element of the subconscious can be brought to the drama: The orchestra can give a sense of what a character is thinking even when he or she is singing about something else. By developing, extending, varying, contrasting, and resolving these representational leitmotifs, Wagner is able to play out the essence of the drama almost without recourse to his singers.

the leitmotif

Leitmotifs in *Tristan* are associated mainly with feelings rather than concrete objects or persons. The Prelude has four such distinctive cells, each of which lends itself to variation and extension.

EXAMPLE 14–2

Notice how both the "Longing" and "Desire" motifs involve chromatic lines, the first descending, the second ascending (see arrows). This sort of linear chromatic motion made it easy for the composer to wind continually through many different keys, not stopping long enough to establish any one as a home base, or tonic*. Wagner's intense use of chromaticism loosened the feeling of key and eventually led to the collapse of tonality as the main organizing force in Western music, as we shall later see (page 354). Here he uses twisting chromatic lines for a specific expressive purpose, to convey a sense of the anxiety and pain to be felt by the ill-fated lovers.

intense chromaticism

As you listen to the Prelude to *Tristan* you can feel the composer trying to draw you into his all-enveloping world of love, longing, and desire. The leitmotifs frequently appear in sequences*, usually moving upward so as to convey a sense of continual longing and rising tension. Cadences are avoided, thereby increasing the restless mood. And dissonances are placed at points of climax to heighten the feeling of pain and anguish. Throughout there is a gradual ebb and flow of intensity that parallels the emotions of the lovers. When the powerful climax of the Prelude finally arrives, it is, however, evasive and strangely unsatisfying. As we shall see, the real climax, and ultimate resolution of the drama, comes only at the end of the opera.

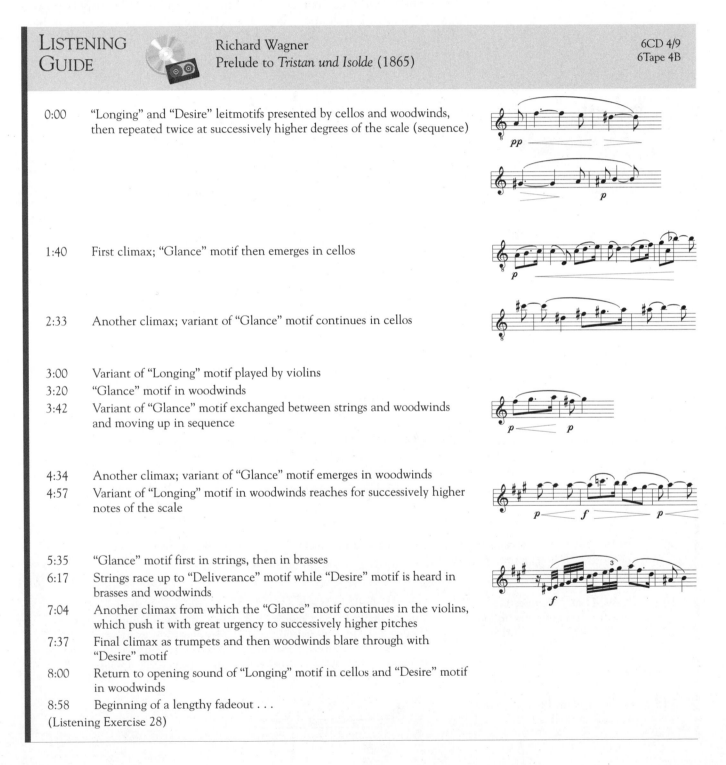

LISTENING GUIDE

Richard Wagner
Prelude to *Tristan und Isolde* (1865)

6CD 4/9
6Tape 4B

0:00	"Longing" and "Desire" leitmotifs presented by cellos and woodwinds, then repeated twice at successively higher degrees of the scale (sequence)
1:40	First climax; "Glance" motif then emerges in cellos
2:33	Another climax; variant of "Glance" motif continues in cellos
3:00	Variant of "Longing" motif played by violins
3:20	"Glance" motif in woodwinds
3:42	Variant of "Glance" motif exchanged between strings and woodwinds and moving up in sequence
4:34	Another climax; variant of "Glance" motif emerges in woodwinds
4:57	Variant of "Longing" motif in woodwinds reaches for successively higher notes of the scale
5:35	"Glance" motif first in strings, then in brasses
6:17	Strings race up to "Deliverance" motif while "Desire" motif is heard in brasses and woodwinds
7:04	Another climax from which the "Glance" motif continues in the violins, which push it with great urgency to successively higher pitches
7:37	Final climax as trumpets and then woodwinds blare through with "Desire" motif
8:00	Return to opening sound of "Longing" motif in cellos and "Desire" motif in woodwinds
8:58	Beginning of a lengthy fadeout . . .

(Listening Exercise 28)

the Liebestod

In the final scene of *Tristan*, Isolde cradles the body of her dying hero and prepares to join him in death. As she sings her justly famous *Liebestod (Love-Death)*, three additional leitmotifs appear, each heard previously in the opera. As in the Prelude, the *Liebestod* is in the form of a great dynamic curve with a sublime climax at the apogee. But now the climax, instead of being frustrated through evasion, reaches its fulfillment as Isolde, in a trancelike state of bliss, joins Tristan in death. First listen to the *Liebestod*, concentrating on the leitmotifs as they are worked out by the voice but even more by the orchestra. Then play it once more, this time just drinking in all of Wagner's divinely inspired sound. If there is such a thing as a transcendental quality about Romantic music, you will experience it here.

LISTENING GUIDE

Richard Wagner
Liebestod, from *Tristan und Isolde* (1865)

6CD 4/10; 6Tape 4B
3CD 3/4; 3Tape 3A

Characters: The lovers Tristan and Isolde
Situation: Tristan's castle in Brittany; Isolde cradles Tristan in her arms as she prepares to join him in death.

0:00	Isolde, gazing at Tristan, slowly sings the "Love-Death" leitmotif, which is then taken up by the orchestra

Mild und leise wie er lächelt,	Oh how tenderly and gently he smiles
Wie das Auge hold er öffnet—	As he opens his eyes—
Seht ihr, Freunde? Seht ihr's nicht?	Do you see, Friends, don't you see it?
Immer lichter wie er leuchtet,	Ever brighter, how he shines,
Stern-umstrahlet hoch sich hebt?	Glowing in starlight raised on high?

1:02	The orchestra continues with the "Love-Death" motif as the singer goes her own way

Seht ihr's nicht?	Do you not see it?
Wie das Herz ihm mutig schwillt,	How his heart proudly swells,
Voll und hehr im Busen ihm quillt?	Full and brave beating in his breast?

1:30	The "Ecstasy" leitmotif enters, not in the voice, but in the high woodwinds and then the violins

Wie den Lippen, wonnig mild	How from his lips, blissfully tender,
Süsser Atem sanft entweht—	Sweet breath gently flutters—
Freunde! Seht!	Do you not see, Friends?

2:08	Reapperance of the ascending, chromatic "Desire" motif from the Prelude

Fühlt und seht ihr's nicht?	Don't you feel and see it?

2:15	"Love-Death" motif returns in voice and orchestra, followed by "Ecstasy" motif and then "Desire" motif in voice

Höre ich nur diese Weise	Do I alone hear this melody
Die so wundervoll und leise,	Which, so wonderfully and gently,
Wonne klagend, alles sagend,	Moaning bliss, expressing all,
Mild versöhnend aus ihm tönend,	Gently forgiving, coming from him
In mich dringet, auf sich schwinget,	Pierces me, soars upwards,
Hold erhallend um mich klinget?	Blessedly echoing all around me?

3:18	"Transcendent Bliss" leitmotif appears in violins

| 3:39 | Tension increases as "Desire" motif rises by chromatic steps | Heller schallend, mich umwallend, Sind es Wellen sanfter Lüfte? Sind es Wolken wonniger Düfte Wie sie schwellen, mich umrauschen, Soll ich atmen, soll ich lauschen? Soll ich schlürfen, untertauchen? Süss in Düften mich verhauchen? In dem wogenden Schwall, in dem tönenden Schall. | Resounding clearly all around me, Are they waves of gentle air? Are they clouds of delightful fragrance? As they swell and envelop me, Should I breathe, should I listen? Should I sip them, plunge beneath them? Breathe my last in such sweet fragrance? In the growing swell, the surging sound. |
| 4:25 | Glorious climax with the "Transcendent Bliss" motif shining forth in the orchestra | In des Welt-Atems wehendem All— Ertrinken, versinken— Unbewusst— Höchste Lust! | In the vastness of the world's spirit To drown, sink down— Unconscious— Supreme bliss! |

The orchestra then fades away into silence as the curtain descends
(Listening Exercise 34)

LATE NINETEENTH-CENTURY OPERA

Verismo Opera

If Wagner's operas center on the deeds of mythical heroes, and Verdi's "domestic operas" on those of the upper middle class, the late nineteenth-century works of Giacomo Puccini (1858–1924) and his competitors focus on the actions of the lower stratum of society. They depict the grimy, everyday life of industrialized nineteenth-century Europe and are tinged with just a hint of eroticism and the threat of violence. This turn to social realism on the musical stage produced what is called *verismo* ("realism") opera. **Verismo opera** was part of a general late-Romantic movement that held that in art and literature the ugly and the vulgar have their place because truth has aesthetic value. The goal for poets like Charles Baudelaire (1821–1867), painters like J.-F. Millet (1814–1875), and novelists like Emile Zola (1840–1902) and Charles Dickens (1812–1870) was to transform the mundane and commonplace into art, to find the poetic and mystical in even the most ordinary of human experience. No more do we hear of gods and goddesses, Nordic giants, or benevolent kings and queens. A gypsy girl who works in a cigarette factory (Carmen in Bizet's *Carmen*, 1875), a jealous clown who stabs his wife (Canio in Leoncavallo's *Pagliacci*, 1892), and a distraught singer who murders the chief of police (Tosca in Puccini's *Tosca*, 1900)—these are the heros and heroines of *verismo* opera.

FIGURE 14–11
Giacomo Puccini.

Giacomo Puccini (1858–1924)

Giacomo Puccini did not have to look far for a profession. He was the scion of four generations of musicians from the northern Italian town of Lucca. His father and his grandfather had both written operas, and before that his forebears had composed religious music for the local cathedral. But Puccini was no child prodigy. For a decade following his graduation from the Milan Conservatory he lived in poverty as he struggled to develop a distinctive operatic style. Not until the age of thirty-five did he score his first triumph, the *verismo* opera *Manon Lescaut* (1893). Thereafter, successes came in rapid succession: *La bohème* (1896), *Tosca*

(1900), *Madama Butterfly* (1904). The heir to Verdi, the king of Italian opera, had been found. Growing famous, wealthy, and a bit complacent, Puccini worked less and less frequently. His last, and some believe his best, opera, *Turandot*, was left unfinished at the time of his death from throat cancer in 1924.

LA BOHÈME (THE BOHEMIAN GIRL, 1896)

the libretto

Puccini's most famous opera is *La bohème*. Indeed, statistics suggest that it is the most performed of all operas. *La bohème* is typical of *versimo* opera, in that the characters are portrayed as living a bohemian life in miserable poverty. The hero, Rodolfo (a poet), and his pals, Schaunard (a musician), Colline (a philosopher), and Marcello (a painter), are starving artists who inhabit an unheated attic on the Left Bank of Paris. The heroine, Mimi (the "bohemian girl"), their neighbor, is a poor, tubercular seamstress. Rodolfo and Mimi meet and fall in love. He grows obsessively jealous while she becomes progressively sickly. They separate for a time, only to return to each other's arms immediately before Mimi's death. In truth, this is not much of a plot, nor is there much character development. The theatrical setup on stage is merely a pretext to allow each of us to feel love, hope, and despair. The words of the singers and their particular dramatic situation, in the last analysis, don't matter. In a singers' opera such as *La bohème* it is the glorious sound of the human voice that carries the moment. When Rodolfo, for example, sings of Mimi's frozen little hand in the aria "Che gelida manina" we escape the cold, hopeless world of a Left Bank attic. The soaring sound of Rodolfo's high tenor voice, not his words, invites us to experience feelings and sensations far beyond the mundane. With the expansive arias of Puccini the golden century of Italian opera, which began with Rossini and embraced all of Verdi, comes to a fitting end.

LISTENING GUIDE

Giacomo Puccini
La bohème (1896)
Aria, "Ah, what a frozen little hand"

6CD 4/11
6Tape 4B

Characters: The poor poet Rodolfo and the equally impoverished seamstress Mimi
Situation: Mimi has knocked on Rodolfo's door to ask for a light for her candle. Charmed by the lovely stranger, he naturally obliges. The wind again blows out Mimi's candle, and amidst the confusion she drops her key. As the two search for it in the darkness, Rodolfo by chance touches her hand and, then holding it, seizes the moment to tell her about himself and his hopes.

0:00	Rodolfo begins conversationally, much like in a recitative	Che gelida manina se la lasci riscaldar. Cercar che giova? Al buio non si trova. Ma per fortuna è una notte di luna, e qui la luna l'abbiamo vicina.	Ah, what a frozen little hand, let me warm it up. What's the good of searching? We won't find it in the dark. But by good luck there is moonlight tonight, and here we have the moon nearby.
	(Mimi tries to withdraw her hand)	Aspetti, signorina, le dirò con due parole	Wait, young lady, I will tell you in two words
1:03	Voice increases in range, volume, and intensity	chi son, e che faccio, come vivo. Vuole? Chi son? Sono un poeta. Che cosa faccio? Scrivo. E come vivo? Vivo!	who I am and what I do, how I live. Would you like this? Who am I? I'm a poet. What do I do? I write. How do I live? I live!

(Rodolfo proceeds to explain who he is and what he does)

1:52	Return to conversational style	In povertà mia lieta scialo da gran signore rime et inni d'amore. Per sogni et per chimere e per castelli in aria, l'anima ho milionaria.	In my delightful poverty I grandiosely scatter rhymes and songs of love. Through dreams and reveries and through castles in the air, I have the soul of a millionaire.
2:30	Voice grows more expansive with longer notes and higher range; orchestra doubles voice in unison	Talor dal mio forziere ruban tutti i gioelli due ladri: gli occhi belli. V'entrar con voi pur ora, ed i miei sogni usati e i bei sogni miei tosto si dileguar! Ma il furto non m'accora,	Sometimes from the strongbox two thieves steal all the jewels: two pretty eyes. They came in with you just now and my usual dreams, my lovely dreams vanish at once! But the theft doesn't bother me
3:24	Orchestra sounds melody alone; then is joined by voice for climactic high note "hope"	poichè v'ha preso stanza la speranza!	because their place has been taken by hope!

(As the music diminishes, Rodolfo asks for a response from Mimi)

Or che mi conoscete,   Now that you know who I am,
parlate voi, deh! parlate.   Tell me about yourself, speak.
Chi siete? Vi piaccia dir!   Who are you? Please speak.

LISTENING EXERCISES

33   Giuseppe Verdi, *La traviata* (1853)   6CD 4/7–8; 6Tape 4B
Act I, Scene 5: Aria "Ah, perhaps he's the one"   3CD 3/3; 3Tape 3A
Recitative "Folly! Folly"
Cabaletta "Always free"

In *La traviata* Verdi has created what is very much a "singers' opera"—the listener's attention is drawn almost entirely to the voices. The orchestra plays a subordinate role, often limited to setting up a solid accompaniment with simple rhythms and regular meters, all in support of the voices. The following questions illuminate the way in which Verdi makes the voice the center of attention, pausing from time to time to enjoy a moment of vocal bravura, yet still keeps the tempo of the opera moving at a rapid pace.

1. (0:00–1:00) What are the meter and the mode at the beginning of this aria?
   a. duple and major   b. duple and minor
   c. triple and major   d. triple and minor
2. (0:12–0:33) What does the orchestra do while Violetta (soprano) sings?
   a. provides simple imitative polyphony
   b. provides simple chordal homophony
3. (0:35–0:58) When the voice repeats the first phrase, does the nature of the accompaniment change? _____
4. (1:24–2:11) Here Violetta sings the expansive refrain introduced previously by Alfredo in Scene 4. The orchestral accompaniment now changes to the "big guitar" effect. How does Verdi create this big guitar in the orchestra?
   a. Strings play pizzicato chords and clarinet plays arpeggios.
   b. Strings play tremolo chords and flute plays arpeggios.
   c. Strings play vibrato chords and flute plays arpeggios.

5. (2:26–5:32) Violetta now sings the second strophe of her aria. When the expansive refrain returns (3:44–4:30), does the orchestra still produce the "big guitar" effect? _____

6CD 4/8; 6Tape 4B; 3CD 3/3; 3Tape 3A

6. During Violetta's accompanied recitative "Folly! Folly!" there is a passage in which she expresses her fear at being merely "a poor woman alone, abandoned in this populated desert that they call Paris" (0:13–0:23). The orchestra helps heighten this feeling of fear by playing:
   a. string tremolo and rising stepwise motion in the bass
   b. string pizzicato and falling stepwise motion in the bass
   c. string *rubato* and rising stepwise motion in the bass

7. After her recitative, and following some vocal fireworks on the word "gioir" ("pleasure"), Violetta launches into her brilliant cabaletta "Sempre libera" ("Always free"). Which number has a clear-cut, regular meter?
   a. the recitative "Folly! Folly!"   b. the aria "Always free"

8. At the end of "Always free" the voice of Alfredo enters (at 2:01) with his familiar refrain "Love that animates the world." Which of the following is true about Alfredo's music?
   a. The tempo speeds up and a guitar accompanies the voice.
   b. The tempo slows down and a harp accompanies the voice.

9. Now Violetta repeats "Always free" (3:17), vowing to pursue pleasure and brushing off Alfredo's feelings of true love. Where does the vocal high point of "Always free" occur—where is the voice pushed to the top of its range?
   a. at the end of the first time Violetta sings the aria (just before Alfredo's voice enters at 2:01)
   b. at the end of the second time she sings it (around 4:40)

---

 34   Richard Wagner   6CD 4/10; 6Tape 4B
        Liebestod, from *Tristan und Isolde* (1865)   3CD 3/4; 3Tape 3A

Isolde's *Liebestod* (Love-Death), which brings *Tristan und Isolde* to a glorious conclusion, is a unique musical composition. It is written for soprano voice—indeed, for a dramatic Wagnerian soprano—with orchestra, yet it is a very different sort of piece from Giuseppe Verdi's aria "Always free" from *La traviata*, which we have previously heard. The following queries begin by asking for specific responses to the music and conclude with a more general question regarding your reaction to the *Liebestod*.

1. Is there an easily perceptible duple or triple meter in the *Liebestod*?

   _____

2. When the soprano sings the "Ecstasy" leitmotif (2:35–2:57) she does so to what for Wagner is exceptionally "square" poetry—lines of 4 + 4 syllables with internal rhyme. (Try saying the German to yourself.)

   Wonne klagend, alles sagend   Moaning bliss, expressing all
   Mild versöhnend aus ihm tönend   Gently forgiving, sounding from within

   What is the course of the soprano line during this couplet?
   a. falls   b. falls in a sequence   c. rises   d. rises in a sequence

3. Immediately after (2:58–3:17), the music rises toward a climax to reflect the sentiment of the next couplet:

In mich dringet, auf sich schwinget,   Pierces me, rises upwards,
Hold erhallend, um mich klinget?   Blessedly echoing all around me?

How is this rising tension brought about in the music?
a. Tremolos are played by the strings.
b. The voice rises up chromatically.
c. There is a gradual crescendo.
d. all of the above

4. As Wagner now builds to another climax (from 3:39 to 4:25) with the "Desire" leitmotif, he suddenly changes dynamics on the word "lauschen" (listen) (at 4:00). Which does he change to?
a. *pianissimo*   b. *fortissimo*

5. (4:45–5:18) How does Wagner musically depict the final words of Isolde "to drown, to sink down, in supreme bliss"?
a. The vocal line falls, then soars up.
b. The vocal line soars up, then falls.
c. The vocal line continually falls.

6. Which leitmotif from the Prelude is heard softly in the oboes (at 5:36) immediately before the final chord?
a. "Longing"   b. "Desire"   c. "Transcendent Bliss"

7. Who has the "last word" (who is heard at the very end of the *Liebestod*)?
a. the voice   b. the orchestra

8. Which musical force could be omitted without serious loss to the music?
a. the voice   b. the orchestra

9. Is the *Liebestod* through-composed (without large-scale repetition), or in *da capo* aria form? _____

10. Do you find this an exceptionally moving musical creation? Are you now a convert to the music of Wagner, a "perfect Wagnerite," to use George Bernard Shaw's phrase? _____

KEY WORDS

Bayreuth Festival Theater	*Gesamtkunstwerk*	*recitativo accompagnato*
bel canto	La Scala	*Ring* cycle
cabaletta	leitmotif	*Singspiel*
diva	*Liebestod*	*verismo* opera
	music drama	

15

LATE ROMANTICISM

When historians speak of "late Romanticism," they refer to the artistic developments that occurred in the West from about 1870 until 1900–1910, from the time of the Franco–Prussian War (1870) until shortly before the outbreak of World War I (1914). Of course, human activity, artistic or otherwise, rarely occurs within tidy chronological units. As we shall see, a strong anti–Romantic movement developed in France as early as the 1880s. Yet while some progressive artists began to turn away from Romanticism at this early date, other, more conservative ones continued to compose in the late Romantic style into the 1940s. Romanticism had a strong hold on the consciousness of the listening public, one that it has not entirely relinquished even today.

During the last decades of the nineteenth century, orchestral music, especially German orchestral music, increasingly came to dominate the European musical scene. The continued growth in the size and color of the orchestra made listening to a symphony orchestra the most powerful aesthetic experience that a citizen of the late nineteenth century could enjoy. Not surprisingly, the force of the ever-larger orchestra affected the development of musical genres. We have seen that Wagner wrote operas in which the instrumental ensemble sometimes overwhelmed and absorbed the voice into its rich orchestral tapestry. Similarly, the orchestra began to infiltrate the realm of the art song, so that now the singer of a *Lied** was often accompanied not merely by a piano but by a full orchestra. So, too, the symphony orchestra expropriated the overture, taking it out of the theater and bringing it into the concert hall. And all the while the traditional four-movement symphony grew longer and more complex, a direct response to the increased number and variety of instruments. Let us review briefly the development of the overture and symphony during the nineteenth century.

THE LATE ROMANTIC OVERTURE AND SYMPHONY

Earlier, in the eighteenth century, an overture usually introduced a theatrical piece, be it an opera or a play. With the advent of Romanticism, however, the custom arose to compose a one-movement work designed to stand by itself and to be performed in the concert hall, not in the theater or opera house. Most of these concert overtures* were programmatic, or descriptive, in nature, like Mendelssohn's Overture to *A Midsummer Night's Dream* (see page 263). Sometimes they were written to help celebrate a special event, such as the dedication of a new concert hall or the accession of a new ruler. Thereafter, they might serve to open any orchestral concert, providing an effective way to capture the audience's attention at the very outset of the program.

the concert overture

The four-movement symphony came into being during the Classical period, in the orchestral works of Haydn and Mozart (see page 187). Throughout the nineteenth century it remained a favorite with audiences everywhere, except in Italy, where opera was a national obsession. Symphonic composers in the Romantic period generally followed the four-movement format inherited from their Classical forebears—fast, slow, minuet or scherzo, fast. But now the third movement might be almost any sort of light, contrasting creation, while the finale increasingly took on a more serious tone. As we have seen (page 242), the movements of a symphony grew in length in the course of the nineteenth century. Perhaps as a consequence of this greater length and seriousness, composers wrote fewer symphonies. Schumann and Brahms composed only four, Mendelssohn five, Tchaikovsky six, Dvořák, Bruckner, and Mahler each nine. No one approached the 40-odd symphonies of Mozart, to say nothing of the 104 of Haydn.

composers write fewer, but longer symphonies

For a Romantic composer contemplating the creation of a symphony, no figure loomed larger than Beethoven. Wagner asked why anyone after Beethoven bothered to write symphonies at all, given the dramatic impact of Beethoven's Third, Fifth, and Ninth. Wagner himself wrote only one, Verdi none. Some composers, notably Berlioz and Liszt, turned to a completely different sort of symphony, the program symphony*, in which an external scenario determined the nature and order of the musical events. But these works sometimes lacked the force, internal unity, and compelling logic of a Beethoven symphony. It was not until the late Romantic period, nearly fifty years after the death of Beethoven, that someone came forth to claim the title of successor to Beethoven the symphonist. That figure was Johannes Brahms.

Johannes Brahms (1833–1897)

Brahms was born in the north German port city of Hamburg in 1833. His father was a street musician who also played double bass well enough to enter the Hamburg city orchestra. Although Johannes's formal education never went beyond primary school, his father saw to it that he had the best training on the piano and in music theory. He was fed a heavy diet of the great masters: Bach's *Well-Tempered Clavier* (see page 138), Beethoven's piano sonatas, and Haydn's chamber music. While he studied these by day, by night he played dance music in brothels and bars on the Hamburg waterfront to supplement the modest family income. He gave his first solo piano recital at the age of fifteen and soon began to compose.

Brahms first came to the public's attention in 1853, when Robert Schumann published a highly laudatory article announcing him to be something of a musical Messiah, the heir apparent of Haydn, Mozart, and Beethoven and their great legacy. Brahms, in turn, embraced both Schumanns, Robert and his wife Clara

FIGURE 15–1
Johannes Brahms.

FIGURE 15–2

Brahms's composing room in Vienna. On the wall, looking down on the piano, is a bust of Beethoven. The spirit of Beethoven loomed large over the entire nineteenth century (see also the cover) and over Brahms in particular.

Clara and Robert Schumann his mentors

(see page 266), as his musical mentors. When Robert was confined to a mental institution in 1854, Brahms moved into the Schumann home for two years to help Clara raise her seven children. Not surprisingly, his respect and affection for Clara ripened into love, despite the fact that she was fourteen years his senior. Yet for whatever reason—they both later destroyed many of their letters to each other—their mutual affection did not culminate in marriage after Robert's death. Brahms remained a bachelor for the duration of his life.

Disappointed first in love and then in his attempts to gain an official position in his native Hamburg, Brahms in 1862 moved to Vienna. He contracted to conduct choral groups from time to time, but for the most part was able to maintain his modest lifestyle—"very un-Wagnerian" he called it—with fees earned as a concert pianist and with royalties accruing from the publication of his ever-growing list of compositions. His fame increased dramatically in 1868 with per-

growing fame

formances of his *German Requiem*, a setting not of the Catholic Mass for the Dead but of texts drawn from the German bible that speak of death, comfort, and peace. Honorary degrees were offered from Cambridge University (1876) and Breslau University (1879). After Wagner's death in 1883, he was generally considered the greatest living German composer. His own death, from liver cancer, came in the spring of 1897. He was buried in the central cemetery of Vienna, thirty feet from the graves of Beethoven and Schubert.

Brahms the conservative

That Brahms should choose Vienna as his home is not surprising. Brahms was very much a musical conservative, one who perpetuated the traditions of the Viennese masters Haydn, Mozart, Beethoven, and Schubert. He acquired and continued to study, like a musicologist, not only the scores of the Classical masters but also those of the Baroque and Renaissance. He wrote canons* in the style of Palestrina and settings of chorale* tunes à la Bach. Sonata–allegro, rondo, and variation—all traditional forms—provided the structural framework for his large-scale compositions.

Brahms's conservative bent is further evident from the fact that he composed no program music, what to other nineteenth-century musicians like Liszt and Berlioz was the very soul of Romantic music. Instead, Brahms chose to write **absolute music,** chamber sonatas, symphonies, overtures, and concertos without any sort of program. His chamber music, especially the F minor piano quintet and the three sonatas for violin and piano, is among the most substantive and inventive ever written—music for the true connoisseur. His four symphonies, two piano concertos, and violin concerto are grand works, worthy successors to those of Beethoven. In these, Brahms did not indulge in unrestrained expression as had Berlioz, Liszt, and Wagner, but maintained a sense of balance by articulating his Romantic feelings within the confines of traditional musical forms. Brahms wrote not a single opera but many works for chorus and nearly two hundred songs, or *Lieder,* for voice and piano. With the songs, however, it is as much the richness of the piano accompaniment as it is the vocal line that carries the day. Brahms could write eminently singable melodies, but he was at heart a contrapuntalist and a "developer" in the tradition of Beethoven.

FIGURE 15–3

The now-bearded and rotund Brahms, cigar in mouth, making his way through the streets of Vienna. This caricature captures the essence of the somewhat eccentric bachelor composer as he heads toward his favorite pub, the Red Hedgehog.

ACADEMIC FESTIVAL OVERTURE (1880)

In 1870 Johannes Brahms wrote: "I shall never compose a symphony! You have no idea how the likes of us feel when we hear the tramp of a giant like him behind us." Brahms, of course, was referring to Beethoven. He did go on to write a symphony—indeed, four of them, each in four movements. They were first performed, in turn, in 1876, 1877, 1883, and 1885. Between the creation of the second and third symphonies, however, Brahms paused to compose two concert overtures. One he called *The Tragic Overture,* because of the somber mood of the work. The other, which he wrote by way of thanks for the honorary Ph.D. he received, he called *Academic Festival Overture.*

Brahms never went to college. As a youth, however, he had lived for a while in the university town of Göttingen, where he drank in the ambience and much of the local brew. When the august University of Breslau conferred on him an honorary doctorate in 1879, it was suggested that he reciprocate by composing a piece to mark the occasion. The overture he created during the summer of 1880, however, was anything but the dignified work the academics expected. It begins solemnly enough, with a march in the tonic minor mode, but becomes progressively more exuberant, even irreverent. What Brahms has done here is to introduce gradually a medley of popular college songs into the musical fabric. And much to the composer's delight, when the overture was first performed under his baton in Breslau on January 4, 1881, the students sang along, substituting their own unprintable texts for the official academic verse. Obviously the students enjoyed themselves. Even today musicians smile, knowing that Brahms chose to stir his potpourri of student songs within the time-honored, and somewhat academic, vessel of sonata–allegro form. The titles of the songs, including the comical freshman initiation tune used as a closing theme and a well-known Latin hymn heard in the coda, are identified in the following Listening Guide.

college songs within an academic form

LISTENING GUIDE

Johannes Brahms
Academic Festival Overture (1880)
Allegro (fast)

6CD 5/1; 6Tape 5A
3CD 3/5; 3Tape 3A

EXPOSITION

0:00   March moving rapidly in a minor key (first theme, part 1)

0:40   Lyrical string playing momentarily interrupts the march

1:08   Return to march, now with emphasis on rhythmic motive

1:48   Trumpets, horns, and trombones enter with first theme, part 2, "We had built a stately house"

2:33   Transition dominated by rhythmic motive from march

3:42   Violins sweep in with second theme, "The Father of the Land"

4:32   Bassoons and then oboes play comical closing theme, "What comes from on high"

DEVELOPMENT

5:15   Fragments of second theme and closing theme
6:11   Retransition

RECAPITULATION

6:29   March in minor key (first theme, part 1)
7:24   Brasses and strings play first theme, part 2, but greatly shortened
7:44   Strings, then woodwinds, play lush second theme
9:00   Full orchestra plays closing theme *fortissimo*

CODA

9:09   Change to triple meter; full orchestra introduces a new melody, the Latin hymn "Gaudeamus igitur"

(Listening Exercise 35)

FIGURES 15–4 AND 15–5

(left) Antonín Dvořák conducting: a painting now hanging in the Dvořák Museum in Prague. (right) 327 East 17th Street, Dvořák's residence in New York City during 1892–1894.

Antonín Dvořák (1841–1904)

"There is no doubt that he is very talented. He is also very poor." Thus Johannes Brahms wrote to the music publisher Simrock in 1876 describing the then-unknown thirty-five-year-old Antonín Dvořák. Dvořák, the son of a butcher, had come from Bohemia, an area of the Czech Republic south of Prague. Young Antonín, too, passed an apprenticeship to be a butcher, but a prosperous uncle saw musical talent in the teenager and sent him to study organ in Prague for a year. Thereafter, for nearly two decades, Dvořák eked out a living as a freelance violist and organist in Prague, playing in dance bands, the opera orchestra, and in church. All the while he composed tirelessly—operas, symphonies, string quartets, and songs, almost all of which went unheard.

Brahms's intervention with the publisher Simrock proved decisive in Dvořák's career. Soon the Czech composer's charming *Slavonic Dances* for piano duet were available in music stores across Europe, and they caught on like wildfire. Simrock's firm got rich from this publication, though Dvořák received only the equivalent of two months of his usual salary. (There was no such thing as artists' royalties at this time; the composer or author simply sold the work for a flat fee to the publisher, who took all risks and kept all revenues.) What Dvořák did receive from his publications was recognition. Commissions from various orchestras and conductors now came like a flood. During the 1880s his symphonies, string quartets, and choral works were heard in London, Berlin, Vienna, Dresden, Leipzig, Moscow, Budapest, and even Cincinnati, which then had a strong Bohemian component to its population.

Brahms helps launch Dvořák's career

In the spring of 1892 Dvořák received an offer he couldn't refuse. He was promised the astonishing sum of $15,000 per year (the equivalent of about $500,000 today) to became the Director of the newly founded National Conservatory of Music in New York City. So on September 17, 1892, Dvořák set sail for America and ultimately took up residence at 327 East 17th Street (see Fig. 15–5). It was here that he began work on his "American" Quartet and his Symphony "From the New World." Instead of returning to Prague that summer, Dvořák and his family traveled by train and carriage to Spillville, Iowa, spending three months among the mainly Czech-speaking people of this rural farming

Dvořák moves to the "New World"

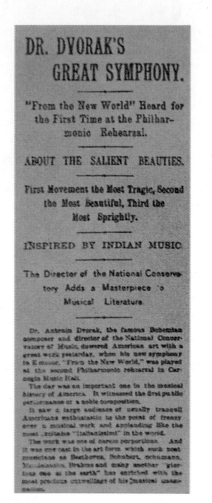

FIGURE 15–6

A review of the premiere of the Symphony "From the New World" in the *New York Herald*, December 16, 1893.

FIGURE 15–7

An autograph sketch of the famous English horn theme from the second movement (*Largo*) of Dvořák's Symphony "From the New World."

community. After two more winters in New York City as Director of the National Conservatory, he returned to his native Bohemia for good. He died in Prague in 1904, the Czechs' most famous and beloved composer.

SYMPHONY "FROM THE NEW WORLD" (1893)

The Symphony "From the New World" in E minor, Dvořák's ninth and last symphony, is by far his best-known work. It received a rousing premiere in New York City, at the newly built Carnegie Hall, on December 16, 1893. As Dvořák wrote to his publisher, Simrock, the following week:

> The success of the symphony was tremendous. The papers write that no composer has ever had such a triumph (see Fig. 15–6). I was in a box. The hall was filled with the best New York audience. The people clapped so much that I had to thank them from the box like a king! You know how glad I am if I can avoid such ovations, but there was no getting out of it, and I had to show myself like-it-or-not.

The title that Dvořák gave to this symphony, "From the New World," might suggest that he placed within it musical elements that are distinctly American. Yet while Dvořák showed a keen interest in the indigenous music of African Americans and Native American Indians, none of the many tuneful melodies heard in this symphony can be identified as a preexisting folk song. They came from Dvořák's own head and heart. And although these melodies, especially those of the famous *Largo*, do possess a "folk style" quality, they may be as much Czech as American in inspiration.

First movement (Adagio: Allegro molto; "Slow: Very Fast"): A satisfying blend of forceful energy and tuneful lyricism mark this opening movement in strict sonata–allegro form. Solo wind instruments—French horn, oboe, and flute—introduce the principal themes, and then leave it to the strings to propel the music forward.

Second movement (Largo; "Slow and broad"): The "emotional soul" of this symphony rests in this second movement, the famous *Largo*. The essence of musical Romanticism can be felt here in the prolonged gestures—as heard in the low brass introduction—and the wealth of beautiful melodies—such as the haunting English horn solo (see Fig. 15–7). This latter tune was soon extracted from the symphony and became a popular American song under the title "Goin' home."

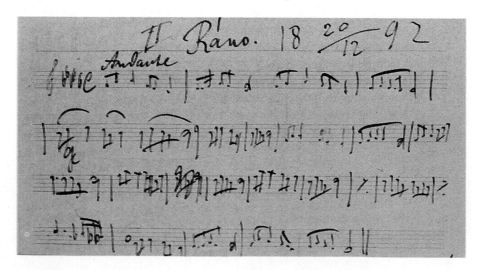

LISTENING GUIDE	Antonín Dvořák Symphony No. 9, "From the New World" (1893) Second movement, *Largo* (Slow and broad)	6CD 5/2 6Tape 5A

(Form: **ABCA**)

A

0:00   Solemn introductory chords by low brass choir, then timpani

0:46   English horn solo, the "Goin' home" melody

1:15   Clarinet joins English horn, then strings join as well

2:29   Introductory chords now played by high woodwinds and French horn, concluded by brasses and timpani

3:04   Strings play and extend "Goin' home" melody

3:55   Melody returns to English horn and is completed by strings and woodwinds

4:38   French horn echoes the melody

B

5:05   Faster tempo and new theme (**B1**) in flute and oboe

5:31   Second new theme (**B2**) in clarinets above bass pizzicato

6:19   Melody **B1** played more insistently by violins

7:12   Melody **B2** played more intensely by violins

C

8:18   Oboe leads chirping of high woodwinds

8:45   Brasses play *fortissimo* recall of first theme of first movement

9:03   Diminuendo and lovely transition back to

A

9:17   English horn brings back "Goin' home" melody

9:45   Pairs of violins and violas play melody but break off, as if choked by emotion

10:20   Solo cello and solo violin play melody, then full strings join

11:01   Quiet, monophonic soliloquy by violins

11:27   Final return and extension of opening chord

Third movement (*Molto vivace*; *"Very fast and lively"*): Dvořák said this scherzo was intended to depict "a feast in the woods where the Indians dance." Yet the only time Dvořák actually heard "live" American Indian music was when he saw a performance of Buffalo Bill's Wild West Show, and there the commercialized songs had little to do with authentic Indian melodies. For most listeners this scherzo is more suggestive of frolicking Bohemian peasants than dancing American Indians.

Fourth movement (*Allegro con fuoco*; *"Fast with fire"*): The stirring finale presents a succession of exciting themes in the brasses while also recalling melodies from the three previous movements, thereby binding the symphony into a satisfying whole.

Although Dvořák tried to conjure up the spirit of American folk music in his Symphony "From the New World," he was above all a proponent of Czech musical culture. In addition to his popular *Slavonic Dances*, he composed such regionally inspired works as *Slavonic Rhapsodies*, *Moravian Duets*, and the *Czech Suite*. In this he was one of many composers of the Romantic era who expressed ethnic sensibilities through music and thereby created a movement historians call musical nationalism.

Musical Nationalism

political nationalism

Musical **nationalism** was not an isolated phenomenon but part of a broad nineteenth-century development that saw various national groups achieve greater political unity and cultural identity. Instead of hundreds of small principalities or city–states owing allegiance to some vague confederation or distant foreign power, Europe was becoming organized into a dozen or so strongly unified, centrally governed nation-states, each with a common language and cultural heritage. After a lengthy struggle, Italy achieved full national unification in 1861, with Rome as the capital. Ten years later a German Empire, under the political leadership of Chancellor Otto von Bismarck (1815–1898), was formally recognized following the German victory over the French in the Franco–Prussian War of 1870. Pride in a national culture and character was likewise felt by smaller groups, like the Czechs, Hungarians, Poles, and Finns, each of which was trying to free itself from more powerful countries such as Germany, Austria, and Russia.

artistic nationalism

Glorification of one's own national group was part of the spirit of the Romantic age. It was manifested in a renewed interest in native languages, like Czech and Hungarian. It was also expressed by giving greater prominence to the folk arts, incorporating them into more "serious" forms of music, literature, poetry, and painting. National color in music was communicated by means of indigenous folk elements—folk songs, native scales and dance rhythms, and local instrumental sounds. It also could be conveyed by the use of national subjects— the life of a national hero, for example—as the program for a symphonic poem or as the libretto for an opera.

FIGURE 15–8

Modest Musorgsky.

Russian Nationalism: Modest Musorgsky (1839–1881)

Russia was one of the first countries to develop its own national style of art music, one distinct and separate from the traditions of German orchestral music and Italian and German opera. An early use of Russian subject matter can be found in Mikhail Glinka's opera *A Life for the Tsar* (1836). Glinka's nationalist spirit was passed to a group of young composers whom contemporaries dubbed "The Mighty Handful" or, less grandiosely, **the Russian Five:** Alexander Borodin (1833–1887), César Cui (1835–1918), Mily Balakirev (1837–1910), Nikolai Rimsky-Korsakov (1844–1908), and Modest Musorgsky (1839–1881). They believed in writing Russian music, free of Western influence, for the Russian people. Of these, the most original and least Western in musical style was Modest Musorgsky.

As with most of the members of "the Russian Five," Musorgsky was not initially destined for a career in music. He was trained to be a military officer, and for a period of four years was commissioned in the Russian army. He resigned his appointment in 1858 in favor of a minor post as a civil servant and more free time to indulge his avocation, musical composition. The next year he said: "I have been a cosmopolitan, but now there's been some sort of regeneration. Everything Russian is becoming dear to me." Unfortunately, his brief, chaotic life was marked by increasing poverty, depression, and alcoholism. During those few periods of creative productivity that Musorgsky enjoyed, he managed to compile a small *oeuvre*, which includes a boldly inventive symphonic poem, *Night on Bald Mountain* (1867), an imaginative set of miniatures for piano, *Pictures at an Exhibition* (1874), and an operatic masterpiece, *Boris Godunov* (1874), based on the life of a popular sixteenth-century Russian tsar. Many of Musorgsky's works were left unfinished at the time of his death in 1881.

"Everything Russian is becoming dear to me"

PICTURES AT AN EXHIBITION (1874)

The genesis of *Pictures at an Exhibition* can be traced to the death of Musorgsky's close friend, the Russian painter and architect Victor Hartmann, who had died suddenly of a heart attack in 1873. As a memorial to Hartmann, an exhibition of his paintings and drawings was mounted in Moscow the next year. Musorgsky was inspired to capture the spirit of Hartmann's works in a series of ten short pieces for piano. To provide unity within the sequence of musical pictures, the composer hit on the idea of incorporating a recurring interlude, which he called "Promenade." This gave the listener the impression of enjoying a leisurely stroll through a gallery, moving from one of Hartmann's paintings to the next each time the Promenade music was heard. Though originally composed as a work for piano, the imaginative sounds of the ten musical pictures begged for orchestration, a task that several composers later undertook. *Pictures at an Exhibition* is best known to us today in the brilliantly orchestrated version by Maurice Ravel, completed in 1922.

inspired by paintings of Victor Hartmann

Promenade. Here the composer projects himself, and by extension the listener, as wandering through an exposition of Hartmann paintings. Immediately, we are transported musically into a world of purely Russian art. The tempo is marked "Fast but resolute, in the Russian manner"; the meter is irregular, as in a folk dance, mixing groups of five beats with those of six; and the melody is built on a folk-influenced scale, called a **pentatonic scale,** which uses only five notes instead of the usual Western scale of seven, here B♭, C, D, F, and G:

EXAMPLE 15–1

Now begins a musical depiction of ten paintings. We focus our gaze on numbers 4 and 10.

Picture 4: Polish Ox-Cart. Hartmann's scene is a view of a rickety ox-cart seen lumbering down a Russian dirt road. The rocking of the cart is suggested by a two-note ostinato*. Notice in this brief composition how music has the capacity to project a sense of time and movement in a way that a painting cannot. Here

music projects a feeling of movement and passing time

FIGURE 15–9

Victor Hartmann's vision *The Great Gate of Kiev*, which inspired the last of the musical paintings in Musorgsky's *Pictures at an Exhibition*. Note the bells in the tower, a motif that is featured prominently at the very end of Musorgsky's musical evocation of this design.

the viewer remains stationary as the cart appears in the distance (*pp*), moves closer and closer by means of a crescendo (reaching *fff*), and slowly disappears as the orchestra is gradually reduced to playing *ppp*. In addition, Musorgsky was aware of an important acoustical phenomenon: Larger sound waves (and hence lower pitches) travel farther than shorter waves (higher pitches). (This is why we hear the bass drum and tubas of an approaching marching band long before we hear the higher trumpets and clarinets.) Thus, in *Polish Ox-Cart* Musorgsky begins and ends with the very lowest sounds (orchestrated with tuba and double basses), to give the impression that the sound comes from a distance and then disappears again into the distance.

Picture 10: The Great Gate of Kiev. The stimulus for the majestic conclusion to *Pictures at an Exhibition* was Hartmann's design for a new and grandiose gate to the ancient city of Kiev, then part of Russia. Musorgsky disposes his thematic material to give the impression of a parade passing beneath the giant gate, and he does so in what is tantamount to rondo form (here **ABABCA**). The majestic vision of the gate (**A**) alternates with religious music for a procession of Russian pilgrims (**B**), and even the composer–viewer walks beneath the gate as the Promenade theme (**C**) appears, before a final return to a panoramic view of the gate (**A**), now with Hartmann's bells ringing triumphantly.

In this climactic final tableau, the full orchestra is able to give more powerful expression to all of the local color and grandeur inherent in Musorgsky's original music for piano, just as Musorgsky's musical creation is a far more powerful artistic statement than was Hartmann's design for the gate of Kiev (Fig. 15–9).

LISTENING GUIDE

Modest Musorgsky
Pictures at an Exhibition (1874)
(orchestrated by Maurice Ravel, 1922)

6CD 5/3–5; 6Tape 5A
3CD 3/6; 3Tape 3B

Promenade

0:00	Solo trumpet begins Promenade theme	
0:07	Full brass respond	
0:15	Trumpet and full brass continue to alternate	
0:30	Full strings and then woodwinds and brass enter	
1:21	Brass briefly restate Promenade theme	

6CD 5/4; 6Tape 5A

Picture 4: *Polish Ox-Cart*

0:00	Solo tuba plays Ox-Cart melody against backdrop of a two-note ostinato	
0:51	Strings and soon full orchestra join in	
1:33	Full orchestra plays Ox-Cart theme (note rattle of tambourine)	
1:54	Tuba returns with Ox-Cart theme	
2:24	Diminuendo and fadeout	

6CD 5/5; 6Tape 5A; 3CD 3/6; 3Tape 3B

Picture 10: *The Great Gate of Kiev*

0:00	A	Gate theme in full brass
1:05	B	Pilgrims appear in woodwind choir
1:35	A	Gate theme in brass, with running scales in strings
2:10	B	Pilgrims reappear in woodwinds
2:42	X	Exotic sounds
3:21	C	Promenade theme returns in trumpet
3:59	A	Gate theme in full glory, with bells added toward the end

(Listening Exercise 36)

LATE ROMANTIC PROGRAM MUSIC

Program music, as we have seen (pages 243–244), was at the very heart of the creative works of the early Romantics, like Berlioz, Mendelssohn, and Liszt. While Brahms, later in the century, held fast to the Classical ideal of absolute music*, most late Romantic composers continued to yield to the allure of music inspired by some sort of extramusical element—a play, an experience with nature, even a painting. The late-nineteenth-century composer who achieved the greatest popular success in writing program music was Peter Tchaikovsky. Tchaikovsky was less a Russian nationalist than a writer of symphonic poems and illustrative ballet music in the then-dominant German orchestral tradition.

Peter Tchaikovsky (1840–1893)

Tchaikovsky was born in 1840 into an upper-middle-class family in provincial Russia. He showed a keen ear for music in his earliest years, and by the age of six could speak fluent French and German (an excellent musical ear and a capacity to learn foreign languages often go hand in hand). As to his career, his parents determined that law would provide the easiest route to fame and fortune. Thus, young Tchaikovsky spent seven years, 1852–1859, at the School of Jurisprudence in St. Petersburg and four more years as a clerk in the Ministry of Justice. Then, like Robert Schumann before him, he realized that it was music, not law, that fired his imagination. He made his way to the St. Petersburg Conservatory of Music, from which he was graduated in 1866. That same year, he went to the newly formed Moscow Conservatory, where he assumed the position of professor of harmony and musical composition.

In truth, it was not his official position in Moscow that supported Tchaikovsky during most of his mature years, but rather a private arrangement with an eccentric patroness, Madame Nadezhda von Meck (Fig. 15–11). This wealthy, music-loving widow furnished him an annual income of six thousand rubles on the condition that she and the composer never meet—a requirement not always easily fulfilled, since the two sometimes resided at the same summer estate. In addition

FIGURE 15–11

Nadezhda von Meck was the widow of an engineer who made a fortune constructing the first railroads in Russia during the 1860s and 1870s. She used her money, in part, to support composers like Tchaikovsky and, later, Claude Debussy.

to this annuity, Tsar Alexander III in 1881 awarded Tchaikovsky an annual pension of three thousand rubles in recognition of his importance to Russian cultural life. Being a man of independent means meant that Tchaikovsky not only was able to travel extensively in Western Europe, and even to America, but could also enjoy the freedom he found so necessary to creative activity.

Tchaikovsky's creative output touched every genre of nineteenth-century music: opera, song, string quartet, piano sonata, concerto, symphony, and symphonic poem. It is, however, his large-scale works for orchestra that have best stood the test of time. Tchaikovsky's musical strengths—sweeping melodies, colorful instrumentations, dramatic contrasts, and grand gestures—could only be fully expressed by a large symphony orchestra. Not surprisingly, he also achieved unparalleled success as a composer of orchestral music for ballet, a type of music in which short bursts of colorful sounds and evocative rhythms are necessary to create distinctly different moods for each new scene. His *Swan Lake* (1876), *Sleeping Beauty* (1889), and *Nutcracker* (1892) are the most popular works in the entire repertoire of grand Romantic ballet, beloved by young and old alike.

Despite his considerable popular success, Tchaikovsky's life was not a happy one. He was a manic–depressive, a neurotic, and a hypochondriac. He was also a homosexual, and this was a time when there was little sympathy for homosexuality or awareness of its biological causes. He died suddenly in 1893, at the age of fifty-three, after drinking unboiled water during an epidemic of cholera.

SYMPHONIC POEM, *ROMEO AND JULIET* (1869)

Tchaikovsky was at his best when writing illustrative music for large orchestra, whether a program symphony, a one-movement symphonic poem*, or music for ballet. He called his most overtly programmatic works sometimes simply "overture," sometimes "overture fantasy," and sometimes "symphonic fantasy." We may broadly group these one-movement programmatic pieces in the general category of symphonic poem. As with Berlioz, Mendelssohn, and Liszt before him, it was the plays of Shakespeare that provided the strongest extramusical stimulation. Of his three symphonic poems based on works of Shakespeare—*Romeo and Juliet* (1869), *The Tempest* (1877), and *Hamlet* (1888)—the earliest is best. Indeed, it was his first masterpiece.

his program music

Just as Mendelssohn captures the spirit, not the letter, of Shakespeare's *Midsummer Night's Dream* (see page 263), so Tchaikovsky offers a free, not literal, presentation of the principal dramatic elements of *Romeo and Juliet*. In fact, he distills these into just three musical themes: the compassionate music of the kindly Friar Laurence, whose plan to unite the lovers goes fatally awry; the fighting music, which represents the feud between the Capulets and Montagues; and the love theme, which expresses the passion of Romeo and Juliet. Once again, it is sonata–allegro form that is the arena in which the musical drama will be played out. The introduction presents the music of Friar Laurence, then anguished dissonant sounds in the strings and French horn, and finally a succession of beautifully mysterious chords with strumming by a harp, as if Friar Laurence, like a medieval bard, were about to narrate a tragic tale. When the exposition begins, we hear angry, percussive music, racing strings, and syncopated cymbal crashes:

themes from Shakespeare's Romeo and Juliet

This is the violent world of the Capulets and Montagues. Soon the fighting sub-
sides and the love theme emerges. As appropriate for a pair of lovers, it is in two
parts, each of which has the capacity to grow and become more passionate when
pushed upward in ascending sequences:

EXAMPLE 15–2A

EXAMPLE 15–2B

The brief development pits the feuding families against the increasingly adamant
pleas of Friar Laurence. The recapitulation, true to sonata form, begins with the
feud music, but moves quickly to an expanded, more ecstatic presentation of the
love theme (part 2 first, then part 1), which is eventually cut off by a noisy return
of the feuding clans. The beginning of the dramatic coda is announced by a foreboding *fortissimo* roll on the timpani. As we hear the steady drumbeats of a funeral procession and fragments of the broken love theme, we know that Romeo and
Juliet are dead. A celestial hymnlike passage (a transformation of the love
theme) suggests the lovers have been united above, a feeling then confirmed by
the return of the love theme in high violins. There only remains to bring the curtain down on the story of the star-crossed lovers, which Tchaikovsky does with
seven *fortissimo* hammer strokes for full orchestra, all on the tonic chord.

Shakespeare wrote *Romeo and Juliet* as a tragedy: "For never was a story of more
woe/Than this of Juliet and her Romeo," say the final lines of the play. By incorporating a "celestial conclusion" into his coda—a hymnlike choir of angelic
woodwinds followed by the transcendent love theme on high in the violins—   *a Romantic ending*
Tchaikovsky has changed the final import of the play. True child of the Romantic age, he suggests that the love-death of Romeo and Juliet was, in fact, not a
tragedy but their spiritual triumph.

LISTENING GUIDE

Peter Tchaikovsky
Symphonic poem, *Romeo and Juliet* (1869)

6CD 5/6
6Tape 5B

INTRODUCTION

0:00   Friar Laurence theme sounding organlike in the woodwinds

0:36   Anguished, dissonant sound in strings and French horn

1:25   Harp alternates with flute solo and woodwinds

2:07   Friar Laurence theme returns with new accompaniment

2:34   Anguished sound returns in strings and French horn

3:23   Harp strumming returns

3:56   Timpani roll and string tremolos build tension; hints of Friar Laurence theme in woodwinds

4:31   Anguished sound again returns, then yields to crescendo on repeating tonic chord

EXPOSITION

5:01   Feud theme in agitated minor; angry rhythmic motive in woodwinds, racing scales in strings

5:48   Crashing syncopations (with cymbal) running against scales

6:19   Gentle transition, with release of tension, to second theme

6:57   Love theme (part 1) played quietly by English horn and viola

7:13   Love theme (part 2) played quietly by strings with mutes

7:51   Love theme (part 1) returns with growing ardor in high woodwinds while French horn plays counterpoint against it

8:51   Lyrical closing section in which cellos and English horn engage in dialogue against backdrop of gently plucked chords in harp

DEVELOPMENT

9:52   Feud theme against which horn soon plays Friar Laurence theme (10:04)

10:11   String syncopations, again against Friar Laurence theme

10:38   Feud theme and Friar Laurence theme continue in opposition

11:23   Cymbal crashes signal climax of development as trumpet blares forth with Friar Laurence theme (11:30)

RECAPITULATION

11:58   Feud theme in woodwinds and brasses against racing strings

12:21   Love theme (part 2) softly in woodwinds

13:00   Love theme (part 1) sounds ecstatically with all its inherent force and sweep

13:41   Love theme begins again in strings, with counterpoint in brasses

14:01   Fragments of Love theme in strings, then brasses

14:28   Love theme begins again but is cut off by Feud theme; syncopated cymbal crashes (14:36)

14:43   Feud theme and Friar Laurence theme build to a climax

15:43   Timpani roll announces coda

CODA

15:52   Timpani beats a funeral march while strings play fragments of Love theme

16:38   Love theme (part 2) transformed into the sound of a heavenly chorale played by woodwinds

17:43   Transcendent Love theme sounds from on high in violins

18:18   Timpani roll and final chords

(Listening Exercise 37)

THE ORCHESTRAL SONG

We began our discussion of Romantic music with two art songs* of Franz Schubert (pages 249–253), and we end it with an orchestral song by Gustav Mahler (1860–1911). This is not an inappropriate framework in which to experience Romantic music, for the nineteenth century was marked throughout by an exceptionally strong union between music and poetry. If poetry had the power to communicate feelings of love, grief, pain, or longing, these typically Romantic sentiments could not fail to be intensified when set to music. Thus, the art song came into being in the early nineteenth century. At about the same time, Beethoven incorporated song into the finale of his Ninth ("Choral") Symphony (1824), as Berlioz and Liszt would also do in their later programmatic symphonies. Naturally, it was only a matter of time before the genres of art song and symphony began to interact and influence each other, producing something new: the orchestral song. In its simplest form the **orchestral song** was an art song in which the full orchestra had replaced the piano as the medium of accompaniment. Yet because the orchestra could supply more color and add a greater number of contrapuntal lines, the orchestral song grew to be longer, denser, and more complex than the piano-supported art song. Berlioz, Brahms, and Wagner all experimented with the orchestral song in various ways, but not until Gustav Mahler did this hybrid musical genre reach maturity.

Gustav Mahler (1860–1911)

Gustav Mahler was born in 1860 into a middle-class Jewish family in Bohemia, then part of the Austrian Empire but now encompassed by the new Czech Republic. At the age of fifteen he was admitted to the prestigious Vienna Conservatory of Music, where he studied musical composition and conducting. Mahler felt his mission in life was to conduct—to interpret—the works of the masters ("suffer for my great masters," he said). Like most young conductors, he began his career in provincial towns, gradually working his way to larger and more important musical centers. His itinerary as resident conductor took him along the following route: Bad Hall (1880), Laibach (1881–1882), Olmütz (1883), Kassel (1883–1884), Prague (1885–1886), Leipzig (1886–1888), Budapest (1888–1891), Hamburg (1891–1897), and finally back to Vienna.

In May 1897 Mahler returned triumphantly to his adopted city as director of the Vienna Court Opera, a position Mozart had once coveted. The next year he also assumed directorship of the Vienna Philharmonic, then and now one of the world's great orchestras. But Mahler was a demanding autocrat—a musical tyrant—in search of an artistic ideal. That he drove himself as hard as he pushed others was little comfort to the singers and instrumentalists who had to endure his wrath during rehearsals. After ten stormy but artistically successful seasons (1897–1907), Mahler was dismissed from the Vienna Opera. About this time he received and accepted a call to come to New York to take charge of the Metropolitan Opera and, eventually, the New York Philharmonic as well. Here, too, there was both controversy and acclaim. And here, too, at least at the Met, his contract was not renewed after two years, though he stayed on longer, until February 1911, with the Philharmonic. He died in Vienna in May 1911 of a lingering streptococcus infection that had attacked his weak heart—a sad end to an obsessive and somewhat tormented life.

FIGURE 15–12

Gustav Mahler.

FIGURE 15–13

Gustav Mahler conducting in the orchestra pit of the Vienna Court Opera. Mahler earned his living as a conductor and was free to devote himself to composition only during the summer months.

Mahler is unique among composers in that as a mature artist he wrote only orchestral songs and symphonies. These he managed to create during the summers when freed of his conducting duties. His five orchestral song cycles* typically contain settings of four, five, or six poems by a single author. *Kindertotenlieder* (*Children's Death Songs*, 1901–1904), for example, is a collection of five songs for voice and orchestra to words by Friedrich Rückert (1788–1866). They express the poet's overwhelming grief on the loss of two young children to scarlet fever. By tragic coincidence, no sooner had Mahler finished setting Rückert's painfully personal memorials than his own eldest daughter died of scarlet fever at the age of four, a loss from which the intensely sensitive composer never recovered.

What is also so unique to Mahler is the extent to which he borrowed from his own orchestral songs when he sat down to compose a symphony. It is as if the songs served as a musical repository or vault to which the composer could return for inspiration while wrestling with the problems of a large, multimovement *songs and symphonies* work for orchestra. Mahler's First Symphony (1889), though entirely instrumental, makes use of melodies already present in his song cycle *Lieder eines fahrenden Gesellen* (*Songs of a Wayfaring Lad*, 1885). His Second (1894), Third (1896), and Fourth (1901) symphonies incorporate various portions of the *Wonderhorn Songs* (1892–1899) as solo vocal parts within the symphony. Symphonies Five (1902) and Six (1904) are again purely instrumental, but once more incorporate preexisting melodies, in this case from *Children's Death Songs* and *Five Rückert Songs* (1901–1902). Altogether Mahler wrote nine symphonies, seven of which make use of his own orchestral songs or other preexisting vocal music.

But to Mahler a symphony was much more than just an extended orchestral song. "The symphony is the world; it must embrace everything," he once said. And so he tried to embrace every sort of music within it. There are folk dances, popular songs, military marches, off-stage bands, bugle calls, and even Gregorian chant at various points in his symphonies. What results is a collage of sound on the grandest scale, one achieved, in part, by employing massive forces and a greatly extended sense of time. Mahler's Symphony No. 2, for example, calls for ten horns and eight trumpets, and lasts an hour and a half. The first performance

---

Life Among the Artists

In 1901 middle-aged Gustav Mahler married the dazzling Viennese beauty Alma Schindler (1879–1964). She was the daughter of a noted Austrian landscape painter and was in her own right a talented pianist and budding composer. As a precondition to their marriage, however, Mahler insisted that Alma give up her own career in music to serve his art. Given this infringement of her liberty and the fact that she was just slightly more than half Mahler's age, it is not surprising that their marriage was not a tranquil one. At one point, in 1910, Mahler consulted the famous Sigmund Freud, father of psychoanalysis, in hopes of coming to a better understanding of himself and his union with Alma. (Freud declined to treat Mahler, apparently for fear of destroying the latter's creative process.) After the composer's death in 1911, Alma went on to have affairs with the conductor Bruno Walter and the painter Oskar Kokoschka (see Fig. 17–2), and later to marry the architect Walter Gropius and the novelist Franz Werfel. Obviously, Alma Schindler had a keen eye for talent. Her tongue was equally sharp, as can be seen in the following extracts from her memoirs *And the Bridge Was Love*, which describe Mahler's work habits at their lakeside summer home in southern Austria.

"Mahler got up at six or six-thirty every day. As soon as he was awake, he rang for the cook, who promptly prepared his breakfast and carried it up a steep, slippery trail to his forest study, two hundred feet above the house. (She was forbidden to use the regular road, lest he meet her on his way up; before work, he could not stand seeing anyone.) The study was a one-room brick hut with a door and three windows, a grand

Alma Schindler Mahler in 1902, shortly after her marriage to Gustav Mahler

piano, a bookshelf with the collected works of Kant and Goethe. No music but Bach's. About noon he came down, changed, and went for a swim. . . . Our afternoons were spent walking. Rain or shine, we walked for three or four hours, or rowed around the gleaming, heat-spewing lake. . . . Often he stopped and stood with the sun burning down on his hatless skull, drew out a notebook, wrote, thought, wrote some more. Sometimes he beat time in the air before writing the notes down. This could go on for an hour or more, with me sitting on a tree trunk or in the grass, not daring to look at him. Mahler made sure that everything in his personal life revolved around his own genius."

---

of his Symphony No. 8 in Munich in 1910 involved 858 singers and 171 instrumentalists. With good reason it has been nicknamed the "Symphony of a Thousand."

"Symphony of a Thousand"

Gustav Mahler was the last in the long line of great German symphonists that extended back through Brahms, Schubert, and Beethoven to Mozart and, ultimately, to Haydn. What had begun as a modest instrumental genre with a limited emotional range had grown in the course of the nineteenth century into a monumental structure, the musical equivalent, in Mahler's view, of the entire cosmos.

ORCHESTRAL SONG, *I AM LOST TO THE WORLD*, FROM THE *FIVE RÜCKERT SONGS* (1901–1902)

It is the everyday world, not the grand cosmos, that concerns Mahler in his setting of Friedrich Rückert's *Ich bin der Welt abhanden gekommen (I Am Lost to the World)*. Rückert was a minor German Romantic poet whose verse, nonetheless, enjoyed favor with Schubert, Schumann, and Brahms because of its structural regularity. During the summers of 1901 and 1902, Mahler chose to set five among the many hundreds of poems by Rückert. The subject of these five verses was dear to the composer because it expresses in various ways his outlook on life and on art.

FIGURE 15–14

Mahler spent his summers at various villas in the Austrian mountains, but he made sure that each was supplied with a "forest hut" where he could go each morning to compose without distraction. The last of these composing chalets, at Alt-Schluderbach, is today one of the more accessible ones.

I Am Lost to the World speaks of the artist's growing remoteness from the travails of everyday life and of withdrawal into a private, heavenly world of music, here signified by the final word *Lied* (song). Although the poem has three stanzas, Mahler chose not a strophic setting*, but a through-composed* one. The first strophe sets the mood of the song as a mournful English horn begins to play a halting melody, one then picked up and extended by the voice. The second stanza moves to a faster tempo and more rapid declamation in the voice, as if the mundane world should be quickly left behind. The final strophe returns to a slow tempo. It also sets the notes of the bass on the beat and on the roots of triads*, all of which help project a settled, satisfied feeling—the self-absorbed poet-composer has withdrawn into the peaceful world of art. Toward the end Mahler shows how music has the capacity to sum up in a few brief sounds the entire progress of the poem, the movement from the dissonance of the world to the peace of the inner self. First the strings (at 6:23) play an extended dissonance (F against E♭), which resolves to a consonance (E♭ against E♭), and this is repeated at the very end (6:39) by the English horn, "dying out expressively" as the composer requests. The desire to escape from this dissonant world into the consonant realm of art has been fulfilled.

I Am Lost to the World has been called Mahler's best orchestral song. That he made use of some of this same music in the beautiful slow movement of his Symphony No. 5 suggests that these musical ideas were important to him and express, as he said at the time, "his very self." Both song and symphony have a certain world-weariness about them, as if Mahler had a premonition that both the artist's life and the Romantic era were coming to an end.

LISTENING GUIDE		Gustav Mahler Orchestral song, *I Am Lost to the World*, from the *Five Rückert Songs* (1901–1902)	6CD 5/7 6Tape 5B

0:00	English horn haltingly rises with the melody		
1:00	Voice enters and extends the melody	Ich bin der Welt abhanden gekommen, mit der ich sonst viele Zeit verdorben; sie hat so lange nichts von mir vernommen, sie mag wohl glauben, ich sei gestorben!	I am lost to the world, in which I've squandered so much time; it has known nothing of me for so long, it may well think that I am dead!
1:56	English horn returns with the melody		
2:34	Triplets in harp; faster tempo, recitative quality in the voice	Es ist mir auch gar nichts daran gelegen, ob sie mich für gestorben hält. Ich kann auch gar nichts sagen dagegen, denn wirklich bin ich gestorben der Welt.	I don't really care, if it takes me for dead. Nor can I contradict, for really I am dead to the world.
3:39	Melody returns in English horn; slow, peaceful conclusion	Ich bin gestorben dem Weltgetümmel und ruh' in einem stillen Gebiet! Ich leb' allein in meinem Himmel, in meinem Lieben, in meinem Lied.	I am dead to the world's commotion, and rest in a world of peace. I live alone in my own heaven, in my love, in my song.
5:47	English horn returns with melody		
6:23	Dissonance–consonance in violins		
6:39	Dissonance–consonance in English horn		

(Listening Exercise 38)

LISTENING EXERCISES

	Johannes Brahms	6CD 5/1; 6Tape 5A
35	*Academic Festival Overture* (1880)	3CD 3/5; 3Tape 3A
	Allegro (fast)	

Somewhat intimidated by the great symphonies of Beethoven, Brahms approached the orchestra tentatively. For years he studied the idiomatic qualities of the instruments and how they might be combined, ultimately making his technique of orchestration a distinctive one. His instrumental hues are not so much sharp primary colors as they are blended complementary ones. Rather than have the clarinets *or* violas play a line as a solo, for example, he is more inclined to put both instruments on the line, thereby creating a less incisive but richer blend of sound. Moreover, he continually changes colors as new instruments move in and out of his dense, usually polyphonic orchestral web. The questions in this exercise deal exclusively with Brahms's particular treatment of the orchestra.

Exposition (0:00–5:14)

1. (0:00–0:39) The marchlike opening sounds somewhat foreboding, in part because of the unusual way the music is distributed among the instruments of the orchestra. Which statement correctly describes Brahms's orchestration here at the beginning?
   a. low strings play staccato against faint cymbal crashes, then French horns respond
   b. high strings play staccato against faint timpani roll, then French horns respond
   c. high woodwinds play staccato with faint timpani roll, then French horns respond

2. After the strings interrupt the march with a calm, mainly stepwise melody (0:40–0:48), that musical line is passed along to which quintessentially Romantic instrument (0:49–0:59)?
   a. flute   b. clarinet   c. French horn

3. (1:45–1:48) The presentation of the first theme, part 2, by the brasses is solemnly introduced by which percussion instrument?
   a. snare drum   b. cymbal   c. timpani

4. The melodious second theme is carried by the violins and violas (3:42–3:58), and later the last two measures of it are repeated again and again, in an imaginative way, by the woodwinds and French horn (4:07–4:17). In what order do the woodwinds present this concluding part of the second theme?
   a. flute, oboe, clarinet, French horn
   b. oboe, clarinet, flute, French horn
   c. clarinet, oboe, flute, French horn

5. The zesty closing theme is presented first by the bassoons and then by the oboes (4:32–4:45). After it is briefly extended, it returns again, now somewhat hidden in the midst of the contrapuntal activity. Which instruments play it now (5:00–5:08)?
   a. middle strings (violas and cellos) playing staccato
   b. high strings (violins) playing staccato
   c. woodwinds playing staccato

Development (5:15–6:28)

6. (5:32–6:08) How would you describe the orchestral texture in the center of the development?
   a. full orchestral texture covering a wide range of audible sonic spectrum
   b. thin orchestral texture covering only the middle range of audible sonic spectrum

7. (6:09–6:28) In the retransition, how would you describe Brahms's handling of the orchestral texture?
   a. The texture gets fuller as more and more instruments are added.
   b. The texture becomes suddenly thin as only a few instruments play.

Recapitulation (6:29–9:08)

8. In the recapitulation, is the lush second theme (7:44–8:00) presented once again by the strings? _____

9. Is the closing theme (8:58–9:08) again presented by the bassoons and then oboes as had been the case in the exposition? _____

Coda (9:09–end)

10. Throughout the brief coda, which brass instrument is the primary carrier of the new coda theme (the Latin hymn "Gaudeamus igitur")? _____

---

36   Modest Musorgsky   6CD 5/3–5; 6Tape 5A
       Pictures at an Exhibition (1874)   3CD 3/6; 3Tape 3B
       (orchestrated by Maurice Ravel, 1922)

This work by Musorgsky is a colorful set of ten musical pictures connected by a musical Promenade. Musorgsky's particular use of scales, rhythms, and textures gives his music a decidedly Russian flavor, one that sometimes sounds exotic to our ears. The following questions deal with the Promenade and two of the ten pictures.

Promenade

1. How would you describe the instrumental color and texture of the beginning of the Promenade?
   a. monophonic trumpet followed by polyphonic brass choir
   b. monophonic trumpet followed by homophonic brass choir

2. (1:21–1:38) What is the texture in the brass choir at the end of the Promenade?
   a. polyphonic   b. homophonic

6CD 5/4; 6Tape 5A

Picture 4: *Polish Ox-Cart*

3. What is the meter of this picture?
   a. duple   b. triple

4. What is the mode?
   a. major   b. minor

5. Which graph (or picture) best represents the dynamic course of this movement?
   a.   b.   c.

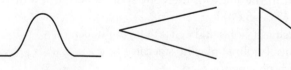

6CD 5/5; 6Tape 5A; 3CD 3/6; 3Tape 3B

Picture 10: *The Great Gate of Kiev*

6. (0:00–1:04) How would you describe the texture and mode at the beginning?
   a. polyphonic and major   b. homophonic and major
   c. polyphonic and minor   d. homophonic and minor

7. (1:05–1:34) When the pilgrims (**B**) return, do the strings provide a counterpoint?
   a. yes   b. no

8. (2:42–3:19) Describe two ways these exotic sounds are created.
   a. _____
   b. _____

9. (3:59–4:50) As the brasses present the Gate theme in the final grand presentation, what do the strings do to fill out the orchestral texture?
   a. play mainly a rapid pizzicato
   b. play mainly a shimmering tremolo
   c. play mainly a nocturne
   d. all of the above

10. Why do you suppose Musorgsky chose not to end his work with the Promenade theme, as he began it? _____

_____

| 37 | Peter Tchaikovsky
Symphonic poem, *Romeo and Juliet* (1869) | 6CD 5/6
6Tape 5B |

Peter Tchaikovsky might be called the quintessential Romantic composer, given his brilliant orchestrations and sweeping, if sometimes sentimental, melodies. Tchaikovsky was not a "developer" in the tradition of Haydn, Beethoven, and Brahms, but usually chose instead to repeat large sections of music. These repetitions he would often partly disguise by means of a new and different orchestration. The following questions focus your attention on various aspects of Tchaikovsky's use of repetition in the symphonic poem *Romeo and Juliet*.

Introduction

1. (0:00–0:35) The opening woodwind passage, which sounds faintly religious, is a musical depiction of the kindly Franciscan monk, Friar Laurence. How would you describe it?
   a. monophonic   b. polyphonic   c. homophonic

0:36–1:05 Anguished dissonances in strings and French horn

2. (1:25–2:06) We hear solo flute and harp strumming. How many times does the harp play its sequence of strumming chords?
   a. once   b. twice   c. three times

3. (2:07–2:33) The Friar Laurence theme now returns. In what way is it different?
   a. Bassoon plays in unison with the melody in woodwinds.
   b. Trumpet plays fanfare against the melody in woodwinds.
   c. Strings provide pizzicato counterpoint to the melody in woodwinds.

2:34–3:04 Repeat of anguished dissonances in strings and horn

4. (3:23–3:55) The harp strumming returns. In what way is it different?
    a. solo flute has been replaced by high violins
    b. flute now plays pizzicato
    c. Friar Laurence theme now heard as a counterpoint

5:01 *Exposition* begins with Feud theme

5. (6:19–6:40) Which sentence best describes what occurs in the transition between the Feud theme and the Love theme?
    a. Woodwinds gradually descend and there is a release of tension.
    b. Strings ascend and there is a release of tension.
    c. Strings descend and there is a release of tension.

6. (7:51–8:10 and again 8:33–8:50) As the Love theme is played passionately by the woodwinds, the French horn provides a counterpoint. How would you describe it?
    a. two-note phrases that gradually ascend by step
    b. two-note phrases that gradually descend by step
    c. three-note phrases that gradually ascend by step

8:51–9:46 Lovely closing section

9:52–11:57 *Development*

7. Is the Love theme anywhere to be heard in the development?
    a. yes   b. no

Recapitulation

8. (11:58–12:21) Has the transition music from the exposition (6:19–6:40) been eliminated here in the recapitulation?
    a. yes   b. no

9. (13:00) When the Love theme returns in its full glory, why does it this time sound so much more passionate and powerful?
    a. because the melody is now played by sweeping strings
    b. because the melody is now played by full brass section
    c. because woodwinds now play the melody louder

10. (13:00–14:00) Does the French horn return again with its counterpoint against the Love theme?
    a. yes   b. no

38	Gustav Mahler	6CD 5/7
	Orchestral song, *I Am Lost to the World*,	6Tape 5B
	from the *Five Rückert Songs* (1901–1902)	

Gustav Mahler's orchestral song *I Am Lost to the World* exploits both the richness of the human voice and the color of the late Romantic orchestra. Listen to this lovely composition and respond to the following questions.

1. At the very beginning, which instrument provides a bass accompaniment below the melody in the English horn?
    a. French horn   b. viola   c. harp

2. Which is the voice that enters?

    a. an alto   b. a tenor   c. a baritone

3. (2:16–2:32) How is the word "gestorben" ("dead") treated?

    a. There is a vocal flourish that is answered by the French horn.

    b. There is a French horn flourish that is answered by the voice.

4. At the end of the second stanza (after "gestorben der Welt"), which musical device is used?

    a. an ascending pizzicato line in the violins

    b. a descending sequence in the violins

    c. an ostinato in the bass

5. For the beginning of the third and final strophe, how would you describe the range of the voice?

    a. falls to the singer's lowest register

    b. continues up to a climax in the singer's highest register

6. The last line of the poem is a fitting epitaph for the entire Romantic era: "in meinem Lieben, in meinem Lied" ("in my love, in my song"). Which is the more correct description of the musical treatment of these two alliterative phrases?

    a. music climaxes on "Lieben" and dies out on "Lied"

    b. starts quietly on "Lieben" and climaxes on "Lied"

7. The movement from dissonance to consonance toward the end, first in the violins (6:23) and then in the English horn (6:39), creates which feeling?

    a. longing and satisfaction   b. a march   c. a waltz

8. This is an orchestral song, and although Mahler later published a version of it with piano accompaniment instead of the orchestra, this later arrangement is not as effective a piece. Which of the following correctly explains why the orchestral version is more successful?

    a. The orchestra can create more colors.

    b. Individual lines of the counterpoint are more audible when assigned to distinctive-sounding instruments.

    c. Winds and strings are better able to sustain pitches than is a piano.

    d. all of the above

9. What role do the brasses play here in Mahler's orchestral song?

_____

10. Is the vocal part of this song strophic or through composed? _____

KEY WORDS

absolute music	orchestral song	Alma Schindler Mahler
Nadezhda von Meck	pentatonic scale	Victor Hartmann
nationalism	the Russian Five	

16

FROM ROMANTIC TO MODERN: IMPRESSIONISM

Romantic music reached its apogee during the late nineteenth century in the grandiose works of Wagner, Tchaikovsky, Brahms, and Mahler. But by 1900 this German-dominated musical empire was in danger of crumbling, shaken by forces both within and without. Some composers outside the mainstream of Romanticism were becoming downright hostile toward the German style, epitomized by the music of Wagner. Not surprisingly, the most powerful anti-German sentiment was felt in France. (France and Germany went to war in 1870 and would do so again in 1914.) After first embracing Wagner during the 1870s and 1880s, the avant-garde of French music had, by the 1890s, turned antagonistic. It began to ridicule the sentimentality of Romanticism in general and the monumental structures of the Germans in particular. German music was said to be too heavy, too pretentious, too bombastic. Wagner's system of obvious leitmotifs* was now deemed overly simplistic—just as clumsy as one of his Nordic giants. True passion, they said, might be expressed in more subtle ways, in something other than sheer volume of sound and epic length.

IMPRESSIONISM IN PAINTING AND MUSIC

The movement that arose in France in opposition to German Romantic music has been given the name **Impressionism.** We are, of course, more familiar with this term as a designation for a school of French painters living and working in Paris during the last decades of the nineteenth century. That group included Claude Monet (1840–1926), Edgar Degas (1834–1917), Camille Pissarro (1830–1903), Alfred Sisley (1839–1899), Auguste Renoir (1841–1919), and the American Mary Cassatt (1844–1926). Impressionist painters were not overtly anti-German like their musical counterparts. There was no need to be, for French painting had a long and secure tradition (Figs. 6–4, 8–7 and 13–14), one not subject to threat of foreign domination. Their rebellion was against the traditional, academic style of painting of their native land.

The Impressionist movement in painting began in the early 1870s when Monet and his colleagues were forbidden to show their canvases in the official Parisian Salon. Consequently, they launched their own exhibition. In the uproar

FIGURE 16–1
The painting that gave its name to an epoch, Claude Monet's *Impression: Sunrise*, was exhibited at the first group exhibition organized by Monet, Renoir, Degas, and Pissarro, in Paris in 1874. The ships, rowboats and other elements in the early morning light are more suggested than fully drawn. Said the critic Louis Leroy derisively of this painting at the time: "Wallpaper in its most embryonic state is more finished than that seascape."

that followed, the artists were jeeringly called "impressionists" for the sometimes-vague quality of their art. The painters accepted the name, partly as an act of defiance against the establishment, and soon the term was universally adopted.

It is ironic that this style of French painting generated such controversy, for no school of painters is now more popular with the general public than the Impressionists. Indeed, judging by museum attendance and the number of books and reproductions sold, there is an almost limitless enthusiasm for the works of Monet, Degas, Renoir, and their associates—precisely the paintings that the artists' contemporaries mocked and jeered. But what is it about the Impressionist style that then caused such a furor?

The Impressionists were the first to turn against representational art, the idea that a painting should exactly represent an object, as in a photograph. Instead, they tried to recreate the impression that the object produced on their senses. The key here is light: The Impressionists saw all objects as awash in vibrant rays of light and sought to capture the aura that the light-bathed object created in the eye of the beholder. To accomplish this they covered their canvases with small, dablike brushstrokes in which light was broken down into spots of color. This creates a sense of constant movement and fluidity. Shapes are not clearly defined but blurred, more suggested than delineated. Minor details disappear. Sunlight is everywhere and everything shimmers (Fig. 16-2).

style of Impressionist painters

As impressions and sensations became paramount for these painters, it is not surprising that they showed an intensified interest in music. What art form is more elusive and suggestive? What medium allows the receiver—the listener—more freedom to interpret the sensations he or she perceives? Painters began to speak in musical terms. Paul Gauguin (1848–1903) referred to the harmonies of line and color as the "music of painting," and Vincent Van Gogh (1853–1890) suggested "using color as the music of tones." Paul Cézanne (1839–1906) painted an "overture" in homage to Wagner, while James Whistler (1834–1903), an

painters and musicians allied

FIGURE 16–2

Claude Monet, *The Bridge at Bougival* (1869). The illuminated clouds, the shadows on the bridge, and the reflection on the water all impart a vibrant sense of light as the rays of the sun project down from the sky and across the bridge.

American who worked in Paris in the 1860s and 1880s, created "nocturnes" and "symphonies." The artist envied the musician's good fortune to work in a medium in which flux and change could be continually expressed—rather than one that required the artist to seize the moment and fix it on canvas. At the same time Claude Debussy, the musician whose work most consistently displayed the Impressionist style in music, found inspiration for his work in the visual arts. He called various collections of his pieces *Sketches*, *Images*, and *Prints*. Rare are the moments in history when the aesthetic aims of painters and musicians were as closely allied.

Claude Debussy (1862–1918)

Claude Debussy was born in 1862 into a modest family living in a small town outside Paris. Since neither of his parents was musical, it came as a surprise when their son demonstrated talent at the keyboard. At the age of ten he was sent off to the Paris Conservatory for lessons in piano, composition, and music theory. Owing to his skills as a performer he was soon engaged for summer work in the household of Nadezhda von Meck, a wealthy patroness of the arts and the principal supporter of Tchaikovsky (see Fig. 15–11). This employment took him, in turn, to Italy, Russia, and Vienna. In 1884 he won the Prix de Rome, an official prize in composition supported by the French government, one that required a three-year stay in Rome. But Debussy was not happy in the Eternal City. He preferred the Bohemian life of Paris, the atmosphere of the bistros and the cafes.

Returning to Paris more or less permanently in 1887, the young Frenchman continued to learn his craft and search for his own independent voice as a composer. He had some minor successes, and yet, as he said in 1893, "There are still things that I am not able to do—create masterpieces, for example." But the next year, in 1894, he did just that. With the completion of *Prélude à L'Après-midi d'un Faune (Prelude to The Afternoon of a Faun)*, he gave to the public what has

FIGURE 16–3

Claude Debussy.

become his most enduring orchestral work. Debussy's later compositions, including his opera *Pelléas et Mélisande* (1902), the orchestral *La Mer* (*The Sea*, 1905), and his two books of *Preludes* for piano, met with less popular favor. Critics complained of a certain formlessness and a lack of melody. Today, with the advantage of a century of hindsight, these works are seen as early beacons pointing straight down the road to musical modernism. *La Mer* has become a staple in the repertoire of every professional orchestra, *Pelléas* is a standing production of every major opera house, and the *Preludes* form part of the required literature for every would-be concert pianist. Illness and the outbreak of World War I (1914) brought Debussy's musical productivity to a virtual standstill. He died of cancer in the spring of 1918 while the guns of the German army were shelling Paris from the north.

PRELUDE TO THE AFTERNOON OF A FAUN (1894)

Debussy spent his time more in the company of poets and painters than with musicians. His orchestral *Prelude to The Afternoon of a Faun*, in fact, was written to precede a staged reading of the poem *The Afternoon of a Faun* by his friend and mentor Stéphane Mallarmé (Fig. 16–4).

Mallarmé was the spiritual leader of a group of versifiers in *fin-du-siècle* Paris called the **Symbolists,** poets whose aesthetic aims were in harmony with those of the Impressionist painters. They worked to create a suggestive verse in which the sound of the word, and the associations that that sound might produce, were more important than the literal meaning of the word. Symbolism is certainly at the heart of Mallarmé's evocative *The Afternoon of a Faun*, which applies suggestive language to an ancient Greek theme. The faun of Mallarmé's poem is not a young deer but a satyr (a mythological beast that is half man, half goat). He spends his days in pursuit of sexual gratification at the expense of the nymphs who inhabit the forest. On this afternoon we see the faun, exhausted from the morning's escapades, reclining on the forest floor in the still air of the midday heat. He contemplates future conquests while piping listlessly on his flute. A passage from the poem suggests the dreamlike mood, vague and elusive, that Debussy was challenged to recreate.

FIGURE 16–4

The poet Stéphane Mallarmé, author of *The Afternoon of a Faun*, as painted by the great predecessor of the Impressionists, Edouard Manet (1832–1883). Mallarmé was a friend and artistic mentor of the composer Debussy.

Symbolist poetry

FIGURE 16–5

Mallarmé's *The Afternoon of a Faun* created something of a sensation among late nineteenth-century French artists. This painting by Ker-Xavier Roussel (1867–1944) is just one of several such representations of the Faun surrounded by woodland nymphs.

No murmur of water in the woodland scene,
Bathed only in the sounds of my flute.
And the only breeze, except for my two pipes,
Blows itself empty long before
It can scatter the sound in an arid rain.
On a horizon unmoved by a ripple
This sound, visible and serene,
Mounts to the heavens, an inspired wisp.

Debussy wisely made no effort to follow Mallarmé's poem closely—the poem is just a succession of feelings, not a narrative program. Debussy, moreover, was no composer of programmatic music like Berlioz or Tchaikovsky. As he said at the time of the first performance in December 1894: "My *Prelude* is really a sequence of mood paintings, throughout which the desire and dreams of the Faun move in the heat of the midday sun." When Mallarmé had heard the music, he, in turn, said the following about Debussy's musical response to the poem: "I never expected anything like it. The music prolongs the emotion of my poem and paints its scenery more passionately than colors could."

Significantly, both musician and poet refer to *Prelude to The Afternoon of a Faun* in terms of painting. But how does one create a painting in music? Here a tableau is depicted by using the distinctive colors of the instruments, especially the woodwinds, to evoke vibrant moods and sensations. The flute has one timbre, the oboe another, the clarinet yet a third. Debussy has said, in effect: Let us focus on the sound-producing capacity of the instruments, let us see what new shades can be elicited from them, let us try new registers, let us try new combinations. Thus a solo flute begins in its lowest register (the pipes of the faun), followed by a harp glissando*, then dabs of color from the French horn. These tonal impressions swirl, dissolve, and reform, but seem not to progress: There is no regular rhythm or discernible meter to push them along. All is languid beauty, a music that is utterly original yet shockingly sensual.

FIGURE 16–6

In 1912 the music of Debussy's *Prelude to The Afternoon of a Faun* was set as a ballet by the famous *Ballets russes* (see page 348). Here the dancer Vaslav Nijinsky assumes the role of the faun.

LISTENING GUIDE

Claude Debussy
Prelude to The Afternoon of a Faun (1894)

6CD 5/8; 6Tape 5B
3CD 3/7; 3Tape 3B

(Form: Ternary **ABA'**)   **A**

0:00	Solo flute plays twisting chromatic line
0:20	Harp glissandos and dabs of color from French horns

0:57	Flute continues with melody, then passes it to oboe
1:37	Crescendo that disappears before it can climax
2:03	Return of melody to flute

B

3:17   Clarinet and then flute play rapid chromatic arabesques

4:15   Crescendo that melts into clarinet solo
5:11   Sweeping Romantic theme in woodwinds

5:50   Sweeping theme repeated in violins, then solo violin

A'

7:05   Solo flute, then oboe return with twisting chromatic line
8:19   Solo flute plays theme again above string tremolo
9:06   Solo viola in low range of instrument plays chromatic line
9:30   Oboe offers complement to the line

CODA

9:54   Ostinato* in harps
10:03   Violins and French horns move up and down in lock step (parallel motion)
10:15   Dabs of sound in various instruments

(Listening Exercise 39)

Debussy's voluptuous *Prelude* creates an entirely new world of musical aesthetics, one very different from the German Romantic school of Mendelssohn, Wagner, and Brahms. Where a composer in the German Romantic tradition asserts a strongly profiled theme, a French Impressionist like Debussy will insinuate a tiny motive. Instead of clear meters and regular rhythms, the Impressionist favors constantly shifting accents that obscure the pulse. Instead of working toward a thunderous climax and a strong cadence, the Impressionist prefers to avoid a climax by placing a diminuendo before the cadence, thereby creating an anticlimax. Instead of moving purposefully along a well-directed harmonic progression, the Impressionist chooses to sit on a single static harmony and let the colorful instruments work their magic. Most important, instead of having musical color reinforce the musical theme, the Impressionist prefers to call on the instruments to demonstrate their sonorities independent of theme. What is radically new about Debussy's music is that beautiful sonorities are allowed simply to exist without having constantly to progress, by means of themes, to some distant goal.

Indeed, with the opening notes of the faun's flute in his *Prelude*, Claude Debussy breathed new life into the art of music, introducing an element of modernism. Think back to the orchestral music of Mozart, Beethoven, Brahms, or Tchaikovsky. When a new theme enters in their works, it is almost invariably presented and carried forward by a new instrument or group of instruments. Instrumental color thus reinforces and gives profile to the theme. The exposition and development of the themes, working in tandem with harmony, in turn create the musical form. With Debussy, on the other hand, color becomes independent of melody. Instruments enter with a distinct color but no easily discernible

German Romanticism vs. French Impressionism

color liberated from melody

FIGURE 16–7

Auguste Renoir, *Le Grenouillère* (1869), a popular outdoor eating and bathing site on the Seine painted many times by both Renoir and Monet. Our present-day love of Impressionist art is due at least in part to the relaxed mood created by the pastel hues and diffused light. Also, because the Impressionists usually painted scenes from everyday life, a deep knowledge of religious symbolism and pictorial conventions is not a pre-condition for enjoyment.

a modern use of color and texture

theme. The instrumental groupings can be more dense or less dense. Thus color and texture begin to replace melody as the primary agents in the creation of musical form. The revolutionary figures of twentieth-century music who use colors and textures exclusively to generate form—among them Varèse, Webern, and Ives (see Chapter 17)—found a precedent for their modernist approach to musical form in the compositions of the Impressionist Claude Debussy.

PRELUDES FOR PIANO (1910, 1913)

Debussy's last and most far-reaching attempt at descriptive writing in music is found in the two books of *Preludes* for piano that he published in 1910 and 1913. Here the challenge to create musical impressions was all the greater, for the piano has a more limited musical palette than the multicolor orchestra. The evocative titles of some of these short pieces allude to their mysterious qualities: *Steps in the Snow, The Sunken Cathedral, What the West Wind Saw,* and *Sounds and*

music as perfume?

Perfumes Swirl in the Night Air. Timbres and textures can be produced in music, and images and events can be suggested, if not actually depicted. But can music really stimulate our sense of smell? Can it create perfume? Presumably not. That Debussy suggests it might shows how intent he was to create an ideal sort of music, one involving all the senses. As he says of this perfect music, "It would involve a mysterious collaboration of the air, of the movement of leaves and of the perfume of flowers along with music; music would serve to bind all these elements in a way so natural that their unity would seem to grow from all of them."

Voiles (Sails, 1910)

Voiles (Sails), from the first book of Preludes, takes us to the sea. In our mind's eye is implanted the vision of a boat resting on becalmed waters. The sails flap listlessly in a fluid descent, mostly in parallel thirds. The hazy, languid atmosphere is created in part by the special scale Debussy employs, the **whole-tone scale.** All the notes of the whole-tone scale are a whole step apart:

FIGURE 16–8
Claude Monet's *Sailboats on the Seine* (1874). The gentle rocking of the boats is suggested by the exaggerated reflections on the water.

EXAMPLE 16–1

Because in the whole-tone scale each note is the same distance from its neighbor, no one pitch is heard as the tonal center—they all seem equally important. The composer can stop on any note of the scale and it will sound no more central, or final, than any other note. The music floats without a tonal anchor. Then, as if impelled by a puff of wind, the boat seems to rock on the now-rippling waters. Debussy creates this gentle rocking by inserting a four-note ostinato* into the texture. Ostinatos are frequently employed by Impressionist composers. They help account for the often static, restful feeling in the harmony. By definition, ostinatos involve repetition rather than dramatic movement.

whole-tone scale

return to ostinatos

EXAMPLE 16–2

Suddenly a gust of wind shakes the ship as the pianist races up the scale in a harplike glissando*. This scale, however, is different from the preceding whole-tone one. It is a pentatonic scale*. There are only five notes within each octave, here the five notes corresponding to the black keys on the piano. We have seen before that the pentatonic scale is often found in folk music (see page 311). Debussy first encountered it in the Indonesian music he heard at the Paris International Exhibit of 1889 (see Fig. 16–12).

EXAMPLE 16–3

Following this energized whirl around the pentatonic scale, the seascape regains its placid demeanor as the whole-tone scale returns and, ultimately, the descending thirds with which the piece began. At the end Debussy directs the pianist to push down and hold the sustaining pedal (the right-most of the three pedals). Once the sustaining pedal is pressed and held, all notes sounded thereafter will blur into a vague haze, similar to the hazes and mists that envelop many Impressionist paintings (see Fig. 16–1).

LISTENING GUIDE

Claude Debussy
Voiles (Sails), from *Preludes*, Book I (1910)

6CD 5/9
6Tape 5B

0:00	Descending parallel thirds using whole-tone scale
0:14	Bass pedal point* enters
1:11	Ostinato enters in middle register
1:40	Ostinato moves into top register
2:14	Harplike glissandos using pentatonic scale
2:28	Chords moving in parallel motion above pedal point
2:51	Glissandos now employing whole-tone scale
3:18	Opening descending thirds return
3:57	Glissandos blur through use of sustaining pedal

La Cathédrale engloutie (The Sunken Cathedral, 1910)
Later in his first book of Preludes for piano, Debussy uses the sustaining pedal to help create another misty image, that of a water-engulfed cathedral. At the outset of *The Sunken Cathedral* the pedal allows high and low chords to sound throughout the measure while other chords move in quarter notes in the middle

register. Here again a wash of sound results (see Ex. 16–4). Notice also that the chords moving in quarter notes do so in what is called a parallel motion. In **parallel motion** all parts move together, locked in step, in the same direction. Parallel motion is the antithesis of counterpoint, the traditional musical technique in which two or more lines usually move in opposite directions to one another. Parallel motion was an innovation of Debussy, and it was one way he expressed his opposition to the German school of Wagner and Brahms, so heavily steeped in counterpoint.

parallel motion, the opposite of counterpoint

EXAMPLE 16–4

By means of these parallel chords, the cathedral slowly rises, "gradually emerging from the fog," as Debussy says in his directions to the pianist. A Gregorian-chant-like theme, which had been suggested at the beginning, now emerges fully formed (2:25). Once again Debussy chooses to construct his melody on an unusual scale:

EXAMPLE 16–5

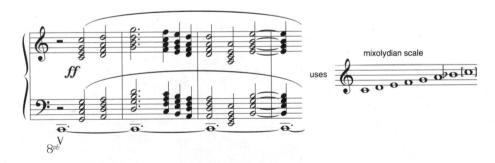

Appropriate for a vision of a medieval cathedral is his selection of one of the old medieval church modes, the **mixolydian scale**, an early type of scalar pattern used in Gregorian chant. In the mixolydian scale, just as in the whole-tone scale and in the pentatonic scale, there is no leading tone* and consequently little pull to the tonic. Soon the pentatonic scale is also heard, as are chords that descend in Debussy's now-familiar parallel motion. This time the chords are all parallel **seventh chords,** four-note chords consisting of a triad with another third on top:

mixolydian scale

EXAMPLE 16–6

parallel seventh chord

Ultimately, the Gregorian chant theme returns in a final statement (5:09), now engulfed by a muddy, undulating bass. The cathedral has once more returned to the depths.

LISTENING GUIDE

Claude Debussy
The Sunken Cathedral, from *Preludes*, Book I (1910)

6CD 5/10
6Tape 5B

| 0:00 | Parallel chords rise from the murky deep |

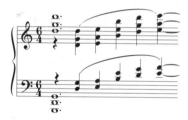

0:40	Slower-moving parallel octaves
1:10	More parallel chords
1:22	Bass begins to move in triplets as the cathedral "rises from the fog"
1:40	Gradual crescendo to a climax
2:04	Bells are sounded as descending parallel octaves
2:25	Gregorian chant theme enters *ff* in parallel chords

3:26	Gradual diminuendo and fadeout
3:50	Quiet melody (on pentatonic scale) enters, grows louder and higher
4:43	Parallel seventh chords, mostly descending
5:09	Murky ostinato enters in the bass as echo of Gregorian chant theme is heard above
6:04	Rising parallel chords as at the beginning
6:19	Final sustained chords

Debussy's *Cathedral* depicts three different views of this mythical church: the cathedral rising from the ocean floor in the early morning mist, sparkling in the radiant light of the noonday sun, and sinking again into the vapors of evening darkness. His method is not dissimilar to that of the painter Claude Monet, who sought to capture, at various times of the day, the effect of fleeting rays of light on the west face of the cathedral of Rouen (Fig. 16–9). While it required a whole set of canvases for Monet to show the effect of light on a single object, the continuous quality of music allowed Debussy to encompass his ever-changing scene within a single composition.

FIGURE 16–9

Three of the thirty paintings of the west façade of the cathedral of Rouen that Claude Monet created between 1892 and 1894. Monet tried to show the facade of the church bathed in different sorts of light, just as Debussy tried to create different musical views of his *Sunken Cathedral*.

THE EXOTIC IN MUSIC

Maurice Ravel (1875–1937), Emmanuel Chabrier (1841–1894), and Paul Dukas (1865–1935), all natives of France, and the Englishman Frederick Delius (1862–1934) are also commonly referred to as Impressionists. Yet their creations are brimming with what might be called the "exotic" in music. This passion for the exotic was part of the widespread movement in the arts at the turn of the century that sought delight in the mysterious and the far-off.

The painters of the period were most obviously affected. Claude Monet felt the attraction of Japanese colors and designs, as can be seen, for example, in his startling portrait of his wife in traditional Japanese costume (Fig. 16–10). Modernists like Pablo Picasso (1881–1973) and Georges Braque (1882–1963) began collecting African art in Paris about this time. Some historians believe that the Cubist movement in painting (see page 342) was born of Picasso's interest in African sculpture and ceremonial masks. Paul Gauguin (1848–1903) followed his passion for non-Western art farthest afield. His love of Oceanic colors and costumes took him to Martinique, Tahiti, and the nearby Marquesas Islands, where he died in 1903 (Fig. 16–11).

a passion for non-Western art

FIGURES 16–10 AND 16–11

(left) Claude Monet, *La Japonaise* (*Madame Camille Monet in Japanese Costume*, 1876). America and Europe began to show an enthusiasm for things Japanese after the opening of trade with Japan in the 1850s. Fashionable Parisian women wore kimonos and furnished their homes with oriental furniture, painted scenes, and other *objets d'art*. (right) The painter Paul Gauguin went farthest afield in a quest for the exotic, spending much of the last twelve years of his life in the South Seas. His painting *Musique barbare* (1892) is a rendering of an Indonesian gamelan orchestra. Three years earlier, Debussy came under the sway of Indonesian music in Paris.

The composer Claude Debussy, of course, had not been immune from the influence of foreign sounds. As we have seen, in 1889 Debussy attended the International Exhibition in Paris, the world's fair for which the Eiffel Tower was constructed (Fig. 16–12). There he not only saw newfangled inventions like electric lighting and electric-powered elevators but he also heard the colorful sounds of a gamelan* orchestra from Java (Indonesia). This stimulus caused him to experiment with the non-Western pentatonic scale and with static, nonfunctional harmonies. It also encouraged him to think differently about time in music—a musician could create a sound and repeat it endlessly without being compelled to move on. Later Debussy would write a piano piece entitled *Pagodas* (1903) and an Egyptian ballet called *Khamma* (1912). In these the influence of authentic Cambodian or Egyptian music is slight. Rather, Debussy drew inspiration from the visual arts of these countries and from what his fancy told him this music ought to sound like. Unlike the painter Gauguin, Debussy's imagination was greater than his will to travel.

The music of Maurice Ravel has many of the same qualities as Debussy's. Ravel's hour-long ballet based on an ancient Greek story, *Daphnis et Chloé* (1912), is full of Impressionist gestures: rippling harp glissandos, parallel descents, ostinatos, shimmering string tremolos, and arabesques for solo flute. Yet Ravel's textures are clearer, his forms more distinct, and his harmonies more inclined to move in purposeful progressions. Ravel, too, had a fondness for the exotic, as can be seen in works such as *Shéhérazade* (1903), which hints at the music of the Middle East, and *Songs of Madagascar* (1926), with their African flavor. We have already seen how Ravel captured the spirit of a seductive Spanish dance in his ever-popular *Bolero* (1928) (pages 8–11).

Two other composers who sought musical inspiration beyond the confines of Europe were Albert Roussel (1869–1937) and Giacomo Puccini (1858–1924; see page 297). In his orchestral *Evocations* (1911) and opera-ballet *Padmâvatî* (1914), Roussel carried to new heights the musical treatment of exotic motifs by making use of Hindu scales from India. Puccini looked for subjects even farther afield, to China, Japan, and the American West, in his operas *Turandot* (1924), *Madam Butterfly* (1904), and *The Girl of the Golden West* (1910).

The love of the exotic, the foreign, and the mysterious were all part of a final expression of Romanticism in the arts. The Romantic writer, beginning with Lord Byron (see page 234), had taught that a free spirit must experience all that the world has to offer. Reality could be found in different forms and in many different lands. The Romantic spirit would go forth to embrace them all. But these distant visions, exotic fantasies, and escapist desires could not last long in the face of global warfare. Such late-Romantic sentiments were soon pushed aside by the grim events of the twentieth century.

FIGURE 16–12

The Cambodian Pagoda at the International Exposition in Paris in 1889. Here Debussy heard the music of Cambodia, China, and Indonesia, and he began to formulate a musical aesthetic different from the prevailing German symphonic tradition.

LISTENING EXERCISE

39   Claude Debussy   6CD 5/8; 6Tape 5B
       Prelude to The Afternoon of a Faun, 1894   3CD 3/7; 3Tape 3B

Debussy, as we have seen, was a master at extracting new sonorities and textures from the traditional Western orchestra. The following questions, therefore, deal mainly with issues of color and texture. Be sure that you have read the entire chapter, as some of the terms employed here appear only toward the end of the discussion of Impressionism in music.

1. (0:00–0:23) What is the musical texture at the beginning?
   a. monophonic   b. polyphonic   c. homophonic
2. (0:57–1:20) When the flute returns with the twisting chromatic line, is the texture the same as it was at the beginning of the piece? _____
3. (1:37–2:03) Here is an instance where Debussy avoids a climax by repeating a motive as it fades away. By continually repeating a motive on the same pitches Debussy is employing
   a. an arpeggio.   b. a pedal point.   c. an ostinato.
4. (1:37–2:03) Which dynamic markings does Debussy prescribe to create this feeling of an evasion and anticlimax?
   a. crescendo–diminuendo   b. diminuendo–crescendo
5. (2:03, 2:18, 2:40, and 7:05) When the flute returns with the twisting chromatic line, which instrument provides a colorful background?
   a. harp   b. French horn   c. English horn
6. Appropriately enough, what is this instrument playing to help create this background "wash of sound"?
   a. chromatic scales   b. pedal points   c. arpeggios
7. (3:21–3:46) Which is a correct description of the music at this point?
   a. Various instruments dart in and out with tiny motives, creating colorful sonorities but a discontinuous texture.
   b. The violins sweep forward with a sensuous, rhythmically free melody based on a whole-tone scale.

8. (5:50–7:02) In this beautiful passage Debussy comes closest to recreating the lush sentimentality more typical of Romantic than Impressionist music. Which statement is *not* correct?
   a. There is a long, sweeping, rhythmically free melody.
   b. The melody is played expressively by the violins.
   c. There is a solo for French horn and then violin at the beginning.
   d. There is a solo for French horn and then violin at the end.
9. A passage with a prominent flute is stated (7:05–7:32) and then repeated at a lower pitch (7:36–8:09), now featuring an oboe. What happens to the texture and orchestration in the course of each of these two passages?
   a. Homophonic texture and unchanging orchestration give way to polyphonic texture and discontinuous orchestration.
   b. Polyphonic texture and discontinuous orchestration give way to homophonic texture and unchanging orchestration.
10. In a typical Romantic work for symphony orchestra, it is usually the strings, particularly the violins, that present and develop most themes. In Debussy's Impressionist *Prelude*, however, the instruments of which family introduce most melodic motives? _____

KEY WORDS

Impressionism	parallel motion	Symbolists
mixolydian scale	seventh chord	whole-tone scale

A checklist of the musical style of Impressionist composers is given on page 67.

THE TWENTIETH CENTURY

17

B y the standards of any age, the twentieth century must be seen as an
eventful, even calamitous, period. Two world wars, a world-wide
depression, the extermination of millions of people, the atomic
bomb, the cold war, biological weapons, and acts of terrorism have
marked its progression. At the same time, scientific advances have
improved the quality and length of life: The automobile and airplane, antibi-
otics, organ transplants, computers, satellite communications, and radio and
television have had a profound impact on our daily lives. Some inventions—the
radio, the magnetic tape recorder, long-playing records, the compact disc, and
now the CD-ROM—have greatly affected our musical culture, bringing serious
music to a much larger segment of the general populace and stimulating the
growth of popular and commercial music in an unprecedented way. Thus, the
tenor of the age has been one of discovery as well as of fear and anxiety brought
about by the constant threat of war, nuclear annihilation, or ethnic cleansing.
During the first half of the twentieth century in particular, scarcely a family in
Europe and America went untouched by the Depression and two world wars. All
of the composers whose works are discussed early in this chapter had their lives
drastically altered by one or the other of the wars and the rise of fascism in
Europe. The anxiety and disjunction that you will feel in much of their music is
an artistic expression of the social upheavals and underlying uncertainties of the
twentieth century.

MODERNISM: DIVERSITY AND EXPERIMENTATION

Given all the good and ill that have marked the last hundred years, it is hardly
surprising to find that in matters of culture the twentieth century has experienced great diversity and what appears to be a corresponding lack of cohesion.
Where is its artistic core? What have been the main artistic currents? What will
be the mainstream for the future?

In previous periods in the history of music, each era seems to have developed
a general musical style that constituted a sort of synthesis of what that age
believed to be the norm, or model, for the music of that time. There was, or
appears to have been, little in the way of radical experimentation with the

experimentation and diversity

accepted notion of what music was to be. The style of Palestrina in the late Renaissance, of Bach and Handel in the late Baroque era, and of Haydn and Mozart in the late Classical period might be seen as representing these musical norms. But in the modern period a consensus has yet to be reached. No one style has emerged as dominant and lasting. We have seen a bewildering variety of styles come and go: atonal music, twelve-tone music, electronic music, chance music, Neo-classicism, and minimalism have all enjoyed favor at one time or another. We will discuss each of these styles in this chapter, but no one of them can be said to be the mainstream of musical modernism. From a vantage point at the end of this century, the last hundred years appears as a time of alienation, fragmentation, experimentation, and diversity. It is the radically experimental quality of this music, and of our culture in general, that allows us to call it modern or avant-garde.

Radical experimentation in music began shortly before World War I (1914–1918). The new music was not a further evolution of the German-dominated symphonic style of late Romanticism but a sharp turning away from it. It renounced the notion that music should be beautiful and pleasing, expressive or elevating, that it should delight or comfort the listener. Instead, it resorted to distortion, even violence, of sound, to shock the listening audience. Arnold Schoenberg's early experiments with dissonance were received with hoots by a hostile public in Vienna in 1913; Igor Stravinsky's dissonant chords and pounding rhythms caused a riot at the first performance of *Le Sacre du printemps* (*The Rite of Spring*) in Paris the same year. The intent of the avant-garde composer was to shake the listener out of a state of cultural complacency, just as the artist of the period offended middle-class sensibilities by means of radical visual distortions.

Indeed, there are clear parallels between the music and the art of the early twentieth century. The increasingly angular melody and discontinuous rhythm of the new music found analogous expression in an artistic style called **Cubism.** A Cubist painting is one in which the artist fractures and dislocates formal reality into geometrical blocks and planes, as in Pablo Picasso's (1881–1973) famous *Les Demoiselles d'Avignon* (1907) (Fig. 17–1), where the female form has been

FIGURES 17–1 AND 17–2

(left) One of the first statements of Cubist art, Picasso's *Les Demoiselles d'Avignon* (1907). The ladies of the evening are depicted by means of geometric shapes on a flat, two-dimensional plane. Like much avant-garde music of the time, Cubist paintings reject the emotionalism and decorative appeal of nineteenth-century art. (right) *The Wind's Bride* (1914) by Oskar Kokoschka—an Expressionist self-portrait of the artist and Alma Mahler (see page 319), with whom the painter lived following the death of the composer Gustav Mahler in 1911. The painter's introspective look into the subconscious has its analogue in Schoenberg's hyperexpressive works written before World War I.

recast into angular, interlocking shapes. During the 1910s and 1920s, Picasso and Stravinsky were friends and occasional artistic collaborators in Paris. So disjointed did the musical line become in the works of Arnold Schoenberg that melody as we know it all but disappeared. At that very time a group of painters working mainly in Germany in a style called Expressionism (see page 355), because they expressed intense internal feelings, so distorted formal reality that objects in their paintings were sometimes barely recognizable. A man and woman are discernible in Oskar Kokoschka's *The Wind's Bride* (1914) (Fig. 17–2), but where is the audience in Wassily Kandinsky's *Concert* (1911) (Fig. 17–3)? Even more shocking art was produced by the Dadaists (a movement begun in Zurich in 1916) and the Surrealists (formed in Paris in 1922), the latter group glorifying the mysteries of the subconscious (Fig. 17–4). Cubism, Expressionism, Dadaism, Surrealism, and later Abstract Expressionism, Optical art, and Pop art are a few of the diverse artistic movements that have left their mark on the twentieth century. Diversity and radical experimentation are hallmarks of modern art no less than they are of modern music.

FIGURES 17–3 AND 17–4

(left) Wassily Kandinsky's *Impression III (Concert)* (1911). Kandinsky was one of the founders of the Expressionist movement, which was centered in Vienna and Munich. This painting of an audience at a concert does not portray a scene so much as it conveys a psychological state, the audience's reaction to the concert. (right) Like the Expressionists, the Surrealists sought to probe the subconscious mind, where unexpected associations might lurk. René Magritte's *Portrait* (1935) calls into question our belief in reality and traditional classification of art by genre. Does the eye in the midst of a piece of ham make this still life a portrait?

TWENTIETH CENTURY MUSICAL STYLE

Despite its diversity, there are, nonetheless, several constant qualities of modern music that create a consistent musical style. These are most forcefully expressed in the elements of melody, harmony, rhythm, and tone color.

Melody: More Angularity and Chromaticism

Music in the Romantic era focused on melody—long sweeping lines that tended to unfold in balanced phrases. The Romantic melody was generally conjunct* in its motion (moving more by steps than by leaps) and built on the notes of the diatonic* scale, though chromatic notes became increasingly frequent toward the end of the nineteenth century. By the early twentieth century, however, this

asymmetrical, angular themes

sort of smooth, controlled melody was becoming out of fashion. The young avant-garde composers now favored themes that were more asymmetrical, fragmented, and angular. They bent over backward to avoid writing conjunct, stepwise lines. Rather than moving up a half-step from C to D♭, for example, they were wont to jump down a major seventh to the D♭ an octave below. Avoiding a simple interval for a more distant one an octave above or below is called **octave displacement** and it is a feature of modern music. So, too, is the heavy use of chromaticism. In the following example by Arnold Schoenberg (1874–1951), notice how the melody makes large leaps where it might more easily move by steps and also how several sharps and flats are introduced to produce a highly chromatic line:

EXAMPLE 17–1

Unlike the melodies of the Romantic period, many of which are song-like in style and therefore easily sung and remembered, there are very few themes in twentieth-century music that the listener goes away humming. In fact, melody per se is less important to the avant-garde composer than is a pulsating rhythm, an unusual texture, or a new sonority.

Harmony: More Dissonance, New Chords, New Systems

Throughout the Baroque, Classical, and Romantic eras, the basic building block of music was the triad*—a consonant, three-note chord. Dissonance was inserted in order to provide tension and variety, but like a hot spice it had to be used sparingly and resolved to a blander consonance. By the late Romantic period, however, composers like Richard Wagner (1813–1883) began to enrich their music with more and more chromaticism. This, in turn, created greater dissonance simply because the added chromatic notes generated more and more chords that were not consonant triads. By the first decade of the twentieth century, some composers, such as Arnold Schoenberg, were using so much chromaticism that the triad all but disappeared. Dissonance became so frequent that it was almost as common as consonance—the exception was becoming the norm. As Igor Stravinsky (1882–1971) said about this reassessment, "Dissonance is now no more an agent of disorder than consonance is a guarantee of security." Hence, the music of the early avant-garde composers took on a harsher, more strident sound, one that has been maintained in modern music, with rare exception, down to the present day. In the course of time we have simply come to accept a greater level of dissonance in the music that we hear, not only in art music but also in popular idioms like film scores and heavy metal rock.

the liberation of dissonance

In addition to creating dissonance by chromatically obscuring the triad, twentieth-century composers created dissonance by means of new chords. This was done mainly by superimposing more thirds on top of the consonant triad. In this way were produced not only the seventh chord* (a seventh chord spans seven letters of the scale, from A to G, for example) but also the **ninth chord** and the **eleventh chord.** The more thirds that were added on top of the basic triad, the more dissonant the sound of the chord:

new chords

EXAMPLE 17–2

eleventh chord

Some composers, including Stravinsky, Béla Bartók (1881–1945), and Aaron Copland (1900–1991), created new dissonant chords by stacking one triad or seventh chord upon another to create a **polychord**. A very dissonant sound is produced if the bottom notes of the two triads are at a dissonant interval from each other, say a major or a minor second away:

polychords

EXAMPLE 17–3

C major triad   D major triad   dissonant polychord

Polychords help create the jarring, clashing sound that is so much a part of modern music.

But perhaps the most challenging harmonic issue facing composers of the twentieth century was the question "What do we do without tonality?" As we have seen, both Richard Wagner and Claude Debussy in different ways moved away from major–minor tonality, a system that had ruled music for nearly two hundred years. Tonality, with its network of closely related keys, provided a structure for music. Without it composers had to find a new basis for structure. The long ostinatos* of Stravinsky and the twelve-tone* method of Schoenberg (both discussed later in the chapter) are modern responses to this need to impose musical structure in the absence of traditional tonality.

Rhythm: New Asymmetrical Rhythms and Irregular Meters

Most art music before the twentieth century, and indeed all of our pop and rock music down to the present day, is built on regular patterns of duple (2/4), triple (3/4), or quadruple (4/4) meter. Romantic music of the previous generation of composers had many qualities to recommend it: direct expression, broad themes, powerful climaxes, and moments of tender lyricism, to name a few. But only rarely was it carried along by an exciting, vital rhythm, staying instead within the comfortable confines of regular accents and duple or triple meter.

At the turn of the century composers of art music began to rebel against the rhythmic and metric regularity that had governed much of nineteenth-century music. In abandoning the traditional structures of rhythm and meter, they were no different from modern poets, like Gertrude Stein (1874–1946) and T. S. Eliot (1888–1965), who dispensed with traditional poetic meters and repeating accents in favor of free verse. Musicians such as Stravinsky and Bartók began to write music in which syncopations and measures with odd numbers of beats made it all but impossible for the listener to feel regular metrical patterns. Accents moved from one pulse to another, meters changed from measure to measure. The following passage from Stravinsky's *Petrushka* (1911) gives a sense of

FIGURE 17–5

The asymmetrical rhythms of modern music find their counterparts in the irregular and ever-changing visual durations in Paul Klee's *Rhythmics* (1930).

how unpredictable modern meter and rhythm can be. Notice how measures with five pulses per unit appear alongside the more traditional measures with two or three, and note how the meter changes for each bar:

EXAMPLE 17–4

polyrhythms and polymeters

In addition, **polyrhythms** (two or more rhythms at once), **polymeters** (two or more meters at once), and rhythmic ostinatos (continually repeating rhythms) now all came into vogue. Each of these is explained in greater detail on pages 351–352. For the moment, it is enough to observe that rhythm in the twentieth century assumed an energy and drive that had not been heard since the Baroque era. But unlike Baroque music, which rejoiced in rhythmic and metric regularity, much of the great force and tension in modern music, its excitement and flamboyance, comes from its irregular rhythms and meters.

Tone Color: New Sounds from New Sources

Twentieth-century composers have created a brave new world of sound. This came about mainly because many musicians were dissatisfied with the string-dominated tone of the Romantic symphony orchestra. The string sound, with its lush vibrato, was thought to be too expressive, perhaps too mushy and sentimental, for the harsh realities of the modern world. So the strings, which had been the traditional melody carriers, relinquished this role to the sharper, crisper woodwinds. Instead of playing a sweeping melody, the violinists might now be *more percussive effects* called on to beat on the strings with the wooden part of the bow or to take their hands and strike the instrument on its sound box. This preference for percussive effects was also expressed in the new importance assigned the instruments of the percussion family. Entire pieces were written for them alone. Instruments such as *new percussion instruments* the xylophone*, glockenspiel*, and celesta* were added to the group (Fig. 3–12), and objects that produced an unfixed pitch, like the cow bell, brake drum, and police siren, were also heard on occasion. The piano, which in the Romantic era had been favored for its lyrical "singing" tone, came to be used as an orchestral instrument prized for the decisive way in which the hammers could be made to bang into the strings. The voice, too, was often asked to abandon its traditional lyrical tone and to replace it with declamatory speech, hisses, whoops, cries, grunts, and other novel sounds. What is more, by mid-century an entirely new way of generating and processing sound had been developed, by means of the electronic synthesizer. This allowed for even more new and different tone colors, ones that could not be produced on traditional acoustical instruments.

Producing new tones in novel ways, whether by new "instruments" or by traditional instruments using new playing techniques, is only part of the story of sound in modern music. A more fundamental development is the new way of *color: an independent element* thinking about musical color, or timbre, as an independent element in music. During the Classical and Romantic periods, sounds of different colors and different volumes had been used mainly as a way to highlight the progress of the themes and thus to articulate the form of a composition. When the second

FIGURE 17–6
Henri Matisse's *The Red Studio* (1911). Here color is not a subordinate element employed to delineate the various objects in the room, but rather an independent element used to intensify the emotional response of the viewer.

theme entered in sonata–allegro form, for example, it was usually assigned to a new instrument to tell the listener that this was, in fact, a new theme; when a final climax was near, more and more instruments, including the powerful brasses, were usually added to increase the level of sound, signaling that the end was close at hand. The use of tone color and volume as mere servants of melody came to an end at the turn of the twentieth century. Claude Debussy (see page 331) was the first to use color, independent of melody, to give form to a work. But this development was carried to radical lengths in the compositions of modernists such as Edgard Varèse (1883–1965), Krzysztof Penderecki (b. 1933), and John Cage (1912–1992), whose pieces sometimes do nothing except progress from bright tones spaced far apart to dark tones densely grouped together. There may be no melody or harmony as we usually think of these, but only clusters or streams of sounds with changing colors. This approach to color and line is, of course, similar to the one followed by avant-garde painters who deconstruct recognizable objects so as to emphasize the emotional power of pure color (see Fig. 17–6).

density of texture: an independent element

THE EARLY AVANT-GARDE: STRAVINSKY, SCHOENBERG, AND BARTÓK

Faced with the extraordinary diversity of modern music, today's conductors and performers have a difficult time selecting a musical repertoire for the listening public. What kinds of modern music should be performed and how much of it? Audiences are notorious for preferring the tried-and-true "chestnuts" of the Classical and Romantic periods to any sort of new or experimental music. The masterpieces by the composers discussed next are not only compelling works of art in themselves, they also have offered answers for other composers in regard to the fundamental question of modern music—how to create cogent new music in a world marked by increasing cultural diversity and artistic fragmentation. All of these works have now become accepted into the standard repertoire of concert music, though not all of the composers have become icons of popular culture like Beethoven or Mozart.

Igor Stravinsky (1882–1971)

an international celebrity

Igor Stravinsky is arguably the most significant composer of the twentieth century, both for the music he produced and for his influence on other composers. He created masterpieces in many different genres: opera, ballet, symphony, church Mass, and cantata. His versatility was such that he could write a ballet for baby elephants (*Circus Polka*, 1942) just as easily as he could set to music a Greek classical drama (*Oedipus Rex*, 1927). Throughout his long life he traveled with the fashionable set of high art. Although reared in St. Petersburg, he later lived in Paris, Venice, Lausanne, New York, and Hollywood. Forced to become an expatriate by the Russian Revolution (1917), he took French citizenship in 1934, and then, having moved to the United States at the outbreak of World War II, became an American citizen in 1945. He counted among his friends the painter Pablo Picasso (1881–1973), the novelist Aldous Huxley (1894–1963), and the poets Dylan Thomas (1914–1953) and T. S. Eliot (1888–1965). On his eightieth birthday, in 1962, he was honored by President John Kennedy at the White House and, later in the same year, by Premier Nikita Khrushchev in the Kremlin. He died in New York in 1971 at the age of eighty-eight.

the Ballets russes

Stravinsky rose to international fame as a composer of ballet music. In 1908 some of his early work caught the attention of the legendary impresario (producer) of Russian opera and ballet, Sergei Diaghilev (1872–1929). Diaghilev wanted to bring Russian ballet to Paris, at that time the artistic capital of the world. So he formed a company, called the **Ballets russes** (Russian ballets), and hired, over the course of time, the most progressive artists he could find: Pablo Picasso and Henri Matisse for scenic designs, George Balanchine (later the

(left) Igor Stravinsky and (right) Sergei Diaghilev. Diaghilev was a cultural impresario who exported Russian art, opera, and ballet to the West. His greatest talent was recognizing and encouraging the genius of artists like Picasso, Matisse, Stravinsky, and Ravel.

force behind the New York City Ballet) as a choreographer, and Debussy, Ravel, and Stravinsky, among others, as composers. Stravinsky soon became the principal composer of the company, and the *Ballets russes* became the focus of his musical activity for the next ten years. Accordingly, the decade 1910–1920 has become known as Stravinsky's Russian ballet period. He would have others—a Neo-classical period (1920–1951) when he returned to classical forms and a smaller orchestra, and a twelve-tone period (1951–1971) during which he adopted the so-called "serial style" of composing (see page 357)—but his fame was made through his early ballets. Motion, whether of dancers or of musical performers, was always foremost in his mind's eye. As Stravinsky said in his autobiography, "I have always had a horror of listening to music with my eyes shut, with nothing for them to do. The sight of the gestures and movements of the various parts of the body . . . is fundamentally necessary if music is to be grasped in its fullness."

his early ballets

The three most important ballets Stravinsky wrote for Diaghilev's company were *The Firebird* (1910), *Petrushka* (1911), and *The Rite of Spring* (1913). All are built around stories taken from Russian folk tales—a legacy of musical nationalism*—and all make use of the large, coloristic orchestra of the late nineteenth century. Unlike symphonic music, however, music for ballet does not explore, or develop, carefully integrated musical themes. Rather, the composer creates a succession of short, independent vignettes designed to express the action being danced and mimed on the stage. The dance of Diaghilev's *Ballets russes* is not the elegant, graceful classical ballet in the French and Russian tradition, the sort that we associate with Tchaikovsky's *Swan Lake* (1877) and *The Nutcracker* (1892). It is a new, modern style of dance influenced by "primitive" Russian folk dancing and folk art; it is heavier, more physical, more driving. Rhythm becomes the driving force of these Russian ballets and in Stravinsky's music in general.

LE SACRE DU PRINTEMPS (THE RITE OF SPRING) (1913)

In a word, the premiere of Stravinsky's *The Rite of Spring* provoked a riot. This opening, the most notorious "first night" in the history of music, took place on an unusually hot evening, May 29, 1913, at the newly built Théâtre Champs-Élysées in Paris. With the very first sounds of the orchestra, many in the packed theater voiced, shouted, and hissed their displeasure. Some called for a doctor, others for two. There were arguments and flying fists as opponents and partisans warred over this Russian brand of modern art. To restore calm, the curtain was lowered momentarily and the house lights were turned on. All in vain. The musicians still could not be heard, and the dancers had difficulty following the pulse of the music. The disorder was experienced first-hand by a visiting critic of the *New York Press*, who reported as follows:

a riot at the premiere

> I was sitting in a box in which I had rented one seat. Three ladies sat in front of me and a young man occupied the place behind me. He stood up during the course of the ballet to enable himself to see more clearly. The intense excitement under which he was laboring, thanks to the potent force of the music, betrayed itself presently when he began to beat rhythmically on the top of my head with his fists. My emotion was so great that I did not feel the blows for some time. They were perfectly synchronized with the beat of the music!

In truth, the violent reaction to *The Rite of Spring* was in part a response to the modernist choreography of Vaslav Nijinsky (see Fig. 16–6). His mode of dance

FIGURE 17–9

Matisse's *Dance* (1911), painted in
Paris two years before Stravinsky's *The
Rite of Spring* had its premiere in the
same city. Like *The Rite of Spring,
Dance* achieves a raw, primitive power
by simplifying and exaggerating a few
basic lines and by intensifying color so
as to heighten emotional response.

was no less "primitive" than Stravinsky's score. But what specifically is there in
Stravinsky's music that so many that night found shocking?

Percussive Orchestra: First, there is a new percussive—one might say "heavy
metal"—approach to the orchestra. The percussion section is enlarged to include
four timpani, a triangle, a tambourine, a guiro*, cymbals, antique cymbals, a bass
drum, and a tam-tam*. Even the string family, the traditional provider of warmth
and richness in the symphony orchestra, is required to play percussively, attack-
ing the strings with repeated down-bows at seemingly random moments of
accent.

Irregular Accents: Stravinsky intensifies the effect of his harsh, metallic sounds
by placing them where they are not expected, on unaccented beats, thereby creating explosive syncopations. Notice in the following example, the famous
beginning of "Augurs of Spring," how the strings accent (>) the second, fourth,
and then first pulses of each four-pulse measure. In this way Stravinsky destroys
ordinary 1, 2, 3, 4 meter and forces us to hear, in succession, groups of 4, 5, 2, 6,
3, 4, and 5 pulses—a conductor's nightmare!

EXAMPLE 17–5

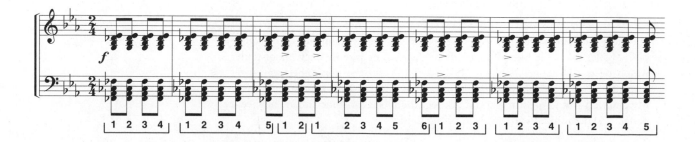

Polyrhythms: The rhythm of *The Rite of Spring* is complex because the composer often superimposes two or more independent rhythms simultaneously. Look at the reduced score given in Ex. 17–6. Every instrument seems to be doing its own thing! In fact, six distinctly different rhythms can be heard.

EXAMPLE 17–6

Ostinato Figures: Notice also in Ex. 17–6 how most of the instruments are playing the same motive over and over at the same pitch level. Such a repeating figure, as we have seen, is called an ostinato*. In this instance we hear multiple ostinatos. Stravinsky was not the first twentieth-century composer to use ostinatos extensively—Debussy had done so earlier in his Impressionist scores (see page 333). But Stravinsky employs them more often and does so for longer spans. In *The Rite of Spring,* ostinatos give the music its incessant, driving quality, especially in the sections with fast tempos.

Polymeters: Not only do individual parts often play separate rhythms, but they sometimes project distinctly different meters, each with a different time signature, either written or implied. Notice in Ex. 17–7 that the oboe plays in 6/8 time, the E♭ clarinet plays in 7/8, while the B♭ clarinet is in 5/8.

EXAMPLE 17–7

Dissonant Polychords: The harsh, biting sound that is heard throughout much of *The Rite of Spring* is often created by having two triads*, or a triad and a seventh chord*, sound at once. When these chords are only a step* or a half step* apart, the resulting polychord is especially dissonant. In Ex. 17–8, the passage from the beginning of "Augurs of Spring," a seventh chord* built on E♭ is played simultaneously with a major triad* built on F♭.

EXAMPLE 17–8

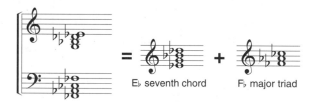

The metallic, sometimes brutal sound of *The Rite of Spring* is appropriate for the story danced on stage. In thirteen scenes it tells of the springtime rituals of primitive tribes in pagan Russia (part 1) and of a sacrificial virgin who dances herself to death as an offering to the god of Spring (part 2). Part 1 begins with an Introduction in which the earth awakens under the warm spring sun. Thereafter comes a succession of scenes depicting pubescent rites danced by the youths of the tribe. In general, the scenes of the adolescent girls are lyrical, with a distinct melody. "Spring Rounds" even makes use of a Russian folk song. On the other hand, the scenes of the adolescent boys, such as "Game of Abduction," are more percussive, even violent, being dominated by dissonance, dense textures, and irregular accents.

Following the *succès de scandale* that attended the premiere of *The Rite of Spring*, Stravinsky immediately removed the music from the ballet itself and had it played as an independent orchestral suite. The music alone was now recognized as an important, if controversial, statement of the musical avant-garde. Later, in 1940, the score of *The Rite of Spring* furnished the music for an important segment of Walt Disney's early full-length animated film, *Fantasia*. Musical modernism had become mainstream.

FIGURE 17–10

As polychords create two or more tonal centers sounding at once, so the Cubist painting *The Violin* (1916), by Juan Gris, refracts the violin and the bow into two and sometimes three simultaneous images.

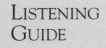

LISTENING GUIDE

Igor Stravinsky
The Rite of Spring (1913)
Introduction and Scenes 1–3

6CD 6/1–4; 6Tape 6A
3CD 3/8–9; 3Tape 3B

Introduction (the awakening of the earth)

0:00   Bassoon writhing in high register

0:20   Other winds (bass clarinet, English horn, another bassoon, high clarinet) gradually enter

1:37   Flutes play in parallel motion

1:53   Writhing woodwinds continue

2:34   Ostinato in bass supports gradual orchestral crescendo

2:57   Bassoon melody returns, clarinet trills

Augurs of Spring: Dances of the Adolescents (youthful dancers pound onto the stage; male and female groups entice one another; attention shifts to more folklike dances of the girls)

0:00   Elemental pounding of dissonant string chords punctuated by blasts from the French horns and trumpets (see Ex. 17–5)

0:46   Bassoons and then trombones play stepwise motive

1:15   *Fortissimo* chords and timpani blows

1:39   French horn plays folklike melody

1:59   Flute plays melody

2:13   Trumpets play new folklike melody

2:47   Gradual orchestral crescendo

(3CD and 3Tape stop here)

Game of Abduction (macho gestures of "kidnapping" a girl)

0:00   Wild, chaotic playing in orchestra peppered with blows on the timpani and blasts from the French horn

0:53   Quickly changing meters; syncopated percussion blows

Spring Rounds (round dances by groups of male and female adolescents)

0:00   Flutes trill while clarinets play in parallel motion

0:26   Low strings set up mournful accompaniment

1:04   Russian folk song played by violins and flutes, then French horn

1:59   Folk song played dissonantly by full orchestra

2:41   Dissonant, syncopated, percussive music for male dancers

2:58   Return of opening flute trill and opening melody

(Listening Exercise 40)

FIGURE 17–11

Arnold Schoenberg, *Self Portrait* (1910).

FIGURE 17–12

This 1909 Viennese theater poster by Oskar Kokoschka shows the Expressionist affinity for the dramatic and grotesque. The effect is created by the use of strong, almost crude, lines and bold contrasting colors.

Arnold Schoenberg and the Second Viennese School

If Paris was the artistic capital of Europe before the First World War, Vienna was second in importance. The city of Mozart and Beethoven was blessed with strong musical traditions and a large, if conservative, audience. But the musical expectations of the Viennese were now challenged by a trio of native composers who were to take modern music on a radically different course: Arnold Schoenberg (1874–1951), Alban Berg (1885–1935), and Anton Webern (1883–1945). The close association of these three innovative musicians has come to be called the "Second Viennese School," the first, of course, being that of Mozart, Haydn, and Beethoven.

Arnold Schoenberg, the leader of this group, almost single-handedly thrust modern music on a reluctant Viennese public. Schoenberg was from a Jewish family of modest circumstances and was largely self-taught as a musician. As a young man he worked as a bank clerk during the day, but studied literature, philosophy, and music at night, becoming a competent performer on the violin and cello. He came to know the music of Brahms, Wagner, and Mahler, mostly by playing their scores and attending concerts. Having "left the world of bank notes for musical notes" at the age of twenty-one, he earned a modest living by conducting a men's chorus, orchestrating operettas—the Viennese counterpart of our Broadway musicals—and giving lessons in music theory and composition. Eventually, his own compositions began to be heard in Vienna, though they were usually not well received.

Schoenberg's earliest works are written in a typical late Romantic style, with rich harmonies, chromatic melodies, expansive forms, and programmatic content. But by 1908 his music had begun to evolve in unexpected directions. Having been strongly influenced by Wagner's chromatic melodies and harmonies, Schoenberg started to compose works in which there was no tonal center. If Wagner could write winding chromatic passages that temporarily obscured the tonality, why not go one step farther and create fully chromatic pieces in which there is no tonality? This Schoenberg did, and in so doing created what is called **atonal music**—music without tonality, music without a key center.

But Schoenberg not only abandoned music with a tonal center—a stable point of reference for the listener—he also dispensed with the triad as the basic building block of music. Earlier, tonal music had unfolded in chord progressions built mainly of consonant triads. Dissonance, which adds an element of tension and anxiety, was carefully controlled and required to resolve to a stable consonance, usually a triad. With Schoenberg's new atonal music, however, dissonance is freed from the necessity of resolving to consonance—it can wander off chromatically to another dissonance and then yet another. We have, in Schoenberg's words, "the emancipation of dissonance." Most listeners today are at first hostile to atonal music, in part because there is no tonal center but more so because it is so highly dissonant. Small wonder that in Schoenberg's day some Viennese musicians refused to play his atonal music, or that when they did the audience's reaction was sometimes violent. (At one concert, March 31, 1913, the police had to be called out to restore order.) Despite the hostility, Schoenberg remained true to his own artistic vision:

Whether one calls oneself conservative or revolutionary, whether one composes in a conventional or progressive manner, whether one tries to imitate old styles or

---

Expressionism and Atonality

Arnold Schoenberg and his students Alban Berg and Anton Webern were not alone in creating a radically new style of art. As we have seen, there appeared at this same time a powerful movement in the visual arts called Expressionism. Expressionism was initially a German–Austrian development that arose in Berlin, Munich, and Vienna. Its aim was not to depict objects as they are seen but to express the strong emotion that the object generated in the artist; not to paint a portrait of an individual but to create an expression of the subject's innermost feelings, anxieties, and fears. In Edvard Munch's early Expressionist painting *The Scream* (1893), the subject cries out to an unsympathetic and uncomprehending audience. Schoenberg's statement in this regard can be taken as a credo for the entire Expressionist movement: "Art is the cry of despair of those who experience in themselves the fate of all Mankind" (1910). Gradually, realistic representations gave way to highly personal and increasingly abstract expression. Artists such as Oskar Kokoschka (1886–1980) and Wassily Kandinsky (1866–1944) used harsh colors, macabre images, and distorted figures to show intense psychological states, sometimes with shocking results (see Figs. 17–3 and 17–12). Schoenberg, a personal friend of both Kokoschka and Kandinsky, was himself a painter and exhibited his works with the Expressionists in 1912 (Figs. 17–11 and 17–13). In fact, the music and art of this movement can be described in rather similar terms. The clashing of strong colors, the disjointed shapes, and the jagged lines of the painters have their counterparts in the harsh dissonances, asymmetrical rhythms, and angular, chromatic melodies of Schoenberg and his followers. It is surely not an accident that Schoenberg moved from tonality to atonality in music (1908–1912) at precisely the time Kandinsky and others turned away from realistic representation to abstract expression.

The Scream, by Edvard Munch

is destined to express new ideas—whether one is a good composer or not—one must be convinced of the infallibility of one's own fantasy and one must believe in one's own inspiration.

PIERROT LUNAIRE (MOONSTRUCK PIERROT) (1912)

Moonstruck Pierrot, Schoenberg's best-known composition, is an exemplary work of Expressionist art. It is a setting for chamber ensemble and female voice of twenty-one poems by Albert Giraud. Here we meet "Moonstruck Pierrot," a white-faced clown from the world of traditional Italian pantomime and puppet shows. Yet in this Expressionist poetry, the fun-loving clown suffers the endless anxiety of a sensitive artist-lover whose only confidant is the moon. Pierrot's inner feelings are projected by means of a new vocal technique invented by Schoenberg called **Sprechstimme**—"speech-voice." *Sprechstimme* requires the vocalist to declaim the text more than sing it. The voice is to produce exact rhythmic values but rises and falls to only approximate pitch levels. This removes all vocal lyricism but adds a new intensity, even an element of hysteria, to the voice, an appropriate feature for this hyperexpressive text.

Poems 6 and 7 of *Moonstruck Pierrot* reveal two different aspects of the clown's feverish state of mind. In number 6 Pierrot offers a hymn of solace to the suffering Madonna; and in number 7 he projects on the face of the moon his own love pains. Each poem is cast as a *rondeau*, an old musical and poetic form character-

Sprechstimme, a new vocal technique

an ever-varying continuum

ized by the use of a refrain (see pages 79–80). Traditionally, composers had used the appearance of a textual refrain to repeat part or all of the melody as well. This helped create a unity of text and music and gave the work formal coherence. But Schoenberg, true to his iconoclastic ways, avoids musical repetition in his atonal works. His music unfolds in an ever-varying continuum, like a stream of consciousness. His dissonances, disjunct rhythms, changing textures, and nonrepeating melodies place unprecedented demands on the listener. Your first reaction to the seemingly formless flow of dissonance in *Moonstruck Pierrot* may be decidedly negative. Yet with repeated listenings the force of the jarring elements of the atonal style begins to lessen and a bizarre, eerie sort of beauty emerges, especially if you are sensitive to the meaning of the text.

LISTENING GUIDE

Arnold Schoenberg
Moonstruck Pierrot (1912)
Number 6, *Madonna*
Number 7, *The Sick Moon*

6CD 6/5–6; 6Tape 6A
3CD 3/10; 3Tape 3B

Number 6, *Madonna*, draws its inspiration from the vision of the sorrowful Mother of Christ at the Cross. The traditional association of the image of the Cross with musical chromaticism, one extending at least back to Bach, may have given rise to the ascending chromatic line, played pizzicato, in the cello. The angular movement of the voice is typical of Schoenberg's atonal melodic line:

| Steig, | O Mut - ter al - ler Schmer zen, auf den Al - tar mei - ner Ver - se! |

Steig, O Mutter aller Schmerzen	**Arise, O Mother of all sorrows**
Auf den Altar meiner Verse!	**On the altar of my verse!**
Blut aus deinen magern Brüsten	Blood from your thin breast
Hat des Schwertes Wut vergossen.	Has spilled the rage of the sword.
Deine ewig frischen Wunden	Your eternally fresh wounds
Gleichen Augen, rot und offen,	Like eyes, red and open,
Steig, O Mutter aller Schmerzen	**Arise, O Mother of all sorrows**
Auf den Altar meiner Verse!	**On the altar of my verse!**
In den abgezehrten Händen	In your thin and wasted hands
Hältst du deines Sohnes Leiche	You hold the body of your Son
Ihn zu zeigen aller Menschheit,	To show him to all mankind,
Doch der Blick der Menschen meidet	Yet the look of men avoids
Dich, **O Mutter aller Schmerzen.**	You, **O Mother of all sorrows.**

Number 7, *Der kranke Mond (The Sick Moon)*, is a soliloquy for voice and accompanying flute. As do the Expressionist painters, here the poet transfers to the object (the moon) the internal feelings of the subject (the artist-Pierrot). Thus, as Pierrot speaks, the moon begins to reflect his inner turmoil, becoming feverish, tormented, death-sick with love. The silvery tones of the flute help evoke an aura of moonlight, "death-sick" as it may be.

Du nächtig todeskranker Mond	**You nocturnal, death-sick moon**
Dort auf des Himmels	**There on heaven's**
schwarzem Pfühl,	**dark couch,**
Dein Blick, so fiebernd übergross	Your look, so feverishly swollen,
Bannt mich wie fremde Melodie.	Charms me like a foreign melody.

An unstillbarem Liebesleid Stirbst du, an Sehnsucht, tief erstickt, **Du nächtig todeskranker Mond** **Dort auf des Himmels** **schwarzem Pfühl.**	In unending pain of love You die, in yearning consumed, **You nocturnal, death-sick moon** **There on heaven's** **dark couch.**
Den Liebsten, der im Sinnenrausch, Gedankenlos zur Liebsten geht, Belustigt deiner Strahlen Spiel, Dein bleiches, qualgebornes Blut, **Du nächtig todeskranker Mond.**	The lover who, in sensual frenzy, Steals to the beloved without a care, Rejoices in your play of light, Your pale, tormented blood, **You nocturnal, death-sick moon.**

Needless to say, this music of the extreme avant-garde did not sit well with the anti-intellectual Nazis who took power in Germany in 1933 and Austria in 1938. Hitler and his National Socialists not only harbored a hatred of Jews, but they also made it virtually impossible for "degenerate" modern art like *Moonstruck Pierrot* to be seen or heard. So Schoenberg fled the German lands, as did thousands of other progressive spirits, including Thomas Mann (1875–1955), Kurt Weill (1900–1950), and Albert Einstein (1879–1955). He ultimately made his way to this country and to Los Angeles, where he died peacefully in 1951 at the age of seventy-six.

SCHOENBERG'S TWELVE-TONE MUSIC

When Arnold Schoenberg and his followers did away with tonal chord progressions and melodies that repeated, they found themselves facing a serious artistic problem: how to write large-scale compositions in the new atonal style. For centuries musical structures, like fugue and sonata–allegro form, had been generated by means of a clear tonal plan and the repetition of broad musical themes. Forms created by repetition were useful to the composer and most welcome to the listener seeking to make sense of a new musical composition. But Schoenberg's chromatic, atonal, nonrepeating melodies made traditional musical forms all but impossible. What other formal plan might be used? If all twelve notes of the chromatic scale are equally important, as is true in atonal music, why choose any one note at a given spot in a piece and not another?

By 1923 Schoenberg had solved the problem of formal anarchy—or absence of form—caused by total chromatic freedom. He had discovered a new way of creating music that he called "composing with twelve tones." **Twelve-tone composition** is a method of writing that employs each of the twelve notes of the chromatic scale set in a fixed, predetermined order. The composer chooses the succession of twelve notes to achieve the desired "melody" and places them in a row. Throughout the composition the twelve notes must come in the same order. Music in which elements such as pitch or timbre come in a fixed series is called **serial music.** In twelve-tone music the twelve-note series may unfold not only as a melody but also as a melody with accompaniment, or simply as a progression of chords, since two or more notes of the row may sound simultaneously. Moreover, in addition to appearing in its basic form, the row might go backward (retrograde*) or upside down (inversion*) or both backward and upside down at the same time (retrograde inversion). While such arrangements might seem wholly

FIGURE 17–13

As a young man Schoenberg was undecided whether his future in the arts lay in music or painting. Like many Expressionist paintings before World War I, his *Red Gaze* (1910) gives a sense of the subject's inner terror.

twelve-tone music

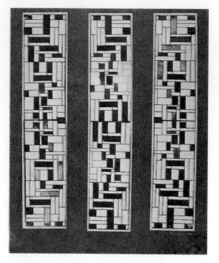

FIGURE 17–14

The same rational processes at work in Schoenberg's twelve-tone music can be seen in Theo van Doesburg's *Composition IV* (1917). Notice the retrograde motion: The pattern proceeding downward from the top left is the same as that upward from the bottom right (see also Fig. 2–8).

artificial and very unmusical, we should remember that composers such as J. S. Bach in the Baroque era and Josquin Desprez in the Renaissance had subjected their melodies to similar permutations. The purpose of Schoenberg's twelve-tone method was to create musical unity by basing each piece on a single, orderly arrangement of twelve tones, thereby guaranteeing the perfect equality of all pitches so that none would seem like a tonal center.

TRIO FROM *SUITE FOR PIANO* (1924)

The first steps along this radical twelve-tone path were tentative and, not surprisingly, the pieces that resulted were short, very short. Among Schoenberg's first serial compositions was his *Suite for Piano*, a collection of seven brief dance movements, including the Minuet and Trio to be discussed here. The tone row for the *Suite*, along with its three permutations, is as follows:

Row													*Retrograde*											
E	F	G	D♭	G♭	E♭	A♭	D	B	C	A	B♭		B♭	A	C	B	D	A♭	E♭	G♭	D♭	G	F	E
1	2	3	4	5	6	7	8	9	10	11	12		12	11	10	9	8	7	6	5	4	3	2	1

Inversion													*Retrograde-inversion*											
E	E♭	D♭	G	D	F	C	F♯	A	G♯	B	B♭		B♭	B	G♯	A	F♯	C	F	D	G	D♭	E♭	E
1	2	3	4	5	6	7	8	9	10	11	12		12	11	10	9	8	7	6	5	4	3	2	1

Schoenberg allows the row or any of its permutations to begin on any pitch, so long as the original sequence of intervals is maintained. Notice in the Trio, for example, that the row itself begins on E but is also allowed to start on B♭ (see Listening Guide). In the second part, measures 6–9, the exact serial progression of the row breaks down slightly. The composer explained this as a "justifiable deviation," owing to the need for tonal variety at this point. Notice as well that the rhythms in which the notes appear may likewise be changed for the sake of variety. As you listen to the Trio, see if you can follow the unfolding of the row and all its permutations. Listen many times—the piece is only thirty-three seconds long! Its aesthetic effect is similar to that of a constructivist painting of an artist like Theo van Doesburg (Fig. 17–14). If you like the painting, you should like Schoenberg's twelve-tone piano piece as well.

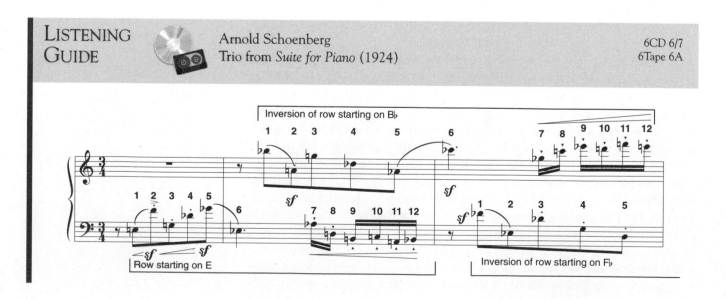

LISTENING GUIDE

Arnold Schoenberg
Trio from *Suite for Piano* (1924)

6CD 6/7
6Tape 6A

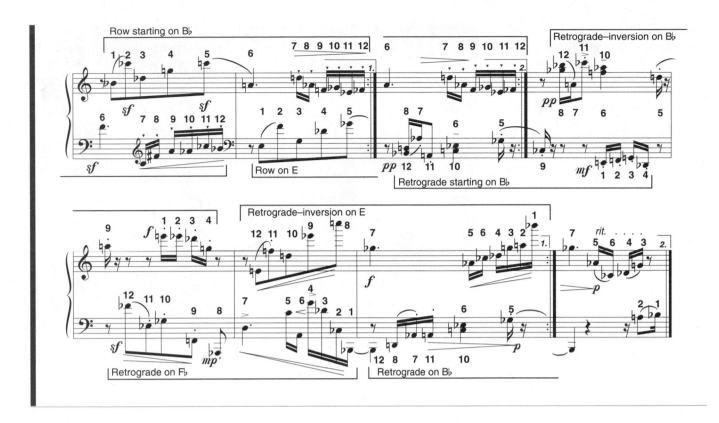

As the years progressed, Schoenberg used his twelve-tone method to construct longer compositions for larger forces. In 1932 he completed most of a full-length opera, *Moses and Aron*, and in 1947 he finished a cantata*, A *Survivor from Warsaw*, that tells of Nazi atrocities in Poland. Both works are twelve-tone in style throughout. But the listening public never embraced Schoenberg's twelve-tone music. The style is still very much that of dissonant, atonal music. For most listeners, it sounds irrational and arbitrary, indeed completely "out of control." Schoenberg, however, remained convinced to the end that time would vindicate this method of composition—that the general listening public would come to appreciate the dissonant universality of twelve-tone music: "One should never forget that contemporaries are not final judges, but are generally overruled by history." So far, history has not ruled in Schoenberg's favor.

Béla Bartók (1881–1945)

The music of the Hungarian composer Béla Bartók is decidedly modern, yet distinctly different in sound from that of Stravinsky or Schoenberg. While it can be atonal, like the music of Schoenberg, it is often highly tuneful, making use of sweeping melodies. And while it is frequently percussive and highly rhythmic, like the motor-driven sounds of Stravinsky, Bartók's rhythmic force derives mainly from folk music. Bartók's creative imagination was fired by folk materials of his native Hungary. He saw the return to the simple, direct style of folk music as a way to counter the tendency in Romantic music toward ostentation and sentimentality.

The life of Béla Bartók was strongly affected by the turbulent events that occurred in Eastern Europe during the first half of the twentieth century. He was

FIGURE 17–15
Béla Bartók.

born in 1881 in Hungary, but in a part of that nation that was later given over to Rumania at the end of World War I. Throughout his life he was an ardent Hungarian nationalist, and chose to develop his obvious musical talents at the Academy of Music in Budapest rather than at the German-dominated Vienna Conservatory, where he had also been admitted. As a student at the Academy in Budapest he studied composition and piano, quickly acquiring a reputation as a concert pianist of the highest quality. By the 1920s he had achieved an international reputation both as a pianist and as a composer of music in the modern vein. His tours even carried him to the western part of the United States, where one newspaper alerted the public to his coming with the following headline: "Hungarian Modernist Advances upon Los Angeles." As both a Hungarian modernist and nationalist, Bartók was an outspoken critic of the supporters of Nazi Germany who gained control of the Hungarian government in the late 1930s. He called the fascists "bandits and assassins," cut off ties with the German firm that published all his music, and banned the performances of his works in Germany and Italy, thereby losing considerable performance fees. Ultimately, in 1940, he fled to the United States. Bartók died of leukemia in New York City in 1945, and not until 1988 were his remains returned, at the request of his sons, to his beloved Hungary.

an ardent anti-Nazi

Bartók and folk music

Béla Bartók is unique among composers in that he was as much interested in musical research, specifically in the study of Eastern European folk music, as he was in musical composition. He traveled from village to village in Hungary, Rumania, Bulgaria, Turkey, and even North Africa using the newly invented recording machine of Thomas Edison (Fig. 17–16). In this way his ear became saturated with the driving rhythms and odd-number meters of peasant dances, as well as the unusual scales on which the folk melodies of Eastern Europe were constructed. If the cosmopolitan Stravinsky took his folk melodies from printed anthologies, Bartók found his among the people.

The musical heritage of Eastern Europe is heard continually throughout Bartók's music, from his first string quartet (1908) to his great final works for orchestra: *Music for Strings, Percussion and Celesta* (1936), *Divertimento for Strings* (1939), and *Concerto for Orchestra* (1943). This last-named work is probably Bartók's best-known composition. Certainly, it is among his most alluring creations.

CONCERTO FOR ORCHESTRA (1943)

The title of this composition, as Bartók wrote in the program notes for its first performance, "is explained by [the work's] tendency to treat the single orchestral instruments in a 'concertante' or soloistic manner." Instead of having one unchanging group function as soloists, as in a Baroque concerto grosso*, Bartók's group of soloists has a continually revolving membership, drawing at various times on different instruments of the orchestra. Now one, now another instrument or combination of instruments steps forward to display its distinctive tonal color against the backdrop of the full orchestra. There are five movements: The first is "written in a more or less regular sonata form," as the composer says, and makes use of the folklike pentatonic* scale; the second is a colorful parade of pairs of instruments; the third is an atmospheric nocturne, an example of what is called Bartók's "night music," in which the woodwinds slither around chromatically above a misty tremolo in the strings; the fourth is an unusual intermezzo; while the fifth is a vigorous peasant dance in sonata–allegro form. Let us focus our attention on the fourth movement, *Intermezzo interrotto (Broken Intermezzo)*.

a modern-day concerto grosso

An **intermezzo** (Italian for "between piece") is a light musical interlude intended to separate and thus break the mood of two more serious surrounding movements. But here, as the title *Broken Intermezzo* indicates, the light intermezzo is itself rudely interrupted by contrasting music. A sophisticated mood is first established by a charming theme in the oboe. As is usual for Bartók, this melody shows the influence of the Hungarian folk song both in its pentatonic construction (the five notes that make up the scale of the melody are B, C♯, E, F♯, and A♯) and in the way it switches back and forth between an even 2/4 and an odd 5/8:

Hungarian melodies

EXAMPLE 17–9

After the tune is passed among several wind instruments, an even more ingratiating melody emerges in the strings. It, too, is Hungarian in style. In fact, it is Bartók's idealized reworking of the song *You Are Lovely, You Are Beautiful, Hungary*.

EXAMPLE 17–10

But the nostalgic vision of the homeland is suddenly interrupted by a new, cruder theme in the clarinet, and it also tells a tale. Bartók took this clarinet melody from the Russian composer Dimitri Shostakovitch's Symphony No. 7, a programmatic work depicting the German invasion of Russia (1942). Bartók borrowed the theme Shostakovitch had written to signify the invading Germans, believing its simple quarter-note descent to be appropriately heavy and trite.

EXAMPLE 17–11

an anti-Nazi work

Thus, Bartók's intermezzo can be heard as an autobiographical work in which, as the composer related to a friend, "the artist declares his love for his native land in a serenade which is suddenly interrupted in a crude and violent manner; he is seized by rough, booted men who even break his instrument." Bartók tells us what he thinks of these "rough, booted men" by surrounding them with rude, jeering noises in the trumpets and woodwinds. Ultimately, he brings back the idyllic vision of the homeland by returning to the opening two themes. The main events of the *Broken Intermezzo* are enumerated in the short Listening Guide that follows. A more detailed description of the piece will emerge as you complete Listening Exercise 41.

LISTENING
GUIDE

Béla Bartók
Concerto for Orchestra (1943)
Fourth movement, *Broken Intermezzo*

6CD 6/8; 6Tape 6A
3CD 3/11; 3Tape 3B

0:00		Four-note introduction
0:06	A	Oboe introduces theme
1:07	B	Violas introduce theme
1:49	A	Oboe briefly plays theme
2:14	C	Clarinet introduces theme (borrowed from Shostakovich)
2:22		Rude noises in trumpets and woodwinds
2:36	C	Parody of theme in violins
2:44		More rude noises
2:52	C	Theme played in inversion by the violins
2:56		More rude noises
3:04	B	Theme returns in violas
3:23	A	Theme returns in English horn, flute, and clarinet

(Listening Exercise 41)

FIGURE 17–17

The American Optical artist Jasper Johns has taken a venerable object and created unexpected effects of light, motion, and color in his *Three Flags* (1958).

THREE AMERICAN EXPERIMENTALISTS: IVES, VARÈSE, AND CAGE

There are times in the history of art when the rejection of a previously dominant system leads to radical experimentation, as new ideas compete to fill a void. In music this happened at the turn of the seventeenth century, when many composers suddenly gave up on imitative polyphony, as well as at the turn of the twentieth century, when tonality and consonance no longer seemed important. Painting, too, experienced an "anything is possible" revolution after the turn of the twentieth century, when it was confirmed that exact photographic reproduction in art was no longer desirable. Just as in this century painters such as Jasper Johns (Fig. 17–17) and Andy Warhol (Fig. 17–25) experimented with a host of new ways that paint, and other substances, could be applied to canvas, so musicians explored ways to arrange pitch, intensity, density, and other musical parameters along new lines.

"anything is possible"

Among the more radical of these exploratory musical thinkers were Charles Ives (1874–1954), Edgar Varèse (1883–1965), and John Cage (1912–1992). Ives sought, among other things, to give new meaning to traditional and popular musical material; Varèse worked to remove the element of pitch from music so as to concentrate on color and texture; and Cage brought noises from the everyday world into the concert hall and asked why these, too, were not music, thereby questioning our very definition of this art. That all three of these experimental composers were American suggests the probing, independent, sometimes scientific quality of American musical thought during the twentieth century.

what is music? what is art?

Charles Ives (1874–1954)

Charles Ives was the greatest, and most eccentric, of American composers. He was born in Danbury, Connecticut, the son of George Ives (1845–1894), a band-

FIGURE 17–18

Young Charles Ives in the baseball uniform of Hopkins Grammar School, New Haven, Connecticut. A better baseball player than student, Ives needed a year of preparatory school before he entered Yale. At Hopkins he studied English, German, Latin, and Greek, but not music.

insurance agent by day

composer by night

leader in the Union Army who had served with General Grant during the Civil War. The senior Ives gave his son a highly unorthodox musical education, at least by European standards. True, there was the obligatory study of the three B's—Bach, Beethoven, and Brahms—along with harmony and counterpoint, as well as lessons on the violin, piano, organ, cornet, and drums. But young Ives was also taught how to "stretch his ears," as he said. In one exercise he was made to sing *Swanee River* in E♭ while his father accompanied him on the piano in the key of C—a useful lesson in polytonality*! And he learned to appreciate new and unusual sounds as his father experimented with violin strings stretched over a clothes press, a piano tuned in quarter tones*, and drinking glasses set at equally small intervals. He was not a product of a music conservatory but spent his time on the ballfield (Fig. 17–18), on the parade ground, and in the church choir loft. The sounds that stuck in his ears were those of marches, popular and patriotic songs, fiddlers' jigs, minstrel tunes, and church hymns.

Since his forebears had gone to Yale, it was decided that Charles should enroll there, too. At Yale he took courses in music with Horatio Parker (1863–1919), a composer of some capability who had been trained in Germany. But Ives's youthful, independent ideas about how music should sound clashed with Parker's traditional European notions of harmony and counterpoint. The student learned to leave his more radical musical experimentations, such as a fugue with a subject entering in four different keys, outside Parker's classroom. Ives became heavily involved in extracurricular activities, including fraternity musicals, and maintained a D+ average (a "gentleman's" mark before the days of grade inflation).

When he graduated with the class of 1898, Charles Ives decided not to pursue music as a profession. He realized that the sort of music he had in his head was not the kind the public would pay to hear. So he headed for New York City, and in 1907 he and a friend formed the company of Ives and Myrick, an agency that sold insurance as a subsidiary of Mutual of New York (MONY). Ives and Myrick grew to become the largest insurance agency in the United States, and in the year in which Ives retired, 1929, had sales of $49 million.

But Charles Ives led two lives: insurance executive by day, frantic composer by night. During the twenty years between his departure from Yale (1898) and the American entry into World War I (1917), Ives wrote the bulk of his 43 works for symphony or band, 41 choral pieces, approximately 75 works for piano solo or various chamber ensembles, and more than 150 songs. Almost without exception they went unheard. Ives made little effort to get his music performed—composition was for him a very private, personal matter. Gradually, however, word of his unusual creations spread among a few influential performers and critics. In 1947 he was awarded the Pulitzer Prize in music for his Third Symphony, one he had written forty years earlier! In his usual gruff, eccentric way, Ives told the members of the Pulitzer committee, "Prizes are for boys. I'm grown up."

THE FOURTH OF JULY (1911–1913)

No piece could be more representative of Ives's distinctly American brand of musical experimentalism than *The Fourth of July*. Ives's own words best capture the panoramic vision of a small-town Fourth of July that inspired this one-movement orchestral work.

> Cannon on the Green, Village Band on Main St., fire crackers, shanks mixed on cornets, strings around big toes, torpedoes, Church-bells, lost finger, fifes, clam-chowder, a prize-fight, drum-corps, burnt shins, parades (in and out of step),

FIGURES 17–19 AND 17–20
(left) Charles Ives as photographed in the 1940s during his retirement. He kept tinkering with his musical compositions to the end of his life. (right) William Harnett's *Music and Good Luck* (1888) creates a satisfying collage by melding various objects from a horse barn and the world of music.

saloons all closed (more drunks than usual), baseball game (Danbury All-Stars vs. Beaver Brook Boys), pistols, mobbed umpire, Red, White and Blue, runaway horse,—and the day ends with the sky-rocket over the Church-steeple, just after the annual explosion sets the Town-Hall on fire.

The Fourth of July is a piece of program music*, but not one in which a succession of musically described events unfold in logical order. Instead, Ives superimposes many musical references to create a giant collage of sound. Marching bands playing in different keys, army buglers, sailors, country fiddlers, and church choirs can all be heard more or less simultaneously. They are depicted musically by the more than fifteen patriotic songs, hymns, sea chanteys, and marches that Ives borrowed, reaching back into the musical memory of his youth. All of these he brings together to produce a jumble of melody, an ear-splitting dissonance, and rhythms of such complexity that they are almost impossible to play. The most oft-quoted tune is *Columbia, the Gem of the Ocean* (see Listening Guide), our unofficial "national anthem" before *The Star-Spangled Banner* was adopted as such in 1931. Snippets of The *Battle Hymn of the Republic*, *The Battle Cry of Freedom*, and *Reveille* can also be heard. Most of the borrowed melodies, however, including *Yankee Doodle* and *Dixie*, are inaudible in the midst of the incredible din of twisted tunes and dissonant harmonies. The cacophony comes to a climax with the burst of a skyrocket toward the end. All of this sounds very wrong, but as Ives instructed his copyist about *The Fourth of July:* "Dear Mr. Price: Please don't try to make things nice! All the wrong notes are right."

What is Ives trying to do in this wild, seemingly chaotic ride through America's past? Above all, he is playing with our musical memories, our nostalgia for the familiar tunes of our youth. He evokes these treasured songs, but then refuses to set them in the traditional tonal, consonant background we remember and expect. Instead, he places the familiar objects in an alien, hyperdissonant environment. In a manner akin to that of an avant-garde artist who reinterprets fragments of reality in surprising ways (see Fig. 17–20), Ives defamiliarizes the familiar. He challenges us to look at the ordinary in a new light, suggesting that truth

a giant collage of sound

a new view of familiar music

may lurk therein. We might prefer the musically familiar and comfortable—the old world of tonality and consonance—but Ives is saying, in effect: What is past is past and will be no more; let us not mourn the loss, but exalt in the possibilities unleashed by a new world of sound.

LISTENING GUIDE

Charles Ives
The Fourth of July (1911–1913)

6CD 6/9; 6Tape 6A
3CD 3/12; 3Tape 3B

O Co - lum - bia, the gem of the o - cean, The home of the brave and the free,——

0:00   Violins play slow variation of *Columbia*
0:36   Basses do the same
0:55   Tuba joins the basses
1:37   Piccolo plays variation of *Columbia*
1:46   Strings play dissonant variation of *Columbia*
2:04   Piccolo plays variation of *Columbia*
3:01   Strings and winds play *Battle Hymn of the Republic*
3:12   Horns play *The Battle Cry of Freedom*
3:20   Horns and trumpet play *Reveille*

3:31   Trombone plays *Columbia*
3:41   A march begins with the entry of the drums
3:51   Piccolo sneaks in phrase of *The Girl I Left Behind Me*
4:01   Orchestral explosion: the fireworks have begun
4:25   March begins again with *Columbia* in the French horns
4:34   Fragments of many tunes are played in various instruments, including *Columbia* (trombones), *Battle Hymn of the Republic* (cornet), *Dixie* (piccolo), and *Yankee Doodle* (piano and xylophone), but most can't be heard
5:27   Pause before the strings carry the skyrocket over the church steeple
5:50   Remnants of the rocket quietly fizzle back to earth

Edgard Varèse (1883–1965)

Passage to a land of new aesthetic frontiers was also the aim of Edgard Varèse, who left the old world of European traditions behind when he emigrated from France to the United States in 1915. An accidental fire caused the loss of some of the scores he had brought with him from Paris. He then destroyed the rest, obliterating in this symbolic act all traces of his European musical past. Significantly, Varèse entitled his first work written in this country *Amériques* (1921), suggesting not only a new geography but also a new world of musical sound. Besides the usual complement of strings, brasses, and woodwinds, *Amériques* also requires a battery of new percussion instruments, including sirens and sleigh bells, most of which had never before been heard in a symphony orchestra. Later

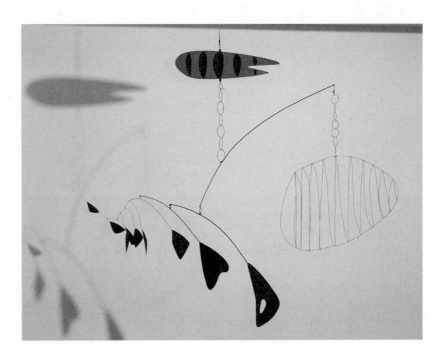

compositions, such as *Hyperprism* (1923) and *Intégrales* (1925), likewise experiment with percussion instruments, to the virtual exclusion of the traditional strings.

Varèse not only uses more percussion instruments than any other composer, but he employs them in a most untraditional way. In earlier centuries, orchestral composers customarily called on the percussion for purposes of accent. By means of taps, thuds, and bangs these instruments helped delineate the main features, and especially climaxes, of the musical structure. Like a spice, they added character, but did not change—and did not constitute—the essence of the musical fare.

IONIZATION (1931)

In *Ionization*, however, Varèse completely turns the musical tables. Now the percussion instruments are everything. Thirteen performers play thirty-seven different instruments, including two sirens, two tam-tams, a gong, cymbals, anvils, three different sizes of bass drum, bongos, snare drums, various Cuban rattles and gourds, slap-sticks, Chinese blocks in three registers, sleigh bells, chimes, a piano, and more. There are no strings, brasses, or woodwinds. Percussive sounds do not reinforce the music—they are the music.

Most important, nearly all the instruments required in *Ionization* generate sounds of indefinite pitch—they produce no one continuous frequency or musical tone. They cannot play melody and harmony. They can, however, set rhythms, show colors, and fill the texture of musical space. Consequently, what Varèse creates is a succession of blocks of sound, each with a distinctive color, texture, and density. These sonic masses collide, interact, and reform, not unlike the changing modules of color within a mobile. *Ionization* reveals to open-minded listeners and composers alike that music is more than just melody and harmony. Compelling works of art can be created by isolating and exploring other parameters, such as color, texture, density, intensity, and registral distribution (highs and lows). It is this discovery that has earned for Varèse a place in the gallery of great

FIGURES 17–21 AND 17–22

(left) Composer Edgard Varèse surrounded by a light sculpture. (right) Just as the composer Edgard Varèse creates interacting "sound masses" of varying color and density, so the American sculptor Alexander Calder, in his mobiles such as *Lobster Trap and Fish Tail* (1939), creates "spatial zones" of different color and density that, on the slightest breath of air, interact in unexpected ways.

color, texture, and density, but no melody or harmony

composers of this century. The novelty of *Ionization* rests in the fact that the ear must focus primarily on nonpitch elements in order to follow the sense of the design.

LISTENING GUIDE		Edgard Varèse *Ionization* (1931)	6CD 6/10 6Tape 6A

0:00	Sound mass 1: shimmer of cymbals, drums, gongs, and sirens
0:33	Sound mass 2: snare drum and tam-tam create sharply defined rhythms, thin texture
0:47	Sound mass 1 returns briefly
1:03	Sound mass 2 expanded, becomes denser as more instruments added
2:08	Siren from sound mass 1 penetrates into sound mass 2
2:19	Sound mass 3: pounding intensity (*fortissimo*), denser texture in low register (bass drums)
3:04	Sound mass 4 (high-sounding anvils) interacts with sound mass 1
3:20	Sound masses 1–4 interact at various levels of intensity (louds and softs)
4:36	Sound mass 5 (piano and chimes) added to the mix
5:30	Fadeout: intensity diminishes, texture thins as accumulated sonority of five sound masses fades away

John Cage (1912–1992)

John Cage was born in Los Angeles, the son of an inventor. He was graduated valedictorian of Los Angeles High School and spent two years at nearby Pomona College before going to Europe to learn more about art, architecture, and music. Arriving in New York in 1942, he worked variously as a wall washer at the YWCA, teacher of music and mycology (the science of mushrooms) at the New School for Social Research, and as music director of a modern dance company.

From his earliest days as a musician, Cage had a special affection for percussion instruments and the unusual sounds they can create. His *First Construction (in Metal)* (1939) has six percussionists play piano, metal thunder-sheets, oxen bells, cowbells, sleigh bells, water gongs, and brake drums, among other things. By 1941 he had collected three hundred percussion objects of this kind—anything that might make an unusual noise when struck or shaken. Cage's tinkering with percussive sounds led him to invent the **prepared piano**: a grand piano outfitted with screws, bolts, washers, erasers, and bits of felt and plastic all inserted between the strings (Fig. 17–24). This transformed the piano into a one-man percussion band that could produce a great variety of sounds and noises—twangs, zaps, rattles, thuds, and the like—no two of which were exactly the same in pitch or color. In creating the prepared piano, Cage was merely going farther along the experimental trail first blazed by his spiritual mentor, Edgard Varèse: "Years ago, after I decided to devote my life to music, I noticed that people distinguished between noises and sounds. I decided to follow Varèse and fight for noises, to be on the side of the underdog."

Cage's glorification of everyday noise began in earnest during the 1950s. Rather than engage in a titanic struggle to shape the elements of music like Beethoven, he decided to sit back, relax, and just let noises occur around him. In creating this sort of purposeless, undirected music, Cage invented what has come to be called chance music, the ultimate in musical experimentation. In

FIGURE 17–23

"I have nothing to say and I am saying it." John Cage.

FIGURE 17–24

John Cage's "prepared piano." By putting spoons, forks, screws, paper clips, and other sundry objects into the strings of the piano, the composer changes the instrument from one producing melodic tones to one generating percussive impacts.

chance music, musical events are not carefully predetermined by the composer but come in an unpredictable sequence as the result of traditionally unmusical activities such as using astrological charts, tossing coins, throwing dice, or shuffling the pages of music any which way. In *Musical Walk* (1958), for example, one or more pianists connect lines and dots in any fashion to create a musical "score" from which to play. Such "scores" only suggest in the most vague way what the musician is to do. The musical "happening" that results is the sort of spontaneous group experience that was to flower during the 1960s. More radical still is Cage's work *0'00"* (1962), which allows the performer total artistic freedom. When performed by Cage himself in 1962, he sliced and prepared vegetables at a table on a stage, put them through a food processor, and then drank the juice, all the while amplifying and broadcasting the sound of these activities around the hall. In a funny way, Cage's attempts to elevate the random, ordinary noise of food processing to the level of art is rather like Andy Warhol's glorification of the Campbell's soup can (Fig. 17–25).

Naturally, music critics called Cage a joker and a charlatan. Most would agree that his "compositions" in and by themselves are not of great musical value. But he did have a philosophy about music that he articulated by means of challenges and indirect questions. By focusing on the chance appearance of ordinary noise, Cage aggressively asks us to ponder the fundamental principles that underlie most Western music. Why must sounds of similar range and color come one after the other, why must music have form and unity, why must it have "meaning," why must it express something, why must it develop and climax, why must it be goal oriented as is so much of human activity in the West?

4'33" (1952)

The "composition" of Cage that causes us to focus on these questions most intently is his *4'33"*. Here one or more performers carrying any sort of instru-

FIGURE 17–25

The *Campbell's Soup Can* (1965) painted by Andy Warhol (1930–1987) asks the fundamental question: What is art?

Electronic Music

One of the universal qualities of modern music, in America as well as Europe, is its insatiable appetite for new sounds. Schoenberg's novel *Sprechstimme** (see page 355) and Varèse's obsession with new percussion instruments are merely two manifestations of this continual search for innovative sonorities. Shortly after World War II, a series of technological developments—including the invention of magnetic tape (tape recording as we know it)—made it possible for progressive composers to dispense with traditional acoustic instruments and write music generated entirely by electronic machines.

The earliest experiments with the electronic creation of sound produced *musique concrète*. **Musique concrète** is so called because the composer works directly, or concretely, with sounds recorded on magnetic tape, not with intermediary symbols (musical notation) and the middlemen (performers). Musical tones or everyday sounds from the real world—a car horn, a dog's bark, a dish falling on the floor—are captured on tape, doctored in some way, and then reassembled to form an unexpected montage of sound. Pierre Schaeffer working in Paris and Edgard Varèse in New York were among the first practitioners of *musique concrète*, Varèse's *Poème électronique* (1958) being a landmark in the history of this sort of synthetic music. The great contribution of *musique concrète* was to show that any sort of sound or noise might serve as building material in a musical composition. The next step, taken in the late 1950s, was to add or mix in sound produced electronically by means of a synthesizer.

An electronic **synthesizer** is a machine that has the capacity to produce, transform, and combine (or synthesize) electronic sounds. A traditional, acoustic musical instrument generates sound by setting a string in motion, by passing pulsating air through a tube, or by striking a skin or some other wooden or metal object. A synthesizer, however, creates sound by means of an oscillator. An **oscillator** is a device that, when activated by an electronic current, pulses back and forth, producing an electronic signal that can be converted by a loudspeaker into sound. Before it passes through a speaker and becomes audible, however, the electronic signal can be modified in various ways: It can be made higher or lower, not just by a tone or semitone, but by every small fraction of an interval in between; its color (timbre) can be changed—a clarinet sound turned into that of a trombone, a violin tone into that of a police whistle—by modifying the waveform and the relative prominence of the overtones*. The synthesizer, then, placed at the fingertips of the user a new range of hitherto-unknown and unimaginable sounds. Equally important, a single electronic keyboard could produce the sounds of many different instruments.

The first synthesizer was built in the 1950s for RCA at a studio in New York City. But it was bulky and awkward to use, making the production of new sounds a time-consuming, costly process. Subsequent developments in microchips and integrated circuitry produced more powerful, flexible, "user-friendly" machines, like the Yamaha SY-22, now a favorite of both "serious" composers and rock performers alike.

The most recent development in electronic music, computer music, couples the computer to the electronic synthesizer. The principle of **computer music** is this: All aspects of musical sound—pitch, duration, color, volume, attack and decay—can be measured and expressed quantitatively in binary numbers. Such numbers can be stored and manipulated by computer and, on command, turned into electrical voltages that can then be pushed through speakers to

(continued)

An early electronic music synthesizer, the RCA Mark II, which occupies walls of a studio in New York City. During the 1950s a composer might spend hours at such a machine trying to generate a mere minute of electronic music.

A composer today can create almost the same music in a fraction of the time with the use of the more modern Yamaha SY-22 electronic synthesizer.

Electronic Music, continued

produce audible sound. (The new technology of CD-ROM simply integrates the retrieval of text and images with the recall of digitally stored sound.) Today the computer-driven synthesizer can produce a tone quality that is almost indistinguishable from the recorded sound of a symphony orchestra, if this is what the electronic composer wishes.

The impact of digital technology on the musical world has been enormous. Electronic music composers can prepare a musical work directly for broadcast on CD or DAT (digital audiotape) without bothering with an orchestra or a listening audience that may be indifferent or even hostile to modern music. Similarly, commercial musicians writing for radio, television, and film can more or less duplicate every nuance of a full ninety-piece orchestra without the enormous expense that orchestral rehearsals and recording sessions usually entail. The "orchestra" that furnishes the soundtracks for the TV shows "Ellen," "Sisters," "The Wonder Years," and "Roseanne," for example, is nothing more than a small group of computers, synthesizers, and mixers in the studio of commercial composer W. G. (Snuffy) Walden near Los Angeles.

The television composer W. G. (Snuffy) Walden at a keyboard synthesizer in his electronic studio near Los Angeles.

ment come out on the stage, seat themselves, open the music, and play nothing. For each of the three carefully timed movements there is no notated music but only the indication *tacet* ("it is silent"). With no organized sound to be heard during the four minutes and thirty-three seconds of silence that follows, the listener gradually becomes aware of the background noise in the hall—a creaking floor, a passing car, a dropped paper clip, an electrical hum. It turns out there is no such thing as absolute silence. Cage asks us to embrace these random, everyday noises—to tune our ears in innocent sonic wonder. Are these sounds not of artistic value too? What is art?

can random noise be music?

Needless to say, we have not filled your tapes and CDs with four minutes and thirty-three seconds of background noise. You can create your own, and John Cage would have liked that. Listen to *4'33"* with the following guide and note what you hear. Perhaps this experiment will make you more aware of how important conscious organization is to the art we call music. If nothing else, Cage makes us realize that music, above all, is a form of communication from one person to the next and that random background noise can do nothing to express or communicate ideas and feelings.

LISTENING GUIDE

John Cage
4'33" (1952)

0:00–0:30	First movement—silence (?)
0:31–2:53	Second movement—silence (?)
2:54–4:33	Third movement—silence (?)

THREE TRADITIONALISTS: SERGEY PROKOFIEV, AARON COPLAND, AND ELLEN TAAFFE ZWILICH

While experimental composers in this century, such as Varèse and Cage, have sought to break with the traditions of Western music, other musicians have tried to extend and invigorate the past by imposing on it modern idioms and styles. In this sense composers like Aaron Copland and Ellen Taaffe Zwilich, to name only two among the traditionalists, are more evolutionary than revolutionary. Their aim is to show that traditional values of form, balance, melodiousness, warmth, emotion, and meaning in music have validity in the modern sonic world. Modernity, of course, could never fully eradicate tradition. The two aesthetics continue to exist side by side. Each offers an ongoing critique of the other, and thereby further identifies and defines itself.

Toward the end of the first World War (1914–1918), a new artistic movement called **Neo-classicism** sought to revive the balanced forms and conjunct melodies of earlier music, specifically of the Baroque and Classical periods. The resourceful Igor Stravinsky turned away from his large-scale, colorful Russian ballets like *The Rite of Spring* to write for a much smaller, leaner orchestra of strings and woodwinds. "I attempted to build a new music on eighteenth-century classicism," he said. This Neo-classical directive of "back to Bach" (and his contemporaries) rejected both the large orchestra and the emotionalism of the Romantics, as well as the extreme sorts of dissonance and atonality being advanced by Arnold Schoenberg and his Second Viennese School (see page 354). Needless to say, the listening public, which had never taken kindly to the experimental works of the radical avant-garde, welcomed the greater simplicity, clarity, and even humor in the Neo-classical style. The earliest and perhaps most enjoyable example of musical Neo-classicism is Sergey Prokofiev's *Classical Symphony* (1917).

FIGURE 17–26

Just as Stravinsky, after the example of Prokofiev, entered a Neo-classical period during the 1920s, so the artist Pablo Picasso painted in a lighter, more transparent Neo-classical style in that decade. Although the figures in his *Mother and Child* (1921–1922) are somewhat extended and abstract, the formal composition of this painting, which harks back to a Madonna and Child of the Renaissance, is classical.

FIGURE 17–27

Sergey Prokofiev.

Sergey Prokofiev (1891–1953)

The career of Sergey Prokofiev is full of contradictions and ironies, caused in part by the place he occupied in Russian history. The son of a well-to-do farm administrator, he fled the Communist Revolution in 1917, only later to celebrate in music the most murderous of the revolutionaries, Joseph Stalin (1879–1953). He was known as the dissonant, atonal "bad boy" of the St. Petersburg Conservatory, where he received his musical education, but later wrote such pleasantly benign works as *Peter and the Wolf* (1936). He thought of himself above all as a serious composer—the author of seven symphonies, six operas and six ballets, five piano concertos, and nine piano sonatas—but today is remembered mainly for his lighter works: the *Classical Symphony, Peter and the Wolf,* and the film scores *Lieutenant Kijé* and *Alexander Nevsky.* He and Joseph Stalin died within minutes of each other on the might of March 5, 1953, but news of Prokofiev's death was withheld for days so as not to deflect attention away from the deceased dictator. No flowers could be bought for the great composer's coffin: The funeral of the supreme murderer, without exaggeration, had claimed them all.

CLASSICAL SYMPHONY (1917)

There is a sense of historical irony present as well in Prokofiev's *Classical Symphony*. It is the irony created by a clash of musical systems and values: those of the eighteenth century against those of the modern world. Prokofiev creates a model of Neo-classicism by invoking the orchestra and the musical forms of Joseph Haydn. He hypothesized: "It seemed to me that had Haydn lived in our day, he would have retained his own style while accepting something new at the same time." The "something new" in this four-movement Neo-classical symphony is the following: a melody that is more disjunct and extended than Haydn would have written, a harmony that slides suddenly to unexpected chords, and a dissonance so biting and so frequent as to be unknown to classical composers. By juxtaposing the classical and the modern in a single work, the composer focuses attention on the question "What makes musical style?" Thus, as we listen to the *Classical Symphony* we enjoy the music in and of itself, but we also think about the interaction of contrasting musical styles. Prokofiev's work is simultaneously art and a critique of art.

a clash of music systems

eighteenth-century form—twentieth-century dissonance

LISTENING GUIDE

Sergey Prokofiev
Classical Symphony (Symphony No. 1; 1917)
First movement, *Allegro* (fast)

6CD 6/11
6Tape 6A

EXPOSITION

0:00   Violins play racing first theme

0:23   Woodwinds lead lively transition
0:55   Violins softly play second theme above bassoon counterpoint

1:28   *Forte* closing theme

DEVELOPMENT

1:44   First theme returns briefly
1:54   Transition material developed and extended to different keys
2:13   *Fortissimo* expansion of second theme
2:38   Closing theme used as retransition*

RECAPITULATION

2:52   First theme returns
3:04   Woodwinds lead transition
3:30   Soft violins bring back second theme above bassoon counterpoint
3:58   *Forte* closing theme
(Listening Exercise 42)

FIGURE 17–28

Aaron Copland conducting one of his scores at a recording session at CBS.

Aaron Copland (1900–1990)

The tradition embodied in the music of Aaron Copland is, simply said, our American musical heritage. He does not reuse materials taken from eighteenth-century Europe but instead employs American hymn tunes, cowboy songs, and jazz idioms. These he sets not in a collage of dissonant atonality, as did his older contemporary, Charles Ives, but in a conservative backdrop of generally consonant harmony.

Copland was born in Brooklyn of Jewish immigrant parents. After a rudimentary musical education in New York City, he set sail for Paris to broaden his artistic horizons. In this he was not alone, for the City of Light at this time attracted young writers, painters, and musicians from across the world, including Stravinsky, Picasso, James Joyce (1882–1941), Gertrude Stein (1874–1946), Ernest Hemingway (1898–1961), and F. Scott Fitzgerald (1896–1940). After three years of study Copland returned to the United States, determined to compose a kind of music that was distinctly American. Like other young expatriate artists during the '20s, Copland had to leave his homeland to learn what was distinctive about it: "In greater or lesser degree, all of us discovered America in Europe."

American subjects

At first Copland sought to forge an American style by incorporating into his music elements of jazz, recognized the world over as a uniquely American creation. His debt to the Jazz Age is especially apparent in his *Piano Concerto* (1926), written two years after George Gershwin's *Rhapsody in Blue for Jazz Band and Piano*. Then, beginning in the late 1930s, Copland turned his attention to a series of projects that had rural and western America as their subjects. The ballet scores *Billy the Kid* (1938) and *Rodeo* (1942) are set in the West and make use of classic cowboy songs like *Goodbye, Old Paint* and *The Old Chisholm Trail*. Another ballet, *Appalachian Spring* (1944), recreates the ambience of the farm country of Pennsylvania, and his single opera, *The Tender Land* (1954), is set in the cornbelt of the Midwest.

his musical style

In these distinctly American works, Copland's musical voice is unique and consistently conservative. He uses folk and popular elements to soften the dissonant harmonies and disjunct melodies of European modernism. Copland's melodies tend to be more stepwise and diatonic than those of other twentieth-century composers, perhaps because Western folk and popular tunes are fundamentally conjunct and without chromaticism. His harmonies are almost always tonal and often slow-moving in a way that can evoke the vastness and grandeur of the American landscape. The triad, too, is still important with Copland, perhaps for its stability and simplicity, but he frequently uses it in a modern way, as we shall see, by having two triads sound simultaneously, creating mildly dissonant polychords. But perhaps the most important component in the distinctive "Copland sound" is his clear, luminous orchestration. He does not mix colors to produce rich Romantic blends, but keeps the four families of instruments (strings, woodwinds, brasses, and percussion) more or less to their own group.

a clear, wide-open sound

And he distributes the instruments of the orchestra so as to construct a solid bass, a very thin middle, and a top of one or two high, clear tones. It is this separation and careful spacing of the instruments that creates the fresh, wide-open sound so pleasing in Copland's music.

The clarity and simplicity of Aaron Copland's music is not accidental. During the Great Depression of the 1930s, he became convinced that the gulf between modern music and the ordinary citizen had become too great—that dissonance and atonality had little to say to most music lovers. "It made no sense to ignore them and to continue writing as if they did not exist. I felt that it was worth the effort to see if I couldn't say what I had to say in the simplest possible terms." Thus, he not only wrote appealing new tonal works like *Fanfare for the Common Man* (1942) but also was attracted to traditional tunes such as *The Gift to Be Simple*, which he uses in *Appalachian Spring*.

music for the common citizen

APPALACHIAN SPRING (1944)

Appalachian Spring is a one-act ballet that tells the story of "a pioneer celebration of spring in a newly built farmhouse in Pennsylvania in the early 1800s." A new bride and her farmer-husband express through dance the anxieties and joys of life in pioneer America. The work was composed in 1944 for the great lady of American choreography, Martha Graham (1893–1991), and it won Copland a Pulitzer Prize the following year. It is divided into eight connected sections that differ in tempo and mood. Copland has provided a brief description of each of these orchestral scenes.

an American ballet

Section 1: "Introduction of the characters one by one, in a suffused light." The quiet beauty of the land at daybreak is revealed as the orchestra slowly spaces out the notes of the tonic and then dominant triad.

EXAMPLE 17–12

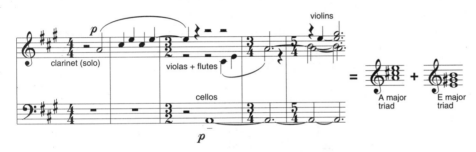

While this simultaneous presentation of two triads should be heard as a polychord, the effect is only mildly dissonant because of the slow, quiet way in which the notes of the two chords are introduced. The serene simplicity of the introduction sets the tone for the entire work.

Section 2: "A sentiment both elated and religious gives the keynote of this scene." The early calm is suddenly broken by a lively dance with a salient rhythm played aggressively in the strings. As the dance proceeds, a more restrained, hymnlike melody emerges in the trumpet.

Section 3: is a dance for the two principals, in ballet parlance a *pas de deux*, accompanied by lyrical writing for strings and winds. *Sections* 4 and 5 are musical depictions of the livelier aspects of country life, with 4 including a toe-tappin' hoedown, while *Section* 6 recalls the quiet calm of the opening of the ballet.

Section 7: "Calm and flowing. Scenes of daily activity for the Bride and her Farmer-husband." For this section Copland chose to make use of a traditional

FIGURE 17–29

A scene from Martha Graham's ballet
Appalachian Spring, with music by
Aaron Copland.

tune of the Shakers, an extreme religious sect that prospered in the Appalachian region in the early nineteenth century and whose members showed their spiritual intensity in frenzied singing, dancing, and shaking. The tune, as Copland
first presents it in the clarinet, is given in example 17–13. Since the action of the
ballet at this point concerns "scenes of daily activity," the original text of the
Shaker song is harmonious with what is occurring on stage:

EXAMPLE 17–13

a Shaker tune

'Tis the gift to be simple,
'Tis the gift to be free,
'Tis the gift to come down where we ought to be,
And when we find ourselves in the place just right,
'Twill be in the valley of love and delight.

Thereafter come five variations in which *The Gift to Be Simple* is not so much
varied as it is clothed in different instrumental attire.

Section 8: "The Bride takes her place among her neighbors." Serenity returns to
the scene as the strings, then the woodwinds, and then the strings and woodwinds together play a slow, mainly stepwise descent "like a prayer." The hymnlike melody from section 2 is heard again in the flute, followed by the quiet landscape music from the beginning of the ballet. Darkness has again descended on
the countryside, leaving the young pioneer couple "strong in their new house"
and secure in their community.

LISTENING GUIDE	Aaron Copland *Appalachian Spring* (1944) Sections 1, 2, 7, and 8	6CD 6/12–15; 6Tape 6B 3CD 3/13; 3Tape 3B

SECTION 1 (track 12; 6Tape 6B)

0:00   Quiet unfolding of triads by clarinet and other instruments

0:45   Soft violin melody descends

1:11   More triads in woodwinds and trumpet

1:36   Oboe and then bassoon solos

2:19   Clarinet plays concluding triad

SECTION 2 (track 13; 6Tape 6B)

0:00   Percussive rhythm (♪♪ ♩ ♪♪ ♩) in strings and rising woodwinds

0:19   Rhythm gels into sprightly dance

0:44   Trumpet plays hymnlike melody above dance

1:13   Rhythmic motive scattered but then played more forcefully

2:09   Hymn heard in strings, with flute counterpoint above

2:36   Rhythmic motive skips away in woodwinds

SECTION 7 (track 14; 6Tape 6B; 3CD 3/13; 3Tape 3B)

0:00   Clarinet presents Shaker tune

0:36   Variation 1: Oboe and bassoon play tune

1:06   Variation 2: Violas play tune at half its previous speed

1:51   Variation 3: Trumpets and trombones play tune

2:16   Variation 4: Woodwinds play tune more slowly

2:31   Variation 5: Final majestic statement of tune by full orchestra

SECTION 8 (track 15; 6Tape 6B)

0:00   Serene, stepwise string music

0:44   Woodwinds continue placid mood

0:58   Strings and winds together play more loudly

1:20   Flute enters with hymnlike tune from section 2

2:14   Clarinet plays triad from the beginning of ballet

2:29   Soft, mild polychords in strings

(Listening Exercise 43)

Ellen Taaffe Zwilich (b. 1939)

Like the late Aaron Copland, Ellen Taaffe Zwilich works to establish connections with past traditions as well as to speak to the general listening public. Her music resonates not so much with American folk and popular music as with the traditional European repertoire of the concert hall. The very titles of her works—

FIGURE 17–30

"I never have to work for themes; they can hit me at any time, and usually do." Ellen Taaffe Zwilich.

Concerto Grosso 1985, Divertimento, and *Song Cycle for Baritone and Piano*—invite comparisons to musical genres favored in the Baroque, Classical, and Romantic periods, respectively. Not surprisingly, at various times her music has been called Neo-baroque, Neo-classical, and Neo-romantic.

The daughter of an airline pilot, Zwilich was born in Miami and educated at Florida State University. She then moved to New York City, where she played violin in the American Symphony Orchestra, studied composition at the Juilliard School, and worked for a time as an usher at Carnegie Hall. Zwilich's big "break" came in 1983, when she became the first woman to win the Pulitzer Prize in music—a contest in which musical scores are judged without knowledge of the name or sex of the candidate. Building on the fame derived from the Pulitzer and an unblemished record of successful premieres, Zwilich has since reached the plateau to which every modern composer aspires: She is now free to devote her time exclusively to composition, living from royalties and, more important, commissions for new works. Institutions such as the New York Philharmonic and the Chicago Symphony Orchestra have paid five-figure sums for a single new piece from her pen. Her aim is always the same: to communicate directly with the audience and thereby show that modern music can be enjoyed by the average listener. As she has said, "Most people have the mistaken impression that classical music is written by dead people."

Among the commissions Ellen Taaffe Zwilich received was one from the Washington Friends of Handel in 1985, to commemorate the three hundredth anniversary of George Frideric Handel's birth. From this resulted a five-movement concerto grosso*, a musical genre from the Baroque period of which Handel was a leading exponent. Zwilich borrows a theme from Handel and gives it a modern profile by making the intervals more chromatic. She then adds other elements of Baroque musical style: a regular rhythmic pulse, a strong polarity between bass and melody, a repeating bass pedal point*, a walking bass*, and a harpsichord*. Yet Zwilich creates a dissonant harmony and demands an intense style of playing that would have shocked Handel. When Handel composed a *Largo,* it was invariably noble and serene. While the body of Zwilich's *Largo* may be festooned with stylistic features from the time of the Baroque master, the heart of her piece pounds with the fearful intensity of the modern age.

LISTENING GUIDE	Ellen Taaffe Zwilich *Concerto Grosso 1985* (1985) Third movement, *Largo* (Slow and broad)	6CD 6/16 6Tape 6B

0:00	Bass pedal point begins
0:05	Melody rises in oboes and violins
0:29	Bass finally begins to "walk" to lower pitches
0:59	Violins play melody *forte*, with dissonant chords added by harpsichord
1:04	French horns provide dissonant melodic counterpoint
1:39	Dissonant chords repeated *forte*
2:10	Cellos play melody above soft dissonant chords in harpsichord
2:42	Cellos and violins play melody above soft dissonant chords and bass pedal point
3:33	Bass and chordal accompaniment become more fragmented
3:52	Violins play melody quietly above fragmented chords

NEW TRENDS: MINIMALISM AND POSTMINIMALISM

Composers at the end of the twentieth century have faced a perplexing question: Where is the mainstream of musical modernism? Should they follow Arnold Schoenberg's dissonant twelve-tone* method and create works in which all aspects of melody and harmony are strictly predetermined? Or should they head in the opposite direction and travel the freely experimental route of John Cage, even though this more chancy path can sometimes lead to musical happenings that border on the silly? Should they recreate the warmth and sentiment of nineteenth-century music, a Neo-romantic sound produced by traditional acoustic instruments? Or should they try to create wholly new sonorities generated electronically by means of synthesizers and computers? One recent trend, which rejects all of these solutions, is a movement in composition called minimalism. Minimalist composers, like their counterparts the minimalist artists (see Fig. 17–31), strive to do away with both time-honored processes and modern technical complexities.

Minimalism is a style of modern music, begun in the late 1960s, that takes a very small amount of musical material and repeats it over and over to form a composition. A three-note melodic cell, a single arpeggio, or two alternating chords is the sort of small, "minimal" element a composer will introduce, reiterate again and again, modify or add to, and then begin to repeat once more. The basic material is usually simple, tonal, and consonant. By repeating these minimal figures incessantly at a steady pulse, the composer creates a hypnotic effect—"trance music" is the name sometimes given this music—where atonality, dissonance, and mathematical systems like those of Schoenberg can never penetrate. Minimalism, in both art and music, has been mainly an American movement. Its most successful musical practitioners are Steve Reich (b. 1936), Philip Glass (b. 1937), and John Adams (b. 1947).

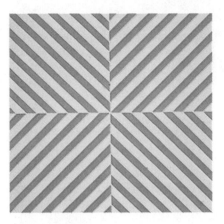

FIGURES 17–31

Frank Stella, *Fez* (1964). Here a single element, an angular stripe, repeats again and again, sometimes running up, sometimes running down. Similarly, a minimalist composer like Steve Reich or Philip Glass may take a simple C major triad and repeat it endlessly, first going up and then down.

John Adams (b. 1947)

John Adams, educated at Harvard and presently living in Berkeley, California, was not the first minimalist composer. Indeed, he is not even a strict minimalist, in that from time to time a warm, traditional-sounding melody will creep into his constantly repeating, minimal patterns. For that reason he might best be termed a "post-minimalist"—a minimalist who blends other materials into the minimal sonorities. Moreover, the two works for which Adams is best known, *Nixon in China* (1987) and *The Death of Klinghofer* (1991), are anything but minimal in size—both are lengthy, three-act operas.

NIXON IN CHINA (1987)

Nixon in China is the result of the collaborative efforts of composer Adams, the poet/librettist Alice Goodman, and the controversial stage director Peter Sellars. The plot concerns the historic seven-day visit (February 21–27, 1972) made by Richard Nixon and Henry Kissinger to China to break the Cold War with the communist bloc of the Far East. To get in tune with these events, Adams and his collaborators read various news magazines and memoirs and watched old television newsreels.

FIGURE 17–32

John Adams.

a visionary villain dominates the opera

At first blush the story of a diplomatic mission to China would seem an unlikely vehicle for operatic success. And why glorify Richard Nixon? Wasn't he the only American president to be forced from office in disgrace? Here the aim is to identify the paradoxes of the man, the discrepancy between public *persona* and private individual, between Nixon's global vision and personal self-doubts. Richard Nixon was, at one and the same time, arguably the most brilliant American president in matters of foreign policy and the most insecure and paranoid of our national leaders.

The aria "News has a kind of mystery" from Act I shows Richard Nixon at both his visionary best and his paranoiac worst. He knows the importance of the mission for world peace, he understands the power of the media to shape world opinion, he grasps the sweep of history, yet he is terrified of those who distrust him, those "rats who chew the sheets." The elements of minimalism—the repeating ostinatos* of thirds and triads, the steady pulse—appear almost entirely in the accompanying instruments. Above this orchestra Adams projects the voice of Nixon, now dramatic, now lyrical. The text-setting is crystal clear. Most surprisingly, words that would seem unsingable, like "It's prime time in the U.S.A.," take on a wholly unexpected excitement as the composer emphasizes the natural rhythms of the English language. This is a libretto full of vivid images and pleasing alliterations. But the success of the opera as a whole belongs only to the composer John Adams. *Nixon in China*, as with any opera, stands or falls on the quality of its music.

LISTENING GUIDE

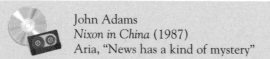

John Adams
Nixon in China (1987)
Aria, "News has a kind of mystery"

6CD 6/17
6Tape 6B

Characters: President Richard Nixon, Chinese Premier Chou En-lai, and Secretary of State Henry Kissinger

Situation: The presidential plane has landed in Peking and the American party disembarks. While Premier Chou En-lai introduces the official Chinese entourage, President Nixon contemplates the importance of his mission, the power of the media in shaping public opinion, the righteousness of the American cause, and the rats who distrust him.

0:00	Ostinato of two low pitches and a single higher pitch	*Nixon:* News has a kind of mystery: When I shook hands with Chou En-lai	
0:25	Trumpets (with mutes) play syncopated chords	On this bare field outside Peking Just now, the world was listening. *Chou:*	May I—
0:48	Ostinatos continue, quietly	*Nixon:* And though we spoke quietly The eyes and ears of history Caught every gesture— *Chou:* *Nixon:* And every word, transforming us As we, transfixed,— *Chou:*	—introduce —the Deputy Minister of Security.
1:33	Syncopated trumpets return	*Nixon:* Made history *Chou:*	May I—
1:54	Ostinatos continue, woodwinds add rapid descents	*Nixon:* On our flight over from Shanghai The countryside looked drab and grey. "Brueghel," Pat said.	

2:10	French horn follows lyrical voice	"We came in peace for all mankind," I said, and I was put in mind Of our Apollo astronauts Simply achieving a great human dream.
2:40	Ostinato in lower strings, trumpets crescendo repeatedly	We live in an unsettled time. Who are our enemies? Who are our friends?
3:08	Bass clarinet and other woodwinds play repeating patterns in this lyrical section	The Eastern Hemisphere Beckoned to us, and we have flown East of the sun, west of the moon Across an ocean of distrust Filled with the bodies of our lost; The earth's Sea of Tranquility.
3:54	Return to ostinato and trumpets heard at the beginning	News! It's prime time in the U.S.A. Yesterday night. They watch us now; The three main networks' colors glow Livid through drapes onto the lawn. Dishes are washed and homework done, The dog and grandma fall asleep A car roars past playing loud pop, Is gone.
4:42	Basses play repeated note, then two-note ostinato	As I look down the road I know America is good At heart. An old cold warrior Piloting towards an unknown shore Through shoals.
5:05	Low instruments play descending syncopated chords; brasses play sinister "wails"	The rats begin to chew The sheets. There's murmuring below. Now there's ingratitiude! My hand Is steady as a rock. A sound Like mourning doves reaches my ears, Nobody is a friend of ours. The nation's heartland skips a beat As our hands shield the spinning globe From the flame-throwers of the mob. We must press on. We know we want— *Kissinger:* *Nixon:* What—Oh yes—.

Mr. President—

LISTENING EXERCISES

Igor Stravinsky
The Rite of Spring (1913)
Introduction and Scene 1

6CD 6/1–2; 6Tape 6A
3CD 3/8–9; 3Tape 3B

Stravinksy, more than any other modern composer before the recent minimalists (see page 379), made use of the musical ostinato—the repetition of a motive, over and over at the same pitch. The ostinato imparts to his music a feeling of kinetic energy continually being recycled and renewed. At the same time, the static quality of a repeating motive allows Stravinsky to work against the functional chord progression* and "goal-oriented" melodic expansion of Romantic music. A stationary musical moment can be maintained and enjoyed in and of itself. The following exercise asks you to focus on the ostinatos heard in the Introduction and Scene 1 of *The Rite of Spring*. Listen to the listed passages, and state if an ostinato is or is not present. Sometimes this will require listening carefully to the inner parts.

Ostinato present? (yes or no)

1. 0:35–0:56 _____   6CD 6/2; 3CD 3/9
2. 2:08–2:20 _____   6. 0:24–0:36 _____
3. 2:34–2:55 _____   7. 1:14–1:22 _____
4. 2:57–3:10 _____   8. 1:23–1:36 _____
5. 3:28–3:34 _____   9. 1:59–2:29 _____

10. Judging from your responses, are there more moments in *The Rite of Spring* making use of an ostinato than those that do not? _____

41	Béla Bartók *Concerto for Orchestra* (1943) Fourth movement, *Broken Intermezzo*	6CD 6/8; 6Tape 6A 3CD 3/11; 3Tape 3B

The fourth movement of Bartók's *Concerto for Orchestra* is entitled *Intermezzo interrotto (Broken Intermezzo)*, and this title may be seen as a metaphor for Bartók's life in his native Hungary, broken or interrupted by the arrival of Nazi troops. The movement incorporates three themes: the first (**A**) is rather light and playful and marked by three staccato notes; the second (**B**) is a lush, lilting Hungarian melody played by the strings; while the third (**C**), representing the German soldiers, is a straight quarter-note descent, spiced with triplets, introduced by the clarinet. The themes are given here. Study them and become familiar with the general outline of each. Then listen to the movement and compile a time log for it. Remember that the movement unfolds **ABACBA,** with the second appearance of **A** being very brief.

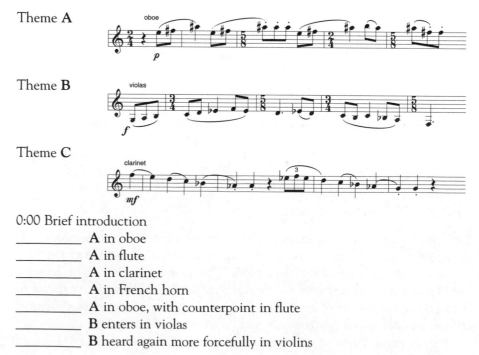

Theme **A**

Theme **B**

Theme **C**

0:00 Brief introduction
_____ **A** in oboe
_____ **A** in flute
_____ **A** in clarinet
_____ **A** in French horn
_____ **A** in oboe, with counterpoint in flute
_____ **B** enters in violas
_____ **B** heard again more forcefully in violins

_____ **A** returns briefly in oboe

_____ **C** enters in clarinet
(rude noises)

_____ **C** in strings varied by means of repeating notes
(more rude noises)

_____ **C** now ascends (rather than descends) in violins
(more rude noises)

_____ **B** returns in strings

_____ **A** returns in English horn

_____ Cadenza by flute

_____ Reminiscences of **A** lead to quiet end

	Sergey Prokofiev	6CD 6/11
42	*Classical Symphony* (Symphony No. 1, 1917)	6Tape 6A
	First movement, *Allegro* (fast)	

As discussed earlier (page 373), Prokofiev's *Classical Symphony* is an object lesson in how an artist might revisit the past in order to clarify the present. For the
listener of this Neo-classical work, the fun rests in identifying what is classical
and what is modern as the music races past.

Listen to the movement once, concentrating on questions of orchestration
and form.

1. Is there a harpsichord in the orchestra? _____
2. Are there tubas and English horns in the orchestra? _____
3. Are there clarinets, French horns, and timpani in the orchestra?
   _____
4. The orchestra from which specific period in the history of music serves as the
   orchestral model for Prokofiev?
   a. Baroque   b. Classical   c. Romantic
5. Which traditional musical form does Prokofiev employ in this movement?
   a. fugue   b. sonata–allegro   c. theme and variations
6. Is there a coda to the movement? _____

Now listen again to the development section, specifically to passages A
(1:54–2:03) and B (2:04–2:13).

7. Which of these two passages represents a moment of heavy dissonance, A or
   B? _____
8. Which of these two passages represents a moment of quick sliding from one
   pitch level to another, A or B? _____

Finally:

9. Identify one moment or passage in this movement (there are many) in
   which the music seems to be strongly in a modern, not eighteenth-century,
   style (give approximate minute and seconds). _____
10. State what it is about the music at the point you identify that creates this
    feeling of modernity. _____

43 Aaron Copland   6CD 6/12–15; 6Tape 6B
  Appalachian Spring (1944)   3CD 3/13; 3Tape 3B
  Sections 1, 2, 7, and 8

The following questions focus on musical themes, textures, and colors. They also ask you to consider the ways in which Copland the conservative softens the sometimes biting sound of twentieth-century music.

Section 1 (6CD 6/12; 6Tape 6B): Introduction

1. Which family of instruments provides the bulk of the soloists for this opening section?
   a. strings b. woodwinds c. brass d. percussion
2. (0:45–1:09) Why does this passage sound more like Romantic music than modern music?
   a. warm, primarily stepwise melody played by violin
   b. lovely French horn call suggests nature
   c. exotic English horn plays stepwise melody
3. (2:19) As the clarinet rises to end the opening section, what do the strings do?
   a. continue with the melody
   b. play a dissonant chord above the clarinet
   c. hold a single note below

Section 2 (6CD 6/13; 6Tape 6B): Joys and anxieties of pioneer life

This section is composed of two musical ideas: an energetic dance theme and a more restrained hymnlike tune (see examples on page 377).

4. The dance theme begins in the strings (at 0:19) and then the hymnlike tune enters in the trumpet (0:43). Which is more percussive and dissonant—hence more modern sounding?
   a. dance theme b. hymnlike theme
5. (1:20–2:07) Now the lively dance theme dominates. Identify three qualities of the music you hear in this passage that are reminiscent of the music of Igor Stravinsky, a composer whom Copland greatly admired.
   a. violent, percussive strokes in the timpani, piano, and xylophone
   b. a rhythmic ostinato in the flutes and harp
   c. a sweeping melody in the cellos
   d. tone clusters in the brasses
   e. strong, irregular accents

Section 7 (6CD 6/14; 6Tape 6B; 3CD 3/13; 3Tape 3B): Variations on a Shaker tune *The Gift to Be Simple* (see Example 17–13 on page 376)

 0:00 Tune in the clarinet
 0:36 Oboe and bassoon present variation 1
 1:06 Violas and then violins present variation 2

6. During variation 2 (1:06–1:41), what do the woodwinds and percussion (piano, harp, and glockenspiel) do?
   a. play a flowing countermelody
   b. establish an ostinato as a sonorous backdrop

7. At the end of variation 2 is a brief transition (1:46) to variation 3 (1:51). Which of the following occurs in this transition?
    a. a rising scale in trombone and trumpet that produces a modulation to a new, higher key
    b. a descending scale in dotted notes in the strings but no modulation

    1:51 Trumpets and trombones present variation 3, against which the violins and violas interject running scales as counterpoint

8. In variation 3 (1:51–2:13) the Shaker tune appears in note values that are played in what speed?
    a. twice as fast as the previous variation
    b. the same as the previous variation
    c. twice as slow as the previous variation

    2:16 Woodwinds quietly carry the tune in variation 4

9. (2:31) The full orchestra offers the fifth and final variation. How would you describe what the strong bass line is doing in this statement?
    a. descending slowly, mainly by step
    b. descending quickly in large intervals
    c. rising slowly, mainly in large intervals

Section 8 (6CD 6/15; 6Tape 6B): "Like a prayer"

This begins with a quiet interlude in which all the strings play a slow, mainly stepwise descent. This is repeated by all the woodwinds (at 0:44) and then by strings and woodwinds together (at 0:58).

10. (2:24–2:50) At the very end the music is warm and glowing, and although polychords are present there is no feeling of harsh dissonance. Why not?
    a. because the polychords are played percussively
    b. because the notes of the polychords enter slowly and quietly, one by one
    c. because the Shaker hymn is heard in the flute

KEY WORDS

atonal music	intermezzo	polymeter
Ballets russes	minimalism	polyrhythm
chance music	*musique concrète*	prepared piano
computer music	Neo-classicism	serial music
Cubism	ninth chord	*Sprechstimme*
electronic music	octave displacement	synthesizer
eleventh chord	oscillator	twelve-tone
Expressionism	polychord	composition

A checklist of musical styles of the twentieth century is given on page 67.

CH. 16 + 17

Study CD'S
↑
extra credit
who, what for mus2

18

AMERICAN POPULAR MUSIC: BLUES, JAZZ, BROADWAY, AND ROCK

W hat is popular music? Is it music for all the people? Is it music more loved or favored than some other types of music and hence "popular," like a movie star or a political figure? Is it a commodity that can be mass produced and sold everywhere, like a pair of blue jeans? Is it a fashionable sort of music whose favored status can quickly fade, like the once-popular miniskirt or bell-bottom pants? With qualifications, we may confidently say "yes" to all of the above. Although lovers of classical music can be just as passionate about Beethoven, for example, as those of rock music can be about the Grateful Dead or R.E.M., obviously, popular music is enjoyed by a much larger segment of society than is more "serious" music. Popular music is heard everywhere—on radio and television, in the supermarket, and in the dentist's office. It is "broadcast" in the literal sense of the word. Popular records, tapes, and CDs outsell classical selections by about nine to one. For the most part, popular music is simple and direct. It requires little or no formal training in music to appreciate. Rarely does popular music aspire to be art. It is made to be enjoyed for the moment without concern about its lasting value.

Popular music is similar, but not identical, to folk music. Folk music, too, is enjoyed by all of society. But, unlike popular music, different folk songs are known to different groups. A cowhand in west Texas or a farmer in Blue Earth, Minnesota, for example, may never have heard the ballads sung by a coal miner in Harlan, Kentucky. Each community and each ethnic group has its own folk music that is passed along from one generation to the next. True folk music is created by the local community. It is never written down, and exists only when sung or played from memory. Popular music, on the other hand, not only is written down but also is intended to be reproduced and sold as a commodity to a mass audience, whether in the form of sheet music or recordings. The homespun folk singer who chants a centuries-old ballad—like *The Streets of Laredo* (see page 30)—is a far cry from the professional pop singer who performs his or her latest hit in Madison Square Garden. Yet from the folk music of both white and black America have sprung our most distinctive genres of popular music: blues, jazz, and rock.

BLUES

Why, where, and how the blues originated is a story that will probably never be fully told. We cannot even hazard a guess as to who gave this style of singing the name "blues," though the expression "the blue devils" had been used to describe a melancholy mood since Shakespeare's time. All that can be said with certainty is that the **blues** are a form of black folk song that originated in the South sometime during the 1880s and 1890s. Like all true folk music, the blues were passed along by oral tradition, one performer learning directly from another without benefit of written music. Comparisons with other forms of folk music suggest that the blues had two immediate ancestors. First and most important was the work song and field holler (or cry) of the black laborers, which bequeathed to the blues a wailing vocal style, a particular scale (see later), and a body of subjects or topics for singing the blues. The second was the Anglo-American folk ballad, which imparted the regular, predictable pattern of chord changes that characterize the blues. Blues were first printed as sheet music in 1912 (*The Memphis Blues* and *The Dallas Blues*), and the first blues recordings, all made by black artists, were cut in 1920.

origins

A singer sings the blues to relieve a melancholy soul, to give vent to feelings of pain and anger. Poverty, loneliness, oppression, family troubles, infidelity, and separation are typical subjects of the blues. The lyrics are arranged in a succession of stanzas, usually three to six to a song, and each stanza is made up of three lines. The second line normally repeats the first, and the third rounds off the idea and concludes with a rhyme. At the end of each line an instrument inserts a short response, called an **instrumental break,** as a way of replying to the cry of the voice. Thus, the blues perpetuates the age-old African performing style of "call and response," the form of which is shown in the following blues stanza:

a succession of three-line stanzas

Call	Response
The moon looks lonesome when	
it's shining through the trees.	(instrumental break)
Yes, the moon looks lonesome,	
shining through the trees.	(instrumental break)
And a man looks lonesome when	
his woman packs up to leave.	(instrumental break)

By the turn of the twentieth century the guitar had become the accompanying instrument favored by blues singers. It could not only supply a solid harmonic support but also provide an expressive "second voice" to answer in the instrumental break after the previous call in the vocal line. "Bending" the guitar strings at the frets produced a whining, mournful sound in keeping with the general feeling of the blues.

guitar accompaniment

The object of the blues is not so much to tell a story, as in the white folk ballad, but to express emotion. The voice sometimes moans and sometimes shouts, it is often raspy or frayed, and it always twists and bends the pitch. Instead of hitting a tone directly, the singer usually approaches it by slide from above or below. In addition, a particular scale, called **blues scale,** is used in place of a major or minor scale. The blues scale has seven notes, but the third, fifth, and seventh are sometimes flat, sometimes natural, and sometimes in between. The three "in

blues scale

between" tones are called **blue notes**. The blues scale is an integral part of virtu-ally all African-American folk music, including the work song and spiritual as well as the blues.

EXAMPLE 18–1

Good blues singers indulge in much spontaneous expression, adding and sub-tracting text and improvising around the basic melody as the spirit moves them. Such liberties are possible because these mournful songs are built above the bedrock of a twelve-bar harmonic pattern that repeats, over and over, one state-ment for each stanza of text. Singing the blues means singing in a slow 4/4 above this simple I–IV–I–V–I chord progression in the following manner[†]:

the twelve-bar blues

Vocal lines:	Line 1		break		Line 2		break		Line 3		break	
Chord:	I ————————————				IV———		I ———		V ———		I ———	
Measure:	1	2	3	4	5	6	7	8	9	10	11	12

Sometimes additional chords are inserted between the basic ones for greater har-monic interest. Yet the simplicity of the pattern is its greatest resource. Thou-sands of tunes have been constructed over this basic harmonic progression, by solo singers, by solo pianists, by Dixieland jazz combos, and by rock 'n' roll bands.

Bessie Smith (1894–1937)

Although there have been and are many great blues singers—Blind Lemon Jefferson, Leadbelly, Muddy Waters, and B. B. King, to name just a few—per-haps the greatest of them all was Bessie Smith, called the "Empress of the Blues." A native of Tennessee, Bessie Smith was "discovered" singing in a bar in Selma, Alabama, and brought to New York to record for Columbia Records. The blues recordings she made between 1924 and 1927 catapulted her to the top of the world of popular music. In her first full year as a recording artist, her disks sold more than two million copies, and she became the highest-paid black artist, male or female, of the day. In fact, all of the great blues singers who achieved recording success during the '20s were women, perhaps because so many of the texts of the blues have to do with male–female relations and are written from the woman's perspective. Tragically, Bessie Smith's career was cut short by a fatal automobile accident in 1937.

Lost Your Head Blues, recorded in 1926, reveals the huge, sweeping voice of Bessie Smith. She was capable of great power, even harshness, one moment, and then in the next breath could deliver a phrase of tender beauty. She could hit a note right on the head if she wanted to, or bend, dip, and glide into the pitch, as she does, for example, on the words "days," "long," and "nights" in the last stanza of *Lost Your Head Blues*. In this recording Bessie is backed by Fletcher Henderson (piano) and Joe Smith (trumpet), and they begin with a four-bar introduction.

FIGURE 18–1

Bessie Smith, the "Empress of the Blues," was a physically powerful woman with an exceptionally flexible, expressive voice.

[†]Chord progressions of this sort are discussed on page 31.

Then the voice enters and the twelve-bar blues harmony starts up, one full statement of the pattern for each of the five stanzas of text. Each time Bessie Smith sings her melody above the repeating bass, she varies it slightly by means of vocal inflections and off-key shadings. Her expressive vocal line, the soulful, improvised responses played by the trumpet, and the repeating twelve-bar harmony carried by the piano are the essence of the blues.

LISTENING GUIDE *Lost Your Head Blues* sung by Bessie Smith (recorded in New York, 1926)

6CD 6/18; 6Tape 6B
3CD 3/14; 3Tape 3B

0:00   Four bar introduction
0:11   Line 1: I was with you baby when you did not have a dime. (trumpet)
        Chords: I ————————————————————————————————
0:22   Line 2: I was with you baby when you did not have a dime. (trumpet)
        Chords: IV ——————————————————— I ———————————
0:32   Line 3: Now since you got plenty money you have throw'd your good gal down. (trumpet)
        Chords: V ——————————————————— I ———————————

(For the next three stanzas the chord changes and instrumental breaks continue as above; in the last stanza the breaks come in the middle of the lines as well as at the end.)

Once ain't for always, two ain't for twice.
Once ain't for always, two ain't for twice.
When you get a good gal, you better treat her nice.

When you were lonesome, I tried to treat you kind.
When you were lonesome, I tried to treat you kind.
But since you've got money, it's done changed your mind.

I'm gonna leave baby, ain't gonna say goodbye.
I'm gonna leave baby, ain't gonna say goodbye.
But I'll write you and tell you the reason why.

Days† are lonesome, nights are long†.
Days are lonesome, nights† are so long.
I'm a good gal, but I've just been treated wrong.

†Note the vocal "slides" here.

(Listening Exercise 44)

The impact of the blues on the popular music of the twentieth century has been enormous. In addition to being in itself a genre of music of great feeling and power, the blues gave to jazz a much-used harmonic pattern and an expressive style of playing. All the jazz greats—from Louis Armstrong (*Gut Bucket Blues*) to Duke Ellington (*Ko-Ko*) to Charlie Parker (*Parker's Mood*) to Wynton Marsalis (*The Majesty of the Blues*)—have improvised around the blues in one style or another. Equally important, it was from the blues and its offspring, rhythm and blues, that rock 'n' roll was born.

influence of the blues

JAZZ

Jazz has been called the only truly American contribution to the world of music. It is a mixture of many different musical streams from the New World, including the marches of John Philip Sousa (1854–1932), the fiddle tunes and jigs of white Appalachia, and, most important, the spirituals and blues of American blacks in the South. The four-square sense of phrasing and strong, regular harmonies of the Anglo-American styles merged with the complex rhythms, percussive sounds, and flexible vocal production of African-American music to produce a dynamic new sound. Jazz originated about 1910 almost simultaneously in many southern and midwestern cities: New Orleans, St. Louis, Kansas City, and Chicago, to name a few. Because its style was different from city to city and because various other styles of jazz would later evolve—swing*, bebop*, cool*, and third-stream* among others—jazz must be defined in rather general terms.

roots

Jazz is lively, energetic music with pulsating rhythms and scintillating syncopations, usually played by a small instrumental ensemble (a combo) or a somewhat larger group (a big band). Jazz tends to be polyphonic, since several instruments play independent lines. And it also includes a strong element of improvisation that gives individual performers the freedom to follow their own flights of musical fancy. Tension and excitement are created as virtuosic soloists play off against a regularly changing harmony and a steady beat provided by the rhythm section (usually drums, piano, and a string bass). During its earliest years, jazz was music meant to be danced to, but today it is heard mostly in supper clubs, cafes, and concert halls. Not only has jazz become the most significant and lasting form of American popular music, producing such figures as Louis Armstrong (1898–1971), Duke Ellington (1899–1974), Benny Goodman (1909–1986), Charlie Parker (1920–1955), and Wynton Marsalis (b. 1961), but it has also influenced the styles of European and American composers of art music, including Debussy, Stravinsky, and Copland.

jazz style

Ragtime: A Precursor of Jazz

Ragtime music was an immediate precursor of jazz and shares with it many of the same rhythmic features. To black musicians, "to rag" meant to play or sing music in a heavily syncopated, jazzy style. Ragtime music originated in brothels, saloons, and dancehalls during the 1890s—the "gay '90s"—and the jaunty, upbeat sound of ragtime captured the spirit of that age. Most rags were written by black pianists who played in houses of ill repute because it was difficult in those years for black musicians to find employment elsewhere. Piano rags, which first began to be published in 1897, took America by storm, more than two thousand titles appearing in print by the end of World War I. Sold as sheet music of a thin page or two, piano rags quickly moved from the saloon into middle-class homes, where musically literate amateurs played them on the parlor piano.

from saloons to parlors

The undisputed "King of Ragtime" was Scott Joplin (1868–1917). The son of a slave, Joplin managed to acquire for himself a solid grounding in classical music while he earned a living playing in honky-tonk bars in and around St. Louis. In 1899 he published *Maple Leaf Rag*, which sold an astonishing one million copies. Though he went on to write other immensely popular rags, such as *The Enter-*

tainer and *Peacherine Rag*, Joplin gradually shed the image of barroom pianist and moved to New York to compose rag-oriented opera.

The *Maple Leaf Rag*, which was all the rage at the turn of the century, is typical of the style of Joplin and his fellow ragtime composers. Its form is similar to that of a traditional military march, consisting of a succession of sixteen-bar units, each of which is repeated. And its harmonies are also European in origin, moving purposefully from chord to chord with slight chromatic inflections—Joplin knew his Schubert and Chopin! But what makes ragtime so infectious is its bouncy, syncopated rhythm. Syncopation, of course, is the momentary displacement of an accent from on the beat to off the beat. In piano ragtime the left hand keeps a regular "um-pah, um-pah" beat, usually in 2/4 meter, while the right hand lays on syncopations against it. In the following example from the *Maple Leaf Rag*, syncopation (S) occurs when long notes (either an eighth note or two sixteenth notes tied together) sound off (between) the steady eighth-note beats of the bass:

EXAMPLE 18–2:

FIGURE 18–2

One of the few surviving photographs of ragtime composer Scott Joplin.

New Orleans (Dixieland) Jazz

Although jazz sprang up almost simultaneously in towns up and down the Mississippi River, its focal point and probable place of origin was New Orleans. Not only was New Orleans the home of many of the early jazz greats—King Oliver (1885–1938), Jelly Roll Morton (1890–1941), and Louis Armstrong (1898–1971)—but it enjoyed an exceptionally lively and varied musical life that encouraged the development of new musical styles as well. Culturally, New Orleans looked more toward France and the Caribbean than it did to the Anglo-American north. The city air was filled not only with opera tunes, marches, and ballroom dances from imperial France but also African-American blues and ragtime and Cuban dance rhythms. The end of the Spanish-American War (1898) brought a flood of used military band instruments into second-hand shops in New Orleans at prices that were affordable even to impoverished blacks. Musicians, black and white alike, found ready employment in ballrooms of the well-to-do, in the bars and brothels of Storyville (a thirty-eight-square-block red-light district in the center of the city), at parades, picnics, weddings, and funerals associated with the many New Orleans societies and fraternal orders. Music was everywhere. Even today in New Orleans bands of various sorts, some good, some bad, can be heard on the streets of the city's French Quarter at almost any hour, day or night.

New Orleans, a musical and cultural melting pot

FIGURE 18–3

FIGURE 18–3

A New Orleans street band in the 1930s. The tradition of playing jazz in the streets of New Orleans, at parades, funerals, and functions of fraternal orders, extends back to the late 1800s and continues today.

Dixieland style

What did the early jazz musicians of New Orleans play? Their repertoire consisted of syncopated or jazzed-up marches and popular songs, ragtime music, and blues. The structure of each of these genres was square and predictable. The rag had phrases (strains) of sixteen bars, many popular songs of the period had four four-bar phrases, and the traditional blues, as we have seen, consisted of a steady stream of twelve-bar units. Within the strict formal confines of these four-, eight-, twelve- and sixteen-bar patterns, the New Orleans jazz combo found a security that allowed the solo instruments the greatest sort of freedom of expression. The melody was usually played in some jazzed-up way by a cornet or trumpet; a clarinet supported this lead instrument and further embellished the tune; a trombone added counterpoint against the melody in a lower range; down below a tuba set the harmonies if the group was marching, but if it did not, that job was handed over to a string bass, piano, banjo, and/or guitar. These same instruments (tuba, string bass, piano, banjo, and guitar), along with the drums, formed the **rhythm section** because they not only set the harmony but also helped the drums give out the beat in a steady fashion.

playing without written music

New Orleans–style bands, then and now, never play from written music. They count, or feel, where they are in the four-, eight-, twelve-, or sixteen-bar phrase; they sense when the chords should change within each phrase; and they improvise and refashion the tune, but always so that it fits the regularly changing chords. Teamwork (each musician has a specific role to play according to his instrument) and individual creativity, precision and spontaneity, regularity and happy abandon are the hallmarks of classic Dixieland jazz.

Louis Armstrong (1898–1971)

The brothels and gambling houses of the red-light district of New Orleans were closed by the U.S. Navy in 1917—the corrupting influence of Sodom and Gomorrah was thought to imperil a large navy base nearby. As a consequence, many places of employment for jazz musicians disappeared and the players began to look elsewhere for work—in New York, Chicago, and even Los Angeles. One of those who eventually made his way to Chicago was Louis "Satchmo" ("Satchelmouth") Armstrong. Armstrong was born in New Orleans in 1898, and in 1923 followed his mentor, King Oliver, to Chicago to join the latter's Creole Jazz Band. By this time Armstrong was already recognized by his peers as the best jazz trumpeter alive. He soon formed his own band in Chicago, The Hot Fives, to make what was to become a series of landmark recordings. When the vogue of classic New Orleans–style jazz gave way to the sound of the swing band around 1930, Armstrong moved to New York, where he "fronted"—played as featured soloist—in a number of large bands. He invented the practice of "scat singing"— singing nonsense syllables in jazz style–and eventually became known as much for the gravelly sound of his voice, in songs such as *Hello Dolly* and *Mack the Knife,* as for his trumpet playing. His last years were spent in almost continual travel, sent around the world by the U.S. State Department as "Ambassador Satchmo." He died at his home in Queens, New York, in 1971.

"Ambassador Satchmo"

Although cut in Chicago, the recordings that Louis Armstrong made with his group The Hot Fives beginning in 1925 are classics of New Orleans–style jazz. In fact, four of the five players in this all-star combo were natives of New Orleans and had played together there. The exception was Lillian Hardin, a pianist and songwriter from Tennessee. *Droppin' Shucks* is Hardin's composition that The Hot Fives play in traditional Dixieland style. The tune here is only sixteen bars long, but it appears seven times, each time varied in some way according to the mood of the players. In a jazz piece of this sort each presentation of the tune is called a **chorus,** whether played by a soloist or the entire ensemble. Although there are three melody instruments here—trumpet, trombone, and clarinet—it is Armstrong's strong, clean trumpet sound that dominates the group. He is also heard as a vocalist in choruses 3 and 4, a jilted lover who has had "shucks" dropped on him by an unfaithful woman, but who is about to drop some of his own.

FIGURE 18–4

Louis Armstrong (seated) with his band The Hot Fives at a recording session sometime during 1925–1926. The songwriter and pianist Lillian Hardin, who became Armstrong's wife, is at the right.

LISTENING GUIDE

Droppin' Shucks, a song by Lillian Hardin,
played by Louis Armstrong's The Hot Fives (recorded in Chicago, 1925)

6CD 6/19
6Tape 6B

0:00	Introduction (minor-key sound)
0:24	Chorus 1—full ensemble
0:48	Chorus 2—piano (Lillian Hardin) and banjo (Johnny St. Cyr)
1:11	Chorus 3—vocal (Louis Armstrong)
1:34	Chorus 4—vocal
1:51	Chorus 5—clarinet (Johnny Dobbs)
2:16	Chorus 6—trombone (Kid Ory)
2:39	Chorus 7—full ensemble

Big Bands and Swing

The recordings of Louis Armstrong and The Hot Fives sold as fast as they could be pressed. Jazz became the rage of the 1920s, just as ragtime had been the craze at the turn of the century. It was, in the words of novelist F. Scott Fitzgerald, the "Jazz Age." So popular did jazz become that it was now performed in ballrooms, large dancehalls, and movie theaters, in addition to the smaller bars and supper clubs where New Orleans–style jazz had its home. And just as the small supper club gradually gave way to the ballroom, so too did the small jazz combo cede pride of place to the big band—for to be heard above the stomping and swaying of many hundreds of pairs of feet, an ensemble larger than the traditional Dixieland combo of five or seven players was needed. Thus was born the big-band *the big band era* era, the glory days of the bands of Benny Goodman (1909–1986), Duke Ellington (1889–1974), Count Basie (1904–1984), and Glenn Miller (1904–1944).

Though not "big" by the standard of today's marching band, the **big band** of the 1930s and 1940s was at least double the size of the New Orleans–style jazz combo. In 1943, for example, Duke Ellington's orchestra consisted of four trumpets, three trombones, five reed players (men who played both clarinet and saxophone), plus a rhythm section of piano, string bass, guitar, and drums—a total of sixteen players (Fig. 18–6). Most big-band compositions were worked out ahead of time and set down in written arrangements called "charts." The fact that jazz musicians now for the first time had to play from written notation suggests that a more disciplined, polished, orchestral sound was desired. The addition of a quintet of saxophones gave the ensemble a more mellow, blended quality. The new sound has little of the sharp bite and wild syncopation of the earlier New Orleans–style jazz. Rather, the music is mellow, bouncy, and flowing. In a word, it "swings." **Swing,** then, can be said to be a popular style of jazz played by a big band in the 1930s and 1940s.

Bebop

The craze for big-band swing jazz reached its peak immediately before and during World War II. It had become, in effect, the popular music of America. Swing jazz was heard at home on the radio, on jukeboxes, at college proms, in hotel *return of the jazz combo* ballrooms, in theaters, and even in New York's Carnegie Hall, the hallowed home of classical music. Then, for reasons that are not fully known, it fell out of favor. One cause was that many of the best young performers found that playing

from written big-band charts limited their freedom and creativity. They wanted to return to a style of playing in which improvisation was more important than composition and where the soloist, not the ensemble, was king. Choosing their playing partners carefully, they worked or "jammed" in small, elite groups in clubs in midtown Manhattan and in Harlem, and in so doing created a new virtuosic style of jazz called bebop.

Bebop is a complex, hard-driving style of jazz played by a small combo without written music. Typically, it involves a quintet of trumpet, saxophone, piano, double bass, and drums. The best players, among them saxophonist Charlie Parker (1920–1955) and trumpeter Dizzy Gillespie (1917–1993), had astonishing technique and played at breakneck speed. Their love was improvisation, and the solos they created were more complex than those heard in either swing or New Orleans–style jazz. They overlaid the melody with so much rapid, jarring embroidery that the tune soon became unrecognizable. They also changed chords more rapidly than earlier jazz players and went to more remote keys. Only the most gifted performers could keep up and "make the changes"—anticipate the changing harmonies and instantly improvise an appropriate melody. Gillespie said that he and Parker intentionally made the harmonies overly difficult to discourage less talented performers from jamming with them. Bebop was for an elite few.

Charlie "Bird" Parker (1920–1955)

Perhaps the most gifted of the bebop artists was Charlie "Yardbird" or "Bird" Parker, the subject of Clint Eastwood's movie *Bird* (1988). Parker was a tragic figure, a drug-addicted, alcoholic, antisocial man whose skills as an improviser and performer, nonetheless, were greater than all other jazz musicians, save Louis Armstrong. Indeed, the lives of Armstrong and Parker make an interesting comparison. Both were born into the extreme poverty of the ghetto, Armstrong in New Orleans and Parker in Kansas City, and both rose to the top of their profession through extraordinary talent and hard work. But Armstrong was an extroverted person who viewed himself as a public entertainer as much as an artist. Parker didn't care whether people liked his music or not, and he managed to alienate everyone around him including, finally, his friend and longtime play-

FIGURES 18–5 AND 18–6

(left) Benny Goodman, the "King of Swing," during a radio broadcast in the early 1940s. (right) Duke Ellington (seated at the piano) and his big band in 1943. Unlike other band leaders of this time, Ellington was as much a composer and arranger as he was a performer.

"far out" improvisations above obscure harmonies

FIGURE 18–7

Charlie "Bird" Parker about 1950. Parker developed a fast, snapping, syncopated style of playing that often sounds like the word "bebop" said quickly.

ing partner Dizzy Gillespie. He died of the effects of his many excesses, alone and broke, at the age of thirty-four. Parker's life may have been a mess, but his rapid, inventive style of playing changed irrevocably the history of jazz.

In 1950 Parker and Gillespie recorded a bebop version of a sentimental love song called *My Melancholy Baby* (1911). Like many popular tunes from the early part of this century, *My Melancholy Baby* is sixteen bars long and divided into four four-measure phrases (here **ABAC**). After a four-bar introduction by pianist Thelonious Monk, Parker plays the tune more or less "straight," with only moderately complex elaborations. But when Dizzy Gillespie enters for the second chorus, the ornamentation becomes more complex by means of running thirty-second notes and continues to do so through the third and final chorus, which Monk and Parker divide. Notice, as you listen to *My Melancholy Baby*, that there is none of the teamwork or intricate counterpoint found in classic Dixieland jazz, where three solo lines would sound simultaneously in the choruses for the full group. Here in bebop are brilliant solos for a single instrument against the backdrop of the rhythm section, but no ensemble improvisation. Try to follow the original tune as each soloist embroiders it.

Although *My Melancholy Baby* is more accessible than most bebop-style jazz, it still has little in the way of a beat. The drummer in bebop, contrary to Dixieland and swing, does not pound the bass drum regularly on beats one and three of the 4/4 measure, but brushes every beat quietly and without accent on the cymbal. And the melody instruments (trumpet and saxophone) constantly shift the accent from one beat to another during their improvisatory solos, confusing the beat. What results is a music more for listening than for dancing. As a consequence, bebop has never achieved a wide popular following. Instead, it serves as a sort of "chamber music" of jazz, a somewhat esoteric style that thrills a small number of aficionados.

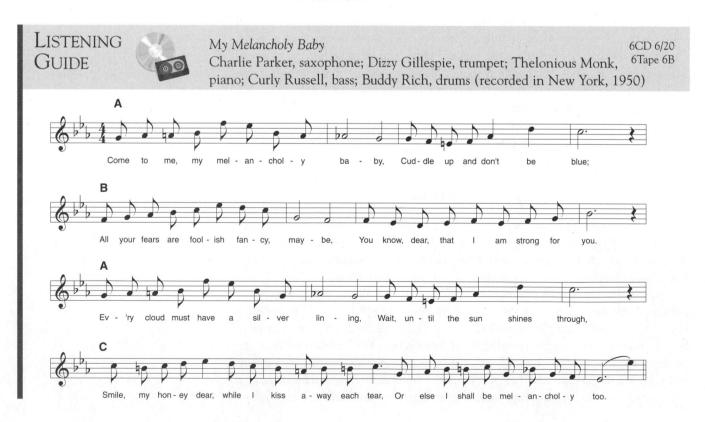

LISTENING GUIDE

My Melancholy Baby   6CD 6/20
Charlie Parker, saxophone; Dizzy Gillespie, trumpet; Thelonious Monk,   6Tape 6B
piano; Curly Russell, bass; Buddy Rich, drums (recorded in New York, 1950)

A
Come to me, my mel-an-chol-y ba-by, Cud-dle up and don't be blue;

B
All your fears are fool-ish fan-cy, may-be, You know, dear, that I am strong for you.

A
Ev-'ry cloud must have a sil-ver lin-ing, Wait, un-til the sun shines through,

C
Smile, my hon-ey dear, while I kiss a-way each tear, Or else I shall be mel-an-chol-y too.

0:00	Four-bar introduction
0:13	Chorus I—**ABAC,** saxophone
1:12	Chorus II—**ABAC,** trumpet (with mute)
2:13	Chorus III—**AB,** piano
2:40	. . . . **AC,** saxophone
3:05	ritard and tag (short coda) by saxophone and trumpet

(Listening Exercise 45)

Jazz Styles since 1950

The heyday of bebop (1945–1955) marked the beginning of a decline in the popularity of jazz. If you couldn't dance to it, why listen? The decade also saw the beginning of a fragmentation and proliferation of jazz styles—no one type of jazz was able to capture the public's imagination. **Cool jazz,** sometimes called "soft bebop" because of its more relaxed, less-frenzied solos, grew out of bebop and gained a modest following in the 1950s. Its main practitioners were trumpeter Miles Davis (1926–1991) and saxophonists Gerry Mulligan (b. 1927) and Stan Getz (1927–1991). Their delivery was soft, gradual, and nonaggressive, a welcome change of pace to the dramatic, hard-driving sound of bebop. The early 'fifties also witnessed the advent of **third-stream jazz,** a mixture of jazz and classical styles. The hope was that the music of one stream (jazz) might blend with that of another (classical) to produce an alternative direction for progressive jazz. The term "third-stream" was first coined by Gunther Schuller (b. 1925), a composer, conductor, and French horn player who in the 1950s moved back and forth between the Metropolitan Opera House and recording "gigs" with Miles Davis. In the 1960s the fragmentation and abstraction begun by Parker and Davis accelerated into the "free jazz" of John Coltrane (1926–1967) and Ornette Coleman (b. 1930).

a multiplicity of styles

By the 1970s, however, jazz was headed in a radically different direction, toward rock. The cause of this about-face, simply said, was money. Jazz recordings—whether in bebop, cool, third-stream, or free-jazz style—were not selling. What was selling was rock. So jazz musicians, driven by economic reality, began to adopt the rhythms of the rock drummer and the simple, repetitious harmonies outlined by the Fender bass guitar. **Jazz-fusion** is the name given this mixture of jazz and rock. Young trumpeters, such as Lou Soloff (b. 1943) and Chuck Mangione (b. 1941), stopped playing like Miles Davis and went off to form jazz-rock bands, such as Blood, Sweat and Tears, Chicago, and the Chuck Mangione Ensemble. They have made great music—and gotten rich—by blending the driving rhythms and harmonies of rock with the big-band brass sounds and the virtuosity of the jazz improviser. The moral of the story, as it pertains to the history of jazz and its listening public, is that any popular music without a catchy tune or a foot-stomping beat won't be popular for long.

a fusion of jazz and rock

Wynton Marsalis (b. 1961)

At present, jazz is enjoying something of a renaissance, simply by returning to its roots—to blues, Dixieland jazz, and the classically elegant sound of Duke Ellington. Appropriately enough, the leader of this revival, Wynton Marsalis, is a native of New Orleans, the birthplace of traditional jazz. Marsalis is the son of

FIGURE 18–8

According to jazz revivalist Wynton Marsalis, "Jazz musicians are making the same mistakes that the classical musicians made. Like modern European classical music, their jazz has become abstract and pessimistic."

pianist Ellis Marsalis and the younger brother of saxophonist Branford Marsalis (leader of the *Tonight Show* band during the early 1990s). He received his first trumpet at the age of six from New Orleans jazz great Al Hirt. To build a virtuosic technique and to "know what makes music great," Marsalis studied the classical repertoire, enrolling at the Juilliard School in New York City in 1980. In 1984 he became the only person to win a Grammy simultaneously as a classical performer (for a recording of the Haydn trumpet concerto) and as a jazz performer (for his album *Think of One*). In the late 1980s Marsalis voiced displeasure with the present repertoire of popular tunes, tunes that had historically provided the basis for jazz improvisations and rearrangments. "Turn on the radio and try to find a pop tune to play with your band. You can't do it. The melodies are static, the chord changes are just the same senseless stuff repeated over and over again." To reinvigorate jazz, he returned to New Orleans rag, stomp*, Dixieland jazz, and blues. He also made himself familiar with the popular ballads that had earlier served Duke Ellington and Charlie Parker so well. *In the Afterglow* is Marsalis's arrangement of a ballad fashionable in the 1920s. In it we hear traditional elements such as eight-plus-eight-bar phrasing and ternary form. Yet we also experience more sophisticated harmonies, including ninth and eleventh chords*, and a smoother style of playing typical of Ellington. The rhythm, too, has a certain freedom that approaches the flexibility of Parker—the beat is sometimes difficult to locate at the ends of phrases, for example. All of this is attributable to Marsalis's obsession with jazz's past. As he says, "Study is the only protection against folly."

LISTENING GUIDE

In the Afterglow
Wynton Marsalis, trumpet; Marcus Roberts, piano; Robert Hurst, bass; Jeff Watts, drums

From album *Marsalis Standard Time* Columbia Records, CD CK 40461, track 10†

(meter: triple; tempo: slow)

0:00	Phrase **a**	A
0:32	Phrase **b**	
1:00	Phrase **c**	B
1:31	Phrase **d**	
1:47	Transition	
1:59	Phrase **a**	A
2:30	Phrase **b**	
3:01	Transition	
3:14	Coda	**CODA**

† Although Wynton Marsalis is very much an activist in music education—witness his four-part *Marsalis on Music* broadcast on PBS—the company that holds the rights to his recordings (SONY) will not license them for educational projects!

BROADWAY

"Broadway" is the name given to a district in New York City, centered at the junction of Broadway and 42nd Street, where more than thirty theaters provide a stage for plays and musicals alike. The Broadway musical has its roots in many diverse forms of popular drama—the Viennese operetta of Johann Strauss, the English operetta of Gilbert and Sullivan, French *opéra comique*, and even traditional Jewish dramatic literature from Eastern Europe. An **operetta** is simply a "light" opera, one involving romance and comedy in equal measure. It differs from opera most fundamentally in that the dialogue is spoken, not sung as recitative. **Musical comedy** is a genre similar to the operetta but even more popular in style. It too uses spoken dialogue, yet its subject matter concerns the proverbial man-in-the-street, his "gal," and their everyday problems. In musical comedy, interest is concentrated in a few carefully placed songs—appealing tunes that make no demands for vocal virtuosity on the leads. The earliest successful operettas on Broadway were written by persons who had received their musical training in Europe, specifically Victor Herbert (*Babes in Toyland*, 1903) and Sigmund Romberg (*The Student Prince*, 1925). The earliest musical comedies, on the other hand, were written by native-born Americans, most notably George M. Cohan (*Little Johnny Jones*, 1906, which included "Give my regards to Broadway") and Jerome Kern (*Showboat*, 1927). The often-revived *Showboat*, with its signal song "Ol' Man River," is especially noteworthy in that it includes strains of uniquely American music, specifically blues, jazz, and the Negro spiritual. These same elements appear in even greater measure in George Gershwin's musically sophisticated *Porgy and Bess* (1935), which the composer called an "American folk opera." The treatment of the African-American experience in these last two shows paved the way for other ethnic subjects in later works, like *Fiddler on the Roof* (Yiddish stories) and *West Side Story* (Puerto Rican immigrants).

the American musical comedy, or musical

The collaboration of composer Richard Rodgers (1902–1979) with lyricist Oscar Hammerstein (1895–1960) marked the beginning of a golden era for the American musical theater. In a span of less than two decades this gifted team produced a succession of blockbuster musicals, beginning with *Oklahoma!* (1943), continuing with *Carousel* (1945), *South Pacific* (1949), and *The King and I* (1951), and concluding with *The Sound of Music* (1959). *Oklahoma!* ran originally for 2,248 performances, *The King and I* for 4,625. Moreover, these were the first musicals in which sales of records, movie rights, and touring companies brought in more money than the box office receipts of the original Broadway production. Rodgers and Hammerstein struck gold by blending tasteful, if sentimental, lyrics with uplifting, if square-cut, melodies. The "Broadway songbooks" performed at home today are filled with such standards as "Oh, what a beautiful mornin'" (*Oklahoma!*), "You'll never walk alone" (*Carousel*), "Some enchanted evening" (*South Pacific*), "Getting to know you" and "Shall we dance?" (*The King and I*), and "Climb ev'ry mountain" (*The Sound of Music*)—all Rodgers and Hammerstein creations.

Rodgers and Hammerstein

Today the Broadway scene is dominated by the megahits of Englishman Andrew Lloyd Webber (*Evita, Cats, Starlight Express, Phantom of the Opera*, and *Sunset Boulevard*), which rely more on dazzling scenic effects and heavily amplified sound than they do on inspired musical invention. These and the equally successful French import *Les Misérables* (1987) have put American musical comedy into a state of temporary eclipse. At the moment Broadway offers more revivals of American musicals (*Damn Yankees, Grease, Pal Joey*, and *Show Boat*) than new productions.

musicals today

FIGURE 18–9

Leonard Bernstein. His podium style was sometimes majestic, more often wild and frenetic, leading to the nickname "Leaping Lenny."

Leonard Bernstein (1918–1990)

One of the most original shows ever mounted on Broadway was Leonard Bernstein's *West Side Story*, a musical as brash and energetic as Bernstein himself. Bernstein was educated at Harvard and at the Curtis Institute in Philadelphia, where he studied conducting. At age twenty-five he vaulted to national prominence as a youthful-looking assistant conductor of the New York Philharmonic. Normally assistant conductors get to do no more than lead an occasional rehearsal and carry the maestro's briefcase. But Bernstein was lucky—on a few hours' notice he was asked to take over for the ailing Bruno Walter and gave an electrifying performance on a coast-to-coast broadcast. Some fifteen years later, Bernstein himself was appointed principal conductor of the Philharmonic, to this day the youngest person to hold that post and the only American-born conductor to do so.

But Bernstein was not merely one of the great conductor-interpreters of this century; he was a protean figure of frenetic energy and diverse talents. As a writer of "serious" music he created symphonies and ballet scores; as a composer in more popular styles he produced a film score (*On the Water Front* starring Marlon Brando) and four musicals (*Wonderful Town, On the Town, Candide,* and *West Side Story*); as a virtuoso pianist he appeared often as a soloist with his own orchestra; as an educator he introduced a generation of youthful Americans to the joys of classical music through his "Young People's Concerts" broadcast nationally on CBS-TV; and as an advocate for the arts he exercised influence on presidents, especially John F. Kennedy. America has never enjoyed a more dynamic musical leader than the lionlike Bernstein.

WEST SIDE STORY (1957)

In *West Side Story* Bernstein takes the age-old story of Romeo and Juliet and gives it modern significance. The feuding Capulets and Montagues are replaced by New York street gangs, one "American" (the "Jets") and one Puerto Rican (the "Sharks"). The scenario crystallized for Bernstein one day during a ride through New York's Spanish Harlem:

> All around, Puerto Rican kids were playing—with a huge causeway as a background in a classic key, pillars, and Roman arches. The contrast between the setting and the kids was striking, fascinating. Right then and there we had our theme for West Side Story—a contemporary setting echoing a classic myth.

a modern-day Romeo and Juliet

The star-crossed lovers are now Tony, former leader of the Jets, and Maria, the sister of the leader of the Sharks and newly arrived from Puerto Rico. They meet at a dance, held not in a Renaissance palazzo but in a high school gym. Juliet's balcony is transformed into Maria's fire escape, and it is here that she and Tony sing the show-stopping duet "Tonight." Ultimately Tony, trying to make peace, causes the death of the leader of the Sharks and is himself killed, leaving Maria to grieve over his body.

West Side Story is a study in dramatic and musical opposites. Fast-paced dances for the gangs are set off against quiet dialogues for the lovers. The gangs' music is dissonant, syncopated, and percussive, much in the style of the musical avant-garde of the early twentieth century (see page 343). The lovers' music, on the other hand, is consonant and melodic, steady in its phrasing and beat. This contrast between the dissonant, syncopated modern style and the melodious Romantic style can be heard in two of the *Symphonic Dances* from *West Side Story*. Both

"Mambo," a dance sequence for the gangs, and "Somewhere," a dream song envisioning a distant place of love and friendship, underscore the mood of the onstage action. *West Side Story* is not a musical comedy but a musical tragedy in which competing forces race headlong toward destruction. By distilling the musical essences of these competing forces, Bernstein captures the energy and tenderness of this timeless tale.

FIGURE 18–10

Still of a dance scene from the 1961 movie version of *West Side Story*. Members of the Jets and the Sharks tauntingly strut their stuff.

LISTENING GUIDE

Leonard Bernstein
Symphonic Dances from *West Side Story* (1957)
"Mambo" and "Somewhere"

6CD 6/21–22
6Tape 6B

Characters: The Jets and the Sharks, Tony and Maria

Situation: Friction between the Jets and the Sharks is felt at a high school dance, where gang members strut to the music of "Mambo"; Tony and Maria meet and express their hopes for love.

"Mambo" (6CD 6/21, 6Tape 6B)

0:00	Introduction
0:10	Fast-moving, syncopated theme
0:37	Percussive blasts from percussion and brasses
1:05	Trumpet solo
2:02	Return of theme leads to climax and then fadeout

(Continued next page)

"Somewhere" (6CD 6/22, 6Tape 6B)

0:00	Cellos tenderly play the melody of the song "Somewhere"
0:29	French horn plays "Somewhere" melody against counterpoint in oboe
0:55	Strings sweep forward with the theme
1:25	Middle strings play "Somewhere" melody against counterpoint in higher violins
1:50	Full orchestra carries melody to a climax and then fadeout

ROCK

Bursting on the scene in the mid-1950s, rock 'n' roll (and its later manifestation, rock) revolutionized popular music in America and indeed throughout the world. Its style is well known to all—the pounding beat, the heavy, amplified guitar sound, the driving bass, and the simple, repetitive harmonies. There is, to be sure, much harmonic repetition, noisy filler, and electronic distortion. But, of course, rock involves much more than just music. The style of dress of the rockers, their sometimes-outrageous behavior, both on and off stage, and their social and political beliefs are just as important to rock culture as is the music they produce. Rock was born as a music of protest and rebellion directed against the established musical and social orders.

rhythm and blues

The origins of rock can be found in a style of music called rhythm and blues that came out of the South around 1950. Like the blues, **rhythm and blues** makes use of the twelve-bar blues pattern, 4/4 meter, and an expressive style of singing. But here the usually slow tempo of the blues is changed to a faster 4/4, upbeats and downbeats are made stronger, a saxophone is added to the basic guitar sound, and the text is shouted as much as sung. All of this produces a raw, driving, highly danceable kind of music. At first rhythm and blues was created and played exclusively by black musicians for a black audience. But as many of these musicians and listeners moved to the urban centers of the North in the 1950s, a white audience began to hear and dance to this energized black music, mostly over the radio. Indeed, the term "rock 'n' roll" was first coined in 1951 by a white disk jockey in Cleveland, Alan Freed, who championed black rhythm and blues—that is the principal reason the new rock 'n' roll Hall of Fame was situated in Cleveland. Soon black artists like Chuck Berry (*Maybellene* and *Roll Over Beethoven*), Bo Diddley (*Bo Diddley*), Fats Domino (*Blueberry Hill*), and Little Richard (*Tutti Frutti* and *Lucille*) found that there was a demand for their music in the white market. And white musicians like Bill Haley (*Rock Around the Clock*), Carl Perkins (*Blue Suede Shoes*), Jerry Lee Lewis (*Great Balls of Fire*), and Elvis Presley (*Jail House Rock*) began to copy the black sound. Perkins, Lewis, and Presley had grown up in the South in the environment of black rhythm and blues. Presley's first manager said that he was simply "looking for a white boy who could sing colored."

Elvis Presley (1935–1977) became the "King of Rock 'n' Roll"; his singing electrified a white audience only then coming to know the sounds of black rhythm and blues. Presley's first hit, *Heartbreak Hotel* (1955), and subsequent *Love Me Tender* (1956) were in the tradition of the white country ballad, though sung in an expressive, throbbing style. But his *Hound Dog* (1956) and *Jail House Rock* (1957) continued the development of hard-driving rhythm and blues. Indeed, *Hound Dog* had been borrowed from blues singer Big Mama Thornton.

FIGURE 18–11

Chuck Berry, one of rock 'n' roll's early stars. Along with Bo Diddley and Little Richard, he transformed rhythm and blues into rock 'n' roll.

Within two years of his first hit, Presley had become a national obsession, his every gyration the object of scrutiny by the media. But the public Elvis was very much a creation of the tabloids and Presley's clever managers. Though on stage he projected an image of the youthful rebel, the hard-guy rocker, exuding sexual confidence and suggestiveness, in reality he was very much a pampered mama's boy and timid about sexual matters. He died young, of drug abuse, a bloated caricature of himself. The sad part is that, in spite of the rhinestones, the Cadillacs, and all the other silliness that attended his life, he was highly musical and blessed with an exceptionally rich and wide-ranging baritone voice. His was by far the best voice of any of the male rock singers, then or now.

By the early 1960s much of the initial energy and freshness of early rock 'n' roll had been lost. Sentimental tunes directed at the hordes of teenagers of the postwar baby boom (*Teenager in Love* and *Teen Angel*, for example) began to dominate the market. But American rock soon received a shot in the arm from an unexpected source, Great Britain. The reason for this is clear. England had recently become infatuated with the sounds of American blues players like Muddy Waters as well as rhythm and blues singers like Chuck Berry and Bo Diddley, some of whom had toured there. As foreign imitators, British pop musicians embraced the new styles with greater fidelity to the original than did their American cousins. The pounding, swaggering style of Mick Jagger and his Rolling Stones is very much in the tradition of "shouting" rhythm and blues from Louisiana and Mississippi. And The Who, led by guitarist Pete Townshend, adopted the same heavy amplification and driving bass, but added more varied chord changes, notably in their "rock opera" *Tommy* (1968). But of all the British groups, the most adaptive and most successful was the Beatles.

The Beatles were formed in Liverpool, England, in 1960 and achieved an overnight success in that country with their first recording (*Love Me Do*, 1962). In 1964 they took America by storm, first with their best-selling single *I Want to Hold Your Hand* and then in person through a sold-out national tour. "Beatlemania" was born. But unlike the equally popular Elvis, a dynamic performer but not a composer, each of the Beatles was a songwriter in his own right. And two of

FIGURE 18–12

The "King Is Dead, Long Live the King." The hysteria surrounding Elvis has diminished only slightly since his death in 1977. Elvis "sightings" are reported almost weekly in the tabloids. One recent television special had him alive and well, living under the F.B.I.'s witness protection program.

FIGURE 18–13

The Beatles's *Sergeant Pepper's Lonely Hearts Club Band* was one of the first to establish "album-oriented" rock, in which tunes in a variety of styles and performing media, from sitar to symphony, are selected and arranged to form a single, unified collection. This revolutionary album required seven hundred hours of recording time in a London studio.

them, bass guitarist Paul McCartney and rhythm guitarist John Lennon, were exceptionally creative. They wrote fresh lyrics and unpredictable tunes that the parents as well as the kids could enjoy. What is most remarkable about the Beatles is the variety of musical styles that they adopted and made their own: rhythm and blues (*Roll Over Beethoven* and *Twist and Shout*), country blues (*Oh, Darling*), church hymns (*Let It Be*), British music-hall songs (*When I'm Sixty-Four*), Broadway show tunes (*The Long and Winding Road*), novelty songs (*Octopus's Garden*), and psychedelic rock (*Lucy in the Sky with Diamonds*). In 1970, after a decade of unprecedented popularity and financial gain, the Beatles disbanded, though each of them ultimately returned, with differing degrees of success, to the field of popular music with his own band.

the Beatles, recreators of all popular styles

While America was held captive to Beatlemania, a newer, softer style of rock music, called folk-rock, emerged on these shores. **Folk-rock** was a mixture of the steady beat of rock with the forms, topics, and styles of singing of the traditional Anglo-American folk ballad (see page 386). The folk ballad had survived in the South and West in the form of the country-western ballad. Folk music, in general, enjoyed a revival, beginning with the Kingston Trio's recording of the ballad *Tom Dooley* (1958) and with the work of Peter, Paul, and Mary, and of Joan Baez. But the sources of the new folk-rock were more city than country, and the primary artists urban Jewish rather than Appalachian Protestant. The labor movement, the civil rights movement, and protests against the Vietnam War were supported by these artists. Bob Dylan, who sang accompanied only by his guitar and harmonica, inaugurated this urban folk style with protest songs such as *Blowin' in the Wind* (1963). Paul Simon, the creative force behind Simon and Garfunkel, started in the footsteps of Dylan but quickly developed his own folk-rock manner with *The Sounds of Silence* (1964), *Bridge over Troubled Water* (1969), and *Slip Slidin' Away* (1977). More recently, Simon has combined the rock beat with the choral sounds of native folk artists of South Africa in his anti-apartheid album *Graceland* (1986). James Taylor, Judy Collins, and Joni Mitchell are three other folksingers who occasionally incorporate rock idioms in their music. The beat is there, but they sing accompanied by the sound of the quieter acoustical guitar rather than an electrically amplified instrument.

folk-rock and protest-rock

Rock (and its progenitor rock 'n' roll) is now nearly fifty years old but shows no signs of losing its popular following. Each time one rock style gets stale, two others emerge to take its place. The last twenty years have seen the rise of acid rock (the Grateful Dead), disco (the Bee Gees), pop-disco (Madonna and Michael Jackson), working-class hard rock (Bruce Springsteen and John Cougar Mellencamp), blues revival (Steve Winwood), rhythm and blues revival (R.E.M.), punk rock (the Clash), symphonic rock (Pink Floyd), Latin rock (Santana), heavy metal rock (Metallica), new wave (Talking Heads), Euro-pop (Enigma), and grunge (Pearl Jam and Nirvana). Yet at the same time the "oldies but goodies" of the mid-1950s keep going strong and are reissued in CD format; Mick Jagger, Pete Townshend, and Eric Clapton enjoy "comeback" tours even though they never really went away; and a six-hour documentary "The Beatles Anthology" was just seen by forty-seven million people on ABC. What began as a youthful rebellion is now the accepted mainstream of American popular music. Only a few extreme styles, like grunge and other types of "alternative rock," exist on the countercultural fringe. A half-century of hearing the "sinful" beat of rock 'n' roll has disarmed even its most militant critics.

from rebellion to mainstream

FIGURE 18–14
R.E.M. began in Athens, Georgia, in the tradition of Southern rhythm and blues, with a mule-kicking drumbeat, a tight ensemble of electric guitars, and regular chord changes. The group's more recent offerings are still hard-driving, but use more electrically synthesized sounds and electrically generated distortion.

LISTENING EXERCISES

44   *Lost Your Head Blues*   6CD 6/18; 6Tape 6B
       sung by Bessie Smith (recorded in New York, 1926)   3CD 3/14; 3Tape 3B

Lost Your Head Blues tells the tale of a "good old gal" who has "just been treated wrong." In a treatment typical of the blues, Bessie Smith belts out five stanzas of text, each with three lines. After each line, trumpeter Joe Smith enters to offer an instrumental comment on the sentiments just expressed by the singer. Complete the following time log by entering the times at which the voice begins each line and the trumpeter begins the instrumental breaks.

Stanza 1

Time	Line	Break
0:11	I was with you baby when you did not have a dime.	__:__
__:__	I was with you baby when you did not have a dime.	__:__
__:__	Now since you got plenty money you have throw'd your good gal down.	__:__

Stanza 2

Time	Line	Break
0:44	Once ain't for always, two ain't for twice.	__:__
__:__	Once ain't for always, two ain't for twice.	__:__
__:__	When you get a good gal, you better treat her nice.	__:__

Stanza 3

Time	Line	Break
1:16	When you were lonesome, I tried to treat you kind.	__:__
__:__	When you were lonesome, I tried to treat you kind.	__:__
__:__	But since you've got money, it's done changed your mind.	__:__

Stanza 4

1:49	I'm gonna leave baby, ain't gonna say goodbye.	:__
:__	I'm gonna leave baby, ain't gonna say goodbye.	:__
:__	But I'll write you and tell you the reason why.	:__

In the final stanza the trumpet is more fully integrated with the voice. Here just listen to the extraordinarily powerful and flexible voice of Bessie Smith.

Stanza 5

2:20   Days are lonesome, nights are long.

Days are lonesome, nights are so long.

I'm a good gal, but I've just been treated wrong.

Bebop-style Jazz   6CD 6/20
My Melancholy Baby   6Tape 6B
Charlie "Bird" Parker, saxophone; Dizzy Gillespie, trumpet
(recorded in New York, 1950)

Bebop is a highly complex style of progressive jazz with difficult chord changes and dizzying flights of instrumental virtuosity. What makes *My Melancholy Baby* easy to follow is the form: a short introduction, three sixteen-bar choruses, and a short coda. The form is made clear to the listener because there is a change to a new solo instrument at the beginning of each chorus. From one chorus to the next, however, the playing becomes progressively more complex and the tune more heavily disguised by ornamentation. The first five questions that follow help illuminate the musical form, while the second five concentrate on aspects of the bass line.

1. (0:00–0:12) Which instrument solos during the introduction?
   a. saxophone   b. trumpet   c. piano
2. (0:13–1:11) What does the piano do during Charlie Parker's solo in chorus 1? _____
3. (1:12–2:12) During the trumpet solo of chorus 2, is Parker's saxophone heard?
   a. yes   b. no
4. (2:13–3:04) During chorus 3, is Gillespie's trumpet heard?
   a. yes   b. no
5. Which of the forms that we have studied is embodied in this piece?
   a. rondo
   b. sonata–allegro
   c. theme and variations
6. Is the bass instrument that plays in this quintet the double bass of the symphony orchestra or the electric bass guitar? _____
7. Does the player use a bow or play pizzicato? _____
8. Which figure more accurately reflects the rhythm of the bass?
   a.   b.
   4/4 ♪♪♪♪♪♪♪♪   or   4/4 ♩ ♫ ♫♫ ♫
9. Which statement correctly describes the bass line?
   a. moves mainly in stepwise motion in regular, even notes
   b. moves by leaps in highly varied rhythms

10. This sort of bass line, then, can be said to be similar to which musical procedure of the Baroque era?
   a. the ostinato* bass
   b. the walking bass*
   c. the pedal point*

---

46   Listening to Contemporary Rock

This book was written as a text for music courses in colleges and universities. Although the author played piano in a rock 'n' roll band many years back, he is certain that you, the college student, are more familiar with the contemporary rock scene than he. This last listening exercise gives you the chance to demonstrate your expertise. Your task is to choose a piece of contemporary rock music, analyze it, and write a brief report. As you listen, you may wish to consider the following questions as a way of focusing your thoughts.

1. What instruments are playing?
2. Are they acoustical musical instruments or electronically amplified ones?
3. Most rock pieces are in a major key and in duple meter. Is yours?
4. Does the voice sing the melody, or tune, alone or is it doubled by one of the instruments?
5. Is the mood and style of the music well suited to this particular text, or might this music be used just as well for another set of lyrics?
6. What do you think is the single most important element in your piece? Is it the text, a catchy melody, a satisfying harmonic pattern, a driving rhythm, or something else?
7. What instrument is playing the bass line? Does the bass stand out in any special way? Is it, for example, played louder than the other parts? If so, why?
8. What about the form of your rock song: Is it through-composed* like Schubert's *Erlking* (page 251) or strophic* like *Lost Your Head Blues* as sung by Bessie Smith (page 389)? Many pop tunes are strophic but each stanza ends with a text refrain. Is yours arranged in this fashion?
9. What do you think is the relationship between music and noise in your piece? Is there any "electronic filler?" If so, what purpose does it serve?
10. How inventive is your work? Is it fresh and innovative, or is it simply a repackaging of the clichés of popular music? Do you think your selection will stand the test of time to become a classic? If so, why; if not, why not?

KEY WORDS

bebop	cool jazz	operetta
big band	folk-rock	ragtime
blue note	instrumental break	rhythm and blues
blues	jazz	rhythm section
blues scale	jazz-fusion	swing
chorus	musical comedy	third-stream jazz

19

CONTRASTS:
WESTERN MUSIC AND
NON-WESTERN MUSIC

Most of the music we have discussed in this book has been Western European art music. It is a musical tradition that originated in Europe and spread both east and west, to Russia and gradually to North and South America. In many ways our operas, concertos, and symphonies have become the international currency of art music. They are heard in many cities throughout the world, east and west, north and south. Symphony orchestras in Tokyo and Rio play the works of Beethoven almost as often as do those in Paris, Rome, St. Louis, and Cleveland. Young students from Korea, China, Taiwan, Singapore, and Japan flood the conservatories of London and New York to develop their considerable talents as performers on Western-style instruments. Added to this is the enormous influence of American and British popular music, which has infiltrated, and in some cases overwhelmed, local traditional musics throughout the world.

But the music of the West, both classical and popular, is by no means the only music of the world. Great masses of people remain wholly or mostly unaffected by it. For example, China, with a quarter of the world's people, India, with 800 million citizens, and Indonesia, the fourth most populous nation on earth, with 200 million inhabitants, all retain their native musical traditions independent of the West, as do the tribes of sub-Saharan Africa. The sounds of each of these cultures are radically different from each other, just as they are all unrelated to the music of Bach, Mozart, and Beethoven. And while we cannot here enjoy anything more than a tantalizing taste of these foreign delights, they will be enough to highlight the ways in which our own art music of the West is different—indeed unique—among the musics of the world.

GAMELAN MUSIC OF BALI

Bali is an island, about the size of Delaware, that belongs to a chain of islands forming the southeast Asian country of Indonesia (see Fig. 19–1). It is a place of swaying palm trees, fertile rice fields, and hundreds of small villages, each with its own vital and distinctive musical tradition. For the more than two million

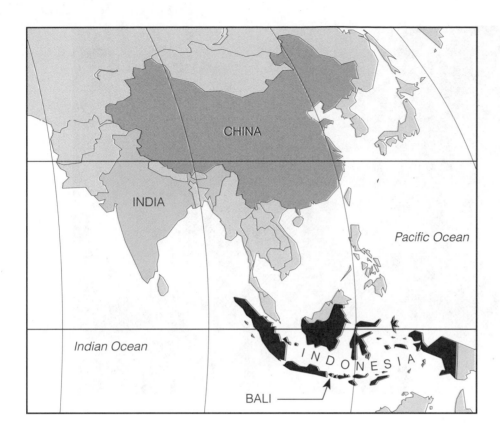

FIGURE 19–1
The subcontinent of Asia, South-East Asia, and the Pacific rim.

inhabitants of Bali, music is an integral part of their daily lives, for music is intimately bound up with religion and folklore. Hindu deities and local spirits must be honored daily in the temple and in the home. Larger ceremonies are invariably celebrated to the accompaniment of music performed by a gamelan.

A **gamelan** is a collection of as many as twenty-five musical instruments played together as an orchestra. The ensemble, however, sounds very unlike our Western orchestra, for the dominant family of the gamelan is not the strings, but percussion: metallophones (xylophone-like instruments with bronze keys and bamboo resonators), tuned gongs, gong-chimes, cymbals, and drums, along with an occasional flute. So, too, the gamelan employs a different approach to generating musical lines. In the Western orchestra a single instrument is responsible for providing a melody or countermelody, or creating a single instrumental color. In gamelan music, however, players of several instruments continually contribute bits of music which, when taken together, form a composite line of distinctive color. In the example that follows, notice how the parts are interlocking and mutually interdependent. It is only their composite sound, not the individual parts, that is conveyed to the ear of the listener. In gamelan music, solos are rare. What sound like solos are actually passages played by small groups. There is a strong commitment to group interaction, with each performer doing his or her part for the benefit of the whole. The effect is that of a well-polished, well-disciplined musical machine—a source of pride for the local village. Indeed, most gamelans are organized as community or village clubs, and they draw heavily on the local populace for performers.

the gamelan—an Indonesian orchestra of percussion instruments

FIGURE 19–2

A Balinese gamelan fronted by a set of gongs tuned to a pentatonic scale.

EXAMPLE 19–1

A striking example of Balinese gamelan music is the piece entitled *Jaya Semara (Victorious Goddess of Love)*. In a way similar to Britten's *The Young Person's Guide to the Orchestra*, *Jaya Semara* begins by exploring the colors and textures of the various instruments and instrumental families of the Balinese orchestra, all the while showing off the extraordinary virtuosity of the performers. Only midway through the piece (at 2:10) does a melody enter and a steady rhythmic pulse assert itself.

oral teaching and learning   As with every piece of Balinese music, *Jaya Semara* was taught to the performers, a group from the town of Denpasar, by a master teacher, or guru. The teacher played and explained each part, bit by bit, until finally the entire composition was learned. Though the music is extraordinarily complex, no notation was used. On Bali, everything is taught, learned, and performed entirely by ear.

LISTENING GUIDE

Jaya Semara (Victorious Goddess of Love)
a piece for Balinese gamelan
(recorded in Denpasar, Bali, Indonesia in 1989 by Michael Tenzer)

Intro CD (35)—Tape (B)

0:00	Full gamelan, with "solos" by high gongs, drums, and then metallophones
0:26	High gongs dominate
0:41	Full gamelan
0:47	High metallophones dominate
1:00	High gongs return
1:24	Single deep gong
1:30	Tempo increases; full gamelan enters
1:37	Drum beat begins
1:47	Drum solo
2:10	Full gamelan with bamboo flute plays repeating melody and ostinato rhythmic patterns
3:17	Tempo increases; then rhythmic patterns break down
3:37	Final gong

MUSIC FOR A CHINESE STRING ORCHESTRA

China is arguably the oldest and richest continuing civilization in the world. Many of the inventions and products that altered the course of Western history—gunpowder, printing, paper, silk, the nautical compass, and the dictionary, for example—were first developed in China. China also has a musical history that extends back thousands of years. A mathematical theory for generating all musical pitches was known in the third century B.C.; orchestras with twenty and more performers played at court during the Ta'ng dynasty (618–907); and full-fledged opera developed during the Yuan period (1271–1368) and continues to be popular today.

In a country with many distinct ethnic groups and over three hundred forms of regional theater, there is, naturally, no one uniform musical style. But a common denominator of all Chinese music is the importance given to the string instruments. They are played alone as solo instruments, and, as in the West, they form the nucleus of the Chinese orchestra. Traditionally the Chinese orchestra is much smaller than its Western counterpart, and the tones it produces are totally different. The **pipa** (a four-string lute), the **qin** (a seven-string zither), and the **erhu** (a two-string fiddle) usually provide the dominant sound. While the strings of the pipa and qin are plucked, those of the erhu (see Fig. 19–3) are made of silk and are played with a bow. A vibrato-rich sound results, a strange, veiled tone of great beauty.

We hear the sound of the erhu prominently in the orchestral piece *The Moon Mirrored in the Pool*, composed by a poor, blind musician from the region of Shangai, Hua Yanjun (1890–1950). As with most Chinese music, here melody is paramount. The task of the player of the erhu and the other bowed instruments is to perform it with great subtlety of color and infinite gradations of pitch. There is little harmony in Chinese music. What there is usually results from two instruments playing different versions of the melody simultaneously. Sometimes the

an ancient art

FIGURE 19–3

The erhu is performed with a bow inserted *between* the two strings. The player continually twists the instrument so that the bow can move from one string to the other.

melody is simply doubled at the octave or in unison with tremolos*, a technique that produces a shimmering effect. Typical of Chinese music, the scale used in *The Moon Mirrored in the Pool* is a pentatonic* one (here G, A, B, D, E, [G]). But these five notes are merely a point of departure for the astonishingly beautiful erhu, which plays as much between pitches as on them.

LISTENING GUIDE

Hua Yanjun (1890–1950)   Intro CD (36)—Tape (B)
The Moon Mirrored in the Pool
(performed by the Central Broadcasting Traditional Instruments Orchestra of China)

0:00	Bamboo flute plays introduction
0:07	Full orchestra introduces melody
0:30	Erhu continues with melody
0:39	Pipa amplifies and extends melody
1:06	Erhu plays variation of melody against background of tremolos on the main notes of the melody
1:42	Crescendo
2:24	Bowed strings play melody with tremolo by plucked strings
2:45	Erhu and pipa play different versions of the melody together
3:16	Prominent "Western-style" bass emerges in low register
3:32	High bowed strings and plucked strings play melody in unison
3:52	Lower bowed strings and plucked strings play melody
4:15	Erhu returns with melody; duple meter accompaniment plucked in background
4:50	Erhu plays fragments of melody

MUSIC FOR THE INDIAN SITAR

Stretching from the towering Himalayan mountains in the north to the tidal mud flats of the south, India is a vast land, full of contrasts: the beauty of the Taj Mahal and the squalor of the urban slums; the wealth of the maharajas and the abject poverty of the untouchables; the jewels on the neck of a prince who, for religious reasons, wears no shoes. It is also a land of many ethnic and religious groups, with the Moslems strong in the north and the Hindus dominating the south. Indian music, too, is divided somewhat along regional lines. What is called **Hindustani-style music** is heard in the north, while **Karnatak-style music** prevails in the south. Among the many differences between the two is the fact that Karnatak music is almost always sung, whereas Hindustani music frequently makes use of an instrument called the sitar.

Hindustani and Karnatak styles

The **sitar** is a large lutelike instrument with as many as twenty strings, some of which are used to play a melody, some simply to vibrate sympathetically with the melody strings, and some to provide a drone*. At each end of the instrument is a large, semicircular gourd that serves as a resonator to amplify the sound of the strings. With this impressive array of strings, the sitar is capable of producing a variety of timbres, dynamic levels, and special effects when in the hands of a gifted performer. A performance on the sitar is invariably accompanied by a **tabla,** a double drum (a drum with a skin stretched over each end). The right-hand end of the tabla is tuned to the tonic, dominant, or subdominant note of the sitar

the sitar and tabla

FIGURE 19–4
Ravi Shankar performing on the sitar.

melody, while the left-hand end can produce almost any low pitch, depending on the amount of pressure the drummer applies. With these two instruments alone, gifted Indian musicians can create a performance that is stunning in its virtuosity and exhilarating in its effect.

Every piece of traditional Indian music makes use of a raga. A **raga** is a basic scale and a basic melodic pattern, but it is more. A raga expresses the feeling, the mood of the piece. It has been called "the mystical expressive force" at the heart of every Indian composition. To the trained ear, *Raga Jogeshwari*, which we shall hear, has the mood of love and pathos. It makes use of a six-note scale that rises and falls as it descends and ascends.

the raga—a scale with a "mystic expressive force"

EXAMPLE 19–2

From the scale of *Raga Jogeshwari* is derived a basic theme that is presented here at the beginning of the piece three times in quick succession. Thereafter the work unfolds in a series of presentations of the theme and increasingly elaborate improvisations on it. As you will hear, not only are the notes of the scale of the raga played, but also microtones between pitches, as the performer manipulates the strings of the sitar to "bend" the pitches. Bending the pitch adds subtlety and expressive power to the music. The texture becomes increasingly saturated with such ornaments, and, toward the end, the tempo increases to heighten the sense of progress.

a melody with microtones

Perhaps more than any other musical culture, Indian music relies exclusively on a single melody for musical expression. There are no contrapuntal lines and no harmony other than the constant drone on the tonic and dominant notes of the melody. For an Indian performer, chords are thought to create too much sound at once and to detract from what is truly important: the expressive nuances of the melody and the intricate rhythmic interplay between the sitar and the tabla.

The performance of *Raga Jogeshwari* that you will hear is by Ravi Shankar, one of India's finest sitar players. Shankar personifies the ideal of Indian music in which composer and performer are one and the same person. Indeed, *Raga Jogeshwari* is his own creation. Yet each new performance of this raga results in a new composition because so much of the performance is improvised. For an Indian musician, composition, improvisation, and performance are three simultaneous manifestations of the urge for creative expression.

LISTENING GUIDE	*Raga Jogeshwari* Gat II (Theme II) (performed by Ravi Shankar, sitar, and Alla Rakha, tabla)	Intro CD (37)—Tape (B)

0:00	Scale of raga played as quick arpeggio
0:08	Sitar presents theme three times against beat in the tabla
0:45	Alternation of the theme with free improvisations
1:17	Ascending and descending improvisations on the scale of the raga
2:11	A strong cadence for the tabla
2:40	More elaborate patterns repeated on successive degrees of the scale
4:18	Tempo increases
4:45	Strumming on the drone strings of the sitar
5:00	Sitar explores half steps that occur naturally in ascending version of the raga
5:50	Tabla mimics rhythmic patterns of the sitar

MUSIC IN SOUTHERN AFRICA

Africa, the second largest continent, is a vast land three times the size of the United States. The Sahara Desert divides it into two racially, culturally, and climatically different zones: Northern Africa, with its historical ties to the Mediterranean region, and Southern Africa (or Black Africa), which includes the whole of tropical Africa. Today Africa is partitioned into no fewer than 53 countries. The boundaries of most of these nations are, however, more or less artificial lines drawn by nineteenth- and early twentieth-century European rulers. Real unity and loyalty in Africa rests within the structure of the tribe. And there are more than a thousand tribes, each possessing its own history and language. Every indigenous group has its particular music as well, and thus there are as many styles of music in Africa as there are peoples. Nevertheless, several commonly held principles can be pointed to as distinctive qualities in the music of Southern (sub-Saharan) Africa.

many tribes, many musics

Music as Social Expression

Music permeates every aspect of African life. It is sung or played while chopping wood, pounding grain, paddling a canoe, harvesting crops, weeding a field, sweeping the house, burying a chief, or stamping letters at the post office. Music keeps the workers together and makes their tasks go faster. When people perform music in the West, others stop and listen. But in Africa something else is always going on when music is being made. Music is thus inseparable from social activity. Each situation, moreover, has its own music, which is heard only in that particular context. People do not sing about chopping wood just for the pleasure of it, outside of the context of chopping wood. In African society, music is part of a holistic experience in which, by means of song and dance, the history and traditions of the community are maintained and renewed.

music inseparable from social activity

Importance of Rhythm

If it is harmony that distinguishes European music, and subtle melodic gradations that characterize Indian music, it is rhythm that marks African music. Rhythms are built into the way Africans relate to one another. The creation and structure of these African rhythms are, however, very different from those of the West.

Western performers invariably start at some beginning point, an opening downbeat*, perhaps one given by a conductor, and are guided by the regular recurrence of downbeats and upbeats. All parts lock onto and play with or against a regulating pulse. In African music, by contrast, the individual parts are far more likely to start independently and to stay that way. There is usually no common downbeat around which the players gravitate. Each part has its own downbeat and its own pulse. In African music, therefore, rhythms are not interdependent and interlocking but truly independent. The performers "play apart" as much as they do together. What is more, not only do African musicians commonly play with independent rhythms and separate downbeats, they also play in different meters simultaneously. We have encountered polymeter* before, specifically in the music of the European avant-garde (see page 346). The difference between the European and African use of polymeter is, again, the absence of a shared downbeat in African music, as can be seen in Ex. 19–3.

many rhythms but no common downbeat

polymeters

EXAMPLE 19–3
Two African drumming patterns, each with its own rhythm and meter

There are always at least two rhythms going on in African music, and this accounts for its complexity. We Westerners perceive it as complex, indeed are often baffled by it, because we can't find a unifying downbeat amid the conflicting meters. We can't find one pulse to which to tap our feet. Africans, on the other hand, rejoice in the dynamic power of a music created by such rhythmic clashes.

delight in rhythmic conflict

Importance of the Drums

Many musical instruments are indigenous to Africa—flutes, whistles, harps, bells, even trumpets—but it is the drum we immediately associate with African culture. Drums are at the heart of almost all group music-making and all dances. Some tribes believe that drums are magical, that they contain the spirits of ancestral drummers. Drum makers sometimes place charms within the drum—pebbles from the yard of the village gossip so as to make the drum talk freely, a bit of skin of a lion to make it roar. African drums come in a staggering variety of shapes and sizes. There are hand drums, stick drums, water drums, slit drums (a hollowed-out log with a long slit on top), drums that are squeezed, and drums that are scraped. Even the human body sometimes functions as a drum when a person slaps the stomach or thigh.

"talking drums"

Despite the many sizes and tone colors of African drums, we tend to think of each drum as producing one and only one sound. But there are many drums that can produce a spectrum of tones. Tension can be placed on the drum head to tighten the skin and thus elevate the pitch. How one strikes and dampens the drum head can also affect pitch. Because native African languages are "tonal" languages, drums have the capacity to imitate speech. In a **tonal language** the precise pitch of a word can determine its meaning; one and the same "sound" can have different meanings depending on the pitch at which it is spoken. By duplicating the speech patterns of the tribe, an African drummer can communicate the salient sounds of the tribal tongue. When such a "talking drum" is present, music and language are one.

Call and Response

The structure of African music is governed in large measure by a principle of performance called "call and response" (see also page 387). In vocal music a lead singer will announce an opening phrase, and the chorus will utter a short, simple reply. The soloist returns, extending and varying the call, to which the chorus responds again in simple, stable fashion. The soloist may enter and depart according to his or her whim. The chorus, however, responds at regular and predictable intervals. Instrumentalists can also engage in call and response. A master drummer, for example, can initiate a conversation with a chorus of subordinates. Sometimes the performing forces are mixed: A vocal soloist may engender a massed instrumental reply.

FIGURES 19–5 AND 19–6

(left) The dondon is a pressure drum, so called because the player can pull on the leather thongs connecting the two heads to raise the pitch. (right) A group of dondon and gongon drummers from Dagomba, Ghana.

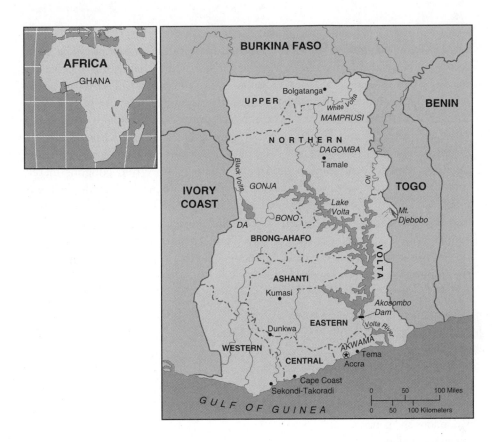

FIGURES 19–7 AND 19–8

(left) The continent of Africa and (right) the country of Ghana situated in the western portion of sub-Saharan Africa.

During the seventeenth and eighteenth centuries, the practice of call and response was carried to the Americas by slaves brought from West Africa. Today it remains an important structural feature of African-American spirituals, blues, gospel, and soul. When James Brown, the "godfather of soul," sings "Get up" and we then hear a collective "Get on up," we have a classic example of African call and response.

A PRAISE-SONG FROM GHANA

Ghana, in the western part of sub-Saharan Africa, is a country somewhat smaller than Texas, with a population of about thirteen million people (see Figs. 19–7 and 19–8). In its northeast corner, north of the Volta River, lies a territory called Dagomba, which supports a people called the Dagombas who speak a language called Dagbani, one of the forty-four official languages of Ghana. The primary musical instruments of the Dagombas are the drums, specifically the dondon and the gongon. The **dondon** (see Figs. 19–5 and 19–6) is a "pressure" drum shaped like an hourglass, with heads at opposite ends. Leather thongs connect the two heads. Pulling on the thongs increases the pressure on the heads and raises the pitch. The **gongon** is a large, barrellike drum that produces a deep tone. By means of a single snare string stretched across the upper part of the face of the drum, it also emits the rattlelike sound of a snare drum*. Both the dondon and the gongon are struck with a stick in a wrist-flicking motion. Five or six dondons and one or two gongons typically constitute the "orchestra" for dance music and praise songs of this region of Ghana.

Kasuan Kura is a praise song of the Dagombas, a song that tells the history of an important member of the tribe. Its structure is call and response. The vocal soloist relates the history of the honored figure while the chorus repeats the name of this esteemed ancestor "Kasuan Kura" throughout. The piece begins with dondon drummers manipulating their instruments to make them speak. Immediately thereafter at (0:02) the gongons enter, recognizable by their snare rattle and deeper sound. The gongons play throughout the song, while the higher-pitched dondons come and go. Whenever dondons and gongons are heard together, complex polyrhythms and polymeters result. When gongons merely support the choral response, a rather simple rhythm in a clear duple meter emerges. Thus two musical conversations develop: one between the solo singer and chorus, and a second between the complex dondon-gongon mixture and the simpler rhythmic texture of the gongons alone. In the course of this short piece the soloist's calls become more elaborate and exuberant, just as the drumming on the dondons grows more excited.

LISTENING GUIDE	The People of Dagomba, Ghana *Kasuan Kura* (recorded in Ghana by John Miller Chernoff)	Intro CD (38)—Tape (B)

0:00	Dondons begin
0:02	Gongons enter
0:12	Solo vocal call accompanied by dondons and gongons
0:16	Choral response accompanied by gongons alone
0:21	Solo call accompanied by dondons and gongons
0:25	Choral response accompanied by gongons alone
0:29	Call and response continues, accompanied as before
1:25	Dondon and gongon patterns become more complex
1:32	Call and response continues to the end

CONTRASTS

From this brief tour of four non-Western musical cultures, it is easy to hear that the beautiful and sometimes exotic sounds of the music of Indonesia, China, India, and Southern Africa are distinctive, indeed unique. Each of these great musical traditions is very different from the others. Yet they also have many things in common that separate them from the musical practices and traditions of the West. The following are among the more important contrasts between Western and non-Western musical practices.

IMPORTANCE OF MELODY AND RHYTHM, AND THE ABSENCE OF HARMONY. Non-Western musics are marked by gradations and subtleties of pitch that are far more sophisticated than those in Western melodies, which tend to move directly from one well-defined pitch to the next. Rhythms, too, are generally more complex and rhythmic interaction between the parts is more complicated. Yet at the same time, harmony as we in the West know it is virtually nonexistent. Of all the musical cultures of the world, only the West has emphasized the simultaneous sounding of several pitches. The harmony that results adds richness and depth to the sound, but often at the expense of melodic and rhythmic features.

IMPROVISATION. Spontaneous improvisation is a musical practice that occurs, to varying degree, in virtually all musical traditions except that of Western classical music. A singer of the Ashanti people in Ghana, Africa, is expected to vary a tribal song and add sections to it, just as the Indian sitar player is expected to ornament and extend a traditional raga, after years of patient study of the ornamental art. A performer's worth is measured in terms of his or her ability to create music that is new and imaginative within the confines of a traditional form. We in the West have a similar type of music, American jazz, but the strong emphasis on improvisation in jazz only serves to show that this style of music is African, not European, in its roots.

ORAL TEACHING AND LEARNING. Each of the musical cultures explored in this chapter relies exclusively on oral transmission, not written notation, as the means by which to communicate music. The Indian guru will teach the secrets of the ragas to the young student by rote. The same is true of the master drummer of Ghana. The master explains and plays, the student imitates and practices, year after year. Musical notation has no place in the process. There is musical notation in India, China, and Bali, but it is usually used in learned discussions of the theory of music, not in practical music-making. This is true everywhere throughout the non-Western world.

IMPORTANCE OF MUSICAL NOTATION IN THE WEST. Western musical culture is the only one to rely on notation as a means of preserving and passing on its musical heritage from one generation to the next. It is also the only culture in which performers play by reading written symbols. Working from notation has advantages and disadvantages. It allows the composer to prescribe in great detail exactly what he or she wishes to express. It is possible to have a very clear and unchanging notion of what a particular work of art is to be. Yet as a result, each successive performance of that work tends to be rather similar to the last—there is little room for spontaneous creativity.

COMPOSER AND PERFORMER AS ONE. The use of musical notation in Western classical music has given extraordinary powers of control and authority to the composer. He or she can dictate every small detail of a composition, and it is up to the performer to carry out precisely these instructions. The performer is very much the servant of the composer. Non-Western cultures have a more balanced relationship between composer and performer. Indeed, the composer and performer, like Ravi Shankar, are usually one and the same person. A piece of music comes into being only at the time of performance. It has no life outside of performance. It is not thought out in advance in someone's head. It is not written down in musical notation. There is no composer and performer, only musician. Similarly, there is no conductor in non-Western cultures, no one who directs but does not produce sound. Even in the large Balinese gamelan, where many instrumental parts have to be coordinated, the leader is one of the performers, usually one of the drummers.

MUSIC AS COMMUNITY RITUAL. Just as we in the West compartmentalize music into producers (composers), middlemen (performers), and consumers (audience), so we tend to think of music as an abstraction. We view art generally as discrete objects divorced from other means of human expression. We speak of a painting or a musical composition as a "work of art." In other cultures music is not an abstract object. Most African languages have no word for the concept of "music," although there are words for poetry, dance, and song. "Music" is thus inseparably bound up with poetry, dance, gesture, pantomime, and other means of expression. As such it serves as a medium to reaffirm the values of the community in daily work and play, and in special rituals. The music for one type of activity or ritual is never heard in the context of another. Religious music, for example, is played only as part of a religious rite. We in the West, by contrast, will often take a sacred Mass of Palestrina, Bach, Mozart, or Beethoven, separate it from church and all religious associations, and perform it as a "work of art" in a concert hall.

CONCERTS AND AUDIENCE RESPONSE. Public performance of music in non-Western cultures occurs in a freer, more relaxed environment. In Africa it is not uncommon to see a group of expert musicians surrounded by people who join in by singing, clapping, playing rattles, and dancing with the music. Concerts in Bali usually occur in open-air pavilions where the audience crowds around, laughs, talks quietly, and encourages the performers. Interaction between the performers and the community is an important part of the music-making process. Prior to the nineteenth century, concerts in the West were similar to this freer, more interactive experience. Not until the Romantic era, when composers made a musical composition a revered "work of art," was the audience required to sit in respectful, meditative silence.

CONCLUSION

The contrasts between Western and non-Western musical traditions have implications that extend far beyond the world of music, for music reflects the way a society thinks and what it values. From the preceding view of non-Western music, we can begin to see how much we have become a society of musical spectators rather than participants. We divorce the individual performers from the group experience. We value a single creator who determines all elements of the musical composition. We have turned away from improvisation and spontaneous creativity, preferring instead precise planning and faithful duplication at the moment of performance. The work of art is given an exalted position. It is fixed in notation and unalterable. It does not grow and evolve to reflect the changing needs and desires of the community. Finally, we have transformed what is at heart an oral and physical means of communication into one of visual relationships through a heavy reliance on musical notation. We have replaced sound with visual symbol. We have also gradually replaced the musician with two individuals, the performer and the composer. More recently, with the advent of computer music in this century, we have replaced the composer with the computer programmer. Today, as arguments about "multiculturalism" swirl around us, even a cursory study of non-Western music suggests why such an experience is important. Not only do we learn something about the music of other people, we find out even more about ourselves.

KEY WORDS

erhu	Karnatak-style music	sitar
dondon	pipa	tabla
gamelan	qin	tonal language
gongon	raga	
Hindustani-style music	• Ravi Shankar	

FOR FURTHER LISTENING

by Timothy Roden and Craig Wright

Medieval Music

Numerous recordings of chant are available, ranging from chants sung in liturgical isolation to complete Mass settings. The funeral chant *Dies irae* was especially favored by nineteenth-century composers when they desired to evoke scenes of demonic activity and death. Several recordings of compositions by Hildegard of Bingen have recently become available.

An excellent survey of music from the period of Leoninus of Machaut is included in *Music of the Gothic Era* recorded by the Early Music Consort of London. The original 3 LP set has been condensed and released on CD (Archiv 415292-2 AH), but the liner notes lack the translations of the text which appear in the booklet accompanying the LPs. *The Art of Courtly Love,* by the same ensemble, offers a survey of secular vocal and instrumental music from Machaut to compositions performed for the Court of Burgundy.

The music of Guillaume Dufay represents the transition between the Medieval traditions of Machaut and the Renaissance style of Josquin. Numerous recordings of music by this prolific composer are available. The chanson and Mass *Se la face ay pale* serve as an excellent introduction. One scholar suggests that Dufay composed the chanson to celebrate the beauty of the Duchess of Savoy in the 1430s and composed the Mass as part of the nuptial celebration for her son twenty years later.

The *EARLY MUSICAL INSTRUMENTS Series* is a six volume video collection which offers an interesting discussion of instrumental sound and construction as well as short performances. This collection is available in many university libraries.

Renaissance

Josquin and Palestrina were the two preeminent composers of the Renaissance (most catalogs simply list Josquin by his first name). While Josquin's *Ave Maria* was the most frequently published motet during the period (a good indicator of its popularity), he composed numerous other famous works including *Missa Hercules Dux Ferrariae* and *Missa Pange lingua*. The former uses a melody based on pitches derived from the vowels of his patron's name while the latter is based on a chant melody. A few perennial favorites by Palestrina include *Missa Papae Marcelli* as well as the motets *Hodie Christus natus est* and *Sicut cervus disiderat*.

Other well-known composers of sacred music during the period include Orlande Lassus (also spelled Lasso), Tomas Luis de Victoria, and the English Tudor composers William Byrd, John Taverner, and Thomas Tallis. The twentieth-century composer Ralph Vaughn-Williams wrote a *Mass in G* which mirrors the style of the English Renaissance. The same composer's famous *Fantasia on Greensleeves* and *Fantasia on a Theme by Thomas Tallis* are based on Renaissance melodies.

In the realm of secular music, there are a plethora of madrigal composers from which to select, a fact which suggests both the popularity of the genre during the period and that composers found it a financially rewarding experience as well as one which extended their reputation. The most famous composers include the Italians Cipriano di Rore, Luca Marenzio, Carlo Gesualdo, and Claudio Monteverdi as well as Thomas Morley and Thomas Weelkes from England. The English composer John Dowland wrote beautiful songs based on lyrics by Elizabethan poets for lute and voice. Clément Janequin and Claudin de Sermisy are the most famous chanson composers from the French Renaissance. Janequin's *La Guerre (The Battle)* is counted, along with Beethoven's *Wellington's Victory* and Tchaikovsky's *1812 Overture*, among those pieces in the history of music that vividly depict in sound famous military battles.

B AROQUE

A number of recordings are available of the motets, sonatas, and organ compositions of Giovanni Gabrieli. One particular recording which has been reissued on CD (CBS MK 42645) predates the more recent emphasis on historical authenticity, but the album, recorded at St. Mark's in Venice, offers a thrilling performance of *In ecclesiis*. Heinrich Schütz, a student of Gabrieli and important German musician, composed a collection of German polychoral motets in the Venetian style entitled *Psalmen Davids*. The English tradition of sacred music from the period is represented by Purcell's anthems, *Te Deum*, and *Music for the Funeral of Queen Mary*.

Like many of life's pleasures, Baroque opera is generally an acquired taste which develops with education and exposure. It is suggested that one read a synopsis of the libretto in a reference work such as *The New Grove Dictionary of Opera* prior to watching a performance. Opera is meant to be seen as well as heard and video performances are recommended as an introduction. All the titles listed below are available on video in many college libraries and selected video stores. In addition to *Orfeo*, Monteverdi's *L'Incoronazione di Poppea (The Coronation of Poppea)* is one of the best examples from the early Baroque period. The operas of George Frideric Handel represent the culmination of the Baroque tradition. *Giulio Cesare* and *Xerxes* are good places to begin. Peter Sellars (the director, not the late comic actor) has produced a video recasting the music of Handel's *Giulio Cesare* into twentieth-century, wartorn Beirut. It's different, but it works. Kiri Te Kanawa recently starred in a lascivious pastiche called *The Sorceress*. Many of Handel's most famous arias were removed from their original operas and placed into this newly created drama which aired on PBS. It is also available on video. The French tradition may be sampled in the operas of Jean Baptiste Lully or Jean-Philippe Rameua, composers for Louis XIV and XV.

The orchestral compositions of the early Baroque emphasized the sonata and concerto. Corelli's works are considered among the best examples and his Concerti Grossi, Op. 6, which includes his famous Christmas Concerto (No. 8), is an excellent introduction. While the four violin concertos that comprise Vivaldi's *The Seasons* are uniformly delightful, almost any of the numerous recordings of his other concertos as well as those of Alessandro Scarlatti will provide an enjoyable listening experience.

Johann Sebastian Bach

Although any selection of Bach's music will omit far more masterpieces than it will contain, it is hoped that this list will inspire readers to explore the rich heritage which this composer bequeathed to humanity. Well-known sacred works include Cantata 4, *Christ lag in Todesbanden* (for Easter Sunday and believed to be Bach's first cantata); Cantata 80, *Ein feste Burg* (cantata for Reformation Sunday and based on Luther's chorale *A mighty fortress is our God*); Cantata 147, *Herz und Mund und Tat und Leben* (composed for the feast of the Visitation of Mary, it contains the famous setting later known as *Jesu, Joy of Man's Desiring*); and the *Christmas Oratorio* which is a collection of six cantatas narrating the Christmas story. Bach's *Mass in B Minor* and *St. Matthew Passion* are two of the greatest artistic achievements of Western civilization.

While a list of compositions for organ should probably begin by stating the obvious, the Toccata and Fugue in D Minor (in which the fugue is inserted into the middle of the toccata), other compositions are also greatly beloved, including the Passacaglia and Fugue in C Minor (one of the few works which has the same theme for both movements), Prelude and Fugue in E-flat Major, "St. Anne" (the three fugue subjects are believed to reflect the divine nature of the Trinity and the initial subject bears an uncanny resemblance to the hymn tune of the same name), and "Wachet auf" from the *Schubler Chorales* (an arrangement for organ of the fourth movement of Cantata 140). Two important collections of fugal writing are *The Art of Fugue* (in which Bach demonstrated every possible fugal technique) and the two volumes of *The Well-Tempered Clavier*. Recordings of the latter are available featuring harpsichord or piano as a solo instrument. Some listeners find it easier to perceive the contrapuntal texture of the fugues in piano recordings. Bach also composed dance suites for the keyboard (Six Partitas, English Suites, and French Suites) and a collection called the *Goldberg Variations*. The latter work was commissioned by a Russian ambassador who suffered from insomnia. This is perhaps the only instance in which a composer desired his audience to go to sleep. For something completely different try finding an old recording of Switched-On Bach by Walter (now Wendy) Carlos. It features numerous keyboard works played on the Moog Synthesizer.

Beside the Brandenburg Concertos, Bach's best known composition for orchestra are the four Orchestral Suites. He also composed other concertos for a variety of instrumental combinations. Any composition by this composer is certain to offer a stimulating and aesthetically pleasing listening experience.

George Frideric Handel

Handel was one of the greatest composer's of choral music in the history of Western music; his mastery of musical drama and effect are well illustrated in the four Coronation Anthems for George II. These have been performed at every English coronation since 1727. There are recordings of *Messiah* to suit every taste, from a large chorus and orchestra (Toronto Symphony and Mendelssohn Choir, Angel CDCB 49027) to an attempt to replicate the "content, sound, and style" of Handel's performance on April 5, 1754 (Academy of Ancient Music, Christopher Hogwood, L'Oiseau-Lyre 411858-4). Boston Baroque, an ensemble conducted by Martin Pearlman, observes the style of the period but uses female voices in the chorus (Telarc CD-80322). One of the best methods to develop an appreciation for this beloved composition is to join a chorus which is preparing it for performance. It is not easy, but the exhilaration which comes from singing the "Hallelujah" chorus for the first time is an enriching experience you will never regret. Other oratorios by Handel include *Israel in Egypt* (the plagues of frogs and flies are graphically depicted) and *Judas Maccabaeus* (which contains several well-known choruses). Later oratorios which followed the Handelian tradition include Joseph Haydn's *The Creation* (the passages relating the creation of light and the rising of the sun are particularly stirring) and Felix Mendelssohn's *Elijah* (the dramatic conflict between the priests of Baal and Elijah is a highlight). The latter two compositions are available in both German and English versions. Both composers expected these works to be performed in English in England, so there is no need to listen to them in German except for reasons of personal preference.

Three orchestral compositions serve as the backbone of Handel's instrumental style: Concerti Grossi (Op. 6), *Water Music*, and *Royal Fireworks Music*. The compositions of Georg Philipp Telemann are another source of excellent late Baroque instrumental music.

CLASSICAL

The youthful Mozart was greatly impressed by the orchestra in Mannheim, a group famous for their discipline and musical effects, especially the crescendo. The music of this "Army of Generals," as the eighteenth-century observer Charles Burney referred to them, can be sampled in the compositions of the Stamitz clan: Johann Wenzel Anton, Carl, and Anton. Johann Sebastian Bach's youngest son, Johann Christian, played a crucial role in the development of Mozart's musical style, especially in the realm of the concerto.

Another important musician whose works are available on recording include another son of J. S. Bach, Carl Philipp Emanuel, who was known as one of the great keyboard virtuosos of the age. His compositions for keyboard as well as orchestra demonstrate an emotional intensity which deeply impressed Haydn after he began composing for the Esterhàzy family.

The operatic tradition prior to the works of Mozart can be sampled in *The Beggar's Opera* (1728) by John Gay, *Orfeo ed Euridice* (1762) by Christoph Gluck, and the farce *La Serva Padrona* (1733) by Giovanni Pergolesi. The first two are available in video performances. Gay's opera served as the basis for Kurt Weil's *Three Penny Opera* (1928) which featured the song "Mack the Knife."

Franz Joseph Haydn

The following symphonies will provide a good introduction to the evolution of Haydn's style. Symphonies 6-8, "Le Matin" (Morning), "Le Midi" (Afternoon) and "Le Soir" (Evening) were the first symphonies Haydn composed for Prince Paul Anton Esterhàzy (1761). Each of these programmatic works were intended to evoke the activities and moods associated with different times of the day. Symphony 44, "Trauer" and 45, "Farewell" (1772) were experiments with the controlled emotionalism associated with the music of C. P. E. Bach, a style which contained the seeds of Romanticism. A decade later, during the winter of 1784–1785, Haydn was commissioned to write six symphonies (82–87) for a Parisian orchestra. The last twenty-two symphonies characterize Haydn's mature style. In his Symphony 85, "La Reine," Haydn based the second movement, in theme and variations form, on an Austrian folk-song. It became a favorite of Queen Marie Antoinette and for that reason received its nickname. While all of the London symphonies (92–104) are works of the highest quality, Symphony 94, "Surprise" and 100, "Military" have always been especially popular. In fact, the "Military" symphony was the most frequently performed work in the genre during the late eighteenth and early nineteenth centuries.

The great variety of Haydn's chamber music may be sampled in the following compositions. In addition to Opus 76, No. 3, the "Emperor" Quartet, of which the second movement is discussed in the text, the six string quartets of Op. 33 are in a popular style. The quartets comprising *The Seven Last Words of our Savior from the Cross* (1786) are in an altogether different vein, having been commissioned by a Spanish church official for a Good Friday service in Cádiz, Spain. Each of the seven slow movements were to provide appropriate reflection subsequent to a ten-minute devotional commentary on each sentence Christ spoke from the cross. The Piano Trio No. 39 in G major (number XV/25 in the catalog of the composer's works) was composed in the summer of 1795. The great Haydn scholar H. C. Robbins Landon observes that in this composition, one of the most popular in Europe after its publication, the sparkling melody of the "Gypsy Rondo" bears a striking similarity to those which Austrian military bands used to entice the peasantry into military service. Potential recruits were so dazzled by the visual and aural spectacle (as well as the generous glasses of Tokay wine) that they would immediately enlist.

Two of Haydn's masses are highly recommended. Both the *Mass in time of War* (also listed under the titles *Missa in tempore belli*, *Kriegsmesse*, and *Paukenmesse*) of 1796 and the *Nelson Mass* (also listed as *Imperial Mass* or *Coronation Mass*) from 1798 are dramatic statements of faith, hope, and fear which were written during the Napoleonic Wars. Comments concerning his influential oratoria *Die Schöpfung (The Creation)*, were included under Handel.

Wolfgang Amadeus Mozart

Mozart wrote his piano concertos in order to showcase his pianistic skills and offer new compositions to draw the public to his concerts; they were generally well received by his audiences. One of the most frequently performed concertos is No. 16 in D minor (K. 466). Another work, "one of his great tragic creations," is the concerto in C minor (No. 20, K. 491). One of Mozart's most beautiful, contemplative melodies—it is called the *Elvira Madigan* theme because it was once used as background music for a film of that name—unfolds in the slow movement of his seventeenth concerto (C major, K. 467). Each concerto has its own unique personality and the joy comes in finding "your" concerto. In a slightly different vein, the clarinet concerto (K. 622), composed two months before his death, is a masterful gem of great lyrical beauty.

The Sonata in C major (K. 545) was composed for beginning students and provides a clear example of sonata and rondo forms. One of his most famous rondos is the concluding movement of the Sonata in A major (K. 331), the "Alla turca." (Other compositions which illustrate the influence the Turkish Janissary ensemble—a military band featuring percussion instruments—had upon composers of the period include the second movement of Haydn's Symphony No. 100, the March from Beethoven's *The Ruins of Athens*, and the fourth movement of his ninth symphony.) A few recordings of Mozart's keyboard music played on period instruments (instruments, or reproductions of instruments, from the period in which the music was written) are available including selections performed by Paul Badura-Skoda on a piano built in 1790 (Skylark 8801 CD) and another by Igor Kipnis on a 1793 fortepiano (Music and Arts CD 660).

Mozart composed only three symphonies in a minor key and two of them are in G minor. While most everyone is familiar with the famous No. 40, No. 25 (K. 183) is equally intense and was featured in the movie *Amadeus*. In addition to his last three symphonies, the "Haffner" (No. 35, K. 385) and "Linz" (No. 36, K. 425) are also quite popular. The less well-known "Prague" Symphony (No. 38, K. 504), however, may well be Mozart's most beautiful.

All of Mozart's operas are available on videocassette. The performance of *Don Giovanni* (1787) conducted by Herbert von Karajan with Samuel Ramey in the title role is musically superb although altering the descent to hell into a trip through "hyperspace" is dramatically disappointing. Peter Sellars (see Handel) also reclothed this opera, turning the Don into a Harlem drug dealer. *Cosi fan Tutte* (1790) is a hilarious comedy as is the *Marriage of Figaro* (1786), while the *Magic Flute* (1791) ranges from solemn to slapstick. The famous aria ("Der Hölle Rache kocht in meinem Herzen") sung by the Queen of the Night is a show-stopper.

Mention Mozart's sacred music and most listeners think of the *Requiem*. However, his rich legacy includes the motet *Ave verum corpus* (K. 618, 1791), the "Laudate Dominum" from *Vesperae solennes de confessore* (K. 339, 1780) and the famous *Exsultate jubilate* (K. 165, 1773). The last work was written for the castrato Venanzio Rauzzini while Mozart and his father traveled through Italy. Two examples of his mass settings are the *Coronation Mass* in C major (K. 317, 1779) and the incomplete Mass in C minor (K. 427, 1783) which, although a religious work, contains some of Mozart's most beautiful, and operatic, vocal writing.

Ludwig van Beethoven

Beethoven's fame as a composer and virtuoso performer was initially established by his piano sonatas. The two "easy" sonatas of Op. 49 are perhaps the simplest examples of Beethoven's treatment of sonata form. The *Waldstein* sonata (Op. 53) is full of the virtuoso fire which made him famous while maintaining a clarity of form easily perceptible to most listeners. The transition into the recapitulation of the first movement is particularly exciting. Beethoven composed *Les Adieux* (Op. 81a) when the Hapsburgs, including his friend and student Archduke Rudolph, fled Vienna when the city fell to Napoleon in 1809. Each of the movements are provided with a title suggesting its mood: "Farewell," "Absence," and "The Return." The *Hammerklavier* Sonata (Op. 106) is one of the most challenging compositions ever written for the instrument. Probably the three most beloved keyboard compositions by Beethoven are the *Moonlight* (Op. 27, no. 2), *Appassionata* (Op. 57), and *Pathétique* (Op. 13) sonatas.

The early (Op. 18) and middle (Op. 59) string quartets provide a good introduction to Beethoven's treatment of the genre. Beethoven related that the inspiration for the second movement of Op. 18, no. 1 was the burial vault scene from Shakespeare's *Romeo and Juliet*. The three *Raxumovsky* quartets of Op. 59 were dedicated to the Russian Ambassador to Vienna, a connoisseur of music, and use Russian themes in two of the movements. His last quartet (Op. 135) concludes with a movement in which the themes are based on the phrases "Muss es sein?" and "Es muss sein!" ("Must it be?" and "It must be!"), ambiguous phrases which have generated a great deal of musicological speculation since Beethoven's death.

Certainly the foundation of Beethoven's reputation rests on his nine symphonies. Every orchestra in existence has made at least one recording of the group and most have made more. Since these works are the staple of the orchestral repertoire, most any recording will be good. Two sets which are of interest: The Hannover Band, conducted by Roy Goodman and Monica Huggett (Nimbus NI 5144/48) is an ensemble of period instruments offering a reasonably full sound and a shimmering wind section; the 1963 recordings by the Berlin Philharmonic Orchestra conducted by Herbert von Karajan (released on CD by Deutsche Grammophon, 429036-2 GX5) appears to be the critical standard by which all other recordings are based. It also has the advantage of being less expensive than most other sets. The complete symphonies conducted by Leonard Bernstein with the Vienna Philharmonic and by George Szell with the Cleveland Orchestra are also highly recommended. Among Beethoven's other compositions for orchestra, the *Leonore* (all three) and *Egmont* Overtures as well as the "Turkish March" from *The Ruins of Athens* are particularly stirring. Of the five piano concertos the fifth has the grandest conception of the form.

OMANTIC

Hector Berlioz

After listening to the complete *Symphonie fantastique*, one can further explore this composer's scintillating orchestral writing in *Harold in Italy* (scenes of Italian life—don't forget he accompanied Italian bandits for a while), *Romeo and Juliet* (scenes from Shakespeare's play), and *Roman Carnival Overture*. His setting of the *Requiem* is full of Romantic intensity and drama, especially the evocation of the final trumpet announcing the last judgment in the "Dies Irae" section.

Frédéric Chopin

Many of Chopin's compositions are well known. Perhaps the most famous works are the Waltz in D-flat major, "Minute" (Op. 64, No. 1) and the Etude in C minor, "Revolutionary" (Op. 10, No. 12). The Etude in A minor (Op. 10, No. 2) is a personal favorite. Many will recognize the famous "Funeral March" which he inserted as the slow movement of the Sonata in B-flat major (Op. 35), while the Grande Valse brilliant (Op. 18) is a true crowd pleaser. Compositions in a more reflective style include the Preludes in E minor and C minor (Op. 28, Nos. 4 and 20), Berceuse (Op. 57), the Nocturne in E-flat (Op. 9, No. 2), and the Prelude in D-flat, "Raindrop" (Op. 28, No. 15). The complete collection of nocturnes (usually a two CD set) makes a great gift for any beginning music lover—if you like lush Romanticism, you'll find it here.

Franz Liszt

Les Préludes (related to a poem by Lamartine, it is a perfect example of thematic transformation), *Mazeppa* (based on a poem by Victor Hugo in which a man—representing the inspired artist—is helplessly strapped to the horse of genius and must go where the beast takes him), and *Tasso* (based on a poem by Lord Byron) are among his most famous symphonic poems. In addition to his *Hungarian Rhapsodies* for piano (familiar to all who have watched Bugs Bunny cartoons), *La campanella* might ring a bell. *Orage* depicts a mountain storm and the B minor piano sonata expands sonata form to encompass three movements rather than one.

Felix Mendelssohn

The collection of character pieces for solo piano entitled *Lieder Ohne Worte (Songs Without Words)* are gems of the genre. Orchestral music inspired by his travels through Europe include his Symphony No. 4, "Italian;" Symphony No. 3, "Scottish;" and *Die Hebriden (Hebrides Overture)*. His Symphony No. 5, "Reformation" was composed for commemorations of the Protestant Reformation and Augsburg Confessions. The fourth movement is based on Luther's chorale melody *Ein feste Burg*. One of the most famous concertos from the period is his Violin Concerto in E minor, written in 1844.

Franz Schubert

Among the composer's best-loved songs are *Gretchen am Spinnrade*, Op. 2, (written when Schubert was seventeen, it is one of the most perfect songs ever composed), *Heidenröslein*, Op. 3, No. 3 (this pleasant folksong can be viewed as an allegory of a rape, the boy blithely deflowering the object of his desire), *Ständchen*, (the fourth song from *Schwanengesang* is a beautiful serenade in which the accompaniment imitates the sounds of a mandolin), and *Ave Maria*, Op. 52, No. 4 (most listeners will be familiar with the song sung to a liturgical text, rather than with Sir Walter's Scott's secular poem). The Symphony No. 8, "Unfinished," is hauntingly beautiful, a perfect example of Romantic melancholy.

Clara and Robert Schumann

Clara Schumann's music has just recently begun to be recorded, so the selection is limited. Robert's lieder include the famous *Dichterliebe (Poet's Love)* cycle as well as such beautiful individual examples as *Widmung (Dedication*, supposedly Clara's favorite song) and *Der Nussbaum (The Nut Tree)*. Many of his piano compositions are collections of character pieces. *Carnaval* includes musical portraits of Clara, Chopin, and Robert's alter egos Florestan and Eusebius. His Piano Concerto in A minor and Symphony No. 4 are staples of the concert repertoire.

Guiseppi Verdi

All of Verdi's operas are widely available on video. A movie version of *La traviata* staring Teresa Stratas and Placido Domingo and directed by Franco Zeffirelli offers an excellent introduction to the opera. It is a visual as well as aural delight and the director's dramatic use of color and light reflects the musical mood. *Rigoletto,* an opera which contrasts love and lust, murder and sacrifice, is one of Verdi's most popular compositions. One of the most spectacular operas to appear on the stage is *Aida,* in which a love triangle is complicated by political considerations (comparable to a U.S. president having an affair with a Russian spy). These three operas are not any better than the others, they just seem to be performed more regularly. As is the case for all operas, it is highly recommended that one read a synopsis of the story prior to watching it. Verdi also composed a *Requiem* featuring soloists, choir, and orchestra. Although a sacred composition, it is a stunning drama about death and judgment.

Richard Wagner

The Ring cycle is the central composition of Wagner's work. For sheer orchestral power the recordings by the Vienna Philharmonic Orchestra conducted by Sir Georg Solti cannot be surpassed. Numerous recordings of orchestral excerpts and overtures provide an excellent introduction to Wagner's music. Two video performances of the cycle are also widely available. The first is a modernistic setting taped at a 1991 performance in Bayreuth conducted by Daniel Barenboim. The second is also a 1991 production by the Metropolitan Opera conducted by James Levine. This latter interpretation returned to the naturalistic, mythological setting originally envisioned by Wagner. In 1953, the comedienne Anna Russell recorded the classic spoof of the Ring cycle at a concert appearance in New York City. It was included on her album *Anna Russell Sings! Again?* Once you are familiar with the rather convoluted plot of the cycle, this recording will give it an unforgettable comic twist. *Der Fliegende Holländer (The Flying Dutchman)* is a dark opera comparable to *Tristan und Isolde* in which the heroine chooses to prove her love through death. *Die Meistersinger von Nürnberg* is a lighter, comic opera set in Medieval Germany. Wagner satirized one of his most vehement critics, Eduard Hanslick, in the character Beckmesser (the name literally translates as "one who continually finds fault"), an individual who judges the songs but has no musical talent of his own.

Giacomo Puccini

If you only go to see only one opera performance during your lifetime, make it *Tosca.* After that experience you will certainly want to see more. Puccini's "instant classic," to employ a favorite oxymoron of movie critics, paints bold characterizations and dramatic situations. Scarpia's aria "Te Deum" is evil incarnate and his murder in Act II must be seen on stage to have its full effect. (The power of this opera is lost on video.) Finally, the opportunity to see a soprano die instantly without a ten minute death aria is worth just about any admission price. For those who prefer extended death soliloquies, don't miss *Madama Butterfly,* a touching opera concerning the hopeless love a Japanese girl has for an American sailor. The moment when Butterfly bids her final farewell to her son is enough to bring tears to any eye.

LATE ROMANTICISM

Symphonies

All four symphonies by Brahms are among the best works ever composed in the genre. They are logically conceived, rhythmically vivacious, and beautifully expressive—what more could Beethoven himself have expected. The only pity is that Brahms did not compose nine. In addition to Dvořák's symphony "From the New World," the eighth is full of Bohemian fire (the second movement is particularly charming). Tchaikovsky's fourth, fifth, and sixth symphonies are justifiably a staple of the concert repertoire. If you enjoy dramatic music featuring brass instruments, don't miss the fourth. His *Manfred Symphony* is a little off the beaten path but worth hearing. For those who wish to wallow in misery, listen to the sixth symphony, the "Pathétique." Bruckner's Symphony No. 4, "Romantic" is an exciting composition. The slow development of the French horn's opening motive into the explosive climax of the first theme is an eminently satisfying experience. Mahler's symphonies, with their dense, elegiac, and complex style have appealed to many in the atomic generation. The best approach to Mahler for beginning listeners is to start with Symphony No. 4 and proceed to Symphony No. 1, before moving on to more expansive works such as Symphony No. 2 (the "Resurrection" symphony), Symphony No. 5 (with its exquisitely beautiful slow movement), and Symphony No. 8 (Symphony of a Thousand"). *Das Lied von der Erde* combines symphony and song into a unique composition. The fourth movement is a beautiful gem and, considering Mahler's expansive style, surprisingly brief.

Concert Overtures and Program Music

Certainly the most famous overture has to be Tchaikovsky's *1812* and it is one of the best "battle" pieces ever composed. For a Russian, Tchaikovsky managed to evoke an excellent portrait of sunny Italy in his *Capriccio Italian*—the joy is infectious. Other important Russian programmatic compositions include Rimsky-Korsakov's *Scheherazade* (loosely suggestive of *A Thousand and One Arabian Nights*) and Musorgsky's *Night on Bald Mountain* (evoking a satanic orgy). In addition to Brahms' *Academic Festival Overture*, the *Tragic Overture* is a moving composition. While not a concert overture, his one-movement *Variations on a Theme by Haydn* (it turns out that the theme was not composed by Haydn, but it doesn't really matter) is a popular work. Brahms' *Hungarian Dances* and Dvořák's *Slavonic Dances* are delightful compositions. One of the most famous examples of Czech nationalist music is Bedřich Smetana's tone poem *The Moldau*. It was so evocative of the Czech spirit that the Nazi's prohibited its performance during World War II.

Concertos

The composers of the late Romantic period have provided some wonderfully moving concertos. Dvořák composed a concerto for the cello and Brahms provided an outstanding example of the genre featuring the violin. Tchaikovsky's Piano Concerto No. 1 and Rachmaninov's Piano Concerto No. 2 are two of the lushest compositions one can experience—the musical equivalent of a rich chocolate dessert.

IMPRESSIONISM

Claude Debussy

Debussy's orchestral compositions are beautifully evocative works in which the composer treats the instruments like a painter with a brush. *Nuages (Clouds)* and *Fête (Festivals)* are highly imaginative compositions as are *La Mer (The Sea)* and *Ibéria*, a work which represents Debussy's idealized vision of Spain (he never visited the country). *Clair de lune* is his most popular composition for the piano. Another keyboard work, *Children's Corner*, is a collection of humorous sketches (he pokes fun at Wagner's *Tristan und Isolde* in the movement *Golliwogg's Cakewalk*). *En blanc et noir (In Black and White)* for solo piano contains fragments of bugle call-like figures and the accompanying poem alludes to the dance of death on the battlefield and those men who (like himself) stand aside in disgrace.

Other Composers

Although Gabriel Fauré predated the Impressionist movement, his compositions display a distinctly Gallic style of instrumental color and mood. Two compositions of great beauty which are easily accessible are his *Requiem* (as opposite an expression of the examples by Mozart, Berlioz, and Verdi as can be imagined) and *Pavane* (a wonderfully gentle composition). In addition to Ravel's *Bolero*, one should experience *La Valse*, which infuses the simple waltz with great orchestral power and rhythm as well as his ballet suite *Daphne et Chloe*, in which he seems to borrow many Impressionist gestures directly from Debussy. Other compositions include *On Hearing the First Cuckoo in Spring* by Frederick Delius and Ottorino Respighi's *I pini di Roma (The Pines of Rome)* and *Feste romane (Roman Festivals)*.

TWENTIETH CENTURY

1900–1918

Stravinsky's three ballets, *Firebird*, *Petrushka*, and *Rite of Spring* have lost none of their sparkling brilliance during the course of the century. (It is interesting to compare *The Rite* with Debussy's ballet *Jeux*. They were composed at the same time, Stravinsky and Debussy discussed their scores with each other during the process of composition, and the works premièred within weeks of each other, yet they sound totally different.) Another example of the influence of "primitivism" during this period is Bartók's composition for the piano, *Allegro barbaro*. Schoenberg's early style is represented by the sextet *Verklärte Nacht (Transfigured Night)* and the melodrama *Erwartung (Expectation)*, works which culminated in the atonal style of *Pierrot lunaire*. The bulk of compositions by Charles Ives were written before the conclusion of World War I. Like Felix Mendelssohn, one of Ives's most beloved works, *Variations on America*, was composed when he was seventeen. It was originally for organ, but was orchestrated by William Schumann. An exceptionally moving composition is the third movement from the *Second Orchestral Set* entitled *From Hannover Square North at the End of a Tragic Day, the Voice of the People Arose*. It was intended to evoke the deep sadness and uncertainty of Americans on the day the Lusitania was sunk (May 7, 1915) with the loss of more than 1,500 lives. With the recent popularity of the movie *Little Women*, listeners might find his Second Piano Sonata of topical interest. The third movement, entitled *The Alcotts*, conveys the innocent vision of America so prevalent in the novel. In addition, the entire composition bears traces of the famous motive from Beethoven's fifth symphony.

Between the Wars

After World War I, Stravinsky's compositions turned toward the Neo-classic aesthetic. *L'Histoire du Soldat (The Soldier's Tale)* was written during the war and illustrates the remarkable change from his early ballets. *Symphony of Psalms, Pulcinella*, and the opera *A Rake's Progress* are interesting Neo-classic works. One of the most compelling examples of Expressionism is Alban Berg's opera *Wozzeck*, a tragedy which, even in this jaded age, causes a visceral response in the audience. (His second opera, *Lulu*, was based on the murders of Jack the Ripper.) Schoenberg's twelve-tone compositions *Suite for Piano* and *Variations for Orchestra* (Op. 31) offer a good introduction to this influential style. In a totally different vein, the music of Ralph Vaughn Williams illustrates the influence of English folk song and hymn tradition. His well-known compositions include *Fantasia on a Theme by Thomas Tallis*, the famous *Fantasia on "Greensleeves"* (derived from his opera *Sir John in Love*, based on Shakespeare's *Merry Wives of Windsor*), and the *Mass in G minor*. An incomplete representation of important American composers from this period includes George Gershwin (*Rhapsody in Blue, Porgy and Bess*), Ruth Crawford Seeger (*String Quartet 1931*), and Henry Cowell (*The Banshee*, a work which predates Cage's experimentation with the prepared piano). The compositions by Aaron Copland are as representative of the American spirit as the paintings of Norman Rockwell. Some of his famous works include *El Salón Mexico, Billy the Kid, Rodeo, Appalachian Spring*, and *Fanfare for the Common Man*. That Copland successfully achieved his desire to write works which appeal to the proverbial "man in the street" is evidenced by the number of television commercials which use his compositions as the soundtrack.

Post World War II

Two late works by the colossi of twentieth-century music include the serialistic *Canticum Sacrum* by Igor Stravinsky (listening to this work and *The Firebird*, one would never guess they were from the same hand) and Schoenberg's cantata *A Survivor from Warsaw*. The latter is a moving account of the atrocities committed by the Nazis in the concentration camps during the Second World War. The audience was stunned at its première in 1947 and the effect has not lessened with the passing of time. Representative electronic compositions include the groundbreaking *Poème électronique* by Varèse (written when the composer was seventy-five), Karlheinz Stockhausen's *Gesang der Jüngling* and *Mikrophonie II*, and Milton Babbitt's *Philomel*. Benjamin Britten's compositions represent a more traditional trend in twentieth-century music. He wrote numerous operas, including *Peter Grimes* and *Billy Budd*. *War Requiem* and *A Ceremony of Carols* exemplify his beautiful and moving choral style. In addition to *Concerto Grosso 1985*, Ellen Taaffe Zwilich's *Double Quartet* is an intense and interesting composition. Two minimalist compositions which serve as a good introduction to the movement are *A Short Ride on a Fast Machine* by John Adams and *Glassworks* by Philip Glass.

Jazz

The core collection of jazz music is compiled on a five CD set entitled *The Smithsonian Collection of Classic Jazz* (revised). It includes selections from all the important jazz movements except jazz-fusion. The accompanying booklet offers a good summary of jazz styles, suggestions for listening to jazz, comments regarding each recording in the set, and a biographical entry on numerous musicians. In recent years collections devoted to single artists and composers have been issued (or reissued) containing some of their most famous recordings. Bessie Smith's recordings are now available on CD (the four volume, 8 CD set *Bessie Smith: the Complete Recordings* are on the Columbia Legacy label). She recorded several versions of *St. Louis Blues* as well as a movie short based on the song. Another blues singer of great power and versatility was Getrude "Ma" Raney. Her songs *Titanic Man Blues* and *Traveling Blues* combine humor and pain in an entertaining and expressive manner. Fletcher Henderson, the pianist in *Lost Your Head Blues*, was famous both for his band and as an arranger for Benny Goodman's big band. *The Fletcher Henderson Story* (Columbia C3K 57596) is a collection of more than sixty of his band's recordings. In addition to the two included on the Smithsonian Collection, *Copenhagen, Sugarfoot Stomp* (1931) and *New King Porter Stomp* (1932) are some of the most exciting jazz recordings ever put on disc. Duke Ellington, one of the most talented and inventive composers of the twentieth century, wrote numerous "hit" songs including *Sophisticated Lady*, *Mood Indigo*, and, in conjunction with Billy Strayhorn, *Take the A Train*. Ellington sought to expand jazz structures into larger forms and wrote several film scores as well as extended instrumental works. One unique work that was recently featured on the PBS special *Marsalis on Music* was his jazz arrangement of Tchaikovsky's Overture to the *Nutcracker*. Many Ellington recordings are readily available. If you are a latent (or just plain late) beatnik and find bebop the coolest form of musical expression, the Smithsonian Collection contains several important recordings including *Ko-Ko*, *Shaw 'Nuff*, and *I Can't Get Started*.

GLOSSARY

absolute music: instrumental music free of a text or any preexisting program

a cappella: a term applied to unaccompanied vocal music; originated in the expression *a cappella Sistina,* "in the Sistine Chapel" of the pope, where instruments were forbidden to accompany the singers

accelerando: a tempo mark indicating "getting faster"

accent: emphasis or stress placed on a musical tone or a chord

accidental: a sharp, flat, or natural sign that alters the pitch of a note a half step

accompagnato: see *recitativo accompagnato*

acoustical instruments: instruments that produce sounds naturally when strings are bowed or plucked, a tube has air passed through it, or percussion instruments are struck

adagio: a tempo mark indicating "slow"

Alberti bass: instead of having the pitches of a chord sound all together, the notes are played in succession to provide a continual stream of sound

aleatoric music: see *chance music*

allegretto: a tempo mark indicating "moderately fast"

allegro: a tempo mark indicating "fast"

allemande: a stately dance in 4/4 meter with gracefully interweaving lines

alto (contralto): the lower of the two female voice parts, the soprano being higher

andante: a tempo mark indicating "moderately moving"

andantino: a tempo mark indicating "moderately moving" yet slightly faster than *andante*

antecedent phrase: the opening, incomplete-sounding phrase of a melody; often followed by a consequent phrase that brings the melody to closure

anthem: a composition for chorus on a sacred subject; similar in design and function to a motet

aria: an elaborate lyrical song for solo voice

arpeggio: the notes of a triad or seventh chord played in direct succession and in a direct line up or down

arioso: a style of singing and a type of song midway between an aria and a recitative

art song: an accompanied song or ayre with artistic aspirations

atonal music: music without tonality, music without a key center; most often associated with the twentieth-century avant-garde style of Arnold Schoenberg

augmentation: the notes of a melody held for longer, usually double, their normal duration

ballad: a traditional song, or folk song, sung by a soloist that tells a tale and is organized by stanzas

ballet: an art form that uses dance and music, along with costumes and scenery, to tell a story and display emotions through expressive gestures and movement

Ballets russes: a Russian ballet company of the early twentieth century led by Sergei Diaghilev

banjo: a five-string plucked folk instrument of African-American origin

bar: see *measure*

baritone: a male voice part of a middle range, between the higher tenor and the lower bass

bass: the lowest male voice range

bass clef: a sign placed on a staff to indicate the notes below middle C

bass drum: a large, low-sounding drum struck with a soft-headed stick

bass viol: see *viola da gamba*

basso continuo: a small ensemble of at least two instrumentalists who provide a foundation for the melody or melodies above; heard almost exclusively in Baroque music

basso ostinato: a motive or phrase in the bass that is repeated again and again

bassoon: a low, double-reed instrument of the woodwind family

Bayreuth Festival House: an opera house in the town of Bayreuth, Germany, constructed exclusively for the music dramas of Richard Wagner

beat: an even pulse in music that divides the passing of time into equal segments

bebop: a complex, hard-driving style of jazz that emerged shortly after World War II; it is played without musical notation by a small ensemble

bel canto: (Italian for "beautiful singing") a style of singing and a type of Italian opera developed in the nineteenth century that features the beautiful tone and brilliant technique of the human voice

big band: a mid- to large-size dance band that emerged in the 1930s to play the style of jazz called swing

binary form: a musical form consisting of two units (**A** and **B**) constructed to balance and complement each other

blue note: the third, fifth, or seventh note of the blues scale that can be altered to be sharper or flatter; helps produce the wail of the blues .

blues: an expressive, soulful style of singing that emerged from the African-American spiritual and work song at the end of the nineteenth century; its texts are strophic, its harmonies simple and repetitive

blues scale: a seven-note scale in which the third, fifth, and seventh pitches are sometimes flat, sometimes natural, and sometimes in between

bolero: a popular, suggestive Spanish dance for a soloist or couple often performed to the accompaniment of castanets

Brandenburg concertos: set of six concerti grossi composed by J. S. Bach between 1711 and 1720, and subsequently dedicated to Margrave Christian Ludwig of Brandenburg

brass family: a group of musical instruments traditionally made of brass and played with a mouthpiece; includes trumpet, trombone, French horn, and tuba

bridge: see *transition*

bugle: a simple brass instrument that evolved from the valveless military trumpet

cabaletta: the concluding fast aria of any two- or three-section operatic scene; a useful mechanism to get the principals off the stage

cadence: a musical resting place at the end of a phrase

cadenza: a showy passage for the soloist appearing near the end of the movement in a concerto; it usually incorporates rapid runs, arpeggios, and snippets of previously heard themes into a fantasylike improvisation

canon (round): a contrapuntal form in which the individual voices enter and each in turn duplicates exactly the melody that the first voice played or sang

cantata: a term originally meaning "something sung"; in its mature state it consists of several movements, including one or more arias, ariosos, and recitatives; cantatas can be on secular subjects, but those of J. S. Bach are primarily sacred in content

caprice: a light, whimsical character piece of the nineteenth century

castrato: a boy or adult singer who had been castrated to keep his voice from changing so that it would remain in the soprano register

celesta: a small percussive keyboard instrument using hammers to strike metal bars, thereby producing a bright, bell-like sound

cello (violoncello): an instrument of the violin family but twice the violin's size; it is played between the legs and produces a rich, lyrical tone

chamber music: music, usually instrumental music, performed in a small concert hall or private residence with just one performer on each part

chamber sonata: see *sonata da camera*

chance music (aleatory music): music that involves an element of chance (rolling dice, choosing cards, etc.) or whimsy on the part of the performers; especially popular with avant-garde composers

chanson: a French term used broadly to indicate a lyrical song from the Middle Ages into the twentieth century

character piece: a brief instrumental work seeking to capture a single mood; a genre much favored by composers of the Romantic era

chorale: the German word for the hymn of the Lutheran church; hence a simple religious melody to be sung by the congregation

chord: two or more simultaneously sounding pitches

chord progression: a succession of chords moving forward in a purposeful fashion

chorus: a group of singers, usually including sopranos, altos, tenors, and basses, with at least two and often many more singers on each vocal part; also, in jazz, a full statement of the tune around which the performers improvise

chromaticism: the frequent presence in melodies and chords of intervals only a half step apart; in a scale, the use of notes not part of the diatonic major or minor pattern

church sonata: see *sonata da chiesa*

clarinet: a single-reed instrument of the woodwind family with a large range and a wide variety of timbres within it

clarino: the high register of the trumpet, two octaves above middle C and up

clavier: a general term for all keyboard instruments including harpsichord, organ, and piano

clef sign: a sign used to indicate the register, or range of pitches, in which an instrument is to play or a singer is to sing

coda: (Italian for "tail") a final and concluding section of a musical composition

col legno: (Italian for "with the wood") an instruction to string players to strike the strings of the instrument not with the horsehair of the bow, but with the wood of it

collegium musicum: a society of amateur musicians (usually associated with a university) dedicated to the performance of music, nowadays music of the Middle Ages, Renaissance, and Baroque era

color (timbre): the character or quality of a musical tone as determined by its harmonics and its attack and decay

comic opera: a genre of opera that originated in the eighteenth century, portraying everyday characters and situations, and using spoken dialogue and simple songs

computer music: the most recent development in electronic music; couples the computer with the electronic synthesizer to imitate the sounds of acoustical instruments and to produce new sounds

concert overture: an independent, one-movement work, usually of programmatic content, originally intended for the concert hall and not designed to precede an opera or play

concertino: the group of instruments that function as soloists in a concerto grosso

concerto: an instrumental genre in which one or more soloists play with and against a larger orchestra

concerto grosso: a three-movement concerto of the Baroque era that pits the sound of a small group of soloists (the concertino) against that of the full orchestra (the tutti)

conjunct motion: melodic motion that proceeds primarily by steps and without leaps

consequent phrase: the second phrase of a two-part melodic unit that brings a melody to a point of repose and closure

consonance: pitches sounding agreeable and stable

continuo: see *basso continuo*

contrabassoon: a larger, lower-sounding version of the bassoon

cool jazz: a style of jazz that emerged in the 1950s that is softer, more relaxed, and less frenzied than bebop

cornet: a brass instrument that looks like a short trumpet; it has a more mellow tone than the trumpet and is most often used in military bands

cornetto: a woodwind instrument that developed during the late Middle Ages and early Renaissance that sounds like a hybrid of a clarinet and trumpet

counterpoint: the harmonious opposition of two or more independent musical lines

courante: a lively dance in 6/4 with an upbeat and frequent changes of metrical accent

crescendo: a gradual increase in the volume of sound

cymbals: a percussion instrument of two metal disks; they are made to crash together to create emphasis and articulation in music

da capo aria: an aria in two sections, with an obligatory return to and repeat of the first; hence an aria in ternary (**ABA**) form

dance suite: a collection of instrumental dances, each with its own distinctive rhythm and character

development: the center-most portion of sonata–allegro form, in which the thematic material of the exposition is developed and extended, transformed, or reduced to its essence; it is often the most confrontational and unstable section of the movement

diatonic: pertaining to the seven notes that make up either the major or the minor scale

Dies irae: a Gregorian chant composed in the thirteenth century and used as the central portion of the Requiem Mass of the Catholic Church

diminished chord: a triad or seventh chord made up entirely of minor thirds and producing a tense, unstable sound

diminuendo: a gradual decrease in volume of sound

diminution: a reduction, usually by half, of all the rhythmic durations in a melody

disjunct motion: melodic motion that moves primarily by leaps rather than by steps

dissonance: a discordant mingling of sounds

diva: (Italian for "goddess") a celebrated female opera singer; a prima donna

dominant chord: the chord built on the fifth degree of the scale

dondon: a two-headed pressure drum indigenous to Southern Africa

dotted note: a note to which an additional duration of fifty percent has been added

double bass: the largest and lowest-pitched instrument in the string family

double counterpoint: counterpoint with two themes that can reverse position, the top theme moving to the bottom and the bottom to the top (also called *invertible counterpoint*)

double exposition form: a form, originating in the concerto of the Classical period, in which first the orchestra and then the soloist present the primary thematic material

downbeat: the first beat of each measure; it is indicated by a downward motion of the conductor's hand and is usually stressed

drone: a continuous sound on one or more fixed pitches

dynamics: the various levels of volume, loud and soft, at which sounds are produced in a musical composition

electronic instruments: machines that produce musical sounds by electronic means, the most widespread instrument being the keyboard synthesizer

electronic music: sounds produced and manipulated by magnetic tape machines, synthesizers, and/or computers

eleventh chord: a chord comprised of five intervals of a third and spanning eleven different letter names of pitches

English horn: an alto oboe, pitched at the interval a fifth below the oboe, much favored by composers of the Romantic era

episode: a passage of free, nonimitative counterpoint found in a fugue

erhu: an ancient two-string Chinese fiddle

étude: (French for "study") a musical composition that aims to improve the technical facility of the performer

exposition: in a fugue, the opening section, in which each voice in turn has the opportunity to present the subject; in sonata–allegro form, the principal section, in which all thematic material is presented

falsetto voice: a high, soprano-like voice produced by adult male singers when they sing in head voice and not in full chest voice

fantasy: a free improvisatory-like composition in which the composer follows his or her whims rather than an established musical form

fermata: in musical notation, a mark indicating that the performer(s) should hold a note or chord for an extended duration

fiddle: a popular term for the violin

figured bass: in musical notation, a numerical shorthand that tells the player which unwritten notes to fill in above the written bass note

finale: the last movement of a multimovement composition, one that usually works to a climax and conclusion

flat: in musical notation, a symbol that lowers a pitch by a half step

flute: a high-sounding member of the woodwind family; the instrument was initially made of wood but more recently, beginning in the nineteenth century, of silver or even platinum

folk-rock: a mixture of the steady beat of rock with the forms, topics, and styles of singing of the traditional Anglo-American folk ballad

folk song: a song originating from an ethnic group and passed from generation to generation by oral tradition rather than written notation

form: the purposeful organization of the artist's materials; in music, the general shape of a composition as perceived by the listener

forte (*f*): in musical notation, a dynamic mark indicating "loud"

fortepiano (pianoforte): the original name of the piano

fortissimo (*ff*): in musical notation, a dynamic mark indicating "very loud"

free counterpoint: counterpoint in which the voices do not all make use of some preexisting subject in imitation

French horn: a brass instrument that plays in the middle range of the brass family; developed from the medieval hunting horn

French overture: a two-part musical form of the Baroque era consisting of a slow first section in duple meter with dotted rhythms and a fast second section with imitative counterpoint

fugato: a short fugue set in some other musical form like sonata–allegro or theme and variations

fugue: a composition for three, four, or five parts played or sung by voices or instruments, which begins with a presentation of a subject in imitation in each part and continues with modulating passages of free counterpoint and further appearances of the subject

full cadence: a cadence that sounds complete, in part because it usually ends on the tonic note

gamelan: the traditional orchestra of Indonesia consisting of as many as twenty-five instruments, mostly gongs, chimes, drums, and metallophones

Gesamtkunstwerk: (German for "total art work") an art form that involves music, poetry, drama, and scenic design; often used in reference to Richard Wagner's music dramas

Gewandhaus Orchestra: the symphony orchestra that originated in the Clothiers' House in Leipzig, Germany, in the eighteenth century

gigue: a fast dance in 6/8 or 12/8 with a constant eighth-note pulse that produces a galloplike effect

glissando: a device of sliding up or down the scale very rapidly

glockenspiel: a percussion instrument made of tuned metal bars that are struck by mallets

gongon: a large barrel-like drum indigenous to Southern Africa

grave: a tempo mark indicating "very slow and grave"

great staff: a large musical staff that combines both the treble and the bass clefs

Gregorian chant (plainsong): a large body of unaccompanied monophonic vocal music, set to Latin texts, composed for the Western Church over the course of fifteen centuries, from the time of the earliest Fathers to the Council of Trent

ground bass: the English term for *basso ostinato*

guiro: a scraped percussion instrument originating in South America and the Caribbean

half cadence: a cadence at which the music does not come to a fully satisfying stop but stands as if suspended on a dominant chord

half step: the smallest musical interval in the Western major or minor scale; the distance between any two adjacent keys on the piano

harmonics: the secondary tones above a fundamental pitch that taken in sum help form the totality of that sound

harmony: the sounds that provide the support and enrichment—an accompaniment—for melody

harp: an ancient plucked-string instrument with a triangular shape

harpsichord: a keyboard instrument, especially popular during the Baroque era, that produces sound by depressing a key that drives a lever upward and forces a pick to pluck a string

Hindustani-style music: the traditional, or classical, music of northern India

homophony: a texture in which all the voices, or lines, move to new pitches at roughly the same time; often referred to in contradistinction to polyphony

horn: a term generally used by musicians to refer to any brass instrument, but most often the French horn

hornpipe: an energetic dance, derived from the country jig, in either 3/2 or 2/4 time

idée fixe: literally a "fixed idea," but more specifically an obsessive musical theme as first used in Hector Berlioz's *Symphonie fantastique*

imitation: the process by which one or more musical voices, or parts, enter and duplicate exactly for a period of time the music presented by the previous voice

imitative counterpoint: a type of counterpoint in which the voices or lines frequently use imitation

incidental music: music to be inserted between the acts or during important scenes of a play to add an extra dimension to the drama

instrumental break: in the blues or in jazz, a short instrumental passage that interrupts and responds to the singing of a voice

intermezzo: (Italian for "between piece") a light musical interlude intended to separate and thus break the mood of two more serious, surrounding movements or operatic acts or scenes

interval: the distance between any two pitches on a musical scale

inversion: the process of inverting the musical intervals in a theme or melody; a melody that ascended by step, now descends by step, and so on

invertible counterpoint: see *double counterpoint*

jazz: a lively, energetic music with pulsating rhythms and scintillating syncopations, usually played by a small instrumental ensemble

jazz-fusion: a mixture of jazz and rock cultivated by American bands in the 1970s

Karnatak-style music: the traditional, or classical, music of southern India

key: a tonal center built on a tonic note and making use of a scale; also, on a keyboard instrument, one of a series of levers that can be depressed to generate sound

key signature: in musical notation, a preplaced set of sharps or flats used to indicate the scale and key

Kyrie: the first portion of the Ordinary of the Mass and hence usually the opening movement in a polyphonic setting of the Mass

La Scala: the principal opera house of the city of Milan, Italy, which opened in 1778

largo: a tempo mark indicating "slow and broad"

leading tone: the pitch a half step below the tonic, which pulls up and into it, especially at cadences

leap: melodic movement not by an interval of just a step but usually by a jump of at least a fourth

legato: in musical notation, an articulation mark indicating that the notes are to be smoothly connected; the opposite of staccato

Leitmotif: a brief, distinctive unit of music designed to represent a character, object, or idea; a term applied to the motives in the music dramas of Richard Wagner

lento: a tempo mark indicating "very slow"

libretto: the text of an opera

Liebestod: (German for "love death") the famous aria sung by the expiring Isolde at the end of Richard Wagner's opera *Tristan und Isolde*

Lied: (German for "song") the genre of art song, for voice and piano accompaniment, that originated in Germany ca. 1800

London symphonies: the twelve symphonies composed by Joseph Haydn for performance in London between 1791 and 1795; Haydn's last twelve symphonies (Nos. 93–104)

lute: a six-string instrument appearing in the West in the late Middle Ages

madrigal: a popular genre of secular vocal music that originated in Italy during the Renaissance, in which usually four or five voices sing love poems

madrigalism: a device, originating in the madrigal, by which key words in a text spark a particularly expressive musical setting

major scale: a seven-note scale that ascends in the following order of whole and half steps: 1-1-½-1-1-1-½

Mass: the central religious service of the Roman Catholic church, one that incorporates singing for spiritual reflection or as accompaniment to sacred acts

measure (bar): a group of beats, or musical pulses; usually the number of beats is fixed and constant so that the measure serves as a continual unit of measurement in music

melisma: in singing, one vowel luxuriously spread out over many notes

melodic sequence: the repetition of a musical motive at successively higher or lower degrees of the scale

melody: a series of notes arranged in order to form a distinctive, recognizable musical unit; it is most often placed in the treble

metallophone: a percussion instrument consisting of keys made of tuned metal bars that are struck by hammers or sticks

meter: the gathering of beats into regular groups

metronome: a mechanical device used by performers to keep a steady tempo

mezzo-soprano: a female vocal range between alto and soprano

middle C: the middle note on the modern piano

minimalism: a style of modern music that takes a very small amount of musical material and repeats it over and over to form a composition

Minnesinger: a type of secular poet-musician that flourished in Germany during the twelfth through fourteenth centuries

minor scale: a seven-note scale that ascends in the following order of whole and half steps: 1-½-1-1-½-1-1

minuet: a moderate dance in 3/4, though actually danced in patterns of six steps, with no upbeat but with highly symmetrical phrasing

mixolydian scale (mixolydian mode): a seven-note scale often used in Gregorian chant, one different from the major and minor scale

mode: a pattern of pitches forming a scale; the two primary modes in Western music are major and minor

moderato: a tempo marking indicating "moderately moving"

modified strophic form: strophic form in which the music is modified briefly to accommodate a particularly expressive word or phrase in the text

modulation: the process in music whereby the tonal center changes from one key to another, from G major to C major, for example

monophony: a musical texture involving only a single line of music with no accompaniment

motet: a composition for choir or larger chorus setting a religious, devotional, or solemn text; often sung *a cappella*

motive: a short, distinctive melodic figure that stands by itself

mouthpiece: a detachable portion of a brass instrument into which the player blows

movement: a large, independent section of a major instrumental work, such as a sonata, dance suite, symphony, quartet, or concerto

music: the rational organization of sounds and silences as they pass through time

music drama: a term used for the mature operas of Richard Wagner

musical comedy: a popular genre of musical theater designed to appeal to a general audience by means of spoken dialogue, songs, and energetic dances

musique concrète: music in which the composer works directly with sounds recorded on magnetic tape, not with musical notation and performers

mute: any device that muffles the sound of a musical instrument; on the trumpet, for example, it is a cup that is placed inside the bell of the instrument

nationalism: a movement in music in the nineteenth century in which composers sought to emphasize indigenous qualities in their music by incorporating folk songs, native scales, dance rhythms, and local instrumental sounds

natural: in muiscal notation, a symbol that cancels a pre-existing sharp or flat

Neo-classicism: a movement in twentieth-century music that seeks to return to the musical forms and aesthetics of the Baroque and Classical periods

ninth chord: a chord spanning nine letters of the scale and constructed by superimposing four intervals of a third

nocturne: a slow, introspective type of piano music with rich harmonies and poignant dissonances that came into favor during the 1820s and 1830s

nonimitative counterpoint: counterpoint with independent lines that do not imitate each other

oboe: an instrument of the woodwind family; the highest-pitched of the double-reed instruments

octave: the interval comprising the first and eighth tones of the major and minor diatonic scale; the sounds are quite similar because the frequency of vibration of the higher pitch is exactly twice that of the lower

octave displacement: a process used in constructing a melody whereby a simple, nearby interval is made more distant, and the melodic line more disjunct, by placing the next note up or down an octave

opera: a dramatic work in which the actors sing some or all of their parts; it usually makes use of elaborate stage sets and costumes

opera buffa: (Italian for "comic opera") an opera on a light, often domestic subject, with tuneful melodies, comic situations, and a happy ending

opera seria: a genre of opera that dominated the stage during the Baroque era, making use of serious historical or mythological subjects, *da capo* arias, and a lengthy overture

operetta: a light opera with spoken dialogue and numerous dances involving comedy and romance in equal measure

ophicleide: a low brass instrument originating in military bands about the time of the French Revolution; the precursor of the tuba

opus: (Latin for "work") the term adopted by composers to enumerate and identify their compositions

oral tradition: the process used in transmission of folk songs and other traditional music in which the material is passed from one generation to the next by singing, or playing, and hearing, without musical notation

oratorio: a large-scale genre of sacred music involving an overture, arias, recitatives, and choruses, but sung, whether in a theater or a church, without costumes or scenery

orchestra: see *symphony orchestra*

orchestral score: a composite of the musical lines of all of the instruments of the orchestra and from which a conductor conducts

orchestral song: a genre of music emerging in the nineteenth century in which the voice is accompanied not merely by a piano but by a full orchestra

orchestral suite: a dance suite written for orchestra

orchestration: the art of assigning to the various instruments of the orchestra, or of a chamber ensemble, the diverse melodies, accompaniments, and counterpoints of a musical composition

Ordinary of the Mass: the five sung portions of the Mass for which the texts are unvariable

organ: an ancient musical instrument constructed mainly of pipes and keys; the player depresses a key that allows air to rush into or over a pipe, thereby producing sound

organum: the name given to the early polyphony of the Western Church from the ninth through the thirteenth centuries

oscillator: a device that, when activated by an electronic current, pulses back and forth to produce an electronic signal that can be converted by a loudspeaker into sound

ostinato: (Italian for "obstinate") a musical figure, motive, melody, harmony, or rhythm that is repeated again and again

overtone: see *harmonics*

overture: an introductory movement, usually for orchestra, that precedes an opera, oratorio, or dance suite

parallel motion: a musical process in which all of the lines or parts move in the same direction, and at the same intervals, for a period of time; the opposite of counterpoint

part: an independent line or voice in a musical composition; also, a section of a composition

pedal point: a note, usually in the bass, sustained or continually repeated for a period of time while the harmonies change around it

pentatonic scale: a five-note scale found often in folk music and non-Western music

phrase: a self-contained portion of a melody, theme, or tune

pianissimo (*pp*): in musical notation, a dynamic mark indicating "very soft"

piano (*p*): in musical notation, a dynamic mark indicating "soft"

piano: a large keyboard instrument that creates sound at various dynamic levels when hammers are struck against strings

piano transcription: the transformation and reduction of an orchestral score, and a piece of orchestral music, onto the great staff for playing at the piano

pianoforte: see *fortepiano*

piccolo: a small flute; the smallest and highest-pitched woodwind instrument

pickup: a note or two coming before the first downbeat of a piece, intending to give a little extra push into that down-beat

pipa: an ancient four-string Chinese lute

pitch: the relative position, high or low, of a musical sound

pizzicato: the process whereby a performer plucks the strings of an instrument rather than bowing them

plainsong: see *Gregorian chant*

point of imitation: a distinctive motive that is sung or played in turn by each voice or instrumental line

polonaise: a stately dance of Polish origins in triple meter without an upbeat and often with an accent on the second of the three beats

polychords: the stacking of one triad or seventh chord on another so they sound simultaneously

polymeters: two or more meters sounding simultaneously

polyphony: a musical texture involving two or more simultaneously sounding lines; the lines are often independent and create counterpoint

polyrhythms: two or more rhythms sounding simultaneously

polytonality: the simultaneous sounding of two keys or tonalities

popular music: a broad category of music designed to please a large section of the general public; sometimes used in contradistinction to more "serious" or more "learned" classical music

prelude: an introductory, improvisatory-like movement that gives the performer a chance to warm up and sets the stage for a more substantive subsequent movement

prepared piano: a piano outfitted with screws, bolts, washers, erasers, and bits of felt and plastic to transform the instrument from a melodic one to a percussive one

prestissimo: in musical notation, a tempo mark indicating "as fast as possible"

presto: in musical notation, a tempo mark indicating "very fast"

prima donna: (Italian for "first lady") the leading female singer in an opera

program music: a piece of instrumental music, usually for symphony orchestra, that seeks to recreate in sound the events and emotions portrayed in some extramusical source: a story, a play, a historical event, an encounter with nature, or even a painting

program symphony: a symphony with the usual three, four or five movements in which the individual movements together tell a tale or depict a succession of specific events or scenes

Proper of the Mass: the sections of the Mass that are sung to texts that vary with each feast day

qin: an ancient seven-string Chinese zither

quadruple meter: music with four beats per measure

quarter tone: the division of the whole tone, or whole step, into quarter tones, a division even smaller than the half tones, or half steps, on the piano

raga: an Indian scale and melodic pattern with a distinctive expressive mood

ragtime: an early type of jazz emerging in the 1890s and characterized by a steady bass and a syncopated, jazzy treble

rebec: a medieval fiddle

recapitulation: in sonata–allegro form, the return to the first theme and the tonic key following the development

recital: a concert of chamber music, usually for a solo performer

recitative: musically heightened speech, often used in an opera, oratorio, or cantata to report dramatic action and advance the plot

recitativo accompagnato: recitative accompanied by the orchestra instead of merely the harpsichord; the opposite of *secco* recitative

recorder: an end-blown wooden flute with seven finger holes played straight out instead of to one side

relative major: the major key in a pair of major and minor keys; relative keys have the same key signature, for example, E♭ major and C minor (both with three flats)

relative minor: the minor key in a pair of major and minor keys; see *relative major*

rest: a silence in music of a specific duration

retransition: the end of the development section where the tonality often becomes stabilized on the dominant in preparation for the return of the tonic (and first theme) at the beginning of the recapitulation

retrograde: a musical process in which a melody is played or sung, not from beginning to end, but starting with the last note and working backward to the first

rhythm: the organization of time in music, dividing up long spans of time into smaller, more easily comprehended units

rhythm and blues: a style of early rock 'n' roll ca. 1950 characterized by a pounding 4/4 beat and a raw, growling style of singing, all set within a twelve-bar blues harmony

rhythm section: the section within a jazz band, usually consisting of drums, double bass, piano, banjo, and/or guitar, that establishes the harmony and rhythm

Ring cycle: a cycle of four interconnected music dramas by Richard Wagner that collectively tell the tale of the Germanic legend *Der Ring des Nibelungen*

ritard: a gradual slowing down of the tempo

ritardando: in musical notation, a tempo mark indicating a slowing down of the tempo

romance: a slow, lyrical piece, or movement within a larger work, for instruments, or instrument and voice, much favored by composers of the Romantic period

rondeau: see *rondo*

rondo: an ancient musical form (surviving into the twentieth century) in which a refrain alternates with contrasting material

rubato: (Italian for "robbed") in musical notation, a tempo mark indicating that the performer may take, or steal, great liberties with the tempo

sackbut: a brass instrument of the late Middle Ages and Renaissance; the precursor of the trombone

Sanctus: the fourth section of the Ordinary of the Mass

sarabande: a slow, elegant dance in 3/4 with a strong accent on the second beat

scale: an arrangement of pitches that ascends and descends in a fixed and unvarying pattern

scherzo: (Italian for "joke") a rapid, jovial work in triple meter often used in place of the minuet as the third movement in a string quartet or symphony

Schubertiade: a social gathering for music and poetry that featured the songs and piano music of Franz Schubert

score: a volume of musical notation involving more than one staff

secco recitative: dry recitative accompanied only by the harpsichord

Sequence: a Gregorian chant, sung during the Proper of the Mass, in which a chorus and a soloist alternate; see also *melodic sequence*

serenade: an instrumental work for a small ensemble originally intended as a light entertainment in the evening

serial music: music in which some important component— pitch, dynamics, rhythm—comes in a continually repeating series; see also *twelve-tone composition*

seventh chord: a chord spanning seven letter names and constructed by superimposing three thirds

sforzando: a sudden, loud attack on one note or chord

sharp: a musical symbol that raises a pitch by a half step

shawm: a double-reed woodwind instrument of the late Middle Ages and Renaissance; the precursor of the oboe

sinfonia: (Italian for "symphony") a one-movement (later three- or four-movement) orchestral work that originated in Italy in the seventeenth century

Singspiel: (German for "singing play") a musical comedy

originating in Germany with spoken dialogue, tuneful songs, and topical humor

sitar: a large lutelike instrument with as many as twenty strings, prominently used in the traditional music of northern India

snare drum: a small drum consisting of a metal cylinder covered with a skin or sheet of plastic that when played with sticks produces the "rat-ta-tat" sound familiar from marching bands

solo: a musical line sung or played by a single performer

solo concerto: a concerto in which an orchestra and a single performer in turn present and develop the musical material in the spirit of harmonious competition

solo sonata: a work, usually in three or four movements, for keyboard or other solo instrument; when a solo melodic instrument played a sonata in the Baroque era it was supported by the *basso continuo*

sonata: originally "something sounded" on an instrument as opposed to something sung (a "cantata"); later a multi-movement work for solo instrument or instrument with keyboard accompaniment

sonata–allegro form: a dramatic musical form of the Classical and Romantic periods involving an exposition, development, and recapitulation, with optional introduction and coda

sonata da camera (chamber sonata): a suite for keyboard or small instrumental ensemble made up of individual dance movements

sonata da chiesa (church sonata): a suite for keyboard or small instrumental ensemble made up of movements indicated only by tempo marks such as *grave, vivace, adagio*; originally intended to be performed in church

song cycle: a collection of several songs united by a common textual theme or literary idea

soprano: the highest female vocal part

Sprechstimme: (German for "speech-voice") a singer declaims, rather than sings, a text at only approximate pitch levels

staccato: a manner of playing in which each note is held only for the shortest possible time

staff: a horizontal grid onto which are put the symbols of musical notation: notes, rests, accidentals, dynamic marks, etc.

stanza: a poetic unit of two or more lines with a consistent meter and rhyme scheme

step: the interval between adjacent pitches in the diatonic or chromatic scale; either a whole step or a half step

stomp: a piece of early jazz in which a distinctive rhythm, with syncopation, is established in the opening bars, as in the opening phrases of "Charleston"

string bass: see *double bass*

string instruments: instruments that produce sound when strings are bowed or plucked; the harp, guitar, and the members of the violin family are all string instruments

string quartet: a standard instrumental ensemble for chamber music consisting of a first and second violin, a viola, and a cello; also the genre of music, usually in three or four movements, composed for this ensemble

strophe: see *stanza*

strophic form: a musical form often used in setting a strophic, or stanzaic, text, such as a hymn or carol; the music is repeated anew for each successive strophe

style: the general surface sound produced by the inner action of the elements of music: melody, rhythm, harmony, color, texture, and form

subdominant chord: the chord built on the fourth, or subdominant, degree of the major or minor scale

subject: the term for the principal theme in a fugue

sustaining pedal: the right-most pedal on the piano; when it is depressed, all dampers are removed from the strings, allowing them to vibrate freely

swing: a mellow, bouncy, flowing style of jazz that originated in the 1930s

syllabic singing: a style of singing in which each syllable of text has one, and only one, note; the opposite of melismatic singing

symphonic poem (tone poem): a one-movement work for orchestra of the Romantic era that gives musical expression to the emotions and events associated with a story, play, political occurrence, personal experience, or encounter with nature

symphony: a genre of instrumental music for orchestra consisting of several movements; also the orchestral ensemble that plays this genre

symphony orchestra: the large instrumental ensemble that plays symphonies, overtures, concertos, and the like

syncopation: a rhythmic device in which the natural accent falling on a strong beat is displaced to a weak beat or between the beats

synthesizer: a machine that has the capacity to produce, transform, and combine (or synthesize) electronic sounds

tabla: a double drum used in the traditional music of northern India

tam-tam: an unpitched gong used in Western orchestras

tempo: the speed at which the beats occur in music

tenor: the highest male vocal range

ternary form: a three-part musical form in which the third section is a repeat of the first, hence **ABA**

terraced dynamics: a term used to describe the sharp, abrupt dynamic contrasts found in the music of the Baroque era

texture: the density and disposition of the musical lines that make up a musical composition; monophonic, homophonic, and polyphonic are the primary musical textures

theme and variations: a musical form in which a theme continually returns but is varied by changing the notes of the melody, the harmony, the rhythm, or some other feature of the music

The Well-Tempered Clavier: two sets of twenty-four preludes and fugues written by J. S. Bach between 1720 and 1742

third-stream jazz: a mixture of jazz and classical styles that originated in the 1950s

through composed: a term used to describe music that exhibits no obvious repetitions or overt musical form from beginning to end

timbre: see *color*

timpani (kettle drums): a percussion instrument consisting usually of two, sometimes four, large drums that can produce a specific pitch when struck with mallets

time signature (meter signature): two numbers, one on top of the other, usually placed at the beginning of the music to tell the performer what note value is carrying the beat and how the beats are to be grouped

toccata: a one-movement composition, free in form, originally for solo keyboard but later for instrumental ensemble as well

tonality: the organization of music around a central tone (the tonic) and the scale built on that tone

tonal language: any language in which the meaning of a word is expressed not only in its phonetic structure but also by the pitch at which it is spoken

tone: a sound with a definite, consistent pitch

tone cluster: a dissonant sounding of several pitches, each only a half step away from the other, in a densely packed chord

tone poem: see *symphonic poem*

tonic: the central pitch around which the melody and harmony gravitate

transition (bridge): in sonata–allegro form the unstable section in which the tonality changes from tonic to dominant (or relative major) in preparation for the appearance of the second theme

treble: the uppermost musical line, voice, or part; the part in which the melody is most often found

treble clef: the sign placed on a staff to indicate the notes above middle C

tremolo: a musical tremor produced on a string instrument by repeating the same pitch with quick up and down strokes of the bow

triad: a chord consisting of three pitches and two intervals of a third

trill: a rapid alternation of two neighboring pitches

trio: an ensemble, vocal or instrumental, with three performers; also, a brief, self-contained composition contrasting with a previous piece, such as a minuet or a polonaise; originally the trio was performed by only three instruments

trio sonata: an ensemble of the Baroque period consisting actually of four performers, two playing upper parts and two on the *basso continuo* instruments

triplet: a group of three notes inserted into the space of two

trombone: a brass instrument of medium to low range that is supplied with a slide, allowing a variety of pitches to sound

troubadour: a kind of secular poet-musician that flourished in southern France during the twelfth and thirteenth centuries

trouvère: a kind of secular poet-musician that flourished in northern France during the thirteenth and early fourteenth centuries

trumpet: a brass instrument of the soprano range

tuba: a brass instrument of the bass range

tune: a simple melody that is easy to sing

tutti: (Italian for "all") the full orchestra or full performing force

twelve-tone composition: a method of composing music, devised by Arnold Schoenberg, that has each of the twelve notes of the chromatic scale sound in a fixed, regularly recurring order

unison: two or more voices or instrumental parts singing or playing the same pitch

upbeat: the beat that occurs with the upward motion of the conductor's hand and immediately before the downbeat

verismo opera: "realism" opera; Italian term for a type of late nineteenth-century opera in which the subject matter concerns the unpleasant realities of everyday life

vibrato: a slight and continual wobbling of the pitch produced on a string instrument or by the human voice

viola: a string instrument; the alto member of the violin family

viola da gamba (bass viol): the lowest member of the viol family; a large six- or seven-string instrument played with a bow and heard primarily in the music of the late Renaissance and Baroque eras

violin: a string instrument; the soprano member of the violin family

virtuosity: extraordinary technical facility possessed by an instrumental performer or singer

vivace: in musical notation, a tempo mark indicating "fast and lively"

vocal ensemble: in opera, a group of four or more solo singers, usually the principals

voice: the vocal instrument of the human body; also a musical line or part

volume: the degree of softness or loudness of a sound

walking bass: a bass line that moves at a moderate pace, mostly in equal note values, and often stepwise up or down the scale

waltz: a popular, triple-meter dance of the late eighteenth and nineteenth centuries

whole step: the predominant interval in the Western major and minor scale; the interval made up of two half steps

whole-tone scale: a six-note scale each pitch of which is a whole tone away from the next

woodwind family: a group of instruments initially constructed of wood; most make their sound with the aid of a single or double reed; includes flute, piccolo, clarinet, oboe, English horn, and bassoon

word painting: the process of depicting the text in music, be it subtly, overtly, or even jokingly, by means of expressive musical devices

xylophone: a percussion instrument consisting of tuned wooden bars, with resonators below, that are struck with mallets

zither: a folk instrument consisting of a wooden box on which are stretched a number of strings of different pitches

CREDITS

Text

83 Marsilio Ficino, "The Golden Age in Florence," in *The Portable Renaissance Reader*, ed. James Bruce Ross and Mary Martin McLaughlin, New York, The Viking Press, 1953, p. 79.

86 Edward Lowinsky, *Music in the Culture of the Renaissance and Other Essays*, ed. Bonnie J. Blackburn, Chicago, The University of Chicago Press, 1989, vol. I, p. 87.

92 Palestrina, *Pope Marcellus Mass*, ed. Lewis Lockwood, New York, W. W. Norton and Company, 1975, p. 12.

117 Walter Kolneder, *Antonio Vivaldi: Documents of his Life and Works*, New York, C. F. Peters Corporation, 1981, p. 43.

140 Christopher Hogwood, *Handel*, London, Thames and Hudson, 1984, p. 71.

158 *Music in the Western World: A History in Documents*, ed. Piero Weiss and Richard Taruskin, New York, Schirmer Books, 1984, p. 299.

159 "Haydn," in *The New Grove Dictionary of Music and Musicians*, ed. Stanley Sadie, London, Macmillan, 1980, vol. VIII, p. 344.

161–162 *The Letters of Mozart and his Family*, ed. Emily Anderson, London, Macmillan, 1938, vol. III, p. 1187.

182 A & M Records, SP–3735.

198 Alfred Einstein, *Mozart: His Character, His Work*, London, Oxford University Press, 1945, p. 300.

212 Conrad Fischer and Erich Koch, *Ludwig van Beethoven*, London, Macmillan, 1958, p. 28.

308 Neil Butterworth, *Dvořák*, London, Monibus Press, 1980, p. 105.

319 Alma Mahler Werfel, *And the Bridge was Love*, New York, Harcourt Brace, 1958, pp. 25–27.

349 Modris Eksteins, *Rites of Spring*, New York, Doubleday, 1989, p. 14.

354–355 Arnold Schoenberg, "The Composition with Twelve Tones," in *Composers on Music*, ed. Sam Morgenstern, New York, Pantheon Books, 1956, p. 380.

364–365 Charles Ives, *The Fourth of July*, ed. John Kirkpatrick, New York, Associated Music Publishers, 1974, p. 1.

Illustrations

cover Bildarchiv preussischer kulturbesitz, Berlin; **2** © Ken Biggs; **3 (top and bottom)** Precision Graphics; **4 (top and bottom)** Precision Graphics; **5** Ken Nahoum Productions, Inc., N.Y.; **6** The Bettmann Archive; **7 (top)** Kevin Hutchinson, Indiana University; **(bottom)** © Joan Marcus 1987; **8 (top)** Eastman School of Music; **(bottom:** Luciana Frassati; **9** Louvre, Musée d'Orsay, © Photo R.M.N.; **10** Bibliothèque Nationale; **15** © 1987 Garry D. McMichael, Photo Researchers; **16** Musée Nationale de l'Art Moderne, Paris; **20** Reuters/Bettmann; **23** Josef and Anni Albers Foundation; **24** Musée Nationale de l'Art Moderne, Paris; **28** The Granger Collection; **30** © Mindy E. Klarman, Photo Researchers; **31** © The Solomon R. Guggenheim Foundation, New York; **33** Musée Nationale de l'Art Moderne, **41 (left)** Picasso, Pablo. *Three Musicians*. Fontainebleau, summer 1921. Oil on canvas, 6'7" × 7'3 3/4" (200.7 × 222.9 cm). Collection, The Museum of Modern Art, New York. Mrs. Simon Guggenheim Fund.; **(right)** © Beth Bergman 1988; **42** Courtesy of Sony Classical; **43 (left)** Courtesy of ICM Artists, Ltd.; **(center)** Courtesy of Sony Classical; **(right)** © Ira Nozik 1987/Jane Davis Inc.; **44 (top)** F. B. Grunzweig, Photo Researchers; **(bottom)** Courtesy of the G. Leblanc Corporation, Kenosha, Wisconsin; **46 (top)** © Martin Reichenthal; **(bottom)** Courtesy of Yamaha Corporation; **47 (left)** The Minnesota Orchestral Association; **(right)** Barrie-Kent Photographers; **48 (top)** University of St. Thomas, M.N.; **(bottom left)** Yale University; **(bottom right)** © 1988 Steve J. Sherman; **49** Precision Graphics; **51** © 1991 Steve J. Sherman; **52** Tate Gallery, London/Art Resource, N.Y.; **56** Courtesy of the Sydney Opera House Trust; **58 (left)** Tate Gallery, London/Art Resource, N.Y.; **(right)**

INDEX